WAY HTML

3rd Edition

Global Structure

Tag		Description
`<!DOCTYPE>`	Document type	Specifies the version of HTML
`<address>` . . . `</address>`	Attribution information	Lists author contact information (footer)
`<body>` . . . `</body>`	Body	Defines or indicates a document's body
`<div>` . . . `</div>`	Logical divisions	Marks divisions in a document
`<h1>` . . . `</h1>`	Headings	Identifies first- through sixth-level headings
`<h2>` . . . `</h2>`		
`<h3>` . . . `</h3>`		
`<h4>` . . . `</h4>`		
`<h5>` . . . `</h5>`		
`<h6>` . . . `</h6>`		
`<head>` . . . `</head>`		Creates a document's head
`<html>` . . . `</html>`		Identifies an HTML document
`<meta>`		Describes aspects of the page's information structure, contents, or relationships to other documents
`<span>` . . . `</span>`	Localized style formatting	Applies style to subparts of a paragraph
`<title>` . . . `</title>`	Document title	Briefly describes document information
`<!- . . . ->`	Comments	Inserts comments; ignored by browser

Describes Document Layout and Structure

Tables

Provides Controls for Table Structure

Tag		Description
`<caption>` . . . `</caption>`	Table caption	Defines the text and location of a table caption
`<col>`	Column properties	Sets the properties of a single column within a column group
`<colgroup>` . . . `</colgroup>`	Column group	Sets the properties for a group of columns
`<table>` . . . `</table>`	Table	Creates a table
`<tbody>` . . . `</tbody>`	Table body	Defines the table body when headers and footers are also defined
`<td>` . . . `</td>`	Table cell	Contains table cell data and formatting controls
`<tfoot>` . . . `</tfoot>`	Table footer	Defines the table footer when headers and body are also defined
`<th>` . . . `</th>`	Table head	Contains the table head data and formatting controls
`<thead>` . . . `</thead>`	Table head	Defines the table header when body and footers are also defined
`<tr>` . . . `</tr>`	Table row	Contains table row data and formatting controls

For Dummies: Bestselling Book Series for Beginners

For Dummies™
BESTSELLING
BOOK SERIES

HTML 4 For Dummies®, 3rd Edition

Cheat Sheet

Text Tags — Adds Structural Information to Text

Tag		Description
`<abbr> . . . </abbr>`	Abbreviation	Identifies expansion for an acronym
`<acronym> . . . </acronym>`	Acronym	Indicates an acronym
`<blockquote> . . . </blockquote>`	Quote style	Sets off long quotations or citations
` `	Force line break	Forces a line break in the on-screen text flow
`<cite> . . . </cite>`	Citation markup	Marks distinctive text for citations
`<code> . . . </code>`	Program code text	Used for code samples
`<del> . . . </del>`	Deleted text	Identifies deleted sections of a Web page
`<dfn> . . . </dfn>`	Defined term	Emphasizes a term about to be defined in the text
`<em> . . . </em>`	Emphasis	Emphasizes enclosed text
`<ins> . . . </ins>`	Inserted text	Identifies newly inserted sections of a Web page
`<kbd> . . . </kbd>`	Keyboard text	Marks text to be entered by the user
`<p> . . . </p>`	Paragraph	Breaks text into content blocks
`<pre> . . . </pre>`	Preformatted text	Keeps spacing, layout of in monospaced font
`<q> . . . </q>`	Quotation markup	Marks a short quotation within a sentence
`<samp> . . . </samp>`	Sample output	Indicates sample output from a program or script
`<strong> . . . </strong>`	Strong emphasis	Provides maximum emphasis to enclosed text
`<sub> . . . </sub>`	Subscript	Renders text smaller and slightly lowered
`<sup> . . . </sup>`	Superscript	Renders text smaller and slightly raised
`<var> . . . </var>`	Variable text	Marks variable or substitution for some other value

Lists — Lay Out Item or Element Sequences in Document Content

Tag		Description
`<dd> . . . </dd>`	Definition description	Marks the definition for a term in a glossary list
`<dir> . . . </dir>`	Directory list	Marks unbulleted list of short elements
`<dl> . . . </dl>`	Definition list	Marks a special format for terms and their definitions
`<dt> . . . </dt>`	Definition term	Marks the term being defined in a glossary list
`<li> . . . </li>`	List item	Marks a member item within a list of any type
`<menu> . . . </menu>`	Menu list	Marks a pickable list of elements
`<ol> . . . </ol>`	Ordered list	Marks a numbered list of elements
`<ul> . . . </ul>`	Unordered list	Marks bulleted list of elements

Hungry Minds™

For Dummies: Bestselling Book Series for Beginners

HTML 4

FOR

DUMMIES®

3RD EDITION

HTML 4 FOR DUMMIES®
3RD EDITION

by Ed Tittel, Natanya Pitts & Chelsea Valentine

Hungry Minds™

Best-Selling Books • Digital Downloads • e-Books • Answer Networks • e-Newsletters • Branded Web Sites • e-Learning

New York, NY ◆ Cleveland, OH ◆ Indianapolis, IN

HTML 4 For Dummies®, 3rd Edition

Published by
Hungry Minds, Inc.
909 Third Avenue
New York, NY 10022
www.hungryminds.com
www.dummies.com

Library of Congress Catalog Card No.: 00-101255

ISBN: 0-7645-0723-0

Printed in the United States of America

10 9 8 7 6 5

3B/RW/QU/QS/IN

Distributed in the United States by Hungry Minds, Inc.

Distributed by CDG Books Canada Inc. for Canada; by Transworld Publishers Limited in the United Kingdom; by IDG Norge Books for Norway; by IDG Sweden Books for Sweden; by IDG Books Australia Publishing Corporation Pty. Ltd. for Australia and New Zealand; by TransQuest Publishers Pte Ltd. for Singapore, Malaysia, Thailand, Indonesia, and Hong Kong; by Gotop Information Inc. for Taiwan; by ICG Muse, Inc. for Japan; by Intersoft for South Africa; by Eyrolles for France; by International Thomson Publishing for Germany, Austria and Switzerland; by Distribuidora Cuspide for Argentina; by LR International for Brazil; by Galileo Libros for Chile; by Ediciones ZETA S.C.R. Ltda. for Peru; by WS Computer Publishing Corporation, Inc., for the Philippines; by Contemporanea de Ediciones for Venezuela; by Express Computer Distributors for the Caribbean and West Indies; by Micronesia Media Distributor, Inc. for Micronesia; by Chips Computadoras S.A. de C.V. for Mexico; by Editorial Norma de Panama S.A. for Panama; by American Bookshops for Finland.

For general information on Hungry Minds' products and services please contact our Customer Care Department within the U.S. at 800-762-2974, outside the U.S. at 317-572-3993 or fax 317-572-4002.

For sales inquiries and reseller information, including discounts, premium and bulk quantity sales, and foreign-language translations, please contact our Customer Care Department at 800-434-3422, fax 317-572-4002, or write to Hungry Minds, Inc., Attn: Customer Care Department, 10475 Crosspoint Boulevard, Indianapolis, IN 46256.

For information on licensing foreign or domestic rights, please contact our Sub-Rights Customer Care Department at 212-884-5000.

For information on using Hungry Minds' products and services in the classroom or for ordering examination copies, please contact our Educational Sales Department at 800-434-2086 or fax 317-572-4005.

For press review copies, author interviews, or other publicity information, please contact our Public Relations Department at 317-572-3168 or fax 317-572-4168.

For authorization to photocopy items for corporate, personal, or educational use, please contact Copyright Clearance Center, 222 Rosewood Drive, Danvers, MA 01923, or fax 978-750-4470.

Hungry Minds is a trademark of Hungry Minds, Inc.

About the Authors

Ed Tittel is a full-time writer/trainer who manages a small gang of technoids at LANWrights, his company in Austin, TX. Ed has been writing for the trade press since 1986, and has worked on nearly 100 books. In addition to this title, Ed has worked on over 30 books for IDG Books Worldwide, including *Networking Windows NT Server For Dummies, XML For Dummies,* 2nd Edition, and *Networking with NetWare For Dummies.*

Ed teaches for Austin Community College, NetWorld + Interop, and The Internet Security Conference (TISC). He also trains on and writes about the Novell and Microsoft certification curriculum and exams. When he's not busy doing all that work stuff, Ed likes to travel, shoot pool, and wrestle with his indefatigable Labrador retriever, Blackie.

You can contact Ed Tittel by e-mail at etittel@lanw.com.

Natanya Pitts is a writer, trainer, and Web guru in Austin, TX. She has extensive experience in the technical training realm, including overseeing the development of the materials for in-class and Web-based training offerings. She also helped establish the Austin Community College Webmaster Certification program and taught in the program for two years.

Natanya has authored, co-authored, or contributed to more than a dozen Web- and Internet-related titles, including *XML For Dummies* (1st and 2nd Editions), *The XML Black Book*, and *XML In Record Time*. Natanya has also taught classes on HTML, Dynamic HTML, and XML at several national conferences (including MacWorld, Networld + Interop, and HP World), as well as at the NASA Ames Research Center.

You can contact Natanya Pitts at natanya@io.com.

Chelsea Valentine is a full-time trainer, writer, Webmaster . . . and the list goes on. She has recently worked on the *XML For Dummies*, 2nd Edition, and the *Hip Pocket Guide for HTML 4.01*, both by IDG Books Worldwide. Chelsea spends most of her days teaching HTML and XML for Austin Community College and in her spare time, she maintains the LANWrights Web site.

While in college, Chelsea worked for LANWrights, helping out any way she could. After graduating from the University of Texas, Chelsea took off to Latin America and then found her way to Washington, D.C. While working for a human rights nonprofit organization, she began working with other nonprofit organizations, teaching them how to get their Web sites up and running. Longing for home, she returned to Austin and picked up where she left off with LANWrights. Now a full-fledged writer and trainer, she fills almost every waking hour working and playing with HTML code.

Authors' Acknowledgments

Because this is the sixth iteration of *HTML For Dummies*, we'd like to start by thanking our many readers for making this book a success. We'd also like to thank them and the IDG editorial team for the feedback that drives the continuing improvement of this book's content. Please, don't stop now — tell us what you want to do with HTML, and what you don't like about this book.

Let me go on by thanking my sterling co-authors, Natanya Pitts and Chelsea Valentine, for their efforts on this revision. I am eternally grateful for your ideas, your hard work, and your experience in reaching an audience of budding Web experts.

Next, we'd like to thank the great teams at LANWrights and IDG for their efforts on this title. At LANWrights, my fervent thanks go to Mary Burmeister, for her services and the time spent on this book. I'd also like to thank Bill Brogden for his outstanding programming efforts on the HTML tool you'll find on the CD that accompanies this book. At IDG, I must thank Kyle Looper and Suzanne Thomas for their outstanding efforts, and Jerelind Charles and Paula Lowell for their marvelous ways with our words. Other folks we need to thank include Regina Snyder and Her Fabulous PLTs for their artful page layouts, and Heather Dismore and the Heather Dismore Media Chorus for their CD production expertise. IDG's Steve Hayes demonstrated extraordinary insight and taste by hiring us again for this edition.

Finally, I'd like to thank my parents, Al and Ceil, for all the great things they did for me, and my sister, Kat, and her family for keeping me plugged into the family side of life. I must also thank my faithful sidekick, Blackie, who's always ready to pull me away from the keyboard — sometimes literally — to explore the great outdoors.

— Ed Tittel

First and foremost I'd like to thank my co-author Ed Tittel for giving me the opportunity to work on this book again. It's been fun! In addition to being a great co-author, you've been a great friend. Special thanks to my beloved husband Robby and my beautiful daughter Alanna. All things are easier because you are a part of my life. Thanks to my parents, Charles and Swanya, for always believing in me and supporting me. And finally thanks to my furry fuzzball Gandalf for keeping me company while I work.

— Natanya Pitts

Thanks to Ed for giving me a chance way back when. Even more importantly, I am thankful to have had the opportunity to work with some of the most talented, kind, and outrageously fun people I know: MaryMary, Dawn, Michael, Bill, and Ed. Thanks to MaryMary for trimming the fat, so to speak, and always making sure I sound good. To my mother and father, I owe you my firstborn (that means you get to do it all over again). Nana, you're the greatest woman on earth. Austin, Kate, Amy, Karl, Chris, Collin, Cameron, Christopher, Isaiah, Markanne, Mary Anne, the list goes on. Now, to the one who makes me want to wake up in the morning: Yes, Sam, I will marry you one day.

— Chelsea Valentine

Publisher's Acknowledgments

We're proud of this book; please send us your comments through our Online Registration Form located at www.dummies.com.

Some of the people who helped bring this book to market include the following:

Acquisitions, Editorial, and Media Development

Project Editor: Kyle Looper, Suzanne Thomas
(Previous Edition: Pat O'Brien)

Acquisitions Editor: Steve Hayes

Copy Editors: Jerelind Charles, Paula Lowell
(Previous Edition: Barry Childs-Helton)

Proof Editor: Teresa Artman

Technical Editors: Frank Baumphrey,
Allan Wyatt

Permissions Editor: Carmen Krikorian

Associate Media Development Specialist:
Megan Decraene

Media Development Manager: Heather Heath
Dismore

Editorial Assistant: Candace Nicholson

Production

Project Coordinator: Regina Snyder

Layout and Graphics: Amy Adrian, Joe Bucki,
Tracy K. Oliver, Jacque Schneider,
Erin Zeltner

Proofreaders: Corey Bowen, Susan Moritz,
Charles Spencer,
York Production Services, Inc.

Indexer: York Production Services, Inc.

General and Administrative

Hungry Minds Technology Publishing Group: Richard Swadley, Vice President and Executive Group Publisher; Bob Ipsen, Vice President and Group Publisher; Joseph Wikert, Vice President and Publisher; Barry Pruett, Vice President and Publisher; Mary Bednarek, Editorial Director; Mary C. Corder, Editorial Director; Andy Cummings, Editorial Director

Hungry Minds Manufacturing: Ivor Parker, Vice President, Manufacturing

Hungry Minds Marketing: John Helmus, Assistant Vice President, Director of Marketing

Hungry Minds Production for Branded Press: Debbie Stailey, Production Director

Hungry Minds Sales: Michael Violano, Vice President, International Sales and Sub Rights

Contents at a Glance

Cartoons at a Glance

By Rich Tennant

"Give him air! Give him air! He'll be okay. He's just been exposed to some raw HTML code. It must have accidently flashed across his screen from the server."

page 185

"Great page, Sue — but let's reconsider the link to www.lycanthropy.com."

page 7

"Gotta hand it to our Web page designer — she found a way to make our pie charts interactive."

page 317

"His text content is fantastic, but lose those harmonic WAV files."

page 341

"... and when you click the fire hydrant, it marks your domain for you."

page 109

"It's a user-coercive search engine. When the user clicks the siphon icon, it installs a proprietary browser and collects the registration fee. Patching into the user's 401(k) was Bill's idea."

page 47

"There's gotta be a more elegant way to prompt for credit card numbers."

page 261

Fax: 978-546-7747
E-mail: richtennant@the5thwave.com
World Wide Web: www.the5thwave.com

Table of Contents

Introduction

● ●

*W*elcome to the wild, wacky, and wonderful possibilities inherent on the World Wide Web, simply referred to as the Web. In this book, we introduce you to the mysteries of the Hypertext Markup Language (HTML), which is used to build Web pages, and initiate you into the still-select, but rapidly growing, community of Web authors.

If you've tried to build your own Web pages before but found it too forbidding, now you can relax. If you can dial a telephone or find your keys in the morning, you too can become an HTML author. (No kidding!)

When we first wrote this book, we took a straightforward approach to the basics of authoring documents for the Web. In this edition, for a new generation of Web page designers, we go after the best of old and new. We keep the amount of technobabble to a minimum and stick with plain English as much as possible. Besides plain talk about hypertext, HTML, and the Web, we include lots of examples, plus tag-by-tag instructions to help you build your very own Web pages with minimum muss and fuss.

We also include a peachy CD with this book that contains each and every HTML example in usable form — plus a number of interesting widgets that you can use to embellish your own documents and astound your friends. For this edition, we add discussions of important topics that have come increasingly to the fore (though not yet to the putting green) in the last few years. Finally, the CD also includes the magnificent and bedazzling source materials for the *HTML 4 For Dummies,* 3rd Edition, Web pages, in which you may find a source of inspiration and raw material for your own use! And we carry on a time-honored tradition upheld by the computer industry generally and IDG Books Worldwide in particular:

Anything silly you may read herein is a *feature, not a bug!*

About This Book

Think of this book as a friendly, approachable guide to taking up the tools of HTML and building readable, attractive pages for the Web. Although HTML isn't hard to learn, it does pack a plethora of details; you need to wrestle with them some while you build your Web pages. Some sample topics you find in this book include

✔ Designing and building Web pages.

✔ Uploading and publishing Web pages for the world to see.

✔ Creating interesting page layouts.

✔ Testing and debugging your Web pages.

Although, at first glance, building Web pages may seem to require years of arduous training, advanced aesthetic capabilities, and ritual ablutions in ice-cold streams, take heart: It just ain't so. If you can tell somebody how to drive across town to your house, you can certainly build a Web document that does what you want it to. The purpose of this book isn't to turn you into a rocket scientist (or, for that matter, a rocket scientist into a Web site); the purpose is to show you all the design and technical elements you need to build a good-looking, readable Web page, and to give you the know-how and confidence to do it!

How to Use This Book

This book tells you how to use HTML 4 to get your page up and running on the World Wide Web. We tell you what's involved in designing and building effective Web documents that can bring your ideas and information to the whole online world — if that's what you want to do — and maybe have some high-tech fun communicating them.

All HTML code appears in monospaced type such as this:

```
<head><title>What's in a Title?</title></head>...
```

When you type HTML tags or other related information, be sure to copy the information exactly as you see it between the angle brackets (< and >) because that's part of the magic that makes HTML work. Other than that, you find out how to marshal and manage the content that makes your pages special, and we tell you exactly what you need to do to mix the elements of HTML with your own work.

The margins of a book don't give us the same room as the vast reaches of cyberspace. Therefore, some long lines of HTML markup, or designations of Web sites (called *URLs,* for *Uniform Resource Locators*), may wrap to the next line after we present them here. Remember that your computer shows such wrapped lines as a *single line of HTML,* or as a single URL — so if you're typing that hunk of code, keep it as one line. Don't insert a hard return if you see one of these wrapped lines. We clue you in that the HTML markup is supposed to be all one line by breaking the line at a slash (to imply "but wait, there's more!") and slightly indenting the overage, as in the following silly example:

```
http://www.infocadabra.transylvania.com/nexus/plexus/lexus/
              praxis/okay/this/is/a/make-
              believe/URL/but/some/real/
              ones/are/SERIOUSLY/long.html
```

 HTML doesn't care if you type tag text in uppercase, lowercase, or both (except for character entities, which must be typed exactly as indicated in Chapter 12). To make your own work look like ours as much as possible, enter all HTML tag text in lowercase only. Those of you who own previous editions of the book may see this as a complete reversal of earlier instructions. That it is! But the keepers of the eternal and ever-magnanimous standard of HTML, the World Wide Web Consortium (W3C), have changed the rules of this game, so we changed our instructions to follow their lead.

Three Presumptuous Assumptions

They say that making assumptions makes a fool out of the person who makes them and the person who is subject to those assumptions (and just who are *They,* anyway? We *assume* we know, but . . . never mind). Even so, practicality demands that we make a few assumptions about you, our gentle reader:

- ✔ You can turn your computer on and off.
- ✔ You know how to use a mouse and a keyboard.
- ✔ You want to build your own Web pages for fun, for profit, or for your job.

In addition, we assume you already have a working connection to the Internet, and one of the many fine Web browsers available by hook, by crook, by download from that same Internet, or from the attached CD. You don't need to be a master logician or a wizard in the arcane arts of programming, nor do you need a Ph.D. in computer science. You don't even need a detailed sense of what's going on in the innards of your computer to deal with the material in this book.

If you can write a sentence and know the difference between a heading and a paragraph, you're better off than 9 out of 10 playground bullies — *and* you can build and publish your own documents on the Web. If you have an active imagination and the ability to communicate what's important to you, even better — you've already mastered the key ingredients necessary to build useful, attractive Web pages. The rest consists of details, and we help you with those!

How This Book Is Organized

This book contains seven major parts, arranged like Russian *Matrioshka,* otherwise known as nesting dolls: All these parts contain three or more chapters, and each chapter contains several modular sections. Any time you need help or information, pick up the book and start anywhere you like, or use the Table of Contents or Index to locate specific topics or key words.

Here is a breakdown of the parts and what you find in each one.

Part I: Getting Started with HTML

This part sets the stage and includes an overview of and introduction to the Web and the software that people use to mine its treasures. This section also explains how the Web works, including the HTML to which this book is devoted, and the server-side software and services that deliver information to end-users (as all of us are when we're not doing battle with the logical innards of our systems).

HTML documents, also called *Web pages,* are the fundamental units of information organization and delivery on the Web. Here, you also discover what HTML is about and how hypertext can enrich ordinary text. Next, you take a walk on the Web side and build your very first HTML document.

Part II: Cranking Out Web Pages

HTML mixes ordinary text with special strings of characters, called *markup,* used to instruct browsers how to display HTML documents. In this part of the book, you find out about markup in general and HTML in particular. This includes an overview of HTML tags and how they work. Then, we tell you all about HTML text pages to help you understand how to include and manage text on a Web page. After that, you find out how to mix graphics in with the text, and how to create pages that can make a good impression on their readers.

By the time you finish Part II, expect to have a good overall idea of what HTML is, what it can do, and how you can use it yourself.

Part III: Formatting Your Data

Part III takes the elements covered in Part II and explains them in far greater detail to help you design and build commercial-grade HTML documents. This includes working with HTML tag syntax and structures, plus working with the kind of presentation controls you need to build complex Web pages. After that, you find out how to make the most of HTML style tags and structures, how to build a variety of lists, and how to include all kinds of keen symbols in the text that appears on-screen in your Web pages.

Part IV: Shaping Your Design

Part IV adds sophistication and elegance to the basics covered in Part III. By the time you read these chapters, you can build complex Web pages of many different kinds. You also find out about how to organize textual and graphical data into a variety of tables; how to create and use clickable images, called image maps, for navigating on your Web site; and how to break your display into individual on-screen areas, called frames, to improve your readers' access to Web document contents and functions.

Part V: Advanced HTML Topics and Techniques

In this part, you go a little beyond the built-in capabilities that HTML 4 delivers to its users, to examine some interesting facilities that sometimes show up in Web pages — but not always. This includes working with HTML forms to request and deliver user input, and working with separate HTML style sheets to control document fonts, formats, and element positioning. Part V also covers how to use special-purpose programs to make your Web pages more interactive to respond to user input that you solicit in Web-based forms.

Part VI: The Part of Tens

In the concluding part of the book, we sum up and distill the very essence of what you now know about the mystic secrets of HTML. Here, you have a chance to review the top do's and don'ts for HTML markup, to rethink document design, and to catch and kill potential bugs and errors in your pages before anybody else sees them.

Part VII: Appendixes

The last part of this book ends with a set of appendixes designed to sum up and further expand on the book's contents. Appendix A is an alphabetical list of HTML tags, designed for easy access and reference. Appendix B is a glossary of the technical terms that appear in this book. Appendix C is a list of HTML-related software tools that your authors think you may find useful. Finally, Appendix D lists the details about what's on the *HTML 4 For Dummies,* 3rd Edition CD-ROM, including a snazzy Java-based HTML lookup tool we built for you our very own selves. As noted in this appendix, the materials on the CD-ROM are organized into modules that correspond to the organization of the book to make it easy for you to find URLs and examples referenced therein.

By the time you make it through all the materials in the book and on the CD, you are pretty well-equipped to build your own Web documents and perhaps even ready to roll out your own Web site!

Icons Used in This Book

This icon signals technical details that are informative and interesting, but not critical to writing HTML. Skip these if you want (but please, come back and read them later).

This icon flags useful information that makes HTML markup, Web page design, or other important stuff even less complicated than you feared it might be.

This icon points out information you shouldn't pass by — don't overlook these gentle reminders (the life, sanity, or page you save could be your own).

Be cautious when you see this icon. It warns you of things you shouldn't do; the bomb is meant to emphasize that the consequences of ignoring these bits of wisdom can be severe.

Text marked with this icon contains information about something that's on this book's CD-ROM.

Where to Go from Here

This is the part where you pick a direction and hit the road! *HTML 4 For Dummies,* 3rd Edition, is a lot like the parable of the six blind men and the elephant: Where you start out doesn't matter; you'll look at lots of different parts as you prepare yourself to build your own Web pages — and each part has a distinctive nature, but the whole is something else again. Don't worry. You'll get it handled. Who cares if anybody else thinks you're just goofing around? We know you're getting ready to have the time of your life.

Enjoy!

Part I
Getting Started with HTML

The 5th Wave — By Rich Tennant

"Great page, Sue—but let's reconsider the link to www.lycanthropy.com."

In this part . . .

This part includes an introduction to the Hypertext Markup Language, aka HTML. It explains a bit of its history and the software that people use to make it work. We cover the basic principles behind the way HTML works, including the markup to which this book is primarily devoted. We take you on a behind-the-scenes tour of a typical Web page, and you find out how to design and build your very first Web page.

Chapter 1

Okay, What's HTML?

• •

• •

*T*he real secret behind the Hypertext Markup Language (HTML) is that nothing's secret. Unlike a computer program you buy in the store (in which you can't generally view the code that makes the program do what it does), the HTML codes that function on any Web page are never more than a click away, just waiting for you to look at them and interpret what's going on. And the format of HTML content is simple, too (just plain-old text characters), which means that you need no special software to generate HTML code — any text editor can do the job.

The challenge of using HTML, however, is in following all its rules. HTML is finicky about how you order its tags and the way you use them, so to produce Web pages that look the way you want them to, you must humor HTML as if it were your rich uncle. HTML is persnickety about how you use it, however, for reasons of sheer practicality: *Some* Web browsers may forgive the omission or misstatement of *certain* HTML elements (tags), but the readers of your Web page could be using who-knows-what browser. The only reliable way to make your Web pages appear and behave consistently (short of magic) is to know the rules for creating HTML documents and to apply them correctly.

HTML tags are what make up HTML. If you've ever viewed the source code for a Web document, you see lots of stuff like this: `<html>` . . . `</html>`. Those are HTML tags (literally), and they make it do its stuff.

This chapter presents the brass tacks: fundamental ideas behind HTML, concepts and operation of hypertext, and some basic principles for building well-structured, readable Web pages. Your mission, should you decide to accept it, is to develop the knack of building well-structured, readable Web pages — and use it to your readers' advantage!

HTML Basics

"What's in a name?" HTML's moniker contains the two concepts that make it work (and make the World Wide Web a phenomenal resource):

- **Hypertext:** The term may sound like science fiction — and you *can* do amazing things with it. Hypertext is a way of creating multimedia documents — and of forging links within or between them.

- **Markup language:** A method of embedding special tags (also known as *elements*) that describe the structure as well as the behavior of a document. (The language you use when a preschooler marks up your wall is something else again.)

The simplicity and power of HTML markup can enable just about anyone to concoct Web documents for private or public use — anyone who plays by the rules, that is. The rules for HTML syntax are discussed in Chapter 4.

Of Links and Sausages

When a Web-head talks excitedly about links, the conversation isn't about breakfast sausage, but rather about sizzling transitions between Web locations — whether within the same document or to different documents elsewhere on the Web. You can do this because HTML offers built-in support for *multimedia links* (links to multimedia files) and *document links* (links to document files). Both types of links work the same way; when you've used one link, you know how to use the others to get around.

Special HTML codes called *tags* allow you to create links (and to perform all your other HTML magic). Put the correct HTML tags around text or graphics to create an *active* (linked) area, and you've already added an intriguing capability. When readers visit your Web site and click an active area, the link transports them to another spot within the same file, to another document in the same Web site, or off to some other Web site. Figure 1-1 shows links to several resources on the *For Dummies* Web site. Each of these links connects to a valuable source of information.

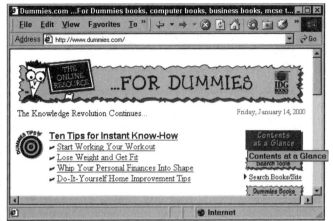

Figure 1-1:
The
Dummies
home page
starts off
with a
sequence of
hyperlinks.

Different browsers use different methods to denote links, but all browsers provide a visual cue that you've selected an active area on the screen. You may see text underlined in a bright color, notice a font change to boldface, or be grabbed by a graphic outlined in a contrasting color. In these and similar cases, you're looking at a portal to another world — or at least another part of the Web.

Your browser's way of saying *Congratulations! You found the link!* may be an *image map* — in which case, your only visual cues are a set of changing numbers in the browser's status line (these correspond to the location of your cursor on screen). Using this kind of link is like playing an adventure game: You're not always sure where you're going, what you'll find after you get there, or whether you just triggered a rolling boulder.

Jumping around inside documents

A hyperlink may connect with another location within the same document; each such location must have a unique name, known as an *internal anchor*. Webmasters often use this kind of link to move readers from a table of contents (at the top of an HTML file) to related sections throughout a document. Also, you can use this approach to jump directly to the start of a document from its end — this beats the heck out of scrolling all the way up through a long file!

Jumping around is a characteristic advantage of hypertext — circumventing the linear nature of the paper documents people have been used to since Gutenberg. The rapid, obvious (well, *modern*) way to navigate within or among documents is to travel by link. Sure, you can do the same thing with a table of contents or an index in a paper book by looking up what you want and flipping pages yourself — a bit of a chore if the book is more than a few hundred pages. Hypertext not only automates the action of moving from one part of a document to another, it makes the jump from page 1 to page 1000 — or to that key document in Kalamazoo — as effortless as the jump from page 9 to page 10. Links are a snap to use (a click, actually) and are easy to create.

Jumping across documents (and services)

After you put together your page the way you want it, you can also use HTML as a kind of cyberglue to link your page to other Web pages, no matter where they reside. This capability stems from the fact that the same hypertext technology that enables Web surfers to jump around inside a document also allows you to point to any other resource available through the Web. You only need to know the Web page's exact URL (address) to enable your reader to go there, so to speak.

Actually, HTML's simple text-tagging technique erases the practical difference between *here* and *there.* With a single click of the mouse (or by selecting the active text field), you *are there,* or the information *is here,* or . . . you get the idea.

Linking to other documents on the Web is a quick way to boost the capabilities of your Web pages and enhance your reader's experience. You create links to distant sites using a combination of hypertext links and *Uniform Resource Locators (URLs)* — the standardized addresses that tell a browser where to go (so politely that it actually goes there). The Web as we know it today springs from the work of individual Web weavers who include links to other documents from their Web sites.

Whenever you want to create a hyperlink to a particular Web page in your HTML document, visit the Web site in your Web browser, highlight the URL in the browser address window, and then use keyboard shortcuts to cut and paste the address from the browser into your hyperlink definition. This is good practice for three reasons:

- ✔ You've checked the site and know it's still there.
- ✔ You save typing time — some URLs can get pretty long.
- ✔ You ensure that you get the reference right.

After you copy a URL into a hyperlink tag, test the URL with your browser to make sure that it takes you where you expect.

URLs can point to — and get you to — a variety of protocols and services on the Internet in addition to other HTML files. You can link to telnet sessions, Wide Area Information Server (WAIS) resources, File Transfer Protocol (FTP) sites, Usenet newsgroups, or even e-mail messages. Individual documents may represent the *content* of the Web, but hyperlinks are the heart of the Web's true nature: They are the strands that make up the Web itself, tying people, ideas, services, and locations together.

The Web has more users now than ever before, but not all of them agree on whether to refer to a Uniform Resource Locator as *a URL* ("a yew-are-ell") or *an URL* ("an earl") — some even split the difference and call it a Ural (as in the mountain range). Just so you know, we're not taking sides; this book uses *a URL* ("a yew-are-ell"), strictly for the sake of technical clarity. (Well, okay, somebody *might* read it aloud in the House of Lords. . . .)

Hypertext Is Everywhere

Although hypertext may seem strange and exotic, you're probably much more familiar with it than you think. Your own desktop computer undoubtedly contains several hypertext applications that you use regularly. For example, if you use Microsoft Office 2000, you use a hypertext application every time you run the Help utility. In addition, as Figure 1-2 shows, this application offers hypertext links to online information.

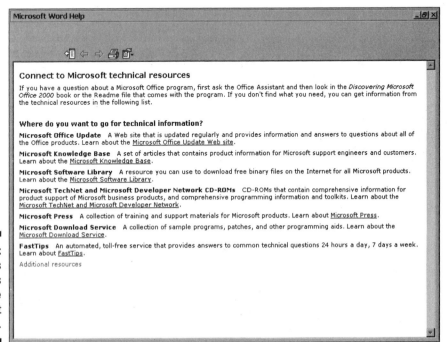

Figure 1-2:
Microsoft's
Windows
Help engine
is hypertext
based.

Notice the buttons above the text area in the help screenshot. These buttons work like the navigation tools for a Web browser; their labels tell whether they take you forward to a list of available links within a document or back to where you've been. The underlined phrases (such as Microsoft Office Update Web site) identify links to text or files associated with the application. In this case, they use genuine HTML links, just like those you encounter within a Web browser.

Hypertext applications have concepts in common with the Web, including some kind of home page (starting point), various navigation tools (shaped arrows and specific commands), multimedia data, and plenty of links to select from. Some of the examples mentioned here, however, support only certain kinds of links; not all of them can navigate the Web like the Office 2000 Help system can. Only access to the Web itself enables users to jump across the Internet and follow links to other Web documents and servers. Enabling this ability is exactly what gives HTML its value — and helps make the Web so popular.

Believe it or not, HTML is unfazed by ancient rivalries between operating systems. Microsoft is switching its Help system over to HTML; UNIX users familiar with FrameMaker or multimedia authoring can find common ground with the Web's hypertext capabilities. And Macintosh users who identified HyperCard and SuperCard as hypertext applications are *absolutely right* (extra credit on that one).

From Text to Multimedia, and Beyond

You're traveling to a wondrous land whose boundaries are . . . oops, wrong medium, though multi*media* capabilities can produce some out-there effects. If you do include nontextual files (such as sound, graphics, and video) in your Web pages, you must employ a certain amount of alchemy. Shipping Web information in *Multipurpose Internet Mail Extension* (MIME) format means that you can bundle multiple attachments within individual files — giving even a mild-mannered Web server the power to deliver multiple forms of data to your browser in a single transfer.

When a MIME file with attachments presents itself to a Web browser, processing begins immediately. The text portion of the incoming file arrives first, containing an HTML page description that lets the browser get right to work building and displaying the page's text. Because the text arrives first, you may see placeholders or icons for graphics when you catch your first glimpse of a Web page. Eventually, graphics or other forms of data replace these placeholders as their related attachments arrive.

As a Web page fills in on your screen — you can make good use of this time lag by reading the text or wishing for faster Internet access — the browser receives attachments in the background. As the attachments arrive, the browser identifies them by file type, or by the descriptive information contained in an attachment tag (as specified by the MIME format or associated Internet Media Type). After the browser knows what kind of file is attached, it can handle playback or display. Table 1-1 lists some common file types used on the Web, including the inevitable alphabet soup (now fortified with explanations!) of filename extensions.

Table 1-1	**Common Sound, Graphics, and Motion Video Formats on the Web**		
Multimedia Type	*Extension*	*Format*	*Explanation*
Graphics	.GIF	Graphics Interchange Format	Compressed graphics format commonly used on CompuServe; easy to render multiplatform. Can be *interleaved* (displayed gradually) or not, depending on how image is created.
Graphics	.JPEG, .JPG	Joint Photographic Experts Group	Highly compressed format for still images, widely used for multiplatform graphics.
Graphics	.PDF	Portable Document Format	Adobe's format for multiplatform document access through its Acrobat software.
Graphics	.PS	PostScript	Adobe's type description language; used to deliver complex documents over the Internet.
Sound and/or video	.RA/.RAM/.RM	RealPlayer media	Used with the RealPlayer add-on audio and/or video for browsers from Real.com.
Sound	.SBI	Sound Blaster Instrument	Used for a single instrument with Sound Blaster cards (multi-instrument: .IBK).

(continued)

Table 1-1 *(continued)*

Multimedia Type	Extension	Format	Explanation
Sound	.SND, .AU	8KHz mulaw	Voice-grade sound format used on work-stations (such as Sun, NeXT, HP9000, and so on).
Sound	.WAV	Microsoft Waveform	Sound format used in Windows for event notification.
Video	.AVI	Audio Video Interleaved	Microsoft Video for Windows standard format; found on many CD-ROMs.
Video	.DVI	Digital Video Interactive	Another motion-video format, also found on CD-ROMs.
Video	.FLI	Flick	Autodesk Animator motion-video format.
Video	.MOV	QuickTime	Apple's motion-video and audio format; originated on the Macintosh, but also available for Windows.
Video	.DCR	Director	A "shocked" (animated) version of a Macromedia Director multimedia file.
Video	.MPEG, .MPG	Motion Picture Experts Group	Full-motion video standard using frame format similar to .JPEG with variable compression capabilities.

Many Web sites contain large amounts of information on file formats and programs; here are two of the best that we turned up by searching on the string "common Internet file formats" at www.excite.com, http://ask.com, and http://about.com:

✔ **Common Internet File Formats:** An annotated list of audio, graphic, and multimedia file formats, compiled by the gurus at Apple.

```
http://til.info.apple.com/techinfo.nsf/artnum/n24464
```

✔ **GRAPHICS:** Maintained by Martin Reddy at the University of Edinburgh, this site contains "everything you ever wanted to know" about graphics and links to additional resources.

```
www.dcs.ed.ac.uk/%7Emxr/gfx/
```

Hyperhelpers: Useful "helper" applications

When referenced by a Web page, nontextual data shows up as attachments to an HTML file. Sometimes the browser itself handles playback or display, as in the case of simple, two-dimensional graphics (including .GIF and .JPEG files). Even so, other applications may handle these (especially for character-mode Web browsers such as Lynx).

When other kinds of files need special handling (beyond the scope of most browsers), the browser hands off these files to other applications for playback or display. Such *helper* or *plug-in* applications have the built-in smarts to handle the formats and the processing needed to deliver, on demand, the contents of a specialized file.

The process normally works something like this:

1. The browser builds a page display that includes an active region (under-lined or outlined in some way) to indicate the attachment of a sound, video, or animation playback.

2. If the user selects the active region (the link), then the browser calls on another application or plug-in to handle playback or display.

3. The helper or plug-in takes over and plays back or displays the file.

4. After the helper completes display or playback, the browser reasserts control, and the user can continue.

A standard part of browser configuration supplies the names and locations of helper programs, or configures specially tailored add-ons called *plug-ins,* to assist the browser when such data arrives. If the browser can't find a helper application or plug-in, it simply won't respond to an attempt to display or play back the requested information. For plug-ins, however, most browsers can recognize what they're missing, and some (such as Navigator or Internet Explorer) will ask you if you want to add the missing plug-in to your current configuration.

For example, RealPlayer is a common sound player plug-in for Web browsers, primarily for PCs running Windows. As part of the configuration that occurs when you install a plug-in, associations between particular file types (such as the .SBI and .WAV file extensions common on the PC) and the plug-in may be automatically established. After this association is created, the browser automatically invokes the plug-in when it encounters files with those extensions. This causes the sounds to play (which, we assume and hope, is a good thing!).

For comprehensive listings of PC, Mac, and UNIX plug-in or helper applications, and links to their sources, start your search at one of the following URLs:

```
http://tucows.myriad.net/acc95.html
```

```
http://wwwhost.cc.utexas.edu/learn/use/helper.html
```

You should also check out both the Netscape and Microsoft sites for information about the latest plug-ins. For example, Netscape has a link to a set of pages labeled Plug-ins in the Web Tools section of its Web site, which is located in the left-hand menu section on the home page at http://home.netscape.com.

Well, okay, helper applications may not send out for pizza or make you a decent cup of coffee, but we've found some useful Windows helpers (visit www.shareware.com for download locations):

✔ **For still graphics:** LView is a good, small graphics viewer that can handle .GIF, .PCX, and .JPEG files. For the compulsively creative, LView supports some intriguing image-editing capabilities.

✔ **For video:** The applications of choice for making your monitor act like a TV are QuickTime for Windows (which plays QuickTime movie-format files), RealPlayer from Real.com, or MPEGplay for .MPEG video files.

✔ **For PostScript viewing:** Ghostview for Windows works with a program called Ghostscript that enables users to view or print PostScript files from any source, including the Web. Because so many documents on the Internet use the PostScript format, Ghostview and Ghostscript are outrageously handy.

A good set of plug-ins or helper applications can make your browser quite effective at bringing the Web's wonders to your desktop. With the right add-ons, your browser can play back, render, or establish friendly relations with just about any multimedia format that lands in your system.

The value of visuals

Without a doubt, graphics add impact and interest to Web pages, but that extra punch comes at a price. You can easily get carried away by the appeal of pictures and plaster them all over your Web page. (And no, size doesn't matter — those innocuous little images that make such cool buttons and on-screen controls have BIG clutter potential if overdone.)

Therefore, heed these caveats when using graphics on your Web pages:

- ✔ **Not everybody who reads your page can see the graphics.** Readers may not see graphics because they use character-mode browsers that can't display them, or because they switch off their graphics displays to improve response time (a common option on most Web browsers to conserve *bandwidth,* the capacity of a system to move data at faster-than-glacial speed). In addition, readers may not see the graphics correctly — 10 percent of the population is colorblind to some extent.

- ✔ **Graphics files (even compressed graphics) can be huge.** Graphics are often 10 or more times bigger than the HTML files to which they belong. Moving graphics takes time and consumes bandwidth. Also, it penalizes users with slower modems (usually the majority) far more than it penalizes those who have speedy (and more expensive) direct connections to the Internet.

Sometimes graphics are essential — for example, a diagram or illustration may be the best and quickest way to explain your material — and certainly an appropriate degree of visual impact can be vital if your home page is where you make a first impression. You can make an even better long-term impression, however, if you're consistently sensitive to the different capabilities and bandwidths of your readers.

We humbly present some rules for using graphics effectively in your Web pages. (One more word to the wise: As you examine the work of others, notice what happens to your attitude when you find that they have violated some or all of these rules.)

- ✔ **Keep your graphics small and uncomplicated whenever possible.** This reduces file sizes and keeps transfer times down.

- ✔ **Use compressed formats (such as .GIF and .JPEG) whenever you can.** Smaller file sizes reduce the graphics overhead.

- ✔ **Create a small version (called a *thumbnail*) of a graphic to include on your Web page:** An easy way to do this is by sizing your image on-screen and then taking a screen shot when you display it in reduced form — usually 100 x 100 pixels or so. If you must use larger, more complex graphics, link thumbnails to full-sized versions. This spares casual readers the impact of downloading large versions every time they access your page (and keeps Internet use under better control, making you a better *netizen!*).

- ✔ **Keep the number of graphical elements on a page to a minimum.** Practically speaking, this means *at most* a half-dozen graphic items per page. Most of these should be compact, icon-like navigation controls; larger images should be content-specific graphics, used sparingly. Here again, your goal is to limit page complexity and to speed transfer times.

Sometimes, the temptation to violate these rules can be nearly overwhelming. If you must break the rules, be sure to run your results past some disinterested (but not *uninterested*!) third parties. Watch them read your pages, if possible, and take heed of their reactions. Listen carefully to any feedback you get, to gauge whether you've merely bent the rules of good graphics or pretty well smithereened 'em.

Remember, not everyone who accesses your pages can see your graphics. For readers who are colorblind, who don't use graphical browsers, or who turn graphics off, try to think of ways to enhance their reading experience without graphics. This may mean supplying alternate text for graphical elements (which appear instead of graphics when users turn graphics off, or which might be placed on a page in addition to graphics for the benefit of those who can't or won't use images in their browsers). It could also mean using tables to organize on-screen text more effectively.

Rules for using multimedia

The problems caused in your HTML files by the size of graphics files (slowing download time and cluttering your page) go *double* for other forms of multimedia. If graphics files are large when compared to HTML text files, then sound and video files are *enormous.* They are also time-dependent; the longer they play, the bigger they are, *and* the longer the browser takes to download them to your computer. Although they're appealing and definitely increase the interest level for some topics, sound and video files don't apply to many topics on the Web. Use them sparingly or skip them, unless your site is an Internet radio show or movie theater. Web usability experts also recommend that you avoid using blinking or animated text, because motion distracts the human eye, an instinctive response intended to help you avoid predators (which are extremely unlikely on Web pages!).

Instead of using sound and video files to enhance your Web site, you have some other options: Java and Flash. Java and Flash are examples of new, faster interactivity tools for the Web that are becoming increasingly prevalent. Java *applets* work with Navigator, Internet Explorer, and other browsers to allow quick display of animated graphics and other special effects. Flash is the name of the Macromedia plug-in that allows Director movies to appear inside Web pages.

Before you go Hollywood in your Web page design, invest a little time in mastering the basics of HTML. Then, when you feel ready to rock with some video tools, check out these URLs for more information:

  ✔ **Java — Sun Microsystems:** www.javasoft.com or java.sun.com
  ✔ **Flash and Director — Macromedia:** www.macromedia.com

Once again, the trick is to make large files available *through links* instead of cramming them onto pages that everyone must download. Label these active regions with the size of the associated file, so people know what they're in for if they choose to download the material. (For example: `Warning! This link points to a 40K sound byte of a shrieking monkey.`)

Using the Web to Bring the Pieces Together

Breeeeeeeee. This is not a test: Before you get too wrapped up in the look of your site, multimedia add-ons, graphics, and such, stand by for an important message from the Emergency Webcast Center. The following paragraph embodies (to the best of our knowledge and experience) the essence of all successful Web pages.

The three most important factors in building good Web pages are content, content, and content (does our point come through clearly here?). If content is well organized, engaging, and linked to interesting places, your Web site can become a potent tool for education and communication. If your Web site is all flash, sharing it can be an exercise in sheer frustration (and humiliation for the Webmaster . . . that's you!). Therefore, if you put your energy into providing high-quality content and link your readers to other high-quality, content-filled pages, your Web site will be a howling success. If you don't, your site will become the electronic equivalent of a ghost town!

Chapter 2

What's in a Page?

*T*he knack for understanding and using HTML lies in knowing how to sepa-rate the two components of the HTML file. Here's the skinny on what makes them different:

✔ **Markup** (as in *markup language* — coincidence? We think not. . . .) gives your page its glitzy capabilities. Markup is made up of *tags*. If you look at an HTML source file and see some text that doesn't show up after your browser displays the page, look for the HTML bracket markers (the less than, ⟨, and greater than, ⟩, signs). These markers surround the tags that control how characters appear on your screen. If you flip through this book, you'll see plenty of examples of these tags.

✔ **Content** is what you want your page to actually *say* (whoa, what a con-cept!). You can stash most of your content in a plain text (ASCII) file with no tagging whatsoever — but tagging or not, it should be good stuff. After you're clear about the statement you want to make, the rest — however high-tech — is purely emphasis.

The really tricky — ah, *interesting* — parts of HTML are the possible combina-tions of markup and content, such as the tags used to give titles to pages or to specify guideposts to help clarify the text for the reader — headers, graph-ics, lists of elements, and so on. But the best place to start building a good Web page is to get really good at telling content apart from markup — to sep-arate the guts from the glitz — so that you can use both to best effect. Therefore, this chapter gives you a guided tour of the components that make up a Web page and offers some pointers on how to assemble them.

Leading with Layout

The human eye and (especially) brain are marvelous instruments, capable of scanning incredible amounts of material and zeroing in on the elements that are most important to the reader. As a Web page designer, your quest is to find the best way to guide the reader to your page's best information quickly, efficiently, and appealingly. Nothing communicates this concern — or lack of it — more clearly than a document's layout.

Layout is the overall arrangement of the elements in a document. Layout isn't just scooting the individual text elements around the page till your eyes water. Instead, layout means taking the time to make some decisions, such as how many elements you want, how to arrange them, and how much white space surrounds them.

The layout of a document — whether a Web page, magazine ad, or résumé — can be a crucial stage of communication: that first impression nobody gets to make twice. Of course, you *have* to look at some documents, regardless of the tedious mess on the page (let's hear it for tax forms!) — but if you have to *attract* an audience, it pays to be layout-literate.

Here's a quick thought-experiment in contrasts: Think of the deadliest textbook you ever slogged (slept?) through — endless pages of text in big blocky paragraphs, maybe an anemic graphic or two wedged in as an afterthought, and just for fun, assume the book was about a topic you like (or *used* to like . . .).

By comparison, think of a recent ad that reached out of a magazine or TV screen and *grabbed* you. Careful work went into the eye-catching images, appealing language, and the arresting combinations of elements. Which of these experiences was less torturous?

An inviting Web page can be as challenging to design as a hot ad (or, for that matter, a really good textbook). Pages that are all pizzazz and no substance tend to disappear quickly or at least get left in the virtual dust; however, pages that stress content at the expense of layout barely attract a yawn, let alone an audience.

Even if you discover antigravity and want to trumpet it to the world, don't assume the world is automatically interested; your page — anyone's, for that matter — joins millions of other sites on the Web in the age-old struggle for attention. A page that's pleasant to read, rich with content, and efficiently gets its point across is a standing invitation to users to visit often — and to link your site to theirs, which means the hits keep coming.

So Much to Say, So Much to Say

Whether you're just a Web-savvy average earthling with choice info to offer the world or an organization with products and services to advertise, you're probably hearing a siren song that calls you to publish online ASAP. Some of that temptation comes from HTML itself; as far as markup languages go, HTML is simple and easy to learn.

Remember that saying about what happens if a kid picks up a hammer ("everything starts to look like a nail")? Nearly everyone who picks up on HTML wants to charge right out and build "killer Web pages" on the fly — an easy way to kill a Web page before it even gets to fly. The usual mistake is to tack on too much of the wrong stuff. Trust us, it won't hurt to step back and do a little analysis and design work before you pick up that hammer.

Who's in the audience?

Creating a Web page is called Web *publishing* for a reason: Knowing your audience is crucial to building a Web page that people can use, enjoy, and want to revisit. If you don't know who's going to visit your Web site, and why they should want to, why build a Web site?

Of course, if you don't care who visits your site, you're not (exactly) alone; most personal pages on the Web are *vanity pages* with "content" that boils down to, "Here's some stuff about me that you must be dying to know but that even bores my mom to tears." A few Web surfers may visit a typical vanity page — once — while everyone else remains blissfully unaware of its presence.

If you have a more (ahem) grown-up reason for building your Web site — and some substantial content to offer — you're two steps closer to a good page. The next questions you need to ask are

- Which "group" of potential visitors do I want to reach?
- What messages are they likely to respond to?
- How do I emphasize my message?

If you aren't blessed with clairvoyance (or a big market-research budget), you must base your Web document design on certain assumptions — educated guesses — about your audience.

Often, advertisements and encyclopedias are designed to reach specific audiences. You could do worse than to shoot for the best of both worlds — the initial interest and impact of an advertisement, but enough depth of content that your audience is likely to react with "Wow — really?" or "I didn't know that!" or (okay, so much for grown-up) "Awesome!"

How can you get to know your audience? Think of the search as a form of hunting and gathering: Identify your target group and then start visiting their haunts, whether in cyberspace or in the real world, to learn their ways and habits. Watch and listen to them. Gather enough information to imagine the world from their point of view, as best you can.

After you recognize the interests of your target group, you also get a sense of their needs and wants. How does your content speak to those needs? Is there a clear niche that it can fill? If so, can you hook them into your content by filling that niche in a way they haven't seen before? If you can — and you deliver solid, usable information to the people in your target group — then your site becomes a resource; they come back for more and spread the word about what you have to offer.

Thus, we come back to the C-word — *content* — and here, be dragons. No matter how long, short, convoluted, or simple your content, we can offer a basic principle to follow safely through the dragon's lair: Form follows function. The following section delves a bit more deeply into this concept.

Design springs from content; form follows function

When we say that form follows function, in effect, we're just talking about good show and tell: If you have content to impart, a good design complements it, and a bad design obscures it. In addition, always remember who your audience is and what point you want to get across and that form should naturally follow function. Use the pointers we provide in the following sections and you'll be designing pages with a point in no time.

Organizing your content

To get your page to speak to your users effectively, you need to know how to organize your content. Therefore, we call upon the fearsome writing skills laid before us long ago — and, verily, the first of these is to create an outline before you start writing (or creating HTML, for that matter).

Outlining your content gives you a potent clue to establishing appropriate links — to your audience as well as to other sites. As you organize your information, consider these pointers:

- ✔ List the topics and major elements in your document.

- ✔ Identify the relationships between your main topics; make notes on what other information sources on the Web may enhance them.

- ✔ Experiment with the order of topics till you find the clearest and most engaging sequence.

- ✔ Assess possible uses for graphics, sound, or other multimedia; pare them down later to no more than the essentials.

- ✔ Consider what visual cues could help your users read and navigate your document (remember, go easy on the graphics where possible).

- ✔ Think of the outline as a blueprint that you'll come back to as you construct the document.

Deciding on your site's goal

The information you put into your Web page and the way you arrange it are both influenced by what you want your page to accomplish. Whether your intent is to inform, educate, persuade, or question, plays a major role in your Web page's design:

- ✔ **If your goal is to inform or educate,** reduce the number of eye-catching displays (too many can be distracting) and make the highlights of your information easy (but not painfully so) to see. See the W3C site for a good example of this at www.w3.org/.

- ✔ **If your goal is to persuade or sell,** try to hook users' attention with compelling visuals and riveting testimonials; follow through with important details about the goods. See the Amazon.com site for a good example of this at www.amazon.com/.

- ✔ **If your goal is to question** a political or social issue, raise that issue early, make your case as succinctly as you can, and provide pointers to additional discussion and related information. See the Human Rights Watch site for a good example of this at www.hrw.org/.

In each case, the goal behind a document strongly conditions its execution and delivery, which affects whether it attracts an audience. Identifying a clear goal and a conscious intent can be just as important as sticking to them.

Emphasizing important information

Your page should emphasize your message but stop short of giving the reader a headache. At the beginning of your document design process, you must answer the question "What am I trying to say?" Approach this task by outlining key ideas or messages that you seek to convey and put the most important ones first. Then follow each main idea with any relevant information to make your case, prove your point, or otherwise substantiate what you say. See Chapter 18 for more information on using style to emphasize content.

If you follow this exercise carefully, much of the content will emerge gracefully from your outline. Important relationships among various elements of your document (and other documents) will also reveal themselves as you work through the outlining process.

Making your site navigable

Information, like water, has a flow — and unless you direct where it's going, all you've got is a puddle. Fortunately, plumbing is available: Web designers customarily use some formal devices to communicate a document's organization, which can give a clueless reader some hope of navigating the information. The word that encompasses these devices is *superstructure*.

Creating superstructure is like giving your readers a can opener so that they can get at your content and be nourished by what they read or view. Not every document needs all the possible elements of superstructure, but most documents — especially longer ones — can benefit from at least some such plumbing. (Some documents cry out for superstructure — if you're an economist who does brain surgery for a hobby, your page just might.)

The elements to create a helpful superstructure are

- **The table of contents (TOC):** After a lifetime of exposure to printed materials, we expect a TOC at the beginning of a document. (Is that so wrong?) Your garden-variety TOC lays out the document's topics and what those topics cover. Using the wonders of HTML, you can put hypertext in your TOC, and whisk users directly from any entry to the information it lists. Your TOC becomes not only a list of topics and an organizational map for your document, but also a convenient navigation tool! *Now* how much would you pay?

- **Common layout and navigation tools for all screens:** Imagine a book in which every page was a different shape, size, or color, and had to be turned in a different direction. (Hurts, doesn't it?) To promote readability and familiarity within your Web site, have mercy. Use layout and navigation tools that work the same wherever your reader finds them: icons to click, text links to accommodate nongraphical browsers, labeled buttons that take the reader forward, back, or to familiar territory (such as the TOC or to your home page). A common look and feel for your pages helps your users navigate. (Consistency may be "the last refuge for the unimaginative," but it does have its uses — save the imagination for your content.)

- **Index or search engine:** Helping users locate key words or individual topics helps them get the best use from your content. Another great aspect about hypertext is that an old-fashioned index may be unnecessary. Because your content is online and accessible to the computer, you can often replace an index with a built-in search engine for your Web pages.

If you include a search tool for keywords in your Web site, make the tool accessible from any document. Chapter 14 covers search engines, including tools to index your documents online.

✔ **A glossary helps manage specialized terms and language:** If you cover a subject that bristles with jargon, technical terms, or other arcane gibberish (beloved of experts and feared by newcomers), include a glossary with your Web pages. Fortunately, HTML includes a text style specifically built for defining terms, which, in turn, helps you to construct a glossary (beloved of beginners and feared by obfuscators) whenever you need one. You still have to come up with the definitions yourself — unless you can find a Web site with a glossary that you can link to your page — which is entirely possible (love that Web!).

Grabbing the audience where they live

Audience attention can be fickle, but countless methods exist for capturing it (some more humane than others). Movie fans may recall a classic bigger-is-better example: the standard demonstration of the THX theater sound system. First, a simple "THX" graphic fills the entire screen, lingering as a sustained orchestral chord (overlaid with a powerful pipe-organ note) starts quietly, builds to a peak over 20 seconds, hits like a jet fighter taking off overhead at 200+ mph, then fades away on a low pedal-tone that seems to sway the entire theater. Having raised the audience nearly out of its seats, the demonstration states coyly, "The audience is listening." (Gee . . . ya think?)

If you're like some advertisers and entertainers, you may yearn to grab your audience with all the subtlety and charm of a hungry T. Rex. But a great effect in a theater may not be feasible — or desirable — on the Web. A grand *ta-daa,* even if technically possible, has two potential drawbacks: Users may not appreciate what it does to their systems (speakers, screens, ears, whatever) and it overwhelms your content (oh, yeah, that . . .).

In fact, your readers have offered you at least some of their attention the moment they get a glimpse of your page. A kinder, gentler grab, if you do it well, can get them interested, get them oriented, and intrigue them enough that they'll want to stay and look around.

Nothing accomplishes a civilized grab as effectively as a tasteful image coupled with a brief, compelling introduction. Include information that tells why your page is important, what it contains, and how to navigate it.

They're after the goods . . . don't get in the way!

After you have your audience's attention, you have to help them find the real content. Make your superstructure visible enough to use but not so elaborate that it bogs down their interest. If you include hyperlinks that direct your visitors to more detailed information, make them few, obvious, and easy to distinguish from the rest of a page. A maze-of-the-month design, layout, or flow of information can hamper easy access to your content, and that can evaporate your visitors' interest.

To make content as accessible as possible, heed these Web design commandments:

- ✔ **Keep your welcome (home) page simple and elegant.**

- ✔ **Use short, direct sentences.**

- ✔ **Keep your focus on the topic(s) at hand.**

- ✔ **Use the superstructure to emphasize your content.**

- ✔ **Include a link to an "About This Site," "Site Overview," or "Site Map" page for those who want to understand the site's structure and function.**

What should your audience remember?

As amazing as the human mind is, it's always filtering information because its storage space is limited. People exposed to new concepts generally remember 10 percent of what they're exposed to — at best. (The wise Web page designer should remember 100 percent of *that* concept.)

Of course, paring down 100 ideas to 10 brilliant insights may not be all you need to do. Sad but true, most people also remember a limited amount of detail. If 10 percent of your concepts stick in your visitors' minds, don't assume they've absorbed 10 percent of your overall content. (So, your visitors are actually only remembering 10 percent of your most important 10 percent — ouch!) You have the best chance of creating a striking Web page (with a memorable 10 percent) if you apply the following principle: Strongly related concepts linger in memory far better than loosely linked or unrelated ones.

Your audience is human, too. Give 'em a break. How many of us can remember the details of 10 full pages out of a hundred in a document we have never seen before, and have looked at for less than an hour? (Show of hands? Anyone?)

As you design your Web documents, keep asking yourself, "Which 10 percent do I want my users to remember?" Use this question as a way to focus on the best 10 percent of your most important ideas. Be hard-nosed; not all of them will make the grade. Then plan to direct your audience's attention to the winners, reinforcing them throughout your Web pages. As with so much else in life, maintaining your focus is the key to successful communication.

Meet the Elements of Page Design

After you have a chance to get comfortable with the design concepts that build good Web pages, you're ready to examine and heft the parts of an HTML document. You may recognize some of these elements right away; they're integral parts of any well-written document. Other components that come with exotic names and concepts — such as hypertext links — are relative newcomers. All are basic building blocks that make up Web pages. After a look at each one, you get into how they affect the flow of information and can influence your choice of design elements.

Tags — they're it

You can always tell an HTML text file apart from an ordinary ASCII file: You see some snippets of its text enclosed in angle brackets (also called the less than, $<$, and greater than, $>$, signs). The snippets aren't for decoration but are the *tags* that make HTML work — and most of them travel in pairs that aren't quite identical. For example, the code that creates a document heading is set apart by two tags: $<h1>$ to mark where it starts and $</h1>$ to mark where it ends. That slash character in the second tag identifies it as an *end tag*. The tags are chunks of code that create an *element* — one of the major parts of your document's structure (such as headings in the case of the $<h1>$ . . .$</h1>$ tags).

After the elements are identified, you can use other tags that identify code chunks (called *attributes*) that help you tell your page how to do its job. For example, some attributes identify pointers that refer to data outside your Web page; others label information that has to be communicated back to a Web server; and others label the code that specifies how to display an on-screen object (for example, the alignment or dimensions of a logo or headline).

HTML tags vary in how many — and which — attributes they demand before they'll work. Some require you to specify particular attributes, and only those; others can take on optional attributes and values; still others abstain from attributes altogether. We let you in on which is which for each element of document design we present in this book; to do less wouldn't be sportsmanlike.

Certain special-purpose attributes provide the endpoints for those nifty links that your visitors will be using to zip around within your site and across documents. These must-have attributes are called *link anchors* (or *anchors,* for short). Link anchors describe the relationship between two named locations in the Web — the source and destination — and tell the system "Yep, that's a link." The endpoints can be in the same document, in different documents, or in different sites. (So, far as we know, they do have to be on the same planet.) See Chapter 13 for more information on links.

In HTML, you indicate the destination of a link by including a *document reference* (if you're linking to some other document), a *location reference* (if the link is closer to home, inside the same document), or a combination of the two (for a specific point inside another document). Chapters 8 and 13 give you a closer look at some linking examples.

Titles (when "this @*&# thing" just won't do)

A Web document isn't really finished till you call it something (preferably something printable) and can easily tell its parts, well, apart. That means a small exercise in creatively writing titles and labels.

Every self-respecting HTML document needs a *title* — not only to save it from anonymity, but also to serve some practical purposes on the Web:

- ✔ A title identifies the document to users. (You'd be surprised how easy it is to overlook the obvious; a title tells them what they're reading.)

- ✔ A title identifies your document in hotlists (or bookmarks), which makes it a navigation or selection tool for Web surfers who use the lists.

- ✔ A title constitutes the brief document description grabbed and spirited away by prowling robots (automated Web site search programs); a useful title makes the entries in search databases more accurate.

- ✔ A title helps you manage your documents, especially if they're complex and voluminous. Think of a title as a small investment that saves you vast amounts of frustration later.

- ✔ And last, but certainly not least, an HTML page without a `<title>` element is an invalid document.

After you title your Web document, at last it has something to put in the window's title bar after you open the document. As a sterling example, Figure 2-1 shows the window for an HTML Style Guide with the title `Style Guide for online hypertext` prominently displayed. (Well, okay, it may not be the most exciting title, but *Titanic* was taken.)

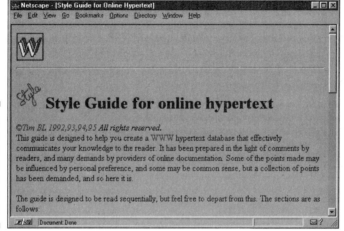

Figure 2-1:
The document's title shows up on the window's title bar.

Labels plain and fancy

Labels are small-scale, optional titles, or subtitles, if you will. We're not talking about the label element; we're talking about the attributes that add additional information to tags. For example, the `alt` attribute that is used with graphics and the `name` attribute used with links. Although labels aren't required, you may find that your document hangs together a lot better if you label (name) its parts. Labeling sections or topic areas in a document is a courtesy to your visitors. In fact, you can go one better if you use labels for links. Suddenly, a courtesy becomes an active navigation aid for users, which can help them feel welcome and encourage them to come back again.

Making a label into a link is pretty straightforward: You use a label's `name=` attribute inside an anchor tag, which directs an HTML link to a named section in your document — which could be the head of the document or another labeled part. Consider the following example:

```
<a name="Mexican Dove">Linda Paloma</a>
```

If you want to link to the `Linda Paloma` area of the document in which it appears, all you need to do is create an HTML link definition by using the anchor's `name` (in this case, `Mexican Dove`). Using an anchor this way also sends a signal to other browsers: If you point to me, refer to me by my anchor's `name` attribute. Simple means and rich results. See Chapter 13 for more information on the anchor tag.

Links: Text, hypertext, and hot

HTML is designed to keep certain vital operations simple — linking, for example. Only one kind of link is available — a one-way association between a source and a target. But you can use that one kind of link in four different ways:

- ✔ **Intradocument linking** moves you from one location to another inside the same document.

- ✔ **Interdocument linking** moves you from one document to another document.

- ✔ **Linking to an agent program** (a program that searches for information) that acts on behalf of the Web server gives your HTML document a way to handle a query or provide a service (such as information gathering).

- ✔ **Linking to a nontext object** gives you a royal road to multimedia, such as graphics, sounds, video, or The Next Big Thing (maybe a hungry T. Rex?).

If you link HTML files to other types of data (for example, sound, graphics, or motion video), suddenly you've done the next best thing to magic: You enable HTML's hypertext capabilities. (Shazam!) Before you know it, you're cooking up links all over the place — inside and outside your document, hooking up to agents, shooting out the electronic tendrils that are the look, feel, and power of the Web.

The world ain't flat; neither is text anymore

If you find it difficult to think about text in nonbook, nonmagazine, nonpaper terms, you're not alone. Although hypertext is an everyday wonder today, nobody imagined it 20 years ago. And even today most people think of *text* as inert words that just sit there, usually on paper, waiting to be read one page at a time. Why? The worldwide legacy of linear text goes back thousands of years, and the Web is still a relatively new phenomenon.

Books in their familiar form still have highly appropriate uses — consider (ahem) the one you're reading — but Web document designers, whether they know it or not, have to fight a nearly overwhelming tendency to make their documents read like books. If you want a truly forceful page, you must discover the ways of the Web and exploit the hypertext capabilities of HTML.

If your Web pages use freshly evolved cybercapabilities — such as multimedia displays and link navigation — in appealing and useful ways, then they not only meet the expectations of your users, but also extend the reach and impact of your content (whoa, there's that word again).

In the sections that follow, as you examine some common techniques for organizing Web documents, you also encounter a species of creature that's never existed before: documents that can exist only on the Web.

Stringing pages together the old-fashioned way

Some pages demand to be read in sequence; many are narratives that build on previous elements (you know — letters, novels, certain congressional reports). Such material lends itself to being strung together in the time-honored page-by-page way, as shown in Figure 2-2. Documents that run to five pages or more — if you believe Tim Berners-Lee in his *Style Guide for Online Hypertext* (which you can view at `www.w3.org/Provider/Style/All.html`) — should use a sequential structure anyway.

Figure 2-2:
Chain pages
together to
read them in
sequence.

But Style Guide for Online Hypertext hold on; here's where it gets intriguing. Hypertext gives you the option of chaining pages together forward *and* backward so that you can easily "turn" pages either way. Other links can make appropriate contributions to this basic structure (such as links to other HTML documents, a glossary, or other points inside your document) without disrupting that comfy, book-like feel.

Pulling rank in HTML hierarchies

If you use another ancient-but-serviceable tool and construct documents from an outline, you may be immediately drawn to arranging your links in a hierarchy. Most outlines start with major ideas, working their way down through levels of divisions that refine and elaborate the details of the content (aha! the C-word again) till, at last, you behold a complete plan of your work. (Well, at least the best ones do it that way.) Figure 2-3 shows a four-level document hierarchy that organizes an entire set of documents — perhaps even a whole Web site.

HTML itself places no limits on how many levels of hierarchies you can build; the only limit is how much complexity you (and your audience) feel you're ready and willing to handle. For both your sakes, keep it simple, Socrates.

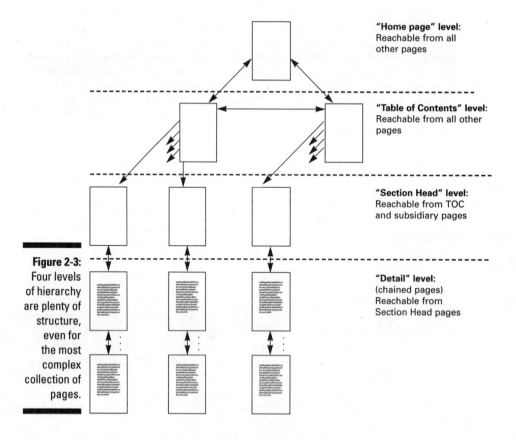

"Home page" level:
Reachable from all other pages

"Table of Contents" level:
Reachable from all other pages

"Section Head" level:
Reachable from TOC and subsidiary pages

"Detail" level:
(chained pages)
Reachable from Section Head pages

Figure 2-3:
Four levels of hierarchy are plenty of structure, even for the most complex collection of pages.

Multiple tracks for multiple audiences

It's more common these days for Web page designers to build documents that encompass different kinds of information to meet the needs of different audiences. HTML makes such an approach possible; you can easily interlink basic introductory documents (such as a tutorial or technical overview) with in-depth reference materials. Your home page can point beginners to a tutorial and lead them through an overview so that they're prepared for the acceleration after you blast them off into the details of your "real" content.

This kind of organization, depicted in Figure 2-4, lets you notify experienced users how to bypass introductory materials and access your in-depth content directly. Such an approach lets you design for multiple audiences without taking on tons of extra work.

The organization in Figure 2-4 departs from that shown earlier in Figures 2-2 and 2-3 — and maybe from that used for the last 500-or-so years. The organization emphasizes links between related documents more than it does the flow of pages within those documents. In fact, the kind of document pictured in Figure 2-4 would probably combine a linear and a hierarchical structure in its page flow. Users would read the tutorial from front to back (or at least a chapter at a time), but they would consult the reference section by topic (and only rarely read all the way through). Welcome to the early future.

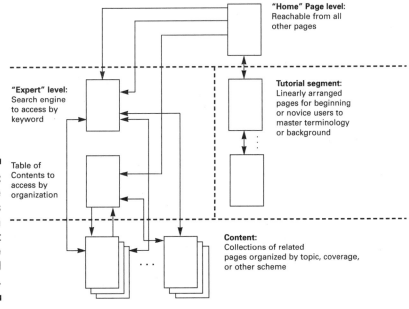

"Home" Page level:
Reachable from all other pages

"Expert" level:
Search engine to access by keyword

Tutorial segment:
Linearly arranged pages for beginning or novice users to master terminology or background

Table of Contents to access by organization

Figure 2-4: Multiple tracks through a document can serve several audiences.

Content:
Collections of related pages organized by topic, coverage, or other scheme

Web wonderland: "Hotlists" and "jump pages"

Some of the best resources we find on the Web are *hotlists* (also called *jump pages*) that are nothing more than lists of annotated references to other documents — with, of course, HTML capabilities. These lists usually relate to one or more specific topics. You can see this kind of document structure in Figure 2-5, which shows a single page that points to multiple pages in various locations. In this example, the picture fails to do justice to the concept. For a better illustration, we think you should open and look at a real Web page — and we just happen to have one handy (so to speak). Fire up your browser and check out the URL listed here: `http://alumni.caltech.edu/~dank/isdn/`. This site (Dan Kegel's collection of ISDN references) is one of the true "seven wonders" of the Web and is a stellar example of what a good hotlist can do!

Welcome back, my friends, to the page that never ends

A type of page that would be unlikely to survive outside the Web solicits input from users, who help create an open-ended document. Users contribute comments, additional text, and hypermedia, or they add to an ongoing narrative. The structure of such a document is hard to predict and, therefore, hard to *de*pict. Suffice it to say that this kind of Web document can grow like a coral colony, more by accretion than by organization or design. But hey, it's an organic experience.

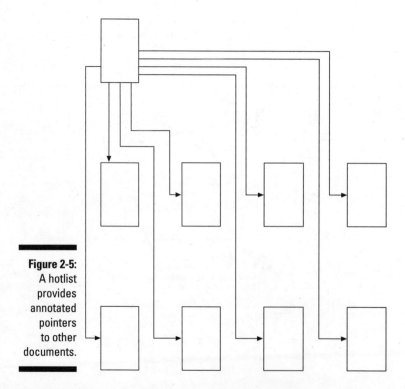

Figure 2-5:
A hotlist
provides
annotated
pointers
to other
documents.

For an example of an open-ended document, consult the following URL: `http://jefferson.village.virginia.edu/wax/`. Waxweb is a hypermedia implementation of a feature-length, independent film, *WAX or the discovery of television among the bees* (David Blair, 85:00, 1991). Waxweb is a large, hypermedia database available over the Internet. It features an authoring interface that lets users collaborate by adding onto the story. Waxweb includes thousands of individual elements, ranging from text to music, motion videos, and video transcriptions of motion picture clips. For users with VRML-capable browsers, Waxweb also offers a pretty nifty three-dimensional VRML implementation.

The only limitations on how you structure a document are those imposed by your need to communicate effectively with your audience. The rest is plumbing — the page-flow and organizational techniques we outline here. As soon as you're familiar with how to use the techniques we outline in this chapter to best effect, it's time to boldly go forth into the world of markup languages.

Chapter 3

Your First HTML Page

• •

In This Chapter

▶ Getting the right tool for the job

▶ Cranking up the Edit-Review cycle

▶ Tinkering with templates

▶ Bracing for what comes next (just kidding)

• •

*T*he deeper you get into the details and capabilities of HTML, the more you may be itching to go out and build a page of your own. This chapter helps you scratch that itch by guiding you through the mechanics of putting together a minimal, but working, HTML page.

An HTML file is basically a plain ASCII text file with a secret identity. Its powers come from special character sequences called markup, which separate the content (the stuff you want to impart to your audience) from the controls (the guides that tell your browser how to display that content). To review the basics of HTML, spin through Chapter 1.

Building good Web pages means understanding how they're put together in the first place and maintained thereafter. In this chapter, we describe creating the text, viewing it in a Web browser, making corrections or changes, and so on — a process we call the Edit-Review cycle. You don't need toe clips to use this particular cycle, but it is (to crank the metaphor) strictly hands-on. The exercises in this chapter should give you a good grip on the process.

Get the Right Tool for the Job

You can find a myriad of tools built specifically to help you create and manage HTML pages, but we think that a plain text editor does the job best. Nothing beats a plain-vanilla text editor for rapid post-creation tweaking or maintenance tasks. We recommend including the text editor of your preference in your HTML toolbox, even if you use a savvy HTML editor, such as Dreamweaver 3, HoTMetaL, HotDog, or FrontPage. Although we have many options available to us for building HTML pages, a plain text editor is still our tool of choice in most circumstances.

If you're reading this book, we assume that you're new to the HTML scene. We strongly suggest that you figure out HTML by using a text editor rather than an HTML editor. HTML editors provide so much help that you really don't find out about the code. See the sidebar in Appendix C to find out why we think it's important for you to know HTML.

For Mac users, SimpleText works well. For UNIX-heads, an ordinary text editor like *vi* is more than adequate for the task. For PC users, a text editor such as NotePad (or its burly cousin WordPad) does the job quite nicely. We base the examples we show in this chapter on the version of Notepad that ships with Windows 95/98 and Windows NT.

For more discussion of HTML tools, consult Appendix C. (The appendix includes a general tool discussion, lists of our personal favorites, plus separate sections for PC, Macintosh, and UNIX users.)

If you absolutely must use a word processor (such as Microsoft Word), be aware that most such programs do not produce plain-text files by default. That's why you have to remember to save any HTML files you create within your program as "text only" or "plain text" with a .html or .htm extension. And no fair using the built-in "Convert to HTML" option either. Word processors were not built to be HTML editors, and the code that they generate can be — to put it nicely — sloppy and icky. You're better off using your handy-dandy text editor and your own HTML knowledge instead.

The Edit-Review Cycle

The process of building an HTML file is cyclical. You start by typing some HTML markup and some plain old text into a file. When you're done typing, you save the file. Then you open the saved file within a Web browser. If you're like most of us, however, the process doesn't end there. When you see what you've wrought, you're likely to find something wrong with your HTML page. To err is human; to edit, even more so — whatever you may have missed, misspelled, or just plain don't like in your page-to-be, you can refine in three simple steps:

1. **Make some changes in the text editor.**

2. **Save the changes in the text editor.**

3. **Open (or refresh) the file in a Web browser to check your work.**

Repeat as often as needed — or until the dinner bell, or till wild horses drag you away from your work. Think we're kidding? (Well, yes, but this activity is habit-forming.)

Time has no meaning when you build or tweak Web pages. Be prepared to lose hours, days, and sometimes even months of your life!

Behold! We bring forth the basic text that any well-formed Web page needs to make it both viewable and legal. Type the following characters into your favorite text editor, and save the resulting file as `test.htm` or `test.html`:

```
<html>
<head>
<title>My very first Web Page!</title>
</head>
<body>
<h2>Daisy's Phone List</h2>
<ul>
   <li>Micky<br>
      555-2290<br><br>
   </li>
   <li>Minnie<br>
      555-1230<br><br>
   </li>
   <li>Donald<br>
      555-4476<br><br>
   </li>
   <li>Goofy<br>
      555-4455<br><br>
   </li>
</ul>
</body>
</html>
```

After you type this material and save the file as `test.html`, open your Web browser and choose File➪Open (in Internet Explorer, you can browse for a file on your hard drive from this option) or Open➪File (Netscape Navigator accepts a local filename here). Depending on the browser you're using, you should get some type of Open dialog box from which you can browse the contents of your computer to find the `test.html` file. Figure 3-1 shows what `test.html` looks like from Internet Explorer.

Notice also that we've typed our HTML using all lowercase letters. We've done this (and suggest that you do, too) because the newest version of HTML (Extensible HTML, or XHTML) is based on the Extensible Markup Language (XML), which requires that you use all lowercase tags.

For quick and easy access, you can type the full path and filename where you would normally enter a URL. In Internet Explorer, you type the path and file-name in the Address box. If you're using Netscape Navigator, you type the path and filename in the Location box.

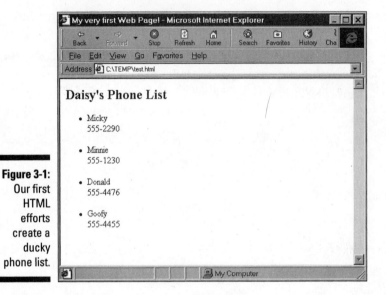

My very first Web Page! - Microsoft Internet Explorer

Back Forward Stop Refresh Home Search Favorites History Cha

File Edit View Go Favorites Help

Address C:\TEMP\test.html

Daisy's Phone List

- Micky
  555-2290

- Minnie
  555-1230

- Donald
  555-4476

- Goofy
  555-4455

My Computer

Figure 3-1:
Our first
HTML
efforts
create a
ducky
phone list.

The text that shows up in the browser's display window is a simple phone list, but don't let its simplicity fool you; a number of classic HTML features are visible. First, notice that the text between the `<title>` and `</title>` tags appears in the title bar at the top of the Internet Explorer window. Also, notice that one of the buttons on that toolbar is labeled "Refresh." From here on out, the Edit-Review cycle works like this:

1. **Switch to the text editor (or open the .htm or .html file you wish to edit). Make the changes you want to make.**

2. **Save the file in the text editor.**

3. **Switch to your Web browser and click the Refresh button.**

4. **Check your most recent efforts (visually and by running them through a validator); if further changes are necessary, go back to Step 1.**

See Chapter 8 for more information on validating your HTML documents.

Trust us, the Edit-Review cycle becomes very familiar, very soon. Even so, two of its steps are often overlooked: (a) saving the file after making changes in the text editor and (b) remembering to refresh the browser display so it shows the most recent version of the file. If you remember to do these things every time, the Edit-Review cycle becomes second nature as you create and maintain your Web pages.

Now to create a creature with a bit more substance, Igor. Return to your text editor, open a fresh document, and operate upon your document until it looks like this one:

```
<html>
<head>
<title>Home Page: The Institute of Silly Research
       (ISR)</title>
</head>
<body>
<h1>Welcome to the ISR!</h1>
The ISR is the world's best-known repository of truly
trifling and insignificant research results. Visit our
pages regularly to keep up with the exciting efforts of
our team of talented scholars, and their magnificent
efforts to extend the boundaries of science and
technology to ever more meaningless ends.
<h2>The ISR Staff</h2>
Dr. Maury Singleton-Smith, PhD, Director<br>
Dr. Gwyneth Gastropolis, PhD, Chief of Research<br>
Dr. Simon Schuster, MD, PhD, Head, Impracticality Dept.<br>
<h2>ISR's Current Projects</h2>
Beyond Charm and Strangeness: The Nerdon<br>
Lukewarm Fusion<br>
Harnessing the Power of Stilton Cheese<br>
The Dancing Louie Louie Masters<br>
<hr>
For more information about the ISR, please contact
<a href="mailto:NERDBOY@ISR.ORG">Dr. Singleton-Smith</a>.
All financial contributions are cheerfully accepted.
</body>
</html>
```

Okay, so you're not really happy about having to type all this text, but you will thank us. Typing the text, rather than cutting and pasting it, will help you *really* learn HTML.

After you type the text, you must save the file. You can save this file, for example, as isr.html. You should already have your Web browser of choice open. Switch to it and open your new file. Presented in full glory is your new HTML Web page. But, maybe you made a mistake. Back up for a second.

As you type the previous text (code), you may find yourself dealing with HTML mistakes (remember to enclose all tags within < and >, and to precede the text for closing tags with a /). You may also find yourself dealing with typos, omissions, and other kinds of content errors. Just remember: Each time you find an error, go back into your text editor, make the necessary changes, and save the file. When you return to your Web browser, refresh the page. You may then contemplate the results of your latest efforts. Keep editing and reviewing, and soon you shall have a page every bit as insignificant and meaningless as the one shown in Figure 3-2.

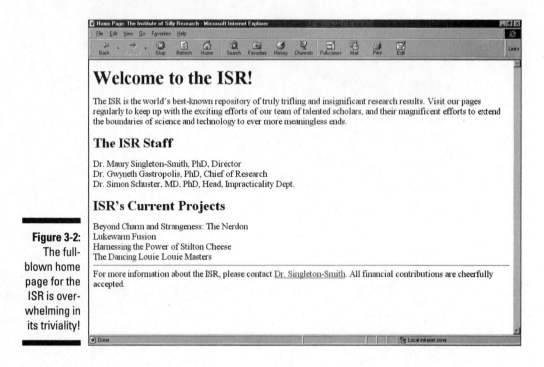

Figure 3-2:
The full-
blown home
page for the
ISR is over-
whelming in
its triviality!

(Hey, who said practice can't be fun?) The real point behind the exercise is to familiarize yourself with creating and editing an HTML document as you build a page to include on a Web site. As you get more adept at it, you can let good habits take care of these operational issues; then you're free to concentrate on the description and the content of your documents. By the time you create a few pages, this process should feel nearly as natural as working on paper.

Part II
Cranking Out Web Pages

The 5th Wave   By Rich Tennant

"It's a user-coercive search engine. When the user clicks the siphon icon, it installs a proprietary browser and collects the registration fee. Patching into the user's 401(k) was Bill's idea."

In this part . . .

In this part of the book, we describe the markup that makes Web pages possible. Next, we show you how ordinary text can be enriched and enlivened in an attractive Web-based presentation. Then, we explain how to add graphics to your pages to create more visual interest. Finally, we take you through some high-impact Web pages to show you just how hot HTML can sizzle!

Chapter 4

Cracking the (HTML) Code

- -

In This Chapter

▶ Scrutinizing HTML tag syntax

▶ Categorizing HTML tags

- -

*I*f you want a no-holds-barred look at HTML markup, you've come to the right place, pilgrim (imagine a John Wayne .WAV file here). In this chapter, we talk some serious turkey about HTML syntax to make sure that you can keep up with all the gory details. We also establish some categories for what HTML can do and group markup tags into meaningful categories (to make them easier to master and use).

So, buckle up, and hold on!

HTML Tags at a Glance

As we discuss in Part I, *HTML tags* are code words that tell a computer program, such as a Web browser or a word processor, how to format the text in an HTML document. When a Web browser or a word processor reads an HTML document, the program finds the formatting by watching for specific words and punctuation — the program assumes everything else is the actual text of your document.

Browsers and word processors assume that you remember the following rules of HTML syntax:

✔ Enclose tags in left and right angle brackets, like this:

```
<head>
```

✔ Tags usually come in *pairs*. For example, `<head>` marks the beginning of a document heading block, and `</head>` marks the end. (Note the use of the forward slash before the tag name. The forward slash tells the browser that this tag is closing.)

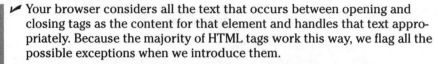

✔ Your browser considers all the text that occurs between opening and closing tags as the content for that element and handles that text appropriately. Because the majority of HTML tags work this way, we flag all the possible exceptions when we introduce them.

✔ Remember that a tag is just a tag; an element includes an opening and closing tag of a tag pair or an empty tag.

✔ HTML has no requirement for text to be uppercase or lowercase.

✔ However, future versions of HTML (such as Extensible HTML, or XHTML) will require tags in lowercase. For future compatibility, we encourage you to write code in lowercase.

✔ Tags can sometimes take attributes to

- Define data sources or destinations

- Specify URLs

- Further specify the characteristics of the text to which a tag is applied

✔ Remember that an attribute is a named characteristic associated with a specific tag.

For example, the `<img>` tag, which you use for placing graphics, can take the following attributes to specify the source and placement of an image on a page:

- `src=` is the source for an image (usually a URL).

- `alt="text"` causes the specified text to display if the browser doesn't show graphics.

- `align=` indicates placement of a graphic.

- `ismap` indicates that the graphic is a clickable image map with one or more links to other locations built onto the image. If it's absent, the image is not a map.

Some attributes take values — in the examples in the previous list, `src`, `alt`, and `align` each require at least one value — whereas others, such as `ismap`, do not. Attributes that don't require values are usually true ("turned on") if present and false ("turned off") when omitted. Also, tags may have default values for required attributes when the attributes are omitted, so be sure to check the HTML specification to determine how such defaults are handled.

At this point, you may already know quite a bit about HTML syntax and layout. But you need to know quite a bit of additional information, some of which we touch on in the preceding bulleted items. This additional material includes a discussion of some goofy characters that aren't part of HTML itself, but which are necessary to explain HTML formally.

Designating syntax conventions

Although we provide formal definitions of the various HTML commands, we use typographical notation in an equally formal way. What this means (in plain language) is that you better pay attention to how we write some things because we intend for the notation to describe how to combine, construct, and use terms.

Describing a formal syntax means using certain characters in a special way in order to show how to treat elements that appear in conjunction with these characters. The formal syntax is nearly identical to the following HTML rules:

- ✔ Angle brackets surround a tag (`<head>`).
- ✔ A forward slash following the left angle bracket denotes a closing tag (`</head>`).
- ✔ An ampersand leads off an entity (which is a character string that represents another string of characters), and a semicolon closes it (`&egrave;`).

For the complete rundown on entities, check out Chapter 12.

Abiding by the HTML rules

In addition to the formal syntax for HTML that we use throughout the book (for HTML is a very finicky language), the markup language itself has some general properties that are worth covering before you encounter the tags directly.

No embedded blanks, please!

All HTML tags require that the characters in a name be contiguous. You can't insert extra blanks within a tag or its surrounding markup without causing that tag to be ignored (which is what browsers do with tags they can't recognize).

This requirement means that `</head>` is a valid closing tag for a document heading, but that none of the following are legal:

```
< /head>
</ head>
</h ead>
</he ad>
</hea d>
</head >
```

We hope that you get the idea: Don't use blanks (spaces) inside tags, except where you use a blank deliberately to separate a tag name from an attribute name (for example, `<img src="sample.gif">` is legal, but `<imgsrc="sample.gif">` is not).

When assigning values to attributes, however, spaces are okay. Therefore, all four of the following variants for this `src` assignment are legal:

```
<img src="sample.gif">
<!-- Previous line: no spaces before or after = sign -->
<img src = "sample.gif">
<!-- Previous line: spaces before and after = sign -->
<img src= "sample.gif">
<!-- Previous line: no space before, one after = sign -->
<img src ="sample.gif">
<!-- Previous line: one space before, none after = sign -->
```

Where one space is legal, multiple spaces are legal. Don't get carried away with what's legal or not, though — try to make your HTML documents as readable as possible and everything else should flow naturally.

We sneaked more HTML markup into the preceding example. After each `<img>` tag line, we inserted readable HTML comments to describe what occurred on the preceding line. The HTML markup to open a comment is the string `<!--`, and the string `-->` ends the comment. As you go through the markup chapters later on in this book, we cover some style guidelines for using comments effectively and correctly.

What's the default?

If a tag can support an attribute, what happens when the attribute isn't present? For `ismap` on the `<img>` tag, for example, you already know that the `ismap` attribute being present means that *the image is a clickable map.* If `ismap` is absent, then *the image is not a clickable map.*

The preceding example is a way of introducing the concept of a *default,* which is not a way of assigning blame, but rather a way of deciding what to assume when some attribute is not supplied for a particular tag. For `ismap`, the default is absent; that is, an image is only assumed to be a clickable map when the `ismap` attribute is explicitly supplied.

But how do images get displayed if the `align` attribute isn't defined? As a quick bit of experimentation shows you, the default for most graphical browsers is to insert the graphic at the left-hand margin. These kinds of defaults are important, too, and we try to tell you what to expect from them as well.

The nesting instinct

Sometimes, inserting one set of markup tags within another is necessary. You may want a few words within a sentence already marked for special emphasis to be the trigger for a hyperlink. For example, the entire heading "Other Important Numbers: Emergency Phone Numbers" draws the readers' attention if it's rendered in boldface, but you only want the words *Emergency Phone Numbers* to be clickable and lead to another HTML document listing relevant emergency numbers.

Enclosing one set of markup within another is called *nesting*. When the nesting instinct strikes you, the best rule is to close first what you opened most recently. For example, the tags `<a href="ephone.html">` . . . `</a>` provide a way of bracketing text linking to another HTML document. If this phrase occurred within strongly emphasized text, `<strong>` . . . `</strong>`, there are two ways you could handle it. The incorrect way to handle this hyperlink is like so:

```
<strong>Other Important Numbers:
<a href="ephone.html">Emergency Phone Numbers</strong></a>
```

The correct way to handle the hyperlink is like so:

```
<strong>Other Important Numbers:
<a href="ephone.html">Emergency Phone Numbers</a></strong>
```

As shown, you close the nested `<a>` tag with its mate before you close out the `<strong>` tag. Some browsers may let you violate this rule, but others may behave unpredictably if you don't open and close tags in the right order. Figure 4-1 shows what this combination of tags looks like. (Notice that the words *Emergency Phone Numbers* are underlined.)

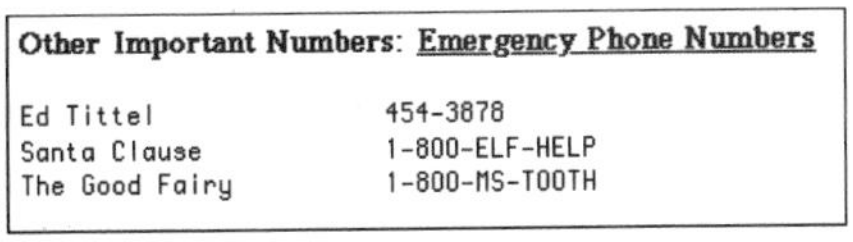

Figure 4-1:
Using
nested tags
to create a
hyperlink
within
strongly
emphasized
text.

Other Important Numbers: Emergency Phone Numbers
Ed Tittel   454-3878
Santa Clause   1-800-ELF-HELP
The Good Fairy   1-800-MS-TOOTH

Nesting just doesn't make sense for some tags. For example, within `<title>` . . . `</title>`, you deal with information that shows up only on a window title, rather than on a particular Web page. Text and layout controls clearly do not apply here (and are cheerfully ignored by some browsers, while making others curl up and die). Note that there are rules as to which tags can be nested within which tags. See the sections on the specific tags throughout this book for details.

Always look back to the left as you start closing tags you already opened. Close the closest one first, then the next closest, and so on. Check the tag details (later on in this book) to find out which tags you can nest within your outermost open tag. If the tag you want to use doesn't appear on the "okay" list, don't try to nest that tag inside the current open ones. Close out what you must close, and then open the tag you need.

Keeping your tags in the right nests keeps your readers' browsers from getting confused! It also makes sure that you hatch only good-looking Web pages.

Okay, you want to know about all these tags we keep twittering about. Gotcha covered:

✔ In most of the following chapters of this book, the chapter begins by introducing you to a group of tags; the rest of that chapter shows you how to spin them. If you read straight through from here to the end of the book, you'll cover the basic everyday stuff first, then the tricky stuff.

✔ Appendix A lists all of the standard HTML tags in alphabetical order. For each tag, we tell you what it does.

Categorizing HTML Tags

Before we take you through the HTML tags throughout this book, we want to introduce them to you grouped by category. These categories help to explain how and when you can use those tags and what functions those tags provide:

✔ **Text tags:** Text tags provide a logical structure for content. This structure may or may not alter that content's display properties. (See Chapter 10.)

✔ **Lists:** You use list tags to define a variety of different lists. (See Chapter 11.)

✔ **Tables:** Table tags define the structure and layout of tables. You can use tables to arrange data or to aid page layout and design. (See Chapter 14.)

✔ **Links:** Link tags create connections, such as hyperlinks, image links, and links to style sheets, between Web resources. (See Chapter 13.)

✔ **Inclusions:** You use these tags to include non-HTML objects, such as Java applets and multimedia files, within Web documents. (See Chapter 17.)

✔ **Style sheet tags:** These HTML elements define how the browser renders content. (See Chapter 18.)

✔ **Presentation tags:** Presentation tags alter the display of content by affecting properties such as font styles and horizontal rules. (See Chapter 9.)

✔ **Frames:** Frame tags define and control frames within the display area of a browser. (See Chapter 16.)

✔ **Forms:** Form tags control the input of data from a user and transmission of that data to a background Common Gateway Interface (CGI) or similar application. (See Chapter 17.)

✔ **Scripts:** You use these tags to embed programming language scripts into Web documents. (See Chapter 17.)

HTML tags give you power over your document at various levels, from managing its structure to controlling the look and feel of its text. In the next section, we take apart some HTML tags and lay them out on the workbench.

Getting the Rundown on Attributes

An attribute is a named characteristic associated with a specific tag. In HTML, attributes typically take one of two forms within a tag:

✔ attribute: Where the name itself provides information about how the tag should behave (for example, ismap in <img> indicates that the graphic is a clickable map). Also, tags may have default values for required attributes when the attributes are omitted.

✔ attribute="value": Where value is typically enclosed in quotes (" ") and may be one of the following kinds of elements:

- **URL:** A uniform resource locator

- **Name:** A user-supplied name, probably for an input field

- **Number:** A user-supplied numeric value

- **Text:** User-supplied text

- **Server:** Server-dependent name (for example, page name defaults)

- **X or Y or Z:** One member of a set of fixed values

- **#rrggbb:** Hexadecimal color notation for a color value

We discuss attributes for individual tags in a section under the tag name. For each one, we provide a definition. We also indicate choices for predefined sets of values or provide an example for open-ended value assignments. In addition, the W3C has kindly provided information about the case-sensitivity to which attribute values are subject. We represent this case sensitivity as follows:

- ✔ [CS]: The value is case sensitive; therefore, browsers interpret "a" and "A" differently.

- ✔ [CI]: The value is case insensitive; therefore, browsers see "a" and "A" as identical.

- ✔ [CN]: The value is not subject to case, because it's a number or a character from the document character set.

- ✔ [CA]: The attribute definition itself conveys case information.

- ✔ [CT]: Consult the type definition in the DTD for details about case sensitivity.

However, there are some commonalities that we think you should be aware of. We list three sets of common attributes for more than 60 percent of all the HTML tags, along with a brief description, to save a few trees and to avoid being redundant. All of these attributes have *implied values,* which means that you don't have to actually list them in your tags unless you want to change those implied values. For example, the implied value for the dir attribute is ltr, which stands for "left to right," the direction the tag and its contents will be read. If, for some reason, you wanted to change the value to rtl ("right to left"), then you would need to include the attribute and that value.

Here are the three sets of attributes (which we explain in more detail immediately afterward):

- ✔ **Core attributes** apply to all HTML tags, without exception. Core attributes provide several ways to label a tag and its content uniquely and to define style information directly to that tag's content.

- ✔ **Language attributes,** which are known in the HTML Document Type Definition (DTD) as i18n attributes, provide ways to associate a specific language code with a tag, and even the direction in which to read the tag's contents (right to left or left to right). Search the W3C site, http://search.w3.org/Public/, for i18n attributes for more information.

- ✔ **Event attributes** name specific events that scripts and programs must recognize and respond to on a Web page (for example onmouseover names the event that occurs when a mouse cursor travels over a specific object onscreen).

Core attributes

HTML's core attributes provide information to help identify, label, or control that tag's contents. These attributes apply to all HTML tags:

- ✔ `id="name"`: A document-wide identifier that you can use to give an HTML element a unique identifier within a document.

- ✔ `class="text"`: A comma-separated list of class names that indicates that the element belongs to a specific class or classes; the most common use for classifying elements is to apply style definitions to them selectively.

- ✔ `style="text"`: Provides rendering information specific to this element, such as the color, size, and font specifics.

- ✔ `title="text"`: Defines an advisory title to display additional help. You can generate balloon text around hyperlinks and graphics using this attribute.

Language attributes

HTML's language attributes apply to most tags (especially those that can contain text inside them) to identify the language in which they appear and to instruct programs or robots in what direction to read a tag's content. By default, the language setting (and its default direction) from the HTML prolog for the document applies here, if these tags are not used — and they seldom are!

- ✔ `dir="LTR"` or `"RTL"`: Indicates the direction the text will be read in — left to right or right to left

- ✔ `lang="name"`: Specifies the language that the element and its contents are written in

Event attributes

The designers of HTML 4.01 included numerous intricate event triggers to support programming and scripting on Web pages. Basically, when an event, such as an `onmouseover`, is tied to an HTML tag it causes a script to run without needing a hyperlink. The user simply performs the event, such as moving a mouse over a tag with the `onmouseover` attribute, and the script is automatically called.

Because you may see intrinsic events listed for many of the tags, we want to warn you ahead of time that events are scripting related. A quick look at intrinsic events shows that:

- You can use the `onreset` and `onsubmit` intrinsic events with the following markup tag: `<form>`.

- You can use the `onload` and `onunload` intrinsic events with the following markup tags: `<frameset>` and `<body>`.

- You can use the `onchange` and `onselect` intrinsic events with the following markup tags: `<input>`, `<select>`, and `<textarea>`.

- You can use the `onblur` and `onfocus` intrinsic events with the following markup tags: `<button>`, `<input>`, `<label>`, `<select>`, and `<textarea>`.

- You can use the `onclick`, `ondblclick`, `onkeydown`, `onkeypress`, `onkeyup`, `onmousedown`, `onmousemove`, `onmouseout`, `onmouseover`, and `onmouseup` intrinsic events with the following markup tags:

```
<a>, <abbr>, <address>, <b>, <big>, <blockquote>, <body>,
<button>, <caption>, <center>, <cite>, <code>, <col>,
<colgroup>, <dd>, <del>, <dfn>, <dir>, <div>, <dl>, <dt>,
<em>, <fieldset>, <form>, <h*>, <hr>, <i>, <img>, <input>,
<ins>, <kbd>, <label>, <legend>, <li>, <link>, <menu>,
<object>, <ol>, <option>, <p>, <pre>, <q>, <s>, <samp>,
<select>, <small>, <span>, <strike>, <strong>, <sub>, <sup>,
<table>, <tbody>, <td>, <textarea>, <tfoot>, <th>, <thead>,
<tr>, <tt>, <u>, <ul>, and <var>.
```

Knowing a lot about intrinsic events keeps you busy for a while. This cool technology helps you add interactivity to Web pages in a relatively simple way and is well worth exploring after you get your feet firmly planted in HTML land. Note that some browsers, namely Netscape, only support a small portion of intrinsic events.

As you examine HTML tags, including attributes, you find that some (the `align` attribute, for example) are *deprecated* — earmarked to be left for dead by future versions of HTML. Coders will have to use style sheet properties to achieve the same effects. We cover style sheet properties in Chapter 18. As always, obsolescence is the cruel-but-just law of the cyber-jungle.

Rather than include code snippets and screen shots, we thought you might like to see HTML at work for yourself. So we included some sample code for every tag, and for attributes where possible, on the CD-ROM. Using your browser, just open the file list under the "Examples" section to see how tag information is rendered. To view the HTML, choose View Source in your browser or open the .HTM file with a text editor. As you read each chapter, you'll be able to identify the examples you want to see.

There's an X in Your Future: XHTML!

The up-and-coming version of HTML has an X in front of it. As we write this book, a replacement for HTML, called XHTML, has been released. In this case, the X stands for XML, and the official designation for this language is "A Reformulation of HTML 4.0 in XML 1.0." You can read more about this work at the W3's page dedicated to the "latest version of HTML" at www.w3.org/MarkUp/.

Basically, XHTML represents the translation and cleanup of HTML markup into an XML-based equivalent. The idea is to maintain the current HTML 4.01 vocabulary of markup tags, but to recast those tags in a more regular and predictable form. Ultimately, this new version is supposed to make everybody's lives easier because XML is much more computer- and Internet-friendly than HTML. For more details on XHTML, and how to switch between HTML and XHTML, please consult Chapter 19.

Chapter 5

Text Pages Are Tried and True

● ●

In This Chapter

▶ Tooling up a document for the first time

▶ Putting templates to work for you

▶ Starting page layout at the top

▶ Writing titles and headings with a purpose

▶ Building better bodies for your pages

▶ Fortifying your paragraphs

▶ Giving your lists the proper structures

▶ Linking to your Web site and beyond

● ●

*B*uilding your first Web page is exciting if you keep this thought firmly in mind: *You can change anything at any time; good Web pages always evolve.* Change is just a keystroke away; nothing is cast in concrete (good thing, too — concrete is murder on a keyboard).

The pressure's off; you can build your own simple, but complete, Web page. Think of it as a prototype for future pages. You can always go back to it later and add bells, whistles, or hungry T. Rexes. You can add whatever's needed to make your Web page the one you want — whether for a business, an academic institution, or a government agency.

Your *look and feel,* which is the way the page looks to the user, combined with your king-sized content, is how your site creates its all-important first impression. The first time a user visits an ugly page with little or no useful content may also be the last time. A Web page is one place where looks and guts matter — fortunately, HTML gives you a way to describe your content so that it looks great in any Web browser.

Remember that the Web itself is a confusing concept to many users. Your Web pages can be pleasing to the eye — and an oasis of clarity — if you follow the KISS approach (Keep It Simple, Sillyhead!). Everything you can do to make your page "intuitively obvious" to a visitor — and keep it that way — makes your viewers happier and keeps them coming back for more.

Chapter 2 presents the basic concepts for a good Web page. It emphasizes efficient form and (especially) worthwhile content over sheer HTML prowess — and brushing up on page layout and information flow before you forge ahead into the nuts and bolts of HTML never hurts. If you used Chapter 3 to create a quickie Web page, revisit your creation with an eye toward using what you discover in this chapter to improve it.

The basics of good Web page design are content, layout, first impression, and KISS (Keep It Simple, Sillyhead!). Be ye mindful of them, and yea, they shall bring you contentment and your visitors, enlightenment.

Templates Build Strong Bones

After you nose around the Web long enough to get a look at some actual Web pages, you probably notice two things about them right away:

✔ Most well-constructed examples of the species contain the following basic elements in some form: *title, heading, body,* and *footer.* (Don't get the title and body basic elements confused with the `<title>` and `<body>` HTML elements in this context.)

✔ Web pages that lack one or more of those basic elements have an uncanny way of frustrating the visitor and inviting a quick departure.

Centuries of print media have predisposed us to look for certain familiar elements of good construction; Web pages that lack them are neither pleasing to the eye nor intuitive to use. Don't let that happen to your work — use this basic template for each HTML document you produce:

```
<html>
<head>
 <title>Your Title</title>
</head>
<body>
<p>
 Your headings and wonderful text and graphics
 go here.
</p>
<address>
 Copyright &copy; 2000, Your Name <br>
 Revised: Revision Date <br>
 URL: <a href = "http://this.page's.url.here">
     http://this.page's.url.here</a>
</address>
</body>
</html>
```

(Note that in this example we use the ⟨address⟩ . . . ⟨/address⟩ tags to create our footer. See the "Finishing with Footers" section later in this chapter for details.)

Starting down the path of enlightenment is really that simple: This template actually works. Figure 5-1 shows what it looks like when viewed with Internet Explorer.

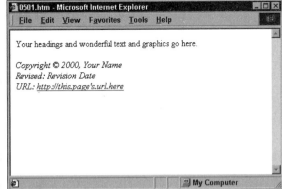

Figure 5-1:
By itself,
a page
template
doesn't look
like much!

Figure 5-1 shows how this particular bit of HTML looks in Internet Explorer 5.0 on a PC running Windows 98 with particular settings. It may look a little different in Internet Explorer on another PC running Windows 98 because no two users' settings are exactly the same.

The bottom line is that no Web page is ever displayed *exactly* the same way from browser to browser and computer to computer. The browser type and version, operating system, and particular user settings all affect the final display of the HTML in the Web browser. These factors mean that you, as the page designer, never have total control over the final look and feel of your Web page for each individual user.

Don't panic! Remember that HTML is a markup language, not a formatting language, and as long as you use it correctly and consistently, your pages will look good in any browser. Coincidentally — NOT! — this book teaches you all you need to know to create pages that look great anywhere.

In case you need a discreet refresher, here's how to view local pages within your browser:

1. **Launch your Web browser.**

2. **Choose File⇨Open (or Open Page, or something similar).**

3. **Navigate through the folders and files on your hard drive until you find the HTML page you want to view.**

   To make it easy to find your HTML files — especially if your disks are as full and cluttered as ours — we recommend that you save all your Web documents in one top-level folder named "Web Docs," "HTML Pages," or another intuitive title.

If you use Navigator, remember to set memory and disk caches to zero so Navigator reloads each new version of your file from the disk, instead of loading from its cache. Other browsers cache pages, too, so be sure to read what you edited — not some older version! When in doubt, click the Reload or Refresh button.

As you can see, this home page is plain and simple — sturdy bones, but not much plumage. It may not cause folks to flock to see it, but that's where your own killer text and understated-but-elegant graphics come in. Although the browsers that most Web surfers use have some form of graphical user interface (GUI), take another look at Chapter 2 before you add that way-cool animated pterodactyl — first and foremost, put your creative energy into high-quality *content*. After you have that, see Chapter 6 for how to add graphics to your Web page (animated flying things are always optional).

Page Layout from Top to Bottom

After you have a basic template, you can start to enhance it. To begin the fun, make sure that your first Web page doesn't occupy more than a single screen. This size limit makes a page much easier to edit and test. You can get more than enough information on a single screen and help your audience avoid unnecessary scrolling, all at the same time.

A *single screen* seems like an easy concept, but is it? A single screen is how much information a browser can display on a monitor without scrolling. We've all seen the message on movie videotapes that says "Formatted to fit your screen." Well, we still haven't figured out how they know how big every screen is, so until we do, this amount varies because not all browsers — or monitors — are created equal. Your users may be running quite an equipment menagerie. Though these differences don't require you to design for lowest-common-denominator systems, we *can* tell you how to avoid one monster mistake: *Don't assume that your users see your page the same way you see it in* your *browser.*

Testing your pages at relatively low resolution (640 x 480 pixels) with several different browsers can help you see your pages through your users' eyes. Getting this view is well worth taking the extra time! Each operating system has a specific way to set monitor resolution. To find out how to set yours, consult your operating system's help file or manual.

You may find it helpful to sketch your design ideas on paper first, or to use a drawing program to create a model of your layout and components. Figure 5-2 offers one such model, showing not only the spatial relationships on the page but also the amounts and locations of the essential breathing room that page designers call *white space*. Although you can leave too much white space on a page, most designers err in the other direction and wind up with far too little, which makes their pages appear cramped and cluttered.

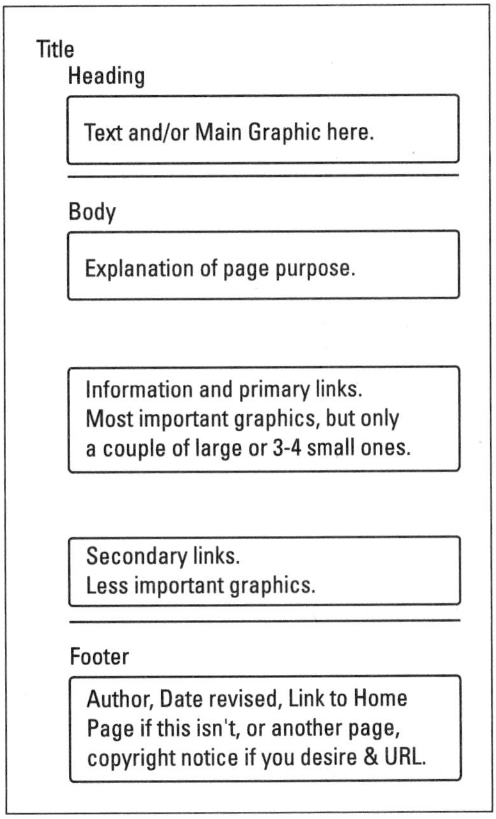

Title
 Heading

┌─────────────────────────────────────┐
│ Text and/or Main Graphic here. │
└─────────────────────────────────────┘

 Body

┌─────────────────────────────────────┐
│ Explanation of page purpose. │
└─────────────────────────────────────┘

┌─────────────────────────────────────┐
│ Information and primary links. │
│ Most important graphics, but only │
│ a couple of large or 3-4 small ones. │
└─────────────────────────────────────┘

┌─────────────────────────────────────┐
│ Secondary links. │
│ Less important graphics. │
└─────────────────────────────────────┘

 Footer

┌─────────────────────────────────────┐
│ Author, Date revised, Link to Home │
│ Page if this isn't, or another page, │
│ copyright notice if you desire & URL.│
└─────────────────────────────────────┘

Figure 5-2: A sketch of basic Web page layout, including white space.

Organize your page so that your viewers can scan through its content quickly and easily:

 ✔ Start with the most important information near the top, in large type, surrounded by plenty of white space.

 ✔ Follow with the less earth-shaking items.

Good page design isn't a space-filling contest. You're trying to hit the highlights and invite closer examination — usually of no more than one topic per page. If you have lots of material or more topics to cover, you can easily make more pages and link them to this one. One good rule comes from professional presenters: *A single slide (or, in this case, screen) should try to convey no more than three to five pieces of related information.*

Rarely will you create a stand-alone Web page; instead, you'll create a group of pages that — when combined — creates an entire Web site. Links are the glue that interconnects a collection of Web pages. Find out more about links in Chapter 13.

What's in a Name? That's Up to You

You normally don't see Web pages titled "Untitled" (or "The page formerly known as . . .," which is almost as bad) for a reason. HTML files use their titles to give search engines (Yahoo!, Excite, AltaVista, and so on) something to grab and put in an index. For indexing purposes, make sure your title contains the most important information a user needs to know about your Web site, distilled to short-but-sweet. After the title piques your visitors' interest and ushers them into your Web site, document headings show them around.

HTML styles, or the users' browser settings, determine the font, page size, and length of line your users see on-screen. Despite the range of possible browsers and monitors, you still have some say-so over the first impression your page makes. With appropriate content and layout, you can make your pages' titles and headings attractive and informative.

To find out all you ever wanted to know — and more — about the markup associated with titles and headings, look at Chapter 8.

Titles — bait the hook with something juicy

Think of your Web page's title as a sort of electronic fishing lure. Many Web indexing search engines — the software robots that relentlessly cruise the Web in search of information — use titles to create index records in *their* databases, pointing the way to *your* pages. Also, most browsers use titles in the name fields of their *hotlist* or *bookmark* sections, which collect URLs that users want to revisit. That means the software robots use your titles to figure out what's on your pages.

Because you want people to find and read your pages, make your titles as concise and descriptive as possible. Try to fit your title on no more than a single line; use an arresting arrangement of keywords to describe the contents of your page (knowing your content thoroughly helps).

Start with the simple stuff: Type a short list of keywords that describe your page best. Then use them in a sentence. Next, delete all conjunctions, adverbs, and unnecessary adjectives. With a little rearranging, what's left should be a pretty good title. Here's an example of constructing a title:

- ✔ **Words:** George, classical guitar player, bicycle racing.
- ✔ **Sentence:** George is a classical guitarist who races bicycles.
- ✔ **Title:** George's classical guitar and bike racing page.

The following shows what this title looks like with some markup around it to describe it as a title:

```
<html>
<head>
  <title>George's classical guitar and bike racing
            page</title>
</head>
...
</html>
```

This title should fit on one line when viewed by most browsers. Test it with several browsers to see how it looks. If it's too long, shorten it!

Web browsers display the content between the `<title>` . . . `</title>` tags in the window's title bar, not at the top of the page as you may expect. Don't panic when you add a title to your document and don't see it appear automatically on the page. Look to the top of your browser window to see it instead.

Headings — here's the beef

Headings are actually a family of specialized critters, some more immediately visible than others. Every Web page needs a *heading section* after its title and various *paragraph headings* within the body of the document. In the print world — for example, in this book — headings take the form of emphasized text that appears just before particular paragraphs. So while we're at it, a closer look at them is in order.

Headings, along with the title, are the most important text in your Web page. They are the first text that users notice. If headings aren't attractive and instantly informative, users may jump to another page with a single click. Well-written headings hook readers and make them want more.

As with the other parts of your Web page, concentrate on content first. Make sure that your headings exhibit consistent, meaningful ties to the paragraphs they introduce, and that they do so throughout your pages. As you mull over and analyze your content, ideas for headings should arise naturally. If they don't, a fresh outline of your content may be just what the doctor ordered.

The neutron-bomb test

A good, strong heading should paraphrase any important concept that you plan to present. If you were to blast all other text out of your document, leaving only the headings, you should be left with a good outline or a detailed table of contents. (Coincidence? We think not.)

If the situation permits, you can make headings humorous and/or refer to a common theme to help catch users' eyes and interest. Try the neutron-bomb test here, too: It's okay if the outline you're left with is entertaining, but does it still do its job? (Well, okay, we admit to using this approach with the headings in this book; it's one ambitious goal of the whole *For Dummies* series.)

A time-honored principle of acting applies here: *Dying is easy; comedy is hard.* Your visitors may have a wide range of funny bones; not all of them may respond to the same stuff. Whether zingers or duds, headings work best if you *use your imagination but keep your audience in mind.*

As a quick and (ahem) modest example, Table 5-1 shows some of the headings from this book in "plain" and "humorous/theme" forms.

Table 5-1	Headings: Plain versus Extra-Crunchy
Plain	*A Bit More Interesting*
Building Documents	Building Better Document Bodies
Building Paragraphs	Building Strong Paragraphs Six Ways
Logos and Icons	Eye-Catchers: Logos, Icons, and Other Gems

Web pages give you some creative space, but not an unlimited amount. You have only a few headings per screen or page; make them count. Keep the structure (and the outline level) of similar headings consistent throughout your pages to help keep your users oriented. Although most browsers recognize at least four levels of headings, most well constructed Web pages use no more than three levels, even for long documents. (Three is a classic "just-right" number — ever hear of a story called *Goldilocks and the Five Bears?* We haven't, either.)

The design-versus-information squabble

As you create headings and assign them levels of importance, you run into two schools of thought about the best way to use them:

✔ **The information school** pontificates that *heading tags should be used in increments or decrements of one and always start with heading 1* (<h1>). This approach gives your content an ordered, standardized structure and makes it easy for Web crawlers to pick out headings for their indexes. This is a practical, logical, dependable approach, which is typically used for informative articles.

✔ **The design school** takes one look at the practical approach and screams, "BORING!" Design advocates want to *use headings to draw attention to content.* For example, putting an <h1> next to an <h3> or an <h4> creates visual interest. This is a wild-eyed, iconoclastic approach, which is typically used for advertisements.

As with most design decisions, the choice is yours. Experiment with heading tags until you arrive at a combination that looks good, tells it like it is, and accurately reflects the mood and purpose of your page.

Too much emphasized text diminishes the overall effect. Use it sparingly — emphasis works better when it remains exceptional. Using too many headings is like crying *wolf!* And look, there's another one! And another one!

Building Better Document Bodies

The *body* of an HTML document is the core of a Web page. It stands between the header and the footer. What you put in the body (its *content*) depends on the type and amount of information you want to put online — and on the audience you want to reach.

Personal Web pages are generally quite different from their business, academic, or government cousins. The most striking differences are in the content and form of their bodies, although the layout for each type may be strikingly similar. The bodies of most personal Web pages contain text for, or pointers to, the following elements:

✔ **Résumé:** Mostly dense text with a picture

✔ **Personal history:** Mostly plain text

✔ **Favorite sports or hobbies:** Text with an occasional picture and links to sports or hobby sites

✔ **Favorite Web sites:** Lists of links to Web sites

Pretty good, as far as it goes. But if you want to do business with that page, it needs some judicious editing and restructuring with the market in mind. Take, for example, the bodies of a commercial artist's Web pages:

✔ **Pictures, pictures, pictures:** Usually small thumbnail-size pictures that link to much larger versions

✔ **Credentials:** A page containing a résumé or a list of shows and exhibits, awards, and other professional activities

✔ **Professional references:** Links to online samples of work on other pages

Government pages are yet another species, often using text in a characteristic fashion (think of an anaconda that's swallowed an elephant). Many of these documents are simply HTML reproductions of long text originals. Some are 100 screens long or more. (Who knows? We may yet see a Virtual Paperwork Reduction Act . . . well, maybe next century.)

Fortunately, you won't need a 200-year life span to download what you need off these pages. Some government Webmasters provide a brief description of their text files along with FTP hyperlinks so you can download such monsters without reading through them on-screen.

The more scrolling required, the slower the experience of reading your Web page becomes. Lots and lots of scrolling means *too much text, already!* and your users may fly away to less wordy climates. It's even been said that 90 percent of scrollable pages never get scrolled. Ouch!

So, how much text is enough, but not too much, to put in the body of your page? The answer, my friend, is blowin' in the minds of your viewers. The better you know their needs and interests (not to say attention spans), the better you can gauge how much text to offer them.

How much text is okay?

If you've ever transcribed someone else's dictation, you know that even five minutes' worth of speaking equals quite a stack of paper. If you can feel the white space shrinking as you work on your Web page, beware: When most Web surfers want to read pages and pages of dense text, they buy the book or download the file and print it. They don't hang around online with the meter running.

Online reading, almost by definition, means keeping your online writing suc-cinct. Many users (especially those who dial in with slower connections) view great globs of text as a waste of bandwidth. Not that your Web pages have to be as hit-and-run as those 30-second video bites that sell beer during the Super Bowl. But a little realism can't hurt: At the current level of Web development, most users are looking for fast ways to find the information they want. They aren't going to dig down through too many strata of text to find it. Your job is to give your readers the fast track to the meat in your pages. Help them cut to the chase by using an appropriate page layout — lean, informative text; and a considerate use of tools such as indexes with hypermedia links.

Composition is a balancing act

The Web-page equivalent of the body beautiful should contain three to five short, well-written paragraphs. Now imagine, if you will, these paragraphs interspersed with moderate-sized headings, enough white space for breath-ing room, and small graphics to add visual interest. *Readers will probably scan them in their entirety.* And love it.

Judicious use of separators and numerous links to other (relevant!) pages can also give your page design more bang for the buck. The idea is to put nothing on your page that doesn't belong there; the result should be a page that's between one and three full screens long. More may be technically possible, but that doesn't always mean *commonly* possible. Hardly anybody has a 33-inch, high-resolution monitor (or a flying car) yet, and both are likely to stay scarce for quite a while.

Pruning leggy pages

Web page benchmark: For any given page, you should be able to count the screens of text on the fingers of one hand. A page that runs to more than five screens of text (or, for that matter, five screens of URL link lists) can bog down your reader's attention. Split it into multiple pages. If your content fero-ciously resists being served in short pages, you can still make a long page readable. Try linking a table of contents (TOC) to each section of the page and providing a link back to the beginning of the page from each section. (If your visitor can travel conveniently, the distance won't seem as long.)

This linking structure does add some structural complexity (it's similar to split-ting a page into multiple files), and it also offers two considerable advantages:

- ✔ Your readers can capture the document as a single file.
- ✔ The HTML file becomes easier to edit.

You want to balance your convenience (as the page's creator) against the penalty (from the user's point of view) of moving a single large chunk of data — moving it takes time! Links add to a page's usability, but (as with all the parts of a Web page) don't overdo it.

Once again, dear friends, we've reached that risky borderland between content and controls (links to other pages can count as both, especially if you're building a longish Web page). When you have a lot of content, make it approachable by including effective controls and only essential ones. If you want your page to rock, *content is King* (thank ya vurry much).

See Chapter 13 for more information on linking pages and for a good example of a TOC in action, check out the W3C HTML 4 Specification site at `www.w3.org/TR/html4/#minitoc`.

The bottom line on page bodies

The rules for creating great Web page bodies are simple and wondrous to behold:

- ✔ Keep layouts consistent to provide continuity for users.
- ✔ Provide plenty of white space and headings for easy scanning.
- ✔ Write short paragraphs and use them sparingly.
- ✔ Use meaningful graphics, but only when absolutely necessary.
- ✔ Make liberal use of hypertext links to additional pages, instead of making your audience scroll, scroll, scroll.
- ✔ Vary the placement of hyperlink words to provide more visual contrast on the page.
- ✔ Write meaningful hyperlink text, not *Click here*. (When confronted with a *Click here*, have you ever thought *Oh, yeah? Why should I?* More on this topic later.)

Building Strong Paragraphs

Web users demand the clearest, most concise text you can muster. Alas, not everyone on the Web is an English professor. For many folks, grammar was a heavy and dolorous subject (and English class was like doing pull-ups in concrete sneakers). Many have never heard of *The Elements of Style* (a slim volume by William Strunk, Jr. and E. B. White) that has eased the pain of writing for generations of students. Nonetheless, two timeless Strunk and White prescriptions are especially healthful for Web page text:

✔ **Omit needless words.** Doing so doesn't mean getting rid of all the details. Just scrutinize your paragraphs and ask, *What can I throw out?*

✔ **Make the paragraph the unit of composition.** Writing one paragraph at a time means not getting stuck on a particular sentence or struggling to turn out a whole page at a time. Often a single paragraph is easier to subdue.

All Web surfers must read *some* language — whether Sanskrit, Mandarin, or High Computerese — and clarity promotes accurate communication, whatever the lingo. To this end, follow these eight steps to build better paragraphs:

1. **Create an outline for your information. See Chapter 2 for more info on outlines.**

2. **Write one paragraph for each significant point; keep the sentences short, direct, and to the point.**

3. **Edit your text mercilessly, omitting all needless words and sentences.**

4. **Proofread and spell check.**

5. **Check your page on a variety of hardware and software setups.**

6. **Ask for volunteers to evaluate your work.**

7. **Revise your text, and then re-edit it as you revise it.**

8. **Solicit comments when you publish online.**

   To find out all you ever wanted to know about soliciting reader response, turn to Chapter 17.

Listward, Ho! Using Lists Online

Provided you don't lose them, lists can be useful (laundry, grocery, mailing) or entertaining (how about those "top-ten lists" on late-night TV?). They're also a simple, effective way to call your viewer's attention to specific items on your Web page.

The most commonly used list structure, the *unordered list*, is actually a lot more ordered than a jumble of vaguely related facts. It implies that several ideas are related without having to assign them a rank or a rigid level of priority (as *numbered lists* normally do). You may know the unordered list by its other name, the *bulleted list*.

A bulleted list is handy for emphasizing several short lines of information. The following shows HTML markup for an unordered list (displayed with Navigator in Figure 5-3).

```
<ul>
<li> This is noticed.</li>
<li> So is this.</li>
<li> And so is this.</li>
</ul>
```

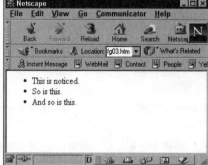

Figure 5-3:
An
unordered
list viewed
with
Navigator.

The following HTML fragment shows the tags for an unordered list in a Web page body. The list serves to emphasize and separate the text lines.

```
You have reached the <i>HTML For Dummies</i> Web Pages,
a charming, and hopefully helpful, addition to the WWW
universe. These pages are designed to aid you in three
key areas:<br>
<ul>
<li> To help you find current information on the Web
 about HTML</li>
<li> To provide working examples and code for all the
 Web tricks in the book</li>
<li> To introduce <i>HTML For Dummies</i> - your
 friendliest resource for HTML material offline!</li>
</ul>
```

Figure 5-4 shows how this text displays in Internet Explorer. The bulleted list definitely emphasizes the body and adds to the visual appeal of the page.

Although the cardinal rule of page layout is still *Keep It Simple, Sillyhead,* some information is simply clearer as a list — even a *nested list* (which produces outline formatting, as we explain in Chapter 11). If you use such structures intelligently and sparingly, that's the impression they'll make.

If you're feeling the symptoms of list-o-mania, Chapter 11 presents the different types of HTML list tags you can use to purge that urge.

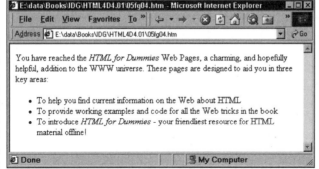

Figure 5-4:
HTML document with bulleted list viewed in Internet Explorer.

Hooking Up Your Pages

Hypermedia links within the body of your pages bring out the power of the Web. To many users, surfing the Web is the ultimate video game. Following links just to see where they go can be interesting and informative.

As a Web page designer and Web weaver, you want users to like your pages well enough to tell others, who tell others, and so on. Therefore, you must provide good links within your own pages and to other Internet resources.

Links come in two flavors — *relative* and *absolute* (also called *full*). They do their work in two distinct places — respectively, inside your Web site and out on the wider Web.

Relative links (to pages within your Web site)

A typical *relative link* in its native habitat looks like this:

```
<a href="ftpstuff.htm">Jump straight to the FTP
page!</a>
```

You can use a link like this one to get around (or show your visitors around) inside your Web site.

How does that link do that?

The URL refers to the directory that contains the Web page itself (which, in turn, calls the reference). In this case, the Web page calls a file (ftpstuff.htm) in the same directory as the current HTML file (whose address is the current URL). Same Web site, same folder; a relative link keeps you close to home (you know, the place where your relatives are).

In jargonese, we'd say it this way: "The reference is relative to the server's document root plus the path in the file system where the current URL is stored." Got that? (We'd never use such language to order a cappuccino.)

The tension of extensions

Normally, when you create links to HTML documents, you'd use the .html extension — all four letters. However, some servers only accept three character extensions, so you can't use .html even if you want to.

Regardless of the number of characters you use in your extensions, remember that file.htm and file.html are *not* the same file but are instead two different files. Always double-check the extension on any file that you link to; be sure the link to it matches the filename exactly. In addition, note that the case of the letters in the filename also matters to most servers, so be consistent when referencing your files.

As a bit of a heads-up, here are some typical cross-platform sticky wickets:

- ✔ If a page resides on a DOS machine that requires an ancient and venerable three-character extension, the server's usual habit is to ignore the fourth letter (the l). This habit is okay unless you're moving pages back and forth from a DOS machine to another computer that supports longer extensions. In this case, standardize on .htm and save yourself the grief.

- ✔ If you upload .htm files from a DOS or Windows computer to a UNIX server, make sure some kindly technical wizard has taught your server to recognize files that end in .htm as valid HTML files).

- ✔ Simple Macintosh text editors (such as SimpleText) don't place default .htm or .html extensions after a filename. Take heed, Mac Webmasters — always add an .html or .htm extension onto each and every Web page you create.

In the past, Web servers required the full four-letter html extension not only for filenames, but also for the links that called them. Today (ah, progress!), you can use either a four- or three-letter extension (html or htm) as long as your naming scheme is *consistent*. But before you dash off to change all your extensions, ask your Webmasters or system administrators about how your server really works, and what extensions it can see and use.

A bit of advice regarding overuse of links: Use them only when they convey needed information; use each specific link only once per page. Users can get irritable if each occurrence of a particular word or phrase on a single page turns out to be a link — especially if all those links take them to exactly the same place.

Absolute links (to the world outside your Web site)

As useful as relative links can be within a page, the whole point of the Web is to establish connections with those realms beyond your own immediate machine. Hence the evolution of the *absolute* (or *full*) link that gives the entire HTTP URL address. A representative of the species looks like this:

```
<a href =
"http://www.lanw.com/html4dum/html4dum.htm">
http://www.lanw.com/html4dum/html4dum.htm</a>
```

You can use absolute URLs for all your links without any noticeable difference in speed, even on a local server. But relative links are shorter to type (which may improve your overall productivity enough so you can go get that cappuccino). Whether using relative or absolute links is better is a debate for the newsgroups or your local UNIX users' group. Might be worth bothering your Webmaster about, though; who wants to put all that work into a link that doesn't link?

When including absolute URLs for links, we strongly recommend that you go on a little hunting trip first: *Link to the resource and capture its URL with your browser.* Then copy and paste this URL into your HTML file. Where URLs are concerned, this technique can stop typographical errors before they start.

The links in your HTML document are what makes your site Web-ready. As you create them, you're primarily concerned with

- ✔ The content of the links within your Web site
- ✔ The links' relationships to one another
- ✔ The links' contribution — not only to your own Web site, but also to the wider Web out there

Chapter 15 gets fancy with Web links, roping such evolved critters as image maps.

Choose your hyperlinks with care

Your home page may have links similar to those shown in Figure 5-5 (from the *HTML For Dummies* home page). Notice which words in the sentence are included in the hyperlink text (highlighted and/or underlined). You must click these words to open the link.

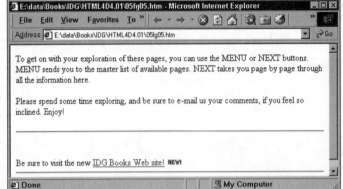

Figure 5-5:
Look at the
pretty
underlined
hyperlink!

The following HTML document fragment shows the tags that make up the innards of the hyperlink in Figure 5-5.

```
<p>
To get on with your exploration of these pages, you can
use the MENU or NEXT buttons. MENU sends you to the
master list of available pages. NEXT takes you page by
page through all the information here.</p>
<p>
Please spend some time exploring, and be sure to e-mail
us your comments, if you feel so inclined. Enjoy!</p>
<hr>
<p></p>
<br>Be sure to visit the new
<a href="http://www.idgbooks.com/">
IDG Books Web site!</a>
<img src="new.gif" height="17" width="32"
align="top">
<hr>
```

Choose all link text and images carefully. Keep the text short and the graphics small. And never, ever use the phrase *click here* for link text. ("Why?" you ask. Because your readers may think you're too lazy or uncaring to write more helpful link text. Can't have that!)

Well-chosen hyperlinks enable your users to quickly scan hyperlink text and choose links without having to read the surrounding text. (Surrounding text is usually included only to provide readers with clarification of the link anyway.) Remember, users are in a hurry to scan your pages and quickly pick out important links; unique wording or graphics can aid this process. Make this job easy by using meaningful hyperlinks, and the overall impression left in the reader's mind is *Nice cyberhospitality. I could come here again.*

Finishing with Footers

Unlike an HTML header and body, a footer is not defined by a specific set of markup tags. By convention, a footer is simply the bottom portion of the page body. Of course, that doesn't mean we can't be authoritative about it. The *Yale C/AIM Web Style Guide* provides a concise statement about the use of footers on your Web pages (http://info.med.yale.edu/caim/manual/index.html):

> "Page footers should always carry basic information about the origin and age of the page. Every Web page needs to bear this basic information, but this repetitive and prosaic information often does not deserve the prominence of being placed at the top of the page."

(**Hint:** Readers may be "reading aloud" in their minds, in which case seeing *My Fantastic Web Site, June 1999, Version 17.2* at the top of every page is at best redundant and at worst an interest-killer.)

Footers may seem pedestrian, but they provide the pedigree of your pages by attributing authorship, contact information, legal status, version/revision information, and a link to your home page. Each footer should contain some or all of the elements listed here:

- Institutional or company affiliation, where appropriate; author's name otherwise
- Phone number
- E-mail address
- Postal mailing address
- Copyright notice
- Date of page's last revision
- Links to the page's URL
- Legal disclaimer or language designating the page as the official communication of the company or institution
- Official company or institutional seal, logo, or other graphic mark
- Hypertext link(s) to home page or to other pages
- Hypertext link(s) to other sections of this page

Your basic home page HTML document already contains the minimum suggested footer information for a home page:

```
<address>
Copyright &copy; 2000, Your Name <br>
Revised: Revision Date <br>
URL: <a href =
        "http://this.page's.url.here">http://this.page's.u
        rl.here</a>
</address>
```

Even though this document is a home page, it contains a link to itself in the URL line. All other local pages in your Web must also contain a link in the footer to a full home-page URL, as in the sterling example just shown. Why? We're glad you asked: If a user saves your page as an HTML file and later wants to know its location, he can find it on the bottom of the page, both visible and as a link. Don't you wish everyone used this technique?

The name of your home page file depends on your Web server software. Some servers require a specific name and extension, such as `index.htm`. Check with your ISP to determine the requirements of the server that houses your Web site. Most likely, one of these formats works:

```
<a href="http://www.servername.net/yourdirectory">
<!-- least desirable -->
<a href="http://www.servername.net/yourdirectory/">
<!-- better -->
<a href="http://www.servername.net/yourdirectory/index.html">
<!-- most desirable -->
```

Government agencies and other public institutions are notorious for big footers because the who and what of their creation has some public importance. So these agencies often include what seems like a staff directory and departmental history in their footers. (At least they're at the bottom of the page!) If you must use a long footer, put a home page link above it so users don't have to scroll so far to find it!

Figure 5-6 illustrates a well-balanced footer for a business-style home page, from the LANWrights home page (ours, as it happens). This footer contains all important footer information (notice the separate contact icon in the upper right of the figure). This footer *doesn't* contain a phone number or snail-mail address, for some practical reasons:

- ✔ On the Net, e-mail rules! Sometimes phone and snail-mail addresses aren't necessary or relevant.

- ✔ For whatever reason (say, your mailroom isn't set up to handle lots of envelopes) you may not want hordes of casual visitors to your page calling you or writing letters to you.

- ✔ In our case, the contact page already includes all this information.

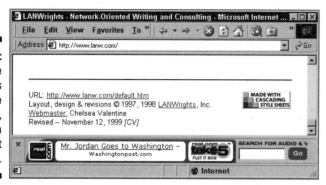

Figure 5-6:
The
LANWrights
home page
footer,
viewed with
Internet
Explorer.

Instead of placing all footer information directly in each page, you may want to put some of it in a page of its own and put a link to that information in the footer instead. The bigger the footer, the handier such a link can be — especially if your information requires a legal disclaimer or other complex language. (Check with your legal representative concerning the fine points of using disclaimers on the Web.)

Catching the copyright

Copyright law hasn't quite caught up with the explosion in electronic publishing on the Web. While you're waiting, it won't hurt you or your organization to put a copyright notice at the bottom of any Web page that you don't want freely copied without attribution to you or without your permission.

The copyright notice shown in Figure 5-6 is standard text except for the copyright symbol. Most browsers can display the copyright symbol © if you use the character entity ©. Otherwise, simulate it with (C) or (c).

For the complete rundown on entities, check out Chapter 12.

Counting coup — versions, dates, times

One of the greatest benefits of publishing on the Web is the ability to change your pages quickly — but why should you even bother to note when you change them? Well, it *is* a courtesy to your users, especially if any of them are the *been there, done that* type. Not only do your users need to know what's up, but you also need to keep track of which version you're publishing so you can be certain to update the old stuff when newer versions are ready.

This (or next?) year's model

If it's appropriate, you may want to use *version numbers* in addition to a revision date. This enables you to refer to a particular page as version 12B, for example, rather than the second revision from December. It's less ambiguous, more direct, and shorter, too!

Placing a revision date in the footer of each page keeps track of its chronology. The format should be March 02, 2000, to avoid confusion. In the United States, this date would be abbreviated 03/02/00. In Europe, this would be read as the 2 March 2000 and abbreviated as 02/03/00. The international ISO 8601 standard date notation is *YYYY-MM-DD* (year, month, day), which would result in 2000-03-02. Use that format for dates if you want to be globally correct.

If, for some reason, you don't want to show a revision date on the page, you'll be happier in the long run if you use HTML comment tags and hide the revision date inside them.

What (or which) time is it?

You may add the time to the date for time-sensitive information. Because users from all over the world can view your information at any time, 24-hour, *UTC* (*Universal Time*, which used to be called GMT — Greenwich Mean Time) is the appropriate format, expressed as *hh:mm:ss* (which is *hour:minute:second,* using two characters for each).

Make sure you note the time as UTC — that is, 18:30:00 UTC or 18:30:00Z for 6:30 p.m. (The *Z* stands for *Zulu* in the NATO radio alphabet and refers to the Zulu or Zero meridian of longitude used for measurement. Now, *there's* an obscure tidbit for *Jeopardy!*)

Fishing for Feedback?

Every well-constructed home page includes a way for users to give feedback to its developer or owner. To solicit feedback, you can choose between an *e-mail link* and a *form.* (Your choice may depend on which of these options your Web service provider makes available.) Of the two, e-mail is simplest, and most generally used on personal home pages. Businesses tend to use forms, fill-in-the-blank screens that prompt users for specific data.

Most custom business forms seek to turn users into paying customers. For more about these specialized tools, see Chapter 17.

One common e-mail approach is to include a special hyperlink (called a `mailto:` link) in the Web page itself so users can send e-mail to the page owner. The link works by starting the browser's e-mail program or another one on the user's computer.

If a mailto: link works for you, go for it. The standard approach is to provide an e-mail address as text inside the <address>... </address> tags. Consider this modest example:

```
E-mail: <a href="mailto:html4dum@lanw.com">
        HTML For Dummies at html4dum@/lanw.com</a>
```

Steady — that's HTML code, all right, but it's translatable. The actual hyperlink is mailto:html4dum@lanw.com. For readers who aren't equipped to use a mailto URL, a second instance of the e-mail address occurs in HTML For Dummies at html4dum@lanw.com to highlight the e-mail address on the page. That way a user can easily print it out or jot it down (on parchment, clay tablets, whatever).

Outside the actual address portion of the link (<a href = "mailto :html4dum"nw.com">...</a>), you can customize the wording to your heart's content. You can also put text in front of it — say, Send kudos or wisecracks to: (or the more demure E-mail: shown in the example, taken from our very own *HTML For Dummies* Web pages).

Using Comments for Posterity (And Sanity)

Do yourself a big favor and *comment* on your HTML documents, overtly and often, by including text in the file that does nothing more than sit there and explain (to the programmer, editor, or tech-support stalwart) what a particular hunk of the page is supposed to do or why it's there. Comments can also explain the relevance of links or identify information that needs updating. Fast-forward to the future: That joyous noise in the background is you, thanking yourself many times over for this valuable resource.

Browsers don't display comments inside HTML documents, a trend that is likely to continue. HTML comment lines are formatted like this:

```
<!-- comment text -->
```

A comment line starts with <!-- and ends with -->. As a general rule, place comments on a line apart from other HTML text. This way you won't interrupt HTML text (because browsers ignore any extra spaces [over one] between HTML tags).

Chapter 6

Grabbing Graphics Gusto

• •

In This Chapter

▶ Adding logos, icons, and other little gems

▶ Building high-impact graphic pages

▶ Transforming graphics into hyperlinks

• •

*T*he Web is both a cooperative and a competitive environment; it relies on interdependence, but it's impatient with boredom. Web sites come and go all the time; many sink without a ripple. Yours can remain afloat and well visited as long as it makes a lasting and positive impression on visitors. This chapter offers some handy hints for keeping your page fresh and vital through the careful and informed use of graphics.

Eye-Catchers: Logos, Icons, and Other Gems

Graphics add color and impact to Web pages for users with GUI browsers, but for most of us, graphics aren't the main point of our Web pages. Unless your Web page focuses primarily on computer graphics as its content, the watchwords are *small, relevant,* and *tasteful,* and use graphics only where they add value. Why small? Well, half that answer is technical (the larger a graphic, the slower it loads) and half is human nature (the only speed acceptable to computer users is instantaneous). That's why small is beautiful!

Speaking of small, fast-loading graphics (and subtle segues), here's where we add some sparkle to the plain-vanilla home page we build in Chapter 5 (you may want to check it out if you haven't already).

So far, the Chapter 5 page has nice-looking headings and simple black bullets next to the list lines (steal a quick look back at Figure 5-4). Because the basic layout is well established, all you need is a few splashes of color in the appropriate places to really spice things up.

Hitting the (red) spot with an <img> tag

Let's pick on that harmless-looking bullet point and turn it red. Adding an image to your HTML document is as simple as inserting a line using the <img> tag:

```
<img src="graphics/dotred.gif">
```

This line contains a *reference* (URL) for a gif file named dotred.gif. In this case, this is a relative reference that points to a file that the Web server expects to find in a subdirectory named graphics — skulking directly beneath the directory where the current page (the page from which the link is called) resides.

Using this particular relative URL to create the red dot causes the Web server to look for a file with the following absolute path:

```
http://www.lanw.com/html4dum/graphics/dotred.gif
```

If you want or need to use absolute URLs, you may use the following image tag with the full URL to link to the red dot:

```
<img src="http://www.lanw.com/html4dum/graphics/dotred.gif">
```

The <img> tag at work

You already know what the <img> tag looks like, now you find out what attributes you can use with it. The <img> tag is an empty tag — one of those tags that is forbidden to have a closing tag — and inserts an image into your HTML document. There are a few attributes you should know about before you jump into the examples.

```
src="url" [CT]
```

This attribute identifies the image file location.

```
longdesc="url" [CT]
```

Longdesc identifies a link to a long description of the image. This description should supplement the short description provided using the alt attribute.

```
name="text" [CI]
```

This attribute names the element so it may be referred to from style sheets or scripts. Although this attribute is included in HTML, it has been included for backwards compatibility. Therefore, you should use the id attribute to identify elements instead.

```
alt="text" [CS]
```

For browsers that cannot display images, this attribute specifies alternate text.

```
align="BOTTOM" "MIDDLE" or "TOP" or "LEFT" or "RIGHT" [CI]
```

align specifies the position of the image with respect to its context. This attribute is deprecated.

```
border="pixels" [CN]
```

This attribute specifies the width of the image border in pixels. The default value for this attribute depends on the user agent. This attribute is deprecated.

```
hspace="pixels" [CN]
```

This attribute specifies the amount of white space to be inserted to the left and right of an image. A default value is not specified. This attribute is deprecated.

```
vspace="pixels" [CN]
```

The vspace attribute specifies the amount of white space to be inserted above and below an image. A default value is not specified. This attribute is deprecated.

```
width="length" [CN]
```

Specifies the width of the image.

```
height="length" [CN]
```

Specifies the height of the image.

Snagging an image from far away

If you want to link to an image file of a red dot (dotred.gif) located on another Web site, you have to use an absolute URL (sometimes called a *full URL*) in the <img> tag, like this:

```
<img src="http://www.someothersite.net/icons/dotred.gif">
```

If you use a full URL to a far away site in a link on your page, then every time a user loads the image, the browser that hosts the Web page actually links to the other remote Web server to retrieve the graphic. This process increases the time needed for the browser to load the file (not a kindly gesture). If the remote location is not online, the browser can't load the image at all (an even unkindlier gesture). Therefore, keeping your graphics in the same place on your own server usually works better and thus helps you avoid getting the unkindliest gesture of all — mass exodus of your visitors.

Some ISPs charge their users for the amount of data — HTML, images, and any other data sent via the Internet — that visitors to their site download on a weekly or monthly basis. If you link to a graphic stored on someone else's Web page, then you add to the amount of information that the other person's site sends out each time *your* Web page is loaded. This practice is unfair — to say the very least — and just plain ol' bad form. If you want to use graphics from someone else's Web site, do the right thing and save a copy to your own Web server and reference it locally.

Absolute URLs do require judicious, careful, and limited use, though that doesn't mean you have to avoid them on pain of cyberwarts. If your site can benefit from links to remote images that change over time (such as a weather map, clock, or Webcam picture), or from a large, complex image in a file too big to park on your server, you may want to try such a link. In the first case, the other site maintains the changing image and your users see it directly from their sites, included in your page. In the second case, you save on server disk space by pointing to a remote location for a multimegabyte picture. (Of course, you may want to warn your users about what they're getting into before you encourage them to click.)

Bottom line: An absolute URL may be good if you're linking to a storm update, but it's too much hassle if all you want is a red dot. So the first principle of linking to graphics is as follows: *Whenever possible, keep 'em small, simple, and handy.*

Chasing small, defenseless graphics around

For a detailed practical example, we invite you to observe how several small, graphic elements are used to navigate the LANWrights Web site. The portion of its HTML document shown in Figure 6-1 uses nine different small graphic elements — *navigation icons* — that take the visitor to other locations throughout the site. Each graphic is less than 1K in size, so the graphics download and display quickly.

Reusing the same graphics on a single Web page doesn't add significant time or disk storage requirements when a user's browser *caches* them (or stores previously viewed images in memory). Therefore, using the same graphical elements repeatedly helps keep load and display times for these images to a minimum. Recycling images makes as much sense for Web pages as recycling physical resources does for the environment!

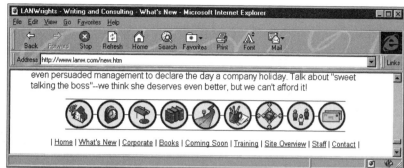

Figure 6-1:
A view of
the
LANWrights
navigation
icons.

Horizontal rules — but colors reign

Separating sections with a colored line graphic can add an extra touch of color to a page. You can accomplish this separation using a simple HTML <hr> tag that goes by the name of *horizontal rule*. However, because <hr>'s only display is as a 3-D line (gray, black, and white to give the 3-D effect), you don't get the same visual impact that a brightly colored line provides.

Using a colored line to bracket an announcement just above footer information sets it apart from surrounding text and makes a grab for the user's attention. When used this way, colored ruler lines are perfect for segmenting pages into eye-pleasing information blocks. You can make these lines with most "paint" programs in any length, thickness, and color combination imaginable (except, maybe, neon paisley, but give it a few years). If you don't mind chasing rainbows, you can actually *find* some on public-access graphic Web sites where they are available for your use, generally with no strings attached. (In fact, feel free to use ours any way you like! You can find a rainbow image on the CD-ROM in the /html4Fd3/graphics directory, named rainbow.gif).

To see a colored line (or two or three) at work in the real Web world, check out another page on the LANWrights site, shown in Figure 6-2. This page uses a burgundy hard rule in a couple different places to divide the page's content — separating header and footer information from the rest of the document's guts.

Rather than list any of the thousands of sites with gifs and jpegs available for download here, we suggest that you search for GIF archives or JPEG archives on one of the many Web search engines, such as www.altavista.com, www.excite.com, or www.yahoo.com.

Figure 6-2:
Colored
hard rules
are both
functional
and fun.

Clicking the HTML editor button that inserts the good old `<hr>` into your document may be quicker and easier than typing a link to the colored line image, especially if you have more than a few of them occurring over many pages. In this case, consider what works best — consistency or punch?

Some Web-searching spiders or agents use the `<hr>` tag to distinguish breaks in text for their indexes. They may not recognize the colored line image as a replacement for the `<hr>` tag. But as always, the spirit of experimentation is alive and well on the Web.

Bored with dots? Have a ball . . .

The standard structure of an HTML unordered list (`<ul>`) places black list dots (bullets) to the left of its elements by default — efficient, but tame. If you want to jazz up the look of your list, you can use small graphical elements for heightened visual appeal.

It just so happens that we have some graphics on hand that use highlights and shadows to convey the impression of a three-dimensional ball. (What a lucky break. . . .) The redball.gif image in the /html4Fd3/graphics directory on the CD-ROM makes a catchy bullet point.

If you alternate shiny balls of different colors — say, red, white, and blue for a political Web page — you increase the eye-catching effects. Each line stands out from the line above it and the line below it. (If you want to try this effect, look for files named whiball.gif and bluball.gif in the same directory on the CD-ROM where you find the red one.)

We generally reserve special effects such as these for home pages and other documents where looks are most important. As always, before you toss in some snazzy spheroids, rainbows, or pterodactyls (how'd they get in there?), study up on how such substitutions may affect your page's all-important relationship with the Web. Speaking of which. . . .

One word of caution about making changes such as replacing list bullets with colored dots: If you use your own images to create snappy lists, the list structure of your document won't fit the standard HTML model. The next section explains why this structure may matter to your Web page.

. . . But please don't confuse the spiders

If you blithely replace <hr> with rainbow lines, or list bullets with festive balls throughout your document, you could run into functional problems: An active spider or agent looking at your page may get confused and not know what to grab. It can deduce that an object following an <li> tag is part of the list it just entered (and can organize its gleanings accordingly), but it's still a pretty simple creature. A spider or agent can't recognize an "imitation list" that uses colored dots as a list at all. If you have a list of items that you want to show up as a list wherever it appears on the Web, use HTML list tags.

The HTML standard sets specifications for unordered or bulleted lists for the sake of consistency — list items in nonsequential order are *supposed* to be set off by a preceding symbol. Style attributes in the HTML 4.01 specification let you set the way you want your numbers or bullets to appear in your lists, as long as they're "normal" bullets. Every browser that adheres to the HTML 4.01 standard should display these bullets in much the same way; they may be a little stodgier, but they'll be consistent. This consistency can't be said about individual images of colored dots — so if you can't decide between the safe-but-plain way and a blatant disregard for HTML conformity, try it both ways and see which you like best. Just don't say we didn't *warn* you.

A solid example of this principle at work is the page on the LANWrights Web site that describes this book's predecessor, *HTML 4 For Dummies*, shown in Figure 6-3.

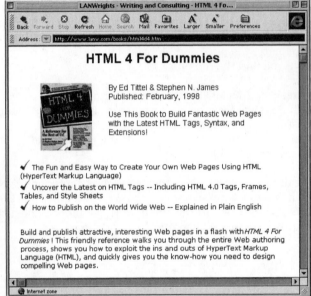

Figure 6-3: A bulleted list using graphics on the LANWrights Web site.

Notice that the "list" of the book's features is marked with graphical checkmarks. These little descriptors, although listed one after the other, won't suffer greatly if a spider or robot doesn't recognize them as a coherent list. The small graphical checkmarks add a splash of color to the page and mark each feature as a unique item. Once again, graphics are both fun and functional. See, we really do try to practice what we preach when we build our own sites.

If you simply want to lighten up and add a little life to your home page with some visual hoopla — and don't mind confusing a few spiders — go for it. This act of rebellion — peppering a line of text with colored dots or other small graphics — is as simple as inserting tagged URLs in the text at the points where you want each graphic to appear. Consider, for example, the following HTML code snippet:

```
<img src="graphics/dotred.gif"> To help you find current
            information on the Web about HTML<br>
```

It creates our familiar red dot with `<img src="graphics/dotred.gif">` and displays it right before *To help you . . .* on-screen. Notice the space between the > and the *To*. Although browsers generally ignore spaces, some

:ape Navigator and Internet Explorer) may recognize a
after text. Such a kindness can help you format sen-
ep images from crowding text.

n the kindness of strangers? Browsers ignore multiple
ler text. Even so, when you're working in and around
cement of spaces *while you're writing the code* can pre-
matting work later on.

vigation — it's a gif

d carefully located icons can help your users quickly
your Web pages. We use the term *icon* here to describe
ge that you can substitute for a unit of text.

are usually small and load quickly. In most instances,
ess: Simply put a standard image-tag with a source URL
you want it to appear.

ll that you don't need to align text next to them (we get
es later in this chapter). The default for most browsers
the bottom of an image.

built to teach a Web-site management class is a conve-
avigation bar isn't a lounge with a nautical motif; it's a
long one side of a page in an HTML document, used for
getting around the site. In the case of our class, we designed the icons to help
our students jump easily to particular modules of the course, or to a set of
navigation instructions. We added these icons to the HTML document using
the following code (note that this is only a portion of the HTML document;
it's not the full document):

```
<body bgcolor="#ffffff">
<p>
<a href="navigate.htm">
<img vspace="1" align="center" border="0"
  src="graphics/nav.gif" alt="Navigation">
</a>
</p>
<p>
<a href="isp.htm">
<img vspace="1" align="center" border="0"
  src="graphics/isp.gif" alt="isp">
</a>
</p>
<p>
<a href="track.htm">
<img vspace="1" align="center" border="0"
  src="graphics/track.gif" ALT="Tracking">
```

```
</a>
</p>
<p>
<a href="search.htm">
<img vspace="1" align="center" border="0"
  src="graphics/search.gif" alt="Searching">
</a>
</p>
</body>
```

This particular set of magic text makes each icon a hyperlink. Click one of these icons and you go directly to the appropriate HTML document — a compact, simple navigation technique that's easy for users with graphical browsers to use. A full-blown implementation of this idea would include an equivalent set of text-based hyperlinks to accommodate a wider range of users, including

✔ Visually impaired users who normally magnify the text

✔ Users who keep graphics turned off to speed download time

The navigation bar (available at `www.lanw.com/training/myw/myw.htm`) appears on the right-hand side of Figure 6-4.

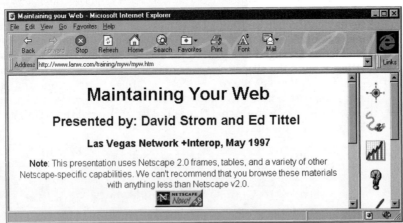

Figure 6-4:
The icons on the right-hand side of the page provide a constant source of navigation in this example site.

Linking with logos — and other graphics

Logos are an art unto themselves. An image that imparts a positive sense of your organization to an audience in a *get-it-got-it-go* manner is a joy (and often a profit) to behold. However, it shouldn't overpower the Web page or overstimulate the user to the point of irritation. Go easy on the size and special effects — especially if you're expecting your logo to do double duty as a hyperlink.

Logos are special-use graphics. However cool it may look, a logo's first goal in life is to identify your business or institution in a memorable, pleasing, eye-catching way. Logos can vary from icon size to much larger — sometimes too large. Complex logos that take too long to load are a waste of time on almost any Web page. Keep It Simple, Sillyhead.

A moderate-size logo at the top of a home page is generally acceptable: big enough to look good, small enough to load fast. Using icon-sized logos in the footer of each Web page is equally acceptable. Remember that text-only browsers and GUI browsers with image loading turned off (for faster page loading) won't display your fantastic logos, anyway. (Yet another argument for good taste.)

Figures 6-5 and 6-6 illustrate the visual effects of using a moderate-size logo gif at the top of a page. The LANWrights logo file is only 4,930 bytes, so it loads in a few seconds. This second image, despite the increase in size, is still only 7,342 bytes.

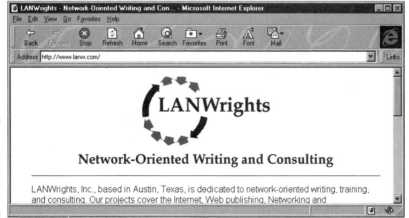

Figure 6-5:
The
LANWrights
logo on the
home page.

Figure 6-5's home page shows the logo used by itself; subsidiary pages combine the logo with an associated navigation icon. Voilá — a visual link between the topic and its related image, as shown in Figure 6-6.

Now we get a little fancy, gathering navigation icons into a table under the LANWrights logo at the top of the home page (shown in Figure 6-7), illustrating the use of tabular graphics as hyperlinks.

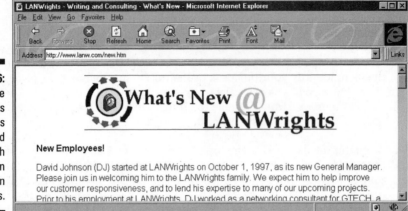

Figure 6-6:
The
LANWrights
logo is
integrated
with
navigation
icons on
other pages.

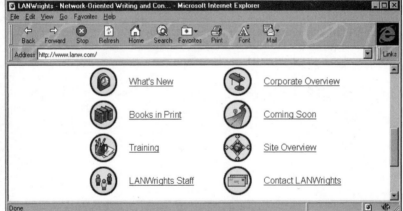

Figure 6-7:
LANWrights
uses
navigation
graphics as
hyperlinks.

Built according to code

Okay, it's time to open this home page for a look at the code that makes it tick. The following lines from the HTML document produced the views you've just been gazing at so intently. (Well, we can hope.) The code is a compact illustration of how to nest an icon image within link-reference tags (between `<a href=>` and `</a>`). In addition, you'll see some table tags. These are discussed in detail in Chapter 14. This code endows an icon with the powers of a hyperlink:

```
<center>
<table width="90%" border="0" cellspacing="4"
  cellpadding="2">
<tr>
<td width="10%"><br></td>
 <td width="15%" height="23">
```

```
<center>
<a href="new.htm">
<img src="graphics/new.gif align="bottom"
 width="51" height="51" border="0"
 alt="What's New!">
</a>
</center>
</td>
<td width="30%">
<a href="new.htm">What's New</a>
</td>
<td width="15%">
<center>
 <a href="corporat.htm">
 <img src="graphics/corporat.gif" width="51"
  height="51" align="bottom" border="0"
  alt="Corporate Services">
 </a>
</center>
</td>
<td width="30%">
<a href="corporat.htm">Corporate Overview</a>
</td>
</tr>
<tr>
<td><br></td>
<td height="23">
<center>
 <a href="books.htm">
 <img src="graphics/books.gif" width="51" height="51"
  align="bottom" alt="Books in Print"
  border="0">
 </a>
</center>
</td>
<td>
<a href="books.htm">Books in Print</a>
</td>
<td>
<center>
 <a href="topress.htm">
 <img src="graphics/comisoon.gif" width="51"
  height="51" align="bottom" alt="Coming Soon"
  border="0">
 </a>
</center>
</td>
<td>
<a href="topress.htm">Coming Soon</a>
</td>
</tr>
<tr>
<td><br></td>
```

```
<td>
<center>
 <a href="training.htm">
 <img src="graphics/training.gif" width="51"
  height="51" align="bottom" border="0"
  alt="Training">
 </a>
</center>
</td>
<td>
<a href="training.htm">Training</a>
</td>
<td>
<center>
 <a href="overview.htm">
 <img src="graphics/wayfind.gif" width="51"
  height="51" align="bottom" alt="Wayfinder"
  border="0">
 </a>
</center>
</td>
<td>
<a href="overview.htm">Site Overview</a>
</td>
</tr>
<tr>
<td><br></td>
<td height="23">
<center>
 <a href="lanwstaf.htm">
 <img src="graphics/staff.gif" width="51" height="51"
  align="bottom" alt="Staff"
  border="0">
 </a>
</center>
</td>
<td>
<a href="lanwstaf.htm">LANWrights Staff</a>
</td>
<td>
<center>
 <a href="lanwcmmt.htm">
 <img src="graphics/contact.gif" width="51"
  height="51" align="bottom" alt="Contact"
  border="0"> </a>
</center>
</td>
<td>
<a href="lanwcmmt.htm">Contact LanWrights</a>
</td>
</tr>
</table>
</center>
```

We know that's a fair-sized chunk of code, but we're talking about some major capabilities here. All the more reason not to leave your graphics-free visitors out in the cold. Funny you should mention that.

Text hyperlinks for the graphics-free user

Notice the use of the alternate text attribute, `alt="text"` that appears within each image tag in the preceding code example. The `alt` attribute tells text-only browsers to ignore the icon and display the associated "text" as a hyperlink instead. No problem.

Some graphical browsers are also equipped to use this handy substitution. If the browser is running with the image display function turned off, it simply displays placeholders where the icons would be and uses the alternate text as the hyperlink. Either way, you've politely provided any graphically challenged visitor to your site (whether speed-demon or DOS curmudgeon) with a way to use the navigation you've so painstakingly defined. For better looks (and, what the heck, greater clarity), we added explicit text definitions in the table cells next to each icon in our previous code sample.

 According to the official HTML 4.01 specification, an HTML page isn't a valid — 100 percent correct — document if you don't have `alt=` attributes for each and every graphic. Yet another argument for taking time out to make your pages accessible to all.

As we put together the LANWrights Web site, we found that a little creative use of icon images as hyperlinks to other pages in the site added not only visual interest, but also convenience for our users. If your Web pages are visually striking and easy to navigate, you get a double reward and then some: Your site stands out and is easy to remember as a nice place to visit.

Rating Sites for Eye Appeal

Just because you can slap together two lines of code and include some graphics doesn't mean you're hip to design aesthetics. However, you can obtain an amateur degree with a little bit of effort. After you create your masterpiece, take a moment to step back and perceive your work. What we mean is to open your new site and take a look at it. Ask yourself the following questions:

- Does anything jump out at me?
- Are my eyes drawn to any one place?
- Does the layout seem smooth and organized?
- Are the navigational aids easy to locate and understand?
- Is the text content superceded by the graphics?
- Does the overall look seem balanced?

You may find that unfocusing your eyes (or even going cross-eyed a bit) to view your creation may help you see shape and balance better than when you're just concentrating on the text. Keep in mind that white space is just as important (and often more important) than graphics. The saying "beauty is in the eye of the beholder" is reasonably true. Everyone has his or her own sense of what he or she likes and dislikes. However, everyone can generally agree that confusion, clutter, and disorganization are not considered advantageous, especially when you're trying to communicate. So, rate your own work on how well it presents its content, how well it's balanced, and how pleasing it is to view. If you think things are too sparse or too dense, your visitors probably will as well. As the author, you need to be pleased with your work. But, don't forget that you're attempting to attract an audience, too.

Chapter 7

High-Impact Pages

In This Chapter

▶ Exploring the good

▶ Recognizing the bad

▶ Avoiding the ugly

*Y*ou know high style when you see an example of classic elegance — *rich results from simple means* — whether it's the understated curve of a sleek fender, a striking-but-simple color scheme, or a musical arrangement with just the right instruments.

Such creations make a high sensory impact with no two-by-fours anywhere in sight. We encourage you to embark on a quest for Web pages that embody classic elegance — not to slavishly imitate or filch, but to learn. This chapter can aid you in your quest.

Graphic Page Layout

At the LANWrights Web site (at `www.lanw.com`), we set out to practice what we preach. We can say, with some pride and a straight face, that the graphic layout of the Web pages you see in this chapter did not occur by accident. (Well, okay, maybe a million monkeys poking randomly at computers might have come up with it — but we had a deadline.) En route to the final layout, we made two discoveries:

- ✔ The approach we used worked pretty well.
- ✔ No matter how practiced you get at it, layout is still a learn-by-doing process.

Here, not necessarily in chronological order, is what we learned:

- If yours is a business site, keep its mission in mind. (Ours focuses on informing visitors about LANWrights services, books, and capabilities.)

- Layout for a business page should shoot for an impression that's conservative enough to be reassuring but lively enough to be interesting. If you use a logo on your home page, make it easy to see right away.

- Add graphics sparingly to brighten the look and enhance visual contrast. Experiment until you find the best locations for them on your page.

- Choose graphics that are relevant, handy to link to, quick to load, and relatively simple. For example, use horizontal rules and highlighted hyperlinks to focus attention.

- Size your graphics to fit the layout and purpose of each page. (Only your home page should look like a home page; don't clone it.) Keep navigation icons small; give them a consistent look and location.

- Use the `alt` attribute to specify alternative text for user agents that cannot display images. (For more information on the `alt` attribute, see Chapter 6.)

- Put additional thought into the design and layout of pages that use larger graphics — the bigger the image, the more thought that's required. Accommodate users of both GUI and text-only browsers so each always has something interesting to look at, regardless of whether graphics are available.

If you follow the sage advice in this book (gathered at great pains and with your best interests at heart), you can do the same as we have — and much more — on your Web pages. Even without the million monkeys — we like monkeys!

Grappling with graphics files

A picture may be worth a thousand words, but which picture? And which thousand words? On a Web page, pictures — the output of graphics files — work more like specialized building blocks. They are both a visual stimulus for your users and a structural element for your page (not to mention a possible navigational aid if you turn them into hyperlinks). To wrestle a graphics file into submission, you have to attack on two distinct levels: size and format. The prize is a visually sophisticated page layout that still supports optimum functionality (or, as the want ads might say of a car, "looks great, runs great").

Inspiration versus appropriation

Everyone needs influences and role models to help inspire original content. Exploring the Web for ideas is surfing with a purpose. When you see a Web page with a layout that you especially like, view the HTML source file to examine its formatting techniques. You can use your browser's Save As feature to save any HTML source to your own hard disk or you can print it, for later study.

At the same time, you can add especially arresting pages to your bookmark file so you can find them again. Most browsers also let you save the images associated with a page to files on your hard disk. However, before you include somebody else's work on your pages, be aware of copyright restrictions — always get the author's permission *in writing* before you use the work of others. (If you're in doubt about whether reusing something is okay, *don't do it!*)

Imitation may be the sincerest form of flattery, but stealing other authors' content — text and images — to use on your Web pages is illegal in most countries (and trying to pass off stolen creativity as original can be as hazardous as it is repugnant). However, discovering new techniques by appreciating and studying the work of others is the way most Web-weavers expand their horizons. Use these techniques to build your own pages, with your own content, in your own unique way.

You don't have to create in a vacuum; you can always e-mail other Web authors and request permission to use something of theirs in your page. Many independent Web authors are happy to help because others helped them find new Web tools and techniques. But it's common courtesy not to assume that someone else's creation is common property.

As e-commerce continues to forge ahead, most corporate Web sites are completely copyrighted, and they take a dim view of anyone who uses things from their site without permission, which they probably won't grant (nothing personal; it's strictly business).

The more commercialized and crowded the Web becomes, the more you need to know and respect the legal boundaries around Web property — others' and your own. Good manners, as well as good design, can be a civilizing influence.

Do I have to . . . do art?

To produce high-quality images for your Web pages, you don't really have to be an artist (besides, not everybody looks good in a beret). You needn't even become a world-beater at using graphics-manipulation programs such as Paint Shop Pro, GraphicConverter, or LView Pro — or, for that matter, the newer programs that pop up almost weekly on the Web. If you plan to work with images regularly, however, we recommend getting fairly adept at one or more of these programs. There are two things to remember about graphics programs: (1) They can be a lot of engrossing fun, and (2) don't forget to eat.

Search for the keywords *graphics editor* on your favorite search engine and you can find links to many useful sites for freeware and shareware graphics tools.

On-screen and in the file — downsize and smile

Graphic images actually have *two* sizes — one visible to the user, one not. First, consider the *on-screen size* of the images themselves, and their impact on the complexity of your document's layout. Second, consider *the size of the graphics files (in bytes)* and how long the files take for users to download.

Modestly, we think you should have another look at our own business site, conveniently represented in Figure 7-1. The original logo file it shows — built in Adobe Illustrator — was a pretty big honker (over 1MB) that filled the entire screen. Problem: Even at today's chip and modem speeds, a megabyte of data can take several *minutes* (in Web terms, an Ice Age) to load over a slow link.

Careful cropping, resizing, and *resampling* (using fewer pixels per inch) brought the file size down to under 5,000 bytes. These changes gave us (to understate somewhat) a *dramatic* improvement in load time: A 5,000-byte file moves in seconds, even over a fairly slow modem. Problem solved.

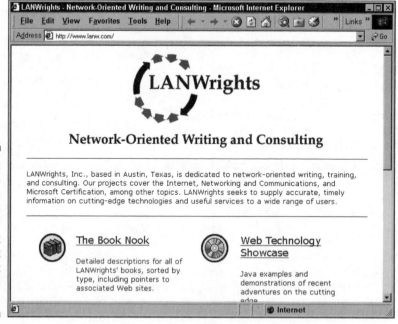

Figure 7-1: The LANWrights logo would choke the fastest Internet feed if not for careful planning.

If you like GUI, then you'll love GIF and JPEG

Not all graphics files are created equal — and even some *formats* for graphics files are clearly "more equal than others" for use on the Web. Although the Web doesn't put much practical restriction on the types of graphic files you can use, two file formats are especially popular. You can recognize them by their distinctive filename extensions: GIF and JPG.

Virtually all GUI browsers have built-in display capabilities that accommodate GIF and JPEG formats; most use external helper applications to display other file types. An advantage also exists when it comes to file transfer: Compressed GIF and JPEG files are the smallest (and therefore the fastest to load) of all commonly used graphics file types.

Most good shareware image-manipulation programs — such as Photoshop, Paint Shop Pro, GraphicConverter, or LView Pro — can load and save files produced in the GIF and JPEG formats.

The graphics programs we mention also support a couple more arcane formats: GIF87a and GIF89a (whether transparent or interlaced). If you work on a Macintosh and are faced with interlaced GIFs, use GifConverter to handle them. (If you're curious about *interlacing* and/or suspect it has nothing to do with hiking boots, take a peek at the handy sidebar we devote to it later in this chapter.)

Whenever you build any image in GIF89a format, however, be sure to test any interlaced images on multiple browsers. Some graphics lend themselves better to interlacing (and to transparency) than others. Now we're back to learning-by-doing; the process is much closer to old-fashioned trial-and-error than it is to an exact science. Testing your images across multiple browsers — on multiple platforms — is a must!

Actually, some graphics are pretty transparent

The GIF89 format also introduced the *transparent background* feature. This feature "turns off" one of the colors in an image displayed by a browser — and allows whatever is behind the image to show through at every point where the color is transparent. Usually, what's back there is a background color, but you can lay images over other images or text as well. To users, your image appears to float on the browser's background instead of atop a square of some other color around the image.

Programs such as giftrans for UNIX and DOS, and Transparency for the Macintosh, create images with transparent backgrounds for browsers that support the GIF89 format. For Windows users, LView for Windows is also worth checking out. Transparent images really add to the visual richness and drama of a Web page.

A new pic's resolution . . .

. . . should be *"I will load fast and refrain from causing eyestrain in the people who look at me."* Lecturing your graphics file on New Year's Eve may not help, but giving it an appropriate degree of resolution will. As you may expect, you perform this miracle by manipulating numbers (that's the only way we postmoderns can *do* magic). The first of these numbers is a ratio: *bits per pixel.* Ask yourself, how many bits does a particular format use to create one pixel?

The more capable graphics programs give you the option of setting the bits-per-pixel ratio. It's a straightforward relationship:

- ✔ Using more bits to create one lowly pixel means you can depict subtler colors and outlines — which sharpens the image but balloons the file.
- ✔ Using fewer bits per pixel reduces the resolution (therefore the quality) of the images rendered by a browser but makes the file smaller and faster to load.

Of course, if you can possibly avoid it, you don't want to use more bits per pixel than most browsers can handle (they'll see the image, all right, but miss the subtlety, which is a waste of bandwidth). Besides, too much subtlety is lost on any Web site visitor who's in a hurry. We're not talking art for art's sake here. However artistic, your Web site graphics are not sitting there to be stared at — unless your visitors are confused, lost, or glazing over (and your page will be too well designed for that, right?).

Settle on a magic bits-per-pixel number for starters. Try storing images with seven (or even five) bits per pixel if you need to show a large image as quickly as possible. For other, smaller graphics, you can practice the balancing act outlined here to find the right mix of resolution and speed.

The second magic figure you can use to reduce the size of a graphic image is the *number of colors* in the picture. A computer "sees" color as information — in particular, instructions that tell it which of those pretty phosphors on the monitor screen to light up. If the file doesn't have to explain the difference between sagebrush green and chartreuse, the instructions are simpler *(just make it light green)* — and voilà, the file is smaller. Here's where the trade-off comes in. Either you can get the color you want *(Why did the logo designer have to make it fuchsia?)* or an image that most of your audience can see *(Neat shade of purple. Where's the info?)* showing up in their browsers. Sometimes practicality means settling for a little of both and all of neither.

Interlacing: Slice and dice for better response time

"What is an interlaced GIF?" you ask. (You *did* ask, right?) Well, call it a way to show order coming out of chaos. An interlaced GIF stores graphic information in a GIF file so a browser can load a low-resolution image on the first of multiple passes — browsers render an image in stages or "passes" — and then fill in the image to its normal resolution on subsequent passes. This method gives images a "Venetian blind" look as your browser draws them.

The load time for images remains the same whether images are interlaced or not, but some browsers load the text of the page with the first pass of the images. This lets users begin scrolling and reading while the browser completes additional image passes. Users get to your information faster, which generally results in happier users!

Check your graphics program documentation to find out whether these techniques are in its arsenal.

A standard GIF image requires 8 bits per pixel, which results in 256 colors. Seven bits of information per pixel produces 128 colors, 5 bits 32 colors, and so on. Some programs, such as Paint Shop Pro (shareware) and Adobe Photoshop (commercial) allow a specific number of colors to be selected. For example, setting the number of colors to 43 results in 7 bits per pixel, but the remaining 85 empty color definitions are set at 0,0,0 (or undefined), which results in a smaller (and faster) graphic than you get if you set the resolution to 7 bits per pixel. Most of these programs also tell you how many unique colors appear in an image and let you manipulate the number of colors until you can achieve the best compromise between size and fidelity.

Rules for using graphics

Keep these rules in mind while you design your Web pages:

- ✔ Sketch your layout with and without graphics.

- ✔ Focus on overall page look and content.

- ✔ KISS your images . . . *Keep It Small and Simple.*

- ✔ Use compressed, interlaced GIFs or JPEGs.

- ✔ Link thumbnail versions of images to larger files instead of dumping megabyte-sized files on your unsuspecting users.

✔ Include the size of image files in the text that describes large images.

✔ Use graphics sparingly for maximum effect.

✔ Don't forget the non-graphical users.

✔ Use images or graphics to enhance text information.

If you understand and can implement all the topics discussed in this chapter, congratulations — you're not an HTML ignoramus. You know enough to design and create well-balanced, attractive, user-friendly Web pages.

Remember, an alternative always exists

Graphics are fun. Every Web designer loves to play with graphics. With that said, please let us say this, too: You should not always use them. Many reasons exist to steer clear of too many graphics. You wouldn't want to scare off any potential viewers, would you? In our minds, two main reasons exist for you to avoid graphics at times.

First, many individuals with disabilities are unable to see and/or understand your graphics. For this reason, the W3C has recently embarked on promoting a high degree of usability for people with disabilities through their Web Accessibility Initiative (WAI). Simple ways exist for you to turn your graphics into readable text — in a manner of speaking. One way is to include the `alt` attribute, which allows authors to include a name or description of the graphic image. This way, text-readers will be able to understand just what is going on. If you're adamantly opposed to using the `alt` attribute, you can instead, just point readers to a text-only version of your Web site.

The second reason we think you should use your graphics carefully, is the tried-and-true tale of bad taste. Don't forget to keep your audience in mind. Readers want to read your pages, not wade through a bunch of graphics to eventually find the content they so desperately want. Remember, Web-time is different than real-time, you only have a few seconds to make an impression and if you forget about your content, users won't hang around for long. Back to the drawing board!

Keep right on going to find out even more fun things to add to your Web pages (sorry, no pterodactyls). The next chapter reveals how to master the intricacies of complex Web pages with élan, panache, and the occasional crêpe suzette. (Who knows? You may want to get that beret, after all!)

Part III
Formatting Your Data

The 5th Wave   By Rich Tennant

"... and when you click the fire hydrant, it marks your domain for you."

In this part . . .

Part III is where you roll up your sleeves and get down and dirty with HTML. In other words, it's time to tackle a variety of HTML tags up close and personal. You begin with the global structure tags that give an HTML document its form and can describe its content. After that, you encounter the presentation tags that allow HTML to manage fonts and text styles.

From there, it's on to the HTML tags for character styles, including ways to label and present various kinds of content and multiple methods for representing computer output and input inside a Web page. After that, you tackle various ways to build lists using HTML and explore some interesting and offbeat uses for this markup. Your next markup adventure involves the numeric and character entities that HTML recognizes. These entities allow you to include many kinds of special characters in Web pages, including alphabets from languages around the world.

Chapter 8

HTML Document Structure

- -

In This Chapter

▶ Identifying HTML versions

▶ Commenting for posterity (or later reference)

▶ Starting an HTML document from the head down

▶ Building an HTML document body

▶ Creating document divisions

▶ Using heading levels

▶ Describing an HTML document to robots and search engines

▶ Naming your HTML documents

▶ Developing an HTML style

- -

*B*uilding a well-formed Web page requires that you use certain HTML tags to describe a document's composition and structure and that you give a Web page a definite title. Certain tags advertise information about the document in which they appear, whereas others define the document's contents and structure. Even within the content, you can use a variety of HTML tags to further subdivide your material and help you organize that content thoroughly and professionally. In this chapter, we tell you about these structure tags and how you can use required tags with optional tags to improve on the bare minimum that HTML itself demands.

The Importance of Document Structure

Whether by design or by default, all HTML documents have a structure of one kind or another. In this section, we tell you more about the tags that help you to create, manage, and identify a document's structure and syntax.

Some tags are necessary to meet basic syntax requirements for a valid, well-formed HTML document. We call these tags *global structure tags* because they define and control the structure that HTML documents can take. Other members of this tag set, although not strictly required, can add a lot to the way a document behaves and help you keep your content better organized. Either way, structure tags define the basic building blocks for HTML documents and are well worth getting to know.

Before we jump in head first, take a look at the three basic parts of an HTML document:

✔ Code containing HTML version information

✔ A declarative header section

✔ A body section containing document content

You can add many other elements to add even more structure, and we get to those shortly. So, hold on to your britches because you're about to begin your first HTML coding experience.

What browsers forgive, a validator may not!

First things first, we need to explain the importance of valid HTML documents. A validator is a type of software program that performs basic quality control on your HTML documents. Validators check the syntax and structure of a document against a model of what the syntax and structure should be to help developers find and fix errors, omissions, and other gotchas.

Where HTML is concerned, such programs are sometimes called HTML validators. The ultimate HTML validator comes from — who else? — the World Wide Web Consortium, fondly abbreviated as W3C. The name of their program is the HTML Validation Service, and you can use it through the Web page at `http://validator.w3.org` to check out your own HTML documents free of charge.

The interesting thing about going through the validator is that you discover that what a Web browser happily lets you get away with, the validator finds fault with — loudly and vociferously, we might add. In other words, most Web browsers are quite indifferent to the requirements built into HTML and cheerfully display so-called HTML documents that aren't worthy of the name!

Today, this is no big deal, because HTML itself doesn't follow a truly strict or regular syntax. (And we're not talking about a tax on booze or cigarettes here; we're talking about a regular, predictable way to describe what HTML markup is and how it works.) In fact, some of what HTML allows is hard for computers to check at all! But beware, the W3C has released a next-generation HTML, the Extensible Hypertext Markup Language (XHTML) 1.0, that is more rigorously defined and extremely well suited to mechanical validation.

XHTML is based on HTML 4, so by learning HTML you're well on your way to understanding XHTML. We cover the current XHTML specification in Chapter 19.

Computer geeks like to talk about code as being *valid.* When code is valid, it passes through a validator program as well formed with no errors, follows all the syntax rules of the elements that must be present in a program, and adheres to the rules whenever optional elements appear. Why not do the same with your HTML documents?

The very model of a valid, well-formed HTML document

You will no doubt discover, if you try, that browsers let you omit almost all the required elements that make up a valid, well-formed HTML document. But because of the shape of things to come, and in the spirit of recommending only the best of practices to you, we present a model for a valid, well-formed HTML document. In our model, required elements appear in boldface and optional elements appear in plain text. We also try to include all the tags that appear in this chapter, just for grins!

Although we highlight the use of optional elements, including them in all your HTML documents is good practice. Just because they're optional doesn't mean they can't save your life — okay that's an exaggeration, but they *can* save you time in the long run!

```
<!DOCTYPE HTML PUBLIC
 "-//W3C//DTD HTML 4.0 Transitional//EN"
 "http://www.w3.org/TR/REC-html40/loose.dtd">
<html>
<head>
<title>The very model of a well-formed HTML document</title>
<base href="http://www.lanw.com">
<style>
body {background color:pink}
h1 {font:14pt Times bold}
p {font: 12 Times; text-align: justify;}
</style>
<meta http-equiv="Resource type" content="document">
<meta http-equiv="Copyright" content="LANWrights, Inc. 2000">
</head> <!-- ends header portion of the document -->
<body> <!-- begins body portion of the document -->
<div>
<h1> A Level One Header</h1>
This is a section of the document.
</div>
<div>
```

```
This is another, longer section of the document.
<p>Notice, the font size does not drop from the default
until the first &lt;p&gt; tag.
Within this section, we can also add a span section. <p>
<span type="text/css" style="font-size: 18pt">
The span text appears in a larger font.
</span>
This text will be back to the original font again, but
with no line break.
</div> <!-- This ends the second division -->
</body> <!-- This ends the body of the document -->
</html> <!-- This ends the entire HTML document -->
```

The page that results from this HTML markup as displayed by Internet Explorer appears in Figure 8-1 and shows the effects of the various document divisions and so forth. (Note that this text may be displayed differently in Netscape Navigator.) The main thing you should notice is that, except for the title, the structure tags don't produce anything on a Web page. Because they work behind the scenes, we call them structure tags!

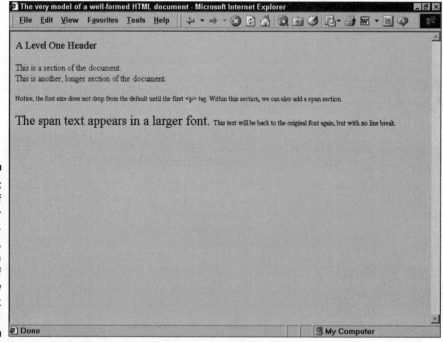

Figure 8-1:
The fruits of our labor didn't produce much, but can be interesting if you know what to look for!

In the following sections, we dissect the previous code — don't worry; it won't be nearly as traumatic as the time you had to dissect your first frog in junior high school.

<!-- . . . --> Comments

When you use the comment tag, the browser ignores the text between the brackets. Use this tag to document your HTML tags and page structures to make notes for future reference or to provide extra information for others who must read your HTML code.

You can use comments to temporarily hide sections of a document. Simply adding a comment tag pair around the text you want to hide keeps the text from being parsed when the document is viewed through a Web browser. (However, if someone views the source code for your document, he or she will be able to see the comments.)

`<!-- . . . -->` is legal within all HTML tags.

Although the results won't appear on-screen, you can enclose any other HTML tags within a pair of comment tags: `<!-- . . . -->`. As the preceding tip indicates, this results in "hiding" the enclosed information from your Web browser. (The text isn't really hidden though; the browser sees the text but ignores it.)

Examples: See file `/html4Fd3/examples/ch08/comment.htm`.

<!DOCTYPE> Document type

`<!DOCTYPE>` specifies the version of HTML used in the document through SGML declaration. All documents should contain a `<!DOCTYPE>` declaration to tell browsers, HTML validation tools (such as the W3C's HTML Validation Service), and other software exactly what version of HTML is used in that document. `<!DOCTYPE>` also

✔ Should be the first element within any HTML document. `<!DOCTYPE>` is not legal within any markup tag. It must appear before the `<html>` tag.

✔ Is a required element in any syntactically valid HTML document. It can only be omitted because most browsers don't require this value to be supplied. (They assume a default value instead.) We recommend that you use this tag.

✔ Can't appear in any other markup tag, and no other tags can be used within it.

DOCTYPE is made up of the following attributes:

```
HTML PUBLIC "version name" "URL"
```

- ✔ HTML identifies the markup language as a version of HTML.

- ✔ PUBLIC identifies the source of the markup language's definition as well known and publicly accessible.

- ✔ "version name" must reference a proper and complete HTML version name. The name of the most typical current English-language version of HTML 4.01 is "-//W3C//DTD HTML 4.01 Transitional//EN".

- ✔ "URL" indicates where a PUBLIC definition resides; it may either be "http://www.w3.org/TR/html4/loose.dtd" for a pretty forgiving, but still official definition of HTML 4.01, or "http://www.w3.org/TR/html4/strict.dtd" for a stricter, less forgiving, entirely official definition of HTML 4.01.

For more information about valid HTML version names and their associated URLs, please visit HTML Help's excellent overview of the <!DOCTYPE> declaration at:

```
www.htmlhelp.com/reference/html40/html/doctype.html
```

Technically, DOCTYPE is an SGML declaration, not an HTML tag. But because it's required at the head of any valid HTML document, we cover it.

Examples: See file /html4Fd3/examples/ch08/doctype.htm.

<address> . . . </address>
Attribution information

<address> . . . </address> encloses credit and reference information about an HTML document, such as the author's name and address, signature files, and contact information. Most browsers display <address> items in an italic font. <address> imposes no major layout changes, but does act much like a character-level style, like the tags discussed in Chapter 10 of this book. But because it delivers important information about a Web document's creator, we cover it here in the discussion of global HTML document structure. <address> is not a required HTML document structure tag.

Use the <address> tag where you want a footer; there is no <footer> markup tag in HTML 4.01. Include this tag at the end of any document to supply author contact information for questions or feedback.

Examples: See file `/html4Fd3/examples/ch08/address.htm`.

<base> Basis for relative addressing

Use the `<base>` tag to define a root-level URL for a collection of Web pages. As long as you put a `<base>` tag in the `<head>` section of an HTML document (which is the only area in which you may legally place it), any URLs that occur within the `<body>` section of the document need include only as much information as is needed to navigate from the `<base>` definition. The `<base>` tag is not a required HTML structure tag. The `<base>` tag is an empty tag, which is a tag that does not require a closing tag.

Take a look at the following attributes:

```
href="URL" [CT]
```

This attribute establishes a base URL for the Web document and defines the basis for relative URLs that may appear elsewhere within the same document.

Example: `<base href="http://www.lanw.com">`

With the tag `<base href="http://www.lanw.com">` in the `<head>` section of a document, any URL in the `<body>` of that document acts like it is appended to that base. URLs for files in the base directory can take the form `href="file.ext"`, and files in a directory named graphics beneath the `http://www.lanw.com` base directory take the form `href="graphics/file.ext"`. This technique is called relative addressing.

```
target="windowname" [CI]
```

Use this attribute on framed Web pages to designate that links should be loaded into a particular window. We cover framed Web pages and use of the target attribute in Chapter 16.

Example: `<base target="menu"> <!--1 loads linked reference into menu window 1-->`

<body> . . . </body> Document body

`<body> . . . </body>` has only one use — it identifies the body of an HTML document, which is where the real document content resides. This explicit structure tag is required for strictly interpreted HTML.

All the individual attributes for the `<body>` tag are deprecated, which means that they won't be supported in future versions of HTML. All such information will be captured through a separate style sheet or in specific style tags within the document itself. You can safely omit any or all of these attributes, which we describe in the following paragraphs:

```
alink="#RRGGBB" or "colorname" [CI]
```

The preceding attribute sets the color for the active (currently selected) link; colors may be set using a six-digit RGB color code preceded by a pound sign or with a recognized color name; if omitted, the browser picks the color for this link. (See `www.w3.org/TR/html4/types.html#h-6.5` for the color names and RGB values.)

Example: `<body alink="teal">` Colors the active link using the color named teal.

```
background="URL" [CT]
```

This attribute points to the URL where an image to be used as the (tiled) background of the document resides.

Example: `<body background = "http://www.lanw.com/graphics/lanwlogo.fig">`

```
bgcolor="#RRGGBB" or "colorname" [CI]
```

The preceding attribute sets the background color, where colors may be set using a six-digit RGB color code preceded by a pound sign, or with the name of a recognized color; if omitted, the browser sets the color to white.

Example: `<body bgcolor="black">`

```
link="#RRGGBB" or "colorname" [CI]
```

This attribute sets the color for unvisited links, using a six-digit RGB code or a specific color name; if omitted, the browser sets the color (usually to blue).

Example: `<body link="#009933">`

```
text="#RRGGBB" or "colorname" [CI]
```

This text sets the color used for textual data, using a six-digit RGB code or a specific color name; if omitted, the browser sets the color to black (#000000).

Example: `<body text="black">`

```
vlink="#RRGGBB" or "colorname" [CI]
```

This attribute sets the color for links that have already been visited (since the last time the cache was refreshed); if omitted, the browser sets the color to purple (#0033FF).

Example: `<body vlink="#FFFF00">` ◁-- pure red -->

Examples: See file /html4Fd3/examples/ch08/body.htm.

`<div>`...`</div>` *Logical division*

`<div>`...`</div>` creates distinct, logical divisions within an HTML document. Use this element to divide a document into separate sections, where each one can have separate style definitions, including alignment values, font choices, text colors, and so forth. Such assignments apply to everything between the opening `<div>` and the closing `</div>` tags.

Take a look at the following attributes:

```
align="LEFT" or "CENTER" or "RIGHT' or "JUSTIFY" [CI]
```

The `align` attribute is deprecated. It specifies the default horizontal alignment for the contents within the `<div>` element. The default value depends on the base text direction. For left to right text, the default value equals `LEFT`.

Example: `<div align="LEFT">`

```
style="text"
```

This attribute supports all standard HTML style properties and values, as described in Chapter 18 of this book. When using the `style` attribute, you must also use the `type` attribute to identify the kind of style sheet language in use (the following example references the notation used for Cascading Style Sheets, or CSS).

Example: `<div type="text/css" style="color:navy">`

Note that the `align` attribute in any element inside `<div>` overrides the `align` value for the `<div>` element itself. You can't use `<div>` in conjunction with `<p>`, because a `<div>` element terminates any preceding paragraph.

Examples: See file /html4Fd3/examples/ch08/div.htm.

<h> . . . </h*> Header levels*

Headers come in different styles and sizes to help you organize your content and make it easier to read. The size and display characteristics for any header level are determined by the browser. But by default, a level 1 heading (<h1>) is larger and more pronounced than a level 2 heading <h2>, and so on. Header tags are by no means required in a document, but they help to organize its contents. Header tags may be numbered from <h1> to <h6>, but you seldom find a document with more than three or four levels of headers in use.

Headers have the following attribute:

```
align="LEFT" or "CENTER" or 'RIGHT' or "JUSTIFY" [CI]
```

The align attribute is deprecated. It sets the alignment of header text on the Web page. The default value depends on the base text direction. For left to right text, LEFT is the default.

Example: <h1 align="CENTER">Test Header 1</h1> <!-- centers this level 1 heading -->

Using headings regularly and consistently helps add structure and divisions to your documents. Some experts recommend not using a subordinate header level unless you plan to use at least two of them beneath a parent level. In other words, don't use a single <h3> . . . </h3> after an <h2> . . . </h2> pair. This practice follows the outlining principle where you don't indent unless you have at least two subtopics under any particular topic. Although we think the occasional exception is okay, this guideline is good for HTML documents.

Examples: See file /html4Fd3/examples/ch08/h.htm.

<head> . . . </head> Document head block

<head> . . . </head> creates a container for all kinds of information that describes an HTML document, including the document's title, search engine information, index information, a next-page pointer, and even links to other HTML documents. <head> . . . </head> is required at the head of an HTML document. Even though many browsers can display documents without a <head> . . . </head> block at the beginning, including one is good practice, especially if you want to establish a base URL for relative page

addressing should you have numerous graphics or hyperlinks to other local documents in your page. In fact, the `<head>` . . . `</head>` tag pair is required to create a valid, well-formed HTML document.

Here is the `<head>` attribute:

```
profile="URL" [CT]
```

It defines the location for a metadictionary, or profile, where a set of applicable profile tags is defined.

Example: `<head profile="http://www.lanw.com/profile.txt">`

Examples: See file `/html4Fd3/examples/ch08/head.htm`.

<html> . . . </html> HTML document

The `<html>` . . . `</html>` tag pair should enclose any entire HTML document as the outermost layer of its overall structure. Its job is to denote where an HTML document begins, and where it ends. The `<html>` . . . `</html>` tag pair is required to create a valid, well-formed HTML document.

Take a look at the following `<html>` attribute:

```
version="URL" [CN]
```

The `version` attribute is deprecated. It specifies a URL for a Document Type Defintion (DTD) to be used to interpret this document, which is usually the same URL that's included in the `<!DOCTYPE>` declaration. If you follow our recommendations for building valid, well-formed HTML, this attribute is unnecessary.

`<html>` . . . `</html>` is not legal within any other markup tags.

The `version` attribute specifies which HTML DTD version governs the current document. This attribute has been deprecated because it's redundant with version information provided in the document type declaration. For more information on DTDs and document type declarations search the W3C site for each at `http://search.w3.org/Public/`.

You can only use the following markup tags within `<html>` . . . `</html>`: `<body>`, `<frameset>`, and `<head>`.

Examples: See file `/html4Fd3/examples/ch08/html.htm`.

<meta> Meta-information

Use the ⟨meta⟩ tag within the ⟨head⟩ element to embed document meta-information (information about information in your document). Such information can be extracted by servers or clients and may be used to identify, index, or catalog specialized document meta-information. This stuff is the kind that Web robots care about a lot, which means that this data is often used to categorize and label your Web pages on a search engine like Yahoo!, Excite, or AltaVista. The ⟨meta⟩ tag is an empty tag.

⟨meta⟩ uses the following attributes:

    name="*text*" [CS]

The preceding attribute names any of several document properties, including its author, publication date, and so on. If this attribute is left out, the name is assumed to be the value set for http-equiv.

Examples: ⟨meta name="author" content="Ed Tittel"⟩

    content="*text*" [CS]

This attribute supplies a value for some named property, or for an http-equiv response header.

    http-equiv="*text*" [CI]

This attribute binds the element to an HTTP response header that will be sent when a robot or browser queries the page for this information. If the HTTP response header format is known to its requester, its contents can be processed. HTTP header names are not case-sensitive. If http-equiv is absent, use the name attribute to identify this meta-information, but it won't show up within an HTTP response header when requested. (That's why we recommend you use this attribute to label your site for public consumption.)

Example: ⟨meta http-equiv="Copyright" content="LANWrights, Inc. -- 1999"⟩

    scheme="*schemename*" [CS]

The preceding identifies the scheme to use to interpret a property's values. This attribute is necessary only when metadata requires interpretation to make sense.

⟨meta⟩ is legal within the ⟨head⟩ markup tag. You can't use any markup tags within ⟨meta⟩; it's an empty tag.

Meta-information makes a site's contents more accessible to spiders and robots for automatic indexing. It also makes information more accessible to programs you use to manage a Web site. No universal `http-equiv` values exist; instead, document designers and robot/agent owners tend to stick to a limited vocabulary of terms. Thus, when a robot/agent declares its support for a specific `http-equiv` value, it quickly spreads around the Web. Some robots record all meta-information so that specialized or focused data searches can use that information, even if it's not standardized. The Web Robots Pages at `http://info.webcrawler.com/mak/projects/robots/robots.html` can tell you more about how these software programs work and how to use the `<meta>` tag to make your site more accessible to them. Also, you can use the Platform for Internet Content Selection (PICS) through the `<meta>` tag to identify content, sign code, aid privacy, or identify intellectual property rights. Details are available at `www.w3.org/PICS/`.

Examples: See file `/html4Fd3/examples/ch08/meta.htm`.

<span> . . . </span> Localized style formatting

This tag applies style information to text within a document on an arbitrary basis. (`<div>` actually requires dividing a document up into separate containers; `<span>` lets you select any chunk of HTML code to which you can apply styles.) Therefore, you should use `<span>` for localized text formatting using the `style` attribute.

`<span>` uses these attributes:

```
align="LEFT" or "CENTER" or "RIGHT" or "JUSTIFY" [CI]
```

The `align` attribute is deprecated. It specifies the default horizontal alignment for contents of the `<span>` element.

```
style="text" [CN]
```

This attribute supports all standard HTML style properties and values, as described in Chapter 18 of this book. When using the `style` attribute, you must also use the `type` attribute to identify the kind of style sheet language in use. (The following example references the notation used for CSS.)

Example: `<span type="text/css" style="color:navy">`

`<span>` is an inline division element. It applies no changes to standard rendering to surrounded content without a `style` attribute definition. You can use `<span>` within paragraphs, unlike `<div>`, but you can't use it to group multiple elements, as you can with `<div>`.

Examples: See file `/html4Fd3/examples/ch08/span.htm`.

<style> . . . </style> Style information

`<style>` . . . `</style>` provides a way to include rendering and display information in an HTML document using standard style sheet notation. CSS1 and CSS2 are the most widely supported standards; most references to style sheets refer to CSS1. Information in the `<style>` tag works with a client's default configuration, as well as any externally referenced style sheets, to define the set of style rules that applies to a given Web page. This material is the subject of Chapter 18 in this book, so please look there for specific examples of HTML markup that uses complex style definitions. The `<style>` tag is by no means required in an HTML document, but it provides a powerful way to control how your documents look and behave.

`<style>` uses these attributes:

```
type="text" [CN]
```

`type` specifies the type of style sheet in use. The type for CSS1 sheets is `text/css`; for CSS2, it's `text/css2`.

```
media= "SCREEN" or "PRINT" or "PROJECTION" or "BRAILLE" or
       "SPEECH" or "TTY" or "TV" or "HANDHELD" or "AURAL"
       or "ALL" [CI]
```

This attribute identifies the ideal environment in which the Web page should be conveyed. The default is `ALL`, and `SCREEN` is used in most cases because Web pages are most often viewed on a computer screen. However, pages designed for presentations should use the `PROJECTION` value, whereas those meant to be read by a text-to-speech reader should use the `SPEECH` value. Currently, this attribute provides information only and doesn't affect the way the style sheet is interpreted or the page is rendered. You may include more than one media type, where each is separated by a comma.

The `<style>` tag should contain only valid style statements in the language indicated by the `type` attribute. Style sheets are now formally part of the HTML 4.01 specification and are supported by Internet Explorer 4.0 and Netscape Navigator 4.0. Older versions of browsers that don't support style sheets ignore style markup.

Example: See file `/html4Fd3/examples/ch08/style.htm`.

<title> . . . </title> Document title

The `<title>` . . . `</title>` tags enclose the title for an HTML document, which normally appears in the title bar in the browser's window. By default, the title is set to the HTML document's filename if a title is not specified. `<title>` . . . `</title>` is legal only within `<head>` . . . `</head>`. You can use only plain text within `<title>` . . . `</title>`, because this text only displays on the title bar of the browser window. The `<title>` tag also takes no attributes.

Try to come up with a useful title for every HTML document you write. An accurate, descriptive title helps the many Web search engines and tools to accurately identify or label your content.

Examples: See file `/html4Fd3/examples/ch08/title.htm`.

Back to the Future

Prior to writing the preceding section, we created an example HTML file that showed all the structure tags in this chapter. If you flip back to the preceding definitions as we explain this file line by line, you can form a pretty good picture of what's going on here.

```
<!DOCTYPE HTML PUBLIC
"-//W3C//DTD HTML 4.01 Transitional//EN"
"http://www.w3.org/TR/html4/loose.dtd">
```

The `DOCTYPE` statement identifies that we're using a public HTML definition known as the transitional HTML 4.01 DTD as defined by the W3C, which resides at the URL that appears in the last line above.

```
<html>
```

The `<html>` tag opens the HTML portion of the document and continues all the way to the end to the closing `</html>` tag.

```
<head>
```

The `<head>` tag opens the HTML document header, which contains all kinds of information that describes this document, as you see in the lines that follow up to the `</head>` tag.

```
<title>The very model of a well-formed HTML
document</title>
```

The text between the two ⟨title⟩ . . . ⟨/title⟩ tags defines the title for the resulting HTML document when viewed in a browser, as a quick jump back to Figure 8-1 confirms.

```
<base href="http://www.lanw.com">
```

This ⟨base⟩ tag identifies the root for all relative references in the body of the document as the LANWrights Web server at http://www.lanw.com.

```
<style>
body {background color:pink}
H1 {font:14pt Times bold}
P {font: 12 Times; text-align: justify;}
</style>
```

This section of code defines a set of styles for the entire body of the HTML document to follow. It sets the page background color to pink, requires level 1 heads to use 14-point Times boldface fonts, and indicates that all text following the first paragraph marker, ⟨p⟩, should be in 12-point Times, and the text aligned for even right- and left-hand margins.

```
<meta http-equiv="Resource type" content="document">
<meta http-equiv="Copyright" content="LANWrights, Inc.
2000">
```

These two ⟨meta⟩ tags are a subset of what you would put on a typical Web page, but they indicate that this file contains an HTML document in the first line and provides a copyright notice for LANWrights, Inc., in the second line.

```
</head> <!-- ends header portion of the document -->
```

This line closes the header portion of the document, followed by an HTML comment that reinforces this point.

```
<body> <!-- begins body portion of the document -->
```

The ⟨body⟩ tag opens the content portion of the document. Except for the text between the two ⟨title⟩ . . . ⟨/title⟩ tags in the ⟨head⟩ section, only text in the ⟨body⟩ . . . ⟨/body⟩ section of an HTML document shows up on-screen.

```
<div>
```

This ⟨div⟩ tag opens the first division in the document, which includes the following header level 1 line and the text line after that.

```
<h1> A Level One Header</h1>
```

This is a level one header that identifies itself as such. In a more normal HTML document, you use header levels to identify various levels of structure within a document (or a division within that document).

```
This is a section of the document.</div>
```

The </div> tag at the end of this line marks the end of the first section of this document, and imposes a paragraph break after this line as a consequence.

```
<div>This is another, longer section of the document.
<p>Notice, the font size does not drop from the default
until the first &lt;p&gt; tag.
Within this section, we can also add a span section. </p>
```

The preceding lines open up a new division within the document, and show the effects of the <p> paragraph style from the <style> section in the document header.

```
<span type = "text/css" style="font-size: 18pt">
The span text appears in a larger font.
</span>
```

Here, we begin a <span> section within a document division, marked by the larger text that appears immediately thereafter. As soon as the </span> tag appears to close this section, the font reverts to its original size setting. But because no paragraph break is implied when a </span> tag appears, the next line follows immediately, with no line break.

```
This text will be back to the original font again, but
with no line break.
</div> <!-- This ends the second division -->
```

The </div> tag closes out the second division of the document.

```
</body> <!-- This ends the body of the document -->
</html> <!-- This ends the entire HTML document -->
```

The </body> tag marks the end of the HTML document's body, and the </html> marks the end of the document itself. Notice that comments after the closing tag are perfectly valid (they're ignored by design).

The best way to understand the importance of HTML's structure tags is to recognize that they define the primary containers for text and other information in an HTML document.

- ✔ DOCTYPE identifies what is to follow.

- ✔ `<head>`, `<title>`, `<style>`, `<meta>`, and `<base>` tags set the style and the stage for what is to come.

- ✔ `<body>`, `<div>`, `<h1>` . . . `<h6>`, and `<span>` tags identify the containers within which you can place the document's content.

Chapter 9

Presentation Controls

● ●

● ●

*H*TML includes a wide range of tags that allow you to manage the way that text appears on-screen. Such tags govern font selection, text styles, colors, and so forth and let you control which way text flows on a page (from left to right, right to left, top to bottom, or bottom to top). As a category, these tags allow you to control what the text in your document looks like, which is why we call them presentation controls. In this chapter, you encounter a variety of such tools.

Style versus Presentation

This section is chock-full of HTML tags that you can use to manage text. These tags allow you to manage everything from the kind of font you instruct the browser to use for your text — which might be something like Times New Roman, Courier, Arial, or some other well-known typeface — to the size and weight of the characters chosen from that font. It also includes a variety of controls for *text styles* (or settings such as bold or italic) and other kinds of related items.

Sounds pretty good, doesn't it? But before you take a spin through these tags, stop to consider this: Except for a single tag (`<bdo>`) that controls the language choice for a text section and the direction in which text displays, all tags in this chapter create text effects that you can control through styles instead.

In fact, many of the tags in this chapter are known as deprecated tags. In ordinary terms, the word *deprecated* refers to something that those in authority disapprove of strongly. In official HTML-speak, a *deprecated tag* is one that is headed for the scrap heap and will probably be abandoned when the next release of HTML is ready.

Therefore, even though these deprecated tags are legal today and most browsers should display them perfectly, we don't recommend that you use them without pausing to consider that a time may come when these tags won't work anymore. If your Web pages live only for a short while or you plan to replace them with newer versions before the new millennium gets too old, you should be okay.

Just to keep you on the straight and narrow, Table 9-1 lists all the tags in this chapter that are deprecated. Surprisingly, this distinction covers the bulk of the tags covered in this chapter.

Table 9-1   Deprecated Presentation Control Tags in HTML 4.01

Tag	What's Deprecated	Explanation
`<basefont>`	tag & attributes	Selects default font
`<center>`	tag	Centers enclosed text
`<font>`	tag & attributes	Selects typeface, size, color
`<hr>`	all attributes	Draws horizontal rule
`<s>`	tag	Strikes through enclosed text
`<strike>`	tag	Strikes through enclosed text
`<u>`	tag	Underlines enclosed text

Here's how to interpret the contents of this table:

- ✔ If the tag is deprecated, it will be phased out with the next release of HTML. If that tag takes attributes, the same goes for them, too.
- ✔ If all attributes are deprecated, the tag will remain in effect, but the attributes will be phased out with the next release of HTML.
- ✔ If some attributes are deprecated, the tag and its other attributes will remain in effect, but the designated attributes will be phased out with the next release of HTML.

In addition to these deprecated tags (which make up more than half the tags covered in this chapter), we don't recommend you use the tags shown in Table 9-2, either. The tags in Table 9-2 also produce effects that you can create more easily by using style sheets or style markup in your HTML documents. (Chapter 18 is where you can find out about this style stuff in HTML.) But because they're not deprecated and we don't recommend their use, we call these tags "nugatory," which means they're trifling, insignificant, or of no worth — we're not referring to their creamy nougat center, either.

Table 9-2	Nugatory Presentation Control Tags in HTML 4.01
Tag	*Explanation*
`<big>`	Increases font size for enclosed text
`<small>`	Decreases font size for enclosed text
`<tt>`	Uses a monospaced font to make the text look like typewriter text

Because you're going to see these tags all over the place in HTML code, and because you may prefer to use these tags' quick-and-dirty capabilities from time to time, we have no choice but to tell you about them. Plus, better you hear about them from us than on the playground or in an alley somewhere.

Whether you succumb to your base desires to use these tags or decide to use style-related markup, remember this: Instead of using these presentation control tags, you can use any of the following techniques:

✔ Reference an external style sheet. In such a style sheet, you can select default fonts and manage font sizes, font styles, and even font colors to your heart's content. You can also control margins, spacing before and after text elements, and more.

✔ Create a `<style>` section in an HTML document's `<head>` section to define the same font characteristics for an entire Web document.

✔ Use the `style` attribute in most HTML tags to control relevant characteristics only for the text associated with the tag you're working on.

We think that managing text presentation in an HTML document is best done with style markup using one of the techniques we describe in the previous bulleted list. However, it's your HTML document, and you can do whatever you like!

Presentation Control Tags

By the time you eliminate all the deprecated tags in Table 9-1 and the nugatory tags in Table 9-2, the only tag that's left is the `<bdo>` tag. If you've already decided to use style sheet markup with your HTML documents, you can skip straight to that tag in the text that follows. Then, when you're done with that tag, you're done with this chapter!

On the other hand, if you want to find out more about a collection of tags you're pretty likely to encounter in most HTML markup that you'll read in other people's Web pages, go ahead and plow through the other tags in this chapter. That way, you'll know what you're missing if you decide to take the style route, or you'll know what to look for if you ever decide to go the other way.

`<b>` . . . `</b>` Bold text

Use of these tags indicates that the enclosed text should appear in boldface type. As such, you can use the `<b>` . . . `</b>` tag pair to provide specific focus or emphasis on words or phrases in paragraph or body text in an HTML document. But style sheets can match the same effects and can better manage character weight and font style. That's why we recommend that you "do it with style" rather than use this tag.

Example: `<b>Hello</b>` displays the word "Hello" in bold type.

Examples: See file `/html4Fd3/examples/ch09/b.htm`.

`<basefont>` Base font

The `<basefont>` tag sets the basic font parameters that are used as the default for any text on a Web page that is not otherwise formatted by a style sheet or by using the `<font>` element directly.

This tag and its attributes are deprecated in HTML 4.01 in favor of style sheet rules. Rather than using the `<basefont>` tag, use style settings to manage font selection within your documents.

The rest of this section describes the `<basefont>` attributes. The attribute appears in code followed by an explanation.

```
color="#RRGGBB" or "colorname" [CI]
```

Defines the color for the base font; you can set colors by using a six-digit RGB color code preceded by a pound sign or with a recognized color name; if this attribute is omitted, the browser picks the color for this font. See `www.w3.org/TR/html4/types.html#h-6.5` for more information on the color names and RGB values.

You cannot use additional tags within `<basefont>` because it's an empty tag, meaning that it stands alone and is forbidden to have a closing tag.

Example: `<basefont color="teal">` sets the base font to the color named teal (RGB value #669999).

```
face="name" [CI]
```

This attribute specifies the base font face; it should be a well-known font family name such as Times New Roman, Courier, and so forth, or one of the generic Cascading Style Sheets (CSS) font families, such as serif, sans serif, monospace, cursive, or fantasy.

Example: `<basefont face="Times New Roman">` sets the base font to the Times New Roman font; if this font is not available on a particular user's machine, the browser substitutes the nearest equivalent font face.

```
size="number" [CN]
```

This attribute defines the size of the base font. The value of `number` can be between 1 and 7, inclusive; the default is 3, and 7 is the largest legal value. Relative font size settings (for example, `<font size="+3">`) are set according to this value throughout the document.

Example: `<basefont size="5">` sets the default font size for the document two sizes larger than the normal default.

Examples: See file `/html4Fd3/examples/ch09/basefont.htm`.

<bdo> . . . </bdo> Bidirectional algorithm

The `<bdo>` . . . `</bdo>` tags name the primary language in use on a document and can establish, alter, or reverse the default algorithm used for display direction. For English and most other European languages, this algorithm is left to right and top to bottom; other languages, such as Japanese and Arabic, use a different algorithm.

The rest of this section describes the `<bdo>` attributes.

```
lang="language-code" [CI]
```

This attribute defines the primary language to be used in the HTML document where it appears. A list of primary language codes appears in ISO Standard 639a, which you can read online at

```
www.oasis-open.org/cover/iso639-2a.html
```

Common language codes include "en" for English, "fr" for French, "de" for German, and so forth.

Example: `<bdo lang="fr">` sets the language to French.

```
dir="LTR" or "RTL" [CI]
```

This attribute specifies the direction of text interpretation for languages that are read from right to left, such as Hebrew, or for languages whose direction of viewing may be unclear. The default is left to right, so you don't usually need to use this attribute except when you include languages that don't adhere to this display direction.

Example: `<bdo lang="he" dir="RTL">` sets the language to Hebrew and the direction to right to left.

Examples: See file `/html4Fd3/examples/ch09/bdo.htm`.

<big> . . . </big> Big text

These tags increase the font of the text enclosed between them to one size larger than the size set in the `<basefont>` tag. Because you can handle these effects more transparently using style-related tags or with an external style sheet, we recommend that you think hard before using this tag pair. The `<big>` tag takes no attributes.

Examples: The HTML markup Mr. `<big>Big</big>` causes "Mr." to appear at the default font size, but "Big" will be one size larger.

Examples: See file `/html4Fd3/examples/ch09/big.htm`.

<center> . . . </center> Centered text

As their name should suggest, the `<center>` . . . `</center>` tags center any text horizontally that occurs between them. The `<center>` tag breaks the current line of text and centers the text between it and the closing `</center>` tag on a new line, even if no other markup to control line breaks is used. The `<center>` tag takes no attributes.

The <center> tag is deprecated and will not be supported in future versions of HTML. Use the align="CENTER" attribute that can be applied to many HTML tags or use style sheets to impose centered alignment on specific tags instead.

Example: <center>This text shows up centered.</center> centers the text on a line by itself.

Example: See file /html4Fd3/examples/ch09/center.htm.

<font> . . . </font> Font appearance

The <font> . . . </font> tag pair sets the size, font, and color of text enclosed between the two tags.

The <font> . . . </font> tag pair — and all the individual attributes for the tag pair — are deprecated in HTML 4.01. Thus, we recommend that you use style sheet rules to achieve the same effects when possible. If you specify a particular font face (called a *font family* in CSS terminology), remember that if users don't have that font installed on their machines, the browser uses a default font instead. For that reason, you should stick to well-known font faces or reference generic fonts instead.

The rest of this section describes the <font> attributes.

```
color="#RRGGBB" or "colorname" [CI]
```

Sets the font color; you can set colors by using a six-digit RGB color code preceded by a pound sign or with a recognized color name; if this attribute is omitted, the browser picks the color for this font.

Example: <font color="teal"> sets the font to the color named teal (RGB value #669999).

```
face="name, name2, name3" [CI]
```

Sets the font face. You can specify a list of font names, separated by commas. If the first font is available on the system, the browser uses it; otherwise, the browser tries the second, and so on. If none of the named fonts is available, the browser uses a default font.

Example: <font face="Times, Times New Roman, Courier"> indicates that the browser should try to use a font named Times first, one named Times New Roman second, and one named Courier third.

```
size="number" [CN]
```

Specifies a font size between 1 and 7 (where 7 is the largest legal value). A plus or minus sign before the number indicates a size relative to the current size setting. Relative font sizes are not cumulative, so using two `<font size="+1">` elements in a row does not increase relative size by 2.

Example: `<font size="+3">` increases the relative size of the font by three settings.

Examples: See file `/html4Fd3/examples/ch09/font.htm`.

<hr> Horizontal rule

The `<hr>` tag draws a horizontal line across the page, usually one or two pixels wide. Use it to separate body text from page footers or to separate areas on a Web page. Note also that you can't use any tags within `<hr>` because it's an empty tag. Some Web browsers (for example, Internet Explorer) accept `color` as an attribute to this tag. The rest of this section covers other attributes.

```
align="LEFT" or "CENTER" or "RIGHT" [CI]
```

The `align` attribute is deprecated. It draws the horizontal rule left aligned, right aligned, or centered, depending on the align type assigned, which can be `LEFT`, `RIGHT`, or `CENTER`. The default is for the rule to be centered, but also for the width to be 100 percent, or the entire width of the display area, so you can't tell how the rule is aligned unless you mess with the size attribute (which is deprecated).

Example: `<hr align="LEFT" width="50%">` left-justifies the rule across half the page width.

```
noshade [CI]
```

The `noshade` attribute is deprecated. It draws the outline of the rule without filling it in or providing any 3-D shading effects (which some browsers also do).

Example: `<hr noshade>` draws a horizontal rule without filling it in or shading it. The lack of shading is most noticeable if you increase the `size` attribute to 10 or so.

```
size="number" [CI]
```

Sets the height of the rule in pixels. This attribute is deprecated in HTML 4.01.

Example: `<hr size="10">` creates a thick horizontal rule that is 10 pixels high.

```
width="number" or "%" [CI]
```

Sets the width of the rule in pixels or as a percentage of window width. To specify a percentage, the number must end with a percent (%) sign. This attribute is deprecated in HTML 4.01.

Example: `<hr width="50%">` centers a horizontal rule that covers half the page width.

Examples: See file `/html4Fd3/examples/ch09/hr.htm`.

`<i> . . . </i>` Italic text

This pair of tags italicizes all text enclosed between them. The `<i>` tag takes no attributes. Use italics sparingly for emphasis or effect; remember that their effectiveness fades quickly with overuse. If you're setting off a citation or quoting from a text resource in your document, use the `<cite>` ... `</cite>` tags instead of the italics tags.

Example: `<i>Mary</i>` displays the word "Mary" in italics.

Examples: See file `/html4Fd3/examples/ch09/html.htm`.

`<s> . . . </s>` Strikethrough

This pair of tags causes all enclosed text to appear with a strikethrough (a fine line, one pixel wide, drawn through the text). This tag causes the same effect as the `<strike>` tag, and both of these tags are deprecated in HTML 4.01 in favor of similar style sheet properties. Strikethrough text is difficult to read on a monitor, so use this tag sparingly. It's most commonly used to show text that has been removed from earlier versions of a document. This tag takes no attributes.

Example: `Three <s>strikes</s> and you're out` causes the word "strikes" to be stricken through.

Examples: See file `/html4Fd3/examples/ch09/s.htm`.

<small> . . . </small> Small text

Using these tags makes the text they enclose one size smaller than the base font size. Although this tag is not deprecated, you can use style sheet rules to achieve the same effects. This tag takes no attributes.

Example: The HTML markup Mr. <small>Little</small> shows "Mr." at the default font size, but "Little" at the next smaller font size.

Examples: See file /html4Fd3/examples/ch09/small.htm.

<strike> . . . </strike> Strikethrough

All text placed between this tag pair appears with a fine line, one pixel wide drawn through it. This tag pair is functionally identical to the <s> . . . </s> tags, and likewise is deprecated. Strikethrough text is difficult to read on a monitor, so use this tag sparingly. It's most commonly used to show text removed from earlier versions of a document. This tag takes no attributes.

Example: Three <strike>strikes</strike> and you're out causes the word "strikes" to be stricken through.

Examples: See file /html4Fd3/examples/ch09/strike.htm.

<tt> . . . </tt> Teletype text

Text enclosed with this tag pair appears in a monospaced (teletype) font, typically some variety of Courier or another serif font. Use these tags to set off monospaced text, where character position is important, or when trying to imitate the look of line-printer or typewriter output. Teletype is often used to indicate computer output. Two similar but already obsolete HTML tag pairs of <kbd> . . . <kbd> and <code> . . . <code> are sometimes used to indicate user input or existing text, respectively.

Example: The HTML markup Type <tt>route</tt> at the command line displays all text except the word "route" in the default typeface, but displays "route" in a monospaced font.

Examples: See file /html4Fd3/examples/ch09/tt.htm.

<u> . . . </u> *Underlined text*

All text enclosed between this tag pair will be underlined. This tag pair is deprecated in HTML 4.01 in favor of similar style sheet properties. Try to avoid this tag because most browsers use underlines to emphasize hyperlinks. Underlining can confuse your users, making them think they see hyperlinks that don't work.

Example: The HTML markup Don't do <u>that</u>! displays all text except the word "that" in the default typeface, but adds an underline to the word "that."

Examples: See file /html4Fd3/examples/ch09/u.htm.

Chapter 10

Text Controls

*H*TML includes an interesting assortment of tags that permit you to flag the way text appears in a document, based on its content or significance. Unlike the tags in Chapter 9, where you operate directly on how the text looks, in this chapter, you operate on text to control how its readers will interpret its meaning.

Text control tags let you handle quotations from other sources, both long and short, and attribution of those sources, whether visible on the document or hidden in the HTML source code. They also let you apply varying degrees of emphasis to the text in your documents. You can even mark text in one version of a document as deleted from a prior version, or added since that prior version was published. Perhaps the most confusing — but potentially most powerful — aspect of text control tags is that you can use HTML markup to distinguish text that originates from a variety of sources, or is destined to be used as input to a computer or other text-driven device. In this chapter, you not only find out how to use these tags, but also when to use certain tags that might otherwise seem indistinguishable from one another.

Separating Form from Content

Although numerous tags in this chapter may produce the same visual effects as tags you can find in Chapter 9, understand that the tags in this chapter try to label the content they embrace, whereas the tags in Chapter 9 simply address the way the text they enclose appears on a Web page.

For example, consider these two one-line fragments of HTML code:

```
Homer's <i>Iliad</i> recounts the Trojan War.
Homer's <cite>Iliad</cite> recounts the Trojan War.
```

Viewed inside a browser, both lines look exactly the same, as long as the defaults are left unchanged. But the meaning of the <cite> tag is quite different from that of the <i> tag — namely, <cite> indicates clearly that what follows it is a citation from a resource of some kind, whereas what follows the <i> could be anything forced into italic text. Humans and browsers can read significance into the <cite> tag and what follows it, whereas the <i> tag carries no such weight of meaning for its readers.

The same is true for many of the other tags covered in this chapter. You can match their appearance quite easily (and perhaps even do so with fewer keystrokes) by using the presentation tags that match their look and feel, but you can't capture the same kind of information with the presentation tags that these text controls can provide.

Using style to emphasize content differences

Perhaps that's why we try to steer you clear of the vast majority of presentation tags in Chapter 9, but recommend the text control tags in this chapter both enthusiastically and forcefully. In fact, we recommend that when you must create documents that require the use of multiple kinds of text that you augment the meaning of these tags with additional changes in their appearance using style markup to underscore their differences.

For example, when creating an online manual for a computer program, you may want to distinguish among three or more kinds of text. You can easily see, for example, that users may need to be able to see and readily understand the differences between:

✔ Text produced by a program to solicit user input

✔ Text that the user needs to enter at the keyboard

✔ Reports that user input causes the program to emit

✔ Error messages that faulty or incomplete user input can provoke

Establishing the right kinds of "look and feel" for each of these kinds of text enables you to cue your readers about what they're seeing, and help them separate what the program will show them from what they must input into that program. You can also help them better understand the kinds of information that the program can provide for them, and help them recognize error messages and take the appropriate action to correct the mistakes that can sometimes cause such messages to appear.

Text control tags

As you work your way through the text control tags in the sections that follow, try to associate each tag with a specific kind of information, or to appreciate the labels for information that using such a tag can deliver. Think of these tags as a way to inform readers of the meaning of the information on the screen, and to separate your thoughts and data from information quoted from other sources. Likewise, some of these tags permit you to clearly separate user input from program output, and even to create distinctions in each of those areas of computer activity as well.

<blockquote> . . . </blockquote> Quote style

Use <blockquote> . . . </blockquote> to set off large chunks of material quoted from external sources, publications, or other materials. When you quote from an external source (more than one line long), use <blockquote> to offset the text from both the left and right margins. Always attribute your sources. For example, use the cite attribute to highlight the actual publication, if applicable.

<blockquote> uses the following attribute:

```
cite="text" [CT]
```

This attribute provides information about the source of the quote between the <blockquote> . . . </blockquote> tags. Rendering directions are not provided for this attribute.

Example: <blockquote cite="The CGI Bible, pg. 115">This optional attribute specifies a URL for processing image events ...</blockquote> associates the page reference with information about the imagemap attribute for the now-obsolete HTML 3.0 <fig> tag.

Examples: See file /html4Fd3/examples/ch10/blockquote.htm.

 Force line break

The <br> tag forces a line break in HTML text, immediately after it occurs.
 is an empty tag. This tag is useful for creating short lines of text, or for text that must be broken in specific places, such as verse.

`<br>` uses the following attribute:

```
clear="LEFT" or "ALL" or "RIGHT" or "NONE" [CI]
```

This attribute is deprecated. LEFT inserts space that aligns the following text with the left margin directly below a left-aligned floating image. ALL places the following text past all floating images. RIGHT inserts space that aligns the following text with the right margin directly below a right-aligned floating image. NONE is the default, which does nothing.

The clear attribute is obsolete and will not be supported in future versions of HTML. To achieve the same effects, use a separate style sheet — `<style>` markup in the document `<head>` section (which affects all uses of the `<br>` tag in the document) — or a specific `<br>` tag to control that paragraph separately.

Example: The HTML markup Go down, Moses`<br clear="ALL">` breaks the line right after the word "Moses," and places any following text past all floating images on the page.

Examples: See file /html4Fd3/examples/ch10/br.htm.

<cite> . . . </cite> Citation emphasis

Use the `<cite>` . . . `</cite>` tags to highlight external resource citations for documents, publications, and so forth. The `<cite>` tag takes no unique attributes.

Example: The HTML markup Homer's `<cite>`Oddysey`</cite>` is the story of an epic journey, sets off the title of that work in a different text style (which most browsers render in italics), whereas the rest of the line appears in plain text.

Examples: See file /html4Fd3/examples/ch10/cite.htm.

<code> . . . </code> Program code text

`<code>` . . . `</code>` is used to enclose programs or samples of code to offset them from normal text. Most browsers use a monospaced font, such as Courier, to set off such text. These tags provide a good way to set off programs, code fragments, or computer output within the body of an HTML document. The `<code>` tag takes no unique attributes.

Example: The HTML markup Enter the string `<code>`route print 172*`</code>` into your batch file. sets off the string "route print 172*" in a monospaced font. It does not break the line, however, either before the opening `<code>` tag, or after the closing `</code>` tag. To set such text off more emphatically, be sure to precede the opening tag with a `<br>` and follow the closing tag with another `<br>`.

Examples: See file /html4Fd3/examples/ch10/code.htm.

<del> . . . </del> Deleted text

Use this pair of tags to mark text as deleted, usually to show changes with respect to a previous version of the Web document in which this markup appears. This kind of tag is only likely to be used when multiple authors share a single document, and deletions must be explicitly marked for approval or feedback from all parties to the document. This reason is why the timing attributes are so inclusive and specific. Use the companion tag pair <ins> . . . </ins> to show where new text is inserted, if necessary.

<del> takes the following attributes:

```
cite="URL" [CT]
```

This line points to another document that describes why the text was deleted.

Example: The markup The <del url="http://www.lanw.com/doc/changes.html">Summary</del> References section contains the list of source materials shows the word "Summary" with a strikethrough line through the term. You must, however, examine the HTML source to read the contents of the cite and datetime attributes for this tag.

```
datetime="YYYY-MM-DDThh:mm:ssTZD" [CS]
```

This attribute marks the time when you changed the document. This attribute's value must use the specific format shown to conform to the ISO8601 time/date specification. The abbreviations shown here match the following date and time information:

- ✔ YYYY = The year
- ✔ MM = The two-digit month — for example, "03" for March
- ✔ DD = The day
- ✔ T = Indicates the beginning of the time section
- ✔ hh = The hour, in military time (0–23 hours), without a.m. or p.m. specifications
- ✔ mm = The minute
- ✔ ss = The second
- ✔ TZD = The time zone
- ✔ Z = The Coordinated Universal Time (UTC)

- +hh:mm = The local time that is hours (hh) and minutes (mm) ahead of the UTC

- -hh:mm = The local time that is hours (hh) and minutes (mm) behind the UTC

Example: The markup The <del datetime="2000-05-10T09:36:00-0600"> Summary</del> References section contains the list of source materials. sets the time of the deletion to May 10, 2000, at 9:36 in the morning, six hours behind Coordinated Universal Time (known in the United States as Central Daylight time).

Examples: See file /html4Fd3/examples/ch10/del.htm.

<dfn> . . . </dfn> Definition of a term

Use <dfn> . . . </dfn> to mark terms when they appear for the first time in a Web document. The text between these opening and closing tags usually appears in italics so users can identify the first occurrence of a term or key phrase. The <dfn> tag takes no unique attributes.

Example: The HTML markup A <dfn>McGuffin</dfn>, according to Alfred Hitchcock, is the central object in a film, around which the plot revolves. sets off the term "McGuffin" in italics in most browsers.

Examples: See file /html4Fd3/examples/ch10/dfn.htm.

<em> . . . </em> Emphasis

The <em> . . . </em> tag pair provides typographic emphasis, usually rendered as italics. Use this tag wherever you need to add mild emphasis to body text. Be sure to use sparingly, both in terms of the number of emphasized words and how often text emphasis occurs. The <em> tag takes no unique attributes.

Example: The HTML markup Push the <em>button</em>, Mr. Chips! sets off the word "button" in italics in most Web browsers.

Examples: See file /html4Fd3/examples/ch10/em.htm.

<ins> . . . </ins> Inserted text

Use this tag pair to mark text that's been added since the prior version of the Web document was published.

<ins> takes the following attributes:

```
cite="URL" [CT]
```

This attribute points to another document that describes why the text was inserted.

Example: The markup The `<ins URL="http://www.lanw.com/ doc/changes.html">References</ins> section contains the list of source materials.` underlines the word "References" in that sentence. To read the contents of the `cite` and `datetime` attributes for this tag, you must examine the HTML source.

```
datetime="YYYY-MM-DDThh:mm:ssTZD" [CS]
```

This attribute marks the time when you changed the document. This attribute's value must use the specific format shown here to conform to the ISO8601 time/date specification. The abbreviations shown match the following date and time information:

- ✔ `YYYY` = The year
- ✔ `MM` = The two-digit month — for example, "03" for March
- ✔ `DD` = The day
- ✔ `T` = Indicates the beginning of the time section
- ✔ `hh` = The hour, in military time (0–23 hours), without a.m. or p.m. specifications
- ✔ `mm` = The minute
- ✔ `ss` = The second
- ✔ `TZD` = The time zone
- ✔ `Z` = The Coordinated Universal Time (UTC)
- ✔ `+hh:mm` = The local time that is hours (`hh`) and minutes (`mm`) ahead of the UTC
- ✔ `-hh:mm` = The local time that is hours (`hh`) and minutes (`mm`) behind the UTC

Example: The markup The `<ins datetime="2000-05-10T09:36:00-0600">References</ins> section contains the list of source materials.` sets the time of insertion to May 10, 2000, at 9:36 in the morning, six hours behind Coordinated Universal Time (known in the United States as Central Daylight time).

Examples: See file `/html4Fd3/examples/ch10/ins.htm`.

<kbd> . . . </kbd> Keyboard text

This pair of tags indicates that enclosed text should be entered at a computer keyboard. `<kbd>` . . . `</kbd>` changes the type style for all the text it contains, typically into a monospaced font like that used in character-mode computer terminal displays. Whenever you want to set off text that the user needs to type in from the body text, use `<kbd>` . . . `</kbd>`. This style is different from `<code>`, which indicates existing program text. It's also different from `<tt>`, which indicates computer output. The `<kbd>` tag takes no unique attributes.

Example: The HTML markup `Enter <kbd>route print 172*</kbd> to show all routes related to networks that begin with 172.` sets the text "route print 172*" in a monospaced font. As with the `<code>` tags, these tags do not force a line break either before the opening `<kbd>` or after the closing `</kbd>` tag. To set off keyboard copy more visibly, use a `<br>` before the opening tag, and another `<br>` after the closing tag.

Examples: See file `/html4Fd3/examples/ch10/kdb.htm`.

<p> . . . </p> Paragraph

The `<p>` tag defines paragraph boundaries for normal text. A line break and carriage return occurs where this tag is placed. The closing tag, `</p>`, is not currently required in HTML 4.01 (it's optional), but is required in Extensible Hypertext Markup Language (XHTML) 1.0, so we recommend using it always. Use paragraphs to break the flow of ideas or information into related chunks. Each idea or concept should appear in its own paragraph for a good writing style.

`<p>` uses the following attribute:

```
align="LEFT" or "CENTER" or "RIGHT" or "JUSTIFY" [CI]
```

The `align` attribute is deprecated. It sets the alignment of the paragraph. The `align` type can be `LEFT`, `CENTER`, `RIGHT`, or `JUSTIFY`. The default alignment depends on the base text direction. For left to right text, the default value is `LEFT`.

The `align` attribute is obsolete, and will not be supported in future versions of HTML. To achieve the same effects, use a separate style sheet — `<style>` markup in the document `<head>` section (which affects all uses of the `<p>` tag in the document) — or a specific `<p>` tag to control that paragraph separately.

Example: The HTML markup `<p>My kingdom for a paragraph.</p>` causes a carriage return and line feed at the beginning and end of the enclosed text.

Examples: See file /html4Fd3/examples/ch10/p.htm.

<pre> . . . </pre> Preformatted text

Enclosing text within a pair of <pre> . . . </pre> tags forces the browser to reproduce the same formatting, indentation, and white space that the original text contains. This feature is useful when you want to reproduce formatted tables or other text, such as code listings, especially when other alternatives (such as table-related tags) may not work for all users' browsers.

<pre> takes the following attribute:

```
width="number" [CN]
```

The width attribute is deprecated. The value set for width specifies the maximum number of characters per line and allows the browser to select appropriate font and indentation settings. Within a <pre> . . . </pre> block, you can break lines by pressing Enter, but try to keep line lengths at 80 characters or less, because <pre> text is typically set in a monospaced font. This tag is great for presenting text-only information, or for reproducing complicated formats where the information is already available in text-only form.

The width attribute is not widely supported.

Example: To conserve space, we don't give any short examples here (preformatted text examples invariably span multiple lines); please consult the examples on the CD, as indicated here.

Examples: See file /html4Fd3/examples/ch10/pre.htm.

<q> . . . </q> Quotation markup

Text placed between <q> . . . </q> tags permits you to highlight short quotations from external resources. When you use a short quote from an external resource, place it within <q> . . . </q> tags. Always attribute your sources. Remember to use the <cite> tag to mention the actual publication, if you want that information to appear on your Web document (entries for the cite attribute for <q> appear only in the HTML source code).

<q> uses the following attribute:

```
cite="text" or "URL" [CT]
```

This attribute provides information about the source of the quote, but that information is only visible in the HTML source code.

Example: The HTML markup `<q cite="Thomas Paine">"Give me lib-erty, or give me death!"</q>` is a worthy sentiment. does not change text appearance by default in most Web browsers; to add effects, you must use style markup to do so.

Examples: See file `/html4Fd3/examples/ch10/q.htm`.

<samp> . . . </samp> Sample output

Use `<samp> . . . </samp>` for sequences of literal characters or to represent output from a program, script, or other data source. The `<samp>` tag takes no unique attributes. In practice, deciding when to use `<samp>` rather than `<code>` or `<kbd>` is sometimes hard. We find this tag largely superfluous on our Web pages, but you may decide to use it if you have to distinguish among a number of different kinds of output in a document.

Example: The HTML markup During the show, the teleprompter read `<samp> Kiss your telephones! </samp>` at one point. causes Salvador Dali's maxim to appear in a monospaced font as part of the body copy. For more separation, add `<br>` tags before and after the `<samp> . . . </samp>` tags. When using multiple kinds of output in an HTML document, consider using style tags to change font selections or text colors to help readers distinguish `<code>`, `<kbd>`, and `<samp>` tagged text.

Examples: See file `/html4Fd3/examples/ch10/samp.htm`.

<strong> . . . </strong> Strong emphasis

Use the `<strong> . . . </strong>` tags to place strong emphasis on key words or phrases within normal body text, lists, and other text elements. This tag is designed to up the emphasis above the `<em> . . . </em>` tags. The `<strong>` tags provide the heaviest degree of inline emphasis available in HTML. Remember that overuse blunts the effect, so use emphatic text controls sparingly. The `<strong>` tag takes no unique attributes.

Example: The HTML markup Do it `<strong>now</strong>`, or I might cry. puts strong emphasis on the word "now." By default, this phrase shows up as bold text (the `<em>` tags produce italics by default).

Examples: See file `/html4Fd3/examples/ch10/strong.htm`.

_{. . .} Subscript

Use these tags to render enclosed text as a subscript, text slightly lower than the surrounding text. This tag is most useful when reproducing scientific or mathematical notation. The `<sub>` tag takes no unique attributes.

Example: The HTML markup H`<sub>`2`</sub>`O reproduces the chemical symbol for water quite nicely.

Examples: See file `/html4Fd3/examples/ch10/sub.htm`.

^{. . .} Superscript

Use these tags to render enclosed text as a superscript, text slightly higher than the surrounding text. This tag is not only useful for mathematical or scientific notation, but also for footnotes, and when working with foreign languages or proper names. The `<sup>` tag takes no unique attributes.

Example: The HTML markup `M<sup>c</sup>Guffin` moves the "c" in McGuffin up from the baseline for other lowercase characters in that line, and reduces character size by one level. It's also useful for numerical exponents such as `2<sup>4</sup>` to represent two raised to the fourth power, or the number 16.

Examples: See file `/html4Fd3/examples/ch10/sup.htm`.

<var> . . . </var> Variable text

Text enclosed between the `<var>` . . . `</var>` tags is meant to highlight variable names or arguments to computer commands. Use this markup to indicate a placeholder for a value the user supplies when entering text at the keyboard (see example).

Example: The HTML markup `When prompted with the <tt>Ready:</tt> string, enter <var>your first name</var> to begin the logon process.` uses monospace text for the `<tt>` prompt and italics for the `<var>` text. You may want to play with styles to make these tags even more distinctive.

Examples: See file `/html4Fd3/examples/ch10/var.htm`.

Mastering Many Forms of Text On-Screen

If you've read the preceding section, with its alphabetical list of text control tags, you've no doubt noticed that four types of tags exist that perform similar functions. In fact, three of these tags produce monospaced text that looks the same when default settings are left unchanged; only the `<var>` tag looks different — it uses italics by default. These four tags are

- `<code>` . . . `</code>`: Meant for display of programs and code fragments
- `<kbd>` . . . `</kbd>`: Meant for display of keyboard input
- `<samp>` . . . `</samp>`: Meant to display literal character sequence or computer output
- `<var>` . . . `</var>`: Meant to display variable names or command arguments, which change with user identity or circumstances

If the content on your Web pages requires that you use two or more of these tags, you'd be well advised to use HTML styles to alter their appearance somewhat so that your readers can tell them apart. This alteration could be something as simple as using the nearly ubiquitous style attribute when invoking both kinds of text, as this code example is meant to illustrate (please assume, for our sake if not for your own, that this HTML markup occurs within the context of a well-formed document):

```
During the logon process, the program prompts you
as follows<br>
<samp>Please enter your first name:</samp>
<p>
Please enter your first name, then strike the Enter
key to continue:<br>
<var>your first name<var>
<samp>[Enter]</samp>
</p>
For someone named Mary, this produces the following
output:<br>
<samp>Please enter your first name:</samp>
<kbd>Mary</kbd>
```

In a typical Web browser (this image comes from Internet Explorer 5.0), this code produces the display shown in Figure 10-1. Please notice how hard it is to separate the various types of text from one another in this display.

Figure 10-1:
Without changing defaults for their appearance, <samp> and <kdb> look exactly alike.

By adding the following markup to the `<head>` section of the preceding HTML markup, you see a big difference in the version of the same text that appears in Figure 10-2, which follows the markup.

```
<style>
samp {font-family:Courier;
  font-weight:900;
  font-size:14 pt}
var {font-family:Arial;
  font-weight:bold;
  color:teal}
kbd {font-family:Lineprinter;
  font-size:12 pt;
  font-style:italic;
  color:red}
</style>
```

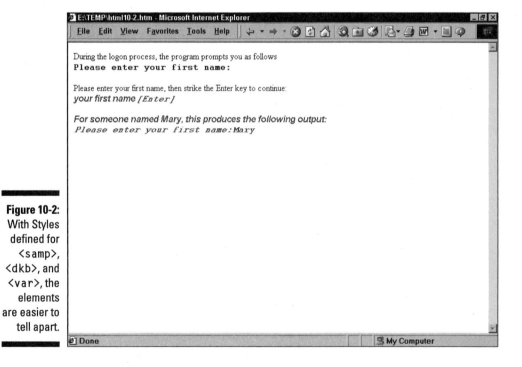

Figure 10-2:
With Styles defined for `<samp>`, `<dkb>`, and `<var>`, the elements are easier to tell apart.

Here, the `<samp>` elements appear in a heavy black Courier font at 14 points, the `<kbd>` elements appear in a 12-point Lineprinter font in red, and the `<var>` elements appear in bold Arial at the default font size in teal. All three elements are now easy to distinguish and even dense text with lots of usage is easy to follow.

The benefit of taking this approach — namely creating a `<style>` . . . `</style>` section in the `<head>` of the document — comes from its application to all instances of the referenced tags in the `<body>` section. Thus, you can use all three tags as often as you like and the style definitions apply to each instance. You can investigate style markup further in Chapter 18 of this book, but hopefully this example helps explain why we keep pushing this concept!

Chapter 11

Listward Ho!

. . . .

In This Chapter
▶ Writing list code
▶ Using lists effectively

. . . .

*L*ists provide a terrific way to deliver information concisely and distinctively. This chapter shows how to code lists and maximize their impact.

Note that many of the tags in this chapter have "optional" closing tags. Although the closing tags are optional, we suggest you get in the habit of including them because in the next generation of HTML (XHTML), closing tags are required.

List Tags

Just like everything else in HTML, you have to know the secret words to create spiffy lists. In the sections that follow, you find all the list-related HTML tags in alphabetical order.

<dd> . . . </dd> Definition description

Material that appears between the `<dd>` . . . `</dd>` tags denotes the descriptive or definition part of a definition list (`<dl>`) element. This element appears indented beneath the term it defines (see the discussion of the `<dt>` tag later in this chapter). The `<dd>` tag may appear by itself, because the closing `</dd>` tag is optional; also, the `<dd>` tag takes no unique attributes. Use this tag for glossaries or other lists where a single term or line needs to be associated with a block of indented text.

Example: See the "Definition list" section later in this chapter.

Examples: See file `/html4Fd3/examples/ch11/defnlist.htm`.

<dir> . . . </dir> Directory list

Use these tags to enclose lists of short elements (usually shorter than 20 characters long), such as filenames or abbreviations. The `<dir>` tag is deprecated in HTML 4.01, and will probably not be continued in the next version of HTML — probably because you can use the unordered list `<ul>` . . . `</ul>` tags to do everything that `<dir>` can do. The `<dir>` tag takes no unique attributes.

Example: See the "Directory list" section later in this chapter.

Examples: See file `/html4Fd3/examples/ch11/dir.htm`.

<dl> . . . </dl> Definition list

`<dl>` . . . `</dl>` encloses a collection of definition items in a definition list. You would usually use the `<dd>` . . . `</dd>` tags for glossaries or other situations in which short, left-aligned terms precede longer blocks of indented text. Browsers usually render definition lists with the term (`<dt>` . . . `</dt>`) in the left margin and the definition (`<dd>` . . . `</dd>`) on one or more lines indented to the right from the term. Use the `<dl>` . . . `</dl>` tags for lists where left-justified elements (for example, terms and definitions) precede longer, indented blocks of text, such as glossaries or a dictionary.

Do not use `<dl>` . . . `</dl>` to create an indented section of text. It is syntactically invalid HTML and may not work as expected.

Examples: See file `/html4Fd3/examples/ch11/defnlist.htm`.

<dt> . . . </dt> Definition term

`<dt>` . . . `</dt>` encloses the term part of a definition entry. Use this tag in situations in which left-justified, short entries pair up with longer blocks of indented text, such as glossaries or definition lists. The `<dt>` tag may appear by itself, because the closing `</dt>` tag is optional; also, the `<dt>` tag takes no unique attributes.

Example: See the "Definition list" section later in this chapter.

Examples: See file `/html4Fd3/examples/ch11/defnlist.htm`.

<li> . . . </li> List item

The `<li>` . . . `</li>` tags enclose an element belonging to one of several HTML list styles. Such elements are treated according to the type of tag within which they appear. This element may be a directory list (`<dir>`), a menu (`<menu>`), an ordered list (`<ol>`), or an unordered list (`<ul>`).

`<li>` takes two attributes, `type` (see the following code) and `value` (discussed later in this section).

```
type="DISC" or "SQUARE" or "CIRCLE"
          or "1" or "a" or "A" or "i" or "I" [Deprecated]
```

When an ordered list (`<ol>`) is used, the `<li>` element will be rendered with a number. You can control that number's appearance with the `type` attribute. Similarly, inside an unordered list (`<ul>`), you can control the type of bullet displayed with `type`. You can't control `<dir>` and `<menu>` this way, because they are not required to be bulleted or numbered. In HTML 4.0, the closing `</li>` tag is optional, but you may want to get in the habit of using it because it's required in the next generation of HTML, XHTML. This markup is deprecated because a style sheet can do everything it can (and more).

Shape types define a named shape for bullets:

- `DISC` uses a filled circular shape for a bullet.
- `SQUARE` uses a filled square shape for a bullet.
- `CIRCLE` uses a circular outline shape for a bullet.

Outline style types define the numbering or labeling scheme that might be used in an outline:

- 1 means to number using Arabic numerals (default starts with "1").
- a means to enumerate using lowercase alpha characters (default starts with "a").
- A means to enumerate using uppercase alpha characters (default starts with "A").
- i means to enumerate using lowercase Roman numerals (default starts with "i").
- I means to enumerate using uppercase Roman numerals (default starts with "I").

```
value="number" [Deprecated]
```

This attribute changes the count of ordered lists as they progress. Use this attribute to reset numbers or resequence parts of lists as needed. This markup is deprecated because a style sheet can do everything the markup can (and more).

Example: See the "Ordered lists" and "Unordered lists" sections later in this chapter.

Examples: See file /html4Fd3/examples/ch11/li.htm.

<menu> . . . </menu> Menu list

These tags enclose a menu list in which each list element is typically a word or short phrase that fits on a single line. This list renders more compactly than most other list types. However, the <menu> tag is deprecated in HTML 4.01 and may not be supported in future versions of HTML. By imposing length restrictions on an unordered list and using styles to force a more compact display, you can replace the functions of this tag without too much effort.

Examples: See file /html4Fd3/examples/ch11/menu.htm.

<ol> . . . </ol> Ordered list

These tags create a list that numbers elements in their order of appearance. The type attribute provides great flexibility in terms of how list elements may be numbered. Ordered lists work well for step-by-step instructions, or other situations where the order of presentation is important.

<ol> takes the type (discussed next) and start (discussed later in this section) attributes.

```
type="1" or "a" or "A" or "i" or "I" [Deprecated]
```

Changes the style of the list, where

- 1 means to number using Arabic numerals (default starts with "1").

- a means to enumerate using lowercase alpha characters (default starts with "a").

- A means to enumerate using uppercase alpha characters (default starts with "A").

- i means to enumerate using lowercase Roman numerals (default starts with "i").

- I means to enumerate using uppercase Roman numerals (default starts with "I").

This markup is deprecated because a style sheet can do everything it can (and more).

```
start="value"
```

This attribute indicates the start value where list numbering or lettering should begin.

Example: See the "Ordered lists" section later in this chapter.

Examples: See file /html4Fd3/examples/ch11/ol.htm.

<ul> . . . </ul> Unordered list

These tags produce bulleted lists of items. The type attribute permits some control over bullet symbols; also, HTML style sheets support nearly any kind of bullet symbols you may want to use. Use bulleted lists when the order in which items appear is not important, or where sequencing plays no role.

<ul> takes the following attribute:

```
type="DISC" or "SQUARE" or "CIRCLE" [Deprecated]
```

Specify a bullet format using the type attribute. The three styles to choose from are DISC for a closed circular bullet, SQUARE for an open square, and CIRCLE for an open bullet.

Example: See the "Unordered lists" section later in this chapter.

Examples: See file /html4Fd3/examples/ch11/ul.htm.

A generic "opening list" attribute

```
compact [Deprecated]
```

This attribute renders a list as compactly as possible by reducing line leading and spacing for short, simple lists. This markup is deprecated because a style sheet can do everything it can (and more). This attribute may be used with all the various list-opening tags — namely, <dir>, <dl>, <menu>, <ol>, and <ul>, but is no longer recommended.

Using List Structures

The preceding section presents the different types of HTML tags that you can use when building a variety of different list types. Now, we can show you a generic example of what it means to build a list structure in HTML.

Here's what's required in an HTML list structure to give you an idea of a simple, one-level list.

Here's a verbal rendition of the set of rules that you could extract from this pseudo-HTML:

- ✔ All types of lists must begin with an opening list tag: <dir>, <dl>, <menu>, <ol>, or <ul>.

- ✔ Any valid list must have one or more list elements: <dt> for the <dl> list type; <li> for the other types: <dir>, <menu>, <ol>, and <ul>. (Don't forget the closing tags.)

- ✔ All types of lists must end with a closing tag that corresponds to the opening tag: </dir>, </dl>, </menu>, </ol>, or </ul>.

What's more, you can mix and match list types, or nest multiple instances of the same type to create "nested lists." Of course, nesting simply means placing one list inside another to model the multiple levels of hierarchy found in most outlines, action plans, or other multileveled lists.

In the sections that follow, you find out about the various list types individually, after which you discover a few interesting combinations.

Unordered lists

The unordered or bulleted list is handy for emphasizing several short lines of information. The following shows HTML markup for an unordered list. A screen shot of this code appears in Figure 11-1.

```
<ul>
<li> You can add as many elements as you need.</li>
<li> You can enter elements as they occur to you.</li>
<li> Some elements can be short.</li>
<li> Other elements can be long enough to become
            tiresome.</li>
</ul>
```

Figure 11-1:
What HTML
calls an
unordered
list, most
people call
a bulleted
list.

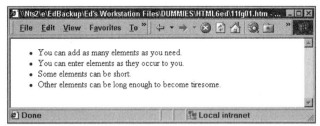

Although you should keep page layouts simple, lists and even nested lists may be needed to display certain information. Use such structures intelligently and sparingly. Notice that a line break occurs when the list begins as the `<ul>` tag is encountered. Each list item gets an automatic line break, and a paragraph break occurs (carriage return plus linefeed) when the `</li>` tag is identified.

The following HTML fragment shows the tags for an unordered list in a Web page body. The list serves to emphasize and separate the text lines.

```
<p>
You have reached the <i>HTML 4 For Dummies</i>
Web Pages, a charming, and hopefully helpful,
addition to the WWW universe. These pages are
designed to aid you in three key areas:
<br>
<ul>
<li>To point out current information about HTML</li>
<li>To provide working examples and code for all
  the Web tricks in the book</li>
<li>To introduce <i>HTML 4 For Dummies</i>
  — your friendliest resource for HTML
  materials!</li>
</ul>
</p>
```

Figure 11-2 shows how this code appears in Internet Explorer. The bulleted list definitely emphasizes the body and adds to the visual appeal of the page.

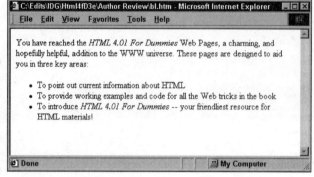

Figure 11-2:
A bulleted list can add visual interest to a Web page.

Ordered lists

An ordered or numbered list is just the thing for delivering step-by-step instructions, explaining an algorithm, or conveying other information where the order of instructions is significant. The following shows HTML markup for an ordered list. A screen shot of this code appears in Figure 11-3.

```
<ol>
<li>Start at the beginning.</li>
<li>Make your way through the middle steps.</li>
<li>More middle elements are good.</li>
<li> Last things come last.</li>
</ol>
```

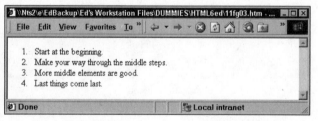

Figure 11-3:
What HTML calls an ordered list, most people call a numbered list.

Directory list

A directory list is a format devised for lists of short elements. You normally use this list for a list of filenames, a bill of materials, or some other list of items, components, or parts. The following HTML markup produces a list of files that also appears in Figure 11-4:

```
<dir>
<li>boot.ini</li>
<li>ntldr</li>
<li>ntdetect.com</li>
</dir>
```

Figure 11-4:
A directory
list works
well for
short lists of
similar
items.

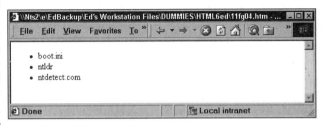

- boot.ini
- ntldr
- ntdetect.com

Remember that the `<dir>` . . . `</dir>` tags are deprecated in HTML 4.01. Nothing is so special about this markup that you can't reproduce it in exactly the same way, by substituting `<ul>` for `<dir>` and `</ul>` for `</dir>`.

Definition list

The definition list is the only list type that uses a different list element tag — namely, `<dt>` — rather than the `<li>` tag used in other list types. Otherwise, its construction is the same as the other list types, as shown in the following HTML markup that is also depicted in Figure 11-5.

```
Here's a brief glossary of list terms:
<dl>
<dt>opening list tag</dt>
<dd>the markup that begins a new list, or that
  indents another level in a nested list.</dd>
<dt>closing list tag</dt>
<dd>the markup that ends a simple single-level list, or that
            outdents to the previous level in a nested
            list.</dd>
<dt>list item</dt>
<dd>the markup that indicates a list element. Lists can con-
            tain an arbitrary number of such items.</dd>
</dl>
```

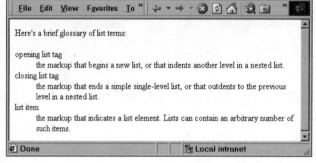

Figure 11-5:
A definition
list groups
terms with
associated
definitions.

Please note that the definition text associated with the <dd> tag is indented to the right of the left margin where the definition terms associated with the <dt> tag appear. Such lists provide a quick-and-dirty way to create annotated lists of items of all kinds, where the items appear with <dd> tags, and the annotations with <dt> tags. Remember, however, that this markup is deprecated, and may no longer be supported in future versions of HTML.

Menu tags

These tags let you create a list in which each element is a word or short phrase that usually fits on a single line. Menu lists usually appear in a more compact format than other types of lists. The following HTML markup is also depicted in Figure 11-6.

```
<h1>Common Edible Mollusks</h1>
<menu>
<li>Cherrystone clam</li>
<li>Green Bearded Mussel</li>
<li>Limpet</li>
<li>Quohog</li>
<li>Razor clam</li>
</menu>
```

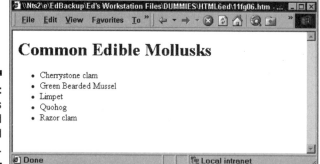

Figure 11-6:
Menu lists
work well
for small
text items.

Remember that the `<menu>` . . . `</menu>` tags are deprecated in HTML 4.01. There's nothing special about this markup that you can't reproduce in exactly the same way, by substituting `<ul>` for `<menu>` and `</ul>` for `</menu>`.

Nested lists

When it comes to representing hierarchical listings of information — such as tables of contents, outlines, and so forth — nesting lists within lists is just the technique to help you master such a job. Robin Cover's "SGML/XML Web Page" starts with a multilevel table of contents that helps keep its hundreds of entries well organized. A nice snippet of this information (which we've edited slightly to make it more compact) appears in Figure 11-7, after the corresponding HTML markup. (Note that this information is copyrighted by Robin Cover and OASIS, 1994-2000.)

```
<ul>
<li><a href="xmlNews.html">XML News: Press Releases</a></li>
<li><a href="xmlSupport.html">XML Industry Support</a></li>
<li><a href="#discussionLists">XML Mailing Lists, Discussion
        Groups, Newsgroups</a></li>
<li><a href="#techDesign">XML: Working Groups, SIGS, Design
        and Development Initiatives</a></li>
<ul>
<li><a href="#saxAPI">SAX - Simple API for XML</a></li>
<li><a href="#xmlLitProg">XML and Literate
        Programming</a></li>
<li><a href="#xmlAndPerl">XML and Perl</a></li>
<li><a href="#xmlAndPython">XML and Python</a></li>
<li><a href="#xmlInMozilla">XML in Mozilla</a></li>
</ul>
</ul>
```

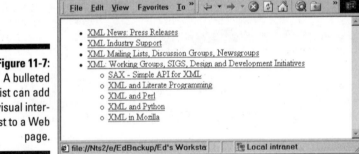

Figure 11-7:
A bulleted list can add visual interest to a Web page.

Notice that this table of contents uses <a> . . . </a> anchor tags to turn the table of contents listings into hyperlinks to the Web pages where the next layer of information resides.

When nesting lists, each sublist occurs within an outer list that's been started with its opening tag but whose closing tag is still pending. You can nest lists arbitrarily as far as HTML itself is concerned, but think about your readers when you start digging down more than three or four layers deep. Just as you will seldom need more than three or four header tags (<h1>, <h2>, <h3>, and <h4>) you should seldom need to nest lists more than three or four levels deep, either.

But because they work equally well in older browsers and in newer ones, and are guaranteed to accommodate readers with visual disabilities (pure text can always be turned into Braille or synthesized into speech), lists represent a powerful way to collect and organize large amounts of information. Especially for tables of contents, outlines, plans, and even textual "site maps" (a list of the titles of all the files in a Web site) nested lists offer a great way to represent and deliver the data to your readers.

Chapter 12

Character Actors

*I*f you've seen the panoply of HTML tags and have gone through examples in Chapter 6 that included strange notations like < or °, maybe these odd locutions aren't as cryptic as they first appear. Hopefully, you now realize that they simply instruct the browser to look up these symbols and replace them with equivalent characters as the browser renders a document. The symbol < produces the less-than sign (<) on your computer screen, and the symbol ° produces the degree symbol (°).

Entities Don't Have to Be an Alien Concept

Instructing a browser to look up entities such as the degree symbol with the string ° may leave you wondering why these contortions are necessary. Here are three important reasons:

✔ Entities let a browser represent characters that it may otherwise interpret as markup.

✔ Entities let a browser represent higher-order ASCII characters (those with codes over 127) without having to fully support higher-order ASCII or non-ASCII character types. Also, these codes support some characters that are even outside the ASCII character set altogether (as is the case with non-Roman alphabet character sets and some widely used diacritical marks).

✔ Entities increase portability of SGML documents.

Okay, so now you know what character and numeric entities are for: They let browsers display symbols that aren't part of the standard ASCII character set — such as © — or display markup elements — such as ‹ and › — without the browser treating them as markup. Consequently, entities let browsers represent a larger range of characters without expanding the actual character set used to write HTML, which helps browsers interpret and display pages faster, which is always a good thing.

As you travel into the land of HTML character and numeric entities, you encounter strange characters and symbols that you may never use. On the other hand, if your native language isn't English, you can probably recognize lots of diacritical marks, accents, and other character modifications that allow you to express yourself correctly!

Producing Entities

Three special characters are part of the code for each and every HTML entity:

- **Ampersand (&):** An & is the browser's first clue that what follows is a code for a character entity instead of ordinary text.

- **Pound sign (#):** If the next character after & is #, the browser knows that what follows is a number that corresponds to the character code for a symbol to be produced on-screen. This kind of code is called a *numeric entity*.

  The next character being anything other than the pound sign tells the browser that the string that follows is a symbol's name and must be looked up in a built-in table of equivalent character symbols. This character is called a *character entity*. Some entities can be represented by both character and numeric entities. For example both © and © are codes for the copyright (©) symbol.

- **Semicolon (;):** When the browser sees a semicolon (;), it knows that it has come to the end of the entity. The browser then uses whatever characters or numbers that follow either the ampersand or the pound sign to perform the right kind of lookup operation and display the requested character symbol. If the browser doesn't recognize the information supplied, most browsers display a question mark (?) or some other odd character.

A couple of things about character and numeric entities may differ from your expectations based on what you know about HTML tags and what you may know about computer character sets:

- Numeric entities are case-sensitive. This means that À is different from à, so you need to reproduce character entities exactly as they appear in Tables 12-1 through 12-8. This accuracy is one reason we prefer using numeric entities — making a mistake is harder.

✔ Numeric codes for reproducing characters within HTML are not ASCII collating sequences; they come from the ISO-Latin-1 character set codes, as shown later in this chapter in Tables 12-1 through 12-8.

If you concentrate on reproducing characters as they appear in Tables 12-1 through 12-8 or copying the numbers that correspond to the ISO-Latin-1 numeric coding scheme, you can produce exactly the right effects on your readers' screens.

You may sometimes encounter problems when trying to represent some of the ISO-Latin-1 character codes in written or printed documentation, as we learned when creating the tables for this chapter. Be prepared to obtain some oddball fonts or symbols to help you overcome this problem, especially for the Icelandic character codes! But what you see in this chapter should indeed be what shows up in your browser when you use the codes you see here. If not, please let us know.

Nothing Ancient about the ISO-Latin-1 HTML

The name of the character set that HTML uses is called ISO-Latin-1. The *ISO* part means that it comes from the International Organization for Standardization's body of official international standards — in fact, all ISO standards have corresponding numeric tags, so ISO-Latin-1 is also known as ISO 8859-1. The *Latin* part means that it comes from the Roman alphabet (A, B, C, and so on), commonly used worldwide to represent text in many different languages. The number *1* refers to the version number for this standard (in other words, this version is the first one of this character set definition).

ISO-Latin-1 distinguishes between two types of entities for characters:

✔ **Character entities:** Collections of characters that represent other characters; for example, < and È show codes that stand for other characters (< and È).

✔ **Numeric entities:** Collections of numbers that represent characters. These are identified by a pound sign (#) that follows the ampersand. For example, < and È show a string of numbers (60 and 200) that stand for characters (< and È).

Table 12-1 illustrates that many more numeric entities exist than character entities. In fact, every character in the ISO-Latin-1 set has a corresponding numeric entity, but this occurrence is not true for all character entities.

As the amount and kind of information presented in Web format has grown, the need for a more extensive character entity set has become apparent. HTML 4.0 (and 4.01) supports such an extended entity set, which includes:

- ✔ Greek characters
- ✔ Special punctuation
- ✔ Letter-like characters
- ✔ Arrows
- ✔ Mathematical characters
- ✔ Special technical characters
- ✔ Playing card suits

See Table 12-9 for a list of other variants of the ISO-Latin character set (versions numbered 1 through 15, with named variants 1 through 10).

Because the support for these other character sets was introduced to HTML 4.0, only browsers that support a full implementation of HTML 4.0 or newer (Navigator 4.0 and Internet Explorer 4.0 and newer versions) can render the character entity codes found in these sets correctly.

The remainder of this chapter includes listings for all the character sets supported by HTML 4.0 (and consequently HTML 4.01). Tables 12-1 through 12-8 include each character's name, applicable entity and numeric codes, and description. We begin with ISO-Latin-1 because it's fully supported by all current and most older browsers, and then continue with HTML 4.0's new character sets. We conclude in Table 12-9 with a list of all known ISO-Latin character sets. Keep in mind that we couldn't get some characters to display correctly because of font restrictions. Therefore, if you don't see a character in the Char column, try using the entity and displaying it in your browser to see what groovy and cool symbol appears.

Table 12-1		The ISO-Latin-1 Character Set	
Char	*Character*	*Numeric*	*Description*
A-Z (capitals)		`&#65;` - `&#90;`	A is `&#65;`, B is `&#66;`, and so on
a-z (lowercase)		`&#97;` - `&#122;`	a is `&#97;`, b is `&#98;`, and so on
0-9 (numerals)		`&#48;` - `&#57;`	0 is `&#48;`, 1 is `&#49;`, and so on
	` `		Em space, not collapsed

Char	*Character*	*Numeric*	*Description*
			En space
			Nonbreaking space
		&#00; - &#08;	Unused
				Horizontal tab

		
	Line feed or new line

		&#11; - &#31;	Unused
		 	Space
!		!	Exclamation mark
"	"	"	Quotation mark
#		#	Number
$		$	Dollar
%		%	Percent
&	&	&	Ampersand
'		'	Apostrophe
(		(	Left parenthesis
)		)	Right parenthesis
*		*	Asterisk
+		+	Plus
,		,	Comma
-		-	Hyphen
.		.	Period (full stop)
/		/	Solidus (slash)
:		:	Colon
;		;	Semicolon
<	<	<	Less than
=		=	Equals
>	>	>	Greater than

(continued)

Table 12-1 *(continued)*

Char	Character	Numeric	Description
?		?	Question mark
@		@	Commercial at
[		[	Left square bracket
\		\	Reverse solidus (backslash)
]		]	Right square bracket
^		^	Caret
_		_	Horizontal bar
`		`	Grave accent
{		{	Left curly brace
|		|	Vertical bar
}		}	Right curly brace
~		~	Tilde
		&#127; - Ÿ	Unused
			Nonbreaking space
¡	¡	¡	Inverted exclamation mark
¢	¢	¢	Cent
£	£	£	Pound sterling
¤	¤	¤	General currency
¥	¥	¥	Yen
»	¦	¦	Broken vertical bar
§	§	§	Section
¨	¨	¨	Umlaut (dieresis)
©	©	©	Copyright
a	ª	ª	Feminine ordinal
«	«	&#171	Left angle quote, guillemet left

Char	*Character*	*Numeric*	*Description*
¬	&not;	&#172;	Not
–	&shy;	&#173;	Soft hyphen
®	&reg;	&#174;	Registered trademark
¯	&macr;	&#175;	Macron accent
°	&deg;	&#176;	Degree
±	&plusmn;	&#177;	Plus or minus
²	&sup2;	&#178;	Superscript two
³	&sup3;	&#179;	Superscript three
´	&acute;	&#180;	Acute accent
>	&micro;	&#181;	Micro
¶	&para;	&#182;	Paragraph
•	&middot;	&#183;	Middle dot
¸	&cedil;	&#184;	Cedilla
1	&sup1;	&#185;	Superscript one
7	&ordm;	&#186;	Masculine ordinal
»	&raquo;	&#187;	Right angle quote, guillemet right
1/4	&frac14;	&#188;	Fraction one-fourth
1/2	&frac12;	&#189;	Fraction one-half
3/4	&frac34;	&#190;	Fraction three-fourths
¿	&iquest;	&#191;	Inverted question mark
À	&Agrave;	&#192;	Capital A, grave accent
Á	&Aacute;	&#193;	Capital A, acute accent
Â	&Acirc;	&#194;	Capital A, circumflex accent
Ã	&Atilde;	&#195;	Capital A, tilde

(continued)

Table 12-1 *(continued)*

Char	Character	Numeric	Description
Ä	Ä	Ä	Capital A, dieresis or umlaut
Å	Å	Å	Capital A, ring
Æ	Æ	Æ	Capital AE diphthong (ligature)
Ç	Ç	Ç	Capital C, cedilla
È	È	È	Capital E, grave accent
É	É	É	Capital E, acute accent
Ê	Ê	Ê	Capital E, circumflex accent
Ë	Ë	Ë	Capital E, dieresis or umlaut
Ì	Ì	Ì	Capital I, grave accent
Í	Í	Í	Capital I, acute accent
Î	Î	Î	Capital I, circumflex accent
Ï	Ï	Ï	Capital I, dieresis or umlaut
Ð	Ð	Ð	Capital ETH, Icelandic
Ñ	Ñ	Ñ	Capital N, tilde
Ò	Ò	Ò	Capital O, grave accent
Ó	Ó	Ó	Capital O, acute accent
Ô	Ô	Ô	Capital O, circumflex accent
Õ	Õ	Õ	Capital O, tilde

Char	Character	Numeric	Description
Ö	`&Ouml;`	`&#214;`	Capital O, dieresis or umlaut
×	`&times;`	`&#215;`	Multiply
Ø	`&Oslash;`	`&#216;`	Capital O, slash
Ù	`&Ugrave;`	`&#217;`	Capital U, grave accent
Ú	`&Uacute;`	`&#218;`	Capital U, acute accent
Û	`&Ucirc;`	`&#219;`	Capital U, circumflex accent
Ü	`&Uuml;`	`&#220;`	Capital U, dieresis or umlaut
Ý	`&Yacute;`	`&#221;`	Capital Y, acute accent
þ	`&THORN;`	`&#222;`	Capital THORN, Icelandic
ß	`&szlig;`	`&#223;`	Small sharp s, German (sz ligature)
à	`&agrave;`	`&#224;`	Small a, grave accent
á	`&aacute;`	`&#225;`	Small a, acute accent
â	`&acirc;`	`&#226;`	Small a, circumflex accent
ã	`&atilde;`	`&#227;`	Small a, tilde
ä	`&auml;`	`&#228;`	Small a, dieresis or umlaut
å	`&aring;`	`&#229;`	Small a, ring
æ	`&aelig;`	`&#230;`	Small ae diphthong (ligature)
ç	`&ccedil;`	`&#231;`	Small c, cedilla
è	`&egrave;`	`&#232;`	Small e, grave accent

(continued)

Table 12-1 *(continued)*

Char	Character	Numeric	Description
é	é	é	Small e, acute accent
ê	ê	ê	Small e, circumflex accent
ë	ë	ë	Small e, dieresis or umlaut
ì	ì	ì	Small i, grave accent
í	í	í	Small i, acute accent
î	î	î	Small i, circumflex accent
ï	ï	ï	Small i, dieresis or umlaut
ð	ð	ð	Small eth, Icelandic
ñ	ñ	ñ	Small n, tilde
ò	ò	ò	Small o, grave accent
ó	ó	ó	Small o, acute accent
ô	ô	ô	Small o, circumflex accent
õ	õ	õ	Small o, tilde
ö	ö	ö	Small o, dieresis or umlaut
÷	÷	÷	Division
ø	ø	ø	Small o, slash
ù	ù	ù	Small u, grave accent
ú	ú	ú	Small u, acute accent
û	û	û	Small u, circumflex accent

Char	Character	Numeric	Description
ü	ü	ü	Small u, dieresis or umlaut
ý	ý	ý	Small y, acute accent
þ	þ	þ	Small thorn, Icelandic
ÿ	ÿ	ÿ	Small y, dieresis or umlaut

Table 12-2		Greek Characters	
Char	**Character**	**Numeric**	**Description**
A	Α	Α	Capital letter alpha
B	Β	Β	Capital letter beta
Γ	Γ	Γ	Capital letter gamma
Δ	Δ	Δ	Capital letter delta
E	Ε	Ε	Capital letter epsilon
Z	Ζ	Ζ	Capital letter zeta
H	Η	Η	Capital letter eta
Θ	Θ	Θ	Capital letter theta
I	Ι	Ι	Capital letter iota
K	Κ	Κ	Capital letter kappa
Λ	Λ	Λ	Capital letter lambda
M	Μ	Μ	Capital letter mu
N	Ν	Ν	Capital letter nu
Ξ	Ξ	Ξ	Capital letter xi
O	Ο	Ο	Capital letter omicron
Π	Π	Π	Capital letter pi
P	Ρ	Ρ	Capital letter rho

(continued)

Table 12-2 *(continued)*

Char	Character	Numeric	Description
Σ	Σ	Σ	Capital letter sigma
Τ	Τ	Τ	Capital letter tau
Υ	Υ	Υ	Capital letter upsilon
Φ	Φ	Φ	Capital letter phi
Χ	Χ	Χ	Capital letter chi
Ψ	Ψ	Ψ	Capital letter psi
Ω	Ω	Ω	Capital letter omega
α	α	α	Small letter alpha
β	β	β	Small letter beta
γ	γ	γ	Small letter gamma
δ	δ	δ	Small letter delta
ε	ε	ε	Small letter epsilon
ζ	ζ	ζ	Small letter zeta
η	η	η	Small letter eta
θ	θ	θ	Small letter theta
ι	ι	ι	Small letter iota
κ	κ	κ	Small letter kappa
λ	λ	λ	Small letter lambda
μ	μ	μ	Small letter mu
ν	ν	ν	Small letter nu
ξ	ξ	ξ	Small letter xi
ο	ο	ο	Small letter omicron
π	π	π	Small letter pi
ρ	ρ	ρ	Small letter rho
ς	ς	ς	Small letter final sigma
σ	σ	σ	Small letter sigma
τ	τ	τ	Small letter tau

Char	Character	Numeric	Description
υ	`&upsilon;`	`&#965;`	Small letter upsilon
φ	`&phi;`	`&#966;`	Small letter phi
χ	`&chi;`	`&#967;`	Small letter chi
ψ	`&psi;`	`&#968;`	Small letter psi
ω	`&omega;`	`&#969;`	Small letter omega
θ	`&thetasym;`	`&#977;`	Small letter theta
ϒ	`&upsih;`	`&#978;`	Upsilon with hook
π	`&piv;`	`&#982;`	Pi

Table 12-3 **Special Punctuation**

Char	Character	Numeric	Description
•	`&bull;`	`&#8226;`	Bullet
...	`&hellip;`	`&#8230;`	Horizontal ellipsis
′	`&prime;`	`&#8242;`	Prime
″	`&Prime;`	`&#8243;`	Double prime
–	`&oline;`	`&#8254;`	Overline
/	`&frasl;`	`&#8260;`	Fraction slash

Table 12-4 **Letter-Like Characters**

Char	Character	Numeric	Description
℘	`&weierp;`	`&#8472;`	Script capital P
ℑ	`&image;`	`&#8465;`	Blackletter capital I
ℜ	`&real;`	`&#8476;`	Blackletter capital R
™	`&trade;`	`&#8482;`	Trademark
ℵ	`&alefsym;`	`&#8501;`	Alef

Table 12-5		Arrow Characters	
Char	*Character*	*Numeric*	*Description*
←	&larr;	&#8592;	Left arrow
↑	&uarr;	&#8593;	Up arrow
→	&rarr;	&#8594;	Right arrow
↓	&darr;	&#8595;	Down arrow
↔	&harr;	&#8596;	Left-right arrow
↵	&crarr;	&#8629;	Down arrow with corner left
⇐	&lArr;	&#8656;	Left double arrow
⇑	&uArr;	&#8657;	Up double arrow
⇒	&rArr;	&#8658;	Right double arrow
⇓	&dArr;	&#8659;	Down double arrow
⇔	&hArr;	&#8660;	Left-right double arrow

Table 12-6		Mathematical Characters	
Char	*Character*	*Numeric*	*Description*
∀	&forall;	&#8704;	For all
∂	&part;	&#8706;	Partial differential
∃	&exist;	&#8707;	There exists
∅	&empty;	&#8709;	Empty set
∆	&nabla;	&#8711;	Nabla
∈	&isin;	&#8712;	Element of
∉	&notin;	&#8713;	Not an element of
∋	&ni;	&#8715;	Contains as member
π	&prod;	&#8719;	n-ary product
Σ	&sum;	&#8721;	n-ary summation
-	&minus;	&#8722;	Minus

Char	Character	Numeric	Description
*	∗	∗	Asterisk operator
√	√	√	Square root
∝	∝	∝	Proportional to
∞	∞	∞	Infinity
∠	∠	∠	Angle
∧	∧	ࢳ	Logical and
∨	∨	ࢴ	Logical or
∪	∪	∪	Union
∫	∫	∫	Integral
∴	∴	∴	Therefore
~	∼	∼	Tilde operator
≅	≅	≅	Approximately equal to
~	≈	≈	Almost equal to
≠	≠	≠	Not equal to
≡	≡	≡	Identical to =
≤	≤	≤	Less than or equal to
≥	≥	≥	Greater than or equal to
⊂	⊂	⊂	Subset of
⊃	⊃	⊃	Superset of
⊄	⊄	⊄	Not a subset of
⊆	⊆	⊆	Subset of or equal to
⊇	⊇	⊇	Superset of or equal to
⊕	⊕	⊕	Circled plus
⊗	⊗	⊗	Circled times
⊥	⊥	⊥	Up tack
•	⋅	⋅	Dot operator

Table 12-7	Technical Characters		
Char	*Character*	*Numeric*	*Description*
⌈	&lceil;	&#8968;	Left ceiling
⌉	&rceil;	&#8969;	Right ceiling
⌊	&lfloor;	&#8970;	Left floor
⌋	&rfloor;	&#8971;	Right floor
〈	&lang;	&#9001;	Left-pointing angle bracket
〉	&rang;	&#9002;	Right-pointing angle bracket

Table 12-8	Playing Card Symbols		
Char	*Character*	*Numeric*	*Description*
♠	&spades;	&#9824;	Black spade suit
♣	&clubs;	&#9827;	Black club suit
♥	&hearts;	&#9829;	Black heart suit
♦	&diams;	&#9830;	Black diamond suit

One thing to note about using this information: If you must frequently work
with character or numeric entities in your documents, using some kind of
HTML editing tool to handle character replacements automatically is easier.
Or look for a file-oriented search-and-replace utility that you can use as a post-
processing step on your files. You can find a variety of search-and-replace
utilities if you look in the HTML Accessories category at www.tucows.com.

In addition to the various character sets mentioned earlier in this chapter,
numerous variants of the ISO-Latin character set have been created, primarily to support developers (and users) who want to read Web pages in languages other than English. As Table 12-9 shows, ten named versions of the
ISO-Latin character sets exist, and 15 versions of ISO-Latin itself, each of
which is aimed at a separate collection of languages. For those who want to
service readers in languages other than English, relief may possibly occur
somewhere in this table!

Table 12-9		ISO 8859 Character Sets
Charset	**Script**	**Languages**
ISO-8859-1	Latin-1	ASCII plus most Western European languages, including Albanian, Afrikaans, Basque, Catalan, Danish, Dutch, English, Faroese, Finnish, Flemish, Galician, German, Icelandic, Irish, Italian, Norwegian, Portuguese, Scottish, Spanish, and Swedish. Omits certain Dutch, French, and German characters.
ISO-8859-2	Latin-2	ASCII plus most Central European languages, including Czech, English, German, Hungarian, Polish, Romanian, Croatian, Slovak, Slovene, and Serbian.
ISO-8859-3	Latin-3	ASCII plus characters required for English, Esperanto, German, Maltese, and Galician.
ISO-8859-4	Latin-4	ASCII plus most Baltic languages, including Latvian, Lithuanian, German, Greenlandic, and Lappish; now superseded by ISO-Latin-6.
ISO-8859-5		ASCII plus Cyrillic characters for Slavic languages, including Byelorussian, Bulgarian, Macedonian, Russian, Serbian, and Ukrainian.
ISO-8859-6		ASCII plus Arabic characters.
ISO-8859-7		ASCII plus Greek characters.
ISO-8859-8		ASCII plus Hebrew.
ISO-8859-9	Latin-5	Latin-1 except that some Turkish symbols replace Icelandic ones.
ISO-8859-10	Latin-6	ASCII plus most Nordic languages, including Latvian, Lithuanian, Inuit, non-Skolt Sami, and Icelandic.
ISO-8859-11		ASCII plus Thai.
ISO-8859-12	Latin-7	ASCII plus Celtic.
ISO-8859-13	Latin-8	ASCII plus the Baltic Rim characters.
ISO-8859-14	Latin-9	ASCII plus Sami (Finnish).
ISO-8859-15	Latin-10	Variation on Latin-1 that includes Euro currency sign, plus extra accented Finnish and French characters.

Appendix C covers HTML-related authoring and editing tools for a variety of platforms. If you want to be a serious Web developer or often need to use character codes in your pages, please check out the tools that are available for your platform. Such tools can save you time and effort and make you a happier, more productive Webmaster.

Part IV

Shaping Your Design

The 5th Wave   By Rich Tennant

"Give him air! Give him air! He'll be okay. He's just been exposed to some raw HTML code. It must have accidently flashed across his screen from the server."

In this part . . .

Here, we cover some of the more interesting and complicated aspects of Web page design. To start, we show you how to combine what you've learned as you approach and appreciate complex Web pages, and we explain how to create complex Web connections. Next, you explore the ins and outs of building and using tables in your Web pages to produce effects that can combine text and graphics in all kinds of interesting ways. Beyond tables come image maps, where you find out how to turn an ordinary digital image into a Website navigation tool. After that, it's time to tackle the joys and sorrows of HTML frames and see what multiple frames can do to your Web site. In short, it's a whirlwind tour of some really snazzy Web stuff!

Chapter 13

Going High-Rise: Linking Complex Pages

In This Chapter

▶ Expanding your home page into a Web

▶ Touring the inside of your documents and local Web

▶ Jumping to remote sites

▶ Analyzing sophisticated Web pages

*J*ust for grins, imagine that you've created a trim, efficient home page, diligently honed by a disciplined use of the KISS (Keep It Simple, Sillyhead) principle. It's nice, it's simple — it fits on one screen. An urge to expand your site overwhelms you. You want your site to compare favorably to all that wonderful stuff you've seen on the Web, right? That's pretty natural — and you don't have to kiss off the KISS principle, either. After all, *simple* is a relative term. (Ever suspect that some people have *very* simple relatives? Just kidding.)

Your single Web page can expand into a full-blown *Web presence* (an ambitious term for a Web site that aspires to greater substance and complexity). But the more pages you add, the harder it gets for your users to find their way around. Although you're expanding your Web site, your most important job is to make your users' journey through it as enjoyable as possible. Okay, pop quiz: *How do you do that?* Killer content? Fast-loading, appropriate graphics? Knockout organization? Easy navigation? Relevant links? Keeping It Simple, Sillyhead? *Right — all of the above.* You *have* been awake the whole time. (If you had to go back and brush up on the last 12 chapters, that's fine too; all quizzes here are open-book.) Now you get to put these principles to use.

This chapter helps you spin a complex Web without getting tangled up. Then, it's virtual road-trip time as we visit some advanced Web sites and comment instructively on their elements and layout.

There's No Place Like Home

Home isn't only your home page, any more than it's only your hometown. Your turf in cyberspace is more like a local system of planets orbiting your home page. Web surfers may arrive from afar to find the information you offer, but even a site of rare and fantastic beauty can put off users if navigating it is too hard. That's why you need a clear mental picture of your site as a fully developed system, well organized and free of drifting junk, *before* you start expanding things.

Organizing in style

If you pay close attention to your content, after a while, it should start to gravitate toward an appropriate style of organization — in fact, it may demand a particular style. Hierarchical style, linear style, and interlinked combinations of these two styles are the standard organizational structures used in most Web sites. These Web structures are illustrated in Figures 13-1, 13-2, and 13-3 (see the next section).

"Webifying" an existing linear document is a straightforward process, but it's a one-way street. A random collection of ideas and concepts, wired up willy-nilly to each other, makes a gawdawful linear document and a reasonably awful Web page. In addition, a random collection of ideas doesn't make much sense to users. When you design and use links — whether within your site or among other Web documents — make sure they are relevant to the content, reflect the organization of your site, and enhance interconnectedness for easy navigation.

Hierarchical structure: So spreads the tree

The *hierarchical* (or *tree*) *structure* is the basis of most Web designs (see Figure 13-1). It's logical, and looks familiar to most computer users (think of hard-disk file trees or GUI help systems), and best of all, easy for users to navigate. It's even easier to use when you put a link back to the home page on each page. It's a reliable structure for your documents, especially if you're just starting your brilliant career as a Webmaster.

Hierarchical information starts abstract and gets specific. A table of contents on your home page represents the most general *(root)* level of the tree structure, getting to the most detailed content as the tree branches out to its outermost leaves.

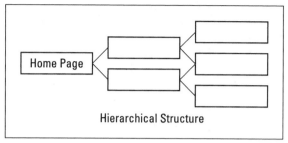

Hierarchical Structure

Figure 13-1:
Hierarchical
structure
looks like a
family tree.

Your content dictates the divisions of the tree. If you try some sample "paths" to particular topics, setting them up as tree branches is easy. For example, if you were building a hierarchical directory to organize information about a company's equipment, you might start at the most abstract level (say, *Equipment,* just to be original). The branches would narrow down to specifics by progressively excluding characteristics.

So, where would you put the hot-red convertible on the Equipment tree? A sample "path" might start from *Equipment* (everything the company uses) and narrow down the characteristics as the tree branches out:

Equipment/Transportation/Cars/Convertibles/In "Howdy, Officer" Red

Our sample "path" could be expanded into a tree with ease, starting with the most general level and indenting our way down to specifics:

Equipment

    Office Furniture

    Transportation

      Business Jets

      Cars

        Minivans

        Convertibles

          In Queasy-Feeling Pink

          In "Howdy, Officer" Red

By sheer coincidence (yeah, right), going from general to specific is exactly the way the "path" of a good old-fashioned DOS command used to work, showing the computer how to navigate the treelike directory structure from the general to the specific. Each level represents a choice: *Go here and not there.*

In HTML, hyperlinks add a new wrinkle to the hierarchy: You can include interesting links between seemingly unrelated branches to better inform your users. For example, if the company has just painted its business jets Queasy-Feeling Pink to match the pink convertibles, you could create a link to the Business Jets page. Your users could jump there with ease and read the exciting details.

The Internet is like a highway — sorry to use the same old cliché — with multiple routes to the same destination. Although linking can be fun, it can also be dangerous if you don't make sure that your links are relevant. For example, if your company has started painting the office furniture pink, a link could help your users jump from Office Furniture to the Queasy-Feeling Pink page. There they could see the color in all its gory, errr. . .glory, read *more* exciting details, and think about selling their stock (just kidding).

The hierarchical structure is reassuringly familiar to a typical user, works much like the index of a book (actively so, if you add some well-chosen links), and can also serve as a table of contents.

Linear structure: You've heard this line before

Simple and *booklike,* but also *rigid* and *confining,* are common descriptions of the linear structure (see Figure 13-2). If your information presents a series of steps — like a slide show — or follows a process from start to finish, linear structure is a fitting choice for your document's organization. A linear structure keeps users on track and out of trouble. When using a linear structure, you can make good use of links to "next page," "previous page," and "top or start page."

If you're using a linear structure to present information such as a tutorial, multipaged document, or a slide show, you might want to provide a link to a downloadable version of your information. Not all of us are lucky enough to have a dedicated connection to the Internet, so save someone time and money by giving him the option of accessing the material offline.

Figure 13-2:
Linear
structure
goes from
start to
finish, one
step at a
time.

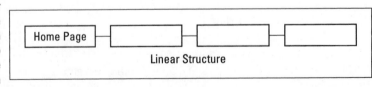

As with the hierarchical structure, effective use of links helps guide and orient your users. Be sure to put links to your home page (or to a starting point) on each page in a linear structure. Without such links, users who drop into the middle of your site can use only their browser's controls to bail out. Of course, if you trap them in this way, they probably *will* talk about your site on the Web, but the talk won't be exactly flattering. (Not to put too fine a point on it, think *roast* and *flame-broil*.)

Careful placement of navigational clues *on each Web page you create* can stop the heartbreak of linklessness. For a characteristically modest example of a good navigational style, check out our LANWrights Web site at www.lanw.com.

The horror of the missing link

Hypertext linking is the most time-consuming part of HTML document development. Do it well and your users will love you forever. Omit it or overdo it, and the consequences are too scary to imagine. (We get into them anyway, later in this chapter. Stay tuned.)

If you have extensive information on related subjects as you compose your text, put a few hyperlinks in it that can take users to specific paragraphs in other pages *(and back again to where they left off)*. But don't get carried away; too many links can interrupt the flow of your text, making the train of thought hard to hang on to and the site easy to get lost in. A lost user is one you may have lost for good.

Keep in mind that readers can enter your Web space from somewhere other than your home page, so make sure to provide navigational clues for *jumped-in* users. You want them to find your home page (or other relevant pages) easily. Otherwise, a user can feel about as welcome as a burglar. Imagine: You get an interesting URL via e-mail from some cohort who says, "Check out this page." You click and find yourself in the middle of the content, blundering around because nobody left you a link to the home page. The idea is to provide viewers with a way out of your pages, but not too soon!

When you build a complex Web structure, always, always, *always* put a link to your home page on each page.

The Web itself is a "web" structure (see Figure 13-3), but it's also a loosely linked environment that allows fantastic freedom of movement and free-flowing design. Paradoxically, providing appropriate structure (without constraining users' freedom to explore) enables you to preserve that spontaneity and make good use of the Web's characteristics.

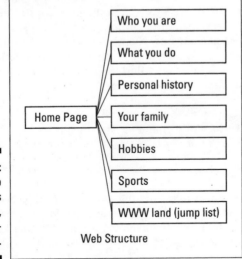

Who you are

What you do

Personal history

Home Page — Your family

Hobbies

Sports

WWW land (jump list)

Web Structure

Figure 13-3:
Web
structure is
rich, varied,
and unpre-
dictable.

It's also a great idea to reproduce the URL for each page in its footer in small type. If you provide this data, users can return to any specific page in your Web by using that URL later, even if they didn't add it to their bookmarks.

It's story (board) time, boys and girls!

As you may recall from Chapter 5, pencil and paper still have their uses. (You *did* sketch your home page, right? Excellent.) Time to pick them up again and draw your Web site's structure. For a schema on the scale of a personal Web page, pencil and paper should do nicely. Larger, more complex sites may require some more specialized and powerful tools. Read on for the details!

First Things First — List 'em Out

Make a list of the major pieces of information you want to include in your Web site. These major points will probably turn into links on your home page and may be similar to the following:

- ✔ Who you are
- ✔ What you do
- ✔ Personal history
- ✔ Your family

✔ Hobbies

✔ Sports

✔ Your adventures in Web land (jump list)

Sketch the Web

In the current example, starting simple, with relatively few topics to consider is good. A combination of structures — hierarchical with some considered Web links — looks appropriate. This structure should look familiar, especially if you've done some file-management housework in your hard disk's directories.

After you complete your sketch, use it to analyze your home page. You'll see some potential links that aren't readily apparent from looking at the HTML. For example, you can hyperlink the "Who you are" page to the "What you do," "Personal history," and "Sports" pages. The "Your family" page is a natural to link to the "Hobbies" and "Sports" pages. And of course, remember to link all these secondary pages directly to the "Home Page." (We know, nag, nag, nag. But mark our words; you'll thank us for it someday.)

All a board — the whole story

A simple sketch of a Web site has its virtues — it fits so nicely on a cocktail napkin — but it can't provide enough information for you to fully visualize your site. Of course, you *could* try conjuring up a detailed mental picture of, say, eight separate pages — right down to all the elements and links specific to each one — in your head. (Hurts, doesn't it?) Save a little on aspirin; prepare a *storyboard* for your pages. A storyboard is essentially a sequence of sketches that looks like the Sunday funnies and shows you how an event develops through time.

You've seen the results of storyboards — every movie, TV show, and comic book gets this treatment before any production takes place. Producing a set of Web pages is a lot like making a TV show, especially if you think of each Web page as a separate scene. Over time, you'll see an entire collection of Web documents and associated materials evolving from your work — resembling a whole season's worth of TV episodes. (And here you thought you were only doing a single show.)

Stick 'em up

To prepare a storyboard, you'll have to abandon the cocktail napkins, but the process is simple: Sketch the layout of each Web page separately, with the URLs for links written on each one. Some Web authors can diagram a small Web on a whiteboard, using colored markers to show different types of links, forms, or other HTML elements.

For more complex Web sites, use a sheet of paper (or a large index card) for each Web page, some string to represent links, and some push pins. Oh, yeah, you'll need a place you can spread out the sketches and move them around — maybe a large bulletin board (no, not a BBS — an actual board covered with cork, like the ones in prehistoric times).

The corkboard method allows complex arrangements that you can change easily. (They don't even disappear if the power goes off. What a concept!) If you attach the text of each Web page to its layout sheet, the storyboard method is also invaluable for identifying potential hypertext links. Whenever you create a Web of more than a handful of pages, do a storyboard. It can save you much more time than it takes initially, and after you finish, you may find it has helped save your sanity as well.

Bringing out the power tools

Of course, some Web authors — practiced adepts of the information age — are more comfortable using software when things start getting complicated. We just happen to have some nifty Web-site management tools on the CD-ROM tucked into this book's back pocket. Some of them work like gang-busters for design and storyboarding, as well as for the maintenance and update phases after your site is fully realized. And here's a hot tip: Commercial software products like Dreamweaver 3 or HotDog Pro often receive favorable mention in this category of tools.

Anchors Bring More to Your Documents

Okay, we *did* say creating Web pages spanning up to three screens wasn't too terrible, *provided* your information demands extra room and you've already put the most important information on the first screen. Under pressure, we'll even admit that it may be okay to expand your home page to more than one screen — if you carefully drop your anchors and don't go overboard on images.

Intra or inter?

You can use two different *anchor tag attributes* for movement within your pages. Each has its own name and method:

- **Intradocument linking** provides viewers with links to specific parts within a particular Web page. Use the `name="text"` anchor to provide the destination for an `href="#label"` tag.

- **Interdocument linking** uses the standard `href="url"` attribute to send users jumping from page to page.

To mark a spot at the top of an HTML page so you can link to that spot later, you use code that looks something like the following:

```
<a name="top"></a>
```

You don't even have to put any text between the `<a>` . . . `</a>` tag because you're just using the tag to mark a particular location in the document, not create a hyperlink. To make a link to this spot, you use this code:

```
<a href="#top">Back to top</a>
```

Notice the pound sign (#) before the word *top* in the `href=` attribute. This nifty mechanism lets the browser know that it needs to look within the current document for the spot named "top" and jump back there when the user clicks the text `Back to top`. Cool huh? We think so, too.

When browsers hit the links

Normally, you must note the important distinction between in*ter*document and in*tra*document linking when you use a browser to follow links. Browsers can show some, ah, *interesting* quirks that you can either exploit or rein in, depending on your site's needs:

- ✔ To jump to a specific location within another page, you can combine interdocument with intradocument linking. To do so, you use the `href="url#label"` attribute.

- ✔ Normally, intradocument linking takes your viewers to places *other* than the default top-of-page. You can land them at the top of the page, safe and sound, if you put a named anchor there and the URL specifies this anchor as the destination of the link.

- ✔ Most browsers, when they follow an interdocument link, land your readers on the first line of a target document. If you want to make sure they get to that first line every time, you may want to place a named anchor that says *Go here and nowhere else.*

- ✔ If you put a named anchor near the bottom of a document, most browsers won't bring it up to the first line on-screen. (More about this dilemma shortly.)

Moral: A nice, tight, relevant linkage can often depend on a savvy use of anchors to bind the browser to your purpose.

Advanced intradocument linking

When you establish an intradocument link, setting an anchor with the `name="text"` attribute provides a destination for the link. If you think users may find a heading within a specific page immediately relevant or important, you can add an anchor tag next to it with a relevant `name` attribute and create a link to it.

Allow us to offer a self-effacing example of how you might use the `name="text"` attribute in anchor tags. Voilà — the LANWrights Corporate Overview page. An HTML line in this document that looks much like the following recurs in four locations, before each of that document's major headings, to speed users' transitions among them:

```
<div align="center">
<a href="#svcs">Services/Capabilities</a>
<a href="#dev">Development/Consulting</a>
<a href="#rate">Rates</a>
</div>
```

This HTML code creates a navigation bar for your intradocument text links and gives you a way to select major headings on the page that may not be visible on-screen just yet. This internal navigation bar is shown in Figure 13-4, just beneath the top-of-page logo.

Figure 13-4:
An internal navigation bar helps users jump around inside a document.

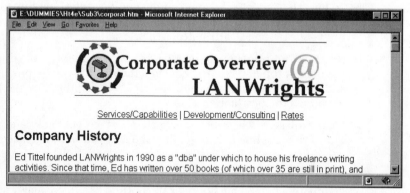

The unique quirks of intradocument linking

You are the captain of your fate, and the author of your page — the one who controls how your information is displayed and how your document is linked. Set your anchors correctly, and your users will go exactly where you say they should go. (For example, if a user selects the text that reads `Services/Capabilities` on the LANWrights page, the result is an instant jump to the "LANWrights Services/Statement of Capabilities" heading.) But beware: Computer programs are nothing if not literalists. If the browser can't find a named anchor, you get the default instead, which is to land at the top of the document. And browsers can get muddled looking for the anchor.

If you put an anchor near (or at) the very bottom of a document, for example, most browsers do *not* bring the named anchor to the first line on the screen. This situation occurs because the browser usually renders a full screen of text, and you've sent it looking for a piece of a full screen. Thus, if the anchor is near the bottom of a document, the link may drop you near the bottom of the screen, rather than the very bottom of the document itself.

Moral: Even absolute power has its limits.

Table of Contents links

You can use intradocument links and the name="text" attribute to create a really jumpin' table of contents (TOC) for long documents. Providing a linked TOC takes a little more time, but it's a great way to impress your users (provided, of course, that you remember to provide a link back to the TOC after each block of text in the destination document).

The following HTML code illustrates how to use the TOC links within a large document:

```
<!-- Make this an anchor for return jumps -->
<p>
<a name="toc">Table of Contents</a>
</p>
<!-- Below are links to the sections 1, 2 and 3 -->
<p>
<a href="#sec1">Section 1.</a><br>
<a href="#sec2">Section 2.</a><br>
<a href="#sec3">Section 3.</a><br>
</p>
<!-- This is a named anchor called "sec1". -->
<a name="sec1"></a>
<h2>CFR Section 1.</h2>
<p>Text of section 1 is here.</p>
<!-- This is a link back to the TOC at the top of
the page -->
<p>
<a href="#toc">(TOC)</a>
</p>
<a name="sec2"></a>
<h2>CFR Section 2.</h2>
<p>Text of section 2 is here.</p>
<p>
<a href="#toc">(TOC)</a>
</p>
<a name="sec3"></a>
<h2>CFR Section 3.</h2>
<p>Text of section 3 is here.</p>
<p>
<a href="#toc">(TOC)</a>
</p>
```

Seeing the (TOC) after each text section may seem strange at first, but your users will quickly become accustomed to this method of intradocument linking (see Figure 13-5). We recommend using this approach for longer, more complex documents or for a collection of related documents, but not for shorter pieces. A ubiquitous TOC in a short document may seem obtrusive to your users.

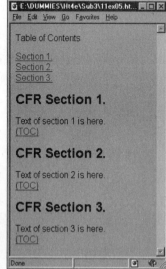

Figure 13-5:
Table of
Contents
and text
links.

If you're thorough, consistent, and a stickler for uniformity, you can use this same general method to link just about anything to anything else within a single HTML document. This linking may look strange when written in HTML, but it works.

To keep the browser from becoming terminally confused, use the "text" part of each name="text" attribute *only once per document*. Otherwise, the browser gives up in frustration and deposits your users at the top of the page (the default for all unrecognized text anchors) yet again.

You should name named anchors with text starting with a character from the set {a–z, A–Z}. They should never be exclusively numeric, for example <a name="12">blah</a>. Be sure to give anchors unique names within any single document. Anchor names are case-sensitive and space sensitive, so name="Three Stooges" is not the same as name="ThreeStooges" is not the same as name="THREESTOOGES". You get the idea.

Jumping to Remote Pages

Yes, you, too, can amaze and amuse your users with the flashiest trick this side of teleportation — hypermedia links that take them from text in your pages directly to other Web sites (oh, yeah, and back again). Although you can't create `name="text"` anchors in text at remote sites, you may be able to use some of the anchors already in place there. If you find a linked TOC at another site, for example, you can reference the same links that it uses.

If you can link to any part of a remote page using your browser, you can copy that link into the text of your Web pages. Just make sure you include the *full* URL in the `href="url"` attribute you use to make the link.

Hypertext links to outside resources

Links to Web sites outside your own Web do require that you mind your *P*s, *Q*s, and URLs if they're going to work properly. Specifically, interdocument links to remote sites require *fully qualified URLs,* such as the following modest example:

```
<p>
URL: <a href="http://www.lanw.com/html4dum/html4dum.htm">
          http://www.lanw.com/html4dum/html4dum.htm</a>
<br>
Text - Copyright &copy; 1995-2000 Ed Tittel &amp;
 Chelsea Valentine.
<br>
Dummies Design and Art - Copyright &copy; 1995-2000
IDG Books Worldwide, Inc. 
<br>
Web Layout - Copyright &copy; 1995-2000
<a href="http://www.lanw.com/">LANWrights</a>
<br>
Revised - April 1, 2000
</p>
```

The two links (you can spot them by their `href` attributes) connect the *HTML 4 For Dummies* home page to itself and to the LANWrights Web site. Wait a minute — why connect the page to itself? Doesn't it *know* where it is?

Well, yes, but there's method in the madness. Including the page's own URL as a link serves two purposes:

- ✔ It shows the user the complete (and correct) URL for your page.

- ✔ It allows direct linking if users save this page's HTML source to their own computers.

All these tags and links make for rough sledding when you're trying to read the actual HTML source code for your page — unless you view them through a browser, that is. We illustrate this very cool technique in Figure 13-6.

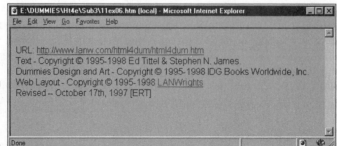

URL: http://www.lanw.com/html4dum/html4dum.htm
Text - Copyright © 1995-1998 Ed Tittel & Stephen N. James.
Dummies Design and Art - Copyright © 1995-1998 IDG Books Worldwide, Inc.
Web Layout - Copyright © 1995-1998 LANWrights
Revised -- October 17th, 1997 [ERT]

Figure 13-6:
External
links.

The browser identifies hypertext words by applying a different color, underlining, or both. You can even specify which; use your browser's preference settings.

Jump pages

The term *jump page* refers to a Web page whose content is primarily a list of URLs that link to other Web pages, usually remote sites. HTML list tags are invaluable for creating visually pleasing (and easily understood) lists of links. Because their content is heavy on the hyperlinks, jump pages (also known as *hotlists*) look and function differently from basic Web pages. A hotlist is great for quick scanning and be-there-yesterday Web travel, but it's not really for general reading (unless your users like stories with seriously sparse description, no characters, and no plot). Think of it as a cyberspaceport.

If you're going to have a hotlist on your site, set it apart by giving it some special visual treatment. Use icon images and spacer lines to separate the list into sections. Carefully choose the words you use for each hyperlink; they should, in effect, sum up or suggest the main point of the information to which the link itself refers.

When you type the URLs for your links, we strongly recommend that you first link to the destination URLs using your browser. Then, highlight, copy, and paste the URL directly into your HTML file to cut down on typos and syntax errors. (That sense of déjà vu does not deceive you; we mention this trick in other chapters.)

A special <link>

The <link> tag provides information that links the current Web page to other Web pages or to other URL resources. When you want to be sure that your Web pages tell browsers and other software about themselves, put a <link> in the <head> . . . </head> section.

The <link> tag is primarily used these days to link style sheets to Web pages. Check out Chapter 18 for more information on this quick but powerful way to assign one style sheet to a multitude of Web pages.

Analyzing Sophisticated Pages

The time has come for you to take a quick look at a complex Web page. In addition to inspecting our captive example, you may want to surf the Web looking for pages that strike your fancy. When you find one, view its source code to see how its author worked the underlying magic. The Web is one of the few places where you can easily look behind the curtain to see how an illusion is created; take full advantage of this opportunity. Ladies and gentlemen, all the way from its smash Broadway run . . .

The LANWrights' home page

Hey, this example isn't about vanity (well, okay, not entirely). LANWrights' own home page illustrates what you can accomplish if you use HTML 4 tags and your imagination (maybe you don't *need* frames anyway). It's eye-catching but not overdone (see Figure 13-7). Its information is arranged nicely and gives users multiple avenues of access. The graphics have neighboring text commands to make the site easy to navigate quickly, both graphically and textually. Users who want to "scan the site" can use the Site Overview section found in the right-hand column to explore the site systematically.

If you want to visit the LANWrights' home page, point your browser to www.lanw.com. View the source code and make a lesson out of it!

The entire home page is less than two screens long. It makes liberal (but not frighteningly so) use of color and blank space to keep the text readable. The graphics load quickly, because each has been designed with only a few colors and simple graphics components. Each link image or image map is repeated in text immediately to the right, a boon to users who don't have GUI browsers.

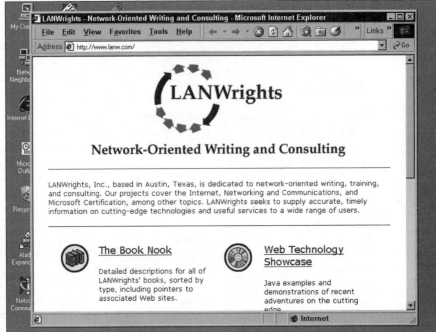

Figure 13-7:
The top of
LANWrights'
home page.

The footer contains much of the requisite information — not the page's URL, however — and makes much of the legal copyright notice that we professionals in the publishing world must hold so near to our hearts. (It *does* deflect a few legal slings and arrows.)

The HTML code for the LANWrights home pages is HTML 4 compliant. It shows some interesting tricks that you may find useful. Its use of `alt` text with images ensures navigation even for non-GUI browsers. It also plays some interesting games with tables, arranging graphics and text elements pleasingly to minimize mnemonic heave-ho, and builds a seductively convenient right-hand column of menu selections. Behold the abbreviated version:

```html
<!-- For brevity, we skipped lots of HTML in the head -->
<!DOCTYPE html PUBLIC "-//W3C//DTD HTML 3.2//EN">
<html>
<head>
<title>LANWrights - Network-Oriented Writing and
          Consulting</title>
</head>
<body bgcolor="#FFFFFF" link="#990033" vlink="#000080">

<center>
<p>
<img src="graphics/lanwlogo.gif" width="240" height="123"
          alt="LANWrights">
```

```
</p>

<p>
<img src="graphics/ntwkori.gif" width="469" height="25"
          alt="Network-Oriented Writing &amp; Consulting">
</p>

<p>
<img src="graphics/line.gif" width="100%" height="1">
</p>
</center>

<p>
<font size="-1">LANWrights, Inc., based in Austin, Texas, is
          dedicated to network-oriented writing, training,
          and consulting. Our projects cover the Internet,
          Networking and Communications, and Microsoft
          Certification, among other topics. LANWrights
          seeks to supply accurate, timely information on
          cutting-edge technologies and useful services to a
          wide range of users.</font>
</p>

<center>
<p>
<img src="graphics/line.gif" width="100%" height="1">
</p>

<table width="97%" border="0" cellpadding="10">

<tr valign="TOP">
<td width="5%" align="CENTER">
<a href="books.htm">
<img src="graphics/books.gif" width="51" height="51" alt="The
          Book Nook" align="RIGHT" border="0">
</a>
</td>
<td width="45%">
<p>
<font size="+1">
<a href="books.htm">The Book Nook</a>
</font>
</p>

<p>
<font size="-1">Detailed descriptions for all of
          LANWrights'books, sorted by type, including point-
          ers to associated Web sites.</font>
</p>
</td>
<td width="5%" align="CENTER">
<a href="showcase.htm">
<img src="graphics/showcase.gif" width="51" height="51"
          alt="Web Technology Showcase" border="0">
```

```
</a>
</td>
<td width="45%">
<p>
<font size="+1">
<a href="showcase.htm">Web Technology Showcase</a>
</font>
</p>

<p>
<font size="-1">Java examples and demonstrations of recent
          adventures on the cutting edge.</font>
</p>
</td>
</tr>

<tr valign="TOP">
<td width="5%" align="CENTER">
<a href="training.htm">
<img src="graphics/training.gif" width="51" height="51"
          alt="Training Center" align="RIGHT" border="0">
</a>
</td>
<td width="45%">
<p>
<a href="training.htm">
<font size="+1">The Training Center</font>
</a>
</p>

<p>
<font size="-1">Read about or sign up for upcoming classroom
          sessions, demo our online training, and learn more
          about licensing our testing and training environ-
          ments.</font>
</p>
</td>
<td width="5%" align="CENTER">
<a href="corporat.htm">
<img src="graphics/corporat.gif" width="51" height="51"
          alt="Coporate Services" border="0">
</a>
</td>
<td width="45%">
<p>
<a href="lanw.htm">
<font size="+1">Corporate HQ</font>
</a>
</p>
```

```
<p>
<font size="-1">Learn more about LANWrights' organization,
            including available services and rates. Read staff
            bios, and find out what's new here.</font>
</p>
</td>
<!-- and so on... -->
```

And that's what the wizard behind the curtain said. As you can see, the HTML arranges the The Book Nook elements in the left-hand column and the Web Technology Showcase elements in the right-hand column. Note the repeated use of the <font> tag to control type size, and the consistent use of alt text to permit words to stand in for graphics where necessary. All these are elements of good design. (After some debate, we took the tail fins and extra chrome off.)

Other sophisticated Web sites

We strongly urge you to explore the Web and view HTML source code for the many exciting sites that abound in Web space. You need to look not only at HTML source for a site's primary page, but also at HTML source for each frame on those sites that use HTML frames. Try right-clicking a frame and see what your browser lets you do. You may be surprised — newer browsers should show you the HTML source code for the frame you selected.

Chapter 14

Using HTML Tables Effectively

*I*n HTML, as in life, tables may seem prosaic, but they're handy for holding things. You can arrange everything from text to images on your pages, efficiently and attractively, in HTML tables. The 3.0 and later versions of both Netscape and Internet Explorer support tables, as do the more recent versions of other, non-commercial browsers, such as Mosaic and Opera.

If your browser doesn't support tables, take it as a sign that upgrade time is here again.

Since the days of HTML 3.2, tables have become standard elements of Web documents. With HTML 4, proprietary extensions from Netscape and Microsoft have given way to official standards. This chapter heralds the new age of HTML 4 tables and gets you started using them.

First, Consider the Alternatives

The traditional approach to tabulating data or organizing content on a page is to use <table> tags. But before you walk down this road, please ask yourself this question, "Do I really have to use a table here?" You can use lists, images, preformatted text, or frames instead of tables. Each of these structures has its good and bad points. The following bulleted list provides a brief description of these items:

✔ **Lists:** Simple to implement and consistently well rendered by every browser available. Lists are sensible alternatives to tables if you want to quickly and easily group information. However, lists don't give you the formatting capabilities of tables, especially for images.

✔ **Images:** You can compose images in grids with borders and colors, but be warned that they may become static and difficult to change. Images also get big and slow!

✔ **Preformatted text:** This choice is the original table markup and an option that still works in a pinch without causing any concern over browser compatibility. However, most browsers generally display preformatted text in a non-proportional font that looks terrible. This option is not recommended when look and feel are important.

✔ **Frames:** These complex constructs may offer an additional dimension to your Web site, but they're not really a replacement for tables.

The preceding alternatives notwithstanding, tables are great for many uses — presenting financial results, organizing lists of related elements (such as dates and birthdays), and giving rowdy elements a defined layout.

HTML <table> Overview

Table markup brings versatility to describing your content. HTML tables offer virtually limitless description possibilities because you can put almost any other HTML tag into a table cell.

For now, follow the KISS principle (Keep It Simple, Sillyhead). We strongly recommend that you stick with basic table elements unless you're developing documents for a private Web server where you *know* your audience is using a particular browser. Sticking to a common denominator (common table elements) is the best way to ensure the widest audience for your work. As you wander awestruck through the rest of this chapter (well, we can hope), eagerly absorbing the basics (and some nifty uses) of HTML tables, pay particular attention to how table constructs nest within each other. If you goof up just one nesting order, your information won't display the way you expect it to!

Every time you add another level to a table, indent the code to offset it from the previous level. Then, when you return to a higher level, decrease your indentation to match previous code at the same level. To demonstrate this healthful and sensible principle, we use this method in all of the examples in this chapter for your rapt perusal.

An obvious-but-important fact is that a table is a visual device that's hard to read aloud to someone who can't see it. If your readership includes users who may be print-handicapped or otherwise visually impaired, provide an alternative form for your table data. Some browsers can produce Braille or convert text to speech, but most aren't able to handle the HTML <table> tag for such conversions. As one solution, many Web sites offer text-only implementations for tables as an alternative. You may want to consider doing the same if it's appropriate for your audience.

HTML Table Markup

The amazing fact is you can put *any* presentational HTML body element into a table cell. You can even nest multiple tables within a single cell — a fun but time-consuming activity that we don't recommend you try just yet. So, if you think that some particular combination of table elements and other elements may work for your table, give it a try. Your idea may work better than you think, or it may not work at all — the only way to be sure is to experiment. Go for what works.

The parts of a <table>

The basic parts of a table are the <table> . . . </table> tag pair that surrounds all of a table's contents, including the <tr> . . . </tr> (table row) tag pair that defines each row within a table, and the <td> . . . </td> (table data) tag pair that defines each cell within each row of a table.

Optional table tags include the <caption> . . . </caption> tag pair, which places contained text above or below a table as a label, and <th> . . . </th> (table header) tag pair, which you can use to label columns in a table. More recently, the <tbody> . . . </tbody> (table body), <thead> . . . </thead> (table head), <tfoot> . . . </tfoot> (table foot), <colgroup> . . . </colgroup> (column group) and <col> (column) tags have been introduced to create snazzier, more structured tables. The following code snippet for a simple HTML table illustrates some of these tags, in the most boring way we can imagine. (Hey, ya gotta play some scales before you jump to the jazzy stuff!)

```
<table>
<caption>The default caption placement (see Figure
        14-1).</caption>
 <tr>
  <th> Header: row 1, column 1</th>
  <th> Header: row 1, column 2</th>
 </tr>
 <tr>
  <td> Cell: row 2, column 1</td>
  <td> Cell: row 2, column 2</td>
 </tr>
</table>
```

If you put the preceding table code in a Web page and view the result in your browser, you'll see something similar to the snazzola table depicted in Figure 14-1 — all bones, no meat. (Bleah!)

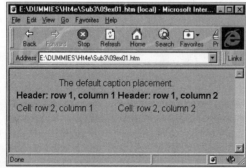

If you're really feeling adventurous, take our first code sample, replace our less-than-exciting content with some of your own (text, images, or whatever you like), save the new code, and view it in your favorite browser. Voilà! You've created a table.

Regardless of how big or small your table is or what content you choose to include within its cells, you need to always include the following tags in every table you create:

- `<table> . . . </table>`
- `<tr> . . . </tr>`
- `<td>. . .</td>`

But wait. After you use this example, you unlock the basic concepts of table-tag layout and nesting techniques. Now that you have this potent knowledge, you can construct a basic table of your own. Before you go forth to rule the world, however, you need to know more about each of these tags and their attributes. Say no more.

The table tag: <table> . . . </table>

The `<table> . . . </table>` tags are like a toy chest; they provide a container for all other table tags. Browsers (ever the sticklers for detail) ignore other table tags if they aren't contained inside `<table> . . . </table>` tags. The `<table> . . . </table>` tag pair accepts the following unique attributes: `summary`, `align`, `border`, `cellpadding`, `cellspacing`, and `width`.

Always include the table closing tag (`</table>`). If you don't, your table may not show up at all; invisible tables aren't really very useful. And as a bonus, you get another warning for no cost: The `align` attribute is deprecated, so watch out, because it may not be in the next version of HTML. If you want to position your table, you should consider using Cascading Style Sheets (CSS) instead.

The table row tag: <tr> . . . </tr>

The `<tr>` . . . `</tr>` (as in *table row*) tags contain the information for all cells within a particular table row. Each tag pair represents a single row, no matter how many cells the row contains. The `<tr>` . . . `</tr>` tag pair accepts only the `align` and `valign` attributes — which, if you specify them, become default alignments that whip all the contents of all cells in the row into line.

The `align` attribute is not deprecated in this instance, so if you are dying to use it, it's okay by us (and the W3C).

The table data tag: <td> . . . </td>

The `<td>` . . . `</td>` *(table data)* tags hold the contents of each cell in a table. If those fussbudget browsers are going to recognize cells as cells, you have to put your cell data within these tags and then, in turn, nest the table data tag within a set of table row tags. Table data tags give your cells some friendly characteristics, such as:

✔ You needn't worry about making each row contain the same number of cells because blank cells on the right complete the short rows.

✔ A cell can contain any HTML tag normally used within the body (`<body>` . . . `</body>`) of an HTML document.

The `<td>` . . . `</td>` tag pair accepts the following attributes: `abbr`, `align`, `axis`, `bgcolor`, `colspan`, `headers`, `height`, `nowrap`, `rowspan`, `valign`, and `width`.

The `width`, `height`, and `nowrap` attributes are deprecated for this tag. You may want to take a look toward CSS to achieve the same effect.

The table header tag: <th> . . . </th>

The *table header* tags (`<th>` . . . `</th>`) display text in boldface with a default center alignment. You can use the `<th>` . . . `</th>` tags within any row of a table, but you most often find and use them in the first row at the top — or head — of a table. Except for their position and egotism, they act just like table data (`<td>` . . . `</td>`) tags and should be treated as such.

The table caption tag: <caption> . . . </caption>

Captions are snobs; `<caption>` . . . `</caption>` tags are designed to exist anywhere inside the `<table>` . . . `</table>` tags but not inside table rows or cells (because then they wouldn't be *captioning* anything) — and they can only occur once. Similar to table cells, captions accommodate any HTML tags that can appear in the body of a document (in other words, inline elements), but only those. By default, captions put themselves at horizontal dead center with respect to a table, wrapping their lines to fit within the table's width. The `<caption>` . . . `</caption>` tag pair accepts the `align` attribute if you ask it nicely.

Many Web page authors take a short cut and use an `<h*>` tag in place of the `<caption>` tag. We know that at work, most of us are under the gun and in a hurry to get our projects on the boss' table. But steer clear of this shortcut because it's a no-no according to the W3C's Accessibility Initiative. To read more about the W3C's guidelines, visit `www.w3.org/WAI/`.

An inline element is any element that controls presentation on an element-by-element basis, and an inline element does not denote structure. In other words, it's a text element, for example the `<b>` . . . `</b>` tag pair is an inline element.

Basic table attributes

Okay, here's where the incantations that create tables get a bit more complicated. You can use several attributes with the different table tags to determine how the table's parts and contents are displayed on-screen. Get to know these critters, use them innovatively, and they repay your attention by making your tables easier on the eye. Here's a quick overview of table attributes; next, we show you how to use them.

align="[left or center or right]" [CI]

The `align` attribute works with all the various table tags to help you control how the browser horizontally aligns the table and its contents. Depending on which tag you add it to, the attribute has a different effect on the final display of the table.

- ✔ Use `align` with the `<caption>` . . . `</caption>` tags to specify how the table's caption needs to be aligned relative to the table itself. The default alignment for a caption is `center`.

- ✔ Use `align` with the `<table>` . . . `</table>` tags to set the table's alignment relative to the rest of the page. The default alignment for a table is `LEFT`, so to center the table or force it to justify to the right, set the value of `align` to `CENTER` or `RIGHT`.

✔ Use align with the ⟨tr⟩ . . . ⟨/tr⟩, ⟨td⟩ . . . ⟨/td⟩, or
⟨th⟩ . . . ⟨/th⟩ tags to define how the content within table cells is
aligned. If you set an alignment for a table row tag, the alignment applies
to all the contents of all the cells or header cells in that row. If you set an
alignment for a single table cell or table header, the alignment only applies
to the content in that single cell or header cell. Finally, if you set the alignment for all the cells in a row and then set the alignment for a cell within
that row, the setting you add to the cell overrides the setting for the row.
Whew! Bet you didn't know one little attribute could do so much.

To show you the align attribute at work, we play with our original, plain-
vanilla table a bit. The HTML has been altered to align the table to the center,
the caption to the right, the contents of the first row to the left, and the contents of the second row to the right. For good measure, the second cell on the
second row has also been aligned to the center.

```
<table align="CENTER">
<caption align="RIGHT">The caption.</caption>
 <tr align="LEFT">
  <th> Header: row 1, column 1</th>
  <th> Header: row 1, column 2</th>
 </tr>
 <tr align="RIGHT">
  <td> Cell: row 2, column 1</td>
  <td align="CENTER"> Cell: row 2, column 2</td>
 </tr>
</table>
```

Figure 14-2 shows how the newly revised markup is displayed in a browser.

Figure 14-2:
The align
attribute
can change
the arrange-
ment of a
table and its
contents.

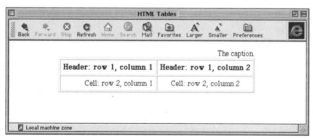

Remember, the align attribute is deprecated for the ⟨table⟩ . . .
⟨/table⟩ tag pair. Take a look at CSS for achieving the same effect.

We add a border to many of the screen shots in this chapter to make it easier
to see each individual cell and the changes different attributes can effect on a
table.

border="number" [CN]

The `border` attribute only works with the `<table>` . . . `</table>` tags. Its job is to let the browser know whether you want a border around your table or not, and if so, how big you want that border to be. This attribute takes a numeric value — `border="5"` for example — that indicates how many pixels wide you want the border to be. If you don't want a border around your table, then specify `border="0"`. If you don't specify a value, `border` defaults to a width of one (1) pixel.

If we change the first line of our plain-Jane table to `<table border="5">`, our table is now well outlined, as shown in Figure 14-3.

Figure 14-3: The border attribute can really box up a table.

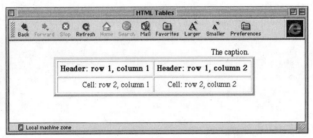

Tables without borders can provide a clean look and feel and help you control unruly text and graphics, but we find the business of building tables to be both tedious and exacting. To make things a bit easier, we suggest you set the border on a table to one (1) while your table is under construction so you can more easily see how the browser is interpreting your rows and columns. After you're done with construction and are satisfied with the results, simply change the one to a zero — and "Bye-bye, border."

cellpadding="number" [CN]

Yet another attribute that you can only use with the `<table>` . . . `</table>` tags, `cellpadding` specifies the amount of space between a cell's perimeter and its contents. Think, cotton padding in a pillow. The default value for this attribute is one (1) pixel but you can make the value as large or small as you like.

This handy-dandy attribute helps you put some space between the content in your cells, making them easier to read. Combined with cell spacing and a well-sized border, cell padding can enhance the visual impact of your tables.

Once again working with our basic table, we add a bit of white space within every cell by changing the opening table tag to `<table cellpadding="5">`. Check out the results for yourself in Figure 14-4.

Figure 14-4:
The cell-
padding
attribute
keeps con-
tent from
being too
close for
comfort.

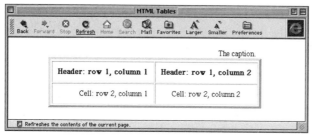

cellspacing="number" [CN]

Use the `cellspacing` attribute within the `<table>` . . . `</table>` tag to determine the amount of space inserted between individual cells in a table. The default value is one (1) pixel between cells. If we set the border on our basic table to five and change the cell padding to five using `<table border="5" cellspacing="5">`, the browser displays the HTML with a bit more space between the cells, as shown in Figure 14-5.

Figure 14-5:
The cell-
spacing
attribute
gives
cells a
bit of
breathing
room.

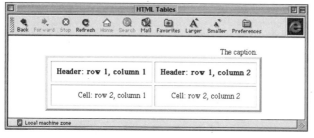

Unless you have your table border set to more than one pixel or the back-ground colors of your table cells set to different colors, you won't be able to see a difference in the display of the `cellspacing` and the `cellpadding` attributes.

summary="text" [CS]

The `<table>` . . . `</table>` tag uses the `summary` attribute to provide a summary of the table's structure and purpose for users using non-visual media such as Braille. This is a fairly new, yet important attribute to include in all your tables. You don't do anything technical here — just in your own words, outline what's in your table. The `summary` attribute is not widely supported.

width="number" or "%" [CN]

If used with <table> . . . </table> tags, the width attribute sets the width of a table in absolute terms (a specific number of pixels) or as a percentage of a browser's display area. You can also use this attribute within <th> . . . </th> or <td> . . . </td> tags — to decree the width of a cell within a table as an absolute number of pixels or else assign it a percentage of the table's width. (Now, that's power!)

Until now, the display of our basic table has only taken up as much of the browser window as was necessary to show all its content. If we change the opening table tag so its width is 75% (<table width="75%">), the table will take up 75% of the browser window's width, as shown in Figure 14-6. If we set the width to 100 (for 100 pixels) — <table width="100"> — the table is forced to be exactly (or absolutely) 100 pixels wide, and the cell contents are wrapped to fit the specific size, as shown in Figure 14-7.

Figure 14-6:
Set a table's width to a percentage to set its size relative to the width of the browser window.

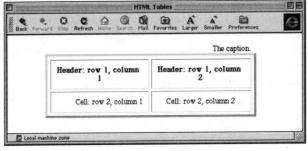

Figure 14-7:
Set a table's width to a pixel size to specify exactly how big you want the table.

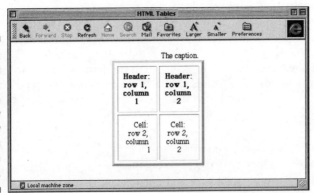

To create tables that are more flexible and accommodate a wider variety of monitor sizes and browser window widths, we highly recommend that you use relative table widths — percentages instead of pixels. If you absolutely must create a table with an absolute width — pixels instead of percentages — don't make it any larger than 550 or 600 pixels. If you violate this restriction, users with small monitors may have to scroll horizontally to read your page, and in the Web world that's a no-no. In fact, it's sure to chase your users away in hordes.

valign="TOP" or "MIDDLE" or "BOTTOM" [CI]

Tuck the valign (*vertical alignment*) attribute within the `<tr>` . . . `</tr>`, `<th>` . . . `</th>`, or `<td>` . . . `</td>` tags to vertically align the contents of the table to the top, middle, or bottom of the cell. In general, valign is a counterpart to align, so you often use them together. The default value for this attribute is MIDDLE. Ten-hut!

nowrap [CI]

If you use nowrap with a table cell or header (`<th>` . . . `</th>` or `<td>` . . . `</td>`), Web browsers will try to display all the text for that particular cell on a single line. This can sometimes produce weird results. Take notice that nowrap is a standalone statement and does not receive an attribute value.

Using this attribute can create extremely wide cells (especially for people who like to write sentences even longer than this one). Be careful! Also, this attribute is deprecated, so don't get too used to using it.

colspan="number" [CN]

Spanning is a key component of HTML tables because it helps you overcome one of the most maddening characteristics of tables: their overwhelming desire to be symmetrical. By way of explanation, think about what may happen if you add another `<th>` . . . `</th>` tag pair to the first row of our basic table — but not to the second row — using this code:

```
<table border="1">
<caption>The caption.</caption>
 <tr>
  <th> Header: row 1, column 1</th>
  <th> Header: row 1, column 2</th>
  <th> Header: row 1, column 3</th>
 </tr>
 <tr>
  <td> Cell: row 2, column 1</td>
  <td> Cell: row 2, column 2</td>
 </tr>
</table>
```

Tables always want to be symmetrical, so the browser automatically adds an empty cell to our second row to serve as a balance for the new cell we added in the first row, as shown in Figure 14-8.

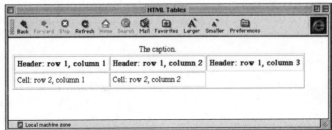

Figure 14-8: Browsers automatically fill in cells if your table code isn't symmetrical.

Not the prettiest picture we've ever seen. What to do, what to do? There's got to be a way to force one cell in a row to act as more than one cell. In fact, there is. Spanning allows you to create a single table cell that can span several rows or columns, depending on your needs. For example, to make the second column of our second row span two columns — act as if two cells in one row — we only need change the table data tag to:

```
<td colspan="2"> Cell: row 2, column 2</td>
```

Ta-da! As Figure 14-9 shows, the single cell now acts as two cells and spans across two columns, filling in the space where the empty cell created by the browser had previously been. It's not magic; it's HTML.

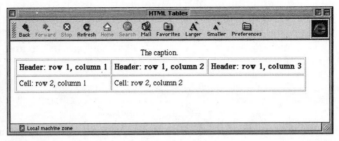

Figure 14-9: The `colspan` attribute helps one cell act as many.

rowspan="number" [CN]

The rowspan attribute is similar to colspan in both form and function — as if their names didn't give that away. If you use rowspan with table data (<td> . . . </td>) or table header (<th> . . . </th>) tags, the cell spans multiple rows — as opposed to multiple columns. In the previous section, we used colspan="2" to force one cell to act as two in the same row to solve the dilemma created by the unbalanced table code example we used. In the same way, we can use `rowspan="2"` with the new table header cell (row 1, column 3) to force the cell to expand down into the second row and make the table symmetrical:

```
<th rowspan="2"> Header: row 1, column 3</th>
```

Check out the results in Figure 14-10.

Figure 14-10:
The
rowspan
attribute
causes one
cell to
expand
down sev-
eral rows.

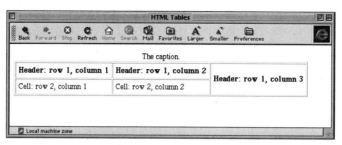

bgcolor="color" [CI]

Remember the `bgcolor` attribute that goes with the `<body>` . . . `</body>` tag pair? `bgcolor` is the same attribute, and it affects the background of table cells in the same way it affects the background of your entire HTML document. Simply add this attribute to any table cell or header to change its background color:

```
<td bgcolor="teal">...</td>
```

There the W3C goes again with deprecating a tag. The `bgcolor` attribute deprecates in favor of using CSS to achieve the same results.

Recent Additions to the Table Family

Recently, the W3C added some functionality to tables by introducing the following tags:

- ✔ `<tbody>` . . . `</tbody>`
- ✔ `<thead>` . . . `</thead>`
- ✔ `<tfoot>` . . . `</tfoot>`
- ✔ `<colgroup>` . . . `</colgroup>`
- ✔ `<col>`

The first three tags allow authors to divide their tables into logical sections. But in the future, that won't be all. Adding structure is important, but it's not the most fun you can have working with HTML. Luckily, the W3C has added a little pizzazz to these three tag pairs. After you separate your table into head, foot, and body sections, the body section is then able to scroll independently of the table head and foot. If you've never created a table before, you may be thinking, so what? But, after you try to fit a multicolumn table into a Web browser — comfortably — you will definitely be singing the same happy song as we are. Although this function is not supported yet, we're all keeping our fingers crossed that browsers will provide support on the next go around.

The last two tags (`<colgroup>` . . . `</colgroup>` and `<col>`) help maintain those pesky columns. With the use of their attributes, you can define uniform behavior for your columns. Another win for tables! Take a look.

The table body tag: <tbody> . . . </tbody>

Table rows may be grouped into a table body section, using the `<tbody>` . . . `</tbody>` tags. As a recent addition to the HTML 4 specification, these tags allow for a division that enables browsers to support scrolling of table bodies independently of the table head and table foot (`<tfoot>` . . . `</tfoot>`). The table body should contain rows of table data. The `<tbody>`. . .`</tbody>` tag must contain at least one table row. Take a look at our example:

```
<table align="CENTER">
<caption align="RIGHT">The caption.</caption>
 <tr align="LEFT">
  <th> Header: row 1, column 1</th>
  <th> Header: row 1, column 2</th>
 </tr>
<tbody>
 <tr align="RIGHT">
  <td> Cell: row 2, column 1</td>
  <td align="CENTER"> Cell: row 2, column 2</td>
 </tr>
</tbody>
</table>
```

The table head tag: <thead> . . . </thead>

Table rows may be grouped into a table head section, using the `<thead>` . . . `</thead>` tag. New to the HTML 4 specification, these tags allow for a division that enables browsers to support scrolling of table bodies independently of the table head and table foot (`<tfoot>` . . . `</tfoot>`). The table head contains information about the table's columns. The `<thead>` . . . `</thead>` tags must contain at least one table row. Take a look at our example:

```
<table align="CENTER">
<caption align="RIGHT">The caption.</caption>
<thead>
 <tr align="LEFT">
  <th> Header: row 1, column 1</th>
  <th> Header: row 1, column 2</th>
 </tr>
</thead>
<tbody>
 <tr align="RIGHT">
  <td> Cell: row 2, column 1</td>
  <td align="CENTER"> Cell: row 2, column 2</td>
 </tr>
</tbody>
</table>
```

If you decide to use one of the logical table dividers — <tfoot>, <thead>, or <tbody> — you need to make sure that all the <tr> tags are contained by them. Don't leave any out to dry!

The table foot tag: <tfoot> . . . </tfoot>

Much like the <thead> . . . </thead> tags, table rows may be grouped into a table footer section, using the <tfoot> . . . </tfoot> tags. New to the HTML 4 specification, these tags allow for a division that enables user agents to support scrolling of table bodies independently of the table head and table foot. The table foot contains information about the table's columns and must contain at least one table row. Be sure to include your footer information before the first instance of the <tbody> . . . </tbody> tags; that way, the browser renders that information before taking a stab at all the content data cells. Take a look at our example:

```
<table align="CENTER">
<caption align="RIGHT">The caption.</caption>
<thead>
 <tr align="LEFT">
  <th> Header: row 1, column 1</th>
  <th> Header: row 1, column 2</th>
 </tr>
</thead>
<tfoot>
 <tr align="LEFT">
  <td> Footer: row 1, column 1</th>
  <td> Footer: row 1, column 2</th>
 </tr>
</tfoot>
<tbody>
 <tr align="RIGHT">
  <td> Cell: row 2, column 1</td>
  <td align="CENTER"> Cell: row 2, column 2</td>
 </tr>
</tbody>
</table>
```

To see a table with a head, foot, and body section, check out Figure 14-11.

Table 14-11:
A table
created
using the
`<thead>`
. . .
`</thead>`,
`<tfoot>`
. . .
`</tfoot>`,
and
`<tbody>`
. . .
`</tbody>`
tags.

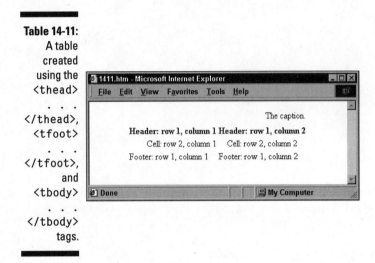

The table colgroup tag: <colgroup> . . . </colgroup>

The `<colgroup>` . . . `</colgroup>` tags create an explicit column group. The number of columns is specified using the `span` attribute or using the `<col>` tag, which is defined shortly. Using the span attribute allows you to specify a uniform width for a group of columns. The `<colgroup>` . . . `</colgroup>` tag pair takes two unique attributes:

```
span="number" [CN]
```

This tag specifies the number of columns in a column group. This attribute is ignored if you specify one or more `<col>` tags within the `<colgroup>` . . . `</colgroup>` tag. The default value is 1.

```
width="%" or "pixels" or "n*" [CN]
```

Defines a default width for each column found within the column group. Using "0*" as the default value assigns a relative value, meaning that the width of each column in the column group is the minimum width necessary to contain the column's contents.

Here is an example using the `<colgroup>` . . . `</colgroup>` tag:

```
<table>
<colgroup span="30" width="15">
</colgroup>
<colgroup span="10" width="45">
</colgroup>
</table>
```

The previous code separates 40 columns into two groups. The first column group contains 30 columns, each with a width of 15 pixels. The second column group contains 10 columns, each with a width of 45 pixels. Easy enough, huh?

The table col tag: <col>

The <col> tag is an *empty tag* — meaning an end tag is forbidden. You use the <col> tag to further define column structure. <col> tag should not be used to group columns — that is a function for the <colgroup> . . . </colgroup> tag — but rather used as a way to support its attributes. After you define a column group and set a uniform width, you can specify a uniform width for a subset of columns using the <col> tag. Take a look at our example:

```
<table>
<colgroup>
  <col width="20">
</colgroup>
<colgroup>
  <col width="20">
  <col width="0*">
</colgroup>
<colgroup>
  <col width="1*">
  <col width="3*" align="char">

</colgroup>
<thead>
<tr>
...
</tr>
...more rows...
</thead>
...table foot and body sections...
</table>
```

If you're shaking your head and saying, "Huh?" you probably want us to explain the previous code. First, the browser allots 20 pixels to columns one and two. Then, the minimal space required for the third column is reserved. The remaining space is divided into four equal portions. Because $1* + 3* = 4$ portions, column four $(1*)$ receives one of the four portions, and column five $(3*)$ receives the remaining three.

Add some flare by using CSS to uniformly style your <col> groups.

Now that you've toured the new tags introduced in HTML 4, we get you back to the basic table tags that you will most likely use when you are constructing tables.

Build Your Own Tables

Building tables by hand is time-consuming, repetitive work, even if you make them out of data instead of wood. So be sure that a tabular form enhances your content. You can simplify your work by carefully planning the layout of your tabular data and by making use of search, replace, copy, and paste functions in your HTML/text editor. Before you start tagging your data to make it totally tabular (is there an echo in here?), consider. . . .

Laying out tabular data for easy display

First, sketch how you want your table to look (give yourself room; your table may be *bigger* than a cocktail napkin). Then, create a small HTML table with only a few rows of data to test your layout. Does the table appear the way you envisioned it? If you're using heads that span multiple columns or rows, you may need to adjust the space they take to fit your data. Finally, test your tables with several browsers to see how they look on each one. Finalize your design before you add the data you want the table to contain.

Multirow and multicolumn spans

Remember to build your tables by rows. If you use `rowspan="3"` in one table row (`<tr> . . .</tr>`), you must account for the extra two rows in the next two rows. For example, consider the following code morsel:

```
<table border=0>
 <tr>
  <td rowspan="3">Letters</td>
  <td>A</td>
 </tr>
 <tr>
  <td>B</td>
 </tr>
 <tr>
  <td>C</td>
 </tr>
</table>
```

The idea is to leave out a cell in each row or column to be assumed ("spanned into," if you prefer) by the `rowspan` or `colspan` cell, as shown in Figure 14-12.

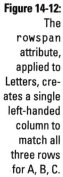

Figure 14-12:
The
rowspan
attribute,
applied to
Letters, cre-
ates a single
left-handed
column to
match all
three rows
for A, B, C.

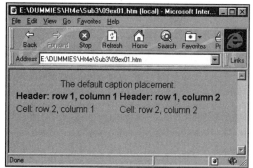

Mixing graphics and tables to add interest

If you want to frighten off a visitor to your Web page, just pack a screen full of dense and impenetrable information — especially numbers. A long, unbroken list of numbers quickly drives away all but the truly masochistic. You can stop the pain: Put those numbers into an attractive table (better yet, *several* tables interspersed with a few well-chosen images). Watch your page's attrac-tiveness and readability soar; hear visitors sigh with relief.

Individual table cells can be surprisingly roomy; you can position graphics in them precisely. If you're moved to put graphics in a table, be sure to:

✔ Select images that are similar in size and looks.

✔ Measure those images to determine their heights and widths in pixels (shareware programs such as Paint Shop Pro and GraphicConverter do this automatically).

✔ Use HTML markup to position these images within their table cells.

We've made extensive use of this particular technique for better controlling graphics throughout the LANWrights Web site.

A short and sweet table keeps the graphics in check and guarantees that the text will always sit nicely to its right.

Two more handy graphics-placement tips: Size your rows and columns of cells that contain images to accommodate the largest graphic and center all graphics in each cell (vertically and horizontally). The result is a consistent, coherent image layout.

Tools automate tedious markup

Most decent/recent HTML editors build tables for you. Many have table wizards that ask you how many rows and columns that you want and then automatically generate the necessary HTML markup. In these same editors, you also find tools that make adding new rows, columns, spans, and background colors as easy as pie.

Likewise, Microsoft Excel now offers a Save as Web Page option in the File menu. You can create your table in Excel — or easily transfer an existing Excel table to HTML — and then use this nifty function to make Excel create the necessary markup automatically.

Let's hear it for progress! So how come we made you learn the details of HTML table markup? Well, what can we say — we're sadists (just kidding).

Actually, none of these tools *fully* automates all the details that can appear within a table. Your artistic touch is still needed to create borders, cell padding, cell spacing, and so on. Besides, no automatic process really understands how to position graphics as precisely as a human designer can (take *that,* soulless machines!). Still, these tools simplify the initial and often tedious creation of table markup. Because you're going to have to tweak your tables by hand anyway, we figured the best way to get started was with a little "manual labor." (You'll thank us later. Honest.)

Some Stunning Table Examples

To find the best uses of tables on the Web . . . well, look around the Web.

We think these popular sites make excellent use of tables in their design:

  ✔ **CNET** — This entire site uses tables for all the complex layout. Often, tables are within tables within tables: www.cnet.com.

✔ **Yahoo!** — The most popular search engine on the Web uses tables to display its front page and all of the navigation items on all results pages: www.yahoo.com.

✔ **Dilbert Zone** — The only engineer on the planet to publicly disparage his boss and still keep his job (wait a minute — didn't he quit and become a cartoonist?). This daily dose of Dilbert is presented entirely by means of tables: www.unitedmedia.com/comics/dilbert.

After you load these documents into your Web browser, take a look at each one's HTML source code (try View⇨Source from your menu bar). Observe how complex the markup is, and mark ye well when the markup looks haphazardly arranged (alas, if only they'd asked us . . .).

Chapter 15

The Map's the Thing!

So you've already deciphered how to insert graphics into HTML documents using the `<img>` tag, eh? And we suspect you've seen other inscriptions that turn graphics into hypertext links within anchor tags (for example, `<a href= . . . ><img src= . . . ></a>`). In this chapter, we show you how to treat a graphic as a collection of selectable regions, each of which points to a different hypertext link or resource.

Where Are You? (Using Clickable Maps)

The geographical maps we're accustomed to identify landmasses and divide them along boundaries into named regions — countries, counties, office parks, whatever. You can use graphics the same way on the Web, divvying up an image so its territories activate different hyperlinks. Users familiar with graphical interfaces have no trouble interacting with buttons, icons, and other kinds of interface controls. Graphical maps add this capability to a single image displayed on a Web page — in Web-speak, an image map, or clickable map. We prefer the latter term because it suggests both the nature of these graphical elements and the way to use them:

▸ **Their nature:** Clickable maps break a graphic into discrete regions that function as a collection of individual hyperlinks. Normally, the regional boundaries are obvious; users simply select whatever portion of the graphic attracts their interest.

▸ **Their use:** Users can select regions by putting the cursor inside the desired region and clicking the mouse. Then it's bon voyage!

Those who have bossed a computer around from a command prompt, word by word, are already hip to a fundamental limitation of clickable maps: They absolutely require a GUI browser. Clickable maps don't work if you can't click 'em (or even see them). The image that represents the map isn't visible in a character-mode browser. Therefore, as a friendly gesture to users with text-only browsers, supplement your clickable maps by implementing alternate navigation methods that don't need pictures.

A typically modest example of a clickable map should save us a thousand words or so. Figure 15-1 shows the home page graphic for *HTML For Dummies*. This graphic features a set of buttons at the bottom, where each button contains a major access category for that set of *HTML For Dummies* pages. As part of a set of Web pages for the current edition of this book, each button acts as the gateway to a page, or set of pages, for each category or topic mentioned. (All together now, "Wow. That is so cool. How do they do it?" Read on, MacDuff!)

Figure 15-1:
The *HTML For Dummies* home page (server version) includes a row of buttons on the bottom.

Cosmic Cartography — Putting Maps on the Web

Because a clickable map is a mode of cybertransportation as well as a nifty picture, building one requires three different processes:

- ✔ **Creating (or selecting) a usable image:** This image can be an existing graphic or a custom-built one. Our *HTML For Dummies* button bar uses five custom-built icons, one for each button.

    If you create your own graphics, don't forget to eat and sleep.

- ✔ **Creating the map file:** This task requires a step-by-step investigation of the image file inside a graphics program that gives you the pixel addresses (coordinates) of each point on the boundary that separates the regions you want to create. (The impatient, lazy, and/or efficient among you may want to use a map-building utility such as the one we mention later in this chapter.)

    Our icons are all about the same size, so working through this process is easy: The image starts in the upper-left corner of the button bar (at vertical location 142, or about the middle of this 285-pixel-high image) and is consistently 143 pixels high. The individual buttons vary slightly in width, producing the following set of coordinates:

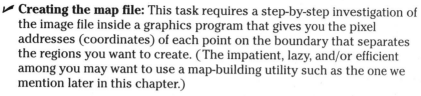

```
(0,142)—(99,142)—(199,142)—(299,142)—(399,142)—
       (499,142)

 | button 1 | button 2 | button 3 | button 4 | button 5

(0,285)—(99,285)—(199,285)—(299,285)—(399,285)—
       (499,285)
```

    Just that easy, just that simple. Unfortunately, the only way to produce this collection of numbers is to view the graphic inside a graphics program that shows pixel coordinates (we used Adobe Photoshop, but you can also use Paint Shop Pro, a widely available shareware graphics program for Windows). The alternative, of course, is to use an image-map construction program. (You haven't peeked ahead yet, have you?)

    Well, okay, we'll tell you about using an image-map tool: It generates a map after you tell it what kind of shapes you're outlining. One example is Tom Boutell's excellent program, called Mapedit, which builds map files at your command. Mapedit is available for Mac, DOS/Windows, and UNIX. Go to `www.boutell.com/mapedit/` to find Mapedit.

- ✔ **Establishing the right HTML information in your page:** You must link an image to both its map file and a CGI script that decodes map coordinates (and uses that information to select an appropriate link to follow).

Our immediate objective is a purposeful meander through the what-for and how-to of making image maps work in your HTML document. Then, we tear aside the veil of secrecy and build a complete back-end CGI script (one that translates the pixel coordinates for a user's map selection into a corresponding HTML link, just like that). But first things first; in this chapter, we cover the general techniques you need for constructing the image map and creating links between map regions and hypertext documents (or other resources). Trust us, that's plenty for now.

Thus, seeker, mark well after you obtain the appropriate image, study the image file for pixel addresses to use in creating map files, and establish a convention to call the script that translates coordinates into links. Only then have you accomplished the epic labors that prepare you to set up a clickable map.

To hail this deed (and protect your sanity), we suggest that you use the same name for the image map as for its related script: Thus, if the image is named ht4menum.gif, the script would be called `ht4menum.map`, or simply `ht4menum`. If your scripts reside in a CGI directory one level down from your HTML files, the URL for this script would then be `/cgi-bin/ht4menum.map`.

Warning: Different maps for different servers

The next quest is to define an appropriate format for your clickable map-to-be. We wish we could report that all servers are happy with just one format. No such luck. The awful truth is, no one image-map definition can meet the demands of all servers.

Et tu, CERN and NCSA?

Even the two most popular httpd servers — CERN and NCSA — differ on clickable map formats. In fact, even though they need more or less the same data to make a clickable map work, they need them in slightly different order and call them by slightly different names. Thus, for the truly stalwart, we provide the gory details in "Building and Linking to CERN Map Files" and "Building and Linking to NCSA Map Files," later in this chapter.

Throughout this chapter, where specific differences between CERN and NCSA requirements exist, we fill you in. If you're not sure whether you're using an httpd server of either variety, you may want to investigate your server's requirements immediately, adjust our examples and recommendations to meet those requirements, and make sure you have your Webmaster's contact info (an e-mail address, if not a phone number).

A babel of servers

Some Web servers, especially if they're not UNIX-based, won't support either CERN or NCSA image-map formats; others support only their proprietary image-map formats. Sometimes, though, a server's native platform can give you a good place to start and some sense of how large your audience may be. For example, the leading Macintosh Web server — WebSTAR — supports the NCSA image-map format, and Windows NT supports more than 20 Web servers.

To make a clickable map work, stay within the requirements of the server on which the map resides. If you don't know those requirements, contact your local Webmaster — or at least, the system administrator for your Web server. That person should be able to set you straight right away and can probably help you find some useful information about how to build clickable maps for your system, above and beyond what we tell you here.

Your maps take shape(s)

As you assemble coordinates to build a clickable map, the process of identifying boundaries may remind you of high school geometry. Both CERN and NCSA image-map definitions recognize the following regions:

- **Circle:** (Specified by the coordinates for a point at the center and the number of pixels for the radius.) Use this to select a circular (or nearly circular) region within an image. To define a circle, you specify where its center is located and its radius. This usually takes the form of something such as `circle, x, y, radius, URL` where `circle` is a keyword that denotes the shape, the `x, y` values specify the center's location, and `radius` defines its radius (in pixels). The URL identifies the Web document where a click in this region takes the user. Also, we hope it's obvious that the values for `x`, `y`, and `radius` need to be numbers.

- **Rectangle:** (Specified by the coordinates for the upper-left and lower-right corners.) Use this to select a square or rectangular region in your image. (We use this style in our button-bar map.) To define a rectangle, provide locations for the upper-left and lower-right corners. Defining a rectangle usually takes the form of `rectangle x1, y1, x2, y2, URL` where `rectangle` is a keyword that denotes the shape, `x1, y1` denotes the upper-left corner, and `x2, y2` denotes the lower-right corner. Here again, `URL` identifies the Web document where a click in this region takes the user.

✔ **Polygon:** (Specified by the coordinates for the point at the vertex of each edge. You remember *vertex* from geometry? We didn't either, but vertex sounds more exotic than *corner* or *intersection of endpoints*.) Simply put, vertices define the points where lines in a polygon come together to define a shape. Creating a polygon usually takes the form `polygon x1, y1, x2, y2, . . .,` `URL` where one pair of `xn, yn` values is necessary for each vertex in the polygon. Once again, `URL` plays the same role: It identifies the Web document where a click in this region takes the user.

Use vertices to outline the boundaries of regularly or irregularly shaped regions that aren't circular or rectangular. Although it takes more effort, the more points you pick to define an outline, the more a region behaves as users expect it to when clicking inside or outside its borders.

✔ **Point:** (Specified by its x and y coordinates.) Use this only when a specific point is easy to select. (A point is usually too small a region on-screen and requires exact control to select — we recommend surrounding a point with a small circle or square so users can be a little sloppy.) We've never actually used a point reference in an image map, except as a vertex for a polygon or rectangle, or the center of a circle. This takes the form `point x, y,` `URL` where `point` is the keyword, and `x, y` denotes its location. Likewise, `URL` indicates the Web document where a click on the point takes the user.

Selecting boundaries for map regions determines the selection of the related links. Even though users may see a nicely shaped graphic to click, you know what really drives the selection: the areas you outline on top of that graphic. For image maps, the upper-left corner of an image resides at coordinates 0, 0, so you can reference any pixel location within an image region by counting to the right to determine the first pixel value (the x coordinate), and down to determine the second pixel value (the y coordinate).

The better a map's regions fit an image, the more the map behaves as users expect — and (given human nature) the more they'll like it! The moral of the story is: Take your time and, when in doubt, pick more points to outline your map, rather than fewer. Even better, use a tool that follows your cursor movement to build the map for you. We mentioned Tom Boutell's Mapedit program earlier; other alternatives abound on the Web. Try out a couple; see what works for you:

✔ For example, a Macintosh image-map tool called MapMaker is available at `www.kickinit.com/mapmaker/download.html`.

✔ And again, Tom Boutell's outstanding PC-based image-map tool, Mapedit, is available at `www.boutell.com/mapedit`.

If you provide either tool with a URL for a graphic you want to map, the tool can guide you through the rest of the process using your very own Web browser. (Now if only we can find a power drill that does that. . . .)

An outstanding general discussion on this topic, entitled "How to Create Clickable Image Maps For Your Web Pages" is available at:

```
http://spider4.spiderlink.com/develop/devimaps.htm
```

Please read it for a slightly different take on this fascinating process.

Building and Linking to CERN Map Files

Here's the first of two sections that grapple with the nuts and bolts of the most popular image-map formats. In this corner . . . the map files for CERN http servers, in a form that looks like this:

```
circle (x,y) r URL
rectangle (x1,y1) (x2,y2) URL
polygon (x1,y1) (x2, y2) (x3,y3) . . . (xn,yn) URL
point (x,y) URL
default URL
```

Okay, so it's a bit anticlimactic. The shapes are pretty much self-evident — except for the polygon, which identifies coordinates for individual points that trace a region's outline. If this sounds like connect-the-dots, you've got the concept! (Whoa, that was waaaay too easy.)

Don't forget to close your polygons; make sure that the last segment fills the gap between your last point and your first. (Here's a really corny mnemonic to help you remember: "Always close the parrot cage or Polly gone.")

Another entry that may seem mysterious is the default URL: It's a fail-safe to prevent blunders by visitors who click randomly to see what happens (which, of course, no one we know ever does). You define a default so nothing much happens if users click an undefined location in the map; they choose the fail-safe. A default can be a script that sends a message back — say, a paean to high school nostalgia, "Click within the lines or stay after school!" Or maybe something kinder, "You have selected an area of the image that is not defined. Please try again."

A CERN map file for the button bar

For our button-bar example, the CERN map is as follows:

```
rectangle (0,142) (98,285) http://www.domain.com/html4dum/
        ftpstuff.htm
rectangle (99,142) (198,285) http://www.domain.com/html4dum/
        contents.htm
rectangle (199,142) (298,285) http://www.domain.com/html4dum/
        search4d.htm
rectangle (299,142) (398,285) http://www.domain.com/html4dum/
        contact.htm
rectangle (399,142) (499,285) http://www.domain.com/html4dum/
        whatsnew.htm
default http://www.domain.com/html4dum/contents.htm
```

Because the menu bar is a collection of rectangular buttons, defining its coordinates is easy. (Why do you think we picked this example?) Then we provide a default link to a `contents` page if somebody insists on staying outside the nice boxes we give them to play in (can't have them wandering the halls). Notice, too, that we use absolute URLs (typing carefully). Absolute URLs make maps easier to debug and relocate.

Is my system ready for CERN map files?

To actually use a map file with the CERN http, your system must already have a program that handles image maps. The name of this program, which is included with the CERN http materials, is htimage. You must have htimage installed if you plan to use image maps on your system. After it's available, you must also know how to invoke htimage. For the purposes of this example, we assume it lives on the directory path `/cgi-bin/`. For details about how to do this on your system, contact your local Webmaster or system administrator. For a sample file that explains how to use htimage on RightClick.Com's system, check out the Help file at:

```
www.rightclick.com/support/ihip.html
```

Building and Linking to NCSA Map Files

Behold NCSA, the other most-popular image-map format. Map files for NCSA servers, though they look much like those for CERN servers, do incorporate some sneaky differences. Have a look at this typical form that NCSA map files are likely to take:

```
circle URL x,y r
rect URL x1,y1 x2,y2
poly URL x1,y1 x2,y2 x3,y3 . . . xn,yn
point URL x,y
default URL
```

The shapes are the same as the CERN varieties and the same kinds of coordinates define them. But names are shorter, and URLs come first (instead of last) in the list of attributes. Here again, defaults work the same way: to provide a handler for people who click outside the image frame. But as you know, computers are literalists; they only read what's there, which gives minor differences in format a larger-than-life effect on compatibility.

An NCSA map file for the button bar

For the *HTML For Dummies* graphic, the NCSA map is as follows:

```
rect http://www.domain.com/html4dum/ftpstuff.htm (0,142)
        (98,285)
rect http://www.domain.com/html4dum/contents.htm (99,142)
        (198,285)
rect http://www.domain.com/html4dum/search4d.htm (199,142)
        (298,285)
rect http://www.domain.com/html4dum/contact.htm (299,142)
        (398,285)
rect http://www.domain.com/html4dum/whatsnew.htm (399,142)
        (499,285)
default http://www.domain.com/html4dum/contents.htm
```

Except for a change in the shape's name (rect instead of rectangle) and reordering the arguments (URLs first, and then coordinates), the map is nearly identical to the CERN variety.

Is my system ready for NCSA map files?

As with CERN, to use a map file with the NCSA httpd, a system must already have a program that handles image maps. The name of this program, which comes with the NCSA httpd materials, is imagemap. If it's not installed, you must have the program installed to use image maps on your system.

If you don't have imagemap yet, or need to check that you have the latest version, version information appears at

```
http://hoohoo.ncsa.uiuc.edu/docs/tutorials/imagemapping.html
```

If the file date is more recent at NCSA, download the new file, rename it to imagemag.c, and recompile. Use the new version instead of the old one.

After you have imagemap available, you must then invoke it on the server. For our example, we assume it lives in the /cgi-bin/ directory. For details about your particular Web server, contact your local Webmaster or system administrator.

Final Touches

Fortunately, formatting your image map isn't all a matter of spotting and accommodating every irritating difference. No matter which type of Web server you use as host for your image maps, they all have a few aspects in common. This happy fact means you can add some classy touches and reasonably expect that most of your users will be able to appreciate them.

Creating and storing map files

Joyous news: You can create a map file with any plain-text editor. Store the map file on the server in a special directory for your map definition files. Contact your system administrator or your Webmaster to find out where this is and if you have write permission. If you don't, you must enlist the administrator's help to get those files installed. For our examples, we use the name, ht4menum.map, and store it in the http://www.domain.com/cgi-bin/ directory, with our other scripts.

Defining a clickable map in your HTML document

After you define a map and store it in the right location, you must bring all three of the magic elements together in an HTML file. Here's how:

```
<a href="http://www.lanw.com/cgi-bin/ht4menum.map">
<img src="graphics/ht4menum.gif" ismap>
</a>
```

Here's what's going on in this series of statements:

- ✔ The opening anchor tag combines the image location, which handles the coordinate-to-URL translation, with a full URL for the map file. Even though you see no space between the name of the program and the file specification, the server still knows what to do.

- ✔ The img tag points to the button-bar graphic but adds an ismap attribute to indicate that it's a clickable map.

- ✔ The closing anchor tag </a> indicates that the graphic specified by src attribute is the target for the map file specified in the opening anchor tag.

There you are! After you make sure that all the right pieces are in place on your CERN server, you can try this, too.

Despite the existence of multiple image-map file formats, you need to create only one image-map file for each image map that you use on your Web pages. Which kind should you use? Only your Webmaster or system administrator knows for sure. But because we don't know what kind you'll use, we told you about the two most common types. You may end up using neither, but if you're not using one or the other, your Webmaster or system administrator should be able to explain the format to you or tell you how to obtain documentation about that format.

"The Map Is Not the Territory"

Alfred Korzybski didn't know about clickable images when he uttered this section's title (in *Manhood of Humanity: The Science and Art of Human Engineering*, in case you're ever asked about it on *Jeopardy!*). Give him a break; it was before computers. But as the twentieth century starts to show up in the rearview mirror, Korzybski's point takes on a new meaning: Because not all users can see an image map, be prepared to show the same set of selections in text that GUI users get in visual form.

Okay, you're game. How? First, consider that what you provide in an image map is a set of choices. You can add an equivalent set of text-based links (choices) near the image. Here's what the HTML for this looks like:

```
<a href="http://www.lanw.com/cgi-bin/html4dum.map">
<img border="0" align="top" src="graphics/ht4menum.gif"
  alt="Navigation Bar" ismap></a><p>
<img align="middle" width="130" height="0"
          src="graphics/space.gif"
  alt=" ">
<b><a href="ftpstuff.htm">FILES</a> &#32;&#124;
<a href="contents.htm">CONTENTS</a> &#32;&#124;
<a href="search4d.htm">SEARCH</a> &#32;&#124;
<a href="contact.htm">CONTACT</a> &#32;&#124;
<a href="whatsnew.htm">NEW</a><br>
<img align="middle" width="240" height="0"
          src="graphics/space.gif"
  alt=" ">
<a href="navigate.htm">HOW TO NAVIGATE</a></b>
<p>
<a href="html4du2.htm">Click here for a non-imagemap ver-
          sion</a></p>
```

As shown in Figure 15-2, this snippet of code creates a text bar (right beneath the graphic) that offers the same choices. Users with graphical browsers won't suffer from this redundancy, and character-mode browsers get a reasonable facsimile of what the graphically advantaged see in living color. We call this mastering the art of compromise!

Figure 15-2:
A text-based bar combined with a button bar keeps everybody in the know.

Of Clickable Maps and URLs

Image links can sometimes play hob with relative URLs within HTML documents. One unforeseen side effect of following links through a map-reading script — to the map and back to the target page — can be a complete mangling of the context within which URLs are addressed. In English, this means it's a really, really, really good idea to use full URLs (instead of relative references) in documents that include clickable maps.

You would be wise (as well as cagey) to consider carefully before using any relative URL reference in documents with clickable maps. Test thoroughly to make sure everything works as it should. Avoiding trouble is, in general, the best way to prevent an encore of the URL Relative Reference Blues!

Mapping on the Client-Side Image!

A client-side image map is a graphical navigation tool that runs within the users' browsers and requires neither a server nor a CGI map file to operate. (Whoa! No visible means of support! How do they do that?) Both Netscape and Microsoft Web browsers support client-side image maps. Creating one is as easy as building a server-side image map.

Building a client-side image map involves

- ✔ Defining the hot-spot areas of the image.
- ✔ Embedding the coordinates in an HTML document.

Possible area definitions include these familiar friends:

- ✔ **Circle** — `<area shape="circle" coords="x,y,x2,y2" href="URL2">`

- ✔ **Rectangle** — `<area shape="rect" coords="x,y,x2,y2" href="URL3">`

- ✔ **Polygon** — `<area shape="poly" coords="x,y,x2,y2,x3,y3,..." href="URL4">`

- ✔ **Default** — `<area shape="default" href="URL5">`

You probably recognize all these types except for `circle`. A circle's area is defined by a central point and a point on the circle's edge (which, as we all fondly remember, defines its radius — and you thought you'd never use geometry). Coordinates are grouped, separated by commas.

Slam a set of `area` tags inside a `map` tag associated with a properly labeled `<img>` tag, and you've built a client-side image map. Notice that we name a client-side image map using the `name` attribute of the `map` tag and reference it with the `usemap` attribute in the `<img>` tag. Here's an example:

```
<img src="HT4MEMU.GIF" usemap="#h4dmap">
<map name="h4dmap">
 <area shape="rect" coords="0,142,98,285" href="http://www.
        domain.com/html4dum/ftpstuff.htm" alt="files">
 <area shape="rect" coords="99,142,198,285" href="http://www.
        domain.com/html4dum/contents.htm" alt="contents">
 <area shape="rect" coords="199,142,298,285" href="http://
        www.domain.com/html4dum/search4d.htm"
        alt="search">
 <area shape="rect" coords="299,142,398,285" href="http://
        www.domain.com/html4dum/contact.htm" alt="con-
        tact">
 <area shape="rect" coords="399,142,499,285" href="http://
        www.domain.com/html4dum/whatsnew.htm" alt="what's
        new">
 <area shape="default" href="http://www.domain.com/html4dum/
        contents.htm" alt="contents">
</map>
```

Given all this flexibility, why use server-side image maps at all? Only one reason: Progress is never uniform. Which is to say, not all browsers support client-side image maps. But any graphical browser that can call a CGI can use a server-side image map. So be wary and au courant if you're switching to the client side of the street.

Character-mode browsers (or GUI browsers with graphics turned off) can't handle image maps of any kind. So, even if you do take the plunge into client-side image maps, always provide a text alternative, just as you would with a server-side equivalent. Either way, the graphically disadvantaged can compensate in another way!

Client-side image maps in action

In yet another revival of school-days skills, masters of the art of cut-and-paste can use simple map constructs just like this one in their own documents. All you need is a file and your trusty cut-and-paste utility. Remember, client-side image maps don't need a map file (that informa-tion is included in the HTML) or a server (the client handles all map processing). If you want to see one in action, load up the front page of the example Web site from the book's CD-ROM.

Chapter 16

HTML Frames

In This Chapter

▶ Introducing HTML frames

▶ Building frames with HTML tags

▶ Framing your Web site

That's right, you've been framed. And you may find you like it. *HTML frames* are so handy they're almost a crime: They delineate, outline, and give structure to HTML documents; they help move information coherently within and among themselves. But wait, there's more! The big fish (the W3C) decided it liked frames so much that they became standard in HTML 4.0. Best of all, today's exciting episode shows you — step-by-step — how you can use frames to make your Web pages get up and wail. And you thought you were just going to see Buffy slay a couple vampires!

As you probably guessed, you always have more to learn about the incredibly cool powers of HTML. Frames are no exception; this chapter gives you a basic understanding of how they work, but practicality demands that we stop there. If you like what you see, and want to ferret out more down-and-dirty details about using frames, check out the following Web sites:

✔ Web Design Group's HTML 4.0 Reference:
   www.htmlhelp.com/reference/html40

✔ Webmonkey's authoring frames articles:
   http://hotwired.lycos.com/webmonkey/authoring/frames

✔ WebReference's frame cheat sheet:
   www.webreference.com/dev/frames/summary.html

✔ HTML 4.01 Specification's frames section:
   www.w3.org/TR/1999/REC-
   html401-19991224/present/frames.html

HTML Frames Overview

So what are frames anyway and why would you want to use them in your Web pages? A single browser window usually holds a single frame that displays a single HTML document. A browser window, however, can hold several frames (which are defined with the <frameset> tag), and can display several HTML documents at one time. Each frame works like a separate browser screen but they are all displayed together in one window. Imagine having three browser windows open (and tiled) at one time and you begin to get the picture. What's really cool is that with frames you can connect the different browser windows and have them work together to display your content. And, for the control freak in all of us, depending on the attributes you give it, a frame can act just like a standard browser screen, or it can be frozen into Elliot Ness untouchability.

To frame the practical question, "Do I really *need* to use the <frameset> tag?" The answer is no. You could, of course, use a table to format your information into areas, complete with borders, on a single browser screen. But remember that tables are static and frames can be dynamic — you can scroll through information within frames, and users may find that appealingly easy to deal with.

With the approval of the HTML 4.0 standard, frames finally become part of the HTML standard, which means that older browsers (anything prior to Versions 3.0 and earlier of just about any major browser) can not handle frames properly. Text-only browsers don't deal well with frames either. To be practical, this means that some of your users may not be able to appreciate the beauty and efficacy of your frames. As long as you're sure users have a frames-compatible browser — the recent versions of both Netscape Navigator and Internet Explorer support frames, as do many of the non-commercial browsers such as Mosaic and Amaya — you can safely use frames on your site. However, if your audience uses a wide variety of browsers, you may want to shy away from frames. Another option is to offer a non-framed version of the same materials so users can pick which version of your pages they want to explore.

Frames have numerous uses, as in the following eye-catching instances:

- A Web page with a fixed logo at the top and a scrolling bottom section

- A page with a fixed top logo, a navigation bar and copyright notice at the bottom, and a scrolling middle section for displaying page contents

- A Web page with side-by-side frames that put a table of contents on the left and a scrolling text frame on the right

✔ A left frame filled with icons linked to different parts of a Web site, where whatever element is displayed in the right frame is based on a selection from the left frame

You find out how to set up these structures a bit later in this chapter. For now, note that frames are flexible without going all rubbery. Frames allow you to keep constant chunks of information on display while your users scroll happily through large amounts of text or dynamic content. But hold on there. Before you jump ahead and start framing everything in sight, get to know the brass tacks — the HTML markup tags — that make frames possible.

HTML Frame Tags

Welcome to HTML Tags for Frames Territory. Here's where we list 'em, discuss their proper syntax and use, and offer some pointers on their good and better uses. After that, it's all up to you and your good taste; hanging some nice frames around your Web site should make it feel homey for your visitors. So we start with basic groundwork (the structure of a document that includes frames) and then trot out the tags you use to make the frames.

The frame document structure

A frame document is simply a normal HTML document in which you replace the `<body>` . . . `</body>` container tags with the `<frameset>` . . . `</frameset>` container tags, which identify the other HTML pages that will show up in the different frames you build on the page. (Simply put: You use `<frameset>` instead of `<body>` as the box to put your content in, and all the content really consists of is `<frame>` tags that point to other, standard Web pages.) The basic frame document starts within the following overall HTML, ah, *framework*. (Couldn't help it. The word seemed so appropriate.)

```
<html>
    <head>
        <title>Don't forget the title</title>
    </head>

<frameset>
Your frame information goes here.
</frameset>

</html>
```

Frame syntax is uncannily similar to the syntax you use within HTML tables. In fact, you can think of frames as movable, dynamically updated tables. After you start using frame-related markup in your own pages, the syntax starts to look pretty straightforward. But getting used to the concepts involved takes some practice.

<frameset> . . . </frameset>

The `<frameset>` `. . .` `</frameset>` tag pair is the main container for any frame. As we mentioned earlier, your basic, red-blooded frame document uses `<frameset>` instead of `<body>` to identify what's going on inside of your main document. After that, framing gets only a little weird:

- ✔ The `<frameset>` tag follows immediately after the `</head>` tag.

- ✔ If any `<body>` tags appear before the `<frameset>` `. . .` `</frameset>` tags, the `<frameset>` `. . .` `</frameset>` tags are ignored — not a good outcome when you're building frames.

- ✔ Between the outermost `<frameset>` `. . .` `</frameset>` tags, you can only nest other `<frameset>` `. . .` `</frameset>` tags, `<frame>` tags, or `<noframes>` tags to define any interior shenanigans. No other HTML is allowed.

To put all this into code perspective, every good frameset starts like this:

```
<frameset>
</frameset>
```

And you thought this was going to be hard. Okay, that's the big box o' frames. Next are the attributes you can put in it. First, the rows attribute looks something like this:

```
rows="n" or "% " or "*, n" or "% " or "*, n" or "% "
        or "*, . . ."
```

(And just try reading *that* aloud.) The rows attribute of the `<frameset>` tag determines two factors: (1) the number of frames that appear vertically (stacked on top of each other) in the browser window and (2) the height of each frame. The rows attribute uses commas to separate the numbers that make up its list of values. The number of elements appearing in the value of the rows attribute determines the number of frames shown up and down the screen. The total height of all the simultaneously displayed frames must equal the height of the browser window; the browser may adjust the rows' height values to make them all fit. (**Hint:** If the text looks like a regiment of ants, you probably have too many frames or a row whose height is a bit cramped.) You can build your rows using any mixture of the following elements:

✔ n: The direct approach — n defines a fixed number of pixels (such as 50 or 250) for the row's height. Seems simple, but be careful: The size of the browser window can vary substantially from one user to another. If you use fixed-pixel values, using one or more relative values (described later in this chapter) with them is good practice. Otherwise, the user's browser can override your specified pixel value to ensure that the total height and width of all the frames equals 100 percent of the user's window. You may not want it to do that; a browser doesn't care about eyestrain. All it knows to do is follow orders and *display all defined frames,* even if mercilessly squashed together and crammed with unreadable text.

✔ value%: This value tells the browser, "Size this frame to a percentage of screen area, between 1 and 100." If the total for all frames is greater than 100 percent, all percentages are reduced to fit the browser window (ants-in-travel-size-sardine-cans again). If the values total less than 100 percent, extra space is added to any relative-sized frames that happen to be hanging around (for example, the next item in this list).

✔ *: A single asterisk (*) character identifies a relative-sized frame. Browsers give a frame defined with the asterisk all remaining space left over after the other frames defined with pixels and percentages are laid out on the screen. If you have several frames that take advantage of this flexible system, the remaining space is divided evenly among them.

✔ value*: If you place a value in front of the *, the frame gets that much more relative space. For instance, an entry such as 3*, * allocates three times as much space to the first frame (¾ of the total on-screen space) as to the second frame (which gets a measly ¼).

Advanced math degrees aren't needed to use these different types of values, but you do need to eyeball the on-screen results of your work carefully. Give 'em extra-severe scrutiny when you mix value types. Following are a couple of examples, each a different way to stack frames on-screen.

✔ **Two vertically stacked frames:** Both pieces of code achieve the exact same results, as shown in Figure 16-1.

```
<frameset rows="20%,80%">
<frameset rows="20%,*">
```

✔ **Three vertically stacked frames:** A mere snippet of HTML code creates three vertically stacked frames, shown in Figure 16-2, using a fixed pixel value (100), a relative value (*), and a percentage value (20%):

```
<frameset rows="100,*,20%">
```

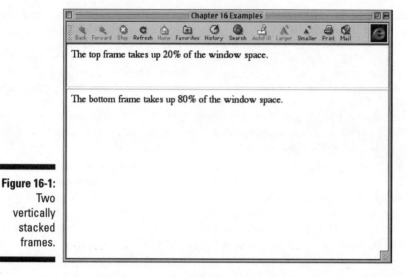

Figure 16-1:
Two
vertically
stacked
frames.

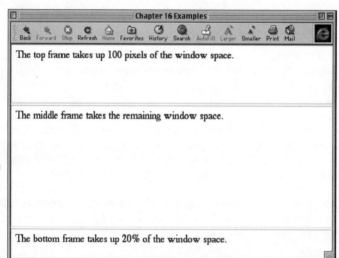

Figure 16-2:
Three
vertically
stacked
frames.

Next, we have the `cols` attribute, which looks something like this:

```
cols="n" or "% " or "*, n" or "% " or "*, n" or "% " or " *,
     ..."
```

The `cols` (for *columns*) attribute is as single-minded as the `rows` attribute; it governs the number of frames that march horizontally across the browser's screen, as well as the width of each frame.

The following example of HTML code displays two frames across the screen, as shown in Figure 16-3; the first one (on the left) gets 20 percent of the available space and the second (on the right) gets the rest:

```
<frameset cols="20%,*">
```

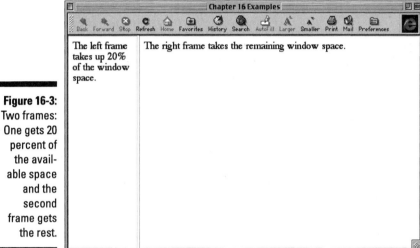

Figure 16-3:
Two frames:
One gets 20
percent of
the avail-
able space
and the
second
frame gets
the rest.

<frame>

If you're going to do frames, go the correct route: A separate <frame> tag must define each separate frame on your Web page. The <frame> tag has no associated end tag; all by its lonesome, the <frame> tag defines the contents, a name, and the attributes for each frame. If you want to display four different HTML pages in frames, you need to create four frames; therefore, you need four <frame> tags. The first <frame> tag defines the top, left-most frame area. The second <frame> tag defines the frame immediately to the right of the first frame, or if the edge of the browser is reached, the frame in the next row. And so on, with no end in sight.

Within each frame that you create, you display a regular Web page. The following is an example of the syntax for a <frame> tag:

```
<frame src="yourstuf.htm" name="Your Frame">
```

You can modify the <frame> tag using any of seven attributes. And here they are, one by one (we thought you'd never ask):

src="url"

The URL that identifies the src (for *source*) attribute points to the source material you want to appear in the frame. Aforesaid source material may be a link, an image, an HTML file, or any other legal URL. If you omit the src attribute, the frame appears blank and may cause the browser to display an error message.

name="window_name"

The name attribute assigns a name to a frame, which is important if you want to click on a hyperlink in one window and have its content appear in another window. Technically, the name attribute is optional; however, we recommend including it for all frames. Each frame needs to have a unique name and all name values must begin with an alphanumeric character.

frameborder="YES" or "NO"

What's a picture without a border? The frameborder attribute enables you to decide for yourself. You can specify whether you want the frames within your frameset to have borders. Borders help your readers differentiate between frames, but they can also get in the way of a seamless page. Your specific implementation of frames is what determines the value you assign to this attribute.

marginwidth="value"

The marginwidth attribute accepts a value of one or more pixels to deter-mine the exact width of the left and right margins of a frame. The margins show up as white space in a browser's display; therefore, you can use this attribute to nicely separate the content in one frame from the content in another. Margins must be one or more pixels wide to keep objects from touching the edges of a frame. (Of course, *some* wiseacres may want to spec-ify margins that leave no space for a document's contents, but they're not allowed to. So there.) The marginwidth attribute is optional, but some margin is always going to be there. If you omit this attribute, the browser sets its own margin widths (usually one or two pixels wide, depending on the browser).

marginheight="value"

The marginheight attribute works like marginwidth — you specify one or more pixels for the height of a frame margin — except this attribute controls the top- and bottom-edge margins of frames instead of the left and right mar-gins. (And the height has to be more than zero — c'mon, you know the rules.)

scrolling="YES" or "NO" or "AUTO"

Merrily users scroll along — but only if they need to. The optional scrolling attribute determines whether a frame displays a scroll bar. A value of YES forces the browser to display a scroll bar on that frame. A NO value keeps scroll bars invisible. The scrolling attribute has a default value of AUTO, which means that scroll bars appear only if more content than fits in the window must be displayed. AUTO is the (very sensible) default, and the wise leave it in place under most circumstances. After all, you can't always determine what size window your users will tack up on their screens to display your framed pages; this way, they get a scroll bar if they need one, nary a one if they don't.

noresize

By default, users can resize frames by dragging a frame edge to a new position. If you have a good reason to say "Don't touch," the noresize attribute sternly forbids a user to resize a frame by, ah, not letting them resize the frame. The noresize attribute is optional and not really a killjoy:

- ✔ If any frame adjacent to the edge of another frame isn't resizable, that entire edge can't move. This unmovable edge affects the resizing of any adjacent frames.

- ✔ If you want your viewers to stay aware of whose site it is and who's paying the bills, noresize can keep your logo or advertising space in view.

- ✔ We don't recommend using the noresize attribute willy-nilly for content frames, but not because it spoils the fun of tweaking them. Its restriction limits the extent to which users can tinker your handcrafted frames (the results of all those display settings) into fitting their screens.

<noframes> . . . </noframes>

You say some of your users are surfing the Web with only the bearskin basics? Give 'em a break: Create some alternative content, put it between a starting <noframes> tag and an ending </noframes> tag, and presto! Frame-challenged browsers can appreciate at least the text part of your site's splendor, and frame-cognizant browsers ignore all tags and data between the <noframes> tags. (Almost lost 'em there. That was close.)

Putting it all together

So after you add all the tags up, the basic code for a solid frameset with two horizontal frames — one right next to each other — looks like this:

```
<frameset cols="20%, *">
 <frame src="frame1_content.html" name="frame1">
 <frame src="frame1_content.html" name="frame2">
 <noframes>
  <body>
   <p>Users who can't view frames see this instead</p>
  </body>
 </noframes>
</frameset>
```

To create two vertical frames — one on top of the other — the opening `<frameset>` tag is:

```
<frameset rows="20%, *">
```

Of course you can add some of the other attributes we discussed just a page or so ago to the `<frame>` tags to tweak the final look and feel of your display. Finally, don't forget that for each frame in your frame document, you need a full-fledged Web document or resource to display. So, a two-frame frameset really requires three HTML documents to work:

✔ The Web page that defines the frameset

✔ The HTML page that shows up in the first frame

✔ The HTML page that takes up residence in the second frame

Targeting frames

Here's the dilemma. You have a frame document with two vertical frames: a skinny one on the left that serves as a navigation document and a wider one on the right where the bulk of the content your users see shows up. You want to create hyperlinks in the document that lives in the skinny frame on the left that, when clicked, cause new Web documents to load in the wide frame on the right. This is actually a common frame dilemma, as illustrated by the layout of a Web-based training site shown in Figure 16-4.

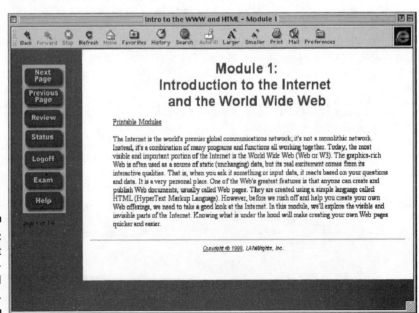

Figure 16-4:
The layout
of a Web-
based
training site.

When you click a hyperlink or a navigation button, the document the link is attached to replaces the one that you just clicked in. So, how do you change the nature of a hyperlink and force documents to show up in a different frame than the one they were called from? Believe it or not, the solution is as simple as adding a single attribute to a hyperlink's anchor (`<a>`) tag.

The `target` attribute gives you control over where the linked page or other resource appears when a user clicks a link in your documents. Of course, you can use the target attribute in other tags — `<area>` and `<form>` to name two — but the attribute really shines when you use it in the `<a>` tag in conjunction with frames.

So, how exactly does targeting work? Normally, when a user clicks a link, the browser displays the new document in a full browser window. Targeting enables you to change that: You can assign names to specific frames — remember the `name` attribute? — and decree that certain documents shall duly appear in the frame that bears the targeted name. (Control freaks, rejoice!)

In the section of this chapter titled "name=`"window_name"`," we explain how to use the `name` attribute to name a frame. Using the `target` attribute to, well, *target* the frame is just as easy: Insert the attribute and its corresponding value (the name of the frame, known inscrutably as the `frame name`) in the `<a>` tag. In the following example, the name of the targeted frame is — you guessed it — frame name:

```
<a href="mypage.html" target="frame name">Targeted Anchor</a>
```

The document referenced by this particular anchor tag loads in the frame defined by this tag:

```
<frame name="frame name">
```

Do you see a trend here? We thought we did.

Any valid frame name specified in a `target` attribute must begin with an alphanumeric character. Well, okay, the exceptions are a few predefined, special-purpose target names that begin with the underscore character (examples coming up). Any targeted frame name that begins with an underscore or a non-alphanumeric character (and *isn't* a special-purpose name) is ignored.

Special-purpose target names include _SELF, _BLANK, _PARENT, and _TOP. Use these different names to determine what the user sees — and where they see it — after that fateful click selects the linked document:

✔ `target= "_SELF"`: Specifying the _SELF target always causes the linked document to load inside the frame in which the user has selected the anchor. All links act this way by default, so you can imagine that every regular anchor tag has an invisible `target="_SELF"` attached to it. Aren't you glad you don't have to type that every time?

✔ `target="_BLANK"`: Specifying the _BLANK target causes the linked document to load inside a new browser window, which is an easy way to force the user's browser to launch another window. The _BLANK attribute can be useful if you want to link to someone else's site. But, still make sure that your site is immediately available to users in the first browser window that never went away. Don't over use _BLANK targets. Visitors to your site won't appreciate new browser windows popping up all the time.

✔ `target="_PARENT"`: Specifying the _PARENT target makes the linked document load in the immediate frameset parent of the document. If the current document in which the _PARENT target appears has no parent, this attribute behaves like the _SELF value.

✔ `target="_TOP"`: Specifying the _TOP target makes the linked document load in the full body of the window. If the current document is already at the top of the document hierarchy, the _TOP target name behaves like _SELF. You can use this attribute to escape from a deeply nested frame. (Oxygen tank optional.)

If you get carried away using frames nested within frames nested within frames, or you link to someone else's framed site only to find their frames loading inside of yours — whew, what a headache — you can use `target="_TOP"` to cancel out your frameset and revert back to a nice, simple, regular HTML page.

A twist on ye' old standard frames: Inline frames

We are the first to admit that a set of frames can be a bit of a pain to build and maintain, but the idea of displaying two or more HTML documents on one Web page is *very* attractive. Don't worry, be happy. You have a middle ground between not using frames and committing to a framed Web site. And the name of this middle ground: inline frames.

Originally an Internet Explorer proprietary tag, inline frames (`<iframe>`) are part of the HTML 4.01 specification. Inline frames are, in our humble opinion, a rather cool addition to the HTML specification because they allow you to stick a frame inside of any HTML document. What's even better is that inline frames float.

What? They float? Basically an inline frame acts as a second browser window — but really isn't — that sits on top of your basic HTML document and is positioned on the page based on the text around it. Adding an inline frame — and its content — to a document is much like adding a graphic to a page, but using a different tag of course.

A single tag controls everything about an inline frame or `<iframe>`. The `<iframe>` is a block element, such as a paragraph or heading, and can live anywhere on a standard Web page. You can use the following attributes with `<iframe>` to create your basic floating frame:

- ✔ **src:** As with a standard `<frame>` tag, the `src` attribute for the `<iframe>` tag identifies the Web resource (HTML pages, graphics, and so on) that lives inside of the floating frame.

- ✔ **name:** This attribute assigns a name to a floating frame so you can target it in hyperlinks.

- ✔ **longdesc:** The `longdesc` attribute includes a long description of the content included in the floating frame. This attribute is for those browsers that don't display or support frames.

- ✔ **width:** As you can imagine, the `width` attribute defines the width of the inline frame.

- ✔ **height:** Once again, it's not a surprise that the `height` attribute defines the height of the inline frame.

- ✔ **align:** The align attribute specifies how the floating frame is aligned horizontally on the page and can take a value of `LEFT`, `CENTER`, `RIGHT`, or `JUSTIFY`.

The `<iframe>` tag also shares these attributes with standard `<frame>` tags:

- ✔ `frameborder`
- ✔ `marginwidth`
- ✔ `marginheight`
- ✔ `scrolling`

This code example creates a floating frame within an HTML document that is 150 pixels high and 200 pixels wide and displays a document named "ad.html":

```
<body>
    <p>Standard paragaraph</p>
    <iframe src="ad.html" name="ad_space" align="LEFT"
     height="150" width="200">
    <p>Another standard paragraph</p>
</body>
```

Isn't it nice how the floating frame just slips right in there between two paragraphs.

If you are intrigued by the idea of floating frames and want to learn more, visit this insightful and humorous tutorial: `http://hotwired.lycos.com /webmonkey/96/37/index2a.html?tw=authoring`.

Framing Your Web

Your Web pages are like pictures waiting to be framed. Even if you provide pure text for your users, you can still use frames behind the scenes to help them navigate within your site.

One important feature of frames is that they let you keep important information on-screen constantly, while other portions of the screen change to reflect new content.

Okay, back to the drawing board: The first requirement for using frames successfully is to visualize your Web page as a collection of frames. Sketch it on a napkin, the back of an envelope, or whatever's handy in the trash can (except maybe that banana peel). As your rough-and-ready diagram takes shape, remember: You need one HTML document to define your sketched-out frame page *and* a separate HTML document for each frame in your sketch.

In the following example, watch closely as the multiple HTML documents needed to construct an image magically come together to build a single, framed Web page. At no time do our hands leave our sleeves — you witness how using frames means creating more (generally smaller) HTML documents. Why the extra work? Two reasons — each frame requires its own HTML document, and such is the price we hardy Web pioneers must pay, slaving tirelessly to provide our users with the best possible Web sites. . . .

Oh, well. With HTML documents, practice makes perfect. Which brings us to the eagerly awaited example. . . .

HTML code for a three-frame page

The following HTML code sets up a top frame 150 pixels high and a bottom frame 100 pixels high. Top and bottom frames are non-scrolling; the bottom frame, a real party pooper, isn't resizable either. The middle frame is set to scrolling to illustrate the scroll bars.

```
<html>
<head>
<title>Three Frame Example</title>
</head>
<frameset rows="150, *, 100">
 <frame src="top.htm" name="top frame" scrolling="no">
 <frame src="middle.htm" name="middle frame"
    scrolling="YES">
 <frame src="bottom.htm" name="bottom frame"
    scrolling="NO" noresize>
</frameset>
</html>
```

Such a three-frame setup is versatile enough to accommodate a hefty range of uses. Here's the HTML code for its top frame (titled Top Frame and coming soon to a Web page near you . . .). And check out that scintillating sample content that appears after the </center> end tag:

```
<html>
 <head>
 <title>Top Frame</title>
 </head>
 <body>
 <center>
  <h2>Top frame text here.</h2>
 </center>
 <p>
   The text you are reading here is in a file named
   top.htm. The file is called by the following line
   in the main.htm document:<br>
   &lt;frame src="top.htm" name="Top Frame"
   scrolling="NO"&gt;
 </p>
 </body>
</html>
```

Okay, next up is the HTML code for the middle frame. Nothing fancy, just a standard HTML document in which you can place any legal HTML tags and other information. (Speaking of which, we include some, ah, dummy content that we have absolute confidence you can improve upon.)

```
<html>
 <head>
 <title>Middle Frame</title>
 </head>
 <body>
 <center>
  <h2>Middle frame text here.</h2>
 </center>
```

```
<p>
  The text you are reading here is in a file named
  middle.htm. The file is called by the following line
  in the main.htm document:<br>
    &lt;frame src="middle.htm" name="Middle Frame"
    scrolling="YES"&gt;
</p>
</body>
</html>
```

Finally, we get to the bottom of this: The following listing shows the HTML code for the bottom frame. This listing is another standard HTML document — but remember, the document is displayed within a fixed-height (100-pixel) frame that can't be resized. As for which content deserves to hang out there, calmly staring your readers in the face . . . that's up to you.

```
<html>
<head>
<title>Bottom Frame</title>
</head>
<body>
<center>
  <h2>Bottom frame text here.</h2>
</center>
<p>
  The text you are reading here is in a file named
  bottom.htm. The file is called by the following line
  in the main.htm document:<br>
    &lt;frame src="bottom.htm" name="Bottom Frame"
    "NO"noresize &gt;
</p>
</body>
</html>
```

For fun, copy each chunk of code for the frameset and related pages into different documents in a text editor, save the four different files with the names we used, and then open `main.htm` in your Web browser to see the cool results. See, frames are both fun and simple, as seen in Figure 16-5. Who can ask for more?

Your job as a Web page author is to make sure that any information you put in a frame is compact or short enough to fit the specified frame space, even if users resize their entire browser screens. If you can't make the information fit the frame, use relative values for the frame height and allow your users to resize as needed.

Of course, no proper exhortation is complete without examples of framed sites in action. Got 'em right here. . . .

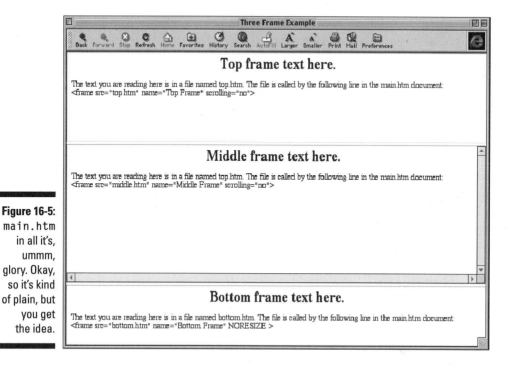

[Browser window titled "Three Frame Example" showing three frames]

Top frame text here.

The text you are reading here is in a file named top.htm. The file is called by the following line in the main.htm document:
<frame src="top.htm" name="Top Frame" scrolling="no">

Middle frame text here.

The text you are reading here is in a file named top.htm. The file is called by the following line in the main.htm document:
<frame src="middle.htm" name="Middle Frame" scrolling="no">

Bottom frame text here.

The text you are reading here is in a file named bottom.htm. The file is called by the following line in the main.htm document:
<frame src="bottom.htm" name="Bottom Frame" NORESIZE >

Figure 16-5:
main.htm
in all it's,
ummm,
glory. Okay,
so it's kind
of plain, but
you get
the idea.

Two stunningly framed Web sites

Because frames are dynamic beasts, capturing them in a picture do them no justice. So, load these URLs in your own frames-enabled browser to see the goods for yourself:

- ✔ EverCom's home page (okay, so the whole page is in Norwegian, but that doesn't stop it from being a great example of frame usage):
  www.evercom.no
- ✔ The Internet Garden: www.internetgarden.co.uk/frameset_1.htm

Part V

Advanced
HTML Topics
and Techniques

The 5th Wave   By Rich Tennant

"There's gotta be a more elegant way to prompt for credit card numbers."

In this part . . .

Part V is where we dare you to peek beyond the limits of accepted standards and tried-and-true technologies to take a look at what gonzo Web artists work with every day — only they do it without a safety net! Here's where you learn what HTML forms are and how they work, how style markup makes it possible to give even humdrum, text-only Web pages some color and pizzazz, and how to make your Web pages solicit input from your users and "talk back" in response to such input. You should find this part to be a real adventure, so be sure to buckle up before you dive in.

Chapter 17

Forms, Feedback, Scripting, and Beyond

· ·

In This Chapter

▶ Using HTML forms to the best of their ability

▶ Understanding the limitations of forms

▶ Gathering the components for an HTML form

▶ Building a form with HTML form tags

▶ Forming good form habits

▶ Introducing CGI

▶ Cheating at CGI

· ·

*W*hen all the pieces come together properly, seeing how the Web brings people and organizations together is easy. At first glance, the Web may look pretty much like a one-way street — that is, an environment in which Webmasters communicate aplenty with Web users, with not much interaction coming back from users at all. But it doesn't have to be that way. HTML forms provide you with the tools you need to build Web pages that allow your users to talk to you.

The Many Uses of HTML Forms

An HTML form is a collection of widgets that help users pass information from a Web page back to your Web server. The business of building HTML forms involves not only writing HTML to make the form widgets appear on the screen, but also looking long and hard at the information you want to collect from your users. Before you can build a form to gather information, you need to figure out what kind of information you're trying to gather. HTML forms have a myriad of uses, two of which are detailed in the following sections.

Forthright feedback

The essence of serving up useful information is relevancy and immediacy. But the best judge of the quality of your information is your audience. Wouldn't it be wonderful if your readers could give you feedback on your Web pages? Then, they can tell you what parts they like, what they don't like, and what other features they'd like to see on your site.

Getting feedback is where HTML forms come into play. In this chapter, you find out how to turn the tables and create HTML that lets your audience communicate with you!

As it turns out, HTML supports a rich variety of input capabilities to let you solicit feedback. In the pages that follow, you discover the tags to use, the controls and inputs they enable, along with some layout considerations for building forms. You also get to see some interesting example forms to help you understand what HTML forms look like and how they behave.

Applications move to the Web with the help of forms

Who would have thought that you'd one day be able to check your e-mail from a Web page, or pay your bills or browse store catalogs online? All of these application-like Web services aren't possible without forms. The only way an online catalog works is if you can type in search parameters to find the items you are looking for and then provide billing and address information so that your products can be shipped to you. Likewise, you can't send e-mail from a Web page without having a place to type your message.

When the Web began, it was used mainly as a way to serve information to people. However, in the last few years, the Web has become a medium for both sending and receiving information. With the help of forms — and some programming on your Web server — Web pages and sites can be interactive; interactivity is the key to building Web-based applications and providing Web-based services.

The same form widgets that you can use to build a feedback form can help you build an online store or other service. As we just mentioned, the HTML form doesn't do all of the work on its own — the form simply gives your Web site visitors a way to send information back to you. You still have to have something — a program or other tool — that interprets the information users send to you and does something with those results.

The behind-the scenes work that makes Web sites respond to the information users send via forms is way beyond the scope of this book. Before you can process user data, you have to get the data, and that's what we're going to show you how to do in this chapter. After you're done, you'll be a form-formin' fool.

On the Limitations of Form (s)

HTML forms were established way back in the HTML 2.0 days — ancient history on the Web, but only a few years in how we measure time. With HTML 4.0, forms gained some new capabilities and a bit of a face-lift, too. But even though forms give users the ability to communicate with Web authors and developers, you'll still find some important limitations when using them. You must be keenly aware of their abilities and limitations before you deploy forms on your site.

Beware of browser!

Most of the newer browsers — Netscape Navigator or Communicator 4.0 (and higher) and Microsoft Internet Explorer (Version 3.0.3 and higher), plus NCSA Mosaic and its variants — already include HTML 4.0-level forms support, but other browsers do not. In fact, you won't know how well your favorite browser handles HTML 4.0 forms until you test your forms with it. If you follow our suggestion and test your pages in multiple browsers, you can immediately observe different levels of robustness and capability when it comes to forms implementations.

The bottom line is that not all browsers support forms equally, but that support is pretty commonplace. Current or modern browser versions have no problem interacting with most form constructs. But don't be surprised if on older browsers, forms don't work as well as they do in newer browsers.

 Assuming that the information your form solicits is important to you, consider adding a File Transfer Protocol (FTP) URL to your page to let users download a file containing a text-only version of the form's content. Adding the FTP URL allows users to complete this form in a text editor and e-mail it to you. Be sure to include an e-mail address inside the form itself. Providing this option allows users who can't deal with forms to provide you with feedback and information. See, nobody gets left out and everyone's happy!

Sorry, servers . . .

Because the Web is a client/server environment, be aware that just because your browser supports forms doesn't automatically imply that the server installed at your site handles them. Unfortunately, keeping up with HTML advancements means that Web servers have to change right along with clients. In other words, your server may not support the input-handling programs necessary to process a form's input after it gets delivered. Or you may not be able to access the right input-handling programs on the server without help from an administrator, even if everything you need is already in place.

However, there is a silver lining in this potentially dark cloud: The most common implementations of the httpd server (the http daemon — the Web server software that handles requests for Web services, including forms, and responds as needed) come from NCSA, the W3C, Microsoft, and Netscape, and run in a variety of environments, including UNIX, Windows, and the Mac OS. All of these industry groups have standardized forms-handling technology and offer useful, robust forms-handling capabilities.

By this point in the evolution of the Web, you probably won't run into a Web server that does not offer some sort of support for forms, either through CGI, server-side includes, some native scripting language, or some other proprietary solution (such as Microsoft Active Server Pages or its Internet Information Server API, also known as ISAPI).

What's in a Form?

When adding forms support to a Web page, you must include special tags to solicit input from users. You surround these tags with text to prompt user responses. You also include tags to gather input and ship it to your Web server, or to other servers that may offer services — such as FTP or e-mail — that your form knows how to query. Here's how the process works:

1. On a particular Web page, you include tags to set up a form and solicit input from users. Some users work their way through this material and provide the information that you want. This essentially amounts to filling out the form that you supply.

2. After users fill out your form, they click a button that directs their input to the program running on the Web server that delivered the form. The click of the button not only sends the user's information to the server, but it also tells the server to start the program that will interpret the information.

3. Assuming that the program is available (installed and running properly, that is), the program accepts the input information. The program then decodes and interprets the contents to guide its further actions.

4. After the input is received and interpreted, the program can do pretty much anything it wants. In practice, this boils down to recognizing key elements in a form's content and custom building an HTML document in response. Building a document isn't required but is a pretty common capability within the majority of forms-handling programs.

5. The custom-built document is delivered to the user in response to the form's content. At this point, additional interaction can occur (if the "return page" includes another form), requested information can be delivered (in response to requests on the form), a simple acknowledgment issued, or so forth.

The information collected from a form can be

- ✔ E-mailed to someone
- ✔ Submitted to a database, such as Oracle, SQL Server, or Access
- ✔ Written to a file

Thus, forms not only provide communication from users to servers, but also provide ongoing interaction between users and servers. This interaction is pretty powerful information and can add a lot of value to your Web pages.

Forms involve two-way communication

Most input-catching programs on a Web server rely on an interface between Web browsers and servers called the Common Gateway Interface (CGI). This interface specifies how browsers send information back to servers. CGI specifies formatting for user-supplied input so that forms-handling programs know what to expect and how to deal with what they receive.

The `action` attribute in a `<form>` tag specifies the URL that indicates a specific CGI script or program that collects the form data that a user entered. Likewise, the `method` attribute describes the way in which input data is delivered to such a forms-handling program.

In this part of the chapter, we concentrate on the input side of HTML forms — building the front end of a form (the part that users see). If you already built the front end and want to build the back end, we suggest you visit one of these quality Web sites that house truckloads of information about building programs to digest form data:

- ✔ The CGI Directory: www.cgidir.com
- ✔ Scripting.com: www.scripting.com
- ✔ CGIFiles.com: www.cgifiles.com

Tag! You're a form . . .

HTML includes several different classes of forms tags (for the details on syntax and usage, go directly to Chapter 4; tell 'em the authors sent you). To begin with, all HTML forms occur within the <form> . . . </form> tags. The <form> tag also includes attributes that specify where and how to deliver input to the appropriate Web server.

All other forms-related tags and text must appear within the <form> . . . </form> tags. (Not just a good idea. It's the law.) These tags include methods for

- Specifying input (the <input> tag and its many attributes).

- Grouping related sets of form controls and fields using the <fieldset> . . . </fieldset> tags.

- Employing <button> . . . </button> tags to create forms controls. (Usually, this markup surrounds graphics of buttons, with alternate text defined by the value of the button's name attribute for non-GUI viewers.)

- Using <label> . . . </label> tags to identify form controls and fields.

- Using <legend> . . . </legend> tags to create captions for sets of related form controls (fieldsets, in other words).

- Setting up large text input areas (the <textarea> . . . </textarea> tags).

- Selecting values from a predefined set of possible inputs in a drop-down menu (the <select> . . . </select> tags).

- Managing the form's content (using the submit attribute for input to deliver the content to the server, or the reset attribute to clear its contents and start over).

Though you can't reach out and touch your users (at least not yet), forms-input tags give you lots of ways to interact by

- Creating text input fields, called text areas, in which users can type whatever they want. Designers can choose either single- or multiline-text input fields and can govern how much text displays on-screen and how much text can be entered into any text area.

- Generating drop-down menus, often called pick lists because they require making one or more selections from a set of predefined choices.

- Creating custom buttons and graphical controls for incorporation into forms.

- Assigning all kinds of labels and captions to individual fields or buttons, or to groups of fields or buttons, as needed.

✔ Creating labeled checkboxes or radio buttons on-screen that users can select to indicate choices. (Checkboxes allow multiple selections and radio buttons allow just one selection.)

These capabilities may sound mild-mannered, but if you combine them with the power to prompt users for input by using surrounding text and graphics, forms are actually a pretty super way to ask for information on a Web page. Which leads us back to the question we asked to kick off this section — what's in a form? Answer: Almost anything you want!

Using Form Tags

As many Web page designers (or housing contractors, for that matter) can tell you, preparing the environment before you start to build is wise. In this case, you're setting up your `<form>` environment to accommodate building a form within your Web page. You can add a form to an existing HTML document or build a whole separate document just to contain your form. We recommend that you add shorter forms (half a screen or less) to existing documents; on the other hand, the big-time forms that take up more than half a screen work best if they have their very own documents and don't have to share.

Setting the <form> environment

The two head-honcho attributes within the `<form>` tag are `method` and `action`. Together, these attributes control how your browser sends information to the Web server and which input-handling program receives the form's contents.

A method to our madness

The `method` attribute indicates how your browser sends information to the server after you submit the form. The `method` attribute takes one of two possible values: `POST` or `GET`.

Of these two methods, we prefer `POST` because it's meticulous but practical: `POST` causes a form's contents to be parsed one element at a time. On the other hand, `GET` joins all field names and their associated values into one long string — which works okay if your long string is a relatively short one. As it happens, UNIX (and most other operating systems) puts a practical, but inconvenient, limit on how long a single string can be; for UNIX, a single string is limited to 255 characters (this sentence can just squeak by as a single string). It's not hard to imagine some heftier strings getting lopped off (truncated), losing important information en route.

For this reason, we use POST as our only method for submitting forms in this book. We recommend that you do the same; unless you're dead certain that the number of characters in a form will never, ever exceed 255.

Lights, camera . . . action

The action attribute supplies the URL for the CGI script or other input-handling program on the server that receives a form's input. This URL can be a fully qualified or simply a relative reference. Either way, you need to make sure the URL points to the right program, in the right location, to do the job you expect.

You also need to make sure that the CGI script or program is executable and that it behaves properly. We reveal these secrets of the ages later in this chapter, apropos of testing HTML documents and related CGI programs.

Given what you now know about the <form> tag and its two main attributes, you should immediately recognize that this snippet of code creates a form that is submitted using the POST method to a program named *form.exe* that lives in the /cgi-bin/ directory:

```
<form method="POST" action="/cgi-bin/form.exe">
    form content goes here
</form>
```

Making an assumption . . .

To standardize handling input, we make two assumptions for all forms' syntax in this chapter:

✔ In every <form> tag, method="POST".

✔ For every action, url="/cgi-bin/form-name" — and when we discuss such creatures, we replace the placeholder form name with the name of the form we're discussing (for example, for the form named *get-inf.html*, we use action="/cgi-bin/get-inf").

Okay, so the forms' syntax is a tad oversimplified for all possible cases; everybody's gotta start somewhere. These conventions make it easy to create sample HTML files to implement the forms in this chapter. (We've also put 'em on the CD-ROM that accompanies this book.)

Incoming! Taking aim with <input> tags

The <input> tag defines the most basic form element — the one you use to gather input. This tag takes at least two attributes — namely type and name. The type attribute indicates what kind of element should appear on the form. The name attribute assigns, well, a name to go with the input field (or with the value that corresponds to the <input> tag).

You use the name attribute to identify the contents of a field in the form information that is ultimately uploaded to the input-handling Web server. In fact, what the server receives from the form is a series of name/value pairs. The name that identifies the value is the string supplied in the name="text" attribute of the <input> tag, and the value is what the user enters or selects for that particular field. Read on — the section titled "A text-oriented <input> example" (catchy, eh?) contains an example that makes all this clear!

Type-casting still works!

The type attribute for the <input> tag can take any of the following values:

- ✔ BUTTON: Creates a button that has no specific use, except to call a script when a user clicks a button built with the <button> tag.

- ✔ CHECKBOX: Produces an on-screen checkbox for users to make multiple selections from a list of choices.

- ✔ FILE: Allows users to upload a file, but for FILE to work, you must provide a list of acceptable file types using the accept attribute.

- ✔ HIDDEN: Sort of a "stealth" attribute because it produces no visible input area. This attribute passes data needed for other uses through the form. For example, this may be an ongoing series of forms based on an earlier interaction during which the user identifies himself or herself — a hidden field contains the name-value pair for that data but doesn't show it on the current form. (Some browsers display these fields at the bottom of a form, and each field has no accompanying label.)

- ✔ IMAGE: Designates a graphic as a selectable item in a form. You can use this to include icons or other graphical symbols.

- ✔ PASSWORD: Same as the TEXT type, but the characters a user types in the form field display as asterisks ("****") or some other masking character, to keep passwords from showing in clear text.

- ✔ RADIO: Nope, this attribute doesn't pick up your favorite FM radio station; it creates a radio button for a range of selections, from which the user may select only one.

- ✔ RESET: Creates a button labeled "reset" in your form. Include this attribute so users can clear a form's contents and start over (to err is human; to reset, a relief). Be sure to place it well away from other controls — you don't want them to clear the form by accident!

- ✔ SUBMIT: Creates a button labeled "submit" (by default, or whatever name you supply for the value attribute for submit) in your form. Not as tyrannical as it sounds, SUBMIT tells the browser to bundle the form data and pass it all to the CGI script indicated by the action attribute. In plain English (remember that?), SUBMIT is the button readers use to send the filled-out form; therefore, a form is useless without an <input type="submit"> tag.

✔ TEXT: Provides a one-line area for text entry. Use this attribute for short fields only (as in the example that follows). For longer text fields, use the `<textarea> . . . </textarea>` tags instead.

These `type` attribute values provide a wide range of input displays and data types for form input. As you look at HTML forms on the Web (and in this book) with a new — dare we say more trained — eye, you can see how effectively you can use these types.

Other <input> attributes

Most of the input tag's remaining attributes exist to modify or qualify the display of the `<input>` tag. Some of these attributes, such as `align` and `src`, only work with specific types of input elements. Here's a list of the attributes du jour that we serve up elsewhere in the book, arrayed in alphabetical order for easy reference:

✔ `align="TOP|MIDDLE|BOTTOM|LEFT|RIGHT"`: For image elements, determines how the graphic is aligned on the form, vis-à-vis the accompanying text.

✔ `checked`: Makes sure that a certain radio button or checkbox is checked when the form is either visited for the first time or after it is reset. Use this attribute to create "default" settings for your forms.

✔ `disabled`: Renders an input element unusable (but the element still displays on-screen).

✔ `maxlength="number"`: Sets the maximum number of characters that a value in a text element can contain.

✔ `readonly`: Neither the contents of the control, nor the control itself, may be modified by the user. Any information already present in this control is automatically submitted with the form. If combined with `hidden`, provides a way to pass "invisible" data along with other form input.

✔ `size="number"`: Sets the number of characters that a text element can display without scrolling.

✔ `src="url"`: Provides a pointer to the source file for an image input element.

✔ `tabindex="number"`: Specifies an element's position in the tabbing order so field-to-field transitions after the user strikes the tab key can be explicitly controlled (default is by order of appearance).

✔ `usemap="filename"`: Identifies a client-side image map used to solicit user input.

✔ `value="text"`: Supplies a default value for a text or hidden element, or supplies the corresponding value for a radio button or checkbox selection. You can also use this attribute to determine the label of a submit or a reset button, for example, `value="Submit to Admin"` for a submit button, or `value="Clear Form"` for a reset button.

A text-oriented <input> example

The `<input>` tag by itself can use all the attributes shown in the previous section. Here's where we observe the tag in its natural habitat in a relatively simple survey form: (Note this is just a partial example; it's not a complete HTML document.)

```
<html>
<head>
<title> Contact Information</title>
<!-- the name of this form is usr-inf.html -->
</head>
<body>
<h3>Reader Contact Information</h3>
<p>Please fill out this form, so we'll know how to get in
touch with you. Thanks!</p>
<form method="POST" action="/cgi-bin/usr-inf">
<p>Please enter your name:</p>
<p>First name: <input name="first" type="TEXT" size="12"
        maxlength="20">
MI: <input name ="MI" type="TEXT" size="3" maxlength="3">
Surname(last name): <input name="surname" type="TEXT"
          size="15" maxlength="25"></p>

<p>Please give us your mailing address:</p>
<p>Address 1: <input name="adr1" type="TEXT" size="30"
        maxlength="45"></p>
<p>Address 2: <input name="adr2" type="TEXT" size="30"
        maxlength="45"></p>
<p>City: <input name="city" type="TEXT" size="15"
        maxlength="30"></p>
<p>State: <input name="state" type="TEXT" size="15"
        maxlength="15">
   ZIP&#47;Postal Code: <input name="zip" type="TEXT"
          size="10" maxlength="10"></p>
<p>Country: <input name="country" type="TEXT" size="15"
        maxlength="15"></p>

<p>Thank you! <input type="SUBMIT"> <input type="RESET"></p>
</form>
<address>
Sample form for <i>HTML 4 For Dummies</i>, 3rd
        Edition<br>2/10/00
          http://www.noplace.com/HTML4D/usr-inf.html
</address>
</body>
</html>
```

Figure 17-1 shows how this HTML form is displayed on our browser. Note the positions of the one-line text boxes immediately after field names and the ability to set these boxes on individual lines (as with Address1 and Address2) or together — as with First name, MI, and Surname(last name). These options make building simple forms that people can actually use very easy (what a concept!).

Being <select>ive

The `<select>` . . . `</select>` tag pair works much like a list; except it builds a drop-down list of `<option>` elements instead of the `<li>` list items. Within the `<select>` tag, the following attributes can occur:

✔ `disabled`: Renders an element unusable but still viewable.

✔ `tabindex="number"`: Identifies an element's position in the tabbing order defined for the page. The idea is to put some explicit controls on the field-to-field transitions that happen if the user strikes the Tab key with a finger or eight-pound sledgehammer (just kidding). The default setting is by order of appearance.

✔ `name="text"`: Provides the name that is passed to the server as the identifying portion of the name/value pair for this element.

✔ `size="number"`: Controls the number of elements that the drop-down list displays. Of course, you can define more than this number of elements, but keeping the list to a reasonable size makes it more manageable on-screen.

✔ `multiple`: Indicates that multiple selections from a list are possible; if this flag isn't present in a `<select>` statement, your users can select only a single element from the pick list.

Building a `<select>` field for your form doesn't take much work. In the following tasty example, you see how easy it is to construct a list of spices from which a user can select and order:

```
<html>

<head>
<title>&lt;select&gt; Spices</title>
<!-- the name of this form is sel-spi.html -->
</head>
  <body>
  <h3>This Month's Spicy Selections!</h3>
<p>Spice up your life. Order from this month's special
          selections.
<br> All items include 2 oz. of the finest condiments, packed
          in tinted glass bottles for best storage.</p>
<hr>
<form method="POST" action="/cgi/sel-spi">
<fieldset>
  <legend>Pepper Selections:</legend>
  <select name="pepper" size="4" multiple>
  <option>Plain-black</option>
  <option>Malabar</option>
  <option>Telicherry</option>
  <option>Green-dried</option>
  <option>Green-pickled</option>
  <option>Red</option>
  <option>White</option>
  </select>
  <p>Please pick a button to indicate how the pepper<br>
          should be delivered:
  <br>Ground <input type="RADIO" name="grind" value="ground">
  <br>Whole <input type="RADIO" name="whole" value="whole">
  <br></p>
</fieldset>
  <hr>
  <p>Imported and Domestic Oregano:</p>
  <select name="oregano" size="4" multiple>
  <option> Italian-whole</option>
  <option> Italian-crumbled</option>
  <option> Greek-whole</option>
  <option> Indian</option>
  <option> Mexican</option>
  <option> Organic-California</option>
  </select>
  <p>Thanks for your order! <input type="SUBMIT" value="Send
          Order">
```

```
<input type="RESET">
</form>
<address>
Sample form for <i>HTML 4 For Dummies</i>, 3rd
        Edition<br>2/10/00
        http://www.noplace.com/HTML4D/usr-inf.html
</address>
</body></html>
```

Figure 17-2 shows what nice results you can get from using <select> elements to provide options for your users to pick from. (Lunch, anyone?)

Notice the radio buttons for specifying whole or ground pepper. By giving both radio buttons the same name attribute, we indicate that the user can choose only one option.

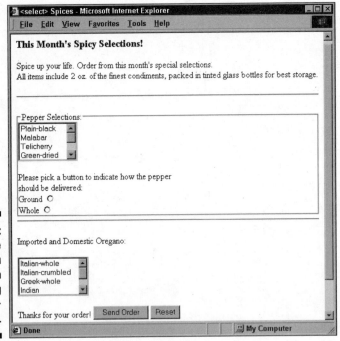

Figure 17-2:
The nice results you can get from using <select> elements.

Adding structure with <fieldset> and <legend> tags

Oftentimes, a form has a variety of different tags, and groups of those tags gather related information. As an example, look back at Figure 17-2. The form can be divided into two separate parts: the pepper selections and the imported and domestic oregano section. Two tags new to HTML 4.0 — `<fieldset>` and `<legend>` — help group related fields and label them. Look at this bit of code from the pepper and oregano example:

```
<form method="POST" action="/cgi/sel-spi">
  <fieldset>
  <legend>Pepper Selections:</legend>
  <select name="pepper" size="4" multiple>
  <option>Plain-black</option>
  <option>Malabar</option>
  <option>Telicherry</option>
  <option>Green-dried</option>
  <option>Green-pickled</option>
  <option>Red</option>
  <option>White</option>
  </select>
  <p>Please pick a button to indicate how the your order
          should be delivered:
  <br>Ground <input type="RADIO" name="grind" value="ground">
  <br>Whole <input type="RADIO" name="whole" value="whole">
  <br></p></fieldset>
```

The `<fieldset>` . . . `</fieldset>` tag pair groups all of the input tags, other HTML tags, and content related to the pepper portion of the form together. The `<legend>` . . . `</legend>` tag pair then identifies the field-set as Pepper Selections. Take one more look back at Figure 17-2 and you see how the Web browser automatically delineates the pepper information by boxing it all together. If you look at the sample code coming up in this chapter, you see the `<fieldset>` and `<legend>` tags at work again. Figure 17-3 shows you how the browser interprets and displays the content shown in the previous code.

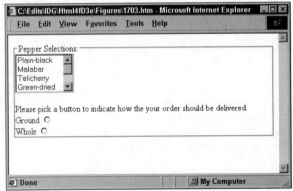

Figure 17-3:
The
`<fieldset>`
and
`<legend>`
tags at
work.

We highly recommend using the `<fieldset>` and `<legend>` tags to group the different portions of your form together because the final visual display really helps users know that they are moving from one set of controls to another. These tags also help break up the monotony of the page without any extra graphics.

<textarea> to wax eloquent (or wane profane)

The `<textarea>` . . . `</textarea>` tags may not give you total artistic freedom, but at least you can use them to create input elements of nearly any size on a form. Any text that appears between these opening and closing tags dutifully appear within the text area you define on-screen. If you leave the text area unmodified, the tags supply the default value delivered by the form — the tags have you covered.

`<textarea>` takes these attributes:

- ✔ `cols="number"`: Specifies the number of characters that can fit onto any one row of the text area; this value also sets the width of the text area on-screen.

- ✔ `disabled`: Makes the element unusable even though it still displays.

- ✔ `name="text"`: Provides the identifier part of the all-important name-value pair delivered to the server.

- ✔ `readonly`: If set, this value prevents users from modifying the text area; any information contained therein automatically is submitted with the form.

✔ `rows="number"`: Specifies the number of lines of text that the text area contains.

✔ `tabindex="number"`: Identifies this element's position in the tabbing order defined for fields on the page so that field-to-field transitions can be explicitly controlled after the user strikes the tab key (default is by order of appearance).

The example that follows shows how you can use a text area to provide your users with space for free-form feedback (whoa, you're a brave little toaster) or specific information as part of a survey-style form:

```
<html>
<head>
<title>&lt;textarea&gt; On Display</title>
  <!-- The name of this form is txt-ara.html -->
</head>
<body>
<h3>The Widget Waffle Iron Survey</h3>
<p>Please fill out the following information so we
  can register your new Widget Waffle Iron.</p>
<hr>
  <form method="POST" action="/cgi/txt-ara">
<fieldset><legend>Model Number</legend>
  <select name="mod-num" size="3">
  <option>102 (Single Belgian)</option>
  <option>103 (Double Belgian)</option>
  <option>104 (Single Heart-shaped)</option>
  <option>105 (Double Heart-shaped)</option>
  <option>204 (Restaurant Waffler)</option>
  <option>297 (Cone Waffler)</option>
  </select>
</fieldset>
  <hr>
  <b>Please complete the following purchase
          information:</b><br>
<p>Serial number: <input name="snum" type="TEXT" size="10"
  maxlength="10"></p>
  <p>Purchase Price: <input name="price" type="TEXT" size="6"
  maxlength="10"></p>
  <p>Location: <input name="location" type="TEXT" size="15"
  maxlength="30"></p>
  <hr>
  <b>Please tell us about yourself:</b>
<p>Male <input name="sex" type="CHECKBOX" value="male">
  Female <input name="sex" type="CHECKBOX"
          value="female"></p>
```

```
  <p>Age:
  under 25 <input name="age" type="CHECKBOX" value="lo">
  25-50 <input name="age" type="CHECKBOX" value="med">
  over 50 <input name="age" type="CHECKBOX" value="hi"></p>
<p>
<hr>
  Please share your favorite waffle recipe with us. If we
like it, we'll include it in our next Widget Waffler cook
book! Here's an example to inspire you.</p>
<p><textarea name="recipe" rows="10" cols="65">
  Banana Waffles
  Ingredients:
  2 c. waffle batter (see Widget Waffler cookbook for recipe)
  2 ripe bananas, peeled, sliced 1/4" thick
  1 tsp. cinnamon
  Preparation:
  Mix ingredients together.
  Preheat Widget Waffler (wait until light goes off).
  Pour 1/2 c. batter in Waffler (wait until light goes off).
  Keep browned waffles warm in oven until ready to serve.
  </textarea></p>
<p>Thank you! <input type="SUBMIT" value="Register now">
<input type="RESET"></p>
</form>
<address>
Sample form for <i>HTML 4 For Dummies</i>, 3rd
          Edition<br>2/10/00
          http://www.noplace.com/HTML4D/usr-inf.html
</address>
</body></html>
```

The screen that results from this HTML document appears in part in Figure 17-4. Notice the use of checkboxes for survey information, coupled with the text input area for recipes. May all your free-form feedback be at least as delightful. (So what time's breakfast?)

If you've read this whole section, you've seen most of the nifty little tricks — we like to call them widgets — that work within forms, but you can't really appreciate what forms can do until you browse the Web to look at what's out there. Our examples barely scratch the surface with a fork; you have a lot more to see. Or is that taste?

Figure 17-4:
The
`<textarea>`
tag in
action.

Form Good Habits and Attitudes

Whenever you create an HTML form, testing it against as many browsers as you possibly can is especially important. Don't be utterly taken in by the graphical side of the Web force; many users still favor character-mode browsers such as Lynx, and they'll miss your site if you miss accommodating them.

Ultimately, the HTML rules regarding layout-versus-content apply to forms: If you can create a clear, readable layout and make a form interesting to your users, you'll probably be a lot happier with the information returned than if you spend extra hours tuning and tweaking graphics elements and precise placement of type, widgets, and fields. Remember, too, that a form's just the front end; a pretty grille and fancy headlights don't make up for befuddled users or under-powered data collection.

Soon, you tackle the demanding-but-rewarding task of building CGI scripts and other input-handling programs for your server. If you're a real glutton for CGI punishment . . . ah, enlightenment, check out these in-depth books on the subject:

✔ *Perl For Dummies,* by Paul E. Hoffman (IDG Books Worldwide, Inc.)

✔ *Perl and CGI for the World Wide Web: Visual Quickstart Guide,* by Elizabeth Castro (Addison-Wesley Publishing Company)

Coming up, we scrutinize some tools that you can use to automate the form and background CGI script-creation process, and then sail bravely into regions of the map labeled "Here be Dragons and Geeks."

Specify CGI and Gate-a-Way with It

Building HTML forms and handling user interaction through Web pages requires action on both sides of the client-server connection. In this book, we concentrate mainly on the client side. It's time to slip quietly across the network connection from client side to server side; here dwells the Common Gateway Interface (CGI).

Along the way, we show you the history and foundations of CGI and cover the basic details of its design and use. We also introduce you to the issues surrounding your choice of a scripting or programming language for CGI, and we introduce you to some prime examples of that species.

You ventured to the client side (and come back alive) if you read Chapter 15's account of clickable image-map files. If this present section seems too much like pidgin geekspeak, skip ahead for the skinny on "How to Cheat at CGI."

A CGI program lets Web pages communicate with applications on the server to provide customized information or to build interactive exchanges between clients and servers.

If you read the previous paragraphs carefully, you notice one important element of CGI programs: They run on the Web server, not on the client side (where you run your browser to access Web-based information). You can't use our CGI programs on your own machine unless it can run Web server software (usually called an HTTP daemon, or more simply, httpd) at the same time that it runs your browser.

Common Gateway: This way to server side

Gateway scripts, or programs, add a powerful capability: true interaction between browsers and servers across the Web. Only your imagination and the tools at hand limit the power. Gateway scripts supply the underlying functions that enable you to work Web magic — perform searches on Web documents, parley with databases that can accept and process data from your forms, get hold of the strategic market intelligence, and customize your Web pages in response to user input.

If you build Web pages, you must manage all this interaction across the Web. That means building the front-end information (and display) that users see and interact with. You also have to pay practical attention to the back-end programming — how else can your system accept, interpret, and respond to all that user input you sweated to get? This coordination does require some effort and some programming, but if you're willing to take the time to learn CGI, you're limited only by the amount of time and energy you have for programming your Web pages.

CGI scripts/programs: Watch your language

Whether you call your server-side creation a program or a script, here's a trade secret: This distinction often describes the tools that you actually use to build the monster. Scripts are built with scripting languages, and programs are built with programming languages. The distinction can be useful:

- A scripting language creates a set of actions and activities that must be performed in the prescribed order each time a script is executed. Like a script read by an actor, scripts are often said to be interpreted.

- Statements written in a programming language are transformed, by a special program called a compiler, into equivalent computer instructions in an executable form that the computer can, well, execute.

Both of these approaches work equally well with the Web's Common Gateway Interface. But we want to keep it simple — we use CGI programs to mean any code creature you conjure up. You can call them whatever you want (although they don't answer to "Fido," "Ralph," or "Hey, you").

CGI retains a fairly pervasive presence on the Web. UNIX-based CERN and NCSA Web servers use it to mediate interaction between servers and programs. Because UNIX was the original Web platform, it sets the model (yet again) for how the Web handles user interaction. Although you can find other platforms that support Web servers — such as Windows NT or the Macintosh operating system — they, too, must follow the standard set for the CERN and NCSA implementations of httpd. Regardless of whether the servers conform to the CERN or NCSA models, all Web servers must provide CGI capabilities — either the real McCoy or a set of functions to match what CGI can do.

You can think of a CGI program as an extension of the core Web server services. In fact, CGI programs are like worker bees that do the dirty work on behalf of the server. The server serves as an intermediary between the client and the CGI program. Being queen bee is good — all those workers jump at your behest. (Whoa. Imagine having a behest!)

The server invokes CGI programs based on information that the browser provides (as in the `<form>` tag, where the action attribute supplies a URL for the particular program that services the form). The browser request sets the stage for a series of information hand-offs and exchanges:

✔ The browser makes a request to a server for a URL, which actually contains the name of a CGI program for the server to run.

✔ The server fields the URL request, figures out that it points to a CGI program (usually by parsing the filename and its extension or through the directory where the file resides), and fires off the CGI program.

✔ The CGI program performs whatever actions it's been built to supply, based on input from the browser request. These actions can include obtaining the date and time from the server's underlying system, accumulating a counter for each visit to a Web page, searching a database, and so on.

✔ The CGI program takes the results of its actions and returns the proper data back to the server; often the program formats these results as a Web page for delivery back to the server (if the content-type is text/html).

✔ The server accepts the results from the CGI program and passes them to the browser, which renders them for display to the user. If this exchange is part of an ongoing, interactive Web session, these results can include additional forms tags to accept further user input, along with a URL for this or another CGI program. Thus, the cycle begins anew.

This method is a rather disjointed way to have a conversation over the Web, but this way does allow information to move in both directions. The real beauty of CGI programs is that they extend a simple Web server in every conceivable direction and make that server's services more valuable.

We're convinced that anything short of an all-CGI volume barely scratches the surface, but for Pete's sake, we've got other fish to fry here. For more information, consult your favorite search engine and use "CGI" or "CGI script" as your search string. You turn up tons of useful references, but we save you at least some hassle by reminding you that we've already pointed you to some truly useful Web site pointers and book references.

Sample CGI Programs to Whet Your Whistle

In the following sections, we examine three different CGI programs. Their code and a great deal of associated information are on the CD-ROM. Each program is available in three versions: AppleScript (for use on an Apple httpd server), Perl (for use on any system that supports a Perl interpreter/compiler), and C (for use on any system that supports a C compiler).

You can find all these examples on the *HTML 4 For Dummies*, 3rd Edition CD that comes with this book.

Example 1: What time is it?

This short Perl program accesses the system time on the server and writes an HTML page with the current time to the user's screen. This program has filenames beginning with "time" in the CGI-bin subdirectory on this CD-ROM.

Example 2: Counting page visits

This AppleScript program establishes a counter that tracks the number of times a page is visited. This kind of tool can provide useful statistics for individuals or organizations curious about how much traffic their pages actually receive. This program has filenames beginning with "counter" in the CGI-bin subdirectory on this CD-ROM.

Example 3: Decoding clickable map coordinates

This C program can distinguish whether the right or left side of a graphic is selected (as well as defining a default to handle if the graphic isn't selected at all). The program shows how a script handles the definitions inside an image map file. This program has filenames beginning with "ismapper" in the compressed CGI files available from the CGI-bin subdirectory on this CD-ROM.

Installing and Using CGIs

Most Web servers are configured to look for CGI programs in a particular directory that's under the server's control. Normal users (including you) probably won't be able to copy CGI scripts into this directory without obtaining help from their friendly neighborhood systems administrator or Webmaster. Before you can install and use any CGI program on a particular server, you want to talk to one of these individuals (if not both), tell them what you want to do, and ask for their help and advice in making it happen.

Don't be nonplussed or surprised if this process takes some time: Systems administrators and Webmasters tend to be chronically busy people. You may have to wait a while to get their attention and then discuss your needs with them. Consider the following as you interact with your Webmaster:

✔ Make your initial approach to your Webmaster by e-mail or a phone call and briefly explain what you want to do. (For example, say something to the effect, "I want to include a counter CGI on my home page to track visitors.") Among other things, you may discover that the wiz already has a CGI available for that very purpose on your server and will simply tell you how to include its reference in the CGI invocation of your home page. (You may not have to use our code at all! But backup is such a comfort.)

✔ Most Webmasters are responsible for the safe and proper operation of the server and/or the Web site on which you want to run a CGI program. Don't be offended if you hear one say, "Well, I need to look your program over first to make sure that it's okay before you can use it." It's the mark of a pro trying to make sure that nobody introduces software that could cripple or compromise the system (saves on headaches and awful language). Don't take it personally if this happens — Webmasters are just doing their jobs, and asking for a review shows you that they care about what happens on their (and your) server, which is actually a good thing!

✔ Finally, the systems administrator or Webmaster can show you how to install and use CGIs more quickly and efficiently than if you try to figure it out for yourself. Be ready to wait your turn to get some time with this person and be ready to listen and learn when your turn comes. You won't be disappointed!

As the sample CGI programs in this chapter illustrate, you find as many ways to skin the proverbial CGI as you find ideas and approaches about how to implement them. We sincerely hope that you can use the tools that we include on this CD-ROM, where you can find C, Perl, and AppleScript versions for all three programs.

How to Cheat at CGI

If CGI doesn't exactly give you a warm, fuzzy feeling, you're not alone. CGI can be difficult, especially if you're not a programmer and don't really want to be. But before you throw out the virtual CGI baby with the cyber-bathwater, let us show you how to cheat at CGI! Here, as promised, are the crib notes.

The secret is to use a forms-designing application to create your forms and the background CGIs automatically. O'Reilly's PolyForm is one great application for this. Answer a few simple questions, click a few buttons, follow the instructions of the semi-intelligent program wizard, and poof! Out comes a form and matching CGI application. No messy code lists, no contortions, no infomercials. And the form really, really works!

Find out more about PolyForm by visiting `http://polyform.oreilly.com`. Unfortunately, for the Apple end of the stick, PolyForm is only available for Windows computers. The good news is many of today's WYSIWYG tools, such as Microsoft FrontPage and Dreamweaver by Macromedia, help you build forms and generate the code to work behind the scenes with the form input. Many of these tools are available for a variety of platforms, and in the next section, we show you how to use Dreamweaver on the Mac to quickly and easily build a form.

Many of the Web development tools that help you work with form input actually use JavaScript or VBScript to process forms on the client-side (a.k.a. the Web browser). Client-side scripting has much to recommend but does have its pitfalls. Before you jump right into working with Web scripting, we recommend that you read through WebMonkey's scripting resources at `http://hotwired.lycos.com/webmonkey/programming`.

I Dream of Forms

Dreamweaver is a great WYSIWYG Web development tool from Macromedia. Dreamweaver helps you build browser-independent and recommendation-compliant HTML in a matter of minutes. You can download a free, 30-day trial of Dreamweaver from the Macromedia Web site at `www.macromedia.com/software/dreamweaver`.

Dreamweaver's graphical interface makes building HTML forms quick and simple. Figure 17-5 shows a basic HTML page displayed in Dreamweaver. To get our form started, we type in some text and specify that it be a second level heading. The box with the dotted-line border delineates where our form controls will reside.

We quickly add three text form fields by choosing Insert⇨Form Object⇨Text Field. Then, we add some text to let users know what kind of information each form field should include, as shown in Figure 17-5.

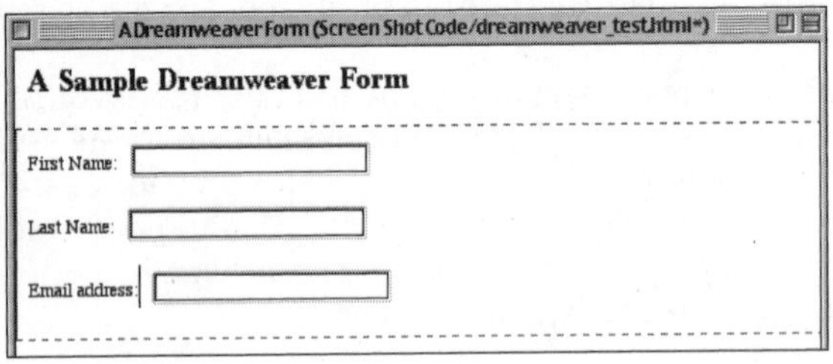

Figure 17-5:
A sample
Dream-
weaver
form.

A Dreamweaver Form (Screen Shot Code/dreamweaver_test.html*)
A Sample Dreamweaver Form
First Name: [   ]
Last Name: [   ]
Email address: [   ]

Remember that a form isn't very useful without a submit button to send its input to the server. A reset button is a nice addition as well. We add both of those to our form using Insert⇨Form Object⇨Button.

Our final touch to the look and feel of our form is to change the label on our reset button to "Clear" and to mark it as a reset button, as shown in Figure 17-6.

Our form looks really good, but it doesn't do much. The power of Dreamweaver comes in here. The form asks for a user's first name, last name, and e-mail address. We want to make sure that the user gives us all three bits of information, and we want to make sure that the e-mail address is really an e-mail address, which is a snap to do with Dreamweaver.

First, we have to give useful names to each input field using the Dreamweaver properties box, as shown in Figure 17-7. We can also set the width of the text field, the maximum number of characters that a user can enter in the field, specify if it is a text field, a multi-line field, or a password field, and provide an initial value for the field — all in the properties box for each field.

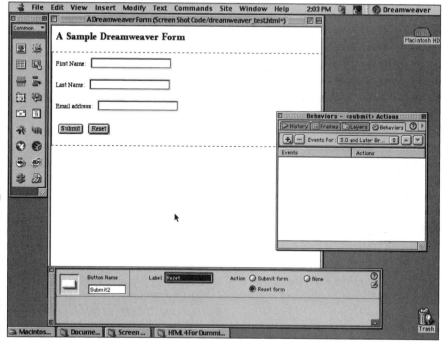

Figure 17-6:
A sample Dream-weaver form with submit and reset buttons.

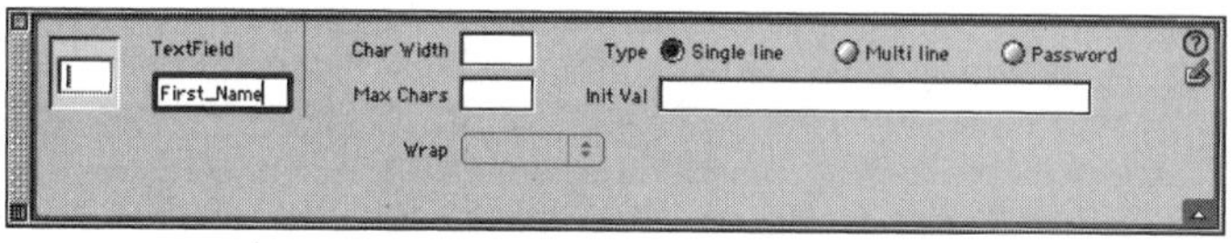

Figure 17-7:
The Dream-weaver properties box.

After we give useful names to each input field — first_name, last_name, and e-mail — we add a *behavior* to the submit button. In Dreamweaver, a behavior simply specifies how the browser should react after a user interacts with the Web page — in this case after the user clicks a button.

We want to make sure that the user enters information into all three fields. In programmer speak, this is called *validating* a form.

To make sure a form is validated before its content is sent to the server, select the submit button, click on the Behaviors tab from the Behaviors window, click on the plus (+) button, and choose Validate Form from the drop-down list, as shown in Figure 17-8.

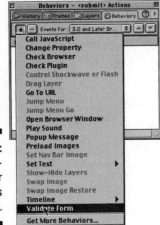

Figure 17-8:
The Dream-
weaver
Behaviors
dialog box.

In the Validate Form dialog box, shown in Figure 17-9, we can specify parameters for each input element that must be satisfied before the form data is considered valid and is passed to the server.

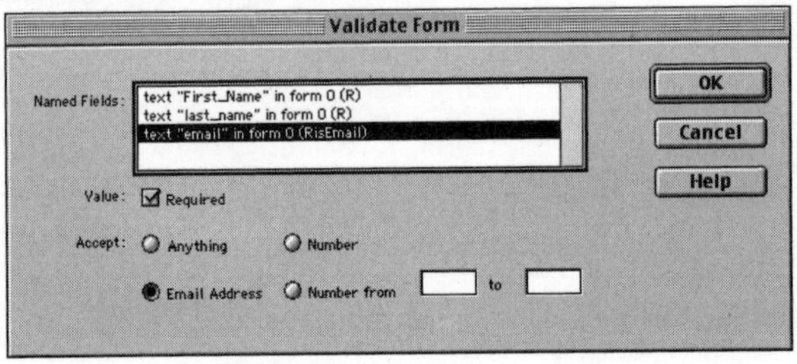

Figure 17-9:
The Dream-
weaver
Validate
Forms
dialog box.

We specify that all three input fields are required — meaning that the fields
must have date input — and that the e-mail field must contain an e-mail
address.

That's it — then we save the file and test the form in our favorite browser. If
we try to submit the form without filling in any data, we get an error message,
as shown in Figure 17-10.

Figure 17-10:
The error
message
that we get
if data is
missing.

If we try to submit the form without including a valid e-mail address in the e-mail field, we get a different error message, as shown in Figure 17-11.

Figure 17-11:
The error
message
we get if
we don't
include a
valid e-mail
address.

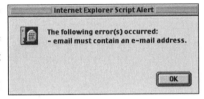

The code that Dreamweaver generates to validate the form content only does part of the job of processing the form. A CGI program of some sort on the Web server still needs to process the user input and respond accordingly to it. The good news is that validating form data isn't the only function Dreamweaver — or other Web development tools — can help you do to help you use forms on your Web pages. This form is just an example. We suggest you take some time to investigate what your favorite WYSIWYG tool can do for you when it comes to using forms.

Chapter 18

Style Is Its Own Reward

● ●

In This Chapter

▶ Introducing Web style

▶ Understanding the basics of CSS1 and CSS2

▶ Finding CSS resources on the Web

● ●

*O*f the various technologies that govern the development and display of Web pages, style sheets are one of the most exciting. Style sheets allow authors to specify layout and design elements — such as fonts, colors, and text indentation. Style sheets give you precise control over how elements appear on a Web page. What's even better is that you can create a single style sheet for an entire Web site to ensure that the layout and display of your content is consistent from page to page. The goal of style sheets is to prevent users' whims — as well as misconfigured browsers — from mangling the display of style-dependent Web documents. And for the last bit of icing on the cake — Web style sheets are easy to build and even easier to integrate into your Web pages.

The gist of how style works on the Web is this: A style sheet's specification combines with users' personal settings to make sure a Web document displays "properly." Of course, the term *properly* is determined by a document's creator, not its viewers — if you don't believe us, ask any artist how he or she feels about his or her work!

Style sheets are important enough that the W3C has devoted an entire section of its Web site to this topic. You can find style sheet information there, plus a collection of links for further study. Look this information up at `www.w3.org/pub/WWW/Style/`.

Before you dive into this chapter expecting to find out how to create and use style sheets, please understand that we don't tell you much about how to make style sheets of your own in this book. Although style sheet syntax is pretty straightforward, the issues surrounding the development and use of style sheets — browser support, interface design, and platform issues to name a few — are more than complex; they're quite advanced and difficult to wrap your brain around. Not that we think you can't tackle them successfully, but creating style sheets isn't for beginners. The real reason we don't cover them in depth here is that we'd have to write a whole book on the subject to do them complete justice. In fact, we've done just that — the book is called *The HTML Style Sheets Design Guide,* by Natanya Pitts, Ed Tittel, and Stephen N. James (published by The Coriolis Group).

Instead, we give an introduction to the concept of style, describe Cascading Style Sheets (CSS), and show you an example style sheet, complete with comments, so you can get a taste of what style sheets are and how they work. We hope our introduction to this new Web technology gives you an idea of what style sheets can do and shows you what direction your site can follow after you master the fundamentals of HTML style.

Of Styles and Style Sheets

If you've worked with desktop publishing applications, you should be familiar with the concept of a style sheet or template. If not, the idea isn't that complicated, so bear with us. (If you belong to the cognoscenti on this subject, see the sidebar "Background investigation reveals . . .") A style sheet defines design and layout information for documents. Usually, style sheets also specify fonts, colors, indentation, kerning, leading, margins, and even page dimensions for any document that invokes them.

In the publishing world, style sheets are indispensable. Style sheets enable numerous people to collaborate. All participants can work at their own systems, independently of other team members. When the pieces of a project are brought together, the final product derives a consistent look and feel (or design and layout, if you prefer "typographically correct" language), because a common template — what style sheets are often called in the print industry — ensures a common definition for the resulting document.

Consistency is a highly desirable characteristic in final products for both print and electronic (online) documents. Therefore, the W3C has made a gallant effort to incorporate such consistency on the Web by introducing style sheets. With the use of Web style sheets, an entire site can look nearly the same on every platform, within any browser that supports style sheets. For Web authors who want to create consistent documents, this uniformity promises a vast improvement over the current, somewhat more chaotic, status quo.

Background investigation reveals...

As you no doubt know, HTML is both a subset and a superset of the Standard Generalized Markup Language (SGML). For more on the history of HTML, read the introductory chapters of this book or take a quick look online at www.w3.org/MarkUp/#historical.

The Document Type Definitions (DTDs) that define how HTML works are based on the same notation as SGML. The original HTML DTDs were designed to separate the description of a document from its actual display, just as SGML strives to separate content from display. In theory, the fact that you define a bit of text as a paragraph should have nothing to do with

wanting the text to be displayed in 12-point Times with an empty line after it. However, over time, HTML DTDs have been modified to include information about display — the <font> tag is a prime example — and have moved away from their SGML roots.

For many standards-obedient programmers, this deviation from the SGML norm is alarming because it violates proper programming and design rules. The advent of Web style sheets may gently lead HTML DTDs and developers back to HTML's SGML roots: tags describe content, and style sheets drive display.

Another issue that arises out of proprietary, non-SGML-compliant HTML extensions is *browser envy*. Since Netscape introduced proprietary markup in 1994, other vendors — such as Microsoft and NCSA — introduced gimmicks and flashy additions to their own browsers. All this work has been expended in hopes that the browsers that can display proprietary Web documents correctly will draw the largest customer bases. This conflict has spawned some exciting and eye-catching HTML, but it has caused more harm than good. Incompatible HTML, stifled competition, and narrow-minded browser development are just some of results of this battle.

Web-based style sheets offer a promising solution to this situation. Style sheets allow proper separation of a document's structure and content from its form and appearance. With the implementation of style sheets, HTML can return to handling document structure and content (and get back to being proper SGML); and style sheets can handle document form and appearance.

The separation of form and content allows authors and users to influence the presentation of documents without losing software or device independence. This separation also lessens the need for new HTML tags, either proprietary or standard, and supports more sophisticated layout or appearance controls. Every possible layout or design element in a document can be defined by an attached — that is, linked — style sheet. Linking style sheets to documents reduces the pressure to add tags and controls directly to HTML.

Cascading Style Sheets (CSS1 and CSS2)

Cascading Style Sheets (CSS) is the official name for the HTML style sheet tool. Currently, CSS is in its second version (CSS2); however, the first version of CSS (CSS1) is better supported by the current Web browsers. CSS1 was a good, solid shot at building a style sheet mechanism for the Web. But, as you may have guessed, it was only a preliminary shot. Changes have already been made to CSS to make it more robust — enter CSS2. In general, CSS1 includes support for:

- Specifying font type, size, color, and effects
- Setting background colors and images
- Controlling many aspects of text layout, including alignment and spacing
- Setting margins and borders
- Controlling list display

CSS2 improves the implementation of many of CSS1's components and expanded on CSS1. CSS2 includes support for:

- Defining aural style sheets for text-to-speech browsers
- Defining table layout and display
- Automatically generating content for counters, footers, and other standard page elements
- Controlling cursor display

Because CSS1 is more effectively supported by browsers — and is therefore more practical to use for real-world development right now — most of our discussions in this chapter focus on CSS1. Rather than exploring the details of CSS1 completely, we discuss its key concepts to help you appreciate its capabilities.

What does the "C" in CSS really mean?

One of CSS1's fundamental features is its assumption that multiple, related style sheets can *cascade*, which means that authors can attach preferred style sheets to Web documents, and readers can still associate their own personal style sheets to those same documents to correct for human or technological handicaps. Thus, a visually handicapped reader could override an author's type distinctions of 10- and 12-point sizes, to accommodate his or her need for 40-point type. Likewise, an older computer's limitations on resolution or display area might override the Web developer's original layouts and type styles.

Basically, CSS contains a set of rules to resolve style conflicts that arise when applying multiple style sheets to the same document. Because conflicts are bound to arise, some method of resolution is essential to make the content of a document appear properly on a user's display.

The specifics of these rules depend on the assignment of a numeric weight to represent the relative importance of each style item. You accomplish this by assigning a value between 1 (least important) and 100 (most important) for a particular style element when it's referenced in a style sheet.

To prevent users' preferences from being completely overridden by a document's author, never set style-item weights to the maximum setting of 100. Keeping the settings low enables users to override settings at will, which is especially helpful for visually handicapped users who may require all characters to be at least 40 point, or who may demand special text-to-speech settings.

The referenced style sheets and their alterations are loaded into memory, and the browser resolves conflicts by applying the definition with the greatest weight and ignoring other definitions.

For example, assume that a document's author creates a style for a level-1 heading, <h1>, using the color red, and assigns a weight of 75. Furthermore, assume that the reader has defined a style for <h1>, colored blue with a weight of 55. In that case, a CSS-enabled browser uses the author's definition, because it has the greater weight.

A very basic style sheet

Style sheets are cool — we know this to be true because we told you they are. So what exactly does a style sheet look like? Here's a very basic one:

```
h1 {color: teal;
    font-family: Arial;
    font-size: 36pt;}

h2 {color: maroon;
    font-family: Arial;
    font-size: 24pt;}

p {color: black;
    font-family: Garamond;
    font-size: 14pt;}
```

But what do all the brackets, colons, and semi-colons really mean? This style sheet creates style rules for these three HTML tags:

- ✔ <h1>: The style rule specifies that all heading level 1 content is displayed in teal, Arial text that is 36 points in size.

- ✔ <h2>: The style rule specifies that all heading level 2 content is displayed in maroon, Arial text that is 24 points in size.

- ✔ <p>: The style rule specifies that all paragraphs are displayed in black, Garamond text that is 14 points in size.

Believe it or not, that's all there really is to building a style sheet. You use CSS syntax — the brackets, semi-colons, colons, and such — to specify how you want different tags (and their content) to be displayed.

Adding style sheets to your Web pages

You can incorporate CSS into a Web document using one or more of four methods:

- ✔ Link a style sheet stored outside of the Web page — called an *external style sheet* — using the <link> tag.

- ✔ Import an external style sheet using the @import command.

- ✔ Build a style sheet directly into a Web page — called an *internal style sheet* — using the <style> tag.

- ✔ Add style information directly to a tag using the style= attribute.

The following code fragment illustrates all four of these methods (refer to the comments to see which is which):

```
<head>
<title>Document title goes here</title>

<!-- the <link> tag links an external style sheet
     to the HTML document -->
<link rel="stylesheet" type="text/css"
 href="http://www.style.org/css/cool.css" title="Cool">

<!-- an internal style sheet resides within
     <style> . . . </style> tags and external style sheets
         can be imported into it with @import -->
<style type="text/css">
@import "http://www.style.org/css/basic.css"
H1 { color: blue }
</style>

</head>
```

```
<body>
 <h1>Headline is blue</h1>

<!-- add style directly to an element with the
     style attribute -->
 <p style="color: green">The paragraph is green.</p>
</body>
```

Other cool style sheet tricks

Other benefits of the CSS implementation of style sheets include:

- **Grouping:** You can group multiple style elements or definitions as follows:

```
h1 {font-size: 12pt;
    line-height: 14pt;
    font-family: Helvetica}
```

- **Inheritance:** Any nested tags inherit the style-sheet definitions assigned to the parent tag, unless you specify otherwise in your style sheet. Take a look at this bit of HTML code:

```
<h1>The headline <em>is</em> important!</h1>
```

If you define <h1> to display in red, the text enclosed by <em> also displays in red — unless you specifically assign <em> another color.

- **Alternative Selectors:** HTML 3.0 and later includes class and id attributes for most HTML tags. You can use these attributes to apply style rules to a limited group of HTML tags. Check out this example:

```
<head>
 <title>Title</title>
 <style type="text/css">
  h1.punk { color: #00FF00 }
 </style>
</head>
<body>
 <h1>Not green</h1>
 <h1 class="punk">Very green</h1>
</body>
```

Notice the style rule h1.punk. The .punk portion of the style rule indicates that this style rule turns the font color to an interesting shade of green — as defined by #00FF00 — for all <h1> tags with the attribute class="punk". If an <h1> element doesn't have the attribute class="punk", the style rule doesn't apply to it.

✔ **Context-Sensitive Selectors:** CSS also supports context-based style definition, which is best described using an example:

```
<style>
 ul ul li  { font-size: small }
 ul ul ul li { font-size: x-small }
</style>
```

In a nutshell, these two style rules specify that the text within the `<li>` in the first code snippet is to be small, and the text within the second code snippet is to be extra small:

```
<ul>
    <ul>
        <li>small text</li>
    </ul>
</ul>

<ul>
    <ul>
        <ul>
            <li>extra small text</li>
        </ul>
    </ul>
</ul>
```

✔ **Comments:** You can add comments inside a style sheet using the common C language syntax: `/* comment */`.

Implementing CSS right now

So you want to use CSS right now, but you don't have the time to learn a new set of syntax rules. Not a problem! Many of the Web page development tools available, such as Dreamweaver (www.macromedia.com) and HomeSite (www.allaire.com), come with built-in CSS support. There are also a whole bunch of development tools designed specifically for building style sheets. Check out the W3C's list at www.w3.org/Style/CSS/#editors.

If you want a truly slick and quick CSS implementation, visit the W3C's core styles page.

The W3C gathered input from the world's foremost style sheet experts and created a pre-built set of style sheets that anyone can use immediately. The W3C Core Styles page at www.w3.org/StyleSheets/Core shows you how to add the style sheets to you pages and provides a nice interface for testing each style sheet before you use it with your pages. If you're looking for a down and dirty way to get started with style sheets, this site is it.

CSS Resources Abound

We whet your whistle and now you're revved up and ready to learn all you can about CSS. We'd be remiss if we didn't clue you in on the best CSS resources available. The good news is that all of these resources are online so they are continually updated. If you're looking for more information about CSS, our top suggestions are:

- The W3C's style sheet resources: `www.w3.org/Style`
- Western Civilisation's CSS tutorial: `www.westciv.com/style_master/academy/css_tutorial/index.html`
- Web Design Group's CSS guide: `www.htmlhelp.com/reference/css`
- WebMonkey's CSS resources: `http://hotwired.lycos.com/webmonkey/authoring/stylesheets`

There are plenty more where these came from, but these are great starting points for learning all you ever wanted to know and more about CSS and style on the Web.

CSS has made a significant impact on the Web. Stay tuned to your favorite Web developer or Internet news provider for the latest updates and implementations. As always, for the latest style sheet specification, turn to the W3C's style sheet pages at `www.w3.org/Style/`.

Chapter 19

XHTML: The Next Generation of HTML

XHTML is another acronym that has recently taken the Web world by storm. It stands for Extensible Hypertext Markup Language. XHTML *is* HTML as an application of XML. In this chapter, our goal is to give you a firm understanding of XHTML and have you writing your own XHTML documents in no time. The concept of XHTML is easy to grasp, and if you play your cards right, maybe one day, people can view your Web pages on their refrigerators!

Dissecting XML

XML was introduced in 1998 as a formal W3C specification — also known as a W3C *Recommendation*. In the creation process, the authors of XML attempted to make up for all of HTML's shortcomings. According to most Web designers, XML seems to be brimming with benefits. Here's a condensed list of our favorite benefits:

✔ **Structured data:** Applications can extract the information they need.

✔ **Data exchange:** Allows you to exchange database contents or other structured information over the Internet.

✔ **XML complements HTML:** You can use XML data in an HTML page. In other words, you can integrate XML information into HTML.

✔ **Self-describing:** You need no prior knowledge of an application.

✔ **Search engines:** Increase in search relevancy because of contextual information found in XML documents.

✔ **Updates:** No need to update the entire site page by page; the Document Object Model (DOM) built into XML documents allows you to access and update individual elements.

✔ **User-selected view of data:** Different users can access different information or present the same information in a variety of ways.

For all the reasons in the previous list — and more — companies are adopting XML as their markup language of choice.

The beginnings of your XML endeavor must begin with the XML document. You have to carefully construct the tags to follow the markup syntax rules outlined by the specification. Then, you have to create a Document Type Definition (DTD) that defines how these tags may interact. The rules outlined by the XML specification are also used for XHTML. Therefore, see the "Converting HTML to XHTML — Easily!" section later in this chapter for details.

Taking in a little history

XHTML (Extensible Hypertext Markup Language) is brand spanking new: The W3C released the formal specification on January 26, 2000. The name sounds futuristic, and that's because it is. X stands for extensible (meaning capable of being extended or added on to), and that letter is stolen from the Extensible Markup Language (XML), which is no accident.

XML has the same parent as HTML: the Standard Generalized Markup Language (SGML). SGML is a *metalanguage* — a language that has the main purpose of talking about other languages — and its primary purpose is to create markup languages. XML is a pared down version of SGML with 10 percent of the complexity and 90 percent of the ability.

XML enables authors to create their own customized tags. In other words, XML provides extensibility — something that HTML, with its predefined tag set, is unable to do. The W3C can add only so many tags to HTML before the language becomes completely unmanageable.

Whereas HTML took some inspiration from SGML (and maybe even plagiarized some aspects), XML is a direct descendent of SGML. What this means for you as a designer, is that with XML, you can create any tag set you like — the sky's the limit.

XML jumped onto the scene in 1996 when SGML celebrated its 10th anniversary. The first official specification — known in W3C terms as a *W3C Recommendation* — was published in February 1998. This got the folks at the W3C thinking and the next thing you knew, they were cooking up ways for average Joes — such as us — to combine our knowledge of HTML with XML, creating a flexible, extensible language for the Web. In walks XHTML.

All of the XML behavioral rules are created in a DTD. With HTML, the DTD was created for you, which explains why you have a predefined tag set to work with. However, with XML you can create your own DTD; therefore, you create your own tag set and the rules that govern that tag set.

This is where the *extensible* comes in. Because you can create your own DTD — and therefore, your own tag set — you have the option of extending that tag set whenever you want. But where does XHTML come in? As we stated earlier, XHTML is HTML as an application of XML.

This means that XHTML follows the XML specification — the syntax rules for creating XML markup — and must be associated with the HTML DTD. The X means that not only can the author work with the predetermined tag set defined in the DTD, but authors can also add any other tags they want — as long as they follow the rules of XML.

We cannot get to the details of XML because that's a whole other book — no really it is! (Check out *XML For Dummies*, 2nd Edition, written by Ed Tittel and Frank Boumphrey and published by IDG Books Worldwide, Inc.)

Ringside with HTML and XHTML

And the winner is . . .

Saying that one language is better than the other is not that easy. However, because XHTML is as easy to code as HTML and provides some extra benefits, why not start using it today? Take a look at some of the reasons we think you need to make the switch:

- **Extensibility:** With HTML, you have to work with a fixed set of tags, providing no variation. Unlike HTML, XHTML can be extended to include new (and by new we mean you create your own) tags and attributes. The addition of new tags and attributes to those that already exist creates many new ways that you can embed content and programming in a Web page. Now, you can mix and match known HTML tags with tags — also known as elements — from other XML languages and your own XML language.

- **Portability:** You've probably already heard of digital phones accessing the Web. But think about those tiny, tiny screens — not to mention disk space — downloading huge Flash graphics. Impossible, right? Well, yes. When working with HTML, you have to create a new page for each different type of browser — tailoring that page to fit the specific needs of each individual browser. XHTML solves this problem while allowing you to work with that same ol' trusty tag set found in HTML.

If you go to the introduction of this chapter, you see a phrase stating "maybe one day, people can view your Web pages on their refrigerators!" When we first decided to include that phrase, we meant it as an exaggerated example — of course. Well, this concept is no longer an exaggeration. To read about Screenfridge visit www.electrolux.com/screenfridge. And you thought we were kidding.

HTML has some limitations

We keep ranting and raving about why XML (and therefore, XHTML) may take home the prize, but we need to reflect on HTML briefly. If you're one of the people who works with HTML (in other words, your audience is still the general public), you probably already know that HTML is a presentation language used to create documents for display on the Web. HTML tags define how text is displayed in your Web browser. Add HTML markup to some text, add some links to graphics, throw in some hyperlinks for good measure, and you have an HTML document.

The idea behind HTML was a modest one. HTML was meant to describe not the page content but rather how that content should be displayed in your browser. Since its introduction to the public, however, HTML has been called on to provide solutions to problems it was never meant to solve. Some of the functions HTML wasn't meant to do include the following:

- Tightly control document display
- Be flexible enough to describe different, specific types of information
- Convey information in a variety of media and formats
- Define complex linking relationships between documents
- Publish a single set of information across a variety of media

Web designers (take us, for example) sometimes catch themselves thinking, "But my heading has to be in 36-point Arial and centered in the first third of the page." Although this sentiment is a bit exaggerated, it's not far from what Web designers expect their HTML to do, leaving them wondering why HTML doesn't live up to their expectations.

Remember, HTML was created not as a page layout markup language but as a document-description markup language. Users are able to describe a document's structure as well as the role each part of the document plays, regardless of how it looks on a monitor.

Today's Web designers want to achieve the same formatting control over their Web documents that they have over printed documents. Web designers want what they see on their screens with their browsers to be exactly what any visitor to their sites will see. Two overarching problems prevent Web designers from achieving this control using HTML:

- ✔ **HTML lacks fine controls.** First and foremost, HTML doesn't include the mechanisms for maintaining fine control. You can't specify the display size of a document or control the size of a browser window. The user's screen size and personal preferences affect these two variables. Although HTML 4.0 includes `<font>` tags to help you manipulate font style, size, and color, users can override your settings with their own.

- ✔ **Browsers' displays vary.** Along with the different versions of the two most common browsers — Internet Explorer and Netscape Navigator — Mosaic, HotJava, and other graphical browsers make it impossible to know exactly which browser and platform are being used to view your pages. And you can't realistically test every Web page on every available browser on every platform just to see what your users will see.

Converting HTML to XHTML — Easily!

If you read this book and understand HTML, you're on the right track. By learning HTML, you have learned the first piece of XHTML. The great feature about XHTML is that if you already know HTML, you know XHTML. The only difference is a few new syntax rules. If you want to take full advantage of XHTML's extensibility, you will have to do some more reading on XML, but that is for a whole other book (specifically, *XML For Dummies*, 2nd Edition).

The good news is that we outline the rules you must follow to create XHTML and combine these rules with what you know of HTML. Now you're off to creating your own XHTML pages. (There's even more good news. We also have an *XHMTL For Dummies* book in the works.)

Just follow a few guidelines and you can convert your HTML to XHTML in seconds. Barring our obvious exaggeration of time, converting an existing HTML document to an XHTML document truly is easy. You have a few rules that you *must* follow — and we mean *absolutely must* follow — before your page is ready to dawn its .xhtml extension.

We know what you must be thinking — what about backward compatibility with browsers. The verdict is in and XHTML is compatible with today's HTML 4 browsers. Can we hear a loud woohoo from everyone please?

Rule by rule, here are the rules you must follow to convert your HTML document to XHTML.

Rule 1: Always nest correctly

Overlapping elements — or tags for that matter — is illegal in XML; therefore, you must nest you tags correctly. Say this with us: *What you open first, you close last.*

If you're shaking your head and saying, "Huh?" here's an example to clear things up.

This is incorrect:

```
<p>What you open <em>first</em>, you must close
        <em>last</p></em>
```

This is correct:

```
<p>What you open <em>first</em>, you must close
        <em>last</em></p>
```

Rule 2: Always include optional ending tags

We admit, sometimes omitting that ending </p> tag is nice. Less typing always sounds good to us. But, get off the couch because omitting ending tags is illegal in XML (and hence XHTML). This rule does not include empty tags, which are forbidden to have a closing tag. The rule goes something like this: If a tag has an optional or required end tag, you must include it in your code.

This is incorrect:

```
<ul>
    <li>list item one
    <li>list item two
</ul>
```

This is correct:

```
<ul>
    <li>list item one</li>
    <li>list item two</li>
</ul>
```

Rule 3: Attribute values must always be quoted

This is another rule that requires a little more effort: Attribute values must always be quoted. You can use both single (') or double (") quotation marks. We (and the W3C) don't care which ones you choose, as long as you choose to include them. (And, so you don't confuse people who view your source code, be consistent and use one or the other.)

This is incorrect:

```
<colgroup span=40 width=15>
...
</colgroup>
```

This is correct:

```
<colgroup span="40" width="15">
...
</colgroup>
```

Rule 4: All element and attribute names must be lowercase

Unlike HTML, XML is case sensitive. For this reason, you must always use lowercase when naming tags and attributes. Note that this does not apply to attribute values — only attribute names and tag names.

This is incorrect:

```
<INPUT TYPE="CHECKBOX" NAME="PET" VALUE="CAT">
```

This is correct:

```
<input type="CHECKBOX" name="PET" value="CAT">
```

Rule 5: Attribute name-value pairs cannot stand alone

In HTML, you find a couple of instances of attributes that are stand-alone text strings, such as compact or checked. These stand-alone strings are not allowed in XML. As a way to work around this problem, there's a simple solution: Stand-alone attributes are set equal to themselves. Although this rule may seem a little silly, it's still another XHTML rule.

This is incorrect:

```
<input type="CHECKBOX" name="PET" value="CAT" checked>
```

This is correct:

```
<input type="CHECKBOX" name="PET" value="CAT"
        checked="checked">
```

Rule 6: Empty elements must end their start tag with />

The easiest way to comply with this rule is to include a /> at the end of all your empty elements. Although that is all you need to follow legal XML, you have an issue with backward compatibility. To ensure that older browsers can understand this construct, include a space before the trailing / and >. You also want to avoid simply adding an end tag, which is legal but not always understood by older browsers.

This is incorrect:

```
<img src="graphic.gif">
```

This is correct:

```
<img src="graphic.gif" />
```

Note the space after the file name and before the trailing />.

Rule 7: You must include a DOCTYPE declaration

The DOCTYPE declaration is what references the DTD. This is not required by browsers, but because you're following XML rules and because you want your page to validate against a DTD, you can't leave it out. The declaration looks like this:

```
<!DOCTYPE html PUBLIC "-//W3C//DTD XHTML 1.0 Strict//EN"
        "DTD/xhtml1-strict.dtd">
```

The DTD must appear before the root element — that is the `<html>` tag — and must follow the previous syntax. We break this rule down:

- Declaration keyword: `<!DOCTYPE`
- Type of document: `html`
- Public identifier keyword: `PUBLIC`
- Public Identifier: `"-//W3C//DTD XHTML 1.0 Strict//EN"`
- DTD file name: `"DTD/xhtml1-strict.dtd">`

The previous example is one of the three DTDs you may choose from; here are the two other options:

```
<!DOCTYPE html PUBLIC "-//W3C//DTD XHTML 1.0
         Transitional//EN"
         "DTD/xhtml1-transitional.dtd">
```

```
<!DOCTYPE html PUBLIC "-//W3C//DTD XHTML 1.0 Frameset//EN"
         "DTD/xhtml1-frameset.dtd">
```

The only difference is the DTD public identifier and filename. To read more about your DTD options, visit the XHTML specification at `www.w3.org/TR/xhtml1/#normative`.

Rule 8: You must include an XHTML namespace

According to the specification, the root element — `<html>` — must include the XML namespace using a `xmlns` attribute. A namespace is a collection of names that are used in XML documents as element types and attribute names. XHTML is using the XHTML collection of names and therefore needs a namespace, which looks like this:

```
<html xmlns="http://www.w3.org/1999/xhtml"></html>
```

Take a look at an example

After you take a look at the following code, you can find some empty tags (`<br />`) and many closing tags (`</p>`) — and that is just the tip of the iceberg. XHTML has many rules and you must follow all of them for your pages to be correct XHTML.

```
<!DOCTYPE html PUBLIC "-//W3C//DTD XHTML 1.0
          Transitional//EN""DTD/xhtml1-transitional.dtd">

<!- This is our root element with a namespace ->

<html xmlns="http://www.w3.org/TR/xhtml1">
<head>
    <title>LANWrights - Network-Oriented Writing and
          Consulting
    </title>
    <link href="lanwstyle.css" type="text/css"
          rel="STYLESHEET" />
</head>

<!- This begins the body of our XHTML document ->

<body>
<center>
    <p><img src="graphics/lanwlogo.gif" width="240"
          height="123" alt="LANWrights" /></p>
    <p><img src="graphics/ntwkori.gif" width="469"
          height="25" alt="Network-Oriented Writing &amp;
          Consulting" /></p>
    <p><img src="graphics/line.gif" width="100%" height="1"
          /></p>
</center>
    <p><font size="-1">LANWrights, Inc., based in Austin,
          Texas, is dedicated to network-oriented writing,
          training, and consulting. Our projects cover the
          Internet, Networking and Communications, and
          Microsoft Certification, among other topics.
          LANWrights seeks to supply accurate, timely infor-
          mation on cutting-edge technologies and useful
          services to a wide range of users.</font></p>
<center>
    <p><img src="graphics/line.gif" width="100%" height="1"
          /></p>

<!- This is our table ->

<table width="97%" border="0" cellpadding="10">
    <tr valign="TOP">
        <td width="5%" align="CENTER"><a href="books.htm"><img
              src="graphics/books.gif" width="51" height="51"
              alt="The Book Nook" align="RIGHT" border="0"
              /></a></td>
        <td width="45%">
          <p><font size="+1"><a href="books.htm">The Book
              Nook</a></font>
          </p>
          <p><font size="-1">Detailed descriptions for all of
              LANWrights' books, sorted by type, including
              pointers to associated Web sites.</font></p>
```

```
      </td>
      <td width="5%" align="CENTER">
       <a href="showcase.htm">
       <img src="graphics/showcase.gif" width="51"
           height="51" alt="Web Technology Showcase"
           border="0" />
       </a>
      </td>
      <td width="45%">
       <p><font size="+1"><a href="showcase.htm">Web
           Technology Showcase</a></font>
       </p>
       <p><font size="-1">Java examples and demonstrations of
           recent adventures on the cutting edge.</font>
       </p>
      </td>
 </tr>
 <tr valign="TOP">
      <td width="5%" align="CENTER">
      <a href="training.htm">
      <img src="graphics/training.gif" width="51" height="51"
          alt="Training Center" align="RIGHT" border="0" />
      </a>
     </td>
      <td width="45%">
       <p>
       <a href="training.htm"><font size="+1">The Training
           Center</font></a>
       </p>
       <p><font size="-1">Read about or sign up for upcoming
           classroom sessions, demo our online training, and
           learn more about licensing our testing and train-
           ing environments.</font></p>
      </td>
      <td width="5%" align="CENTER">
       <a href="corporat.htm">
       <img src="graphics/corporat.gif" width="51"
           height="51" alt="Coporate Services" border="0"
           /></a>
      </td>
      <td width="45%">
       <p><a href="lanw.htm"><font size="+1">Corporate
           HQ</font></a>
       </p>
       <p><font size="-1">Learn more about LANWrights' orga-
           nization, including available services and rates.
           Read staff bios, and find out what's new
           here.</font></p>
      </td>
 </tr>
 <tr valign="TOP">
```

(continued)

```
        <td width="5%" align="CENTER"><a href="exam.htm"><img
            src="graphics/testprep.gif" width="51" height="51"
            border="0" alt="Certification Central" /></a></td>
        <td width="45%">
          <p><a href="exam.htm"><font size="+1">Certification
            Central</font></a>
          </p>
          <p><font size="-1">Learn about preparing to pass exams
            required for Microsoft, Novell, or Java certifica-
            tions. Covers the Exam Prep, Exam Cram, and CT
            Guide series, including errata and practice
            tests.</font></p>
        </td>
        <td width="5%" align="MIDDLE">
          <a href="overview.htm">
          <img src="graphics/wayfind.gif" width="51" height="51"
            alt="Site Overview" border="0" /></a>
        </td>
        <td width="45%">
          <p><a href="overview.htm"><font size="+1">Site
            Overview</font></a>
          </p>
          <p><font size="-1">A bird's-eye view of our Web site.
            From here, you can jump to any other section or
            page on the site.</font></p>
        </td>
      </tr>
</table>

<!- Whew! That was the end of our table ->

<p><br />
<img src="graphics/line.gif" width="100%" height="2" />
</p>
</center>
<p class="address">
        <a href="http://www.w3.org/Style/css/">
        <img src="graphics/css.gif" align="right" border="0"
                alt="Made With Cascading Style Sheets" />
        </a>
        <font face="ARIAL">URL:
                <a href="default.htm">http://www.lanw.com/
                default.htm<br />
        </a> Layout, design &amp; revisions &#169; 1997, 1998
        <a href="default.htm">LANWrights</a>, Inc.<br />
        <a href="mailto:webmaster@lanw.com">Webmaster:</a>
            Chelsea Valentine<br />
        Revised — February 14, 2000<i>[CV]</i></font></p>
</body>
</html>
```

Doing It with HTML Tidy

The folks at the W3C want to help you out. Well, really, David Raggett wants to help you out.

We all make mistakes when creating — and editing — HTML. With this in mind, David Raggett created a simple tool to fix these mistakes automatically and tidy up sloppy editing into nicely laid out markup. His tool is called HTML Tidy, which is a free utility offered on the W3C Web site. Luckily for us, Raggett added some XHTML features to HTML Tidy, so now this tool takes a look at your HTML page, cleans it up, and then outputs it in XHTML. HTML Tidy can even help you identify where you need to pay further attention to making your pages more accessible to people with disabilities.

To read more about Tidy, visit www.w3.org/People/Raggett/tidy.

You can download the DOS or the Windows version, TidyGUI. You can also visit a Web front-end created by Peter Wiggin. Visit the URL listed here (http://webreview.com/1999/07/16/feature/xhtml.cgi), enter your URL, and then see your page magically convert before your very eyes.

Part VI
The Part of Tens

The 5th Wave — By Rich Tennant

"Gotta hand it to our Web page designer - she found a way to make our pie charts interactive."

In this part . . .

Here, we cover the do's and don'ts for HTML markup, help you rethink your views on document design, and help you catch potential bugs and errors in your Web pages. Enjoy!

Chapter 20

Ten HTML Do's and Don'ts

*B*y itself, HTML is neither excessively complex nor overwhelmingly difficult. As some high-tech wags (including a few rocket scientists) have put it, "This ain't rocket science!" Nevertheless, a few important do's and don'ts can make or break the Web pages you build with HTML. Consider these humble admonishments as guidelines to help you make the most of HTML without losing touch with your users or watching your page blow up on the pad.

If some of the fundamental points that we made throughout this book seem to be cropping up here, too (especially regarding proper and improper use of HTML), it's no accident. Heed ye well the prescriptions and avoid ye the maledictions. But hey, we know they're your pages and you can do what you want with them. Your users will decide the ultimate outcome. (We'd *never* say, "We told you so!" Nope. Not us.)

Never Lose Sight of Your Content

So we return to the crucial question of payload: the content of your page. Why? Well, as Darrell Royal (legendary football coach of the University of Texas Longhorns in the '60s and '70s) is rumored to have said to his players, "Dance with who brung ya." In normal English (as opposed to Texan), we think this phrase means that you should *stick with the people who've supported you all along* and give your loyalty to those who've given it to you.

We're not sure what this means for football, but for Web pages it means keeping faith with your users and keeping content paramount. If you don't have strong, solid, informative content, users quickly get that empty feeling that starts to gnaw when a Web page is content-free. Then they'll be off to richer hunting grounds on the Web, looking for content to satisfy their hunger. Above all, *place your most important content on your site's major pages.* Save the frills and supplementary materials for the secondary pages. The short statement of this principle for HTML is, "Tags are important, but *what's between the tags* — the content — is what really counts." For a refresher course on making your content the very best it can possibly be, take a spin through Chapter 2.

Structure Your Documents and Your Site

Providing users with a clear road map and guiding them through your content is as important for a single home page as it is for an online encyclopedia. When longer or more complex documents grow into a full-fledged Web site, a road map becomes even more important. This map ideally takes the form of (yep, you guessed it) a flow chart that shows page organization and links. If you like pictures with a purpose, the chart could appear in graphic form on an orientation page for your site.

We're strong advocates of top-down page design: Don't start writing content or placing tags until you understand what you want to say and how you want to organize your materials. Then start the construction of any HTML document, or collection of documents, with a paper and pencil (or whatever modeling tool you like best). Sketch out the relationships within the content and the relationships among your pages. Know where you're building before you roll out the heavy equipment.

Good content flows from good organization. It helps you stay on track during page design, testing, delivery, and maintenance. And organization helps your users find their way through your site. Need we say more? Well, yes, don't forget that *organization changes with time.* Revisit and critique your organization and structure on a regular basis, and don't be afraid to change either one to keep up with changes in your content or focus.

Keep Track of Those Tags

While you're building documents, forgetting to use closing tags is often easy, even when they're required (for example, the `</a>` that closes the opening anchor tag `<a>`). Even when you're testing your pages, some browsers can be a little too forgiving; compensating for a lack of correctness and leading you into a false sense of security. The Web is no place to depend on the kindness of strangers; scrutinize your tags to head off possible problems from other browsers that may not be quite so understanding (or lax, as the case may be).

As for the claims some vendors of HTML-authoring tools make ("You don't even have to know any HTML!"), all we can say is, "Uh-huh, surrre." HTML itself is still a big part of what makes Web pages work; if you understand it, you can troubleshoot with a minimum amount of fuss. Also, ensuring that your page's inner workings are correct and complete is something only *you* can do for your documents, whether you build them yourself or a program builds them for you.

We could go on ad infinitum about this subject, but we'll exercise some mercy and confine our remarks to the most pertinent:

- **Keep track of tags yourself while you write or edit HTML by hand.** If you open a tag — be it an anchor, a text area, or whatever — create the closing tag for it right then and there, even if you have content to add. Most HTML editors do this task for you.

- **Use a syntax-checker to validate your work during the testing process.** Syntax checkers are automatic tools that find missing tags — and other ways to drive you crazy! Use these tools whether you build pages by hand or with software assistance. Here's the URL for the W3C's own HTML validator: `http://validator.w3.org/`.

- **Obtain and use as many browsers as you can when testing pages.** This step not only alerts you to missing tags, but it can also point out potential design flaws or browser dependencies (covered in a section later in this chapter). This exercise also emphasizes the importance of alternate text information, which is why we always check our pages with Lynx (a character-only browser).

- **Always follow HTML document syntax and layout rules.** Just because most browsers don't require tags like `<html>`, `<head>`, and `<body>` doesn't mean you should omit them; it just means that browsers don't give a hoot if you do. But browsers per se are not your audience. Your users (and, for that matter future browsers) may indeed care — the spiders will, for sure. (Note that the <head> and <body> tags are required in XHTML.)

Although HTML isn't exactly a programming language, it still makes sense to treat it like one. Therefore, following formats and syntax helps avoid trouble, and careful testing and rechecking of your work ensures a high degree of quality, compliance with standards, and a relatively trouble-free Web site.

Make the Most from the Least

More is not always better, especially when it comes to Web pages. Try to design and build your pages using minimal ornaments and simple layouts. Don't overload pages with graphics; add as many levels of headings as you can fit, and make sure your content is easy to read and follow. Make sure any hyperlinks you include connect your users to useful information that adds value to your site. Gratuitous links are nobody's friend; if you're tempted to link to a Webcam that shows a dripping faucet, resist, resist.

Remember that structure and images exist to *highlight* content. The more elaborate your structure — or the more bells, whistles, and dinosaur growls dominate a page — the more the extra elements can distract visitors from your content. Therefore, use structure and graphics sparingly, wisely, and as carefully as possible. Anything more can be an obstacle to content delivery. Go easy on the animations, links, and layout tags, or risk having your message (even your page) devoured by a hungry T. Rex.

Build Attractive Pages

When users visit Web pages with a consistent framework that focuses on content — and supplements (but doesn't trample) that content with graphics and links — they're likely to feel welcome. Making those Web pages pretty and easy to navigate only adds to a site's basic appeal, and makes your cyber-campers even happier. If you need inspiration, cruise the Web and look for layouts and graphics that work for you. If you take the time to analyze what you like, you can work from other people's design principles without having to steal details from their layouts or looks (which isn't a good idea anyway).

As you design your Web documents, start with a fundamental page layout. Pick a small but interesting set of graphical symbols or icons and adopt a consistent navigation style. Use graphics sparingly (yes, you've heard this before), and make them as small as possible — reducing size, number of colors, shading, and so on, while retaining eye appeal. When you've worked up simple, consistent navigation tools for your site, label them clearly and use them throughout your site. You can make your pages appealing, informative, and powerfully inviting if you're willing to invest the time and effort.

Avoid Browser Dependencies

When you're building Web pages, the temptation to view the Web in terms of your favorite browser is hard to avoid, which is why you should always remember that users view the Web in general (and your pages in particular) from many perspectives — through many different browsers.

During the design and writing phases, you'll probably ping-pong between HTML and a browser's-eye view of your work. At this point in the process, we recommend switching from one browser to another, testing your pages among a group of browsers (including at least one character-mode browser). This step helps balance how you imagine your pages and helps keep you focused on content.

During testing and maintenance, you must browse your pages from many different points of view. Make sure to work from multiple platforms; test on different size screens; try both graphical and character-mode browsers on each page. Such testing takes time but repays that investment with pages that are easy for everyone to read and follow. It also helps viewers who come at your materials from a platform other than your own, and helps your pages achieve true independence from any one platform or browser. Why limit your options?

If several pages on your site use the same basic HTML, create a single template for those pages. Test the template with as many browsers as you can find. After you're sure the template is browser-independent, use it to create other pages. This practice helps you ensure that every page looks good, regardless of which browser a visitor may be using, and puts you on your way to real HTML enlightenment.

Think Evolution, Not Revolution

Over time, Web pages change and grow. Keep a fresh eye on your work, and keep recruiting fresh eyes from the ranks of those who haven't seen your work before, to avoid what we call "organic acceptance."

This concept is best explained by the analogy of your face and the mirror: You see it every day; you know it intimately, so you aren't as sensitive as someone else to the impact of changes over time. Then you see yourself on video, or in a photograph, or through the eyes of an old friend. At that point, changes obvious to the world are obvious to you as you exclaim, "I've gone completely gray!" or "My spare tire could mount on a semi!" or "Who the heck is *that?*"

As with the rest of life, changes to Web pages are usually evolutionary, not revolutionary. They proceed with small daily steps; big radical leaps are rare. Nevertheless, you must stay sensitive to the supporting infrastructure and readability of your content as pages evolve. Maybe the lack of on-screen links to each section of your Product Catalog didn't matter when you had only three products — but now that you have 25, it's a different story. You've probably heard the phrase "form follows function;" in Web terms, the structure of your site needs to follow changes in its content. If you regularly reevaluate your site's effectiveness at communicating its contents, you'll know when it's time to make changes, whether large or small.

At this point is where user feedback is crucial. If you don't get feedback through forms or other means of communication, go out and aggressively solicit info from your users. If you're not sure how you're doing, consider this: If you don't ask, how can you tell?

Navigating Your Wild and Woolly Web

Users who view the splendor of your site don't want to be told, "You can't get there from here." Aids to navigation are vital amenities on a quality Web site. In Chapter 7, for example, we introduce the concept of a *navigation bar* — a consistent graphical place to put buttons that help users get from A to B. By judicious use of links and careful observation of what constitutes a "screenful" of text, you can help your users minimize (or even avoid) scrolling. Text anchors make it easy to move to "previous" or "next" screens, as well as to "top," "index," and "bottom" in any document. It appears that easy to the user.

We believe pretty strongly in the *low scroll* rule: That is, users should have to scroll *no more than one* screen in either direction from a point of focus or entry without encountering a navigation aid to let them jump (not scroll) to the next point of interest.

We don't believe that navigation bars are required, nor that the names for controls should always be the same. However, we do believe that the more control you give users over their reading, the better they like it. The longer a document gets, the more important such controls become; they work best if they occur about every thirty lines in longer documents (or in a separate, always visible frame, if you use HTML frames).

Beat the Two-Dimensional Text Trap

Conditioned by centuries of printed material and the linear nature of books, our mind-sets can always use adjustment. The nonlinear potentials of hypermedia give the Web a new definition of what constitutes a document. Of course, the temptation is to pack your page full of these capabilities until it resembles a Pony Express dynamite shipment and gallops off in all directions at once. To avoid this situation, judge your hypermedia according to whether they add interest, expand on your content, or make a serious — and relevant — impact on the user. Within these constraints, this kind of material can vastly improve any user's experience of your site.

Stepping intelligently outside old-fashioned linear thinking can improve your users' experience of your site and make your information more accessible to your audience, which is why we encourage careful use of document indexes, cross references, links to related documents, and other tools to help users navigate within your site. Keep thinking about the impact of links as you look at other people's Web materials; it's the quickest way to shake free of the linear text trap. (The printing press was high-tech for its day, but that *was* 500 years ago!) If you're looking for a model for your site's behavior, don't think about your new trifold, four-color brochure, however eye-popping it may be; think about how your customer-service people interact with new customers on the telephone. (*What can I do to help you today?*)

Overcome Inertia through Constant Vigilance

Finally, when dealing with your Web materials post-publication, remember that goofing off after finishing a big job is only human. Maintenance may not be nearly as heroic, inspiring, or remarkable as creation; however, it represents most of the activity that's needed to keep a living document alive and well. Sites that aren't maintained often become ghost sites; users stop visiting when developers stop working on them. Never fear — a little work and attention to detail keeps the dust off of your pages.

If you start with something valuable and keep adding value, a site appreciates over time. Start with something valuable and leave it alone, and it soon becomes stale and loses value. Consider your site from the viewpoint of a master aircraft mechanic: Correct maintenance is a real, vital, and ongoing accomplishment, without which you risk a crash. A Web site, as a vehicle for important information, deserves the same regular attention; the work of maintaining it requires discipline and respect.

Keeping up with constant change translates into creating (and adhering to) a regular maintenance schedule. Make it somebody's job to spend time on a site regularly, and check to make sure the job's getting done. If someone is set to handle regular site updates, changes, and improvements, they should start flogging other participants to give them things to do when scheduled site maintenance rolls around. The next thing you know, everybody's involved in keeping information fresh — just as they should be. This activity keeps your visitors coming back for more!

Chapter 21

Ten Design Desiderata

*I*t's a familiar refrain from other chapters: Before you can design and build a Web site that works, you have to know exactly what you want to communicate (the content) and to whom (the audience). Remember that content is your site's king, queen, and big kahuna. To help keep the crown steady, we'd like to suggest a bevy of design desiderata to consider when you lay out your Web pages. Consider the principles in this chapter as Big Kahuna Content's court and cabinet: As long as they play a supporting, not a starring, role, they add value and appeal without getting you into too much trouble.

Create Standard Layout Elements

As you build or renovate a site, focus your design efforts on a common layout for your pages. The elements of a common layout may include text links, graphical controls, or a combination of both. In addition, your layout may contain frequently used icons (or other graphical conventions such as logos) and styles for page headings and footers. Ambitious designers may have to build style sheets to keep everything straight; regardless of complexity, governing layout and typography for your site's pages is up to you. If you choose to use HTML frames, establish a set of framing rules to lay out common page areas and elements.

Headings can incorporate text, navigation, graphics, and other information that works best if it's consistent on all pages. Footers should include contact information and a unique URL for reference, preceded by a horizontal rule or graphical line (or packaged in their own compact frames).

Whatever your final layout looks like, make it as attractive as you can (without making it distracting) and apply it consistently. From a user's point of view, such reassuring touches help create a welcome feeling of familiarity across your pages and make it easier to navigate around your site. For some solid examples of good-looking, consistent site layout, have a look at the family of CNET sites, including `www.cnet.com`, `http://home.cnet.com/webbuilding/0-3880.html`, and `www.news.com`.

Build a Graphical Vocabulary

Web sites speak in pictures partly because they save a lot of words. If you use graphics for navigation, keep icons or buttons small and simple. The smaller a graphic (in file size, not necessarily in number of pixels), the faster it downloads, which saves your users time on their way to your content.

Building a small, consistent set of graphical symbols (what we call a vocabulary) also improves browser efficiency: Most browsers cache graphics so they don't have to download them after they first appear in a particular session. Reusing an existing graphic rather than downloading a new one is much faster. An added benefit of keeping a graphics vocabulary small is that users can quickly become accustomed to your graphical conventions and don't have to work through making sense of a new set of graphics on each new page. Result: Content is easier to see.

Supply `alt="text"` definitions for graphical elements when you reference them. Doing so keeps users with character-mode browsers (or users who surf with graphics turned off) from being left in the lurch. Such graphical elements should be simple enough that a single word or short phrase can substitute for, yet still deliver, the same meaning and impact as the graphic itself does.

Use White Space

Although content may be the acknowledged potentate of Web pages, you can have too much of a good thing. Nothing obscures words like too many words. Even though limiting the scrolling a user has to do is laudable, don't muddle the text by eliminating headings and paragraph breaks; try dropping in a little empty space.

White space is the term used by page designers to describe the space on a page that's unoccupied by things such as graphics and text. Even if your background is navy blue, you'll still have "white" space (well, okay, blue space in this case). The human eyes need to rest now and then; a certain amount of white space is critical for your site to function well. In general, the more complex the images or content, the more positive the effect of white space on a page.

Be sure to give your content and images room to breathe by leaving at least 20 percent of any screen unoccupied. You can build white space into your documents by using alignment attributes to place your graphics, using headings to separate regions of text and graphics, or building a style sheet that controls line spacing and white space for all kinds of tags. Whatever method you use, give readers plenty of room to follow your lead through your pages!

Format for Impact

HTML includes a variety of character tags — whether descriptive (`<em>`, `<strong>`, `<cite>`, and so on) or physical (`<i>`, `<b>`, `<tt>`, and so on). These tools can give you ways to set particular words apart from the others in a sentence or paragraph. You can employ larger fonts and text styles to make your headings look different from ordinary text. When you use these controls, however, remember that emphasis and impact are relative terms. In fact, the less you use such tags, the more impact they have. In the wake of Cascading Style Sheets (CSS), we think working with style attributes may often make more sense than using character tags to achieve a consistent look throughout your site. However, the tags work well if you have a really unique-but-relevant item to include — say, a snippet of text that mimics a newspaper:

```
900 Bags of T. Rex Chow Missing from Local Warehouse
City officials were stunned Tuesday to find the Hungry Dino
          Pet Food Store's main distribution center opened
          like a sardine can . . .Several cars were damaged
          in the incident.
```

Character handling can be a nice effect — whether descriptive, stylistic, or physical — but overusing it can blunt any document's overall impact. Be sure to use such controls only where impact is critical. Too much **boldface**, *italicized*, or underlined text is hard to read on a computer screen. Be kind to your users (and their eyes) by limiting your use of character formatting. Keep It Simple, Sillyhead.

While you're deciding how to emphasize your chosen text elements, be aware that certain browsers provide wider options for descriptive tags than for physical tags, and that style definitions have the widest latitude of all. Physical tags are often associated with certain fonts (for example, monospaced Courier is typical for `<tt>`). Browsers often display descriptive tags (for example, `<b>`) the same way they display physical tags (for example, `<strong>`) — in fact, those two particular tags produce the same effect in most browsers: boldface text. Some browsers (especially the graphical ones) provide other options for representing descriptive tags — such as different fonts or text colors.

Style tags give designers complete control over text appearance and layout, but can be overridden by savvy users or may not be supported by older browsers. Bottom line: Consider which aspect of your text — appearance or emphasis — is more important to your message. If it's appearance, use a physical style; if it's emphasis, use a logical style or a style sheet.

Enhance (Don't Curb) Content with Graphics

If a picture is worth a thousand words, are a thousand words worth a picture? (All together, now: Which thousand words? Which picture?) When you combine text and graphics in your Web pages, emphasize the relationship between them. Graphics can be useful for diagramming complex ideas, representing physical objects or other tangible phenomena, and compressing large amounts of content into a small space. Text that surrounds an image needs to play off the image, to use it as a point of reference, and to refer back to key elements or components as they're discussed. Thus, the methods you use to identify graphical elements — such as labels and captions — are almost as important as the graphic itself. Careful integration of text and graphics enhances content. (Take another look at that "newspaper" snippet in the previous section. Imagine it illustrated with a simple graphic — say, a picture of the building with its roof opened like a can or a Volkswagen half squashed with a reptilian footprint on it . . .).

Graphics can pull double duty, both enhancing the look and feel of your page and adding significant content. Some graphics that work overtime to play both roles include navigational aids (such as buttons and arrows) as well as diagrams and charts. If you use a graphic to provide content as well as splash of color, include appropriate alternative text as well.

Rules for using graphics also apply to any other hypermedia on your Web pages. Beyond their novelty, effects such as sound (including music), animation, or video can deliver striking content. To create great impact without distraction, integrate them carefully — and sparingly — with your text.

The Web offers unprecedented expressive options — for example, educators have new ways to engage students' interest. Instead of using only text to explain, say, a leitmotif (a musical phrase with a specific referent), a teacher could define, and then discuss, a musical phrase from a symphony or string quartet as a leitmotif, setting up a hyperlink that plays the phrase on command. (A beginners' version could highlight the sequence of notes on a musical staff as the file plays.) Likewise, a discussion of film-editing techniques (such as dissolves) could include examples taken from the work of classic directors.

If you plan to quote the creative work of others in your Web site, make sure you know — and heed — any applicable copyright restrictions. Getting written permission is often a good idea. Just assuming you can use a creative work without asking is a bad idea.

Whatever materials appear in or through your Web pages should be solidly integrated and share a common focus. These characteristics apply as strongly to hypermedia as they do to text, but all of the Web's possibilities to enhance content should be fully exploited.

Make Effective Use of Hypermedia

The key ingredient in effective use of hypermedia (linked pages, graphics, and other Web elements) is relevance. How well does the linked document relate to the content on the page that links to it? If (for example) you make a link to the Dallas Cowboys Web page from a page about the Wild West because both mention cowboys, you'll lose your readers in a heartbeat. A link to a site about Buffalo Bill or Jesse James, on the other hand, is right on target. (Moral: Rein in those free associations, pardner.)

In addition to making effective hyperlinks, a Web designer must also understand the potential bottlenecks that some users face. Not all browsers come to a site with identical capabilities or settings. The more a user needs to interact with hypermedia to appreciate a page, the fewer users will be equipped to get the whole point.

Effective use of hypermedia, therefore, implies asking your users for informed consent before inflicting the whole cornucopia of effects on them. For graphics, this courtesy means preparing thumbnails of large images, labeling them with file sizes, and using the miniature on-screen versions as hyperlinks so users can request to download a full-sized image. Users who decide to pull down a full-color image of The Last Supper cannot complain when they already know it's a 1.2MB file that may take several minutes to download. By the same token, "decorating" your Web page by putting 2MB-worth of a photo-realistic T. Rex smack in the middle of every visitor's screen — without asking permission — means committing every visitor to a long wait, even those who merely wanted information. (Irritating? You ain't seen ferocious yet . . .).

This courtesy applies equally to sounds, video, and other kinds of hypermedia that travel (a) in very large files and (b) very slowly over phone lines. Remember to ask for informed consent from your users, and you can be sure that only those individuals who can stand the wait will be subjected to delivery delays.

Aid Navigation Wherever Possible

The Web can be a confusing place for new or infrequent visitors. The more you can do to help your users out, the more likely they are to return to your pages, time and time again. Put some steering gear on that Web page — outlines, tables of contents, indexes, or search engines — so your users can not only find their way around your materials, but also recognize your site as friendly territory.

Form Good Opinions

We think no Web site is complete without an interactive HTML form to ask users for their feedback. Feedback not only gives you a chance to see your work from somebody else's perspective, but also serves as a valuable source of input and ideas to enhance and improve your content. This practice is akin to asking for directions when you're lost. Remember, "Assuming isn't knowing; nothing beats knowing, and you can't know if you don't ask."

Know when to split

As pages get larger, or as your content grows oversized, you may come to a point where a single, long document functions better as a collection of smaller documents.

How do you decide when it's time to split things up? Weigh the convenience of a single page against the lengthy download that may tag along with it. A single, long document takes longer to download and read than any individual smaller one, but an individual document may have to be downloaded on the spot each time a user requests it. The question then becomes, "One long wait or several short ones?"

The answer lies in the content. If your document is something that's touched quickly and then exited immediately, delivering information in small chunks makes sense. The only people who suffer delays are those who choose to read many pages; in-and-outers don't have to wait long. If your document is something designed to be downloaded and perused in detail, keeping large amounts of information within a single document — and letting your readers know you've set it up that way — may make sense.

By using your materials frequently yourself (make sure you test them over a slow link as well as a fast one) and by asking users for feedback, you can strike a happy medium between these extremes. The happier the medium, the happier the users — and the more receptive they may be to your content.

Add value for value

Obtaining feedback from users is incredibly valuable and makes HTML forms all the more worthwhile. But you're missing half the benefit if it's good only for you; responding to that feedback in a visible, obvious way can make the experience as good for the respondents as it should be for you.

Publicly acknowledging feedback that causes change is a good idea, whether for reasons good or ill. On many sites (and maybe on yours, too), a "What's New" page that links to the home page is a good place to make such acknowledgments. We also believe in acknowledging strong opinions by e-mail or letter — this method is often a relatively flame-retardant way to let respondents know that you heard what they said and to thank them for their input.

If you cultivate your users as allies and confederates, they help improve and enhance your content. Such improvements, in turn, can lead to improved business or maybe just to improved communications. Either way, by giving valuable information and acknowledging the value of other people's contributions, you create a superior site. And the more superior sites exist, the greater the total value of the Web itself!

Chapter 22

Ten Ways to Kill Web Bugs

In This Chapter

▶ Avoiding markup and spelling faux pas

▶ Keeping those links hot and fresh

▶ Gathering beta testers to check, double-check, and triple-check your site

▶ Applying user feedback to keep your site bug free

*A*fter you put the finishing touches on a set of pages (but before you post them on the Web for the world to see) is the time to put them through their paces. Testing is the best way to control your content's quality. Thorough testing should include content review, a complete analysis of HTML syntax and semantics, checks on links, and a series of sanity checks to make doubly sure that what you built is what you really wanted. Read on for some gems of testing wisdom (torn from a wealth of Web adventures) — as we seek to rid your Web pages of bugs, errors, gaucheries, and lurking infelicities.

Make a List and Check It — Twice

Your design should include a road map that tells you what's where in every individual HTML document in your site, and the relationships among them. If you're unusually perceptive, you diligently kept this map up-to-date as you moved from design to implementation (and in our experience, things always change when you go down this path). If you're merely as smart as the rest of us, don't berate yourself — go forth and update thy map now. Be sure to include all intra- and inter-document links.

Such a road map can act as the foundation for a test plan. Yep, that's right — effective testing isn't random. Investigate and check every page and every link systematically. You want to make sure that everything works as you think it does — and that what you built has some relationship (however surprising) to what you designed. Your site's road map also defines your list of things to check; as you go through the testing process, you'll check it (at least) twice. (Red suit and reindeer harness optional.)

Master the Mechanics of Text

By the time any collection of Web pages comes together, you're typically looking at thousands of words, if not more. Yet many Web pages are published without even a cursory spell check, which is why we suggest — no, demand — that you include a spell check as a step in testing and checking your materials. (Okay, we don't have a gun to your head, but you *know* it's for your own good.) Many HTML development tools have built-in spell-check utilities. Even if you only use these tools occasionally and hack out the majority of your HTML by hand, take advantage of such HTML-aware checkers before posting your documents to the Web. (For a handy illustration of why this step matters, try keeping a log of the spelling and grammar errors you encounter during your Web travels. Be sure to include a note on how those gaffes reflect on the people who created the page.)

You can use your favorite word processor to spell check your pages. Before you check them, add HTML markup to your custom dictionary, and pretty soon, the spell-checker runs more smoothly — getting stuck only on URLs and other strange strings that occur from time to time in HTML files.

If you'd prefer a fashionably up-to-date approach, try one of the several HTML-based spell-checking services now available on the Web. We like the one at the Doctor HTML site, which you can find online at www2.imagiware.com/RxHTML/.

If Doctor HTML's spell-checker doesn't work for you, visit a search engine, such as www.yahoo.com, and use *web page spell check* as a search string. Or, in Yahoo!, you can choose the *Computers and Internet⇨Information and Documentation⇨Data Formats⇨HTML⇨Validation and Checkers* category to find a list of spell-check tools (as well as few other really cool testing and maintenance tools) made specifically for Web pages.

One way or another, persist until you root out all typos and misspellings. Your users, intent on your content, may not know to thank you for your impeccable use of language — but if they don't trip over any errors while exploring your work, they'll have a higher opinion of your pages (and of the pages' creator). Even if they don't know why. Call it stealth diplomacy.

Lack of Live Links — A Loathsome Legacy

In an unscientific and random sample we undertook as a spot check, users told us that their positive impressions of a particular site are proportional to how many working links they find there. The moral of this survey: Always check your links. This step is as true after you publish your pages as it is before they're open to the public. Nothing is more irritating to users than when a link to some Web resource on a page that they're dying to read produces the dreaded 404 Server not found error, instead of "the good stuff."

Link checks are as indispensable to page maintenance as they are to testing. If you're long on twenty-first-century street smarts, hire a robot to do the job for you: They work really long hours (no coffee breaks), don't charge much, and faithfully check every last link in your site (or beyond, if you let them).

We're rather fond of a robot named MOMspider, created by Roy Fielding of the W3C. Visit the MOMspider site at www.ics.uci.edu/WebSoft/ MOMspider. This spider takes a bit of work to use, but you can set it to check only local links, and it does a bang-up job of catching stale links before users do. If you don't like this tool, utilize a search engine and search for words such as *link check* or *robot*. You'll find lots to choose from! The best thing about robots is that you can schedule them to do their jobs at regular intervals: They always show up on time, always do a good job, and never complain (though we haven't yet found one that brings homemade cookies or remembers birthdays).

If a URL points to one page that immediately points to another, that doesn't mean you can leave that link alone. If your link-checking shows a pointer to a pointer, do yourself (and your users) a favor by updating the URL to point *directly* to the content's real location. You save users time, reduce bogus traffic on the Internet, and generate good cyberkarma.

If you must leave a URL active even after it has become passé, you can instruct newer browsers to jump straight from the old page to the new one by including the following HTML command in the old document's <head> section:

```
<meta http-equiv="refresh" content="0" url="newurlhere">
```

This nifty line of code tells a browser (if sufficiently new) that it should refresh the page. The delay before switching to the new page is specified by the value of the content attribute, and the destination URL by the value of the url= attribute. If you must build such a page, be sure to include a plain-vanilla link in its <body> section, too, so users with older browsers can follow the link manually, instead of automatically. Getting there may not be half the fun, but it's the whole objective.

Look for Trouble in All the Right Places

You and a limited group of users should test your site before you let the rest of the world know about it. This process is called *beta-testing*, and it's a bona fide, five-star *must* for a well-rounded Web site, especially if you're building it for business use. When the time comes to beta-test your site, bring in as rowdy and refractory a crowd as you can possibly find. If you have picky customers (or colleagues who are pushy, opinionated, or argumentative), be comforted to know that you have found a higher calling for them: Such people make ideal beta-testers — provided you can get them to cooperate.

Beta-testers use your pages in ways you never imagined possible. They interpret your content to mean things you never intended in a million years. They drive you crazy and crawl all over your cherished beliefs and principles. And they do all this before your users do! Trust us, it's a blessing in disguise.

These colleagues also find gotchas, big and small, that you never knew existed. They catch typos that word processors couldn't. They tell you things you left out and things that you should have omitted. They give you a fresh perspective on your Web pages, and they help you to see them from extreme points of view.

The results of all this suffering, believe it or not, are positive. Your pages emerge clearer, more direct, and more correct than they would have if you tried to test them by yourself. (If you don't believe us, of course, you *could* try skipping this step. And when real users start banging on your site, forgive us if we don't watch.)

Covering All the Bases

If you're an individual user with a simple home page or a collection of facts and figures about your private obsession, this particular step may not apply. But go ahead and read along anyway — it just might come in handy down the road.

If your pages express views and content that represent an organization, chances are oh, *about 100 percent* that you should subject your pages to some kind of peer-and-management review before publishing them to the world. In fact, we recommend that you build reviews into each step along the way as you build your site — starting by getting knowledgeable feedback on such ground-zero aspects as the overall design, writing copy for each page, and the final assembly of your pages into a functioning site. These reviews help you avoid potential stumbling blocks. If you have any doubts about copyright matters, references, logo usage, or other important details, you may want to get the legal department involved (if you don't have one, you may want to consider a little consulting investment).

Building a sign-off process into reviews so you can prove that responsible parties reviewed and approved your materials may be a good idea. We hope you don't have to be that formal about publishing your Web pages, but it's far, far better to be safe than sorry. (So is this process best called *covering the bases,* or covering, ah, something else? You decide.)

Use the Best Tools of the Testing Trade

When you grind through your completed Web pages, checking your links and your HTML, remember that automated help is available. If you visit the W3C HTML validator at `http://validator.w3.org`, you'll be well on your way to finding computerized assistance to make your HTML pure as air, clean as the driven snow, and standards-compliant as, ah, *really well-written HTML*. (Do we know how to mix a metaphor, or what?)

Likewise, investigating the Web spiders discussed earlier in the chapter is a good idea; use them regularly to check links on your pages. (Spiders? Ewww! Relax; it's another name for *robot*.) These faithful creatures tell you if something isn't current, so you know where to start looking for links that need fixing. While you're at it, make link-checking part of your maintenance routine. The most painless way is to schedule and use a spider at regular intervals! (Arachnophobia — what's that?)

Foster Feedback

Even after you publish your site, the testing isn't over. (Are you having flashbacks to high school and college yet? We know we are.) You may not think of user feedback as a form (or consequence) of testing, but it represents the best reality-check that your Web pages are ever likely to get, which is why doing everything you can — including offering prizes or other tangible inducements — to get users to fill out HTML forms on your Web site is a good idea.

This reality-check is also why reading *all* the feedback you get is even better. Go out and solicit as much as you can handle (don't worry; you'll soon have more). But the best idea of all is to carefully consider the feedback that you read and then implement the ideas that actually bid fair to improve your Web offerings.

Make the Most of Your Audience

Asking for feedback is an important step toward developing a relationship with your users. Even the most finicky and picky of users can be an incredible asset: Who better to pick over your newest pages and to point out those small, subtle errors or flaws that they revel in finding? Your pages will have contributed mightily to the advance of human society by actually finding a legitimate use for the universal human delight in nitpicking. And your users develop a real stake in boosting the success of your site. Working with your users can mean that some become more involved in your work, helping guide the content of your Web pages (if not the rest of your professional or obsessional life). Who could ask for more? Put it this way: You may yet find out, and it could be remarkably helpful.

Part VII
Appendixes

The 5th Wave   By Rich Tennant

IF BOB DYLAN HAD PURSUED A CAREER IN RESEARCH

"His text content is fantastic, but lose those harmonic WAV files."

In this part . . .

The appendixes in this part are multifarious and magnificent. In Appendix A, you find a concise overview of HTML 4.01 syntax and markup codes. Its worthy successor, Appendix B, provides a glossary to help explain and defuse all the items of techno-babble that we were unable to avoid throughout the rest of the book. Appendix C explores some powerful and useful HTML tools that we keep in our Webmaster's toolbox and present for your consideration. Finally, Appendix D closes the show by detailing all the keen programs and examples that appear on the CD-ROM that accompanies this book.

These appendixes are like the instructions that come with a Christmas bicycle: You don't always have to read them, but they're handy to keep around if you should ever need 'em! Just remember, when it comes to building your own Web pages, "some assembly is required!" Have fun!

Appendix A

HTML 4 Tags

• •

*K*eeping track of the bountiful bevy of HTML tags can often be tricky, even for experienced Webmasters. To make your HTML coding life a bit easier, we include Table A-1, which lists the following information:

✔ **Name:** The name of the tag.

✔ **Start tag and end tag syntax information:** If the tag is listed with the letter O, the start or end tag is optional. If the tag is listed with a F in the end tag column, the end tag is forbidden.

✔ **Empty:** If the tag is listed with the letter E, the tag is an empty tag and is forbidden to have an end tag.

✔ **Deprecated:** If the tag is listed with a D, then the tag has been deprecated — the tag will soon be omitted from future HTML specifications.

✔ **Description:** A description of the tag.

| Table A-1 | | | | HTML Tags | |
Name	*Start Tag*	*End Tag*	*Empty*	*Deprecated*	*Description*
a					Anchor
abbr					Abbreviated form (for example, WWW, HTTP)
acronym					Indicates an acronym
address					Information on author
applet				D	Java applet
area	F	E			Client-side image map area
b					Bold text style
base	F	E			Document base URI
basefont	F	E	D		Base font size

(continued)

Table A-1 *(continued)*

Name	Start Tag	End Tag	Empty	Deprecated	Description
bdo					I18N BiDi override
big					Large text style
blockquote					Long quotation
body	O	O			Document body
br		F	E		Forced line break
button					Push button
caption					Table caption
center				D	Shorthand for DIV align=center
cite					Citation
code					Computer code fragment
col		F	E		Table column
colgroup		O			Table column group
dd		O			Definition description
del					Deleted text
dfn					Instance definition
dir				D	Directory list
div					Generic language/style container
dl					Definition list
dt		O			Definition term
em					Emphasis
fieldset					Form control group
font				D	Local change to font
form					Interactive form
frame		F	E		Subwindow
frameset					Window subdivision

Name	Start Tag	End Tag	Empty	Deprecated	Description
h1					Heading 1
h2					Heading 2
h3					Heading 3
h4					Heading 4
h5					Heading 5
h6					Heading 6
head	O	O			Document head
hr		F	E		Horizontal rule
html	O	O			Document root element
i					Italic text style
iframe					Inline subwindow
img		F	E		Embedded image
input		F	E		Form control
ins					Inserted text
isindex		F	E	D	Single line prompt
kbd					Text to be entered by the user
label					Form field label text
legend					Fieldset legend
li		O			List item
link		F	E		A media-independent link
map					Client-side image map
menu				D	Menu list
meta		F	E		Generic meta-information
noframes					Alternate content container for non frame-based rendering

(continued)

Table A-1 *(continued)*

Name	Start Tag	End Tag	Empty	Deprecated	Description
noscript					Alternate content container for non script-based rendering
object					Generic embedded object
ol					Ordered list
optgroup					Option group
option		O			Selectable choice
p		O			Paragraph
param		F	E		Named property value
pre					Preformatted text
q					Short inline quotation
s				D	Strikethrough text style
samp					Sample program output, scripts, and so on
script					Script statements
select					Option selector
small					Small text style
span					Generic language/style container
strike				D	Strikethrough text
strong					Strong emphasis
style					Style info
sub					Subscript
sup					Superscript
table					Table
tbody	O	O			Table body
td		O			Table data cell

Name	Start Tag	End Tag	Empty	Deprecated	Description
textarea					Multi-line text field
tfoot		O			Table footer
th		O			Table header cell
thead		O			Table header
title					Document title
tr		O			Table row
tt					Teletype or mono-spaced text style
u				D	Underlined text style
ul					Unordered list
var					Instance of a variable or program argument

Appendix B

Glossary

● ●

absolute: When used to modify pathnames or URLs, a full and complete file specification (as opposed to a relative one). An absolute specification includes a host identifier, a complete volume, and path specification.

anchor: In HTML, an anchor is tagged text or a graphic element that acts as a link to another location inside or outside a given document, or an anchor may be a location in a document that acts as the destination for an incoming link. The latter definition is most commonly how we use it in this book.

animation: A computerized process of creating moving images by rapidly advancing from one still image to the next.

ASCII (American Standard Code for Information Interchange): A binary encoding method for character data that translates symbols, letters, and numbers into digital form.

attribute: In HTML tags, an attribute is a named characteristic associated with a specific tag. Some attributes are required, whereas others are optional. Some attributes also take values (if so, the syntax is `attribute="value"`) or not, depending on the particular tag and attribute involved. (Chapter 6 provides tag information, including attributes, in alphabetical order).

bandwidth: Technically, bandwidth is the range of electrical frequencies a device can handle; more often, bandwidth is used as a measure of a communication technology's carrying capacity.

bookmark: A reference from a saved list of URLs kept by the Netscape Web browser. Bookmarks allow quick loading of a Web site without retyping the URL. Bookmarks work the same as Microsoft Internet Explorer Favorites.

browser: A Web access program that can request HTML documents from Web servers and render such documents on a user's display device. See also *client*.

bugs: Small, verminous creatures that sometimes show up in software in the form of major or minor errors, mistakes, and gotchas. Bugs got their name from insects found in antiquated tube-based computers of the late 1950s and early 1960s that were attracted to the glow of the filament in a tube.

C: A programming language developed at AT&T Bell Laboratories, C remains the implementation language for UNIX and the UNIX programmer's language of choice.

cache: When used in reference to Web pages, cache is a process performed by a computer system that stores frequently accessed Web pages in memory so the computer doesn't have to reload the page every time you visit it.

case sensitive: Means that the way you type computer input is significant; for instance, HTML tags can be typed in any mixture of upper- and lowercase, but because HTML character entities are case sensitive, you must type the characters exactly as reproduced in this book. However, to comply with the XHTML specification, we suggest you write all your tags in lowercase only.

CERN (Conseil Européen pour la Recherche Nucléaire): Agency that established the High-Energy Physics Laboratory in Geneva, Switzerland, now known as the birthplace of the World Wide Web. CERN is commonly used as a name for the laboratory itself.

character entity: A way of reproducing strange and wonderful characters within HTML, character entities take the form `&string;` where the ampersand (&) and semicolon are mandatory metacharacters, and `string` names the character to be reproduced in the browser. Because character entities are case sensitive, the string between the ampersand and the semicolon must be reproduced exactly as written in Chapter 7 of this book.

clickable map: An image in an HTML file that offers graphical Web navigation. The file contains linked regions that point to specific URLs after a user clicks them.

client: The end-user side of the client/server arrangement; typically, "client" refers to a consumer (rather than a provider) of network services; a Web browser is therefore a client program that talks to Web servers.

client/server: A computing model that divides computing into two separate roles, usually connected by a network. The client works on the end-user's side of the connection and manages user interaction and display (input, output, and related processing); the server works elsewhere on the network and manages data-intensive or shared-processing activities, such as serving up the collections of documents and programs that a Web server typically manages.

client-side image map: The same as a server-side image map, except that the hot-spot definitions are stored within the HTML document on the client side, rather than in a map file stored on the server.

common controls: For designing HTML documents, most experts recommend using a set of consistent navigation controls throughout a document (or collection of documents) to provide a consistent frame of reference for document navigation.

Common Gateway Interface (CGI): The specification that governs how Web browsers communicate with and request services from Web servers; also the format and syntax for passing information from browsers to servers via HTML forms or document-based queries. The current version of CGI is 1.1.

content: For HTML, content is its raison d'être; although form is important, content is why users access Web documents and why they come back for more.

convention: An agreed-upon set of rules and approaches that allows systems to communicate with one another and work together.

CSS1 (Cascading Style Sheets Level 1): A style sheet standard that lets authors attach preferred style sheets to Web documents, while allowing readers to associate their own personal styles to those same documents.

CSS2 (Cascading Style Sheets Level 2): The second version of CSS. See also _CSS1 (Cascading Style Sheets Level 1)._

default: In general computer-speak, a selection made automatically in a program if the user specifies no explicit selection. For HTML, the default is the value assigned to an attribute if none is supplied.

deprecated: The term we use to earmark an HTML tag or attribute that is to be left for dead by future versions of HTML.

directory path: Device and directory names needed to locate a particular file in a given file system; for HTML, UNIX-style directory paths usually apply.

document: The basic unit of HTML information, a document refers to the entire contents of any single HTML file. Because this definition doesn't always correspond to normal notions of a document, we refer to what can formally be called HTML documents more or less interchangeably with Web pages, which is how browsers render such documents for display.

document headings: The class of HTML tags that we refer to as ⟨h*⟩. Document headings allow authors to insert headings of various sizes and weights (from one to six) to add structure to a document's content. As structural elements, headings identify the beginning of a new concept or idea.

document reference: In HTML, the document reference is used to indicate that the destination of a link is in another document.

document type declaration: Tells the processor where to locate the DTD and contains declarations for the particular document.

DoD (Department of Defense): The folks who paid the bills for and operated the earliest versions of the Internet, and one of the more prominent institutions to adopt SGML.

DOS (Disk Operating System): The underlying control program used to make some Intel-based PCs run. MS-DOS by Microsoft is the most widely used implementation of DOS and provides the scaffolding atop which its 3.x versions of Windows run. See also *operating system.*

DTD (Document Type Definition): A formal SGML specification for a document, a DTD lays out the structural elements and markup definitions to be used to create instances of documents.

element: A section of a document defined by a start- and end-tag or an empty tag.

e-mail: An abbreviation for electronic mail, e-mail is the preferred method for exchanging information between users on the Internet (and other networked systems).

empty tag: An HTML tag that does not require the use of a closing tag. In fact, the use of a closing tag in empty tags is forbidden.

entity: A character string that represents another string of characters.

error message: Information delivered by a program to a user, usually to inform him or her that the process hasn't worked properly, if at all. Error messages are an ill-appreciated art form and contain some of the funniest and most opaque language we've ever seen (also, the most tragic for their unfortunate recipients).

external style sheet: A style sheet that resides outside of the Web document in a separate, external file.

footer: The concluding part of an HTML document, the footer should contain contact, version, date, and attribution information to help identify a document and its authors. Most people use the `<address>` . . . `</address>` tag pair to identify this information.

forms: In HTML, forms are built on special markup that lets browsers solicit data from users and then deliver that data to specially designated input-handling programs on a Web server. Briefly, forms provide a mechanism to let users interact with servers on the Web.

front end: In the client/server model, the front end refers to the client side; the front end is where the user views and interacts with information from a server; for the Web, browsers provide the front end that communicates with Web servers on the back end.

FTP (File Transfer Protocol): An Internet file transfer service based on the TCP/IP protocols, FTP provides a way to copy files to and from FTP servers elsewhere on a network.

GIF (Graphic Interchange Format): One of a set of commonly used graphics formats within Web documents, because of its compressed format and compact nature.

graphics: In HTML documents, graphics are files that belong to one of a restricted family of types (usually .GIF or .JPG) that are referenced via URLs for inline display on Web pages.

GUI (Graphical User Interface): Pronounced "gooey," GUIs make graphical Web browsers possible; they create a visually oriented interface that makes it easy for users to interact with computerized information of all kinds.

heading: For HTML, a heading is a markup tag used to add document structure. Sometimes the term refers to the initial portion of an HTML document between the `<head>` . . . `</head>` tags, where titles and context definitions are commonly supplied.

helper applications: Today, browsers can display multiple graphics files (and sometimes other kinds of data); sometimes, browsers must pass particular files — for instance, motion picture or sound files — over to other applications that know how to render the data they contain. Such programs are called helper applications because they help the browser deliver Web information to users.

hexadecimal: A numbering system composed of six letters and ten numbers that is used to condense binary numbers. In HTML, hexadecimal numbering is used with tags and their attributes to denote what colors should comprise backgrounds and other elements in a Web page.

hierarchical structure: A way of organizing Web pages using links that make some pages subordinate to others. (See also *tree structured* for another description of this kind of organization.)

hot list: A Web page that consists of a series of links to other pages, usually annotated with information about what's available on each link. Hot lists act like switchboards to content information and are usually organized around a particular topic or area of interest. Also called jump pages.

HTML (Hypertext Markup Language): The SGML-derived markup language used to create Web pages. Not quite a programming language, HTML nevertheless provides a rich lexicon and syntax for designing and creating useful hypertext documents for the Web.

HTTP (Hypertext Transfer Protocol): The Internet protocol used to manage communication between Web clients (browsers) and servers.

httpd (http daemon): The name of the collection of programs that runs on a Web server to provide Web services. In UNIX-speak, a daemon is a program that runs all the time, listening for service requests of a particular type; thus, an httpd is a program that runs all the time on a Web server, ready to field and handle Web service requests.

hyperlink: A shorthand term for hypertext link. (See also *hypertext link*.)

hypermedia: Any of a variety of computer media — including text, graphics, video, sound, and so on — available through hypertext links on the Web.

hypertext: A method of organizing text, graphics, and other kinds of data for computer use that lets individual data elements point to one another; a non-linear method of organizing information, especially text.

hypertext link: In HTML, a hypertext link is defined by special markup that creates a user-selectable document element that can be selected to change the user's focus from one document (or part of a document) to another.

image map: A synonym for clickable image, which refers to an overlaid collection of pixel coordinates for a graphic that can be used to locate a user's selection of a region on a graphic, in turn used to select a related hypertext link for further Web navigation.

inline element: Any element that controls presentation on an element-by-element basis, and an inline element does not denote structure. In other words, it's a text element, for example the <b> . . . </b> tag pair is an inline element.

internal anchor: A type of link that connects within the same document.

input-handling program: For Web services, a program that runs on a Web server designated by the action attribute of an HTML <form> tag; its job is to field, interpret, and respond to user input from a browser, typically by custom-building an HTML document in response to some user request.

internal style sheet: A style sheet that resides inside of the Web document in which you're working.

Internet: A worldwide collection of networks that began with technology and equipment funded by the U.S. Department of Defense in the 1970s. Today, it links users in nearly every country, speaking nearly every known language.

ISP (Internet Service Provider): An organization that provides individuals or other organizations with access to the Internet, usually for a fee. ISPs usually offer a variety of communications options for their customers, ranging from analog telephone lines, to a variety of higher-bandwidth leased lines, to ISDN and other digital communications services.

IP (Internet Protocol): IP is the specific networking protocol of the same name used to tie computers together over the Internet; IP is also used as a synonym for the whole TCP/IP protocol suite. See also *TCP/IP*.

ISO (International Organization of Standardization): The granddaddy of standards organizations worldwide, the ISO is made up of standards bodies from countries all over the world. Most important communications and computing standards — such as the telecommunications and character code standards mentioned in this book — are the subject of ISO standards.

Java: An object-oriented, platform-independent, secure, and compact programming language designed for Web application deployment. Most system vendors support Java, which was created by Sun Microsystems.

JPEG (or JPG): JPEG stands for Joint Photographic Experts' Group; an industry association that defined a highly compressible format for images designed for complex color still images (such as photographs). JPEG files take the extension .JPG. Today, .JPG is one graphics format of choice for Web use, particularly for complex images.

layout: The overall arrangement of the elements in a document.

linear text: Shorthand for old-fashioned documents that work like this book: by placing one page after the other, ad infinitum, in a straight line. Even though such books have indexes, pointers, cross-references, and other attempts to add linkage, such devices can be employed only by manipulating the physical book (rather than by clicking your mouse).

link: For HTML, a link is a pointer in one part of a document that can transport users to another part of the same document, or to another document entirely. This capability puts the "hyper" into hypertext. In other words, a link is a one-to-one relationship/association between two concepts or ideas.

list element: An item in an HTML list structure tagged with <li> (list item) tag.

list tags: HTML tags for a variety of list styles, including ordered lists `<ol>`, unordered lists `<ul>`, menus `<menu>`, glossary lists `<dl>`, or directory lists `<dir>`.

Lynx: A widely used UNIX-based character-mode Web browser, useful for checking a Web page before "going live" with it.

Macintosh: A type of PC created by Apple Computer in 1984 that first commercially introduced the graphical user interface (GUI), complete with a mouse, icons, and windows. Microsoft Windows uses design elements similar to those of the Macintosh operating system. The Mac operating system is the most popular alternative to Windows.

maintenance: The process of regularly inspecting, testing, and updating the contents of Web pages; also, an attitude that such activities are both inevitable and advisable.

map file: Pixel coordinates that correspond to the boundaries of regions that users may select when using a graphic for Web navigation. This file must be created using a graphics program to determine regions and their boundaries, and then stored on the Web server that provides the coordinate translation and URL selection services.

markup: A way of embedding special characters (metacharacters) within a text file that instructs a computer program how to handle the file's contents.

markup language: A formal set of special characters and related capabilities used to define a specific method for handling the display of files that include markup; HTML is a markup language, which is a subset of SGML, used to design and create Web pages.

MIME (Multipurpose Internet Mail Extensions): HTTP communications of Web information over the Internet rely on a special variant of MIME formats to convey Web documents and related files between servers and users. The same technology is used to convey attached files with e-mail messages.

modem: An acronym for modulator/demodulator, a modem is a piece of hardware that converts between analog forms for voice and data used in the telephone system and digital forms used in computers. In other words, a modem lets your computer communicate using the telephone system.

Mosaic: A powerful, graphical Web browser originally developed at NCSA, now widely licensed and used in several browser implementations.

MPEG or MPG: An acronym for Motion Picture Experts' Group, .MPEG is a highly compressed format designed for moving pictures or other multiframe-per-second media (such as video). .MPEG not only provides high compression ratios (up to 200 to 1), but it also updates only elements that have changed on-screen from one frame to the next, making it extraordinarily efficient. .MPEG is the file extension that denotes files using this format, but .MPG is the three-letter equivalent used on DOS and Windows 3.x systems (which can't handle four-letter file extensions).

multimedia: A method of combining text, sound, graphics, and full-motion or animated video within a single compound computer document.

navigation: In the context of the Web, navigation refers to the use of hyperlinks to move within or between HTML documents and other Web-accessible resources.

navigation bar: A way of arranging a series of hypertext links on a single line of a Web page to provide a set of navigation controls for an HTML document or a set of HTML documents.

NCSA (National Center for Supercomputing Applications): A research unit of the University of Illinois at Urbana, where the original Mosaic browser was built and where NCSA httpd code is maintained and distributed.

nesting: In computer terms, one structure that occurs within another is said to be nested; in HTML, nesting happens most commonly with list structures that may be freely nested within one another, regardless of type.

numeric entity: A special markup element that reproduces a particular character from the ISO-Latin-1 character set. A numeric entity takes the form &#nnn; where nnn is the one-, two- or three-digit numeric code that corresponds to a particular character. (Chapter 7 contains a complete list of these codes.)

online: A term that indicates information, activity, or communications located on or taking place in, an electronic, networked computing environment (such as the Internet). The opposite of online is offline, which is what your computer is as soon as you disconnect from the Internet.

operating system: The underlying control program on a computer that makes the hardware run and supports the execution of one or more applications. DOS, Windows, UNIX, and OS/2 are all examples of operating systems.

pages: The generic term for the HTML documents that Web users view on their browsers.

PDF (Portable Document Format): The rich, typographically correct document format of Adobe, used to provide multiplatform document access through its Acrobat software as a more powerful alternative to HTML.

Perl: A powerful, compact programming language that draws from languages such as C, Pascal, sed, awk, and BASIC; Perl is the language of choice for CGI programs, partly because of its portability and the many platforms it currently supports, and partly because of its ability to exploit operating system services quickly and easily.

physical character tags: Any of a series of HTML markup tags that specifically control character styles — bold (<b>) and italic (<i>) — or typeface (<tt>) for typewriter font.

plug in: Hardware or software added to a system that adds a specific feature such as plug-ins that allow Netscape Navigator to play video.

relative: When applied to URLs, a relative address provides an abbreviated document address that may be combined with the <base> element to create a complete address or is the complete address for a local file found in the same directory

resource: Any HTML document, capability, or other item or service available via the Web. URLs point to resources.

robot: A special Web-traveling program that wanders widely, following and recording URLs and related titles for future reference in search engines.

screen: The glowing part on the front of your computer monitor where you see the Web do its thing (and anything else your computer may like to show you).

scripting language: A special kind of programming language that a computer reads and executes at the same time (which means that the computer figures out what to do with the language when it appears in a document or at the time that it's used. JavaScript is a common scripting language associated with Web use).

search engine: A special Web program that searches the contents of a database of available Web pages and other resources to provide information that relates to specific topics or keywords, which a user supplies.

search tools: Any of a number of programs (see Chapter 16) that can permit HTML documents to become searchable, using the <isindex> tag to inform the browser of the need for a search window, and behind-the-scenes indexing and anchoring schemes to let users locate particular sections of or items within a document.

server: A computer on a network whose job is to listen for particular service requests and to respond to those that it knows how to satisfy.

SGML (Standard Generalized Markup Language): An ISO standard document definition, specification, and creation mechanism that makes platform and display differences across multiple computers irrelevant to the delivery and rendering of documents.

shareware: Software, available by various means, that users can run for free for a trial period. After that trial period expires, users must register and purchase the software, or they must discontinue its use.

specification: A formal document that describes the capabilities, functions, and interfaces for a specific piece of software, a markup language, or a communications protocol.

spider: A Web-traversing program that tirelessly investigates Web pages and their links, while storing information about its travels for inclusion in the databases typically used by search engines. Also called Web spider and Webcrawler.

style sheet: A file that holds the layout settings for a certain category of a document. Style sheets, like templates, contain settings for headers and footers, tabs, margins, fonts, columns, and more.

superstructure: In HTML documents, superstructure refers to the layout and navigational elements used to create a consistent look and feel for Web pages belonging to a document set.

syntax: Literally, the formal rules for how to speak. But in this book, we use syntax to describe the rules that govern how HTML markup looks and behaves within HTML documents. The real syntax definition for HTML comes from the SGML Document Type Definition (DTD).

syntax checker: A program that checks a particular HTML document's markup against the rules that govern its use; a recommended part of the testing regimen for all HTML documents.

tag: The formal name for a piece of HTML markup that signals a command of sorts, usually enclosed in angle brackets ($<$ $>$).

TCP/IP (Transmission Control Protocol/Internet Protocol): The name for the suite of protocols and services used to manage network communications and applications over the Internet. TCP, a reliable, connection-oriented protocol, usually guarantees delivery across a network; IP is the specific networking protocol that ties computers together over the Internet. (IP also serves as a synonym for the whole TCP/IP protocol suite.)

Telnet: The Internet protocol and service that lets you take a smart computer (your own, probably) and make it emulate a dumb terminal over the network. Briefly, Telnet is a way of running programs and using capabilities on other computers across the Internet.

template: Literally, a model to imitate, we use the term template in this book to describe the skeleton of a Web page, including the HTML for its heading and footer, and a consistent layout and set of navigation elements.

test plan: The series of steps and elements to be followed in conducting a formal test of software or other computerized systems; we strongly recommend that you write — and use — a test plan as a part of your Web publication process.

text controls: Any of a number of HTML tags, including both physical and logical markup, text controls provide a method of managing the way that text appears within an HTML document.

thumbnail: A miniature rendering of a graphical image, used as a link to the full-size version.

title: The text supplied to a Web page's title bar when displayed, used as data in many Web search engines.

tree structure(d) (See also *hierarchical structure***):** Computer scientists like to think of hierarchies in graphical terms, which makes them look like upside-down trees (single root at the top, multiple branches below). File systems and genealogies are examples of tree-structured organizations that we all know, but they abound in the computer world. This structure also works well for certain Web document sets, especially larger, more complex ones.

UNIX: The operating system of choice for the Internet community at large and the Web community, too, UNIX offers the broadest range of tools, utilities, and programming libraries for Web server use.

URI (Uniform Resource Identifier): Any of a class of objects that identify resources available to the Web.

URL (Uniform Resource Locator): The primary naming scheme used to identify Web resources, URLs define the protocols to use, the domain name of the Web server where a resource resides, the port address to use for communication, and a directory path to access named Web files or resources.

URL-encoded text: A method for passing information requests and URL specification to Web servers from browsers, URL encoding replaces spaces with plus signs (+) and substitutes special hex codes for a range of otherwise unreproducible characters. This method is used to pass document queries from browsers to servers (for the details, please consult Chapter 12).

Usenet: An Internet protocol and service that provides access to a vast array of named newsgroups, where users congregate to exchange information and materials related to specific topics or concerns.

valid: Code that follows all the syntax rules defined in a document type definition, allowing the document to pass through a validator program with no errors.

WAIS (Wide-Area Information Service): A collection of programs that implement a specific protocol for information retrieval, able to index large-scale collections of data round the Internet. WAIS provides content-oriented query services to WAIS clients and is one of the more powerful Internet search tools available.

Web: Also called the World Wide Web, WWW, or W3. The complete collection of all Web servers available on the Internet, which comes as close to containing the "sum of human knowledge" as anything we've ever seen.

Web pages: Synonym for HTML documents, we use Web pages in this book to refer to sets of related, interlinked HTML documents, usually produced by a single author or organization.

Web server: A computer, usually on the Internet, that plays host to httpd and related Web-service software.

Web site: An addressed location, usually on the Internet, that provides access to the set of Web pages that correspond to the URL for a given site; thus a Web site consists of a Web server and a named collection of Web documents, both accessible through a single URL.

well-formed document: An HTML document that adheres to the rules that make it easy for a computer to interpret.

white space: The "breathing room" on a page, white space refers to parts of a display or document unoccupied by text or other visual elements. A certain amount of white space is essential to make documents attractive and readable.

WYSIWYG (What You See Is What You Get): A term used to describe text editors or other layout tools (such as HTML authoring tools) that attempt to show their users on-screen what final, finished documents will look like.

XHTML (Extensible Hypertext Markup Language): The reformulation of HTML 4.0 as an application of XML 1.0.

XML (Extensible Markup Language): A system for defining, validating, and sharing document formats.

Appendix C

Tools of the Trade

● ●

In This Appendix

▶ Finding an HTML tool for every platform

▶ Identifying exactly the right HTML editor

▶ Authoring systems for the Web

▶ Using non-HTML tools for HTML purposes

● ●

*S*tone Age HTML was created using only simple text editors, with each and every tag composed by hand. Today, hand-coding HTML is no longer the only way to do it — although some authors still like to boast that they only hand-code. The latest generation of HTML editors declares that you can "build Web pages without knowing HTML." Amazing . . . or maybe not.

HTML editors are intended to make Web page creation easier, but editors that claim to do "all the work for you" make us a little nervous. Imagine that someone gives you a word processor that claims to know English grammar and writes your documents for you. You wouldn't expect that word processor to write the way you prefer, and you wouldn't stake your reputation on its output without checking and tweaking the results. (We know our humble editors sometimes cringe at the suggestions made by the Microsoft Word grammar checker.) You should be just as demanding, careful, and skeptical about your HTML authoring program as your word processor. Fortunately for you, we're demanding, careful, and skeptical people, too!

Although an HTML editor may make creating your Web pages easier, that doesn't mean it's the only tool you need to publish and maintain your Web site. Nope, one tool just won't do the trick. Instead, you need an entire collection — fondly referred to in the "biz" as a Webmaster's toolbox. In addition to your HTML editor, you need an FTP tool to upload your files to a Web server, as well as validation and maintenance tools to help you check your pages twice and keep them ship-shape. This appendix reviews and recommends the latest HTML authoring tools — as well as other tools you'll find in any professional Webmaster's well-stocked toolbox. You may be surprised to find that some of these tools may already be on your system quietly waiting to help you create stupendous Web pages.

Why you need to know HTML

You have a boatload of reasons why you need to know HTML, despite what any HTML-editor marketing gadfly may tell you. We can write an entire book about this, but never mind. Here's a brief rundown of our arguments instead:

✔ You must know what HTML can and can't do. HTML has many capabilities, but just as many limitations. If you don't know HTML, you won't be completely aware of either side of this puzzle. For instance, even with the latest HTML 4 markup, you can't be sure that a complicated table, image, or text format will look exactly as you expect it to. You must contend with many variables — different browser types and versions, user preferences, and more. On the flip side, if your editor doesn't support the latest HTML attributes, you won't know anything about them, much less be able to use them in your pages. Generally, ignorance is a bad thing. This statement is doubly true for HTML.

✔ You need to know HTML to identify problems and fix them. To figure out what's wrong with a page, you must know what's right. Your pages may look great in an editor or even in your browser of choice, but chances are they won't always be that way. Broken links, corrupted files, and new tags and interpretations can all change the way HTML looks. If you can't identify errors or changes because you can't recognize them for what they are, you won't be able to troubleshoot your pages without the help of a professional, and we don't come cheap (but we can be had!).

✔ You must know HTML to know what tags to use. What's the difference between `<strong>` and `<b>`? The tags look the same, but one is logical and the other is physical. One conveys meaning whereas the other creates only a textual effect. If you don't know HTML, you simply see boldface text. Another more extreme example is using `<pre>` to create columnar data instead of the `<table>` tag because you don't know about table markup. Although you can build a page in a variety of ways, usually there's only one best way. If you know HTML, you can figure out the best way to meet your needs.

✔ You need to know HTML to implement the latest cool stuff. That HTML editor you invested so much time and money in may not support frames, but what if you want frames on your pages? If you know HTML, the solution is simple: Dust off your text editor and code the frames by hand. If you don't know HTML, you must wait until a new version of the editor — presumably, one that supports frames — is released. In short, if you don't know the HTML tags, your pages are limited to the ones that your editor supports.

We know that you bought *HTML 4 For Dummies*, 3rd Edition, because you're interested in learning HTML and therefore won't fall prey to the attractive promises of the many editors out there and give up learning HTML because you think you can skip it. Take it from us: You need to know HTML, even if your editor does 99 percent of the work.

We told you what kind of tools you need, and in this chapter, we recommend some of our favorites. Until you see a good toolbox in action, you can't truly understand how all these products can work together to create and maintain HTML pages. We devote the remaining sections of the chapter to a good, hard look at the different Webmaster tools — editors, FTP tools, and maintenance tools — organized by type. The first of those sections — HTML Editors — is further divided by platform — Windows, Mac, and UNIX — and for each platform, we list the best tool, the most popular tool, and a good inexpensive — m'kay cheap — tool. The remaining sections just list quality tools because many are available on multiple platforms or are Web-based. So roll up those virtual sleeves and get ready to build your very own Webmaster's toolbox.

Keep in mind that shareware editors aren't as multifunctional as those that cost real money (as opposed to Monopoly money — kidding). If you write a lot of HTML and manage a large site (or more than one site), you may need to invest in an editor that can handle many different tasks. Most of the major software players, including companies such as Macromedia, Adobe Systems, Symantec Corp., and Microsoft, have jumped into the HTML editor fray.

Making an HTML Editor Work for You

Although this book explains how to create and maintain HTML pages with nothing more complicated than a pocketknife and a ball of string, we don't think you should snub all HTML editors. But we do want you to understand that the editors are just tools, and like every other tool you use, HTML editors are no substitute for knowledge. An HTML editor is only a helping hand when you apply what you know. Because HTML editors seem to have multiplied as quickly as rabbits, here are a few tips on how to locate and choose a good one.

At the very least, an HTML editor needs to

- Be easy to understand and use.
- Accurately preview HTML without using an external browser.
- Comply with HTML 4.
- Upgrade as HTML changes.
- Support image map creation.
- Check local links for accuracy.
- Support HTML validation and spell checking.
- Enable you to see and tweak your HTML code directly.

An exceptional HTML editor also:

- Provides site map information.
- Provides pixel-level control over object and text placement.
- Supports style sheet creation.

✔ Supports the Extensible Markup Language (XML).

✔ Accommodates Common Gateway Interface (CGI) scripts, Java applets, and scripting.

Keep in mind that two different kinds of HTML editors exist: helpers and WYSIWYG editors. An HTML helper does exactly what it sounds like: It helps you create HTML; it doesn't do all the work for you. Usually, a helper application displays "raw" HTML — tags and all (shocking though this may seem) — and such tools often color tags to help you differentiate them from your content. Helpers usually include an HTML-aware spell checker that knows your tags aren't just misspelled words, and helpers also incorporate other functionality to make HTML development easier and more fun. In our opinion, no Webmaster's toolbox is complete without a good HTML helper.

WYSIWYG stands for "What You See Is What You Get" and editors that fall into this category usually create HTML for you and hide its R-rated nakedness from you along the way. These tools look much like word processors or page layout programs and are designed to do quite a bit of the work for you. Although WYSIWYG editors can make your life easier and can save you from hours of endless coding — after all, you do have a life, right? — once again, we stress that you don't want to let this kind of editor substitute for your own know-how. Instead, use WYSIWYG editors for initial design work on your pages — with a WYSIWYG editor you can create a complex table in under a minute flat — and use your helper to refine and tweak your HTML code directly.

Often the best, most popular, and least expensive HTML editor for a particular platform is neither helpers nor editors but may be a combination of the two. As we review our selections for each platform in this category, note that both kinds of editors may be listed.

Although we believe that the different tools we list here are of high quality and are part of a many Webmaster's toolboxes, we do know that our opinions and needs may not match yours exactly — no, as hard as we try, we can't read your mind (yet). If you find yourself still looking for bliss, you can find more information on the latest and greatest Web page development tools on many Web sites. Our favorite is TUCOWS — The Ultimate Collection of Winsock Software — at www.tucows.com. The developers of the TUCOWS site review all the tools they list, and if a tool isn't up to snuff, it doesn't get listed; it's as simple as that. TUCOWS has been around for a long time — in Web years that is — and we've never known it to lead us astray.

Windows Web authoring systems

It seems as if every programmer and company is trying to produce a better mousetrap for Windows Web authoring. Some of the systems we surveyed appear to be well constructed and low on bugs, but we think that it's more fun to cover the cheesy, buggy ones instead. (If you believe that, we have a deal for you on some swampland in . . . never mind.) We won't waste your time or ours by discussing anything but the best of what we could find. The following sections describe the (most widely acknowledged) best in this category.

Dreaming of Dreamweaver and home, home on the HomeSite

Unlike many other HTML editors, Dreamweaver is relatively new on the scene — at least in Web years. Released for the first time in early 1998, Dreamweaver is quickly becoming the professional Webmaster's tool of choice. The folks at Macromedia, best known for their Director multimedia authoring system, went to great lengths to research the needs of established Web professionals and created a product that meets all their needs. Dreamweaver is a WYSIWYG tool that can not only help you build the simplest of pages, but it also includes tools for creating Dynamic HTML — motion and more on the screen — even if you don't know the first thing about scripting. For a firsthand look at a high-end Web site that Dreamweaver was used to create, visit `www.dhtmlzone.com` and take a look at the tutorial portion of the site. You'll be amazed, we promise.

Macromedia recently introduced Dreamweaver 3, extending this already powerful editor's capabilities. Now, with XML support and better site management tools, Dreamweaver promises to be the Web designer's editor of choice. Not to mention it has an easy-to-follow-and-learn dialog box that allows authors to style Web pages using Cascading Style Sheets (CSS) without ever knowing what a style rule is!

Although Dreamweaver is a WYSIWYG tool, it comes with another popular HTML editor, Allaire's HomeSite. HomeSite is an advanced HTML helper that allows you to manipulate your HTML code by hand as well as manage your Web site. HomeSite is an extremely feature-rich HTML editor for both the beginner and the professional. You edit the HTML directly and also instantly get a browser view by clicking a tab.

HomeSite color-codes the HTML to help you with your editing. HomeSite uses drag-and-drop and right mouse-click menus. The integrated spell checker, and global search and replace can check your spelling and update entire projects, folders, and files simultaneously. You can use the image and thumbnail viewers to browse image libraries directly in your editor.

HomeSite even has customizable toolbars and menus. Add to that an extensive online help system to access documentation on HTML and other popular scripting languages, and you have an impressive system. But there's even more. HomeSite helps you with your project management, provides for link verification, internally validates your HTML, and opens and uploads your files to your remote Web server.

You can open a Web page in both Dreamweaver and HomeSite, and the changes you make to your page in one program are automatically registered in the other. This two-in-one combination of a WYSIWYG tool and a helper is a direct reflection of what the pros have figured out — you don't need just one kind of HTML editor, you need both. Finally, Dreamweaver and HomeSite both create solid HTML that plays by the official HTML 4.0 rules so you don't have to worry about the quality of your HTML. If you create code by hand and Dreamweaver is concerned about its validity, Dreamweaver will warn you that you made a booboo and will correct it for you if you so desire. About the only task Dreamweaver doesn't do is make your coffee in the morning.

With all this functionality, rest assured Dreamweaver doesn't come cheap. Dreamweaver is priced in the $300 range, but that price includes a HomeSite license, quality documentation, tutorials, and an all-around tool that you can use for many aspects of Web development. Also, Macromedia is loyal to its customers, and after you buy a copy of Dreamweaver, upgrades are available at minimal cost. In addition, you have all the power of an established multimedia company behind the product. What more can you ask for?

To find out more about Dreamweaver, point your Web browser at www.macromedia.com/software/dreamweaver. If you're only interested in HomeSite, visit www.allaire.com/Products/HomeSite.

Voted most popular: Microsoft FrontPage 2000

FrontPage 2000 is the Microsoft commercial Web-authoring system for Windows 95/98/2000 and Windows NT/2000. Since Microsoft bought FrontPage from Vermeer Technologies, Inc., in January 1996, Microsoft has made FrontPage its premier personal Web authoring, publishing, and maintenance tool for Windows. As we predicted, this product has become the most widely used tool of its kind on the Internet.

Within FrontPage, each Web site is in its own project folder so you can develop and manage multiple sites. Enhanced drag-and-drop features let you drag Microsoft Office files into the FrontPage Explorer or move hyperlinks, tables, and images within the FrontPage Editor. The "Verify all links" feature automatically verifies that all hyperlinks are valid — within and outside your Web site. This feature even corrects all link errors within your site for you. FrontPage 98 also supports database connectivity, ActiveX controls, Java applets, plus VBScript and JavaScript creation and insertion, tables, frames, and HTML 4.0, plus the Microsoft version of Dynamic HTML. Breathe!

As if all of this wasn't enough, the FrontPage Bonus Pack includes a powerful image editor that you can use to create and edit graphics for your Web documents. The Bonus Pack includes more than 500 tools and effects and works with PhotoShop-compatible plug-in products, such as Kai's Power Tools from MetaTools, Inc. Image Composer includes more than 600 royalty-free Web-ready images. You may also download the free Microsoft GIF Animator to animate your own Image Composer images and make your Web site really jump on the screen.

As a bonus for Microsoft Office users, the FrontPage interface also allows you to use any document created with Microsoft Office 97 or 2000 because it works like other Office applications. FrontPage uses the shared spelling checker, global Find and Replace, and the Microsoft Thesaurus. Now, you can't quite say "FrontPage, create my Web site" into your PC's microphone, walk off, have an espresso, and come back to view the finished work. But, if you apply the knowledge of planning and preparation from earlier chapters in this book, you should be able to have an outstanding Web site created, tested, and running on your ISP's Web server in very little time by using FrontPage.

For more information about FrontPage 2000, check out the Microsoft Web site at www.microsoft.com/frontpage.

Good 'n' cheap: HotDog express

Sausage Software is the purveyor of HotDog Professional — and for more involved site creations, HotDog Webmaster Suite. Just as its predecessors, HotDog continues to grab massive accolades from users and editors alike. Although HotDog Pro — the bigger, badder, and more expensive version of the little gem, HotDog Junior — has more bells and whistles and is more widely used, we know many people that prefer the Junior version.

Not only does HotDog Professional assist with the HTML editing process and help you produce flawless HTML, but it's also smart enough to recognize if it has the latest set of extensions installed and goes out and downloads them for you if it's not in synch with the most current set. We've heard of smart programs before, but HotDog Professional is one of the only HTML editors we know of that has the brains to recognize it needs an HTML Document Type Definition (DTD) tune-up, and then goes out and grabs the changes for itself! Keeping up with changes to draft HTML standards and DTDs is a snap, as well as tracking release of standards as soon as they go official. And if all these features weren't enough, the Junior and Professional versions list at $39.95 and $129.95 respectively.

To find out more about HotDog Junior and Professional and download working copies, visit www.sausage.com.

Macintosh Web authoring systems

You can download a plethora of excellent HTML authoring tools for the Macintosh from numerous online sites. Most of these Macintosh products ship with very good to pretty good documentation, and some even have online or balloon help. (For non-Mac heads, balloon help is pop up information that takes the form of cute little balloons that appear if you run your mouse over a portion of the program's interface.) Thankfully, these tools are easy to learn because they use familiar Macintosh word processing or text-editor models and the Macintosh menu system.

Best of the breed: Macromedia Dreamweaver

Dreamweaver wins hands down as the best Web development tool for the Macintosh. (Sound familiar? We liked it for the PC, too. What can we say? We *really* like Dreamweaver.) All that can be said about the Windows version of this excellent tool can also be said for the Macintosh version. Macromedia is truly Mac-user friendly and has committed to continued development of this product. That cute little iMac has definitely won hearts at Macromedia.

Instead of working with HomeSite, Dreamweaver for the Macintosh interacts directly with the most popular HTML text editor available, BBEdit. Almost a legend in the Mac world and the preferred tool for any Mac programming nerd, BBEdit is also a powerful tool for Web page development. As a helper, BBEdit is HTML-aware and supports tag color-coding, site management, HTML validation, HTML-aware spell checking, and more. You can launch BBEdit directly from Dreamweaver, and any changes you make in a document open in both applications will reflect in the other. This close relationship with BBEdit is one of the reasons that Dreamweaver has become so popular with Macintosh Web gurus. If you've used BBEdit and appreciate its power as part of your Web arsenal, you'll love Dreamweaver. If you've haven't used either and you're a Mac Web head, we recommend you acquire them both immediately. Once again, Dreamweaver for the Mac is not an inexpensive solution, also weighing in at about $300, but it's worth every cent. Dreamweaver is an investment you'll never regret!

To read more about Dreamweaver visit `www.macromedia.com/software/ dreamweaver`.

Good 'n' cheap: BBEdit Lite

As its name suggests, BBEdit Lite is a limited version of the BBEdit package we raved about earlier in our discussion of Dreamweaver. From the folks at Bare Bones Software, BBEdit Lite is a Macintosh text editor that comes complete with a set of HTML extensions to make Web page development easier.

These HTML extensions for BBEdit Lite are quite extensive and provide a well-rounded HTML authoring system. Tools of this kind can cause an editor to open a standard text file and automatically save the file with HTML tags. The two sets of extensions for BBEdit Lite — BBEdit HTML Extensions by Charles Bellver and BBEdit HTML Tools by Lindsay Davies — come with the editor so you don't have to do any extra installation along the way.

Although BBEdit Lite doesn't include all the functionality that its big brother BBEdit does, you find that using BBEdit Lite gives you access to most, if not all, of the HTML authoring functions you ever need — even for the most complex Web pages. BBEdit Lite also addicts you to the BBEdit way of life, and we predict that soon you'll be using the full-blown version of BBEdit. It's all a conspiracy, didn't you know? Seriously though, to download a copy of BBEdit Lite, simply point your Web browser at `www.barebones.com`.

UNIX Web authoring systems

Outstanding new HTML authoring tools for UNIX-based systems continue to find their way onto the Web. Some are still being tested, but the current crop looks promising, especially certain graphical editing tools. For those of you who happen to like text-only, EMACS is still alive and well, and supports numerous HTML modes that can liven it up considerably. To top things off, you can convert or filter almost any file type into or out of HTML using one of the myriad HTML utility programs available for UNIX.

The UNIX mindset is one of sharing resources; so nearly all UNIX-based HTML authoring systems are freeware. Even commercial UNIX packages typically offer a freeware version for download and evaluation. But free and shareware UNIX HTML authoring tools aren't supported the same way as recently released commercial products. Thankfully, UNIX packages don't cost much, either. These tools are usually easy to figure out because they use familiar text editor metaphors or they act as add-ins to your own UNIX text editors. Either way, if you've ever used any kind of editor, you can learn one of these HTML tools easily.

Best of the breed: HoTMetaL Pro

HoTMetaL Pro is SoftQuad's commercial HTML editor. HoTMetaL requires you to edit a document with its embedded HTML codes visible, and then hands the code off to your browser for display. HoTMetaL Pro supports all HTML 4 tags and can handle definitions for custom markup (which makes extending for the occasional bit of proprietary markup that is sometimes needed very easy). HoTMetaL can open lots of document formats — Lotus WordPro/AmiPro; Microsoft Word for Macintosh, Windows, and DOS; RTF (Rich Text Format); and WordPerfect for DOS, Windows, and Macintosh — and convert them to HTML.

HoTMetaL performs both syntax checking and HTML validation. With syntax (rules) checking turned on, HoTMetaL helps you enter only valid HTML. If you select HTML validation, it checks your document for conformance to your choice of any of a number of HTML DTDs. The HTML validation also provides a list of all nonstandard tags in your document to alert you to possible incompatibilities with browsers that don't support such markup.

To find out more about HoTMetaL, visit the Web site at `www.softquad.com/products/hotmetal/`.

Most popular: EMACS modes and templates

The old tried-and-true UNIX EMACS editor has several add-in macro systems (modes) available to help you create HTML documents. These modes vary in their features but generally are basic in their approach. Modes save you from typing each tag in its entirety and provide pick lists from which you can choose the markup you want.

EMACS users will understand this section, but everyone else will think it's written in E-Greek. But then, EMACS is a foreign language to most non-UNIX computer users.

Various EMACS macro packages are available for editing HTML documents. The first and oldest is Marc Andreesen's html-mode.el, which was written while he was at the University of Illinois. (Andreesen was the primary designer of Mosaic and Netscape Navigator.) Heiko Muenkel at the University of Hannover, Germany, added pull-down menus (hm — html-menus.el) and template handling (tmpl-minor-mode.el), which is up to Version 4.15.

Nelson Minar of the Santa Fe Institute wrote and continues to improve html-helper-mode.el, which supports Lucid EMACS menu bar and font-lock capabilities and runs under GNU EMACS, Epoch, and Lucid EMACS.

Generally speaking, the various forms of HTML modes display text and HTML tags alike in fixed-size fonts. By using the hilit.el package, tags and references can be colored differently from text. The HTML modes do not support in-line graphics. However, more recent versions of HTML mode can call a Mosaic or Navigator process to display pages in a browser view.

All these HTML modes work primarily from direct keyboard commands that create paired begin/end HTML tags with an entry point available between the tags. You can select a segment of text, and tags are inserted around it. None of these modes checks the validity of tags or suggests possible tag usage. However, html-helper-mode and tmpl-minor-mode provide templates for entering multiple fields inside link tags.

For EMACS users, these modes may be just the thing for creating HTML documents. Using modes can make HTML tagging easier and less prone to error than manual tag entry. You must still know what tags to use, however, and where to use them. You can obtain information and copies of Muenkel's and Minar's packages, respectively, at

```
www.tnt.uni-hannover.de/js/~muenkel/software/own/hm—html-menus
www.santafe.edu/~nelson/tools
```

Good 'n' cheap: A.S.H.E.

A.S.H.E. — A Simple HTML Editor — was written using the C language, Motif, and NCSA HTML Widgets. A.S.H.E. is a stand-alone, plain-text HTML editor. The emphasis in A.S.H.E. is *Simple*. If you understand the UNIX environment, you can learn A.S.H.E. fairly quickly. A.S.H.E. provides active hyperlinks, supports multiple windows, prints text or postscript, and offers automatic file backup. The menu bar is well-designed with File, Edit, HTML, Styles, and Lists menus. A.S.H.E. provides a unique user Message Area while displaying the HTML code in a browser screen view. Unfortunately, it only works under Motif on Sun workstations and requires the NCSA HTML Widget library. A.S.H.E provides simple but adequate HTML assistance for users of Motif. If that sounds like it's up your alley, please give A.S.H.E. a try!

The A.S.H.E. beta version was created by John R. Punin, Department of Computer Science. Rochester Polytechnic Institute, Troy, New York (e-mail:). You can download it from

```
ftp://ftp.cs.rpi.edu/pub/puninj/ASHE/ASHE-1.1/src/
                ashe-1.1.tar.Z
```

Lists of UNIX helper and filter programs are available at:

```
www.utoronto.ca/webdocs/HTMLdocs/UNIXTOOLS/unix_doc_man.html
www.w3.org/Tools/Word_proc_filters.html
```

The Doctor Is In: Page Checkups

So you write a bunch of HTML, and you think you're done. Not by a long shot — at least, not if you want to avoid being a laughingstock on the Web. Before all these great tools were available, an occasional misspelled word or broken link was acceptable, but now you have no excuse for such boo-boos. Before you post pages for public display, you must perform three important checks:

- ✔ HTML validation
- ✔ Links to other pages
- ✔ Spell checking

Lots of different tools can do one or more of these jobs; many are available for free on the Web. You can find a number of stand-alone utilities as well, not to mention those already embedded in HTML editors. As we said, you no longer have a valid excuse for mistakes.

HTML validation: Bad code is bad news

The majority of browsers are forgiving of markup errors. Most don't even require an <html> tag to identify an HTML page, and instead look only for an .HTML or .HTM file extension to identify a document as readable. Just because the real world is that way, doesn't make it right. You may see a day when browsers can't afford to be so forgiving, and that day is drawing closer as HTML becomes more complicated and precise. Get the code right from the beginning and save yourself a bunch of trouble later on.

HTML validation is built into many HTML editors, and although not many stand-alone HTML validation applications exist, the W3C has put together a free, Web-based validation system available at http://validator.w3.org.

This validation tool lets you choose which HTML or Extensible HTML (XHTML) DTD (version) you want to check your document against and provides you with a variety of different outputs depending on your preference. You can choose a terse output that only lists the line numbers in your document with boo-boos and a brief description of the error, or a verbose output that goes into great detail about why each and every error is an error and even includes links to the relevant information in the HTML specification.

We strongly recommend that you don't ever, ever, ever — have we made our point yet — post a page on the Web without running it through this validator. If your HTML is correct, your pages will look better on a variety of Web browsers, and your users will be happier — even if they don't know exactly why.

Of cars hew kin spill (but spell check those pages anyway)

What is the biggest problem with checking HTML pages for spelling errors? The tags themselves are misspellings, according to *Webster's* and most other dictionaries. Sitting and clicking the Ignore key for each and every new tag can make spell checking tedious. After your eyes glaze over, you're more apt to miss real misspellings. Once again, many editors include HTML-aware spell checkers that skip markup and check just the text. Because so many editors support this option, few stand-alone utilities are available, or any dedicated online spell checkers that we could find.

Doctor HTML is an HTML checking tool that performs several different checks, including spell checks, on any HTML document or on an entire site. To investigate this utility and try its analytical skills, please visit this Web site:

```
www2.imagiware.com/RxHTML
```

Regardless of how you do it, even if it means cutting and pasting text from a browser to a word processor, you must check your pages for spelling errors. Bad spelling is often considered to be an indicator of intelligence and abilities, and we wouldn't want anyone to underestimate you.

Don't lose the connection: Link checking

If you think spelling errors are embarrassing, here's something that's even worse: broken hyperlinks. Hyperlinks make the Web what it is; if you have broken links on your site, that's borderline blasphemous. Seriously, if your text promises a link to a great resource or page but produces the dreaded

`404 Object Not Found` error after that link is clicked, users will be disappointed and may not ever revisit your site. The worst broken link is one that points to a resource in your own pages. You can't be held responsible for what others do to their sites, but you are 100 percent accountable for your own site. Don't let broken links happen to you!

As with the other checks, many HTML editors include built-in local link checkers, and some editors even scour the Web for you to check external links. In addition, the majority of Web servers also offer this feature. Checking external links isn't as simple as it sounds because a program must work over an active Internet connection to query each link. This checking can be processor intensive, and you should check external links only during off-peak hours, such as early morning, to avoid tying up other Web servers as well. A number of scripts and utilities are available on the Web to help you test your links.

MOMSpider was one of the first link checkers available to Web authors. This link checker is written in Perl and runs on virtually any UNIX machine. The nice feature about MOMSpider is that it needn't reside on the same computer as the site it checks; so even if you don't serve your Web from UNIX, you can still check links from MOMSpider on a remote system.

Anyone who has some knowledge of Perl can easily configure MOMSpider to create custom output and to check both internal and external links on a site. Don't fret; if you don't know Perl, you can easily find a programmer who can adjust a MOMSpider in his or her sleep for a nominal fee. Many ISPs run a MOMSpider on your site for a low monthly fee and cheerfully handle the configuration and implementation for you.

To find out more about MOMSpider, visit the official site at `www.ics.uci.edu/pub/websoft/MOMspider`.

Web-Site Garage: An all-around checker

We stumbled across a great Web site not too long ago that adds a powerful punch to your Web arsenal: Web-Site Garage. This Web-based Web page-checking tool is a gem that you can't afford to be without. This site checks your HTML, spelling, download time, and many other aspects of the mechanics under the hood of your Web pages to help you fine-tune your code. The site analyzes a page and flags code that may potentially cause problems in particular browsers or Web graphics that can be made smaller. You can find out how long a page may take to download over a variety of connections and find out if your pages are accessible or not. To drive your page in for an inspection and tune-up, visit `http://websitegarage.netscape.com/`.

Other Useful Tools and Utilities

You find helpful tools and utilities to create Web pages in the most unexpected places sometimes. The word processor on your computer right now may double as an HTML editor — or a converter in the very least. Other application-like page layout programs and database tools may also have HTML functionality, even if their primary focus isn't creation of Web pages. Finally, you find certain utilities whose only purpose in life is to convert documents from a particular format — such as RTF — into HTML. Although you may be able to live without some of these tools in your Webmaster's toolbox, you may find that they can be quite useful at times and are worth a second look.

Word processors as HTML editors

If you're joined at the hip to Microsoft Word or Corel WordPerfect, you may want to try their built-in HTML-editing and site-management features. These features provide adequate HTML assistance but aren't really in the same ballpark with better stand-alone WYSIWYG Web development and HTML editing systems. If you already own one of these word processing programs, however, their Web functionality is free. For now, you may want to use your favorite one for text and for Web development.

For example, Word 97/2000 for Windows has a nice WYSIWYG editing window with a good number of functions in its toolbar. This program is adequate for a word processor turned Web document editor. However, who knows what Microsoft will do in the long-term with both Word 97/2000 and FrontPage contending for the role of Web document development systems. Why worry about that now? If you own one, try it out for Web development.

Keep in mind that word processors may not create HTML that is 100 percent standard; instead Web pages that these tools create can be erratic and clumsy. If you have long documents that have been developed in a particular word processor that need to be converted to HTML, doing a first-stage conversion in the processor itself may be easier, but do any final clean up and tweaking in a full-fledged HTML editor.

See the following sites for their respective information on Microsoft Word 97/2000 for Windows, Corel WordPerfect 8.0 for Windows:

```
www.microsoft.com/office
www.corel.com/Office2000/index.htm
```

Filters and file converters for Windows

Several of the current crop of HTML editors, word processors, and page layout programs support automatically converting existing text documents into HTML. They work quickly and easily. For example, if you use Word for Windows, simply open a standard Word document, save the file in HTML format via the Save As command, and the file is converted. Most of the text formatting that really counts, including headings, is transformed into HTML. However, you may have files saved in a particular format for a specific application that doesn't support this automatic conversion. If that's the case, you may need a stand-alone converter to help you along.

The following stand-alone converter is an example of the numerous converters available on every conceivable computer platform to convert virtually every file format to HTML and sometimes back again. HTML Transit imports and converts a large number of file formats. If you have many highly formatted files that you want to convert to HTML for Web display, check into HTML Transit.

HTML Transit, from InfoAccess, Inc., reads the structure of the source document, recognizing elements such as headings, subheads, bullets, images, and so on. HTML Transit then creates a default template based on this structure that becomes the foundation for one-button generation of HTML documents. HTML Transit offers direct translation of all major word processing formats and all major graphics formats.

HTML Transit is based on over a decade of electronic publishing experience by InfoAccess (formerly OWL International), which produced the industry's first commercially available hypertext product ten years ago. Their $45,000 GUIDE Professional Publisher was the model for HTML Transit's template-based architecture.

With a well-formatted word processor or page layout file and HTML Transit, you may not need an HTML editor at all. Although HTML Transit is a bit expensive, it may be just what you're looking for. Have a look for yourself at

`www.infoaccess.com`

Appendix D

About the CD-ROM

- -

*I*n this section of the book, we explain what you find on the *HTML 4 For Dummies,* 3rd Edition CD-ROM. In a nutshell, it contains the following goodies:

- ✔ A collection of Web documents built specifically to help you find your way around the book's materials.

- ✔ A hotlist of all URLs mentioned in the book to make it easy for you to access any of the Web resources we mention.

- ✔ Copies of all the HTML examples, easily accessible by chapter number.

- ✔ A hyperlinked table of contents for the book to help you find your way around its many topics and treasures.

- ✔ A collection of Common Gateway Interface (CGI) programs, built especially for you, to help add functionality to your own Web server (and to provide what we hope are sterling examples of the art of CGI programming).

System Requirements

Make sure that your computer meets the minimum system requirements listed in this handy section. If your computer doesn't match up to most of these requirements, you may have problems using the contents of the CD-ROM. Avoid the heartbreak of obsolescence; look before you load.

- ✔ A PC with a 486 or faster processor, or a Mac OS computer with a 68030 or faster processor.

- ✔ Microsoft Windows 95 or later, Windows NT 4 or later, or Mac OS system software 7.5 or later.

- ✔ At least 16MB of total RAM installed on your computer. For best performance, we recommend at least 32MB of RAM installed.

- ✔ At least 325MB of hard drive space available to install all the software from this CD-ROM. (You need less space if you don't install every program.)

> ✔ A CD-ROM drive — double speed (2x) or faster.
>
> ✔ A monitor capable of displaying at least 256 colors or grayscale.
>
> ✔ A modem with a speed of at least 33,600 bps.

If you need more information on the basics, check out *PCs For Dummies*, 7th Edition, by Dan Gookin; *Macs For Dummies*, 6th Edition, by David Pogue; *Windows 98 For Dummies*, *Windows 95 For Dummies*, all by Andy Rathbone (all published by IDG Books Worldwide, Inc.).

How to Use the Web Pages and Examples

Regardless of what platform and operating system you run, you can view all of the CD material straight from the CD-ROM. To do so, however, you must have a Web browser installed on your system. We included both Windows and Mac versions of the two mainstream browsers on the CD. Before you try to view the CD content, be sure you have one of these browsers installed if you don't already have a browser of some kind on your system. To browse the CD-ROM contents, just do the following:

1. **Launch your Web browser.**

2. **Using the Open File command in your browser's File menu, open the file** `\html4fd3\html4dum.htm\` **from the CD-ROM.**

This page serves as the home page for the CD-ROM; it connects you to all other files. Although you won't be able to edit any of the files on the CD itself, you can make changes to them and save them elsewhere on your hard disk or a floppy disk. If you plan to modify any Web pages, examples, or templates, save them to your local drive before you do so. The simplest way to modify the contents is to copy the `html4fd3` folder to your hard drive, which transfers the entire directory structure from the CD-ROM to your computer. (You'll need about 2MB of drive space to accommodate it, so we suggest you check your available disk space before you actually copy the files over to your hard disk.)

Chapter 15 makes several references to the CD-ROM's image maps and navigation buttons that don't match what you'll see on the CD-ROM 's Web pages. After the chapters were all written, we decided to revamp the CD-ROM format to update the CD materials and make them more useful to you. So no, you aren't seeing things; the CD-ROM Web pages are different from the screen shots in Chapter 15. Even though we've changed our style a bit, the examples in Chapter 15 are still valid. If you want to see them at work visit `www.lanw.com/html4dum/h4d3e/html4dum.htm` and view the source to see the full set of HTML elements at work behind the pages. Our new CD-ROM format does use client-side image maps, so if you want to see a second set of image map examples, view the source on just about any CD-ROM Web page.

The HTML 4 For Dummies Files

The top level of the *HTML 4 For Dummies* CD-ROM directory includes the following items:

- ✔ The html4fd3 folder
- ✔ Folders containing installers for shareware, freeware, evaluation versions, and trial programs
- ✔ A License Agreement text file
- ✔ A Read Me file

The html4fd3 folder contains all the HTML files in the book; the software folders are chock-full of shareware, freeware, evaluation versions, and trial versions that introduce you to some of the best HTML editors in the business (they're software, so you don't have to invite them out to dinner). License.txt includes some important end-user information, and Readme.txt is a text-only version of this appendix (just in case your book grows legs and happens to wander away somewhere).

To give you an idea of what's in each folder, we cover the files within them according to their home directory — and subdirectory when necessary. The html4fd3 directory contains the majority of *HTML 4 For Dummies,* 3rd Edition files. Nearly every file in this directory ends with the extension .htm, indicating that it is an HTML document.

All in all, the best way to explore the *HTML 4 For Dummies,* 3rd Edition Web pages is to fire up your browser and point it at the file named html4dum.htm (the home page for the whole collection). For a complete, linked, graphical overview of all the files on the CD-ROM, open menu.htm and behold! Table D-1 lists and describes the remaining top-level HTML.

Table D-1	The html4fd3 Directory File Listing
File	*Description*
applet.htm	Starts the HTML context applet
contact.htm	List of e-mail, home-page, and biography page links for the authors
copy.htm	Important copyright information

(continued)

Table D-1 *(continued)*

File	Description
html4dum.htm	The *HTML 4 For Dummies* home page
menu.htm	A bird's-eye view of the entire page collection
wayfind.htm	HTML navigation information

The html4fd3 directory has eight subdirectories whose names indicate what you find within them.

- ✔ contents: Contains files listing the book contents by chapter
- ✔ examples: Contains files listing the book examples by chapter
- ✔ graphics: Contains all the graphics used with the *HTML 4 For Dummies*, 3rd Edition Web pages
- ✔ h4dftp: Contains compressed versions of all the Dummies files
- ✔ cgi-bin: Contains AppleScript, C, and Perl CGI scripts
- ✔ templates: Contains a collection of templates to get you started
- ✔ urls: Contains files that list the book's URLs by chapter

- ✔ applet: Contains the files that are needed to run the HTML context applet. Do not modify these files. They are necessary for the applet to function properly.

For you list enthusiasts who need to know more about the files lurking within the subdirectories, the following list unveils them in greater detail:

- ✔ **html4fd3/contents:** The file default.htm within the contents of the subdirectory includes a hyperlinked listing of all the chapter titles. Click a chapter title to view a list of its contents. The other files in the subdirectory are named chnncont.htm (where nn is a two-digit number between 0 and 9) and are keyed to the chapters of the book. For example, ch01cont.htm contains the contents listing for Chapter 1. The easiest way to navigate through these pages is to choose a chapter from default.htm to view a chapter's contents. To return to the list of chapter titles, choose "Book Contents" from the bottom image map (or text provided for navigation).

- ✔ **html4fd3/examples:** The file default.htm within the contents of the subdirectory includes a hyperlinked listing of all the chapter titles. The examples folder is further broken down into subfolders that contain the individual HTML example documents for each chapter. Click a chapter title in default.htm to view a listing of the examples included for the chapter. To view a specific example, click the example name. Each example includes the code listing from the book and shows the final rendering of the example by a Web browser when possible.

Note: The easiest way to navigate through these pages is to choose a chapter from `default.htm` to view a listing of the chapter's examples and select the example you would like to see. When you finish with a particular example, press the Back button in your browser windows to return to the list of examples by chapter. To return to the list of chapter titles, choose "`Book Examples`" from the bottom image map (or text navigation).

✔ **html4fd3/graphics:** This is the graphics subdirectory for the graphics used in the HTML documents for the *HTML 4 For Dummies* pages themselves. As its name implies, this folder houses all the `gif` image files in our Web page. If we used an image on a Web page (except in the templates pages) you can find it here. All we can say further is *Help yourself!*

✔ **html4fd3/h4dftp:** To make transferring our file collections easier, we include a Web page where you'll find links to download a compressed version of the CGI, `html4fd3`, and template folders. Each one is available as a `zip` (PC), `sea.hqx` (Macintosh), and `tar` (UNIX) archive; you should be able to get at them regardless of the operating system you use.

✔ **html4fd3/cgi-bin:** This folder contains three subfolders (`AppleScript`, `C`, and `Perl`), each of which holds unarchived versions of the CD-ROM's CGI files.

✔ **html4fd3/templates:** For your pleasure and convenience, we include a few simple templates to get you started on your HTML authoring adventures. The folder's main page, `default.htm`, gives you a complete rundown on each template. The `graphics` subdirectory within the `templates` folder contains all the graphics we used in creating the templates. As we said before, Help yourself!

✔ **html4fd3/urls:** The file `default.htm` within the `urls` subdirectory includes a hyperlinked listing of all the chapter titles. Click a chapter title to view a list the URLs we included in it. The other files in the subdirectory are named `chnnurls.htm` (where nn is a number between 0 and 9) and are keyed to the chapters of the book. The easiest way to navigate through these pages is to choose a chapter from `default.htm` to view a chapter's URLs. To return to the listing of chapter titles, choose "`Book URLs`" from the bottom image map (or text provided for navigation).

Working with templates

Nothing is so simple that it can't benefit from a few well-chosen shortcuts. Building a Web page may not be quite like falling off a log, but we've put some template files on this book's CD-ROM to help you get your feet wet. Try using one as a starting point for your own Web page design. Simply copy it to your hard drive, give it a few tweaks to reflect your own interests, and then edit it to kick-start the Edit-Review cycle. A couple trips around the block on that cycle and your file will soon look like a Web page!

Whenever you want to use a template as a point of departure for your work, save it under a different name as soon as you open it in your text editor. That way, you won't have to recopy the files from the CD-ROM each time you want to reuse the same template.

The Software

In addition to the nifty files, examples, and scripts described in the previous section, we also include a small software collection on the CD-ROM. Heft and try out these evaluation and shareware versions of Webmaster tools that might fit your needs. Fear not the compatibility dragon; the CD is a multiplatform hybrid format. You have access to only those packages that can run on the platform you currently use (clever, eh?). To see the other tools, you must load the CD into a computer that uses a different operating system (of course it has to be one of the platforms the CD itself supports . . . but you knew that). Table D-2 lists all of the software you can find on the CD-ROM along with information about the vendor that produces it.

Shareware programs are fully functional, free trial versions of copyrighted programs. If you like particular programs, register with their authors for a nominal fee and receive licenses, enhanced versions, and technical support. Freeware programs are free, copyrighted games, applications, and utilities. You can copy them to as many PCs as you like — free — but they have no technical support. GNU software is governed by its own license, which is included inside the folder of the GNU software. There are no restrictions on distribution of this software. See the GNU license for more details. Trial, demo, or evaluation versions are usually limited either by time or functionality (such as being unable to save projects).

Table D-2	Software Included on the CD-ROM	
Software	*Vendor*	*Software Type (Platform)*
CSE HTML Validator Lite v2.00	AI Internet Solutions	Lite version (95/98/2000/NT)
CSE HTML Validator Professional v4.04	AI Internet Solutions	Demo version (95/98/2000/NT)
Agile HTML Editor v1.20	Agilic Corporation Limited	Shareware (95/98/2000/NT)

Software	Vendor	Software Type (Platform)
Dreamweaver 3.0	Macromedia, Inc	Trial version (95/98/2000/NT/Mac)
FrontPage 2000	Microsoft Corporation	45-day Trial (95/98/2000/NT)
Fusion 5.0	NetObjects	Trial version (95/98/2000/NT)
HTML Tidy	Dave Raggett	Freeware (95/98/2000/NT/Mac)
HotDog Professional v5.5	Sausage Software	Trial version (95/98/2000/NT)
HomeSite 4.5 for Windows Evaluation	Allaire Corporation	30-day Evaluation version (95/98/2000/NT)
ColdFusion Express	Allaire Corporation	Freeware (95/98/2000/NT)
Internet Explorer 5.0	Microsoft Corporation	Commercial version (95/98/2000/NT/Mac)
Netscape Communicator 4.7	Netscape Communications	Commercial verison (95/98/2000/NT/Mac)
40tude HTML v3.1	Softwareentwicklung Marcus Moennig	Evaluation version (95/98/2000/NT)
BBEdit Lite v4.6	BareBones Software, Inc.	Freeware (Mac)
BBEdit 5.1.1	BareBones Software, Inc.	Demo version (Mac)

If You've Got Problems (Of the CD Kind)

We tried our level best to compile programs that work on most computers with the minimum system requirements. Alas, your computer may differ, and some programs may not work properly for some reason. (Check the label. Was your system reverse-engineered from a UFO?)

The two likeliest problems are (1) you may not have enough memory (RAM) for the programs that you want to use, or (2) you may have other programs running that are affecting installation or running of a program. If you get error messages like Not enough memory or Setup cannot continue, try one or more of these methods and then try using the software again:

- ✔ **Turn off any antivirus software that you have running on your computer.** Installers sometimes mimic virus activity and may make your computer incorrectly believe that it is being infected by a virus.

- ✔ **Close all running programs.** The more programs you're running, the less memory is available to other programs. Installers also typically update files and programs; if you keep other programs running, installation may not work properly.

- ✔ **In Windows, close the CD-ROM interface and run demos or installations directly from Windows Explorer.** The interface itself can tie up system memory or even conflict with certain kinds of interactive demos. Use Windows Explorer to browse the files on the CD-ROM and launch installers or demos.

- ✔ **Have your local computer store add more RAM to your computer.** This is, admittedly, a drastic and somewhat expensive step, but be of good cheer: More RAM is almost always a good thing. However, if you have a Windows 95 PC or a Mac OS computer with a PowerPC chip, adding more memory can really help the speed of your computer and enable more programs to run at the same time.

If you still have trouble installing the items from the CD-ROM, please call the Hungry Minds Customer Care phone number: 800-762-2974 (outside the United States: 317-572-3393).

Index

Notes

Hungry Minds, Inc.,
End-User License Agreement

READ THIS. You should carefully read these terms and conditions before opening the software packet(s) included with this book ("Book"). This is a license agreement ("Agreement") between you and Hungry Minds, Inc. ("HMI"). By opening the accompanying software packet(s), you acknowledge that you have read and accept the following terms and conditions. If you do not agree and do not want to be bound by such terms and conditions, promptly return the Book and the unopened software packet(s) to the place you obtained them for a full refund.

1. **License Grant.** HMI grants to you (either an individual or entity) a nonexclusive license to use one copy of the enclosed software program(s) (collectively, the "Software") solely for your own personal or business purposes on a single computer (whether a standard computer or a workstation component of a multi-user network). The Software is in use on a computer when it is loaded into temporary memory (RAM) or installed into permanent memory (hard disk, CD-ROM, or other storage device). HMI reserves all rights not expressly granted herein.

2. **Ownership.** HMI is the owner of all right, title, and interest, including copyright, in and to the compilation of the Software recorded on the disk(s) or CD-ROM ("Software Media"). Copyright to the individual programs recorded on the Software Media is owned by the author or other authorized copyright owner of each program. Ownership of the Software and all proprietary rights relating thereto remain with HMI and its licensers.

3. **Restrictions On Use and Transfer.**

   (a) You may only (i) make one copy of the Software for backup or archival purposes, or (ii) transfer the Software to a single hard disk, provided that you keep the original for backup or archival purposes. You may not (i) rent or lease the Software, (ii) copy or reproduce the Software through a LAN or other network system or through any computer subscriber system or bulletin-board system, or (iii) modify, adapt, or create derivative works based on the Software.

   (b) You may not reverse engineer, decompile, or disassemble the Software. You may transfer the Software and user documentation on a permanent basis, provided that the transferee agrees to accept the terms and conditions of this Agreement and you retain no copies. If the Software is an update or has been updated, any transfer must include the most recent update and all prior versions.

4. **Restrictions on Use of Individual Programs.** You must follow the individual requirements and restrictions detailed for each individual program in Appendix D of this Book. These limitations are also contained in the individual license agreements recorded on the Software Media. These limitations may include a requirement that after using the program for a specified period of time, the user must pay a registration fee or discontinue use. By opening the Software packet(s), you will be agreeing to abide by the licenses and restrictions for these individual programs that are detailed in Appendix D and on the Software Media. None of the material on this Software Media or listed in this Book may ever be redistributed, in original or modified form, for commercial purposes.

5. Limited Warranty.

(a) HMI warrants that the Software and Software Media are free from defects in materials and workmanship under normal use for a period of sixty (60) days from the date of purchase of this Book. If HMI receives notification within the warranty period of defects in materials or workmanship, HMI will replace the defective Software Media.

(b) HMI AND THE AUTHOR OF THE BOOK DISCLAIM ALL OTHER WARRANTIES, EXPRESS OR IMPLIED, INCLUDING WITHOUT LIMITATION IMPLIED WARRANTIES OF MERCHANTABILITY AND FITNESS FOR A PARTICULAR PURPOSE, WITH RESPECT TO THE SOFTWARE, THE PROGRAMS, THE SOURCE CODE CONTAINED THEREIN, AND/OR THE TECHNIQUES DESCRIBED IN THIS BOOK. HMI DOES NOT WARRANT THAT THE FUNCTIONS CONTAINED IN THE SOFTWARE WILL MEET YOUR REQUIREMENTS OR THAT THE OPERATION OF THE SOFTWARE WILL BE ERROR FREE.

(c) This limited warranty gives you specific legal rights, and you may have other rights that vary from jurisdiction to jurisdiction.

6. Remedies.

(a) HMI's entire liability and your exclusive remedy for defects in materials and workmanship shall be limited to replacement of the Software Media, which may be returned to HMI with a copy of your receipt at the following address: Software Media Fulfillment Department, Attn.: *HTML 4 For Dummies,* 3rd Edition, Hungry Minds, Inc., 10475 Crosspoint Blvd., Indianapolis, IN 46256, or call 1-800-762-2974. Please allow four to six weeks for delivery. This Limited Warranty is void if failure of the Software Media has resulted from accident, abuse, or misapplication. Any replacement Software Media will be warranted for the remainder of the original warranty period or thirty (30) days, whichever is longer.

(b) In no event shall HMI or the author be liable for any damages whatsoever (including without limitation damages for loss of business profits, business interruption, loss of business information, or any other pecuniary loss) arising from the use of or inability to use the Book or the Software, even if HMI has been advised of the possibility of such damages.

(c) Because some jurisdictions do not allow the exclusion or limitation of liability for consequential or incidental damages, the above limitation or exclusion may not apply to you.

7. U.S. Government Restricted Rights. Use, duplication, or disclosure of the Software for or on behalf of the United States of America, its agencies and/or instrumentalities (the "U.S. Government") is subject to restrictions as stated in paragraph (c)(1)(ii) of the Rights in Technical Data and Computer Software clause of DFARS 252.227-7013, and in subparagraphs (a) through (d) of the Commercial Computer–Restricted Rights clause at FAR 52.227-19, and in similar clauses in the NASA FAR supplement, when applicable.

8. General. This Agreement constitutes the entire understanding of the parties and revokes and supersedes all prior agreements, oral or written, between them and may not be modified or amended except in a writing signed by both parties hereto that specifically refers to this Agreement. This Agreement shall take precedence over any other documents that may be in conflict herewith. If any one or more provisions contained in this Agreement are held by any court or tribunal to be invalid, illegal, or otherwise unenforceable, each and every other provision shall remain in full force and effect.

Notes

Notes

Backyard Homesteading

ALL-IN-ONE

by Todd Brock with

Bob Beckstrom, Howland Blackiston, Cathy Cromell,
Rik DeGunther, Suzanne DeJohn, Owen E. Dell, The Editors
of the National Gardening Association, Kelly Ewing,
Philip Giroux, Theresa A. Husarik, Amelia Jeanroy,
Rob Ludlow, Marty Nachel, Charlie Nardozzi,
Emily Nolan, Cheryl K. Smith, Paul Simon,
Lance Walheim, Karen Ward, Marni Wasserman,
CN, Ann Whitman, Kimberley Willis, Dave Zook

for
dummies®
A Wiley Brand

Backyard Homesteading All-in-One For Dummies®

Published by: **John Wiley & Sons, Inc.**, 111 River Street, Hoboken, NJ 07030-5774, www.wiley.com

Copyright © 2019 by John Wiley & Sons, Inc., Hoboken, New Jersey

Published simultaneously in Canada

Contents at a Glance

Recipes at a Glance

Freezing

Pickling

Pressure Canning

Water-Bath Canning

Table of Contents

Introduction

Feeding your family with what comes from your little piece of land. Making your own. Doing it yourself. Buying less. Being more self-sufficient. That's what backyard homesteading is all about.

A lot goes into backyard homesteading. It's a hobby for some, and a lifestyle for many. And it's increasing in popularity, as people from all types of backgrounds feel an urge to reconnect with a simpler time, the earth, and their roots. There was a time when families who grew their own vegetables, preserved their own food, and raised their own chickens weren't the least bit extraordinary. But those activities fell out of favor as society continued its never-ending search for bigger, faster, easier. Now these activities are returning to a mainstream society that lost sight of their value.

If you've considered joining that growing movement — even with just the smallest of steps — *Backyard Homesteading All-In-One For Dummies* is for you. Here, you learn how to get started, how to succeed, and how to make the homesteading spirit an integral part of your everyday life.

About This Book

Backyard Homesteading All-In-One For Dummies breaks down the various components most often associated with backyard homesteading: growing food, preserving the harvest, making your own food and other products, raising animals, and building items that help you keep doing those other things. The goal is to walk you through each topic step by step so you can start from scratch if you're a newbie, or brush up with a quick reference if you already have some experience.

As you read, you'll find the following:

>> Background information and special considerations to factor in before you embark on a new aspect of homesteading

>> Recommended tools, equipment, and gear to do the job correctly and safely

>> Potential problems to look for and how to avoid or resolve them

>> Assembly instructions and building plans that give you a solid baseline for a project, but can usually be adapted or modified to suit your unique situation

>> Recipes that help you get started in the kitchen, but are by no means the extent of what you can do with what comes out of your garden

This book is your entry guide to the world of backyard homesteading, a launching point for a lifelong adventure that will evolve along with you the longer you pursue it.

Foolish Assumptions

In compiling the content for this book, some general assumptions have been made about you, the reader:

>> You have enough property to make homesteading a worthwhile endeavor. You can homestead on acres of rolling pasture or in a small backyard in a suburban neighborhood. If you live in a high-rise apartment with a tiny balcony, though, you can adapt bits of information in this book, but "backyard homesteading" might be a stretch.

>> You have some experience with gardening and are interested in growing food beyond a single potted tomato plant or one modest vegetable bed.

>> You know your way around the kitchen and can follow the basic conventions of recipes, even if more advanced techniques such as pressure canning, pickling, and fermenting are new to you.

>> You have an interest in being more self-sufficient by utilizing your own property and skills to produce things you and your family will consume.

>> You are at least modestly handy or willing to become so. No one expects you to be able to build your own pole barn after reading this book, but homesteaders are typically resourceful folks who aren't afraid to roll up their sleeves and tackle whatever is required to do the job.

Icons Used in This Book

TIP

The Tip icon marks tips (duh!) and shortcuts that you can use to make your efforts as a homesteader easier.

REMEMBER

Remember icons mark the information that's especially important to know. To discover the most important information in each chapter, skim through these icons.

TECHNICAL STUFF

The Technical Stuff icon marks information of a highly technical nature that you can normally skip.

WARNING

The Warning icon tells you to watch out! It highlights important safety information or marks other details that may save you considerable headaches.

Beyond the Book

Often, you'll need to recall a specific piece of information at a time when this book isn't handy. An accompanying cheat sheet online can be accessed anytime by any Internet-ready device.

You can go to www.dummies.com/cheatsheet/backyardhomesteadingaio for a comprehensive planting guideline, perfect for when you're planning or laying out your garden at the beginning of the season. You'll also find a quick step-by-step refresher on the steps for both water-bath canning and pressure canning, easy to call up when you're in the kitchen ready to get to work on a batch of tomato sauce. And a convenient chicken coop checklist helps you ensure that the structure you're either looking at purchasing or thinking about building will fit the needs of your flock.

Where to Go from Here

Instructions for various homesteading techniques and projects can be found throughout the book. If you're starting a garden from scratch, though, Book 1, Chapter 1 is the best place to begin. If you already have a garden up and running and want to start canning and preserving, go right to Book 2.

Book 3 is loaded with recipes that help you expand your homesteading horizons to fermenting food, brewing beer, and baking bread. Considering backyard bees or chickens? Book 4 has you covered with no need to read the previous minibooks.

Book 5 details miscellaneous projects and step-by-step building plans for a few larger specialty builds, too.

1

Creating a Garden

Contents at a Glance

Chapter **1**

Planning Your Garden

A lush, bountiful vegetable garden is the centerpiece of any backyard homestead. Everyone loves good food. And what better way to have fresh, tasty, and nutritious food than to grow it yourself? You don't have to be a farmer to do so either. Whether you have a plot of land in the yard that's tilled to grow vegetables, a few vegetables planted amongst your flowers and shrubs, or containers loaded with attractive, edible choices, growing your own food is a satisfying and rewarding activity.

But vegetable gardening isn't just about taste. It's about safe food that's produced close to home. It's about knowing what has been sprayed on that food. It's about feeding your friends and family nutritious food high in vitamins and *antioxidants* (cancer-fighting compounds). It's about connecting with your neighbors and community as you experiment with ethnic dishes using exotic ingredients grown in your not-so-exotic backyard. It's about reducing pollution and global warming by not buying produce that's shipped hundreds of miles to your local grocery store. Finally, it's about getting in touch with nature and reclaiming your ability to grow some of your own food, even if it's a container of basil, to be more self-reliant in your little corner of the world. (And that's pretty much why you're interested in backyard homesteading to begin with, right?)

This chapter is all about conceptualizing the garden that your homestead will be built around.

Determining Location and Size

When considering where to plop down your plot, think of these three main elements, which are necessary for the perfect spot: site, sun, and soil. The following sections describe each of these and give you some things to think about when surveying your yard for the best possible spot for your plot. Figure 1-1 puts some of these ideas into visual perspective.

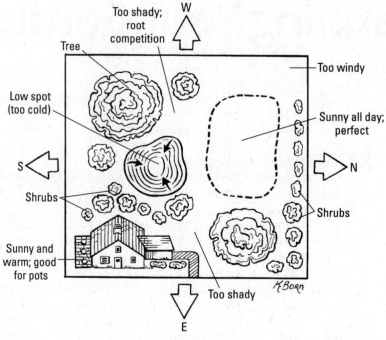

FIGURE 1-1:
A sample yard with possible (and impossible) sites for a vegetable garden.

Illustration by Kathryn Born

REMEMBER

Don't be discouraged if you lack the ideal garden spot — few gardeners have one. Just try to make the most of what you have.

Acclimating to your conditions

The first step in planting wisely is understanding your region's climate, as well as your landscape's particular attributes. Then you can effectively match plants to planting sites.

Don't use geographic proximity alone to evaluate climate. Two places near each other geographically can have very different climates if one is high on a mountainside and the other is on the valley floor, for example. Also, widely separated regions can have similar climates.

USDA Plant Hardiness Zone Map

Low winter temperatures limit where most plants will grow. After compiling weather data collected over many years, the U.S. Department of Agriculture (USDA) divided North America, Europe, and China into 11 zones. Each zone represents an expected average annual minimum temperature.

On the USDA Plant Hardiness Zone Map for North America (see Figure 1-2), each of the 11 zones is 10°F warmer or colder in an average winter than the adjacent zone. The warmest zone, Zone 11, records an average low annual temperature of 40°F or higher. In Zone 1, the lowest average annual temperature drops to minus 50°F or colder. Brrr!

Zones 2 through 10 on some North American maps are further subdivided into *a* and *b* regions. The lowest average annual temperature in Zone 5a, for example, is 5°F warmer than the temperature in Zone 5b. When choosing plants that are just barely hardy in your zone, knowing whether your garden falls into the *a* or *b* category can ease your decision. After a few years of personal weather observation in your own garden, you'll have a pretty clear idea of what to expect for winter low temperatures too.

TIP

Most books, catalogs, magazines, and plant labels use the USDA zone system. For a color version, which may be a bit easier to read, visit the U.S. National Arboretum website, which offers a map of North America and individual regions at www.usna.usda.gov/Hardzone/index.html.

REMEMBER

The USDA map is based on a single factor: a region's average minimum winter temperature. Many other factors affect a plant's ability to thrive in a particular environment, so use the map only as a guideline.

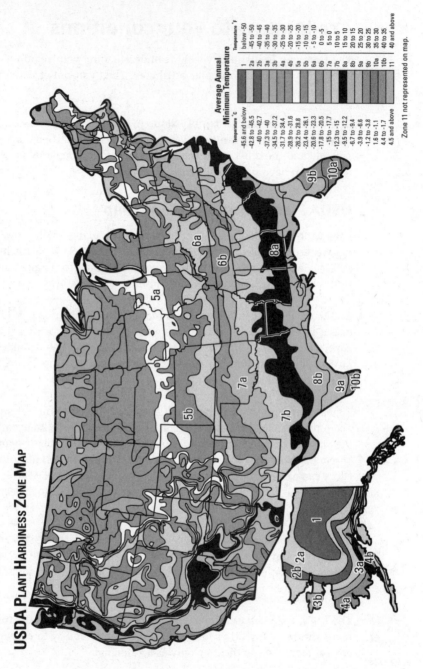

USDA PLANT HARDINESS ZONE MAP

Average Annual Minimum Temperature			
Temperature °c			Temperature °F
-45.6 and below	■	1	below -50
-42.8 to -45.5	■	2a	-45 to -50
-40 to -42.7	■	2b	-40 to -45
-37.3 to -40	■	3a	-35 to -40
-34.5 to -37.2	■	3b	-30 to -35
-31.7 to -34.4	■	4a	-25 to -30
-28.9 to -31.6	■	4b	-20 to -25
-26.2 to -28.8	■	5a	-15 to -20
-23.4 to -26.1	■	5b	-10 to -15
-20.6 to -23.3	■	6a	- 5 to -10
-17.8 to -20.5	■	6b	0 to -5
-15 to -17.7	■	7a	5 to 0
-12.3 to -15	■	7b	10 to 5
-9.5 to -12.2	■	8a	15 to 10
-6.7 to -9.4	■	8b	20 to 15
-3.9 to -6.6	■	9a	25 to 20
-1.2 to -3.8	■	9b	30 to 25
1.6 to -1.1	■	10a	35 to 30
4.4 to -1.7	■	10b	40 to 35
4.5 and above	■	11	40 and above

Zone 11 not represented on map.

FIGURE 1-2:
The USDA Plant Hardiness Zone Map indicates each zone's expected average annual minimum temperature.

AHS Heat Zone Map

To help gardeners in warm climates, the American Horticultural Society developed the AHS Heat Zone Map. This map divides the United States into 12 zones based on the average number of *heat days* each year — days that reach temperatures of 86°F or higher. Zone 1 has fewer than one heat day per year; Zone 12 has more than 210.

Order your own color poster of the AHS Heat Zone Map by calling the society at (800) 777-7931, ext. 137. Or visit the American Horticulture Society's website at `www.ahs.org/publications/heat_zone_map.htm` for more information and a downloadable map. The site also offers a Heat Zone Finder to locate your particular heat zone by zip code.

Sunset map

In an attempt to take total climate into consideration when evaluating plant hardiness, Sunset Publishing created Sunset's Garden Climate Zones, a map that divides the country into 24 zones. This map is especially useful to gardeners in the western United States, where mountains, deserts, and coastal areas create wildly diverse climates, sometimes within a few miles of each other.

Although most national plant suppliers and references use the USDA zone map, regional garden centers and growers in the western half of the country often refer to the Sunset map. View it at `www.sunset.com/sunset/garden/article/1,20633,845218,00.html`.

Factoring in microclimates

Within larger climates, smaller pockets exist that differ somewhat from the prevailing weather around them. These *microclimates* occur wherever a building, body of water, dense shrubs, or hillside modifies the larger climate.

Microclimates may be very small, such as the sunny side of your house or the shady side under a tree, or as large as a village. A town on the shore of Lake Michigan has a different microclimate than a town just 20 miles inland, for example. Common microclimates around your property may include the following:

» **North side of the house:** Cool and shady year-round

» **South side of the house:** Hot and sunny all day; often dry

» **East side of the house:** Warm morning sun and cool afternoon shade

» **West side of the house:** Morning shade and hot afternoon sun

» **Top of a hill:** Exposed to wind and sun; soil dries quickly

» **Bottom of a hill:** Collects cold air and may be poorly drained due to precipitation that runs down the slope

No doubt you can find other examples on your site as you closely observe the patterns of sun, water, wind, and temperature throughout the year.

TIP

Plan your landscape and gardens to take advantage of microclimates. Use wind-sheltered areas to protect tender plants from drying winter winds in cold climates and hot, dry winds in arid places. Put plants such as phlox and lilac, which are prone to leaf disease, in breezy garden spots as a natural way to prevent infections. Avoid putting frost-tender plants at the bottoms of hills, where pockets of cold air form.

REMEMBER

Urban environments typically experience higher temperatures than suburban or rural areas thanks to so many massive heat absorbers such as roofs, steel and glass buildings, concrete, billboards, and asphalt-paved surfaces. And that doesn't even begin to account for all the waste heat generated by human sources such as cars, air conditioners, and factories. The urban homesteader needs to consider all of these additional factors that could make their microclimate even more of a challenge.

Considering different sites

Choosing a site is the important first step in planning a vegetable garden. This may sound like a tough choice to make, but don't worry; a lot of the decision is based on good old common sense. When you're considering a site for your garden, remember these considerations:

>> **Keep it close to home.** Plant your garden where you'll walk by it daily so that you remember to care for it. Also, a vegetable garden is a place people like to gather, so keep it close to a pathway.

Vegetable gardens used to be relegated to some forlorn location out back. Unfortunately, if it's out of sight, it's out of mind. But most homesteaders prefer to plant vegetables front and center — even in the front yard. That way you get to see the fruits of your labor and remember what chores need to be done. Plus, it's a great way to engage the neighbors as they stroll by and admire your plants. You may even be inspired to share a tomato with them.

>> **Make it easy to access.** If you need to bring in soil, compost, mulch, or wood by truck or car, make sure your garden can be easily reached by a vehicle. Otherwise you'll end up working way too hard to cart these essentials from one end of the yard to the other.

>> **Have a water source close by.** Try to locate your garden as close as you can to an outdoor faucet. Hauling hundreds of feet of hose around the yard to water the garden will cause only more work and frustration. And, hey, isn't gardening supposed to be fun?

>> **Keep it flat.** You can garden on a slight slope, and, in fact, a south-facing one is ideal since it warms up faster in spring. However, too severe a slope could lead to erosion problems. To avoid having to build terraces like those at Machu Picchu, plant your garden on flat ground.

REMEMBER

How big is too big for a veggie garden? If you're a first-time gardener, a size of 100 square feet is plenty of space to take care of. However, if you want to produce food for storing and sharing, a 20-foot-by-30-foot plot (600 square feet) is a great size. You can produce an abundance of different vegetables and still keep the plot looking good.

Speaking of upkeep, keep the following in mind when deciding how large to make your garden: If the soil is in good condition, a novice gardener can keep up with a 600-square-foot garden by devoting about a half-hour each day the first month of the season; in late spring through summer, a good half-hour of work every two to three days should keep the garden productive and looking good. Keep in mind that the smaller the garden, the less time it'll take to keep it looking great. Plus, after it's established, the garden will take less time to get up and running in the spring.

Letting the sun shine on your plot

REMEMBER

Vegetables need enough sun to produce at their best. Fruiting vegetables, such as tomatoes, peppers, beans, squash, melons, cucumbers, and eggplant, need at least six hours of direct sun a day for good yields. The amount of sun doesn't have to be continuous though. You can have three hours in the morning with some shade midday and then three more hours in the late afternoon.

However, if your little piece of heaven gets less than six hours of sun, don't give up. You have some options:

>> Crops where you eat the leaves, such as lettuce, arugula, pac choi, and spinach, produce reasonably well in a partially shaded location where the sun shines directly on the plants for three to four hours a day.

>> Root crops such as carrots, potatoes, and beets need more light than leafy vegetables, but they may do well getting only four to six hours of sun a day.

TIP

If you don't have enough sun to grow all the fruiting crops that you want, such as tomatoes and peppers, consider supplementing with a movable garden. Plant some crops in containers and move them to the sunniest spots in your yard throughout the year.

Keep in mind that sun and shade patterns change with the seasons. A site that's sunny in midsummer may later be shaded by trees, buildings, and the longer shadows of late fall and early spring. If you live in a mild-winter climate, such as parts of the southeastern and southwestern United States where it's possible to grow vegetables nearly year-round, choosing a spot that's sunny in winter as well as in summer is important. In general, sites that have clear southern exposure are sunniest in winter (refer to Figure 1-1).

You can have multiple vegetable garden plots around your yard matching the conditions with the vegetables you're growing. If your only sunny spot is a strip of ground along the front of the house, plant a row of peppers and tomatoes. If you have a perfect location near a backdoor, but it gets only morning sun, plant lettuce and greens in that plot.

If shade in your garden comes from nearby trees and shrubs, your vegetable plants will compete for water and nutrients as well as for light. Tree roots extend slightly beyond the *drip line,* the outer foliage reach of the tree. If possible, keep your garden out of the *root zones* (the areas that extend from the drip lines to the trunks) of surrounding trees and shrubs. If avoiding root zones isn't possible, give the vegetables more water and be sure to fertilize to compensate.

Checking your soil's drainage

After you've checked the site location and sun levels of your prospective garden, you need to focus on the third element of the big three: the soil. Ideally you have rich, loamy, well-drained soil with few. Unfortunately, that type of soil is a rarity. But a key that's even more essential to good soil is proper water drainage. Plant roots need air as well as water, and water-logged soils are low in air content. Puddles of water on the soil surface after a rain indicate poor drainage.

TIP

One way to check your soil's drainage is to dig a hole about 10 inches deep and fill it with water. Let the water drain and then fill the hole again the following day. Time how long it takes for the water to drain away. If water remains in the hole more than 8 to 10 hours after the second filling, your soil drainage needs improvement.

Soils made primarily of clay tend to be considered *heavy.* Heavy soils usually aren't as well drained as sandy soils. Adding lots of organic matter to your soil can improve soil drainage. Or you also can build raised beds on a poorly drained site.

But slow water drainage isn't always a bad thing. Soil also can be *too* well drained. Very sandy soil dries out quickly and needs frequent watering during dry spells. Again, adding lots of organic matter to sandy soil increases the amount of water it can hold.

If you encounter a lot of big rocks in your soil, you may want to look for another spot. Or consider going the raised-bed route. You can improve soils that have a lot of clay or that are too sandy, but very rocky soil can be a real headache. In fact, it can be impossible to garden in.

WARNING

Don't plant your garden near or on top of the leach lines of a septic system, for obvious reasons. And keep away from underground utilities. If you have questions, call your local utility company to locate underground lines. If you're unsure what's below ground, visit www.call811.com to have lines or pipes identified for free.

Deciding On a Layout

Designing a vegetable garden is a little bit of art and a little bit of science. Practically speaking, plants must be spaced properly so they have room to grow and arranged so taller vegetables don't shade lower-growing types. Different planting techniques fit the growth habits of different kinds of vegetables. You also should think about the paths between rows and plants. Will you have enough room to harvest, weed, and water, for example?

Your garden needs to make the most of the space you've got. Homesteaders tend to do some serious multitasking with every square foot of land they have to work with, but not everything can happen on the same patch of dirt. If your homesteading efforts will also include raising chickens, for example, you'll need to give your flock ample room for them to spread their wings, too.

A thoughtful garden layout is critical, even if it evolves (and it probably will) over time.

Looking at hills, rows, or raised beds

Before you sketch a plan, you need to decide how to arrange the plants in your garden. You can use three basic planting arrangements:

>> **In rows:** Planting vegetables in rows is the typical farmer technique. Any vegetable can be planted in straight rows, but this arrangement works best with types that need quite a bit of room, such as tomatoes, beans, cabbages, corn, potatoes, peppers, and summer squash.

>> **In hills:** Hills are typically used for vining crops such as cucumbers, melons, pumpkins, and winter squash. You can create a 1-foot-wide, flat-topped mound for heavy soil, or you can create a circle at ground level for sandy soil. You then surround the soil with a moatlike ring for watering. Two or three evenly spaced plants are grown on each hill. Space your hills the recommended distance used for rows of that vegetable.

>> **In raised beds:** Raised beds are kind of like wide, flat-topped rows. They're usually at least 2 feet wide and raised at least 6 inches high, but any planting area that's raised above the surrounding ground level is a raised bed. Almost any vegetable can benefit from being grown on a raised bed, but smaller vegetables and root crops, such as lettuce, beets, carrots, onions, spinach, and radishes, really thrive with this type planting. On top of the raised bed you can grow plants in rows or with broadcast seeding.

A raised bed can be *temporary*, with the soil piled 5 or 6 inches high. Or you can build a *permanent raised bed* with wood, stone, or masonry sides, as shown in Figure 1-3. And refer to Book 5, Chapter 1 for instructions on building your own easy raised garden beds.

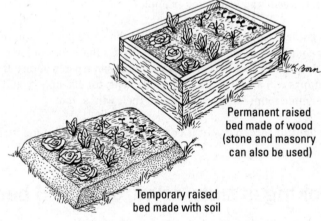

FIGURE 1-3:
Raised beds can be made with soil alone, or with wood, stone, or masonry sides.

Permanent raised bed made of wood (stone and masonry can also be used)

Temporary raised bed made with soil

Illustration by Kathryn Born

Raised beds have several advantages, including the following:

>> **They rise above soil problems.** If you have bad soil or poor drainage, raised beds are for you. You can amend the garden soil in the raised bed with compost or the same sterile potting soil you use for containers. And because you don't step on the beds as you work, the soil is more likely to stay light and fluffy, providing the perfect conditions for root growth — especially for root crops such as carrots and beets.

>> **They warm up quickly.** Because more of the soil in raised beds is exposed to the sun, the soil warms early and dries out faster, allowing for early planting and extended harvest seasons.

If you're in a hot climate and have sandy soil, raised beds may not be for you, because they'll dry out and heat up too much.

>> **They reduce your work.** By growing your vegetables in raised beds, you can maximize your fertilizing and watering so that more nutrients and water are actually used by the plants rather than wasted in the pathways.

>> **They're easy on your back and knees.** If you design the beds properly (about 18 to 24 inches high and no wider than 4 feet), raised beds can make vegetable gardening a lot more comfortable. You can sit on the edge and easily reach into the bed to weed or harvest. You can even cap the edge to make it more benchlike.

>> **They're attractive.** You can make raised beds in almost any shape you like — rectangle, square, triangle, circle. Just keep the width less than 4 feet so you can easily reach the center of the bed without stepping on the soil.

Never use pressure-treated wood or creosote-treated railroad ties to construct raised beds. These woods have been treated with chemicals, and although they'll last a long time, research has shown that some of these chemicals leach into the soil and can adversely affect your plants. The risk of poisoning your soil and crops is simply too great and far outweighs any benefits that might come with treated wood.

The one possible downside of permanent raised beds is turning the soil. Lifting a tiller onto the bed can be difficult, so they may be best turned by hand with an iron fork or with a minitiller. There's more on tilling — including a gardening strategy that avoids it altogether — in Chapter 3 of this minibook.

In dry areas such as the desert Southwest, the traditional bed isn't raised — it's sunken. These *waffle beds* are created by digging into the soil about 6 inches deep and making a small wall of soil around the outside edge of the bed. This design allows the bed to catch any summer rains, protects young plants from the drying winds, and concentrates water where the vegetables grow.

Spacing your plantings properly

After you know what you're planting and how to arrange the plants, it's time to talk spacing. Make a list of the different types of vegetables that you want to grow, and then pay attention to these columns in the guide to planting in Chapter 4 of this minibook:

- » **Plants/Seeds per 100 ft. of Row:** This column tells you how many plants/how much seed you need to purchase.

- » **Spacing between Rows/Beds (Inches):** This column includes the ideal distance you should leave between rows or beds of different vegetables. This is usually a little more than the distance you should leave between plants.

- » **Spacing between Plants (Inches):** In this column, you find the ideal distance to allow between individual vegetable plants within a row or planting bed.

- » **Average Yield per 10 ft. of Row:** This column shows you how much you can expect to harvest.

TIP

If you're growing in raised beds, you can plant a little closer together than the guidelines suggest because you'll be concentrating fertilizer and water in a smaller space.

WARNING

Even though closer planting is possible, don't plant so close that plants have to compete with each other for food, water, and light. If you do, you'll eventually get smaller harvests or lower-quality vegetables.

Following the paths

You can get so involved in the beds, rows, hills, and vegetable varieties that you forget about the paths between everything. Keep the paths at least 2 to 3 feet wide so you can easily walk on them. For larger gardens, consider a few main paths that are wide enough for a garden cart.

Sketching it out

After you determine the location and dimensions of your garden, you need to sketch out a simple garden plan. A functional drawing is fine; it doesn't have to be a work of art. All you need is a piece of graph paper and a pencil, a list of vegetables you want to grow, and maybe a seed catalog or two. Then just grab your pencil and graph paper and start drawing. First, draw the garden to scale. Leave space from the edge of the paper, draw in the first row, leave room for a path, and then create your next row. Continue filling in the rows with your favorite crops, taking into account the space requirements of the crops you want to grow; whether you want to plant in rows, beds, or hills; and how much of each vegetable you want to harvest.

REMEMBER

Here are a few things to keep in mind as you sketch out your garden plan:

>> **You can't plant everything.** Choose your crops carefully, and grow only what you like to eat. And grow only how much you think you can eat. Eating broccoli for breakfast, lunch, and dinner can get old fast.

>> **Not all plants have it made in the shade.** Tall crops such as corn should be placed where they won't shade other vegetables. The north end of the garden is usually best.

>> **These roots aren't made for walking.** Plan your garden with walkways so you can get to plants easily without damaging roots.

TIP

Planning on paper helps you purchase the correct number of seeds or transplants and use space more efficiently. It's a good way to see the possibilities for *succession planting* (following one crop with another) and *interplanting* (planting a quick maturing crop next to a slower-maturing one and harvesting the former before it competes for space). For example, you might see that you can follow your early peas with a crop of late broccoli, and you'll be ready with transplants in July. Or you might see that there's space to tuck a few lettuce plants among your tomatoes while the vines are still small. You can find out more about these techniques in Chapter 5 of this minibook.

Thinking Outside the Garden Bed

Not all of your crops have to be planted in the ground. Generations of resourceful gardeners and homesteaders have used various techniques to maximize their planting space well beyond the actual square footage of earth they have to work with. Keep them in mind as you plan your garden, and you may magically find room for a bunch more plants, a few more rows, maybe even a whole additional crop!

Going vertical

If you're short on space in your garden or want to plant more than you really have room for, go vertical! You can save space and energy by trellising, fencing, or caging certain vegetables. And by incorporating these vertical growers into your initial design, you can often free up more planting space in your beds. For example, one cucumber plant can take up 15 square feet or more when left sprawling on the ground. Grow your cukes on a trellis, and you can have four plants in that same amount of space.

Vertical gardening can create the additional space needed to help urban home-steaders grow a larger and more abundant vegetable garden, but the same techniques can help suburban gardeners and rural homesteaders maximize the output of a garden of any size!

Climbing vegetables, such as peas and pole beans, need fences or poles to grow on. These devices also save space. Set up a teepee of 6- to 8-foot poles, attach chicken wire to fence posts, or train the plants on an A-frame. (If you use the teepee method, wind some twine around the poles at 6-inch intervals to give the vines something to cling to or wind around.)

Cucumbers, melons, and even some squash love to vine and ramble. You can direct their energy by growing them on a trellis. Place the trellis on an angle, such as an A-frame design (shown in Figure 1-4), instead of straight up and down.

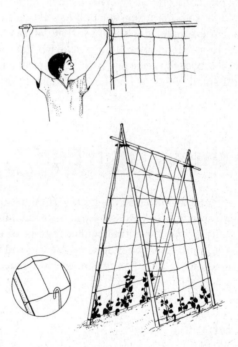

FIGURE 1-4:
An A-frame.

REMEMBER

If you're growing vines with heavy fruits, such as melons or squash, make sure that the trellis is very sturdy. You can find step-by-step instructions for building your own trellises and such in Book 5, Chapter 1.

Tomatoes, peppers, and eggplants all can be caged or staked with a pole to keep them growing upright, elevate their fruits off the ground (which can help prevent disease and damage from slugs, mice, and other ground- dwelling critters), and give you more produce in less space. Commercial growers tie wire or twine between fence posts and weave the growing tomato plants through it. Also, 4- to 5-foot-high wire cages made of hog fencing or concrete reinforcing wire work well. Secure the cages with a tall stake pounded into the ground to prevent them from blowing over.

REMEMBER

Keep in mind that sun exposure is important for good vegetable production. Locate your trellises, teepees, or other vertical structure where the foliage will receive good sunlight without shading other areas of the garden.

Container vegetables

You can grow almost any vegetable in a container. Whether you're strapped for space in your beds, want to locate certain crops close to a patio or porch, or just want to add some architectural interest to your homestead landscape, containers offer all kinds of possibilities.

In most cases, pots that are bigger (in terms of width and volume) are better, especially for growing large plants such as tomatoes. Lots of root space means that your vegetables are less likely to get cramped; they'll also be easier to water and fertilize.

Pots made of porous materials such as clay dry out faster than those made of plastic or wood, so you must water the plants in them more frequently, especially in hot or windy climates.

REMEMBER

You're not limited to pricey ceramic pots from the garden superstore! Wooden window boxes, affordable plastic flowerpots, and hanging baskets offer alternatives. Of course, any kind of container at all can add a touch of creative whimsy with some plants growing in it: an old boot, a rusted-out galvanized bucket, a chicken feeder, a vintage wheelbarrow, or even an old bathtub can be turned into a planter by an imaginative gardener.

WARNING

All the pots you use for growing vegetables should have drainage holes; fortunately, almost all store-bought pots do. If you repurpose something else as a container, you may need to add a drainage hole so the plant roots don't drown.

REMEMBER

Don't fill your pot with soil from your garden — even if your garden has the very best soil on the planet. It's too heavy and too dirty (you know, weed seeds, bugs, bacteria — stuff that you don't want in your pots), and it may not drain properly in a pot. Instead, use potting soil.

Vegetable breeders have long had container gardeners in mind. They breed many small-space varieties (of even the most sprawling plants) that are ideal for growing in pots. The following list contains the most common vegetables to grow in containers, but try anything with the words *compact, bush, baby, midget, dwarf, tiny,* or *teeny* in the name:

>> **Beans:** Bush varieties such as 'Provider' and 'Derby' are best; you can grow three to four plants in a 12-inch pot. You can grow pole types in a long narrow box, but you have to attach some type of trellis.

>> **Beets:** Any variety grows well in a pot, and smaller varieties such as 'Red Ace 'even grow well in smaller pots. However, make sure your pot is big and deep enough (at least 12 inches); beets don't like to be crowded.

>> **Carrots:** Carrots are a perfect vegetable to grow in a pot. Start with a baby variety such as 'Little Fingers', 'Short 'n Sweet', or T'humbelina'. If you water diligently, you can get a bumper harvest in pots as shallow as 6 to 8 inches deep. Longer varieties need deeper pots. After thinning, you should end up with 20 or so carrots per 12-inch pot.

>> **Cole crops — broccoli, cabbage, cauliflower, and so on:** All the cole crops grow well in containers as long as your pots are big enough; try planting three or four plants in a half barrel.

>> **Cucumbers:** You can't go wrong growing small cucumber types such as 'Bush Pickle' and 'Salad Bush'. Plant large-growing varieties in bigger pots and slip a sturdy wire cylinder into the outside edge of the pot for the plants to climb on.

>> **Eggplant:** An eggplant's purple foliage and compact habit are perfect for pots; any variety works as long the container is at least 5 gallons. Plant one eggplant per 5-gallon pot. If a plant gets floppy, push a small stake in the pot to support the plant.

>> **Lettuce and other greens:** Lettuce and greens may be the ultimate container vegetables. The size of your pot doesn't really matter — just sprinkle some seeds in it, keep the soil moist, and then get out your salad bowl for a great harvest. You can harvest the whole plant or snip off just what you need.

>> **Melons:** Melons aren't ideal container subjects; they're wild and unruly. But through the magic of modern science, some dwarf varieties, such as 'Bush Sugar Baby' watermelon, grow well in containers. Plant one to two plants in a big pot (at least 5 gallons) and let the vines sprawl over the edges, supporting the fruit if necessary. And don't let up on water and fertilizer.

>> **Onions:** Green onions — scallions or bunching onions if you prefer to call them that — grow well in containers. Just buy a bag of sets, plant them 2- to 3-inches deep, and you're in business. You can grow onions to full bulb size; just make sure that you use a big pot (preferably 5 gallons) and give them plenty of room to grow.

>> **Peas:** Go with dwarf pea varieties such as 'Green Arrow' and 'Maestro', English peas, 'Sugar Bon' snap pea, or 'Dwarf Grey Sugar' snow pea. Any variety larger than that needs a trellis. Planting six plants in a 12-inch pot should be fine.

>> **Peppers:** You can grow any pepper variety in a pot, but the bigger the pot the better. Small-fruited varieties such as 'Serrano' and 'Black Pearl' peppers produce so much colorful fruit that their containers become showpieces. A 5-gallon pot should hold one to two plants.

>> **Potatoes:** Potatoes are fun vegetables to grow in a container. Just place 8 to 10 inches of potting soil in a big pot (at least a 5-gallon size). Plant two to three potato eyes 2 to 3 inches from the bottom of the pot, and then water them in. After the plants start to grow, cover the stems with more soil (leaving the very top exposed) until the pot is full. In a couple of months, you can harvest a pot full of spuds.

>> **Radishes:** Growing radishes is quick and easy even in the smallest container. Scatter some seeds in the top of a pot, keep the soil moist, and you'll have radishes in less than a month.

>> **Squash:** Use a 5-gallon pot (or even larger) to grow space-saving winter squash varieties such as 'Cornell Bush Delicata', 'Papaya Pear', or 'Table King'. Plant three seeds in each pot and thin to the healthiest plant.

>> **Tomatoes:** Try your favorite dwarf indeterminate variety, such as 'Bush Big Boy' in a container that's at least 5 gallons (bigger is better), but be ready to stake or cage tall plants. Or you can grow dwarf varieties such as 'Patio', 'Tiny Tim', and 'Window Box Roma', which fit perfectly in pots, even smaller sizes.

Most herbs grow well in containers.

Vertical containers

After you wrap your head around the idea of growing things non-horizontally outside the garden bed, and warm up to the concept of growing some of your crops in containers, the next logical step is to take your containers vertical, too, and utilize all of that wall and fence space for growing.

Here is a list of some popular vertical gardening products:

>> **Vertical containers:** Many interesting containers that are made for hanging on a fence, wall, or post are on the market now. Imagine a wall filled with flowering containers of cascading plants, or a monoculture of salad greens!

>> **Pot hangers for containers:** Some garden centers now sell attractive pot hangers from which a terra-cotta pot can be hung on a post, wall, or fence. These hangers can be used to create a multitiered garden of radishes, chard, kohlrabi, lettuce, or other small greens. Other half-round containers are made for attaching to a wall or fence and make great use of limited space in city gardens.

>> **Planter walls:** Manufacturers now include options for planting vertically along both freestanding and retaining walls. Another option to consider when building retaining walls is to divide the wall height and include a terraced area for planting between the walls (see Figure 1-5). For instance, instead of building an 8-foot-high wall, build two 4-foot-high walls with a 2-foot-wide planter between the two wall structures.

FIGURE 1-5: Example of a modular planter wall.

Illustration by Kathryn Born

>> **Straddling containers:** Numerous products are available that (like a saddle) can straddle both sides of your balcony railing, even along the top of a fence. The Steckling plants container designed by German designer Michael Hilgers is one example of a modern design that has a look of a simple circular planter (see Figure 1-6, left), whereas more traditional balcony containers are boxier like window planters (see Figure 1-6, right).

>> **Wall hanging pocket gardens:** Wall hanging pocket gardens (see Figure 1-7) are simple pocket planters which can easily hang and affix to walls, rails, and fences and can be used indoors or outside. They all come with simple

fasteners and anchors that work on masonry, drywall, sheetrock, wood, and metal walls.

» **Stacking planters:** Imagine picking the fruit from a stand of strawberries 3 feet high! Stacking planters are specifically designed so that when you stack them, they create a column of multiple and interconnected growing facets that may be suspended or just left freestanding. Nancy Jane's Stacking Planters are one product specifically designed so that when you stack them, they create a column of multiple and interconnected growing facets that may be suspended or just left freestanding. Check them out at www.gardensupplyinc.com.

FIGURE 1-6:
Different types of straddling containers.

Illustration by Kathryn Born

FIGURE 1-7:
A wall hanging pocket garden.

Illustration by Kathryn Born

PALLET GARDENING: HOW DOES IT STACK UP?

Shipping pallets are being reused extensively in the garden today (see the figure), often being reconstructed into vertical garden features which are great for small or tight spaces. (You can remove and relocate some of the planks to form a series of tiered horizontal planter boxes along your pallet garden.) But many pallets are made with treated wood, and the chemicals used in that process may slowly leach into the soil over time. As cool as pallet gardens are, you shouldn't use them for vegetable gardens because the pallet wood may have been chemically treated, even if it might not look like it. Save the pallet garden for flowering annuals or other non-edibles only.

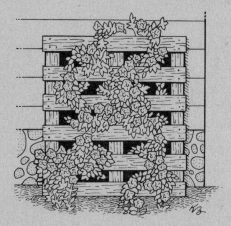

Illustration by Kathryn Born

Keeping Critters Out

A discussion of garden planning wouldn't be complete without considering the animals that may plague your gardens: deer, rabbits, groundhogs, and the like. Some of these larger critters can quickly eliminate an entire plant — or row of plants. Deer, rabbits, and woodchucks can consume a whole garden! The best way to deter these animals from helping themselves to your homestead is to figure out up front how you're going to keep them out, rather than wait until you already have a problem.

We'll deal with how to install various types of fencing in Chapter 3 of this minibook. Here, for your garden planning purposes, we'll limit ourselves to which members of the wild kingdom you need to be on the lookout for, and on guard against. (Animals are ordered from most to least damaging to a vegetable garden.)

Deer

Deer are among the most troublesome of garden pests. They live in wooded areas but also in suburban and urban locales, and in many places their numbers are increasing. When food is scarce, they eat just about anything. A deer or two can ravage an entire garden overnight.

To identify deer damage, look closely at affected plants. Deer don't have upper front teeth, so when they eat, they tear plant tissue rather than cutting it, leaving ragged edges. Deer prefer tender new growth when it's available, but eat buds and twigs in winter. They tend to feed on the edges of wooded areas so that they can duck for cover if threatened.

Deer can reach as high as 6 feet, so if you see damage at eye level, you're probably dealing with a deer, not a mutant rabbit. Look for telltale hoofprints and piles of deer scat (usually rounded pellets with a dimple on one end, about the size and shape of a chocolate-covered peanut or small black olive). Deer are most likely to visit gardens when other food sources are scarce, especially in late winter and early spring.

Fencing is the most common deer deterrent. But be prepared to think big (and potentially expensive). You might be surprised how high (and effortlessly) deer can jump. A 6-foot fence won't cut it; make it at least 8 feet high.

TIP

You can even make a 5-foot-fence more deerproof by using taller posts and attaching strands of wire above the fence, such as at 7 feet and 10 feet.

Consider slanting your fence outward, as shown in Figure 1-8. Deer are less likely to jump a wide fence, apparently intimidated about jumping when they can't tell how much distance they have to clear or how much space they'll have once they land. A slanted fence can be just 4 to 5 feet high and still be quite effective, but it does take up more yardspace.

Some gardeners rely on a double fence of sorts, with a 5- or 6-foot fence surrounding their garden, and a much shorter fence (or even a row of stakes with string run between them) just outside it. This visual barrier can confuse deer, who have poor depth perception, and encourage them to look elsewhere for their meal. Deer are creatures of habit; some gardeners find they can remove this outer barrier after the deer in their area change their travel pattern. If deer return, it's easy enough to reinstall the short outer fence.

Illustration by Kathryn Born

Electric fencing or netting is the answer for other gardeners. Not intended to be a physical barrier, electric fencing uses a strong shock to convince deer that entering the garden is too painful to be worth the trouble. Some electric fences are solar powered, and some use scented bait to attract deer to the fence, where they touch an electrified strand and learn to avoid contact.

These are a few other tactics gardeners use to dissuade deer, from the ultra-practical to the super-weird.

» **Scare tactics:** Motion-detector-activated sprinklers may deter deer for a short time. (Just be sure to turn them off before you venture into the garden.) Playing a radio in the garden at night may work for a few days, but the deer will catch on quickly, and if they're hungry enough, they won't care.

» **Row covers:** In early spring, spread row-cover fabric over tender new growth, supporting the covers with wire cages or hoops if necessary. These row covers can deter the deer long enough to give your plants a head start and allow time for their natural wild food plants to become plentiful. Refer to Chapter 7 of this minibook for info on row covers.

>> **Sprays:** Some gardeners swear by predator urine (which repels by scent) along with a bad-tasting hot pepper spray. But if you continually use the same deterrent, the deer will get used to it and ignore it.

>> **Soap:** Hang bars of soap from low tree branches or from stakes so that the bars are about 30 inches off the ground. Fragrant, tallow-based soaps such as Irish Spring work best.

>> **Hair:** Ask your barber or hairdresser if you can have some hair trimmings. Human hair hung in mesh bags about 3 feet off the ground may deter deer. Dog hair may work for some, too.

>> **Homemade repellent:** Use spray repellents on foliage. One recipe: Mix three raw eggs in a gallon of water and spray the mixture on plants. This substance apparently smells worse to the deer than it does to you.

REMEMBER

Many plants are touted as deer resistant, but if deer are hungry enough, they'll eat just about anything. Still, if you live in an area where deer pressure is high, including plants such as catmint, hellebore, and yarrow increases the likelihood that at least something in your garden will survive.

Rabbits

Some homesteaders choose to raise rabbits (see Book 4, Chapter 3), but most prefer to keep Peter Cottontail and his friends away from their crops.

Rabbits are homebodies. They tend to stake out a rather small territory — 10 acres or less — and not wander elsewhere. They make their homes in natural cavities in trees, in other animals' abandoned burrows, in brush piles, and under buildings. They nibble the foliage of almost any plant, returning again and again, day and night, to finish the job.

Unlike deer, rabbits have both upper and lower front teeth, and you can identify their damage by a clean, angled cut on the ends of leaves and twigs. If you suspect rabbits, look for their droppings, which are round or slightly flattened; think marbles or M&Ms. The individual pellets are smaller and rounder than the more elongated deer scat.

Rabbits tend to eat vegetables and flowers in spring and summer. The best way to keep rabbits away from your plants is to fence them out. Because they burrow, a fence must also extend underground. Choose a 4-foot-high, chicken-wire fence with 1-inch mesh. Bury the bottom foot of the fence, bending the lowest 6 inches into a right angle facing outward.

Some folks have luck using hair gathered from hair salons and dog groomers as a repellent. Sprinkle it around the boundary of a garden and replenish it every few weeks. Most commercial spray repellents are not suitable for use on vegetables, as they affect the plants' taste, to both the rabbits and you.

Groundhogs

These slow-moving rodents, also called woodchucks and whistlepigs, live in an extensive system of underground dens and tunnels, and they defy you to find all their tunnel entrances. A tunnel can extend nearly 70 feet. If you see a mound of excavated earth surrounding a foot-wide hole, you're probably looking at the entrance to a groundhog tunnel.

Groundhogs generally stay within about 100 feet of their dens, venturing out morning and evening to find food: your tender veggies. They favor beans, squash, peas, and brassicas (the genus of plants that include broccoli, cabbage, and cauliflower) and they can mow down a row of seedlings overnight. They also gnaw and claw woody plants.

If you suspect groundhogs, scan your landscape in the morning and evening hours. They are relatively bold, and you may catch a culprit red-handed. Here are some deterrents:

>> **Fencing:** Groundhogs can climb up almost as well as they can dig down, so use a sturdy 4- or 5-foot fence, and bury the bottom 18 inches underground. Bend the top of the fence outward so that a groundhog falls over backward if it attempts to climb over. Two strands of electric fence — one 4 inches above the ground and the other 8 inches high — may also keep them out.

>> **Repellents:** Hot pepper wax sprays may act as deterrents; groundhogs don't seem to be fazed by other repellent sprays.

Gophers

These burrowing rodents live in underground tunnel systems extending as far as 200 yards. They feast underground on plant roots and bulbs, occasionally emerging to eat aboveground parts of those plants located near the tunnel openings. Most gopher species live in the western two thirds of the country; one species is native to the Southeast. (If you live in New England, don't blame your garden problems on gophers.)

The telltale sign of gophers is a collection of fan-shaped soil mounds, with new mounds appearing daily. You won't see a tunnel entrance; the critters keep the entrances plugged with soil.

Gophers are difficult to scare or repel. Castor oil sprayed on the garden may repel them. If gophers are a serious problem, you may want to go to the trouble of lining the sides and bottom of your garden at a depth of 2 feet with hardware cloth to keep the gophers out. (See Figure 1-9.) Gopher-resistant wire baskets, which can be placed in planting holes before planting, are commercially available. For persistent problems, use traps.

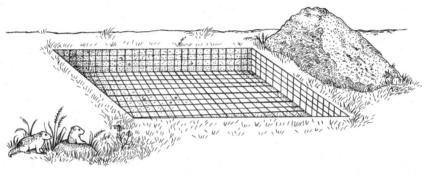

FIGURE 1-9:
Buried fencing is the safest and most effective way to deter digging animals such as gophers.

Illustration by Kathryn Born

TIP

Research has shown that vibrating devices such as large whirligigs stuck in the ground near tunnels have little effect. Apparently, gophers in a home landscape even get used to the sounds and vibrations of mechanical equipment such as lawn mowers. So don't waste your money on these devices.

Mice and voles

Mice and voles look similar. Both are small rodents, but the tail of a vole is much shorter than that of a mouse. Mice are fond of young seedlings, especially those growing in a greenhouse on a cold winter day; they're omnivores, though, and eat almost anything. (They can be particularly problematic for backyard chicken-keepers, as we discuss in Book 4, Chapter 4.) Voles, on the other hand, are almost exclusively herbivores and are the more troublesome pest for gardeners.

Voles create extensive networks of tunnels that, if located under your garden or lawn, can cause root damage. Chewed root vegetables probably are the work of voles. Look for the tiny, 1/8-inch-wide chisel marks left by their incisors. Damage to stored vegetables, on the other hand, probably is the work of mice.

Voles are hard to control, but you can discourage them by keeping grass mowed and your yard free of weeds. (More on why and how to control weeds in Chapter 5 of this minibook.) Surround valuable plantings with a fence made of 1/4-inch hardware cloth buried 6 inches deep and rising at least a foot off the ground. Keep the perimeter mowed and free of plant debris.

Raccoons

Raccoons like to eat pretty much anything. They seem to appear out of nowhere to pilfer your fruit and corn just before you get out to harvest it. They also eat grubs and, like skunks, dig up your lawn to find them, damaging plants in the process.

Repellents and motion-detector-activated sprinklers may provide enough protection to allow your crops to ripen. Controlling grubs in the lawn can also help. A low, two-strand electric fence, described in the "Groundhogs" section, might keep raccoons out of your vegetable garden.

You might also consider a 5-foot wire-mesh fence specially modified to use the raccoon's body weight against it. Bury the bottom 12 inches of fence, curving the material away from the garden, allowing 4 feet of fence to stand aboveground. But leave the top 18 inches unattached to support posts; if a raccoon attempts to climb the fence, it will bend back down under the animal's weight.

Squirrels

Squirrels are so bold, it's likely that you'll catch them in the act of digging in your garden. These agile, fearless creatures can cause quite a problem, eating fruits, nuts, berries, seedlings, and bark. . . even pilfering softball-sized tomatoes!

You can't get rid of squirrels permanently. If you evict your current residents, new ones will come to take their place. You can try deterrents such as spraying bad-tasting sprays on favorite plants, however.

For some crops, you can cover newly planted beds with chicken wire; the plants will grow right through it in spring. Motion detector–activated sprinklers can offer short-term help.

WARNING

Despite advice you may have heard, don't use mothballs in the garden as a squirrel deterrent. You don't want this potential carcinogen contaminating your soil.

Birds

Birds in the yard are a mixed blessing. You appreciate their appetite for insects, but when they nibble on the tomatoes and devour the ripe blueberries, they cross the line into nuisance territory. You can keep birds away from your plants by draping bird netting or row covers over them, but this solution isn't always practical.

To keep birds from eating seeds or pulling up newly sprouted plants, protect your seedbed with a bird tunnel (see Figure 1-10) or a floating row cover. By the time the plants outgrow the cover, they're no longer appetizing to birds.

FIGURE 1-10:
Covering seedlings with a portable bird tunnel is a sure way to keep birds away.

Illustration by Kathryn Born

Noise, fluttering objects, and anything resembling a predator can startle birds. Try bordering your garden with strings tied to stakes and fastening aluminum pie plates or unwanted CDs to the string. The noise and flashing of the sun on the shiny surfaces can scare birds away. Or instead of string, use only a thin nylon line, which will vibrate and hum in the breeze.

Flash, or *scare, tape* is effective. Available in long rolls, this lightweight iridescent ribbon is cut to size and can be hung anywhere birds are a nuisance. The streamers flutter in even a slight breeze, scaring away birds with both noise and bright reflected light.

You can use the modern version of the scarecrow: balloons and kites with images of predators, such as owls and hawks. Place them in the garden to convince birds that their enemy is on guard.

TIP

Birds catch on quickly, so change your scare tactics regularly.

Assembling Tools

You've probably heard this saying at least a hundred times: "Use the right tool for the job."

When planning a new vegetable garden, however, you may find that knowing which tools to pick is often confusing. You can spend hundreds of dollars buying tools for every imaginable use, but you may end up spending more time in your tool shed than in your garden. So when you're selecting your tools, it's best to start simple — here are the ten essential tools. And keep in mind that even these tools may not be appropriate for all garden situations.

TIP

To keep your metal hand tools functioning for years, clean and store them properly. After you're finished using a tool, wash all soil off it. Yearly, sharpen the blades of weeders, spades, and shovels; oil wooden handles with linseed oil; and tighten any nuts and screws on the handles.

Watering hoses and cans

Even if you have a fully-operational irrigation system (you'll find options in Chapter 3 of this minibook), there will be times when it's best to water by hand with a good old-fashioned hose and watering can. (One of these times is when caring for seedlings and new plants, as discussed in Chapter 4 of this minibook.)

Rubber hoses are less likely to kink than vinyl or nylon hoses, but they tend to be much heavier to move around. Whatever material you choose, be sure to get a hose that's long enough to reach plants in all areas of your garden without having to shoot water across the beds to reach distant plants. Choose a hose that has brass fittings and a washer integrated into the hose; these elements make the hose less likely to fail after prolonged use.

Watering cans can be made of simple, inexpensive, brightly colored plastic or high-end, fancy galvanized metal. Plastic is lighter, but galvanized metal is rust-proof and more attractive. Watering cans also come in different sizes, so try a few out for comfort before buying. Make sure you can easily remove the sprinkler head, or rose, for cleaning.

TIP

For watering tender seedlings, buy a can with an oval rose that points upward and applies water with less pressure. The traditional round rose is better for watering more mature plants.

Hand trowels

Hand trowels are essential for digging in containers, window boxes, and small raised beds. The wider-bladed hand trowels, which are scoop shaped and rounded on the end, are easier to use to loosen soil than the narrower-bladed, V-pointed ones. These narrower blades are better for digging tough weeds, such as dandelions.

Hand trowel blades usually are made of steel or plastic. Steel blades are more durable, but plastic blades are lighter. Although stainless steel versions are more expensive than plastic ones, they're easier to clean and easier to find if you lose them. The handles may be steel, wooden, or plastic. Choose a trowel that's forged as one piece of metal or that has secure attachments between the blade and handle.

Try different hand trowels before buying, choosing one that feels comfortable and that fits your hand well. Ergonomic versions of hand trowels have forearm supports and cushioned grips.

Hand cultivators

A *three-pronged hand cultivator* is a handy tool to break up soil clods, smooth seed beds, and work in granular fertilizer. Plus, after you plant your small container or raised bed, the weeds will come whether you like it or not; a cultivator serves as a great tool to remove these young weeds as they germinate. When you're digging a planting hole, a hand cultivator breaks up the soil more easily than a hand trowel.

As with a hand trowel, be sure to choose a hand cultivator that feels comfortable in your hand and that has a handle securely fastened to the blade. The steel-bladed types are the most durable.

Garden hoes

Hoes are available for all occasions — hoes for digging furrows, hoes for weeding, hoes for wide rows, hoes for tight rows, hoes that scuffle, hoes that oscillate, and even hoes for specific vegetables such as the onion hoe. What you need largely depends on the design of your garden. The best hoes have long hardwood handles and single-forged steel blades strongly attached to their handles. Here are three favorites:

>> **Common garden hoe:** This classic hoe has a broad, straight, 6-inch steel blade that's good for all types of gardening, including digging, weeding, chopping, hilling, and cultivating. Longer- and narrower-bladed versions, such as the collinear hoe, are good for weeding in tight spots.

>> **Oscillating hoe (also known as a stirrup hoe):** This hoe, shown in Figure 1-11, is primarily used for weeding. Unlike other hoes — which cut weeds on the pull stroke — this hoe cuts weeds on the pull stroke *and* the push stroke, enabling you to weed faster. The 4- to 7-inch-wide steel stirrup is hinged so it moves back and forth, digging about 1/4 inch deep into the soil and scalping off young weeds. This hoe works well in gardens with clearly defined rows and spaces between plants.

>> **Tined hoe:** This hoe has 3 or 4 steel tines attached to the bottom of a 5- to 6-inch-diameter steel head. Tined hoes are good for weeding, cultivating, digging, chopping, hilling, and breaking up soil clods. They're lighter, more versatile, and easier to use than common hoes.

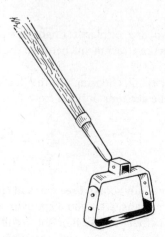

FIGURE 1-11:
An oscillating hoe.

Spades and shovels

Spades and shovels are two of the most commonly used gardening tools. The difference between the two is simple: A *spade* is designed for digging, and a *shovel* is designed for scooping and throwing. Shovels traditionally have rounded and pointed blades, whereas spades have flat, straight, almost rectangular blades. A good shovel is essential in any garden for spreading compost, manure, or fertilizer. A spade is essential for edging or breaking new ground. However, many gardeners use spades for anything from cutting open fertilizer bags to hammering in stakes. Good spades are rugged.

Both spades and shovels come in short- and long-handled versions. A long handle gives you more leverage when digging holes, so keep that in mind if you're purchasing a new spade. Choose a spade or a shovel that has a single piece of metal attached to a wooden handle with either a single socket or a single socket that runs 1 foot up the handle (referred to as a *solid-strap* connection). These models are heavier, but they're much more durable.

TIP

To get a more comfortable grip on long-handled tools such as spades and shovels, try low-cost foam grippers that fit on the handles. These grippers make the diameter of a handle larger and more cushioned, reducing the amount of blistering and cramping in your hands. They're available at local garden centers or on the Internet.

Garden forks

As handy as a spade is for turning fresh garden soil, an *iron fork* (also called a garden fork, a spading fork, a digging fork, or even a border fork) is a better tool for turning beds that have been worked before. The fork digs into the soil as deep as

12 inches, and at the same time breaks up clods and loosens and aerates the soil better than a spade. Iron forks look similar to short-handled spades except that they have three to four iron tines on their heads. The best ones are those forged from one piece of steel with hardwood handles firmly attached. They're great not only for turning soil but also for turning compost piles and digging root crops, such as potatoes and carrots.

One tool you may want to consider is the *broadfork*. With two long handles and a series of deep curved tines between them (see Figure 1-12), the gardener steps onto the crossbar of the broadfork (sometimes called a U-fork or *grelinette*), using body weight to till and break up garden beds without destroying the soil's structure.

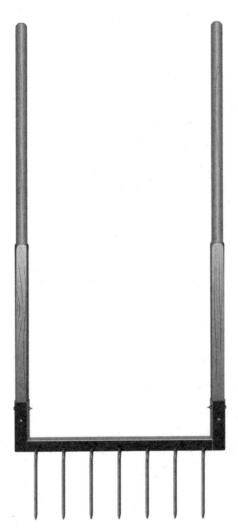

FIGURE 1-12:
A broadfork uses body weight to efficiently break up garden soil.

TIP

A heavy-duty broadfork can be quite expensive; many gardeners get by with a conventional pitchfork. Some even roll up their sleeves (and ingenuity) to make their own broadfork!

Garden rakes

After you dig soil, you need to level it, break up soil clods, and smooth the seedbeds (especially if you're growing raised beds). An *iron rake* is the right tool for the job even though you may use it for this purpose only a few times a year. A 14-inch-diameter, iron-toothed rake should have a long, wooden handle that's securely attached to a metal head. You can flip the metal head over to really smooth a seedbed flat. For a lightweight but less durable version of an iron rake, try an aluminum rake.

Buckets, wagons, and baskets

You may not have a 1,000-square-foot garden. But you still need to carry seeds, tools, fertilizer, produce, and other items around. Here are three essential containers:

>> **Buckets:** For fertilizers, potting soil, and hand tools, a 5-gallon plastic bucket is the perfect container. You can probably get one free from a construction site; just make sure to clean it out well. For a more durable but smaller bucket, buy one made from galvanized steel.

>> **Wagons:** For bulkier items, such as flats of seedlings, use a child's old red wagon. Wagons are great for moving plants and small bags of fertilizer in your garden, and the lip on the wagon bed helps hold these items in place when you cover bumpy ground. If you're interested in a wagon to move yourself (and not just equipment) around the garden, try a wagon with a seat. This type of wagon usually has a swiveling seat and is perched on four pneumatic tires, allowing you to sit and push yourself through the garden as you work (see Figure 1-13). It has storage space under the seat as well.

>> **Baskets:** To gather all that great produce you grow and harvest, invest in a wire or wicker basket. Wire baskets are easier to use because you can wash the produce while it's still in the basket. Wicker and wooden baskets, though less durable than metal, are more aesthetically pleasing and stylish in your garden. Piling your produce in either basket is a lot more functional than trying to balance zucchinis in your arms while carrying them from your garden to your kitchen.

FIGURE 1-13:
A wagon with a seat and storage space is useful in the garden.

Wheelbarrows and garden carts

Invariably you need to move heavy items such as soil and fertilizer from one spot to another in your yard or garden. The two main options for moving stuff that's "larger than a bread box" are wheelbarrows and garden carts. The basic difference between the two vehicles is the wheels. *Wheelbarrows* have one or two wheels and an oval tray; *garden carts* have two wheels and a boxy rectangular wooden tray.

Wheelbarrows are maneuverable in tight places, can turn on a dime, and are easy to dump. A contractor-type wheelbarrow has a deeper box and is worth the extra investment because of its superior quality. For a lightweight wheelbarrow, try one with a box made out of plastic.

Garden carts are better balanced, can carry larger loads, and are easier to push than wheelbarrows. A larger-sized garden cart can easily handle loads of compost, soil, rocks, and bales of hay. Some garden carts even have removable back panels that make dumping easier.

Power tillers

The old-fashioned rear- or front-tined *power tiller* was designed to help large-scale gardeners save time breaking ground in their gardens. The large power tillers (more than a 5-horsepower engine) are best if you have 1,000 square feet or more to till. They also can be indispensable tools for forming raised beds and breaking sod.

If you need to use a large tiller only once a year, consider renting one from a local rental store.

Because home gardens have become smaller, tiller manufacturers have responded by designing a new group of tillers called *minitillers* (see Figure 1-14). These two-cycle, 1- to 2-horsepower tillers weigh only 20 to 30 pounds, are easy to handle, and can till in tight places. They not only have tilling tines but also come with other attachments such as lawn aerators, edgers, and lawn dethatchers.

FIGURE 1-14:
A minitiller is perfect for smaller home gardens.

Illustration by Kathryn Born

Minitillers work best in previously worked, loamy soil without large stones. Unlike their larger cousins, minitillers are easy to handle when you're weeding between rows of vegetables and close to plants. However, they aren't good for breaking new ground or tilling stony or heavily weeded areas in your garden. Because they're lightweight, they till raised beds and small gardens very well. Electric models are available if you don't like the noise and smell of a two-cycle engine.

Chapter **2**

Deciding What to Grow

Few things are better than fresh fruits and vegetables, and growing your own can be very rewarding. You may want to grow just enough for yourself, or you may decide to grow extra so you can pocket a little cash. And if you have animals, you may want to raise crops to feed them.

As you plan your garden, you need to consider how much of your day you want to devote to caring for crops, how long you want the growing season to last, which types of crops you want to grow, what kind of soil you have, and how to supplement the soil so it makes for a perfect environment. This chapter helps you answer some of those questions and describes common fruits and vegetables and how best to grow them.

Understanding Veggie Varieties

Before you go drooling over the luscious veggies in catalogs, in garden centers, and online, it's good to know a little about the varieties you can choose from. If you select your veggie varieties before you design your garden (as laid out in Chapter 1 of this minibook), you can ensure that you have the proper amount of space and the best growing conditions.

A *variety* is a selection of a particular type of vegetable that has certain predictable, desirable traits. These traits may include the following:

>> **Adaptation:** Some varieties are particularly well adapted to certain areas and climates. For example, some tomato varieties produce good-tasting fruit in the cool, foggy coastal climates of the Pacific Northwest. And certain bean varieties are better adapted to the hot, dry deserts of the American southwest.

>> **Appearance:** You can choose from a rainbow of fruit and leaf colors, such as purple peppers, yellow chard, and orange tomatoes. Leaf textures and shapes range from frilly to smooth to puckered. The flowers of some vegetables, such as okra and eggplant, are attractive in their own right. You get the idea. The more beautiful the vegetables, the more beautiful the vegetable garden — and the more stunning the food.

>> **Cooking and storage characteristics:** Certain varieties of beans and peas, for example, freeze better than others. Some winter squash varieties may be stored for months, but others need to be eaten immediately.

>> **Days to maturity (or days to harvest):** Days to maturity refers to the number of days it takes (under normal conditions) for a vegetable planted from seed (or from transplants) to mature and produce a crop. This number is especially important for vegetable gardeners who live in short-summer climates. Average days to maturity are listed for each type of vegetable in Chapter 4 of this minibook.

>> **Extended harvest season:** A certain variety of corn, for example, may ripen early or late in the season. By planting varieties that ripen at different times, you can start harvesting as early as 60 days after seeding and continue for five or six weeks. Seed catalogs and packages often describe varieties as early season, midseason, or late season in relationship to other varieties of the same vegetable.

>> **Pest resistance:** Many vegetable varieties are resistant to specific diseases or pests — a very important trait in many areas. Some tomato varieties, in particular, have outstanding disease resistance. See Chapter 6 of this mini-book for more on pest control.

>> **Plant size:** The trend in vegetable breeding is to go small. Tomato, cucumber, and even winter squash varieties are available in dwarf sizes. These varieties are perfect for container growing or small-space gardens.

>> **Taste:** Choose a flavor and you can find a vegetable that stars in it. You can grow fruity tomatoes, super-sweet varieties of corn, bitter melons, and spicy peppers. You'll discover flavors for every taste bud.

To realize the scope of your vegetable variety possibilities, it's important to note that you can categorize a variety as a hybrid, an open-pollinated, or an heirloom variety. Here's what these terms mean:

>> **Hybrid:** Hybrid seeds (also known as F-1 hybrids) are the result of a cross of selected groups of plants of the same kind, called inbred lines. (A cross is when pollen from one flower fertilizes a flower from another similar plant, resulting in seed.) Hybrid seeds generally are more expensive than open-pollinated seeds, and they can't be saved and planted the next year because the offspring won't have the same characteristics as the parents. If you did plant them next year, you'd get a mix of characteristics — some desirable and some not. The plants are uniform, but they often lack a diversity of shapes, colors, sizes, and flavors. However, hybrid plants are more vigorous, productive, and widely adapted than other varieties.

>> **Open-pollinated:** Open-pollinated varieties basically are inbred lines allowed to pollinate each other in open fields. They produce offspring that are similar to their parents. Before the arrival of hybrids, all vegetable varieties were open-pollinated. Some gardeners like these varieties for their flavor, their diversity, and the fact that they can save the seeds each year to replant. The resulting offspring are pretty predictable, but they don't provide the consistency of hybrids.

>> **Heirloom:** Any open-pollinated variety that's at least 50 years old is generally considered an heirloom. Heirlooms are enjoying quite a revival because of the variety of colors, tastes, and forms that are available. They're worth trying, but keep in mind that some varieties may not have the disease resistance and wide adaptability that hybrids generally have.

Deciding How Much to Grow

Just because you have a bit of land for growing veggies doesn't necessarily mean you're interested in taking on the task of planting, tending, and harvesting crops on the whole plot. That's a lot of work for a homesteader! But maybe you do want to do it. Maybe you have dreams of raising enough to sell to the local grocery stores and farmer's markets and of lining your pockets with some extra cash. Or maybe you have dreams of becoming a full-fledged, full-time farmer, and you need to get your feet wet on a smaller scale before taking the giant plunge.

Before you plant your first seed or seedling, you need to determine how much to grow to suit your purposes, and think about the time you have available for managing your crop or garden. You may be surprised at how much you can grow in a small space. Sometimes, the smaller the space, the more attention you can give, and thus the more yield you get.

Supplementing your grocery needs and sharing with friends

Have you ever added up how much you spend on fruits and veggies per year? Wouldn't it be cool if you could reduce or even eliminate that expenditure? Well, with a little bit of acreage, a little knowledge, and a little work, that's very possible.

As far as the amount of space you need, you may hear all kinds of suggestions. One source says with 500 square feet, you can grow 90 percent of a person's annual vegetable requirements; however, your results will undoubtedly vary.

If your intention is not only to feed yourself but also to treat your relatives, friends, neighbors, and coworkers, you need a few more plants. Or you may just be content to share any overabundance that grows from what you've planned for yourself. Many plants produce all their fruit within the span of a few weeks, so if your freezer is getting just a little too full of grated zucchini, share the wealth!

To determine how much you'll need, ask yourself how much your family consumes: How big is your family? Do the little ones even like vegetables? A couple of tomato plants may be sufficient for a family of two who mostly uses tomatoes as a garnish or maybe as an accent in sandwiches, but for a family who loves and eats salads at every dinner, you want to go with several plants. Chat with neighbors, the county extension agent, and the people at the seed stores for advice. You'll most likely go through a few seasons of trial and error before getting the garden size right.

Selling at the market

If you have enough land and time, planting a lot more, with the intention of selling to local markets — or setting up a table at the various farmer's markets that crop up in the summertime — can very well give you some well-deserved pocket money, as well as a little fun socializing with the people who come to visit. To get an idea of just how much you should plant, ask neighbors for suggestions, inquire at your local cooperative extension office, or even chat with farmers at the farmer's markets (which can give you planting ideas for next year).

WARNING

A lot of rules and regulations come with selling food to the general public, and each state defines its requirements. If you operate as a produce stand — you handle only raw, unprocessed fruits and vegetables as opposed to selling prepared food — you may get away with anything from very limited rules to having a food handler's certificate or specific equipment (such as refrigeration) at your booth.

Going all the way to a subsistence-level operation

Being completely self-sufficient — growing enough to meet your basic needs — requires a bit more work. You have to be diligent about caring for the plants, dealing with pests, and so on, and you'll be spending more of your time out in the field than inside enjoying a warm fire or a cold beer.

Although being able to fend for yourself may seem like a romantic concept, you may want to read about some of the hardships American pioneers and homesteaders faced. And no, I don't mean using buffalo chips for fuel, repairing broken wagon wheels, building houses out of sod, and using oxen-drawn plows, because in this day and age, most of those problems are a thing of the past. But you may still face droughts or insect infestations that may mean little or no food one year. Of course, today, you'll always have a backup in place (a grocery store nearby) to run to if your crops fail.

For a subsistence-level operation, you freeze, dry, or can fruits and veggies to preserve them for the off-season. The freezer is definitely an advantage you have over the homesteaders. Instead of having to dry veggies or smoke meats, you can simply toss things in the freezer and have at them as needed, well outside the growing season. (See Book 2 for more about enjoying the fruits of your labor.)

REMEMBER

You'll probably have to do a few seasons of trial and error until you find out just how much you need to plant. That means estimating what your family consumes in a year and planting what you think will cover that, adding a little extra as a buffer in case some of the plants fail. You may even consider growing a bit more than you'll consume so you can harvest the seeds, dry them, and use them the next season. Then see where you stand at the end of the winter when it's time to start the growing all over again. If you find that you misestimated, adjust accordingly.

Even with all this calculation, you may not be able to be completely self-sufficient. You may get the plants right, but if you want to eat meat, you may need to find a good butcher. Or perhaps you want to do some bartering for something your neighbor grows, exchanging some corn for some okra. Or how about trading some tomatoes for some fresh goat's milk?

Succeeding with Vegetables

With so many options for veggies to pour your time, money, and heart into, the possibilities may seem endless. Some limitations that can help you make your decision are the amount of space you actually have to devote to crops, the quality of your soil, and the growing season, although certain varieties may be able to compensate for those shortcomings. The ultimate decision may come down to what you like to eat.

Although what grows well may vary according to your soil and your skills, this section lists veggies that homesteaders typically grow pretty well. Whatever you plant, and however many you decide on, you should probably plant at least two plants so that if something doesn't mesh with one, you have a backup plant. Some plants even require partners so they can pollinate each other.

Because your livelihood doesn't depend on having a successful crop, feel free to experiment with what and how much you plant. As you become more confident about both what grows well in your area and how much time and effort you can afford to invest, you can expand or contract your garden as needed.

Cucumbers, melons, and squashes

Cucumbers, melons, and squashes are all members of the cucumber family. They all have in common their love of heat, their capability to grow long stems (and vine to great lengths), and the fact that they have separate male and female flowers on the same plant. These viners need someone to play Cupid and bring pollen from the male flower to the female flower to produce fruit. If you're trying out beekeeping, as explored in Book 4, Chapters 1 and 2, they'll handle this job happily.

This large family of vegetables is known for producing lots of fruits and taking up lots of room in the process. However, modern plant breeders have responded to the need for smaller, space-saving vegetable plants by breeding bush (nonvining) varieties of some favorite cucumber-family crops.

Cucumbers

Cucumber varieties usually are categorized two ways: slicers and picklers. Slicing-cucumber varieties are long, smooth-skinned cucumbers that tend to be larger, a darker shade of green, and have thicker skin with fewer bumps (spines) than pickling varieties, which are short and prickly. Slicing cucumbers are the ones you're probably most familiar with from grocery stores; they're great in salads and other recipes, but they're also super for munching. You can use pickling varieties the same ways you use slicing varieties, and they're great when eaten fresh. But if you want to make pickles, the pickling varieties have better textures for it than the slicers.

The easiest cucumber varieties to grow are the hybrid bush types. These varieties, such as 'Salad Bush', are good producers, are disease resistant, and produce a small vining plant that can grow in a container. Bush types don't produce as many cucumbers as larger vining varieties, nor do they produce them all summer long. But if you have a small family, a few bush varieties should be plenty.

TIP

You'll see some cucumber varieties labeled as *burpless.* This thin-skinned cucumber type has a long, slender shape and a mild flavor that isn't bitter. It's said to produce less intestinal gas than other varieties, which clearly explains where it got its name.

Melons

Most gardeners are familiar with the two most popular types of melons: muskmelons (also known as cantaloupes) and watermelons. But more and more exotic melon types continue to show up in produce markets and seed catalogs. These exotic types include crenshaw, honeydew, and charentais. They're similar to muskmelons, but they offer a tropical, juicy flavor.

Watermelons come in the traditional "let's have a picnic" oblong shape as well as the more compact, round shape (also called an icebox shape). Yellow-fleshed and seedless watermelon varieties also are available. Most muskmelons tend to weigh between 2 and 5 pounds, but watermelons can run from 8 pounds to between 20 and 30 pounds.

WARNING

Seedless watermelon varieties may germinate more slowly than other varieties, especially in cool soils (below 65 degrees Fahrenheit). So wait until the soil is warm before seeding and give them a few more days than the other watermelon varieties to germinate.

Summer squash

Although many varieties of squash are available, a couple consistently show up in gardens because of their ease of growing and their tastiness and familiarity to the consumer. Squashes come in two basic varieties: summer and winter. Summer squashes are those with a soft skin that you pick and eat all summer.

Summer squashes thrive in warm weather and have a soft, pliable shell. Of the several varieties that abound in the summer squash class, the most popular is the zucchini. It's a prolific plant, and its fruit is versatile — you can eat it raw in salads, steam or grill it as a side dish, or even use it as an ingredient in a sweet, cinnamony bread!

Unless you really like zucchini, or unless you plan to sell the things and have a reliable recipient, don't plant more than a few plants. They'll yield dozens of veggies throughout a season. Their mission in life is to produce offspring, so if you keep picking the vegetables, the plants will keep trying to be fruitful and prosper. An old gardening joke says it's "against the law to plant more than two" because of how prolific this plant is. Really!

Bush zucchini also grows well in plant pots. Say you have a nice long deck that would benefit from some beautiful vegetation. Consider planting a zucchini plant or two in containers and placing them on that deck. Zucchinis are nice-looking plants, and if placed up on the deck and away from the soil (and the insect and the other wildlife pests), they may thrive even more than they do in the garden. Harvesting is even a little easier — just walk out on the deck every morning and pick off whatever veggie is ready!

Zucchini is one of those plants that pretty much grows itself. Toss two or three seeds directly into the soil (which you've mixed with fertilizer or compost) in late spring. Give them plenty of water and add organic fertilizer every four weeks or so. When the seedlings are about 4 inches tall, gently pinch off the weaker leaves.

Harvest the zucchini fruits when they're still small, maybe about 7 inches long (the size of a typical pickle). If you let them go, they continue to grow and can get downright huge — baseball bat-sized! Smaller fruits are more tender and contain fewer seeds. Of course, if a zucchini gets too big, you can grind it up for zucchini bread or consider feeding it to your critters — they'll love you for it.

Winter squash

Winter squashes favor the cooler months and last much longer in storage than summer varieties. Unlike summer squashes, winter squashes have a hard shell.

Many varieties of winter squash are available, and each type has its own amazing characteristics and tastes. Of all the possibilities, the most popular are pumpkins, butternut squash, and spaghetti squash.

Winter squashes are known for being easy to grow. Simply plant seeds in separate mounds about a yard apart and keep only the strongest seedlings — this practice keeps the plants strong and healthy.

After about 14 to 20 weeks, winter squashes are usually mature and ready to be harvested. Cut them off the vine, leaving at least 2 inches of stem. Store them in a dry place until you're ready to do something with them.

Legumes, the nitrogen-fixers

Legumes are plants that grow fruit in pods and help *fix* their own nitrogen — that is, they provide luxurious homes for beneficial bacteria that take nitrogen gas from the air and turn it into something the plants can use. In many cases, you don't have to fertilize the plants with nitrogen at all. These plants are also good to use in crop rotations because they return some nitrogen to the soil just by being planted there. The most popular legumes for small farmers are peas and beans.

Peas

Peas freeze and dry well, and with some peas, such as snap and sugar peas, you can even eat the pods. Peas are a cool-weather crop, so you should plant anywhere from late winter (provided your soil is workable) to early summer; then plant again in late summer/early fall. They don't do well in the heat of the summer.

TIP

To extend your harvest of fresh peas, try planting some in one area and then planting some in another area a couple of weeks later.

Because peas like a higher soil pH (lower acidity) than most vegetables, they benefit from having a little lime added to the soil along with compost or other fertilizer. (More on soil pH in Chapter 3 of this minibook.)

Plant legume seeds every 2 inches or so, and give the plants something to climb up, such as small sticks or fancy metal or plastic poles from your local garden store.

Some varieties can grow and climb very tall, which means they produce shade and can interfere with other plants around them. A good plan is to use the space around the pea plants for smaller, shade-tolerant plants, such as radishes.

Green beans

Green beans come in bush varieties, which stand up on their own, and pole varieties, which need some sort of support to lean on. Plant pole varieties from seed about 4 to 6 inches apart; bush varieties should be 2 to 4 inches apart.

Harvest green beans regularly to encourage the growth of more beans. Pods should be about 3 inches long. Hold the stem with one hand while picking the pods off carefully with the other. Do the picking in the morning, when the beans are still tender but after the dew has dried off. Picking from wet plants can spread *bacterial blight*, a disease that threatens the bean plant.

As with peas, you can plant a bed of green beans every couple of weeks to extend the harvest throughout the summer.

Tomatoes and peppers: The not-so-deadly nightshades

The nightshades are staples in most home gardens, and their fruits are both tasty and healthy. Tomatoes and peppers are nightshades, as are eggplants and tobacco. (Potatoes are nightshades as well, but are included later, in the "Root crops and tubers" section.)

Tomatoes aren't poisonous as people once believed, but the leaves and stems of plants in this category can be toxic. Take care not to feed the green parts to the animals.

Tomatoes

If you grow only one type of vegetable, tomatoes are a good choice — they're easy and yummy. In foods, they go with pretty much everything, and very few earthly delights can beat that. Tomatoes contain lycopene, which has been linked to prostate health and can help with some other forms of cancer and heart disease.

Tomatoes contain flavonoids (flavor pieces), some of which can be activated only with alcohol! If you cook tomatoes with white wine, you can unlock these things and get a better flavor.

After you've tasted a fresh-from-the-garden-tomato, you'll never be happy with a store-bought tomato again. Tomatoes you get in the store are picked before they're completely ripe so they'll last through the time it takes to get them from the farms to the shelves. These tomatoes do turn red, but turning red and ripening aren't the same thing. Vine-ripened tomatoes are the tastiest because as they ripen on the vine, they continue to get nutrients — and sugar — from the plant.

Bush tomatoes, the kind that don't ramble very far from the roots, set all the tomatoes at once. They have a short harvest season, but if you're canning, the bush tomato is a good kind to plant. Of course, they're not-so-good if you intend to eat fresh tomatoes all summer. Planting both varieties can ensure you have both fresh tomatoes all summer and canned tomatoes to enjoy in the winter.

Hundreds of varieties of tomatoes are available, from the itty bitty grape tomatoes to the massive beefsteak tomatoes, so-named because one slice can cover an entire sandwich. Plum or paste varieties such as the Roma are ideal for canning and sauces. Plant several types and find out which you like the best.

Start tomato seeds inside, six to eight weeks before the last killing frost. Starting them early gives them a chance to get big enough to be planted outside as soon as conditions allow. If you don't have a greenhouse where you can control temperatures, a good way to get the tomato plants started is to put them on top of your water heater. That gives them the warm and dark environment seeds like. Move them into the light as soon as they sprout.

Staking the plants has many benefits. It gets the vegetables off the ground, provides better air circulation, gives bugs fewer places to access the plant, and reduces the potential that a vegetable will rot on the ground. If you're going to stake the plants so they can climb, put the stakes in the ground first to protect the young roots. Put a little fertilizer in the soil as you plant the plants. An initial dose of fertilizer is enough, with maybe a little topical application later.

WARNING

If you treat a tomato plant too well by giving it lots of water and fertilizer, you'll end up with a beautiful plant that bears little fruit. What another plant may consider a good amount of nitrogen, the tomato sees as something to beef up its green parts. The ideal tomato plant is a little scraggly with beautiful, healthy fruits.

Pick your tomatoes as soon as they ripen, and you can get fruits all summer. As soon as the first frost comes, the plants are done. (Anything left on the vine turns to slime.) If you still have some green tomatoes when a frost is threatening, pick them off the vine and put them in a window. They won't ripen anymore, but they'll get red and soft.

Peppers

Peppers come in a ton of varieties as well as a rainbow of colors. They can be hot or sweet, round or oblong, with colors including ivory, purple, bright red, yellow, orange, or even brown. Of course, although brown peppers taste fine, they may not be the most aesthetically pleasing things to put in salads.

All peppers are green peppers first. When they ripen, they turn into their other color. That means green peppers aren't technically all the way ripe. (Other plants work that way, too. Olives, for instance, start out green, and you can pick and eat green ones, but the ripe ones are black.) Green peppers have a specific flavor; when they ripen to their final color, their flavor also changes: They tend to get sweeter. Fully ripe peppers also have more vitamin C.

Peppers are related to tomatoes, so growing and caring for them is pretty much the same (see the preceding section). Too much fertilizer results in beautiful, healthy, green plants with little or no peppers. Prepare the bed, put in a little fertilizer and maybe compost, and put in the already-started plants.

Corn

You can choose among three basic types of corn:

>> **Sweet corn:** This is the stuff that goes to backyard barbeques. It doesn't store well and is best if eaten right away, because as soon as you pick it, the sugar enzymes start to turn into starch. The longer it sits, the less sweet it becomes. Plant two to three varieties a few weeks apart to extend the harvest.

>> **Field corn:** This corn grows really tall (up to 12 feet high) and has little or no sugar in it. Its purpose in life is to be grown, dried, and then ground into corn meal or used in animal feed.

>> **Popcorn:** Yes, you can grow your own popcorn. If you have kids, it could be kind of fun. But for as cheap as you can get ready-to-pop corn, growing it may not be worthwhile.

Corn plants are considered a heavy feeder, meaning they really abuse the soil they grow in. They leach out any nutrients they can. Corn plants especially suck out a lot of nitrogen, so fertilize relatively often.

TIP

For best results, plant a block of corn instead of rows. With corn, the pollen has to fall from the tassel onto the ear shoot in order to produce a mature ear. With a block (kind of a square area, maybe four rows planted with corn for about 5 feet), the plants can more easily cross-pollinate each other. The plants in the middle of the block get the most benefits, yielding the better ears of corn.

Corn likes a lot of water, but not from above, which washes away the pollen needed to make the ears. The best watering method is a drip system. In its simplest form, you simply lay a hose along the rows, cut small holes in the hose, and turn the water on at a low pressure.

Leaf crops and cruciferous veggies

In leaf crops, the leaves are the tastiest and most nutritious parts. Also in this section is a subcategory called *cole crops,* or *crucifers,* vegetables that belong in the mustard family, such as cabbage, Brussels sprouts, broccoli, cauliflower, collards, kale, kohlrabi, turnips, and watercress. All are delicious, but this section simply focuses on some of the more common and easy ones.

Lettuce and spinach

Lettuce and spinach are so good, and the animals love them, too. The main types of lettuce are leaf lettuce, butterhead (bibb is a popular variety), Romaine (also known as *cos*), crisphead (such as iceberg), and stem (or asparagus) lettuce. Spinach comes in three main varieties: savoy (what's sold in most supermarkets), smooth-leaf (which has larger leaves than savoy and is typically grown for canning and freezing), and semi-savoy (a hybrid between the two).

Lettuce and spinach favor cooler temperatures, so plant them in late spring or early summer. They like small amounts of water, administered often. Cut the leaves whenever you think they're big enough. The plant has a shallow root system, so be careful when you harvest — don't tug too hard or the whole plant could come up.

Lettuce and spinach are easy to grow, but they grow in such a way that slugs like to hang out in the leaves. Some other common pests include aphids (watch for a gathering of these guys on the underside of the leaves) and foliage rot, caused by too much water and too-hot temperatures.

Cabbage

With the many varieties of cabbage around, you should really try growing at least one. Green cabbage is by far the most popular, but others such as red or savoy can also be a nutritious and tasty addition to your diet. Cabbage contains vitamin C, and all sorts of good stuff are in sauerkraut, which is simply fermented cabbage; it boosts the immune system, helps fight cancer, and helps your digestive system run smoothly.

Cabbage likes cooler temperatures, and you can grow it either in the spring (plant six weeks after the last frost) or fall (plant eight weeks before the first frost). The trick to getting good plants is rich soil, good fertilization, and plenty of water.

TIP

To help warm up the soil more quickly for the spring planting, lay black plastic on the ground and poke a few evenly spaced holes where you'll then put the seeds.

The appearance of a head of cabbage doesn't necessarily mean it's ready for harvest. Give it a little squeeze, and don't harvest until the head is nice and firm and dense. Cut it from the base of the plant.

Broccoli

Broccoli is one of the easiest cole crops to grow. Modern broccoli varieties have been bred to form one large main head. This head is simply a tight cluster of flower buds. Once the main head is cut off, multiple side branches and mini heads form along the plant. In most areas, the side branches and mini heads continue to form until the plant is killed by frost, insects, or disease. So from one plant, you can harvest right through summer, fall, and winter (if your climate is warm enough).

REMEMBER

Choosing the right broccoli variety for your garden depends on a number of factors, including where you live and what you plan to do with the crop. Here are a few guidelines to follow when choosing a broccoli variety:

>> If you plan to stock up for the winter by freezing broccoli heads, choose a variety with large heads that mature mostly at the same time. Try 'Green Magic' or 'Premium Crop'.

>> Broccoli, like all cole crops, thrives in cool weather. Warm weather makes the heads flower too quickly, resulting in a bitter flavor. Gardeners in warm climates should choose varieties that withstand heat or mature early, before the heat of summer. 'Packman' is a good choice.

>> If you want a long, steady production of small but tender side shoots, choose an old-fashioned variety with good side-shoot production, such as 'DeCicco'.

> **»** If you live in a humid climate (such as Dallas) or a coastal area that has lots of fog and mist (such as San Francisco), broccoli heads can rot before maturing. Choose varieties with added disease resistance and tightly clustered flower heads that shed water easily, such as 'Arcadia'.

Brussels sprouts

Brussels sprouts are sweet and tender and delicious when steamed. They're very similar to cabbages and can cause a not-so-pleasant fragrance when cooked.

These plants do well in warmer temperature, so you should plant them in early to mid-summer. They do their growing during the heat of the summer, so be sure to keep them good and watered.

When the buds (or sprouts) get to be around 1 inch in diameter, you can pick or cut them off. As soon as the leaves start turning yellow, the plant is at the end of its growing season, and you should pick any remaining sprouts.

For best results, pinch the growth off the top of the plants after they're at least 2 feet high. This allows the plant to concentrate its energy on the buds in the lower part, making those buds denser.

Root crops and tubers

Root crops are those whose roots or underground bulb is the tasty thing you eat. Several plants fall into this category. The easiest to grow are the radish, onion, and carrot, but others include turnips, beets, parsnips, artichokes, leeks, garlic, and sweet potatoes. This section includes some popular root crops and *tubers,* which are enlarged underground stems.

Beets

Beets grow best in cool, moist conditions. Two weeks before the average date of your last frost, prepare a raised bed by working in a 2- to 3-inch layer of composted manure. Then sow seeds ½ inch deep and 2 inches apart. Cover the seeds with soil, and keep them well watered. Plant seeds again every two weeks into summer to ensure a continual supply of beets. (See Chapter 5 of this minibook for more on this succession planting technique.)

TIP

Beet seeds are actually tiny dried up fruits with many seeds inside. For this reason, one seed produces many plants. These plants really need to be thinned early. After the seedlings stand 2 to 3 inches tall, thin them to 2 inches apart; thin the seedlings to 4 inches apart a month later. Because many beet plants grow in the same area, try snipping off the seedlings that you don't want with scissors instead of pulling them out and disturbing the roots. Use the thinned greens in salad mixes to add color and flavor.

WARNING

Thinning root crops is essential if you want the roots to grow into beets, carrots, onions . . . whatever. If they don't have adequate space, you'll get a small vegetable or no vegetable forming in the roots.

Harvest the roots when they're golf-ball sized and the most tender. To see whether the beet is large enough to harvest, brush the soil off around the beet root; beets grow right at the surface of the soil, so it's easy to see the tops of the roots. But make sure you leave some beets to experience the cool weather that produces the sweetest fruits.

Carrots

Carrots are a great source of vitamin A, which aids in eyesight, builds the immune system, and promotes bone growth. They're a cool-season crop, and they need a lot of water, so they probably won't do so well in a dry climate. The best temperatures for growing carrots are between 60 and 70 degrees. You sow carrot seeds directly into the soil.

Potatoes

Potatoes, like tomatoes, are a member of the nightshade family. These tubers can be eaten at various stages of maturity, all of which are tasty and healthy, from the young *new potatoes* to the fully mature.

Potatoes need a soil that isn't sopping wet, but they can stand cooler temperatures, so an early spring planting works for them. Start plants by planting *seed potatoes* — use only certified ones that you get from a nursery to ensure they're disease free. A couple of weeks before you intend to plant, set these special potatoes somewhere that's warm and well-lit. When planting day comes, cut the now-sprouting seed potatoes into small chunks, making sure each chunk has at least one eye, and let the chunks sit for a day or two.

Mix the soil with some compost and put the chunks in the ground, maybe 15 inches apart. Give the plant a lot of water while it's growing, stopping at the end of the season, when the foliage starts to turn yellow and die. Let the tubers sit and mature for a couple of weeks and then harvest.

Too much organic matter can be damaging to potato plants and can cause a disease called *scab,* which makes them aesthetically unappealing but doesn't ruin their nutritional benefits.

Radishes

Radishes are some of the easiest vegetables to start out with. They do well in all climates and mature really quickly, going from seed to table in as little as four weeks. And because they grow so quickly, the bugs usually don't have a chance to infest them.

Mix compost into the soil prior to planting, and then all you have to do is provide sufficient water. Instead of planting in rows, spread seeds out in a small patch (1 or 2 square feet). Harvest as soon as they get to be a size that looks good. If they get too big, they become woody, and after the plant goes to seed, the radishes aren't worth eating.

WARNING

Don't plant radishes where dairy goats can get into them, and don't feed them to the goats. Radishes negatively affect the taste of the milk.

Garlic

If any vegetable has experienced a renaissance lately, it has to be garlic (*Allium sativum*). Now the chic ingredient in many gourmet restaurants and touted as a major medicinal herb to cure everything from earaches to high cholesterol, garlic also is a key ingredient in some insect and animal repellents.

Many also believe that garlic is difficult to grow. That isn't true. Even though you could grow your own garlic from bulbs bought in grocery stores, most of those varieties are adapted to a California climate. Unless you live in central California where most garlic is commercially grown, it's best to select varieties from catalogs and local garden centers.

Garlic likes cool weather conditions and requires a long time to mature its bulbs. For gardeners in cold areas or areas with hot summers, fall is the best time to plant garlic. For gardeners with mild summers and winters, garlic also can be planted in spring. Garlic needs well-drained soil — if the crop fails, it's usually due to the cloves rotting in wet, cool soil. Fertilize the beds as you would for onions.

After harvest, let the bulbs *cure* (toughen their skins) in a warm, dry, airy place for a few weeks. Garlic flavor is enhanced in storage; cloves often taste best after stored for a few months.

Onions

The first year you grow an onion, the plant forms a bulb. The second year, the plant goes to seed if you haven't harvested the bulb, so you can save the seeds but the bulb is no longer useful as a food product. Thus, the plant lives for only two seasons.

The length of the day determines when onions form a bulb, so certain types of onions work best for certain parts of the country:

>> **Long-day onions,** such as 'Walla Walla', are better suited to gardens in the northern half of the U.S.

>> **Day-neutral onions,** such as 'Stockton Red', do well anywhere.

>> **Short-day onions,** such as 'Vidalia', grow better in the southern part of the U.S.

If you're starting onions from seed, plant them in April so the plants have a chance to get strong before the warm weather and amount of daylight triggers the bulbs to begin forming. If you're using seedlings or sets (small bulbs), wait about another month so the colder weather doesn't stimulate seed development instead of bulb development.

When most of the tops have fallen over, the onions are ready for harvest. Pull the bulbs out of the ground, rinse them off, and let them dry out for a couple of days. Then cut the tops and roots and let them sit another day or two. Now they're ready to eat or store for later.

Leeks

Cousin to the onion, the leek is a little easier to digest and makes a great addition to many recipes where you'd otherwise use onions.

Leeks are a cool-weather crop, and they like full sun and well-drained soil. They need a reliable watering schedule — about 1 inch per week — or the stems get too tough. To get them to grow large, succulent, and white, blanch the lower part of the stem by piling dirt around the stalk as it develops. In midsummer, start removing the top half of the leaves to encourage stalk growth.

They're typically ready to harvest in the fall, when they're about as thick as a finger.

Stem crops

Asparagus, rhubarb, and celery are three types of plants whose edible parts are the stems. Other stem crops include hay and alfalfa, but because this section concerns vegetables and because celery isn't very easy to grow, the only ones discussed here are asparagus and rhubarb.

Asparagus

Unlike most other vegetables, asparagus is a perennial plant, meaning it comes back year after year. In other words, you have to plant it only once. If you care for it properly, it may last 15 years or more.

You usually have to wait a couple of years before the plant bears any edible shoots. In the first and second seasons, the plant concentrates on building up a stable root system. Around the third season, you finally see spears that you can harvest.

Wait until the spears are about 3/8 of an inch or more in diameter before you harvest them. Make a cut just below the ground to enable the cut to properly heal, or snap off the spears at soil level. You can expect to get eight to ten sprouts per plant the first harvest year and more as the plant continues to mature.

WARNING

Never take everything when you harvest asparagus; instead, plant extras and pick what you want without depleting the whole crop. Leaving some makes for a healthier crop.

TIP

Asparagus does especially well in moist environments. Plant them on banks of a canal, creek, or river you have running through your property and benefit from healthy plants that also help keep bank erosion down.

Rhubarb

Another hardy cool-weather plant, rhubarb is drought resistant and can do well in most soils, but it loves well-drained soils enhanced with organic matter.

To get the best stalk growth, remove flowers as they appear. Don't harvest the stalks until their third year. In the first two years, the stalks and leaves are nourishing the roots. Beginning the third year and ever after, the stalks may be picked all at once or individually over the next four to six weeks. After the stalks are cut, you can remove the leaves.

WARNING

The leaves of rhubarb are toxic, so don't feed them to animals.

Planting Other Small-Scale Crops

Besides vegetables, other crops may do well on your backyard homestead and add some joy to your menus or those of your friends and neighbors. If you have the space and an interest in making a little money on the side, you can grow these flowers, fruits, and nuts and market them to local restaurants or grocery stores. You may even get a booth at a farmer's market or set up your own roadside stand. (Be sure to check with local laws to be sure you're legally selling your wares.)

Letting business bloom with flower gardens

Who doesn't like the beauty of colorful and fragrant flowers adorning the land-scape around the house? Besides adding to the aesthetics of your own outside look, you may consider growing flowers to either grace your own table (or desk or bureau top) or provide the materials for drying or pressing for subsequent use in crafts. Or you can sell fresh flowers to the local flower shop.

Although the staples such as roses, carnations, and daffodils are popular and often in high demand in local floral shops, you may find an even more lucrative side business in growing exotics such as lilies or orchids.

Ask around. See what the local flower shops are lacking, and find out whether they're open to accepting product from a local homesteader.

Aiming higher with fruit- and nut-bearing trees

Not everybody can grow fruit and nut trees, but if your soil supports them, they can be a lot of fun. Fruits and nuts are a great way to supplement your own diet as well as your income. The best way to figure out what you can grow is to check with a local nursery.

Fruit trees

How cool is it to go out into your backyard, pick a fruit, and then take a bite, tast-ing a tremendously sweet, healthy snack?

You can choose fruit trees in dwarf, semi-dwarf, or standard sizes. If you choose a fruit that requires cross-pollination, such as apples or plums, you need at least two trees.

You should prune, water, and fertilize your tree to keep it as healthy as you can so it produces the best (and most) fruit. Bees are a godsend for pollinating the flowers.

After you have a good, reliable supply of fruit, contact local grocery stores or even consider setting up a booth at the summer farmer's market or a roadside stand.

Nuts

Historically shunned by the average dieter for being high in calories and fat, nuts are welcomed with open arms by hikers and backpackers and others who regularly do some moderate to heavy exercise. However, people are reconsidering the health benefits of nuts for daily consumption. They're high in protein and rich in fiber, and they contain antioxidants. The fats they provide are the healthy ones — the much lauded omega-3s — so there's definitely a market for nuts.

Several varieties of nuts work on a small farm operation. Growing up, I was regularly treated to English walnuts from the big old tree in my backyard. Nuts grow better in loamy or sandy soils and don't do as well in soils with a lot of clay.

Prune, water, and fertilize your tree as needed. A new tree takes three to four years to be mature enough to produce nuts, and after the nuts start coming, they'll continue every year until the tree dies.

Another idea for using the nut tree is to sell the wood. A lot of nut tree wood is used in smoking. For instance, people often use hickory tree wood in smoking bacon.

WARNING

The black walnut tree produces *juglone,* a substance that can be toxic to plants growing around the tree's base. Avoid planting sensitive plants such as tomatoes, peppers, cabbage, or eggplant nearby.

Growing berries and grapes: Fruit bushes and vines

Growing berries yourself means the fruits can be more natural — there'll be no pesticide residues or preservatives — but that also means they need to be eaten, dried, frozen, or baked within a few days of picking. Homegrown berries can be a lot cheaper than store-bought ones — you may even sell them to the store!

Blueberries

Blueberries thrive in full sun and grow on handsome, perennial shrubs that range in height from 2 to 6 feet, depending on the type. You can choose from *low-bush* (1 to 2 feet tall), *half-high* (2 to 4 feet tall), and *high-bush* varieties (5 to 6 feet tall) that can fit into many locations in your yard. They have pretty white flowers followed by large clusters of tasty, blue fruit. Berries appear the second year after planting. The attractive green leaves turn bright shades of red, orange, and yellow before dropping in the fall. Blueberries make an excellent foundation plant grown up against the house or grouped to form a hedge between properties.

REMEMBER

Blueberries must be grown in acidic soil (with a pH level between 4.5 and 5.5), so if you don't have that kind of soil, you need to make some adjustments. Amending your soil with a lot of peat moss and some sulfur is one easy way to lower the soil pH; see Chapter 2 of this minibook for more on soil pH and amending your soil.

Plant at least two different blueberry varieties to ensure good pollination and fruit set. Variety selection is the key to success. Blueberries grow best in areas with cold winters and mild summers. In hot-summer areas of the South, grow blueberry types that are adapted to the heat, such as Southern blueberries or rabbit-eye blueberries. In cooler climates, all other blueberry types are fine to plant.

Raspberries

Raspberries are versatile. Peach melba wouldn't be the same without them, and raspberries make a beautiful jam or preserve. And who doesn't like raspberry vinaigrette, adding a hint of sweetness to a salad?

These berries grow in the wild. Have you ever taken a hike — or even a walk in a city center — and seen wild raspberries growing by the side of the road or trail? Well, that goes to show you how easy they are to grow in your own yard. Only the nastiest of soils disallow a raspberry bush.

Raspberries are typically started from a crown: An established plant throws out underground shoots, and those shoots periodically throw a stem and leaf up out of the ground, a new plant called a *crown.* Be sure to get crowns from a place that can certify the crowns are disease free — most home and garden stores are a good bet. Then harvest as you see the berries appear. It takes a raspberry bush two to three years to produce berries.

Strawberries

Fresh strawberries are one of life's little treats. You can put them on waffles, on cold cereal, or into the blender to make strawberry or strawberry-banana milk-shakes. You can make jam or even bake them into muffins. And don't forget just dipping your hand into a bowl and eating them au naturel!

Strawberries come in two basic types:

>> **June-bearing:** These are usually the better-quality berries. They set all at once, giving you gobs of berries at one time. If your intention is to make jams, these are the ones to use.

>> **Everbearing:** This type produces a few berries at a time, but in a more extended growing season. If you want to have berries as snacks or as additions to your desserts, these are the ones.

Strawberries, like raspberries, do better if started from an established plant. In a process called *daughtering,* a strawberry plant sends out aboveground shoots. Plant one of these daughters directly in the ground and wait for berries.

The way to keep the strawberry plant healthy is to periodically prune back the older or weaker, scrawnier parts of the plant, allowing the newer or stronger parts to thrive.

WARNING

Don't plant strawberries where you've planted nightshades (tomatoes, peppers, potatoes, or eggplants). Nightshades can harbor *verticillium wilt*, a serious strawberry disease.

Growing Herbs for and in the Kitchen

If you decide you don't have the time to invest in a garden or a larger crop but still want to grow something, you can always plant some herbs in small pots and keep them indoors. If you have a few well-lit windows, these plants can supply you with exotic flavorings year-round. Here are some of the easiest to get, in Table 2-1, but there are tons of others.

TABLE 2-1 Types of Herbs and Their Uses

Herb	Uses
Anise	Has the scent and flavor of licorice; very good in salads and baking.
Basil	Probably the most popular homegrown herb. Used in many foods, especially pesto and tomato-based recipes.
Caraway	Use it to flavor rye bread. It's also good in coleslaw and Hungarian-style dishes and meat stews.
Catnip	Cats go into a hypnotic trance when they get a whiff of catnip; it's like marijuana for cats, although it's a harmless treat for them.
Chives	An onion-like plant that's popular with baked potatoes.
Cilantro	Use cilantro in foods such as chili, salsa, and pico de gallo. (Note: The seed, coriander, is common in Indian curries; ground, it's in many baked goods.)
Dill	Seriously yummy with potatoes (consider sour cream and dill dip with potato chips, in potato salad, or on baked potatoes), in sauerkraut, or with pork roast.
Fennel	Has an anise-like flavor that becomes delicate when cooked. Use it in salads, in cheese spreads, or on vegetables or fish.
Lavender	Dry and use it in sachets and perfumes; the fragrance is amazing.
Marjoram	Good in cooking — sprinkle it over sliced tomatoes or baked fish. Also use it in perfume.
Oregano	Adds that extra spark to Italian-style recipes, especially pizza, lasagne, or good old-fashioned spaghetti

Herb	Uses
Parsley	High in vitamins A and C, this herb is versatile. Use it as a garnish; to flavor soups, meats, or pastas; or in ethnic foods such as tabbouleh or parsley pesto.
Mint	Besides the food-related uses of mint (tea is one of the biggies), mint's a good plant to grow and place strategically to ward off mice.
Rosemary	Rub a pork roast with rosemary before cooking — seriously yummy.
Sage	Add sage to stuffing or sprinkle it on baked fish and most meats, especially poultry, rabbit, and pork.
Savory	Comes in a summer and a winter variety (summer is sweeter); both are used to flavor meats and vegetables.
Tarragon	Similar to anise. Use it in salads, sauces, and marinades.
Thyme	Especially good in slow-cooking beef dishes, clam chowder, or poultry stuffing.

TIP

Indoor herbs do better if they're well ventilated and away from cooking fumes. Typically, the bushy, perennial herbs — rosemary, thyme, oregano, sage, and winter savory — perform better indoors than those with soft stems, such as mint and tarragon.

Get seeds or starts at a local nursery and ask the salesperson for suggestions. He or she may suggest something you've never heard of but that turns out to be just right for your favorite recipe. Use your herbs fresh or dry them for later use.

Scented geraniums make wonderful, fragrant herbal roommates, as do lemon verbena, basil, coriander, and some varieties of lavender.

TIP

Plant dill, fennel, and parsley, and you may end up with caterpillars from the black swallowtail butterfly. You may want to plant extra so you can transfer all the caterpillars to a single plant and still have some herbs for yourself.

Chapter **3**

Preparing to Plant

The work you put into your garden beds *before* you plant may be more important than anything you do after plants are in the ground. Sure, meticulous prep won't ensure a bountiful harvest. But skipping the important advance work will guarantee less-than-spectacular results.

Gardening wisdom says that to grow healthy plants, what you need to do is build healthy soil. And that's a big part of what this chapter is about: getting the ground ready for gardening. You'll do that by clearing your garden space, figuring out what you have to work with already in terms of soil, adjusting your soil to optimize growing conditions, and preparing it for actual planting.

But it's also the ideal time to think ahead to things such as how you'll water your plants, enclose areas of the garden that you want protected or just partitioned off from the rest of the yard, and get around the garden as you maintain your homestead. All of these things are easier to add now while your garden is still a blank slate.

This chapter helps get you ready for long-term gardening success without putting a single plant or seed in the dirt.

Razing Your Garden Spot

After you choose a good sunny spot for your vegetable garden and draw a plan on paper (see Chapter 1 of this minibook if you haven't completed this early-stage conceptual work), you need to clean up the area so the soil will be easier to work. You can clear your garden area any time during the year, but the season before planting works best — clear in the fall for spring planting, clear in the spring for summer or fall planting. You can clear the area the day before you plant, but you may have more weed problems later.

If you already have an established garden, clean up any debris in fall or winter, depending on where you live, and till the ground before planting.

REMEMBER

Here are the basics of initially clearing a garden spot:

1. **Outline the areas of your garden plot that you want to clear.**

   You outline the areas depending on how you want the plots to be shaped. Follow these guidelines:

   - To get your edges straight for a square or rectangular vegetable plot, stretch a string between sticks and mark the line with a trickle of ground white limestone, available at garden centers, or marking spray paint.

   - For a round garden, use a hose or rope to lay out the area, adjusting the position to create a smooth curve.

   - If you want several individual beds separated by permanent paths, outline each bed independently so you don't waste time improving soil that you'll never use. But if you think that you may change your garden layout from season to season or year to year, work the entire area within the outline. (For more on adding walkways, see the section titled "Planning for Pathways" at the end of this chapter.)

2. **Clear the surface by first removing plants, weeds, brush, and rock. If necessary, mow the site to cut back the grass and weeds close to the surface of the soil.**

   See the section "Killing weeds and aggressive grasses," for details on removing weeds.

3. **Dig out the roots of small trees and tough weeds with a hoe, shovel, or pick ax.**

4. **After the vegetation is manageable, remove any sod.**

   See the section "Stripping sod" for details on how to do this.

Killing weeds and aggressive grasses

If your garden area contains a lot of perennial weeds, such as quack grass or is lawn composed of vigorous grasses (such as Bermuda grass), make sure that you first kill those weeds or grasses. You can pull out or mulch seedlings (see Chapter 5 in this minibook for more on mulches and weeding), but many aggressive weeds and turf spread by underground roots as well as seeds. Those underground roots can haunt you for eons.

If you have an existing garden, you have to be diligent about weeding, or you may need to start all over again with tilling and removing as much of the weed's root system as you can.

You can kill weeds and aggressive grasses two ways:

>> **Hand dig and sift:** For a small garden, dig up the earth and carefully sift the soil, removing sod and root parts that may come back next year as weeds (see the tip on sifting compost in Chapter 5 of this minibook).

>> **Apply a covering:** An easy, chemical-free way to clear your garden is to cover it with clear or black plastic, cardboard, or even old rugs. After a month under these impermeable coverings, existing plants die from the lack of sunlight. You must plan ahead to use this method. It may not look pretty, but it works like a charm — especially on annual weeds. For perennial weeds, you may need to dig out their roots, too, after applying the plastic.

You can buy plastic in rolls at hardware stores or home improvement centers. Check department stores for old pieces of cardboard (big appliance boxes cover a large area and are nice and thick) and carpet stores for old rugs. Use the thickest plastic or cardboard you can find — it should be at least 2 millimeters, but 4 millimeters is even better.

Controlling weeds and grasses by applying a covering to your garden area is easy. Just follow these steps:

1. **Spread the covering over your entire garden area, securing the edges with spare rocks, bricks, or boards.**

    Let neighboring pieces overlap by several inches so no light can penetrate. If you're using old rugs, place them nap side down.

2. **After a month, remove the covering and strip off any grass or weeds.**

    Use a shovel to cut off any grass or weeds at the root level (just below the soil surface). If they aren't too thick, rototill them into the ground.

3. Wet the area and wait about 10 days for weeds to sprout.

Leave the covering off; you want weeds to sprout. You should get some growth because you haven't removed weed seeds.

4. Use a hoe to kill the weeds.

Hoeing the weeds down is sufficient to kill annual weeds, but if you have perennial weeds, you need to dig out the roots. Check out the National Gardening Association's Weed Library (www.garden.org/weedlibrary) for help identifying the weeds in your garden.

TIP

For an organic approach to killing weeds and building your garden soil, try a no-till layered garden technique (see Figure 3-1). It's like making lasagna. The season before planting, lay a layer of black-and-white newspaper three to four sheets thick over the garden area. Water the paper to keep it in place. Cover the newspaper with a 6-inch layer of hay or straw. Top that with 1- to 2-inch layer of compost. By the next planting season, the layers will have killed the grass and most of the annual and perennial weeds in your garden. You can hand pull any tenacious perennial weeds that survived. Earthworms will have munched up much of the newspaper, turning it into valuable compost. You can plant your seedlings right into the mulched layers, and they'll grow like weeds — but even better.

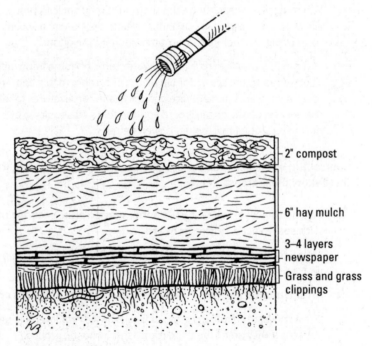

FIGURE 3-1: Creating a no-till layered garden.

- 2" compost
- 6" hay mulch
- 3–4 layers newspaper
- Grass and grass clippings

Stripping sod

If you don't want to try the techniques in the preceding section, you can immediately remove the lawn grass by stripping the *sod* (grass and roots) before planting. If your lawn consists of bluegrass and other less-spreading grasses, you can strip the sod without first killing the grass; most lawns in the northern United States consist of these types of grasses.

You should kill weedier grasses, such as Bermuda grass, before you strip the sod (see the preceding section for details on killing weedier grass). Stripping sod takes a lot of effort, but it works. Just follow these steps, and have your wheelbarrow or garden cart handy:

1. **Water the area that you want to clear for 15 minutes for each of the 2 days prior to digging up your sod.**

   Stripping sod is easier when the ground is slightly moist.

2. **Starting at one end of your plot, slip a spade under the grass and slide it under the sod.**

   TIP

   An easier method is to precut the sod into square or rectangular sections and then loosen each section with a spade. Either way, don't dig too deep; you just want to remove the sod and 1 to 2 inches of roots. You also can use a rented sod stripper to cut the sod into rows that you roll up and remove.

3. **Pivot your spade up and let the sod flip off the spade and back onto the ground. Use your spade to slice off the sod section, toss the sod into a wheelbarrow or garden cart, and take it to a compost pile.**

   TIP

   If your sod has healthy grass with few weeds, and you don't want to compost it, use it to patch bare spots in your lawn. Keep it well watered, and it should root and blend in with the existing grasses.

4. **Repeat Steps 2 and 3 until your garden is cleared of sod.**

These steps should clear all the grass in your garden. You'll get new growth only if you have an aggressive grass such as Bermuda and don't kill all the roots.

Analyzing and Improving Your Soil

After clearing your garden area, you need to take a close look at your soil — give it a good squeeze, have it tested, amend it, and then work it out to make sure it's in shipshape. Good soil gives vegetable roots a balance of all the things they need: moisture, nutrients, and air. And knowing your soil type enables you to counteract problems that you may face when gardening on that piece of land.

Distinguishing different types of soil

Three main types of soil exist, with a lot of variations in between. Hard clay is at one end of the spectrum; soft, sandy soil is at the other end; and loam is in the middle. Being familiar with your soil helps you know what to expect when gardening. Clay soil tends to have a lot of natural fertility but is heavy to work with and doesn't drain water well. Sandy soil, on the other hand, drains water well (maybe too well) but doesn't have a lot of natural fertility. Loam, the ideal soil, is somewhere in between the two.

Here are general characteristics of the three basic types of soil:

>> **Sandy soil** is composed of mostly large mineral particles. Water moves through this soil quickly, taking nutrients with it. Sandy soil is well aerated, quick to dry out and warm up, and often lacks the nutrients that vegetables need.

>> **Clay soil** consists of mainly small particles that cling tightly together and hold water and nutrients. It's slow to dry out and warm up, and has poor aeration, but it's fertile when it can be worked.

>> **Loam soil** is a happy mixture of large and small particles. It's well aerated and drains properly, but it can still hold water and nutrients. This is *the* soil to have for a great vegetable garden.

TIP

To find out what type of soil you have, grab a handful of moist soil and squeeze it, as shown in Figure 3-2. Then use these guidelines to determine what type of soil you're working with:

>> **Sandy soil** falls apart and doesn't hold together in a ball when you let go. It feels gritty when you rub it between your fingers.

>> **Clay soil** oozes through your fingers as you squeeze it and stays in a slippery wad when you let go. Rubbing clay soil between your fingers feels slippery.

>> **Loam soil** usually stays together after you squeeze it, but it falls apart easily when you poke it with your finger.

If you have sandy or clay soil, don't despair; you can improve your soil and make it more like loam. Check out the section "Adding organic matter (aka the dead stuff)," later in this chapter, for details.

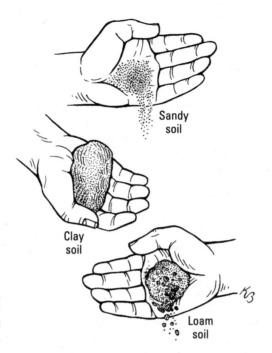

FIGURE 3-2:
Squeeze your soil
to find out what
type you have.

Testing your soil

Vegetables are picky about soil chemistry. Too much of this nutrient or too little of that nutrient, and you have problems. For example, when tomatoes grow in soil that's deficient in calcium; they develop blossom-end rot. Yuck. Sometimes too much of a nutrient, such as nitrogen, causes lots of leaf growth on plants (such as peppers) but few fruits. Getting the levels just right is important for the best harvest.

In addition to nutrient levels, soil pH also is an important factor in plant growth. The right pH enables vegetables to use nutrients from the soil. Soil is rated on a pH scale, with a pH of 1 being most acidic and a pH of 14 being most alkaline. If your soil's pH isn't within a suitable range, plants can't take up nutrients — such as phosphorus and potassium — even if they're present in the soil in high amounts. On the other hand, if the pH is too low, the solubility of certain minerals, such as manganese, may increase to toxic levels.

REMEMBER

Most vegetables grow well in a slightly acidic soil with a pH between 6 and 7. Potatoes, including sweet potatoes, prefer a slightly more acidic soil, in the 5 to 6 range. But in general, if you aim for a soil pH between 6 and 7, your vegetables should grow well.

Preparing to Plant

The only way to find out whether your soil will be to your vegetables' liking is to test it. Don't worry; analyzing your soil isn't complicated, and you don't need a lab coat. Here are two ways that you can test your soil:

>> **Use a do-it-yourself kit.** This basic pH test measures your soil's acidity and alkalinity and sometimes major nutrient content. Buy a kit at a nursery, follow the instructions, and voilà — you know your soil's pH. However, the test gives you only a rough picture of the pH and nutrient levels in your soil. You may want to know more about your soil.

>> **Have a soil lab do a test for you.** A complete soil test is a good investment because a soil lab can thoroughly analyze your soil. Here's what you can find out from a soil lab's test in addition to the pH level:

- **Your soil's nutrient content:** If you know your soil's nutrient content, you can determine how much and what kind of fertilizer to use. In fact, many soil tests tell you exactly how much fertilizer to add; see Chapter 5 of this minibook for more on fertilizer.

- **Soil problems specific to your geographic region:** A soil test may help you identify local problems. The soil lab should then give you a recommendation for a type and amount of fertilizer to add to your soil. For example, in dry-summer areas, you may have salty soil; the remedy is to add *gypsum,* a readily available mineral soil additive.

Soil labs charge around $20 to $30 for their basic services. Your local Cooperative Extension Service office or a private soil lab can conduct a complete and reliable soil test. To locate a private lab, look in the phone book under *soil testing* (or search the Internet for soil test labs around the country). You also can ask your Cooperative Extension Service office for recommendations.

TIP

Fall is a good time to test soil because labs aren't as busy. It's also a good time to add many *amendments* (materials that improve your soil's fertility and workability) to your soil because they break down slowly.

To prepare a soil sample to use with a do-it-yourself kit or to send to a soil lab, follow these steps:

1. **Fill a cup with soil from the top 4 to 6 inches of soil from your vegetable garden, and then place the soil in a plastic bag.**

2. **Dig six to eight similar samples from different parts of your plot.**

3. **Mix all the cups of soil together; place two cups of the combined soil in a plastic bag — that's your soil sample.**

After you've collected your sample, consult the instructions from your soil test kit or the testing lab.

REMEMBER

If you're testing a soil imbalance — a known problem that you've identified in either pH or nutrients — you may want to test your soil every year because changes in pH and most nutrients are gradual. A home testing kit is a good way to test a pH imbalance. For nutrients, you may want to do a yearly test at a lab until the imbalance (high or low levels of a nutrient) is fixed. To maintain balanced soil, test it every three to five years.

Adjusting soil pH

Most garden soils have a pH between 5.5 and 8.0. This number helps you determine when and how to adjust your soil's pH level. The following guidelines help you interpret this number:

>> If the number is below 6, the soil is too acidic, and you need to add ground limestone.

>> If the measurement is above 7.5, the soil is too alkaline for most vegetables, and you need to add soil sulfur.

The following sections explain how to figure out how much lime or sulfur to add to your soil and how to apply the materials.

Calculating how much lime or sulfur you need

All Cooperative Extension Service offices, any soil lab, and many lawn and garden centers have charts showing how much lime or sulfur to add to correct a pH imbalance. The charts tell you how many pounds of material to add per 1,000 square feet, so you need to measure the size of your vegetable garden first. Then use Tables 3-1 and 3-2 to figure out how much lime or sulfur you need to add to your soil.

TABLE 3-1 **Pounds of Limestone Needed to Raise pH (per 1,000 Square Feet)**

pH	Number of Pounds for Sandy Soil	Number of Pounds for Loam Soil	Number of Pounds for Clay Soil
4.0–6.5	60	161	230
4.5–6.5	50	130	190
5.0–6.5	40	100	150
5.5–6.5	30	80	100
6.0–6.5	15	40	60

TABLE 3-2   **Pounds of Sulfur Needed to Lower pH (per 1,000 Square Feet)**

pH	Number of Pounds for Sandy Soil	Number of Pounds for Loam Soil	Number of Pounds for Clay Soil
8.5–6.5	45	60	70
8.0–6.5	30	35	45
7.5–6.5	10	20	25
7.0–6.5	2	4	7

REMEMBER

In general, soils in climates with high rainfall — such as east of the Mississippi River (particularly east of the Appalachian Mountains) or in the Pacific Northwest — tend to be acidic. West of the Mississippi, where less rainfall occurs, soils are more alkaline. But regardless of where you live in the United States, you should easily be able to find the lime or sulfur that you need at your local garden center.

Applying lime or sulfur to your soil

The best way to apply sulfur and limestone to your soil is to use a *drop spreader* (the same machine you may use to apply lawn fertilizer). This simple machine doesn't cost very much, and it helps you spread the material more evenly. Some nurseries may even loan you a spreader or allow you to rent one inexpensively. You also can spread these materials by hand if you're careful and wear gloves. No matter how you spread the materials, make sure that you work the soil well afterward.

You can purchase and apply different types of limestone to your soil. The type you use may depend on the type of nutrients your soil needs:

>> **Dolomitic limestone** contains magnesium as well as calcium. Magnesium is one of the nutrients that a soil lab may test for, and even though it isn't in the top three (nitrogen, phosphorus, and potassium), it's as important as calcium for plant growth. Use dolomitic limestone to adjust the pH if your soil test shows that your soil is low in magnesium.

>> **Pulverized limestone** is the most common and inexpensive acid neutralizer. Use this limestone if you don't need to add magnesium to your soil.

>> **Pelletized pulverized limestone** is a little more expensive than ordinary pulverized limestone, but it's cleaner, less dusty, and easier to use than both dolomitic and powdered limestone.

Sulfur usually comes in only powdered form or mixed with other nutrients such as ammonium sulfate.

REMEMBER

Your soil uses limestone and sulfur most efficiently when it's tilled into the soil to a depth of 4 to 6 inches.

Adding organic matter (aka the dead stuff)

If you're like most people, your garden doesn't have perfect loam soil. So to fix that mucky clay or loose sand, you need to add *organic matter* — once-living stuff such as compost, sawdust, animal manure, ground bark, grass clippings, and leaf mold (composted tree leaves). You can't change your soil type (clay, sand, or loam), but adding organic matter makes your soil more like loam, which is perfect for vegetable roots. Even if you have loam soil, you still should add organic matter to your soil every year.

WHAT IS ORGANIC GARDENING?

Organic gardening has become a household term in the past 20 years or so. Many people are choosing organically grown produce from the grocery store because they feel it's safer and healthier. Because organic produce costs more than conventionally grown produce, it's a good idea to grow your own.

Organic gardening, in many ways, is just good, simple gardening practices and common sense. Some of the basic facets of organic gardening include the following, covered more in-depth in Chapters 4, 5, and 6 of this minibook:

- Feeding the soil — not just the plants — with organic fertilizers, manure, and organic matter
- Rotating crops
- Planting a diverse group of crops
- Solving pest problems by planting disease-resistant varieties
- Using barriers (covers that keep bugs away from plants)
- Releasing beneficial insects
- Using the least harmful biological and plant-based sprays

The USDA now has a certification program for organic farms, and the fertilizers and pesticides that can be used on these certified farms are widely available at local garden centers and through the mail. But you don't have to be certified to grow plants organically. A good philosophy is to emphasize compost and soil-building practices and to use sprays only as a last resort (and even then use only organic ones).

Preparing to Plant

Organic matter improves garden soil in the following ways:

>> It helps loosen and aerate clay soil.

>> It improves the water- and nutrient-holding capacity of sandy soil.

>> It provides the once-living material that attracts microorganisms, beneficial fungi, worms, and other soil-borne critters that improve the health of your vegetables.

REMEMBER

Work some organic matter into your soil before you plant each season. If you're using unfinished (raw) organic matter such as leaves or undecomposed manure, add it to your soil at least 1 month before planting. That way it will break down before you plant. Add finished compost and manures just before planting.

Follow these steps to add organic matter to your garden soil (for information on the best kinds of organic matter, see the following sections):

1. **Add a 1- to 2-inch layer of organic matter to the area where you intend to plant your vegetables.**

   Go for the higher end (2 inches) if your garden is new or if your soil is heavy clay or very sandy. Use less if you've grown there for years or if your soil is loamy and fertile.

   You need 3 cubic yards of compost to spread a 1-inch layer over 1,000 square feet.

TIP

2. **Work in the organic matter to a depth of at least 6 inches.**

   There's nothing glamorous about spreading manure. The best way to spread organic matter is with a wheelbarrow and a shovel. Work it into the soil with a shovel, iron fork, or rototiller.

The best choice: compost

The best organic material to add to your soil is compost. Composting breaks down yard waste, agricultural waste, wood scraps, and even sludge into a crumbly soil–like material called *humus*.

Compost is usually clean, easy to use, and available. You can buy it in bags or have it delivered by the truckload. Most waste disposal sites make compost and sell it relatively cheap. You also can make your own compost; see Chapter 5 of this minibook for details.

Other organic materials, such as sawdust and manure

Using organic materials other than compost — such as sawdust and manure — is fine, but these materials present a few problems that compost doesn't. Here are some advantages and disadvantages:

>> **Sawdust** adds organic matter to your soil, which eventually breaks down and forms humus. However, the sawdust also robs the soil of nitrogen when it decomposes, so you have to add more fertilizer to compensate.

>> **Livestock manure** improves your soil's nitrogen level. However, livestock diets often include lots of hay that's full of weed seeds, which may germinate in your vegetable garden. Some manures (such as horse manure) add organic matter and some nutrients to your soil, but they're also loaded with bedding materials (such as dried hay) that cause the same problem that adding sawdust causes.

TIP

If you use manure, make sure it's *fully composted* — that is, it has been sitting around for a year or two, so it's decomposed and the salts have leached out. Too much salt in the soil can be harmful to plants. Good-quality compost or fully decomposed manure should have a dark brown color, an earthy smell, and little original material visible.

Turning Your Soil

After adding nutrients and amendments to your soil, you need to mix them up. Turning your soil to mix the amendments enables them to break down faster and be available where the roots can use them.

If your soil is dry, water well, and let it sit for a few days before digging. Then, to determine whether your soil is ready to turn, take a handful of soil and squeeze it. The soil should crumble easily in your hand with a flick of your finger; if water drips out, it's too wet.

WARNING

Don't work soil that's too wet. Working soil that's too wet ruins the soil structure — after it dries, the soil is hard to work and even harder to grow roots in.

The easiest way to turn your soil, especially in large plots, is with a *rototiller* (or *tiller*, for short). You can rent or borrow a tiller, or if you're serious about this vegetable-garden business, buy one. Tillers with rear tines and power-driven wheels allow you to really lean into the machines and use your weight to till deeper. If you have a small (less than 100 square feet) vegetable plot, consider using a minitiller (see Chapter 1 for more details on this tool) or hand dig it if you're up for a little exercise. If you use a rototiller, adjust the tines so the initial pass over your soil is fairly shallow (a few inches deep). As the soil loosens, set the tines deeper with successive passes (crisscrossing at 90–degree angles) until the top 8 to 12 inches of soil are loosened.

To turn your soil by hand, use a straight spade and a digging fork. You can either dig your garden to one spade's depth, about 1 foot, or *double dig* (that is, work your soil to a greater depth), going down 20 to 24 inches. After turning the soil, level the area with a steel rake, breaking up clods and discarding any rocks. Although double digging takes more effort, it enables roots to penetrate deeper to find water and nutrients. If you're double digging, dig the upper part of the soil with a straight spade to remove the sod and loosen the *subsoil* (usually any soil below 8 to 12 inches) with a spade. Replace the original topsoil often when you loosen the subsoil.

WARNING

Don't overtill your soil. Tilling to mix amendments or loosen the soil in spring or fall is fine, but using the tiller repeatedly in summer to weed or turn beds ruins the soil structure and causes the organic matter (the good stuff) to break down too fast. In the case of tilling, more isn't necessarily better.

SAYING YES TO NO-TILL GARDENING

A large percentage of gardeners adhere to a strict no-till policy. A rototiller makes the work of mixing soil easier, but it also tends to destroy the soil structure — the intricate network of thousands upon thousands of particles of sand, silt, clay, and organic matter that make up your dirt. That structure determines the soil's capability to hold the water, nutrients, and air that your plants need to grow. The relentless machinery of a rototiller is devastatingly effective — maybe too effective — at breaking down that life-giving structure.

No-till gardening is increasing in popularity among gardeners looking to adopt more organic practices. Fewer amendments are needed to help build back the soil quality; no rototiller means no fossil fuel consumption and air pollution; and turning soil by hand allows the beneficial bacteria, fungi, micro-organisms, and earthworms in your soil to live and continue to do their important jobs.

Converting your garden to a true no-till garden can be a lengthy process that takes multiple seasons and lots of patience and discipline, but devotees say it results in a dramatically healthier garden with stronger plants and even far fewer weeds!

Looking Ahead at Watering Options

You can water your vegetable garden several different ways. This section discusses some of the basic techniques, from the simple — furrows and basins — to the more complicated — drip irrigation and harvesting systems.

It's a good idea to consider how you'll water your garden before you actually plant your garden. Some of these ideas are easier to plan for and implement when the beds are a blank canvas rather than work around tender young seedlings or maturing plants already in the ground.

TIP

You can measure water flow by attaching an inexpensive *flowmeter* (available at hardware and garden supply stores) to your outdoor spigot. To figure out the flow rate at the spigot, turn off all the spigots and read your water meter. Then turn on the spigot serving the hose line for 1 minute. Reread the meter to find out how much water flows through the hose in 1 minute. You need about 60 gallons per 100 square feet of garden to get 1 inch of water.

Furrows

Furrows are shallow trenches between raised beds that channel water to plant roots. This watering method is based on an old farmer technique of planting on narrow raised mounds or beds and then using furrows to water. The beds can be 1 to 3 feet apart — the wider apart they are, however, the more water you need to add. You can use a hoe to dig a furrow at planting time and then plant the seeds or transplants on top of the raised beds, in between the furrows.

When you're ready to water, fill the furrows completely with water and then wait a while, or fill them more than once so the water penetrates down as well as sideways into the raised soil. Poke around with your finger to make sure the water has penetrated the bed.

Furrows work best on level or slightly sloping ground; otherwise, the water moves too fast down the furrows without sinking in. This watering technique traditionally has been used in arid areas with clay soil, such as the Southwest, where little natural rain falls during the growing season and streams or ground water can be used in the garden. Furrows don't work well in sandy soil because the water soaks in before it can reach the end of the furrow.

WARNING

Furrows aren't the most efficient way to water. Here are a few reasons:

>> It takes time for the water to run from one end of a mound or bed to the other.

>> The beginning of a row always gets more water than the end.

>> You have to move your hose around a lot to fill each furrow.

>> Water is wasted through evaporation as it's sitting in the furrow.

Basins

A *basin* is a donutlike depression around a vegetable plant that you fill with water — almost like a circular furrow. You make a basin in a 2-foot-diameter circle around the plant. Plastic basins that fit underneath plants such as tomatoes and eggplants are sold commercially. These basins concentrate the water around the roots of the plant.

WARNING

Homemade basins work particularly well for watering sprawling plants such as melons and squash early in the season. After the plants mature, however, their roots grow out of the diameter of the basin, and the method is no longer effective.

Hoses

Watering with a hose is probably the most common way that gardeners water. It's simple, and some might say therapeutic. Who hasn't seen a gardener after a long day at work come home and take some time to hose down the garden with a cup of coffee or drink in hand?

However, watering with a hose isn't the ideal watering system and probably is best for watering containers; for watering individual, large plants such as tomatoes; and when used in conjunction with the basin method (explained in the preceding section). In these situations, you can be sure that you're applying the right amount of water to your plants.

Unless you check the amount of water you're applying by digging the soil after watering, you may not water your garden evenly with a hose. Some areas may have lots of water, whereas other areas may just have water on the surface. Also, like overhead sprinklers (described in the next section), a hose is a more wasteful way of watering because much of the water falls in pathways or on the lawn around your garden.

REMEMBER

The best way to water your vegetable garden with a hose is to leave the hose running at a trickle in a basin near each plant until the water has soaked down at least 6 inches deep.

Sprinklers

A sprinkler, shown in Figure 3-3, is effective for watering vegetables planted in sandy soil that absorbs water quickly. It's also an effective way to water a large garden when you're pressed for time. Just set up the sprinkler, and based on the amount of time it takes to water to 6 inches deep (see Chapter 5 in this minibook for details on knowing when your vegetables need a drink), you can set a timer and go about other business.

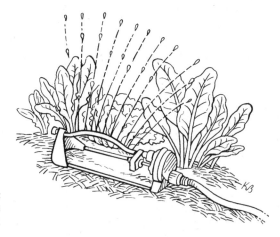

FIGURE 3-3:
Watering with
a sprinkler.

However, if you have heavy clay soil that absorbs water slowly or if your garden is on a slope, the water may run off and not sink into the soil where the plants need it. Instead, it's best to use drip irrigation (see the next section) so the water soaks into the ground.

For vegetable gardens, portable-type sprinklers (versus in-ground permanent sprinklers used in lawns) are best. You can move them around in your garden to cover a certain area or the whole garden. Some sprinklers throw water back and forth, whereas others send it in a circular direction. Choose the type that best suits your garden design.

TIP

Constantly wetting the foliage of vegetable plants can encourage disease problems. So when you use a sprinkler, water in the morning so the foliage can dry before nightfall and so you lose less water to evaporation.

As taller plants such as corn and tomatoes grow, sprinklers tend to be less effective because the water hits the foliage, damaging it and not thoroughly watering the rest of the garden. Some gardeners use watering towers that have an overhead sprinkler attached to the top. You position the sprinkler a few feet above the plants, hook it up to a hose, and sprinkle the garden. However, even these

Preparing to Plant

sprinklers prove to be less effective when plants reach above 4 to 5 feet tall. For these taller plants, it's best to choose one of the other watering methods described in this chapter.

WARNING

Frequent, shallow waterings do more harm than good. They cause roots to develop mainly in the upper few inches of the soil, where they're susceptible to drying out. Instead, go for occasional, deep waterings. Deep waterings allow moisture to penetrate deeply into the soil. The roots will follow the water, and the plant will be deep rooted and less likely to be affected by dry conditions. You'll water less frequently; maybe deeply once per week.

Soaker-hose irrigation

A *soaker-hose irrigation system* consists of a rubber hose perforated with tiny pores that leak water, as shown in Figure 3-4. You can lay the hose between rows or curve it around plants, similar to how you use a drip irrigation system (described in the following section). Water leaks out of the hose and onto the soil, leaving your plant foliage dry and reducing evaporation.

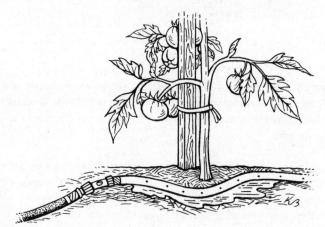

FIGURE 3-4:
Watering with a soaker hose.

REMEMBER

Using a soaker-hose system is easier than using a drip irrigation system because it involves fewer parts and no nozzles. Its primary limitation is that it works best on flat terrain, often delivering water unevenly on sloped or bumpy gardens. It also may clog over time and not deliver water evenly along the hose.

Drip irrigation

A *drip irrigation system* provides water slowly through holes, or *emitters*, in flexible plastic pipes. Many different drip irrigation systems are available; they can consist of a single pipe with flexible lines running off it, or a series of pipes. You weave these pipes — which are connected to a water supply, a filter, and often a pressure regulator — along rows of plants so the water flows directly to the roots of your vegetables, as shown in Figure 3-5.

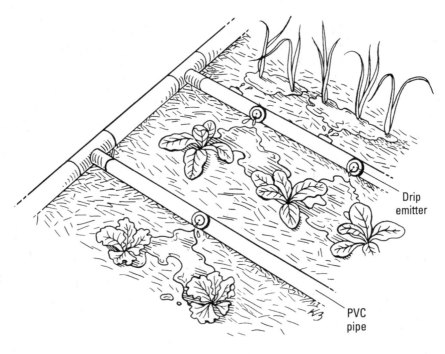

FIGURE 3-5:
Watering with drip irrigation.

Drip emitter

PVC pipe

This watering technique is the most effective and efficient way to water vegetables because water drips right to the roots of the plants and little water is wasted on pathways, in between plants, and in between rows. Drip irrigation works well even if your garden is on a slope, which poses problems for most other systems.

WARNING

The downside to drip irrigation is that it's more costly than the other methods listed in this chapter; it's also more involved to set up and take down at the end of the season. Drip irrigation is best for those gardeners who are into technology, who don't have lots of time to water, and who live in water-restricted areas.

You can wet an entire bed from one end to the other at each watering with drip emitters. You snap the emitters in the pipes wherever you want them, or you can buy a pipe with emitters already evenly spaced along the length of the pipe. The moisture radiates sideways underground and wets the soil between emitters.

TIP

As an alternative to emitters, you may want to use *microsprinklers*, which are tiny sprinklers that hook to plastic pipes like drip emitters. They're usually supported by 12- to 24-inch stakes and cover various-sized areas of soil with a fine spray of water. They're particularly useful for watering closely spaced vegetables such as lettuce and root crops, or for watering germinating seeds.

Most nurseries sell drip irrigation systems, but you also can purchase them online. Emitters and microsprinklers are available with different application rates, varying by the number of gallons applied per hour. Pressure-compensating emitters apply water consistently from one end of the line to the other, regardless of pressure changes due to uneven ground.

Follow these steps to set up a drip irrigation system in your garden:

1. **Lay the pipe (or pipes — depending on the system) on top of the soil and cover the pipe with plastic mulch, or bury the pipe a few inches below the surface of the soil.**

   Most people like to keep the pipe close to the surface so they can check it for clogs and fix breaks.

2. **If your pipe doesn't already have emitters in it, snap emitters in the pipe wherever you want them.**

   Position the emitters so they're close to the bases of your plants.

3. **Run the drip system for at least several hours a day (two to four hours).**

   Watch the system carefully the first few times that you water. Dig around in your garden to see how far the water travels over a given time period, and then adjust your watering schedule in the future.

WARNING

If you live in an area where the soil freezes, don't leave your drip irrigation system or soaker hoses outside in the winter because they may burst. Instead, drain the water out, roll up the tubing, and store it in your garage.

Harvesting rainwater in a barrel

One of the simplest ways to collect water is by installing a rain barrel under a downspout of your gutters (see Figure 3-6). This method is safe, easy, and quite productive. For example, ½ inch of rain hitting a 1,000 square foot roof will yield more than 300 gallons of water. Commercial rain barrels are attractive, too. Some look like old whiskey barrels, while others are shaped like giant urns. They can be nice additions to your yard. Here's what you'll need to get started:

>> **Gutters:** It's clear you'll need gutters on part of your roof to collect the rain water hitting it. Although a cost investment at first, they will pay for

themselves in water savings later on. Ideally, place the downspout so that it connects to the gutters on that side of the roof closest to the garden.

» **Barrels and cisterns:** Although a simple 60-gallon rain barrel is great for collecting water, sometimes you might get hundreds of gallons of rain in a single day! It's hard to just let that water go to waste, especially if you're gardening in a dry climate. You can connect a few barrels together to save more water or use a cistern. Cisterns are large above or below ground vessels that hold hundreds of gallons of water. They may not be practical for the average urban homeowner, but are something to consider when building or buying a home in a dry climate.

» **Screens:** Water coming off the roof collects leaves, pine needles, and other debris. Place a heavy-duty, removable screen at the end of the downspout to catch these materials before they enter the barrel. This will prevent clogging the outflow spigots in the rain barrel. Clean them out periodically to allow the water to flow through.

» **Hoses:** After you have all the pieces in place, you'll need a way to get the water to the garden. You could simply dip your watering can in the barrel and hand water. Also, many commercial rain barrels have spigots where you can attach a hose and run it to the garden. As long as the barrel is higher than the garden, gravity will feed the water through the hose and onto your plants.

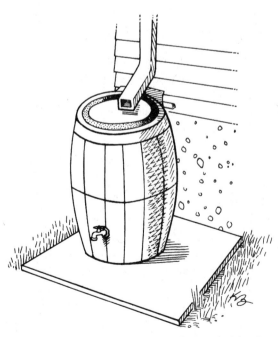

FIGURE 3-6:
A rain barrel.

Illustration by Kathryn Born

THE BLACK AND WHITE OF GRAYWATER SYSTEMS

One way to harvest and re-use water that has seen a recent uptick in popularity is the installation of a graywater system. A *graywater system* uses secondhand water from your washing machine, sinks, and possibly tubs and showers (never toilets). The water is collected with a system of pipes throughout the house and delivered to landscape plantings, often after being stored temporarily in an underground cistern. If graywater irrigation is legal where you live (it isn't everywhere), it can be a great way to recycle water in certain areas of the landscape. Although you can irrigate ornamentals and even fruit trees with graywater, health reasons prohibit its use on vegetables or other edible crops. Even though experts claim that there are no documented cases of anyone becoming sick from contact with graywater, you shouldn't ignore the possible health risks. Because of the potential for problems, graywater can't be allowed to appear on the surface of the ground and can't be applied through overhead sprinklers or garden hoses. Homesteaders may love the repurposing concept of a graywater system, but it's simply not compatible with crops you'll be harvesting to eat.

Fencing It In

Your property needs boundaries around it and pathways within it. Even sprawling ranches under the western sky have fences around them and a dusty road or two through the sagebrush. In your backyard homestead, fences and walls define areas. For many homesteaders, it's helpful to have the chickens' part of the yard partitioned off from, say, the vegetable garden. Fences can help you form a basic infrastructure. Installing them (or at least planning for them) early in the process of creating a homestead — before things are planted or your animals are scurrying about — can be a logistical lifesaver.

Most fences are variations on a basic design: posts buried in the ground; horizontal rails installed between them; and some kind of fencing attached to the rails — pickets, boards attached vertically, boards attached horizontally, lattice, wire mesh, solid panels, siding materials, bamboo, or wood worked into decorative designs.

Six feet is standard for side and back yards, but may not be high enough if you have a raised deck or if neighboring houses are close to your property line. You may have to build an 8-foot fence (check your local zoning laws first, though) or solid screen of tall bushes. For front-yard fences, 3 to 4 feet is sufficient for defining your property line. Short fences are also usually adequate for sectioning off just a portion of your homestead. If you have a corner lot with fences along both streets, make sure that neither fence blocks views of traffic. Check your local zoning ordinances for other restrictions, and be sure to discuss the fence with your neighbor.

TIP

If deer are a concern in your area, your garden beds could become a giant salad bar for Bambi. A fence meant to keep deer out needs to be 8 feet tall. Or angled strategically. Or electrified. Or even paired with a second fence. Check out Chapter 1 of this minibook for more tips to help keep unwanted critters out of your homestead.

Building the fence

If you have a few weekends, some vacation time, or lots of helpers in the family, you may enjoy building your own fence. The experience offers an excellent opportunity to practice basic carpentry skills. For a basic wood fence, follow the steps in this section.

Laying out post hole locations

Start by laying out the locations for your post hole:

1. **Stretch a string along the fence line.**

   Align it with the centers — not the edges — of the post positions.

2. **Establish the post spacing.**

   Posts are typically spaced 5 to 8 feet apart, depending on the size of framing members, weight of the fencing material, and length of prefabricated fence panels, if you use them. If possible, choose a spacing that divides evenly into the total fence length.

   TIP

   Don't forget to put in posts for the gate. Try to make fence *bays* (sections between posts) equal on either side of the gate. If you end up with an odd-sized bay, get rid of it by readjusting the post spacing or changing the overall fence length. If neither solution works, split the odd-sized bay dimension in half and place the shorter bays at each end of the fence.

3. **Mark the ground.**

   Starting at the uphill end of the fence and holding a tape measure as close to level as possible (rather than laying it on sloping ground), mark the center of each post location with spray paint, a swatch of cloth with a nail through the center, or a pinch of flour. To align the mark with the stringline, hold a *plumb bob* (a string with a weight on the end) against the string or hold a level vertically against it, without deflecting the string.

Installing posts

Use the following instructions, shown in Figure 3-7, to install the posts.

1. **Temporarily move the stringline out of the way.**

2. **Determine post hole size.**

Plan 12-inch diameter holes for 4x4 posts set in concrete; 8-inch diameter for posts set in alternating layers of gravel and earth (a technique used in regions with severe winters and firm soils). If you use larger posts, expand the hole accordingly.

The hole depth should be equal to ⅓ the fence height, plus 6 inches for a layer of gravel at the bottom of the hole. A 6-foot (72-inch) fence, for example, requires a 30-inch hole — 24 inches for the buried portion of the post, plus 6 inches for gravel. Add another 12 inches (for a hole that's 42 inches deep) for gate posts and corner posts.

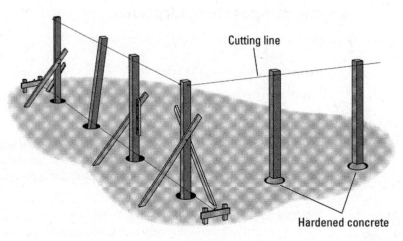

Cutting line

Hardened concrete

Installing fence posts

FIGURE 3-7:
Use stringlines to align fence posts and mark them for trimming.

3. **Dig holes.**

No way around it, this is hard work. For just a few holes, use a *clamshell digger* (hand tool that resembles a large pair of tongs). For long fences, rent a *power auger* (a gas-powered, hand-held machine with a screw-type blade) or hire an excavator. If you rent an auger, specify an 8-, 12-, or 14-inch diameter blade. Whichever tool you use, have a 6-foot long digging bar handy to dislodge rocks and loosen hard soil. Keep the sides of each hole plumb — don't flare the top of the hole; if anything, flare the bottom to increase stability.

A power auger generates tremendous *torque* (twisting force) and requires two strong people to operate the beast, especially one with a large-diameter blade.

4. **Place 6 inches of gravel or crushed rock in the bottom of each hole.**

5. **Restring lines.**

   Move the stringline position from the post centers to the post edges (either side). For 4x4 posts, for example, move the stringline over 2 inches (1¾ inches if you use *surfaced* (that is, planed or smooth) posts, which are 3½ inches thick).

6. **Set the corner or end posts in place first.**

   Set each one in its hole, burying the bottom 2 inches in the gravel. Align the post with the stringline(s), using a level to make sure that the post is plumb. Brace the post by driving stakes diagonally into the ground along two adjacent sides. Nail the stakes to the post with duplex nails — 8d nails for 1-by stakes; 16d for 2-by stakes, again checking with a level to make sure the post is plumb.

   If the posts aren't pressure-treated with preservatives for ground contact, apply preservative to the portion that will be buried by soaking the end of each post in preservative. Use a brush to reach undipped areas.

7. **String a line between the end posts near the top.**

8. **Set the remaining posts in their holes.**

   Align them to both stringlines and brace them, using a level to make sure they're plumb.

9. **Backfill the holes.**

   If you use concrete, mix enough for one or two holes at a time. Shovel the concrete carefully around each post and jab a stick or metal rod into the concrete several times to consolidate it. Using a trowel or shovel, mound the top of the concrete to keep water from settling around the post.

   If you backfill with alternating layers of gravel and soil, pack each layer firmly to a 2- or 3-inch thickness, using a pipe or rod. Mound the top layer of soil to shed water away from the post.

Posts with *mortises* (holes) cut into them to receive rails, or with decorative tops, must all be set to the same level — you can't trim the tops to level them. To do this, install the higher end post first. Attach temporary *cleats* (short pieces of wood that straddle the hole) to opposite sides of the post to keep it from sinking into the hole. Install the other end post at the same level, using a water level or builder's level to keep them aligned. Brace both posts securely. Then, measure down an equal distance from the top of each post, tack nails at those points, and stretch a line between the nails. Install the remaining posts so that all of the tops are an equal distance above the stringline.

Building the framework

To build a framework for your fence, follow these steps (see Figure 3-8):

1. **Trim the post tops.**

   After the concrete sets, mark and trim the tops of the posts so that they are all level. If the ground is fairly level, simply start with the post at the highest point of the fence. Mark that post where the top rail rests on top of the post. Using a string level, transfer this mark to the other end post. String a *chalkline* (a string coated with chalk) between the two marks and snap the line to transfer chalk marks to the other posts at the same level. Using a square and pencil, extend the mark around the four sides of each post. Cut along these marks.

   If the ground slopes gently, take trial measurements at several posts and refer to your plans to determine the best level for cutting. If the ground slopes steeply, step the fence down the slope by marking only a few posts level with each other and then lowering the marking level a few inches for the next few posts, and so on.

WARNING

   Making horizontal cuts with a circular power saw is dangerous. If you don't have experience making such cuts, use a handsaw. If you do have experience, stand on a sturdy stepladder or bench, and wear safety glasses.

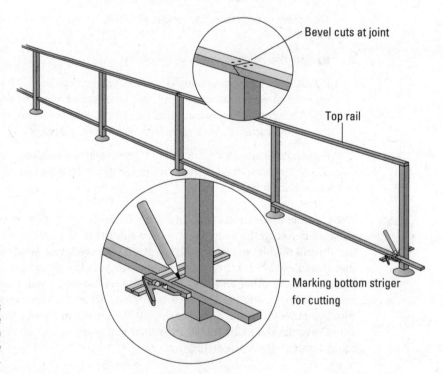

Bevel cuts at joint

Top rail

Marking bottom striger for cutting

FIGURE 3-8:
After the concrete hardens, attach the fence rails to the posts.

2. Install the top rail.

Use 2x4s or 2x6s long enough to connect at least three posts. Take measurements, along a level line, at the *bottoms* of posts (the tops may be out of line). Plan joints over the centers of posts. After cutting each board, secure it to each post with at least two 16d galvanized spiral-shank nails — drill pilot holes for nailing near the ends of boards. You may need to pull post tops into alignment before nailing.

TIP

As boards shrink, joints open up. When joining boards end-to-end, cut the ends at a 30-degree *bevel* (angle, as viewed from the edge — refer to Figure 5-2) so that each board slightly overlaps the previous board. As the joint opens up, the beveled ends appear to touch each other from most viewing angles.

3. Install bottom rails between the posts.

Mark the rail locations on each post by measuring *down* from the top rail (which should be level), not up from the ground. Cut 2x4s to fit between the posts at these marks. Install them by drilling pilot holes and toenailing each end to the post with two 16d galvanized spiral-shank nails.

4. Install kickboards.

To fill the gaps below bottom rails and make the fence stronger, install a 1-by board, set on edge, under each bottom rail, as shown in Figure 3-9. Cut it to fit between the posts. If it's too wide for the gap, excavate some soil or trim the bottom of the board to the same contour as the ground. Toenail it to the posts with 8d galvanized common nails (drill pilot holes first).

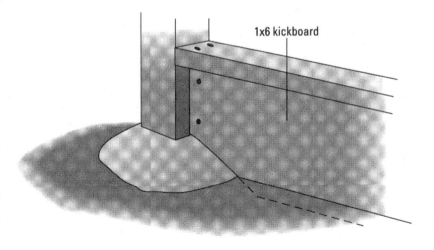

1x6 kickboard

FIGURE 3-9:
A kickboard secures the bottom of the fence and is relatively easy to replace if the wood rots.

Installing the fencing

With the basic framework of the fence in place, you can now finish it with the individual boards or panels that provide separation and privacy in and around your homestead:

1. **Install nailers, as needed.**

   If you install boards or panels between the rails, you may need to attach *nailers* (strips of wood) along the bottom of the top rail and top of the bottom rail to nail the fencing to — and perhaps along the posts, as well.

   WARNING

   Avoid a fence design that depends on too many nailers. They create more joints for moisture to get trapped in — which encourages rot — and provide weaker support than the frame itself.

2. **Attach the boards or panels to the framework or nailers.**

   Attach 1-by boards with 8d galvanized box nails. Attach lattice screening with galvanized deck screws.

   For pickets or other vertical boards with uniform spacing, make a spacer to speed up installation — see Figure 3-10. *Rip* (saw along the board's length) a board to the same width as the required spacing, long enough to extend from top rail to bottom rail. Attach a small cleat to the back side of the spacer, flush with the top edge, as a hanger. After installing each board, hang the spacer beside it, butt the next board against the spacer, and nail the board in place. Use a straightedge or stringline to keep the tops level.

   TIP

   Rent a pneumatic nailer to speed up installation of the fencing. The rental agency provides operating and safety instructions.

3. **Trim the top edge.**

   If you attach boards to the edge of the rails (rather than below the top rail), the tops may not be even (unless you used a straightedge or stringline to keep them level, as with a picket fence). Snap a chalkline along the length of the fence (shown in Figure 3-11), at the finished height, and cut along the line. If you use a power saw, nail a cleat along the fence to guide the saw.

4. **Add decorative trim.**

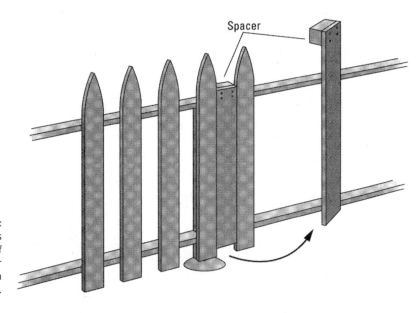

FIGURE 3-10:
Installing pickets is less tedious if you use a spacer to align each picket.

Spacer

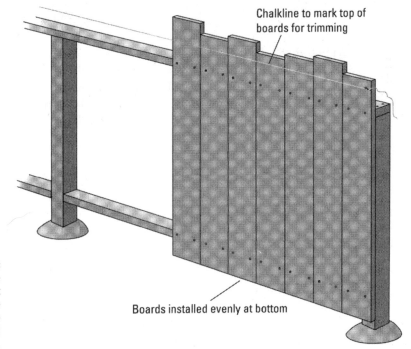

Chalkline to mark top of boards for trimming

FIGURE 3-11:
For a simple board fence (not pickets), trim the top of the fence after installing all of the boards.

Boards installed evenly at bottom

Applying the finish

Allow the wood to season for a week or two and apply a sealer (for natural color) or water-repellent stain to the fence. If you paint the fence, wait several weeks for the wood to season. Apply white-pigmented shellac to exposed knots to keep resin from bleeding through the paint. Then prime the fence (use oil-based primer for redwood and cedar, or latex for other woods) and finish it with one or two coats of latex paint.

Planning for Pathways

After you have the boundaries of your homestead and the areas within it established with fences, think about how you'll move throughout the property. Pathways connect the various areas within your homestead with one another and make it easier to get from Point A to Point B. Base them on where you need to walk, but also allow them to meander slightly to take advantage of views and attractive garden settings; you do want to enjoy the time you spend in your homestead, too! (Avoid low areas with poor drainage and steep inclines, though.)

Make paths at least 36 inches wide; two people walking side-by-side require a 48-inch width. Also consider the pathways that will see a lot of back-and-forth traffic from wheelbarrows and garden carts. As far as the pathway's walking surface, consider stepping stones, gravel, crushed stone, or good old wood chips. Know that you'll need to replenish them once or twice a year.

Chapter **4**

Planting

A re you ready to plant some vegetables? Now the fun really starts. You can plant vegetables two different ways — from seed or by transplant:

» When planting seeds, you either sow the seeds indoors and then transplant the young seedlings in your garden (when the time is right, of course), or you sow the seeds directly in your garden.

» To skip the seed process, you purchase young *transplants* (seedlings ready to be transplanted) at your local nursery or through the mail and then plant them directly into your garden.

Both methods have their advantages, and timing is critical to success. You can plant seeds quickly and without much thought. But working deliberately and carefully — whether planting indoors or out — pays off in sturdier, more vigorous plants. This chapter guides you through the planting process and gives you information about correct seed spacing, planting depth, soil and germinating conditions, and fertilizing so you produce strong-growing, vigorous plants. It also covers how to plant transplants, whether you grow them yourself or buy them.

Timing Your Planting Wisely

As the saying goes, "Timing is everything." This axiom is especially important for vegetable gardening, so file it where you can't forget it. Remembering it will save you lots of heartache and disappointment. For example, if you plant tomatoes too early, the plants will sit there like bumps on a log, not growing and possibly rotting in cold, wet soil or turning mushy and black after they've been zapped by frost. Plant lettuce too late, and it'll produce more flowers than leaves, and the leaves you harvest will be tough and bitter. There are examples like this for every vegetable; just know that planting at the wrong time of year is a recipe for disaster.

If you follow the rhythms of nature and plant when conditions are perfect for proper growth, growing vegetables is a breeze. But how are you supposed to know about these rhythms? Start tapping your foot, because the following sections will have you moving like Fred Astaire.

Some like it cool, some like it hot

Vegetables can be divided into the following two categories based on the temperature conditions in which they grow best:

>> **Cool-season vegetables:** These vegetables, such as lettuce, spinach, peas, potatoes, broccoli, and cabbage, grow best in the cool weather of spring and fall. As vegetables go, they're fairly hardy and survive despite freezing temperatures. In most areas, cool-season vegetables are usually planted in early spring so they mature before the onset of hot weather, or in late summer to early fall for maturation in the cool months of fall or early winter. However, in areas where summers are very cool and winters are mild, such as in coastal areas of the western United States and the far north, cool season vegetables can be grown year-round and may be the only vegetables that can thrive in this climate.

WARNING

What happens if you plant a cool-season vegetable when it's too warm? Not a lot of good. Lettuce will *bolt,* meaning it starts to flower before you get a chance to harvest it. In other words, instead of producing tender, crisp leaves, lettuce will send out a tall flower spike. Any leaves that are left on the plant will be bitter-tasting and tough. Broccoli will form loose clusters of yellow flowers instead of forming nice tight heads. And peas won't properly fill their pods with sweet, succulent peas. You get the idea!

>> **Warm-season vegetables:** These vegetables, such as beans, tomatoes, peppers, cucumbers, melons, squash, okra, and corn, like it hot and grow best in the warm months of summer. They need warm soil and air temperatures to grow their best; if they're planted while the weather is still too cool, they'll suffer and not grow. Because freezing temperatures kill these vegetables,

they're usually planted after the threat of frost in spring. In warm areas, they also can be planted in late summer for a fall harvest.

To push along warm-season veggies, wait until the soil and air are the proper temperature. Or consider using season extenders to trap heat around the plants. Season extenders also help in cool summer climates such as the Pacific Northwest, where the weather rarely gets warm enough even in summer to ripen heat-loving vegetables such as melons. (Chapter 7 of this minibook has more ideas on season-extending techniques.)

Frost dates and the length of the growing season

You should know two important weather dates for your area if you want to grow vegetables successfully:

>> The average date of the last frost in spring

>> The average date of the first frost in fall

These frost dates tell you several important things:

>> **When to plant:** Cool-season vegetables are generally planted four to six weeks before the last spring frost. Fall planting of cool-season vegetables is less dependent on frost dates, but it's usually done eight to twelve weeks before the first fall frost. Warm-season vegetables are planted after the last spring frost or in late summer in warm areas for a fall harvest.

>> **When to protect warm-season vegetables:** Frosts kill warm-season vegetables. So the closer you plant to the last frost of spring, the more important it is to protect plants. And as the fall frost gets closer, so does the end of your summer vegetable season — unless, of course, you protect your plants. See how to provide frost protection in Chapter 7 of this minibook.

>> **The length of your growing season:** Your *growing season* is the number of days between the average date of the last frost in spring and the average date of the first frost in fall. The length of the growing season can range from less than 100 days in northern or cold winter climates to 365 days in frost-free southern climes. Many warm-season vegetables need long, warm growing seasons to properly mature, so they're difficult, if not impossible, to grow where growing seasons are short.

How are you to know whether your growing season is long enough? If you check mail-order seed catalogs or even individual seed packets, each variety will have the number of days to harvest or days to maturity (usually posted in

Planting

parentheses next to the variety name). This number tells you how many days it takes for that vegetable to grow from seed (or transplant) to harvest. If your growing season is only 100 days long and you want to grow a melon or other warm-season vegetable that takes 120 frost-free days to mature, you have a problem. The plant will probably be killed by frost before the fruit is mature. In areas with short growing seasons, it's usually best to go with early ripening varieties (which have the shortest number of days to harvest).

TIP

However, you also can find many effective ways to extend your growing season, such as starting seeds indoors or planting under *floating row covers* (blanketlike materials that drape over plants, creating warm, greenhouselike conditions underneath). Various methods of extending growing seasons are covered in Chapter 7 of this minibook.

There you have it; now you know why frost dates are so important. But how do you find out dates for your area? Easy. Ask a local nursery worker or contact your local Cooperative Extension office (look in the phone book under *county government*). You also can check Table 4-1, which lists frost dates for major cities around the country. Double-check online sources due to continuing climate changes.

TABLE 4-1   **First and Last Frost Dates**

City	Last Frost Date	First Frost Date	Length of Season
Birmingham, Alabama	March 29	November 6	221 days
Mobile, Alabama	February 27	November 26	272 days
Juneau, Alaska	May 16	September 26	133 days
Flagstaff, Arizona	June 13	September 21	99 days
Phoenix, Arizona	February 5	December 15	308 days
Tucson, Arizona	February 28	November 29	273 days
Fayetteville, Arkansas	April 21	October 17	179 days
Little Rock, Arkansas	March 23	November 9	230 days
Fresno, California	February 22	November 25	273 days
Los Angeles, California	None likely	None likely	365 days
San Bernardino, California	February 23	December 8	294 days
San Francisco, California	January 8	January 5	362 days
Sacramento, California	February 14	December 1	287 days
San Jose, California	January 22	December 25	338 days

City	Last Frost Date	First Frost Date	Length of Season
San Diego, California	None	None	365 days
Santa Rosa, California	March 26	November 19	236 days
Denver, Colorado	May 3	October 8	157 days
Durango, Colorado	June 4	September 18	105 days
Hartford, Connecticut	April 25	October 10	167 days
New Haven, Connecticut	April 15	October 27	195 days
Dover, Delaware	April 9	October 28	202 days
Wilmington, Delaware	April 13	October 29	198 days
Washington, DC	April 10	October 31	203 days
Jacksonville, Florida	February 14	December 14	303 days
Miami, Florida	None	None	365 days
Orlando, Florida	January 31	December 17	320 days
Tallahassee, Florida	March 12	November 14	246 days
Atlanta, Georgia	March 13	November 12	243 days
Savannah, Georgia	March 10	November 15	250 days
Boise, Idaho	May 8	October 9	153 days
Pocatello, Idaho	May 20	September 20	122 days
Chicago, Illinois	April 14	November 2	201 days
Indianapolis, Indiana	April 18	October 22	186 days
Cedar Rapids, Iowa	April 29	October 7	161 days
Des Moines, Iowa	April 19	October 17	180 days
Manhattan, Kansas	April 23	October 16	176 days
Wichita, Kansas	April 13	October 23	193 days
Lexington, Kentucky	April 17	October 25	190 days
Louisville, Kentucky	April 1	November 7	220 days
New Orleans, Louisiana	February 20	December 5	288 days
Portland, Maine	May 10	September 30	143 days
Baltimore, Maryland	March 26	November 13	231 days
Amherst, Massachusetts	May 9	September 29	142 days

(continued)

TABLE 4-1 *(continued)*

City	Last Frost Date	First Frost Date	Length of Season
Boston, Massachusetts	April 6	November 10	217 days
Detroit, Michigan	April 24	October 22	181 days
Marquette, Michigan	May 12	October 19	159 days
Minneapolis–St. Paul, Minnesota	April 30	October 13	166 days
Duluth, Minnesota	May 21	September 21	122 days
Columbus, Mississippi	March 27	October 29	215 days
Jackson, Mississippi	March 17	November 9	236 days
Jefferson City, Missouri	April 26	October 16	173 days
St. Louis, Missouri	April 3	November 6	217 days
Billings, Montana	May 12	September 23	133 days
Helena, Montana	May 18	September 18	122 days
Lincoln, Nebraska	March 13	November 13	180 days
North Platte, Nebraska	May 11	September 24	136 days
Las Vegas, Nevada	March 7	November 21	259 days
Concord, New Hampshire	May 23	September 22	121 days
Newark, New Jersey	April 4	November 10	219 days
Trenton, New Jersey	April 6	November 7	214 days
Albuquerque, New Mexico	April 16	October 29	196 days
Los Alamos, New Mexico	May 8	October 13	157 days
Albany, New York	May 7	September 29	144 days
New York, New York	April 1	November 11	223 days
Rochester, New York	May 3	October 15	164 days
Syracuse, New York	April 28	October 16	170 days
Asheville, North Carolina	April 10	October 24	195 days
Charlotte, North Carolina	March 21	November 15	239 days
Raleigh, North Carolina	April 11	October 27	198 days
Fargo, North Dakota	May 13	September 27	137 days
Akron, Ohio	May 3	October 18	168 days

City	Last Frost Date	First Frost Date	Length of Season
Cincinnati, Ohio	April 14	October 27	195 days
Columbus, Ohio	April 26	October 17	173 days
Oklahoma City, Oklahoma	March 28	November 7	224 days
Tulsa, Oklahoma	March 30	November 4	218 days
Ashland, Oregon	May 13	October 12	152 days
Pendleton, Oregon	April 15	October 21	188 days
Portland, Oregon	April 3	November 7	217 days
Allentown, Pennsylvania	April 21	October 18	179 days
Pittsburgh, Pennsylvania	April 16	November 3	201 days
State College, Pennsylvania	April 27	October 15	170 days
Kingston, Rhode Island	May 8	September 30	144 days
Charleston, South Carolina	March 11	November 20	253 days
Columbia, South Carolina	April 4	November 2	211 days
Memphis, Tennessee	March 23	November 7	228 days
Nashville, Tennessee	April 5	October 29	207 days
Amarillo, Texas	April 14	October 29	197 days
Dallas, Texas	March 18	November 12	239 days
Houston, Texas	February 4	December 10	309 days
Cedar City, Utah	May 20	October 2	134 days
Salt Lake City, Utah	April 12	November 1	203 days
Burlington, Vermont	May 11	October 1	142 days
Norfolk, Virginia	March 23	November 17	239 days
Richmond, Virginia	April 10	October 26	198 days
Seattle, Washington	March 24	November 11	232 days
Spokane, Washington	May 4	October 5	153 days
Parkersburg, West Virginia	April 25	October 18	175 days
Green Bay, Wisconsin	May 12	October 2	143 days
Milwaukee, Wisconsin	May 5	October 9	156 days
Cheyenne, Wyoming	May 20	September 27	130 days

REMEMBER

Frost dates are important, but you also have to take them with a grain of salt. After all, these dates are averages, meaning that half the time the frost will actually come earlier than the average date and half the time it will occur later. You also should know that frost dates are usually given for large areas, such as your city or county. If you live in a cold spot in the bottom of a valley, frosts may come days earlier in fall and days later in spring. Similarly, if you live in a warm spot or you garden in a microclimate, your frost may come later in fall and stop earlier in spring. You're sure to find out all about your area as you become a more seasoned vegetable gardener and unearth the nuances of your own yard. One thing you'll discover for sure is that you can't predict the weather.

Listening to your evening weather forecast is one of the best ways to find out whether frosts are expected in your area. But you also can do a little predicting yourself by going outside late in the evening and checking conditions. If the fall or early spring sky is clear and full of stars, and the wind is still, conditions are right for a frost. If you need to protect plants, do so at that time. Frost-protection techniques are covered in Chapter 7 of this minibook.

Choosing Seeds or Transplants

Whether you choose to grow vegetables from seeds or transplants, each planting method has its own advantages. Here are some advantages to starting from seed:

- **A wider choice of varieties:** Your local garden store or nursery may carry only three or four varieties of tomato transplants but offer a great selection of seeds. And mail-order seed catalogs offer hundreds of varieties of seeds and specialty types, such as organically grown seed.

- **Healthy plants:** You don't have to settle for plants that are *leggy* (tall, weak, spindly stems) or *root-bound* (roots crammed into a small pot) and that may have been hanging out at the nursery too long. Such plants usually don't get off to a fast start when you plant them in the ground. Also, when you start from seed, you don't have to worry about introducing any insects or diseases into your garden that may be lurking on nursery-grown transplants.

- **Reduced cost:** Especially if you have a large garden, starting from seed can save you some dough. A six-pack of seedlings may cost you $3.00, whereas for the same price you can buy a seed packet with 100 seeds.

- **A lot of fun:** The excitement of seeing those first seedlings push through the soil is something special. Two feet of snow may be on the ground outside, but by sowing seeds indoors, you can enjoy a little spring.

The advantages to growing seeds stack up pretty impressively. But planting nursery-grown transplants has a major benefit as well — convenience and immediate gratification. Growing plants from seeds takes time and diligence, but going with nursery transplants gives you an instant garden. And if you have problems with transplants, you can always buy more. If you have problems with the special seed varieties you started, it's usually too late to start them again indoors, so you're out of luck growing that variety that year.

REMEMBER

Growing seeds is like taking care of a new pet. You have to check on seeds every day, maybe several times a day, to make sure they're happy. Unless a reliable neighbor or friend can care for your seedlings, say goodbye to your winter trip to the Caribbean. Also, you have to think in advance of what you'll be growing and need to start indoors. In this harried world, it's often easier to decide a week or so before planting what vegetable varieties you need and to buy transplants than to plan months in advance to start seeds. Plus, you have to store unused seeds somewhere where you won't forget them next winter. A metal tin in a cool, dark part of the house is best.

After you consider the advantages of each planting method, you need to make sure that you time your planting for the most productive results. Keep reading for full details on starting veggies from seeds and growing veggies from transplants.

Deciding on Your Seeding Method and Decoding a Seed Packet

Suppose you decide to grow your veggies from seeds. Now what? You have another choice to make: Will you start your seeds indoors or outdoors? If you plant seeds indoors, you have to transplant them into your garden later. With *direct seeding*, you skip the indoor step and sow the seeds directly into your garden. Which option should you choose? Probably both, if you're serious about growing vegetables. But consider these points when making your choice:

TIP

>> **Starting indoors gives you a jump on the growing season.** If you start at the right time (remember, timing is everything), you can have vigorous seedlings that are ready to go into the ground at the ideal time. In areas with short growing seasons, starting seedlings indoors really gives you a head start.

The best candidates for an early start are plants that tolerate root disturbance and benefit from a jump on the season. These veggies include broccoli, Brussels sprouts, cabbage, cauliflower, celery, eggplant, leeks, lettuce, onions, peppers, and tomatoes. Another group of vegetables that have to be transplanted carefully but do benefit from an early start include cucumbers, melons, and squash.

Planting

>> Seeds are easier to start indoors. You have more control indoors, enabling you to more easily provide the perfect conditions for hard-to-germinate or very small seeds. You can provide the ideal temperature, moisture, and fertility so your seedlings grow strong and sturdy.

>> **Some vegetables don't like to be transplanted and are better sown directly in the ground.** These vegetables include many of the root crops, such as carrots, beets, turnips, and parsnips. They're cold-hardy vegetables, so you can direct seed them pretty early anyway. Crops such as corn, beans, and peas also are pretty finicky about transplanting and grow better when you sow them directly in the ground. (Sowing seeds outdoors is explored in detail later in this chapter.)

REMEMBER

No matter your decision, the seed packet you buy to start your vegetables indoors or to plant directly in the ground is loaded with useful information. You still want to use a good book (like this one!) to get all the nitty-gritty details, but much of the information you need to plant your seeds is right on the packet. Consider some things your seed packet can tell you:

>> The name or description should indicate whether it's a hybrid or open-pollinated variety (see Chapter 2 of this minibook for more on understanding vegetable varieties) and whether the seed is treated with a fungicide.

>> The description tells you the high points about the variety, including yields, disease resistance, and suggestions for use. Remember to read with a critical eye, because companies can make all varieties sound fabulous.

>> Cultural information tells you information such as when to plant, days to germination, mature plant size, days to maturity, and plant spacing.

>> The packing date tells you the year in which the seeds were packed. Always buy this year's seeds for best germination. Even though many 1- to two-year-old seeds will still grow well, you shouldn't be paying full price for them, and your results may not be optimal.

Starting Seeds Indoors

To start seeds indoors, all you need is a container, soil, seeds, moisture, warmth, and light. The timing may vary depending on the specific vegetable, but here are the basic steps for planting seeds indoors:

1. **Sow the seeds in containers filled with sterile soil (which garden centers call a *germinating mix*).**

   Keep the seeds in a warm place until *germination* (when the first shoots start to push through the soil).

2. **After the seeds germinate, move the seedlings to a well-lit location (preferably under lights).**

   While your seedlings are growing in their well-lit location, be sure to keep them moist.

3. **Thin crowded seedlings.**

   When the seedlings' heights are three times the diameter of your pot, transplant the seedlings to a larger container.

4. **Acclimate the seedlings to outdoor conditions.**

   Adapting your seedlings to the weather conditions in the great outdoors is called *hardening off.*

5. **Plant the seedlings in your garden.**

Here's a little more detail to help your seeds off to the best start possible.

Picking a pot to plant in

Any container that holds several inches of soil and that you can punch drainage holes in is suitable for growing seedlings. Several low-cost possibilities include milk cartons, paper or Styrofoam cups, cottage-cheese containers, and home-made wooden *flats*, which are shallow, wide, seedling trays. Flats enable you to start many seedlings in a small space, which is helpful when you water or move the plants. After you plant the seeds in the flats, the seedlings stay there until planting time.

Garden stores and most mail-order garden catalogs sell a wide variety of plastic, fiber, peat, and Styrofoam flats and containers that satisfy just about any budget. You can even purchase pots made out of cow manure. Yum. Figure 4-1 shows you some flats that you can buy, along with the appropriate lights.

WARNING

You can use individual peat pots for plants such as cucumbers, which don't like to have their roots disturbed during transplanting. Similarly, for gardeners who put a premium on convenience, premade growing cubes (compressed peat pots that expand when soaked in water) are a good idea. The idea behind a peat pot is that once planted (pot and all) in the garden, the plants' roots grow through the sides of the wet pot, and as the season progresses, the peat naturally breaks down and disappears. But in the real world, the peat sometimes doesn't break down. In the fall when you pull up your plants, the peat pots may still be intact and some roots constricted in the pots. If you still want to give peat pots and cubes a try, follow the guidelines in the later section "Making the big move to the ground."

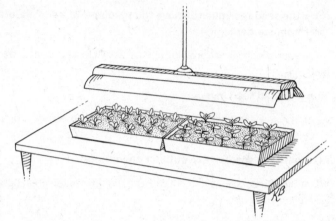

FIGURE 4-1:
Seed-starting flats
and lighting that
plants love.

REMEMBER

Before you sow any seeds, sterilize your flats and pots (especially ones that you've used before) to prevent the fungus called *damping off* from killing your seedlings. (See the later sidebar "Dealing with damping off" for more on this soil-borne disease.) Dip the containers in a solution of 9 parts water to 1 part household bleach and then rinse them in clear running water.

Using a mix that doesn't include soil

The most practical seed-starting mediums for gardeners are the commercially prepared soilless or peatlite mixes that are sold in most garden stores as *potting soil* or *germinating mix*. As the name implies, the mix doesn't contain any true soil. Instead, it's usually a combination of peat moss, vermiculite or perlite, ground limestone (which brings the pH to proper levels, as discussed in Chapter 3 of this minibook), fertilizer, and sometimes compost, which is good for plant growth. Potting soil is lightweight, is free of disease organisms that may be present in true garden soil, and holds moisture well but at the same time offers good aeration and drainage.

WARNING

Don't use garden soil to start seeds indoors. Garden soil isn't light enough (that is, it doesn't have enough air spaces) and may contain insects or diseases that can kill your tender seedlings.

Sowing your seeds

After you've chosen the proper container and soilless soil (or *growing medium*), follow these steps to sow your seeds:

1. **Fill a container with moistened growing medium to within ½ inch of the top of the container.**

Soilless mixes are dusty and difficult to wet initially. Pour the mix into a plastic bag, and then add enough warm water to moisten the mix but not turn it into a drippy mud pie. Mix the water and growing medium with your hands or a strong wooden spoon, closing off the opening of the bag as much as possible to keep the dust in. Remove the soil from the bag and place it in the container. Gently firm down the medium with a flat piece of wood, such as a ruler.

2. **If you're planting seeds in a flat, follow these directions to sow your seeds:**

Make shallow *furrows* (rowlike impressions) with a blunt stick or by pressing the narrow edge of a ruler into the medium. Then sow the seeds according to these guidelines:

- Sow small seeds, such as lettuce seed, at about five to eight seeds per inch if you intend to transplant them into different containers soon after they come up. Sow larger seeds, such as melons, at three to four seeds per inch.

- Sow seeds more sparingly, at three to four seeds per inch, if you intend to thin and leave them in the same container (rather than transplant into a larger container).

Either method — transplanting the seeds into a new container or leaving them in the same container — works fine; it's just a matter of what pots and room you have. Transplanting into individual pots takes up more room but allows larger plants such as tomatoes more room for their roots to grow. Smaller plants, such as lettuce, grow fine when thinned and left in their original containers.

You can *broadcast* (randomly spread) seeds rather than plant them in rowlike trenches, but row planting and thinning are easier.

3. **If you're planting seeds in individual containers, here's how you sow:**

- Put two to four seeds in each container.

- Later, thin the seedlings, leaving the strongest one.

4. **After sowing the seeds at the correct depth (see the appendix), cover them with fine potting soil or vermiculite.**

TIP

Label each row or container because many seedlings look alike. You can purchase labels from a nursery or through a mail-order catalog, or you can use old ones from previously purchased nursery transplants. Using a waterproof pen, record the type of vegetable, the variety, and the date that the seed was planted.

Planting

5. **Water the seeds gently with a mister or spray bottle.**

A stronger stream of water can wash seeds into one section of the container or move them too deeply into the soil.

6. **Cover the container with a sheet of clear plastic or a plastic bag to hold in the moisture.**

If necessary, use small stakes to prop up the plastic so it doesn't rest on top of the soil.

7. **Place the planted containers in a warm spot.**

The cooler the temperature, the longer it takes for the plants to emerge, so keep 'em warm and toasty! Some warm spots include the top of your refrigerator or near your furnace. But be careful how you water around electrical appliances. You also can buy heating cables or mats that keep the soil warm from below. Follow the package instructions carefully.

Never put containers in direct sun; the plastic cover holds in the heat, cooking your seeds to death.

8. **Check the containers daily to make sure they're still moist but not so wet that they mold.**

If you see signs of mold, loosen the cover and let air in; the mold should disappear. You also can hook up a small fan to gently blow across the seedlings (without the plastic cover on), keeping the soil on the dry side. However, be careful not to dry out the seedlings.

9. **As soon as you see the first green shoots emerge, remove the plastic cover and move your seedlings to a spot that provides plenty of light and the proper growing conditions for that vegetable.**

Until seedlings emerge from the soil, light is unnecessary, with the exception of lettuce and celery seeds. Sow these seeds by lightly pressing them into the soil or covering them very lightly with ⅛ inch of fine potting soil, and then place the containers in a bright spot or position them under a 40-watt incandescent light.

Providing the right amount of light and heat

The light that your young seedlings receive is one of the most important factors in good growth. Placing the seedlings in a south–facing window is one option but not always the best one. Even in a sunny window, plants get only a fraction of the light that they would get outside. Windowsill plants often get tall and spindly because they get too warm in relation to the light they receive.

REMEMBER

Try to keep your seedlings on the cool side — 60 to 65 degrees Fahrenheit (75 degrees maximum) — to encourage slower growth; cooler temperatures give you sturdy, stocky plants that transplant well. Although a 10- to 15-degree drop in temperature at night is beneficial, a windowsill can get pretty chilly at night when it's wintry outside. Place a blanket between the plants and the glass to keep windowsill seedlings warm on frosty nights, or move plants away from the window at night.

Growing seedlings under fluorescent lights is a good way to keep light-hungry plants happy. Ordinary cool-white, 40-watt fluorescent bulbs are fine for starting seedlings. If possible, set up your lights near a window so the plants can receive both natural and artificial light. The more expensive grow lights that you can purchase at a nursery or through a mail-order seed catalog produce the broader spectrum light that plants need for flowering and fruiting (although your seedlings will be in the garden before they're ready to flower).

TIP

No matter what kind of light you have, use one set of lights (usually two bulbs to a set) for every 1-foot-width of seedling-growing area and keep the bulbs 2 to 4 inches from the tops of the seedlings at all times. Keep the lights on for no more than 16 hours per day so the plants can get their natural rest period. Inexpensive timers that turn the lights on and off automatically are available at nurseries and hardware stores.

Watering your seedlings

Water fragile seedlings carefully, or you risk uprooting them. Mist them with a gentle spray, or water them from the bottom by setting your container in a pan of water just long enough for the soil surface to wet (keeping them in water longer than this can damage the plants' roots). After the surface is wet, remove the container from the water and let it drain. Keep the soil surface lightly moist but not soggy. Always water with lukewarm water, and try to do so early in the morning, if possible. This way the foliage can dry off quickly during the day to avoid disease problems.

As your plants get sturdier, you can water with a sprinkling can that has a *rose,* a nozzle that breaks the water into many fine streams. After the plants grow their first set of true leaves (the first leaves to open as the seed germinates are called *seedling leaves,* and the next set are *true leaves*) and have a bigger root system, let the soil dry out slightly between waterings.

WARNING

Give the plants enough water at one time so that some of it runs out the drainage holes in the bottom of the container, but never leave the container sitting in water. Overwatering promotes damping-off disease (see the sidebar "Dealing with damping off") and decreases the amount of air in the soil, resulting in a weaker root system.

Planting

With soilless mixes, you may have a difficult time deciding when to water, because the soil looks dry on the surface even though plenty of moisture is still present. To check whether the soil has moisture, take a small amount of soil off the top ½ inch of mix and squeeze it between your fingers. If you can squeeze out any water, hold off watering. The difference in a container's weight when the soil is moist compared to when it's dry can also indicate when to water. Dry soil is very light. Finally, wilted seedlings also are a sure sign that you've waited too long to water (unless, of course, your plants have damping off).

Certain types of containers require more frequent watering. For example, soil in clay pots dries out faster than soil in plastic pots. Peat pots dry out fast and are difficult to rewet. Try putting your peat pots or growing-cubes in a tray and packing moist peat moss between them to keep them from drying out too quickly.

TIP

Self-watering seed starting kits that reduce the need for checking your seedlings daily for dryness are now available. These kits have a reservoir of water in the bottom of the tray that wicks into the pots when the soil is dry. See the appendix for companies carrying seed starting supplies.

DEALING WITH DAMPING OFF

One day you're admiring your strong, healthy seedlings, and the next day you're gaping in dismay at the sight of them toppled over and dying. The attacker is called *damping off*, which is a fungus that infects young seedlings, sometimes even before they have a chance to emerge from the soil. If you examine infected seedlings closely, you usually can see that part of the stem near the soil line is sunken, shriveled, and water soaked. Sometimes a white mold also forms on the stem.

Damping off is one of the most common problems that seed-starters face, but fortunately you can control it with good sanitation and cultural practices (proper watering, fertilizing, and lighting). Sterilizing containers with a bleach solution and using sterile potting soil go a long way toward preventing problems. Wet potting soil and high nitrogen encourage this fungus, so avoid overwatering, and use a well-drained germinating mix that's low in nitrogen. Or consider using fertilizer only after the seedlings develop their first true leaves. Sowing seeds thinly to allow good air circulation also can help. Many seeds come coated with a fungicide that helps prevent damping off.

If you notice seedlings in one portion of a container beginning to wither, cut them off and remove the soil around them as quickly as possible. Then do whatever you can to make conditions less favorable for the fungus (basically, let the soil dry more). With luck, you'll be able to save the rest of the batch.

Thinning and transplanting indoors

After seedlings develop their first set of true leaves (or when onions or leeks, which send up a single blade, are 2 inches tall), you need to thin them or move them from shallow flats to larger quarters. Thinning is an important step, and timing is crucial. If you let your seedlings grow too large in a small container, their growth is stunted. And if you don't space them out at all, you end up with weak plants.

To thin plants that will continue growing in the same container, snip out extra seedlings at the soil line with a pair of scissors, as shown in Figure 4-2. If you try to pull these seedlings out, you may disturb the roots of the plants that are staying. Also be sure to snip out any weak or misshapen plants. The appendix explains how much space to leave between different types of vegetable seedlings.

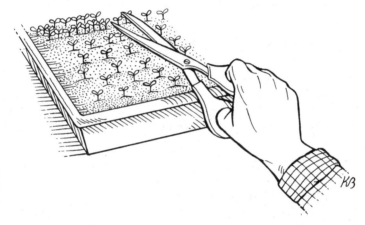

FIGURE 4-2:
Thin seedlings at the soil line with scissors.

To move seedlings to a new container, first fill a larger container (plastic six-packs, 4-inch pots, or peat pots) with moist potting soil. Poke holes in the soil large enough to put the seedling roots in — the eraser end of a pencil is a good tool for this. Dig around the plants carefully by using the blade of a table knife or a small stick, such as a plant label, and then lift the seedlings out of the soil. Always hold the seedlings by the tips of their leaves; otherwise, you can easily crush their delicate stems or injure their growing tips. Set the plants in the new container, slightly deeper than they were growing before. Firm the soil gently around the roots, water well, and keep the plants out of direct sun for a day or two until they adjust to their new pots.

Feeding your seedlings

Regular fertilizing helps produce strong, healthy plants. Some potting soils already have fertilizer mixed in, and in that case you don't have to add more. For other types, use a diluted water-soluble fertilizer to one-third strength (usually

1 teaspoon of fertilizer per gallon of water) to water your seedlings. Water with the solution once a week. For more on fertilizers, see Chapter 5 of this minibook.

Transplanting Indoor Seedlings and Starter Plants

After you nurture your seedlings indoors for a good four to eight weeks, and when the weather's right for planting, you're ready to transplant the seedlings outdoors. Or maybe you haven't grown seedlings at all, but you want to buy some starter plants at a nursery and get them in the ground. Both scenarios are examined in the following sections.

Buying starter plants

If you don't start your transplants from seeds at home, you can buy them at a nursery or garden center. You can find seedlings of almost every type and size around planting time. However, the range of varieties available will be greater if you start your own transplants from seed.

Follow these tips when buying starter plants:

» **Choose healthy-looking plants.** Tomatoes, for example, should have a stocky stem, be about 4- to 6-inches tall, and sport dark-green foliage.

» **Avoid large, crowded, spindly plants in small containers.** The roots of these types of plants are often bound up and have no room to grow. You can check the roots for yourself by gently removing the transplants from their containers (if you aren't sure how to do this, see "Making the big move to the ground," later in this chapter). If you see a dense mat of roots around the outside of the *root ball* (the soil with roots growing in it), the plants probably have been in the pot too long.

» **Buy plants at the optimum size.** Plants with four to six leaves and short, stocky stems are usually best. In general, younger plants are better than tall, older plants that most likely were stressed at one point or another.

» **Avoid plants that are already flowering and have fruit on them.** Plants with flowers and fruits never produce well.

WARNING

You can sometimes buy large tomato plants in 1-gallon or larger pots — sometimes they even have tomatoes on them. But beware, these large plants rarely grow well after you get them home. You'll likely have better luck with smaller transplants that can get off to a running start.

You can buy vegetable transplants locally, but many mail-order seed companies now also offer a wide range of vegetable varieties as small plants or plugs. The plants usually are in good shape. They offer a wider selection than you can find in garden centers, you don't have to drive around to find the best transplants, and they ship plants to you at the appropriate planting time for your region.

Toughening up all types of transplants

Vegetable seedlings that are grown indoors at home or purchased from a greenhouse or nursery in spring need to acclimate gradually to the brighter light and cooler temperatures of the outside world. This process, called *hardening off*, slows plant growth, causing the plants to store more food internally and increase the thickness of their outer leaf layers. Basically, hardening off toughens up transplants for the cold, cruel, outside world.

To harden off your transplants, follow these steps:

1. **A week or two before you intend to set plants out in your garden, stop fertilizing and reduce the amount of water you give them.**

   Give plants just enough water so they don't wilt.

2. **Take your plants outside for a short time.**

   Give the plants a half hour of filtered sunlight — setting them under an arbor or open-branched tree — during the warmest part of the day. If the weather is windy, put the plants in a spot where they're sheltered, or construct a windbreak out of pieces of wood.

3. **Gradually increase the amount of time that the plants spend outside and the intensity of the light that they're exposed to.**

   You want to increase the amount of time your plants are outside so that by day seven, they're out all day. Move them into progressively sunnier locations during the week so they get used to their future condition in the ground. However, make sure that you bring the plants in every night.

Another option is to move your plants to a cold frame (see Chapter 7 of this minibook to learn more or Book 5, Chapter 1 to build one), and then you can open the cold frame more each day and close it at night. Plants that are raised in a cold frame from the time that they're young seedlings will need much less hardening off.

WARNING

Don't overharden your plants. Certain crops, such as cabbage and broccoli, can quickly *bolt* (flower before they're supposed to) if seedlings older than three weeks are repeatedly exposed to temperatures lower than 40 degrees for a couple of weeks.

Planting

Making the big move to the ground

Before transplanting your homegrown seedlings or nursery-bought transplants, you need to prepare your soil and sculpt beds or rows, and your garden must be ready to plant (see Chapter 3 of this minibook for more prep work). If you're worried about keeping the rows straight, use string and stakes as described in the later section "Row planting."

Choose a calm, cloudy day to transplant, if possible. Late afternoon is a good time because plants can recover from the shock of transplanting without sitting in the midday heat and sun. Your garden soil should be moist, but not soggy. If the weather has been dry, water the planting area the day before you plant. Moisten the soil in your flats or pots so it holds together around the plants' roots when you remove the plants from their containers.

TIP

When setting out plants in biodegradable peat pots, make slits down the sides of the pots or gently tear the sides to enable the roots to push through. Also, tear off the lip (top) of the pot so it doesn't stick up above the soil surface and pull moisture out of the soil. If you're using premade growing blocks encased in netting, cut off the netting before planting.

To transplant seedlings, follow these steps:

1. **Use a hoe, spade, or trowel to make a small hole in your garden for each seedling.**

    The hole should be deep enough so the transplant is at the same depth in the ground as it was in the pot (except for tomatoes). Make the hole twice as wide as the root ball.

2. **Unpot a seedling (unless it's in a peat pot) by turning its pot upside down and cupping the seedling with your hand.**

    Be sure to keep the root mass and soil intact. If the seedling doesn't come out easily, gently tap on the edge of the pot or gently press on the bottom of each cell of the flat with your fingers. Whatever you do, don't yank out a plant by its stem.

3. **Check the root ball's condition.**

    If the roots are wound around the outside of the pot, work them loose with your fingers so they can grow out into the soil. Unwind larger roots and break smaller ones (this won't hurt them) so they all point outward. Try to keep as much of the original soil intact as possible.

4. **Mix a diluted liquid fertilizer into the soil of the planting hole to help the plants get off to a fast start.**

Reduce the recommended strength on the fertilizer container by half. For example, if it says apply 1 tablespoon per gallon of water, use only ½ tablespoon.

5. **Put each prepared seedling into the holes that you made.**

TIP

Most young vegetables should be planted at the same soil level as they were in the pot, as shown in Figure 4-3. For some vegetables, such as tomatoes, you can sink the seedling a little deeper. They grow extra roots along the lower portion of their stems and thrive with this treatment.

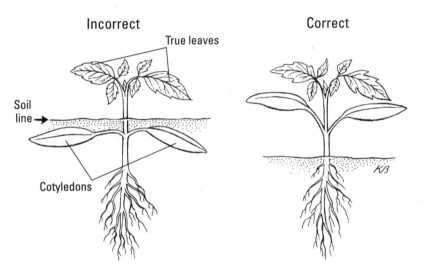

Incorrect   Correct

True leaves

Soil line →

Cotyledons

FIGURE 4-3:
Plant vegetable seedlings at the correct depth.

6. **After firming the soil around the roots with your hands, form a shallow soil basin around the base of the transplant.**

The soil basin serves as a moat around the seedling to hold water. When you water or it rains, the moisture stays in the moat and drains to where the roots are located. Chapter 3 of this minibook provides more information on soil basins.

7. **Depending on the conditions, water the bed that day or the next.**

If the weather has been dry or if the soil is sandy, you may want to water the entire bed; if it's rainy or the soil is already very wet, wait until tomorrow to water.

8. **Keep the bed moist while the seedlings get established and begin to grow strongly.**

In extreme hot, dry weather, provide temporary shade for transplants with paper tents or wooden shingles pushed into the ground on the south or west side of the plants.

REMEMBER

If you don't get an ideal transplanting day and the weather is hot and sunny, shade the plants until the sun goes down. And don't be alarmed if your plants look a little droopy after you set them out; they'll soon recover. Cabbage seedlings can droop and look almost dead, for example, and be up and growing in a day or two.

Sowing Seeds Directly in Your Garden

Unless you live in an area where summers are really short, some vegetables are better off sown directly in a garden rather than as transplants. Large-seeded, fast-growing vegetables — such as corn, melons, squash, beans, and peas — usually languish if they're grown in containers for even a day or two too long. Plants sown directly in the ground usually surpass these seedlings if both are planted at the same time. (Even if you live in a short-season area, you can help speed new plants along. See Chapter 7 of this minibook for information on extending your growing season.)

The following sections describe different methods for planting seeds right into your garden and show you how to thin seedlings carefully.

Deciding on a seed-planting method

You can plant seeds in a variety of patterns: single rows, wide rows, beds, raised beds, or hills. The method you choose depends on your climate, your tools, and your taste. You can find out more about these planting methods in Chapter 3 of this minibook. Whichever method you choose, here are a few basic principles to keep in mind when planting seeds:

>> **Make sure that the soil has dried out sufficiently before you work it, and be sure that the soil is warm enough for the seeds that you want to plant.** Pea seeds, for example, germinate in soil as cool as 40 degrees, and you can plant them as soon as you can work the soil in spring. Squash seeds, on the other hand, need warmth. If your soil temperature is much below 65 degrees, the seeds are likely to rot in the ground before they sprout. (See the appendix for a list of appropriate soil temperatures for different kinds of seeds.) The best way to determine the temperature of your soil is to use a soil thermometer, which you can buy at a garden store.

>> **Immediately before planting seeds, loosen your garden soil with a hoe or shovel to a depth of 6 inches.** Rake over the area to create a smooth planting surface. Don't walk over areas where you'll be sowing seeds; stay in the pathways. Compacting the soil makes it difficult for seedlings to emerge and send down their roots.

>> **Sow seeds at the proper planting depth.** A seed planted too deeply uses up its supply of stored nutrients before the seedling can push its way to the surface; a seed planted too shallow may dry out. A general rule is to plant seeds to depths that are two to three times their diameters, but the appendix gives recommended planting depths for different kinds of seeds. Also try to sow at a uniform depth because seedlings are more likely to emerge at the same time, enabling you to see where your plants are when you do your first weeding.

WARNING

>> **Water newly planted seeds carefully.** Use a watering can with a rose (nozzle with multiple holes) or a hose with a *breaker attachment* (a nozzle that breaks the stream into a gentle spray). A strong stream of water can wash seeds out of a bed or too deeply into the ground. Keep the seeds moist but not soggy until the seeds germinate. Heavy soils often form a crust as they dry out, making it difficult for the seedlings to break through. A moist surface helps prevent crusting, as does covering seeds with vermiculite or sand, instead of soil alone. If the weather is dry after you sow the seeds, gently water the seeded area every two days or so.

The following sections explain the basic methods for planting your seeds.

Row planting

The first step when row planting is to mark the placement of a row within your garden. A planting line consisting of a simple string and stakes enables you to easily lay out rows. Make a *furrow*, or trench, at the correct depth along the row. To make a shallow furrow, lay a rake or hoe underneath your string marker, and press the handle into the soil. You can make deeper furrows (ones that can be used for watering, too) by dragging the corner of your hoe across the soil surface, using the string as your guideline.

Sow seeds more thickly than you want the final spacing of the crops to be to ensure an adequate number of plants; some seeds may fail to sprout. Thinning rows is less of a chore if you space seeds as evenly as possible. Large seeds such as peas and beans are easy to space at precise intervals, but evenly spacing small seeds can be a real challenge.

Cover the seeds with fine soil and then firm them in with the back of a hoe to make sure that all the seeds are in contact with the soil. Water gently.

TIP

If you're planting long rows of corn, beans, or peas that will be furrow-irrigated (see Chapter 3 of this minibook), fill the furrows with water first and then push the large seeds into the top of raised beds.

Wide row planting

You can plant more seeds in less space and get higher yields by using the wide row planting method. (Figure 4-4 compares wide rows and straight single rows.) This method not only saves space but also allows you to concentrate watering, weeding, and fertilizing in a smaller area. Follow these steps for wide row planting:

1. **Choose the location and width of your row, usually 10 to 16 inches wide, and then smooth the soil until it's level.**

   You may want to run strings along the outside edges of the row to clearly designate the planting area.

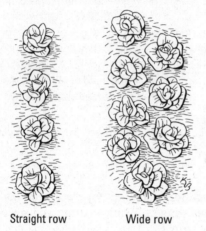

FIGURE 4-4:
Straight
single rows
versus wide rows.

Straight row   Wide row

2. **Sprinkle seeds over the entire row — with most crops, try to land the seeds about ½ to 1 inch apart (for peas and beans, 1½ to 2 inches).**

   Pat the seeds down with the back of a hoe.

3. **Use a rake to lift soil from the side of the row to cover the seeds, and gently smooth the soil covering the seeds to the same depth throughout the row.**

   Cover small seeds (such as carrot and lettuce seeds) with a thin layer of potting soil. Then pat the potting soil down again to bring the added soil into firm contact with the seeds.

TIP

4. **Water the seeds gently.**

   Keep the soil moist by gently watering a few times a week or when you see that the top layer of soil is drying out.

Raised bed planting

Planting raised beds is essentially the same as planting wide rows. If you don't have permanent beds, mark the dimensions and smooth out the soil. You can broadcast sow (sprinkle by hand) in single rows with a few inches between rows, as shown in Figure 4-5, or you can plant individual seeds at the proper distance apart.

FIGURE 4-5:
Broadcasting
seeds in a
raised bed.

Hill planting

Plant seeds for vining crops that spread out — such as squash, melons, or cucumbers — in hills or circular groups, as shown in Figure 4-6. Loosen and level the soil in a 1-foot-diameter area, and then plant five to six seeds close together. After the second set of true leaves form, keep the two strongest seedlings (the ones that are the biggest and sport the most leaves) and thin out the remaining seedlings by cutting them with scissors (see the next section for details).

FIGURE 4-6:
Sow vining crop
seeds in hills.

TIP

If your soil is heavy, you may want to plant in a *raised hill* (also called a *mound*). The raised soil warms up more quickly than the surrounding soil and drains better. But be careful in midsummer not to let the mound dry out. You can easily construct a soil basin around the mound for watering (see Chapter 3 of this minibook).

Thinning seedlings in your garden

Soon after seedlings grow their second set of true leaves, you need to thin them out. Don't neglect this important step; crowded seedlings turn into weak, spindly plants that don't produce well. Separate the plants by hand or with a narrow hoe.

REMEMBER

When you thin plants, either discard the extra seedlings or move them to another part of your garden. Newly transplanted seedlings need extra attention until they get established. Shade them from the hot sun for a day or two and be sure to keep them well watered. Lettuce is one of the easiest vegetables to move when it's small. Root crops such as beets and carrots transplant poorly, as do beans and peas.

You can thin some crops in stages, with delicious results. Carrots, lettuce, and beets are all good candidates for gradual thinning. If you've ever tasted beet greens cooked up with tender, marble-sized beets still attached, you know what a real treat they are. Start thinning carrot, lettuce, and beet seedlings when they're 1 to 2 inches apart. After the plants grow to 6 to 8 inches tall, pull up every other one and enjoy them. Leave a final 4- to 6-inch spacing for larger plants to develop.

Planting Guidelines

The best way to plan your garden is to start by deciding how much produce you want. For example, if you like lettuce, 25 heads will take approximately 25 feet of row. The recommended distances between rows in Table A-1 tell you how much space to leave between crops.

Use the information in Table 4-2 as a general guideline. You may choose to vary the distance between rows, for example, depending on the method of planting or cultivating. You usually can hand-hoe weeds between rows adequately in 18- or 24-inch-wide pathways; rototilling is faster, but pathways should be 30 or 36 inches wide to do so. If you garden intensively, such as in raised beds, you can space plants closer than indicated in the chart.

The days to maturity and the yield figures are averages. Depending on weather, soil fertility, pests, and weed pressure, yield and maturities in your garden can vary greatly. Just remember, you can always find friends, relatives, and bunnies who'd love some fresh, homegrown produce.

TABLE 4-2   **Planting Guide**

Crop	Seed/Plants per 100 ft Row	Frost Tolerance	Planting Depth (Inches)	Spacing between Rows (Inches)	Spacing between Plants (Inches)	Soil Temp for Germination*	Average Days to Germination	Average Days to Maturity	Average Yield per 10 ft Row
Asparagus	1 oz/65	Very hardy (R)	6 (crowns)	36–48	18	50–95 (75)	7–21	2 years	3 lb
Beans, snap (bush)	½ lb (seeds only)	Tender	1–1½	18–24	3–4	60–95 (85)	6–14	45–60	12 lb
Beans, snap (pole)	½ lb (seeds only)	Tender	1–1½	36–48	4–6	60–95 (85)	6–14	60–70	15 lb
Beans, lima (bush)	½ lb (seeds only)	Very tender	1–1½	18–24	3–4	60–85 (80)	7–12	65–80	2.5 lb, shelled
Beans, lima (pole)	¼ lb (seeds only)	Very tender	1–1½	36–48	12–18	60–85 (80)	7–12	85–90	5 lb, shelled
Beets	1 oz (seeds only)	Hardy	½	15–24	2	40–95 (85)	7–10	50–60	12 lb
Broccoli	¼ oz/45	Very hardy (P)	¼	24–36	14–24	40–95 (85)	3–10	60–80	10 lb
Brussels sprouts	¼ oz/55	Very hardy (P)	¼	24–36	14–24	40–95 (85)	3–10	90–100	7.5 lb
Cabbage	¼ oz/55	Very hardy (P)	¼	24–36	14–24	40–95 (85)	4–10	60–90	18 lb
Carrots	½ oz (seeds only)	Hardy	¼	15–24	2	40–95 (80)	10–17	70–80	15 lb
Cauliflower	¼ oz/55	Hardy (P)	¼	24–36	14–24	40–95 (80)	4–10	70–90	10 lb
Celery	¹⁄₆₄ oz/200	Hardy	⅛	30–36	6	40–75 (70)	9–21	125	18 stalks
Chinese cabbage	¼ oz/65	Hardy (P)	¼	18–30	8–12	40–105 (80)	4–10	65–70	8 heads

(continued)

TABLE 4-2 *(continued)*

Crop	Seed/Plants per 100 ft Row	Frost Tolerance	Planting Depth (Inches)	Spacing between Rows (Inches)	Spacing between Plants (Inches)	Soil Temp for Germination*	Average Days to Germination	Average Days to Maturity	Average Yield per 10 ft Row
Corn	3–4 oz (seeds only)	Tender	2	24–36	12–18	50–95 (95)	6–10	70–90	1 dozen
Cucumbers	½oz/30–40	Very tender	1	48–72	24–48	60–105 (95)	6–10	50–70	12 lb
Eggplant	⅛ oz/50	Very tender (P)	¼–½	24–36	18–24	65–95 (85)	7–14	80–90	10 lb
Leeks	½oz/300	Very hardy	½–1	12–18	2–4	45–70 (75)	7–12	130–150	12 lb
Lettuce, heading	¼oz/120	Very hardy	¼–½	18–24	6–10	32–75 (75)	4–10	70–75	10 heads
Lettuce, leaf	¼oz/400	Very hardy	¼–½	15–18	2–3	32–75 (75)	4–10	40–50	5 lb
Muskmelon	½ oz/50	Very tender	1	60–96	24–36	65–105 (95)	4–8	85–100	5 fruits
Okra	2 oz/50	Very tender	1	36–42	12–24	60–105 (95)	7–14	55–65	10 lb
Onion, seed	1 oz/300	Very hardy	½	15–24	3–4	32–95 (80)	7–12	90–120	16 lb
Onion, sets	400–600 (no seeds)	Very hardy	1–3	15–24	3–4	NA	NA	80–120	10 lb
Parsley	¼oz/150	Hardy	¼–½	15–24	6–8	50–90 (75)	14–28	70–90	4 lb
Parsnips	½ oz (seeds only)	Hardy	½	18–30	3–4	32–85 (70)	15–25	120–170	10 lb
Peas	1 lb (seeds only)	Very hardy	2	18–36	1	40–85 (75)	6–15	55–90	4 lb
Peppers	⅛ oz/50	Very tender	¼	24–36	18–24	60–95 (85)	10–20	60–90	30 lb
Potatoes	6–10 lb seed potatoes	Very hardy (R)	4	30–36	8–10	NA	NA	75–100	10 lb

Crop	Seed/ Plants per 100 ft Row	Frost Tolerance	Planting Depth (Inches)	Spacing between Rows (Inches)	Spacing between Plants (Inches)	Soil Temp for Germination*	Average Days to Germination	Average Days to Maturity	Average Yield per 10 ft Row
Pumpkins	½ oz/25	Very tender	1–2	60–96	36–48	65–105 (95)	6–10	75–100	10 lb
Radishes	1 oz (seeds only)	Hardy	½	14–24	1	40–95 (80)	3–10	25–40	10 bunches
Rhubarb	20 (no seeds)	Very hardy (R)	4	36–48	48	NA	NA	2 years	7 lb
Southern peas	½ lb (seeds only)	Very tender	½–1	24–36	4–6	60–95 (85)	7–10	60–70	4 lb
Spinach	1 oz/300	Very hardy	¾	14–24	3–4	32–75 (70)	6–14	40–60	4–5 lb
Squash, summer	1 oz/40	Tender	1	36–60	18–36	65–105 (95)	3–12	50–60	25 lb
Squash, winter	½ oz/35	Very tender	1	60–96	24–48	65–105 (95)	6–10	85–100	15 lb
Sweet potatoes	75–100 (no seeds)	Very tender (P)	NA	36–48	12–16	NA	NA	100–130	10 lb
Swiss chard	1 oz/50	Hardy	½	12–15	24–36	40–95 (75)	5–16	50–60	50–75 lb
Tomatoes	⅛ oz/50	Tender	½	24–48	18–36	50–95 (80)	6–14	70–90	80 lb
Turnips	½ oz (seeds only)	Very hardy	½	14–24	2–3	40–105 (80)	3–10	30–60	5–10 lb
Watermelon	1 oz/20	Very tender	1	72–96	36–72	65–105 (95)	3–12	80–100	4 fruits

P — plants; R — roots; NA — not applicable; Very hardy — plant outside four to six weeks before average last spring frost date; Hardy — plant outside two to three weeks before average last spring frost date; Tender — plant outside on average date of last spring frost; Very tender — plant outside one to two weeks after average last spring frost date

*Range of germination temperature in degrees Fahrenheit; optimum germination in parentheses

Planting

Chapter **5**

Growing Your Garden

After planting your garden, you need to keep your vegetables growing vigorously until harvest. Maintaining your vegetable garden is similar to running a long-distance road race. After you're off and running, the key is to pace yourself for the entire race and not burn out in the beginning.

You must have lots of enthusiasm to prepare the soil and plant, but you also have to be consistent about checking plants, watering, fertilizing, and harvesting (among other tasks) to get the best results. If you lose interest in your garden halfway through the growing season, your harvest may be small or poor. Don't worry though; your garden won't require all your time — just some of it each week.

This chapter serves as a checklist of sorts of the things you should be doing throughout the growing season to keep your vegetables happy as you work toward the all-important harvest.

Introducing Your Inner Gardener to the Watering Basics

Even though Mother Nature is often very generous with rain, she still sometimes leaves gardens with a dry spell. Flooding isn't good for your garden, but neither is drought. If your plants don't have adequate water at the right times, they can easily die.

It's a good idea to think about how you'll water your garden plants even in the garden planning stages (as discussed in Chapter 1 of this minibook). But now that everything is in the ground, you need to actually *do* the watering.

Following guidelines for watering seeds and plants

Different crops have different water needs. Some vegetables, such as celery, are real water lovers and prefer to have moist soil around their roots at all times. Shallow-rooted crops (such as onions and cabbage) need more careful watering during dry spells than deeper-rooted crops (such as tomatoes) that can pull water from greater depths.

REMEMBER

You also need to keep in mind a plant's growth stage when watering. Here are some general watering guidelines for different growth stages:

>> **Seedlings and germinating seeds:** Seedlings with small root systems near the soil surface and germinating seeds benefit from frequent, gentle watering, which enables them to sprout and emerge quickly. Water once a day to a few inches deep if it doesn't rain. (Chapter 4 of this minibook has more details on seedlings and transplants.)

>> **Transplants:** Water transplants when they're first planted in the garden and then every few days after that to 6 inches deep or so. Watering frequently helps the roots recover from transplant shock.

>> **Established plants:** Plants that have been in your garden for a few weeks and that are beyond transplant shock need to be watered deeply. Try to wet the soil at least 6 inches deep. Watering to this depth encourages roots to penetrate deeply, where they're less susceptible to drought. Give the soil a chance to dry out slightly (three to six days if it doesn't rain) before watering thoroughly again.

TIP

When you're advised to water to a certain number of inches, don't feel like you have to guess when you've hit the mark; you can dig into the soil with a trowel to see how far the water has penetrated.

In the following sections, you'll learn when to quench your veggies' thirst and get information on different watering methods.

Knowing when your veggies need a drink

In general, most vegetables use about 1 inch of water per week (1 to 2 inches in hot, windy, dry climates). If you don't get water from rainfall, you have to supply it. Here are some general guidelines for determining when your plants need water:

>> **Your finger is the best indicator of when the soil has dried sufficiently to re-water.** Dig down several inches into the soil; if the soil is dry to your touch 3 to 4 inches down, it's time to water.

>> **Wilting plants can be a sign that your soil needs water.** *Wilting* is when the leaves or stems of a plant droop, bend over, and look limp. These symptoms, however, can be misleading at times. Some plants, such as tomatoes, peppers, and eggplants, tend to droop slightly during the heat of the day, even if the soil has enough moisture. If your plants don't stand tall and proud and the soil feels dry, add water and watch them perk up fast.

WARNING

Overwatering also causes plants to wilt, so check the soil before watering. If the soil is waterlogged, roots die from lack of air. With fewer roots, plants can no longer take up the water they need from the soil, and so they wilt. Damage from insects and disease also cause wilting.

>> **Each vegetable has a critical period when you need to be especially careful about watering.** If you slack off during these times, your crop may be ruined. Table 5-1 shows the important watering periods for different types of vegetables.

TABLE 5-1

Critical Watering Periods for Vegetables

Vegetable	Important Watering Stage
Bean, lima	When flowering and forming pods
Bean, snap	When flowering and forming pods
Broccoli	When forming a head
Brussels sprouts	When forming sprouts
Cabbage	When forming a head
Carrots	When forming roots
Cauliflower	When forming a head

(continued)

TABLE 5-1 *(continued)*

Vegetable	Important Watering Stage
Corn, sweet	When silking, tasseling, and forming ears
Cucumber	When flowering and developing fruit
Eggplant	From flowering through harvest
Lettuce	When true leaves form
Melon	During fruit set and early development
Onion, dry	During bulb enlargement
Pea	When flowering and during seed enlargement
Pepper	From flowering through harvest
Potato	When tubers set and enlarge
Pumpkin	When fruits form
Radish	When forming roots
Spinach	When true leaves form
Squash, summer	When forming buds and flowering
Swiss chard	When true leaves form
Tomato	From flowering through harvest
Turnip	When forming roots

Digging Into Composting

A beneficial, soil-like substance, *compost* is a mixture of decayed and decaying organic matter that improves soil structure and provides nutrients for plants. *Composting* is a method for you to copy nature's process, speeding it up if you so choose, to ultimately reap a rich mound of soil-enhancing compost for your landscape.

For gardeners, compost is sometimes called "black gold." You can add finished compost to the garden or around plants at any time. Doing so is considered by many to be the single most beneficial thing you can do for your garden.

Perhaps best of all, it's easy: you can't fail at composting. Isn't that a nice thing to know at the start of a project? Organic matter will rot no matter what you do. Fuss over it daily or ignore it for months; it doesn't matter. So, dig right in and enjoy the process!

Why not just add raw organic matter to your garden instead of composting it? When you compost the materials first, the final product is uniform in color, nutrients, and texture; is odor free; and contains fewer viable weed seeds and potential disease organisms (depending on how it was composted). Your plants will be happy with you for treating them so well.

You can buy compost in bulk (back the truck right up) or bagged, depending on where you live. The following sections explain these options. For many gardeners, making their own compost is the best solution. For information, head to the section "Compost happens: making your own."

Buying bagged compost

Bagged compost is the easiest form to buy, especially if you have a small yard or container garden. Look for the words "certified organic," the "OMRI Listed" seal, or some other indication that the contents are approved for organic growing and don't come from contaminated sources, such as sewage sludge. (OMRI — the Organic Materials Review Institute, or OMRI — certifies products that meet the National Organic Standards.)

Buying compost in bulk

For larger quantities of compost, buy in bulk. The price is less in quantity, and you can check the quality of the compost as well. Many private companies, municipalities, and community groups make and sell compost. Often, they even deliver the compost to your yard for a fee.

TIP

Use these tips to evaluate bulk compost:

>> **Consider the source.** Before buying the compost, ask about the primary, organic-matter sources that were used to make the compost. Compost made from yard waste (leaves and grass clippings) is considered to be the safest and best. Other compost may contain ingredients that had contaminants, such as herbicides from agricultural crop residues and heavy metals from municipal wastes, which may affect the growth of your plants or accumulate toxins in your soil. Ask if the finished product is tested for contaminants.

>> **Look at the color and texture.** Finished compost should look dark and have a crumbly texture without any large pieces of undecomposed organic matter, such as branches or pieces of wood.

>> **Squeeze it.** If water oozes out when you squeeze a handful of the material, it's too wet; if it blows away easily, it's too dry.

>> **Give it a whiff.** The smell should be earthy, without a strong ammonia or sour smell.

Compost happens: making your own

Making your own compost is probably the simplest way to ensure high-quality compost and save some money. The process really isn't as complicated as you may think; the many commercial composting bins and containers on the market (see Figure 5-1) make composting a mess-free, hassle-free process. For steps on building your own compost bin, refer to Book 5, Chapter 1.)

FIGURE 5-1:
Commercial composters.

Wire composter   High-rise composter   Tumbler composter

Building a good compost pile involves much more than just tossing organic materials in a pile in the corner of your yard, though many people use this technique with varied success. Because, you know, everything does eventually rot. But to compost correctly, you need to have a good size for your pile, add the right types and amount of materials, and provide the correct amount of moisture.

REMEMBER

Here are the characteristics of a well-made pile:

>> It heats up quickly — a sign that the decay organisms are at work.

>> Decomposition proceeds at a rapid rate.

>> The pile doesn't give off any bad odors.

>> The organisms that do all the decay work take up carbon and nitrogen (the stuff they feed on and break down) in proportion to their needs.

You can easily come up with the correct amounts of materials for a compost pile by building the pile in layers. Just follow these steps:

1. **Choose a well-drained spot in your yard.**

   If you build your compost pile on a naturally wet spot, the layers will become too wet and inhibit the decomposition process.

2. **Create a 4- to 6-inch layer of brown materials that are rich in carbon.**

   These brown materials include roots and stalks of old plants, old grass clippings, dried hay, and leaves. The more finely chopped these materials are, the more surface area that decay organisms can attack, and the faster the materials decompose.

3. **Add a thin layer of green materials that are high in nitrogen.**

   Green materials include green grass clippings, kitchen vegetable scraps, a 2- to 4-inch layer of manure, or a light, even coating of blood meal, cottonseed meal, or organic fertilizer high in nitrogen.

4. **Repeat the green and brown layers (Steps 2 and 3) until the pile is no more than 5 feet high.**

   If a pile is higher than 5 feet, too little oxygen reaches the center of the pile, enabling some nasty anaerobic decay organisms to take over and produce bad odors. Five feet is a good maximum width for the pile as well.

WARNING

Here are a few additional ways to ensure success in your compost pile:

>> **Moisten each layer of your compost pile lightly with a watering can as you build it.** However, don't let the pile get soggy.

>> **Cover each layer with a few inches of garden soil.** The soil covers any material in the nitrogen layer that may attract flies, such as household garbage.

>> **Add a dusting of ground limestone or wood ashes on the carbon layer.** This dusting keeps the compost's pH around the 6 to 7 mark that your plants like.

Avoiding materials that don't belong in a compost pile

WARNING

A well-made pile heats up enough to kill off many insects and disease organisms, but the heating isn't uniform enough to be relied on to kill everything that you want it to. So don't add the following materials to your pile:

>> **Diseased or infected plant material:** Disease organisms may survive the composting process and stick around to reinfect your plants when you apply the finished compost.

QUICK AND EASY COMPOST RECIPES

To make the most compost in the shortest time, try some of these proven recipes. For each recipe, mix the ingredients thoroughly, and follow the directions earlier in this chapter. Depending on the weather and compost ingredients, you should have finished compost within one to two months.

- **Recipe 1:** Use 4 parts kitchen scraps from fruits and vegetables, 2 parts chicken or cow manure, 1 part shredded newspaper (black ink only), and 1 part shredded dry leaves.

- **Recipe 2:** Use 2 parts kitchen scraps, 1 part chicken manure, and 1 part shredded leaves.

- **Recipe 3:** Use 2 parts grass clippings, 1 part chicken manure, and 1 part shredded leaves.

>> **Weeds that have gone to seed:** The heat may not be high enough to kill the weed seeds. And then those weeds will show up in your garden.

>> **Pieces of aggressive weeds such as quack grass or Bermuda grass:** Even a small piece of a root can produce a new plant.

>> **Grass clippings from lawns treated with herbicides:** Some herbicides may not break down during the composting process.

>> **Meat scraps and fats:** They break down slowly and may attract animals to the pile.

>> **Dog or cat feces:** They may carry diseases that can be transmitted to humans.

Moistening and turning your compost pile

After you build your compost pile, the decay process begins, causing the center of the pile to heat up. Proper moisture helps decay organisms to work properly. Following are some ways to keep your compost pile moist:

>> Water the pile as needed. To determine whether you need to water, dig about 1 foot into the pile and see if it's moist.

WARNING

» Be careful not to overwater your pile. It's easy to do. The water seeps in and tends not to evaporate readily, so people think the pile is dry when it's not.

» If there's a long dry spell or if you live in a dry-summer area, water the entire pile to keep it lightly moist.

» Make a depression in the top of the pile to collect rainfall.

You also must turn the pile periodically to aerate it, prevent it from overheating, and ensure that all the material decomposes uniformly. You can turn your compost pile by forking the material from the outside of the pile to the center or by moving the pile from one area to another. If you made a pile out of wire fencing, simply unhook the ends, pull the fencing apart, and move the cylinder a few feet away from the pile. Then fork the materials from the pile into the empty wire cylinder.

TIP

How often you turn the pile and how quickly the compost is done depend on how quickly decay takes place. For example, green, succulent organic material — such as fresh grass clippings — decays faster than dried plant material; cool fall temperatures or a spell of rainy days that turn the pile soggy slow things down. Follow these guidelines for deciding when to turn your pile:

» If you added only shredded material, the pile may be ready for turning in a week.

» If the pile contains a lot of big pieces of organic material, wait several weeks before turning.

» If the pile heats up and then cools, turn it.

» Turning the pile two to three times throughout the process is plenty.

You can tell that decay has set in if your pile starts to smell bad. If smells occur, hold your nose and fix things by spreading out the pile and reconstructing it.

Your compost is ready for use when the interior of the pile is no longer hot and all the material in the pile has broken down into a uniform, dark crumbly substance; this process takes about 1 to 2 months. To determine whether the pile is no longer hot, feel the interior of the pile with your hand. If you're squeamish, use a compost thermometer (which is available at garden centers).

WORKING WITH WORMS AS COMPOSTING COMPANIONS

Vermicomposting is a composting method that employs certain worm species to consume and convert organic matter into a useful soil amendment and organic fertilizer. *Castings* (a refined term for worm poop) resemble grains of black soil or coffee grounds. In your worm bin, castings blend with partially decomposed food scraps and worm bedding to form *vermicompost*.

Vermicompost has many benefits similar to those of "regular" compost, and can contain up to 11 times more calcium, magnesium, nitrogen, phosphorus, and potassium than plain soil. When added to soil, vermicompost improves aeration, water retention, porosity, and microbial activity. Vermicompost also suppresses diseases in plants and enhances plant growth.

Only a few worm species, such as the red wiggler, are suitable for vermicomposting, and should be purchased from worm suppliers rather than obtained from bait shops or dug up from the yard. Many practitioners of vermicomposting house their worms in a bin made from a pair of plastic storage totes (shown here) with one lid used as a drip tray and with aeration holes drilled in the sides. The bins are filled a foot deep with moist bedding comprised of native soil, newspaper, or cardboard. Food scraps are then added regularly; the worms will eat half their body weight daily. Every four months or so, the bedding is changed and the castings are harvested for use in the garden just like conventional compost.

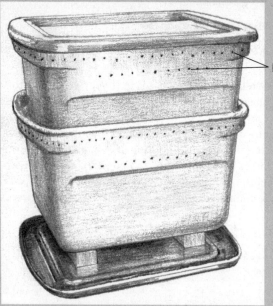

Holes for aeration

Fertilizing Your Vegetable Garden

Even if you have the healthiest soil around, growing vegetables is an intensive process that strips many important nutrients from the soil. So you need to add some fertilizer to your soil to keep it in optimum shape to feed your plants.

How much fertilizer you add depends on the soil and the plants you're growing. So it's difficult to generalize across the board on what type of fertilizer to choose and how much to apply. Soil tests are a great way to know what to add. Refer to Chapter 3 of this minibook for more on soil tests.

Examining a fertilizer label

REMEMBER

Commercial fertilizers are labeled with three numbers that indicate the fertilizer's nutrient content (see Figure 5-2). The first number indicates the percentage of nitrogen (N), the second number shows the percentage of phosphate (the type of phosphorus, P2O5), and the third number represents the percentage of potash (the form of potassium used, K2O).

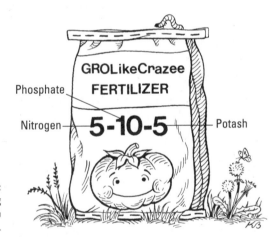

Phosphate — GROLikeCrazee FERTILIZER

Nitrogen — 5-10-5 — Potash

FIGURE 5-2:
A fertilizer bag is labeled with nutrient content.

TIP

When talking fertilizer, the abbreviation is NPK. A good way to remember what the NPK numbers refer to is the saying, *"Up, down, and all around:"*

>> **N:** Nitrogen, the first number, helps the top growth, or what the plant sends *up*.

>> **P:** The second number is for the amount of phosphorus in the mix, and it deals with root growth, or what the plant sends *down*.

>> **K:** The final number represents potassium, which deals with the general health of the plant or the *all-around* health.

For example, a 5-10-5 fertilizer contains 5 percent nitrogen, 10 percent phosphate, and 5 percent potash, and it's called a *complete fertilizer* because it contains some of each type of nutrient. In contrast, bone meal has an analysis of 4-12-0. It's a good source of phosphate for root growth but doesn't provide any potash for the plant's all-around health.

Choosing a fertilizer

Most home gardeners can grow a perfectly beautiful and productive garden using organic principles. In the last 20 years, an explosion of organic products (such as fertilizers) has hit the market, making gardening with this method much more accessible.

Organic fertilizers

Organic fertilizers — animal and green manure, blood meal, fish emulsion, cottonseed meal, granite dust, and rock phosphate — have several advantages:

>> Many organic fertilizers contribute organic matter to your soil, improving its structure, feeding soil microbes, fighting fungal and bacterial diseases, and contributing micronutrients.

>> Most organic fertilizers supply a slow but steady diet for plants.

>> Some organic fertilizers, such as manure and compost, may be inexpensive — or free if you create them yourself.

>> Complete organic fertilizers, such as 5-5-5, are now more widely available and have higher concentrations of nutrients than in the past, making them easy-to-use alternatives to chemical fertilizers.

WARNING

However, it's not all sun and roses when using organic fertilizers. Here are some disadvantages:

>> Some organic fertilizers, such as manures and compost, are bulky and difficult to store and transport.

>> Their slow release of nutrients, in some cases dependent on the action of soil microorganisms, may take too long to remedy a dire situation when an adequate nutrient supply is needed.

>> Many organic fertilizers are lower in nutrient content than their chemical equivalents, and the contents may vary depending on the weather and conditions where the fertilizers were produced. So you may not be exactly sure how much to put on your garden.

Chemical fertilizers

Chemical fertilizers are synthetically manufactured. They include elements such as sodium nitrate, potassium chloride, and superphosphate. Chemical fertilizers come in liquid, granular, powder, or pellet form. You can fertilize when you water with a watering can, using a liquid fertilizer. Or you can sprinkle some granular fertilizer around each plant.

WARNING

Chemical fertilizers are widely available, less expensive than organic fertilizers, quick acting, and easy to use, but many believe that the disadvantages of using chemical fertilizers far outweigh the advantages. Here's why:

>> **Chemical fertilizers add no organic matter to your soil and contribute nothing to improving soil structure.** In fact, some research suggests that chemical fertilizers actually harm the microorganisms in the soil, making the soil less able to support long-term plant growth.

>> **Chemical fertilizers are concentrated and fast acting, but they have no long-term benefits for your soil.** It's like taking a vitamin for your health versus eating a good meal.

>> **Manufacturing chemical fertilizers requires large amounts of energy, usually supplied by nonrenewable resources.** This massive use of energy increases pollution, global warming, and our carbon footprint. Even though some commercial organic fertilizers, such as rock phosphate and green sand, also are manufactured and require energy inputs, home gardeners can instead choose to use locally made compost and manures to get the nutrients they need for their gardens.

Side-dressing

Depending on the crops you grow and the type of soil you have, you may need to add repeat doses of fertilizer throughout the growing season — a practice called *side-dressing.* For example, because sandy soils don't hold nutrients well, giving plants small, regular fertilizer applications ensures a steady supply of nutrients.

Fertilizers and techniques that work well for side-dressing

Granular organic fertilizers, such as 5-5-5, are a good choice for side-dressing most root and fruiting crops. Use 1 to 2 tablespoons per plant, or 1 to 2 pounds for every 25 feet in a row.

Depending on plant spacing, side-dress either in a narrow furrow down a row or around each individual plant (refer to Figure 5-3). In either case, spread granular fertilizer (which is easier to use than liquid fertilizer) at least 6 to 8 inches away from plant stems. Rake the fertilizer into the soil and then water.

FIGURE 5-3:
Ways to fertilize vegetable plants.

TIP

For leafy green crops, fish emulsion is a quick-acting, highly soluble organic source of nitrogen that gives your greens a boost, especially if they're turning a pale green color. You can add micronutrients to this fertilizer by mixing it with seaweed. Add this liquid fertilizer to your watering can following the directions on the label. As you water, pour this solution around the bases of the plants and on the leaves.

Knowing when to side-dress

WARNING

Too much fertilizer can be more harmful than too little. Excess fertilizer accumulates in the soil in the form of salts and damages plant roots. So be sure that growing conditions enable plants to use the fertilizer that you apply. For example, don't add fertilizer during a dry spell if you can't irrigate your garden, because without adequate soil moisture, roots can't take up nutrients. And if cool weather causes your plants to grow slowly and need less fertilizer, go easy on the fertilizer until the temperature warms up or you'll be wasting it.

The kind of plants that you grow makes a difference in how often you side-dress. Plants that take a long time to mature (such as tomatoes and eggplants) and heavy feeders (such as corn) generally benefit more from side-dressing than quick-maturing crops that fix their own nitrogen — such as lettuce, or legumes such as peas and beans. See Table 5-2 for some general side-dressing guidelines.

TABLE 5-2   Deciding When to Side-Dress Your Vegetables

Vegetable	When to Side-Dress
Beans, green	Not necessary
Beet greens	Two weeks after leaves appear
Beets	When tops are 4 to 5 inches high; go light on nitrogen, which encourages leaf growth
Broccoli	Three weeks after transplant; go light on nitrogen
Brussels sprouts	Three weeks after transplant; again when sprouts begin to appear
Cabbage	Four to six weeks after planting
Carrots	Three weeks after plants are well established and no longer seedlings
Cauliflower	Four to six weeks after planting
Celery	Three weeks after setting out; again six weeks later
Corn, sweet	Three weeks after planting; again when plants are 8 to 10 inches high; again when tassels appear
Cucumbers	When they first begin to *run* (form vines and sprawl); again when blossoms set
Eggplant	Three weeks after planting
Kale	When plants are 6 to 8 inches tall
Lettuce, head	Three weeks after transplant; again when heads form
Lettuce, leaf	Three weeks after germination
Melons	When they begin to run; again a week after blossom set; again three weeks later
Onions	Three weeks after planting; again when tops are 6 to 8 inches tall; again when bulbs start to swell
Peas, English	Not necessary

(continued)

TABLE 5-2 *(continued)*

Vegetable	When to Side-Dress
Peppers, sweet and hot	Three weeks after transplant; again after first fruit set
Potatoes	When plants bloom
Pumpkin	When plants start to run; again at blossom set
Radishes	Not necessary
Spinach	When plants are about 3 to 4 inches tall
Squash, summer	When plants are about 6 inches tall; again when they bloom
Squash, winter	When plants start to run; again at blossom set
Swiss chard	Three weeks after germination
Tomatoes	Two to three weeks after transplant; again before first picking; again two weeks after first picking; go light on nitrogen

Keeping Your Plants Cozy and Weed Free with Mulch

Mulch is any material, organic or inorganic, that you place over the surface of soil, usually directly over the root zone of growing plants. It has many benefits depending on the type used. Mulch suppresses weeds, holds in moisture, modifies soil temperature, lessens the chances of certain diseases attacking your plants, and adds an attractive look to your garden.

REMEMBER

Some people use compost as a mulch, but remember that compost has a different purpose than mulch. Compost is added and mixed into the soil to add nutrients and increase the workability of soil (water-holding capacity, aeration, and so on). Mulch generally doesn't add nutrients, but it helps hold in the ones already in the soil and prevents undesirables from attacking your growing plants.

You can choose from two basic types of mulch: organic and inorganic. For vegetable growers, each type of mulch has a unique purpose, as described in the following sections.

Spreading organic mulch

Organic mulch can include grass clippings, compost, leaf mold, pine needles, shredded bark, nut shells, cotton gin waste, straw hay, grain and fruit byproducts, composed manure, mushroom compost, peat moss, and sawdust. Some of these mulches are easier to find in different parts of the country. You can even use newspaper as an organic mulch; black-and-white newspaper print is perfectly safe to use in your garden, and most colored inks are soybean based and biodegradable.

REMEMBER

Generally, a 2- to 4-inch layer of organic mulch, spread evenly on the ground beneath your plants, is sufficient. However, you may have to replenish the mulch during the growing season, especially in hot summer areas, because many organic mulches break down quickly.

Using organic mulch in your vegetable garden has many benefits:

>> Organic mulch conserves water by reducing the soil temperature and evaporation. It also keeps the soil cool by buffering direct sunlight.

>> It prevents wild fluctuations in soil moisture levels that can really spell disaster in hot weather.

>> It smothers weed seeds and prevents them from germinating. Any weeds that do come up in loose mulch are easy to pull.

>> As the mulch breaks down, it adds nutrients and improves the texture of the soil that it covers.

>> Organic mulch looks good and makes the ground tidy and clean.

WARNING

The following list includes some of the downsides of organic mulches. As minor as they are, they may lead you to choose one type of organic mulch over another:

>> **Bark mulches, such as pine, are quite acidic.** So if you use them, keep a close eye on the pH level of your soil and correct it accordingly. Avoid the trendy artificially colored mulches around veggies, because they may contain potentially harmful chemicals that can leach into your soil.

>> **Grass clippings decay quickly and must be replenished often.** Fortunately, grass clippings are usually pretty abundant. But if the grass goes to seed before you cut it, you may end up with grass growing in your vegetable garden. Also, make sure that no *herbicides* (weed killers) have been used on your lawn because the residue can damage or kill vegetables; if you have your lawn treated regularly, use another type of mulch. Likewise, hay mulch often has weed seeds in it, so use cleaner straw mulch if available.

» **Some organic mulches — such as fresh sawdust — rob nitrogen from the soil as they break down.** You may have to add supplemental nitrogen to your vegetables if they grow mysteriously slow or start to turn yellow.

» **Some organic mulches, such as peat moss or leaves, can pack down or get hard and crusty when exposed to weather.** Water may not penetrate these mulches, running off the soil instead of soaking into the roots. Avoid peat moss; or at least mix it with another organic mulch such as sawdust.

» **Some lightweight mulches, such as straw or cocoa hulls, can blow around in the wind.** You may want to avoid them if you live in a windy area.

» **Organic mulch, which keeps the soil cool, may slow the growth and maturity of warm-season crops such as tomatoes and melons.** This cooling can be especially problematic in areas with cool summers. However in very hot-summer areas of the country, organic mulches work to keep the roots of even warm-season crops cool and healthy.

» **Composted manures may burn young vegetables if used as mulch because the manures vary in the amount of nitrogen they contain.** If you want to use composted manure, mix it with three times the volume of another organic mulch before applying it.

You can purchase organic mulches such as shredded bark, compost, and leaf mold in bags or sometimes in bulk from nurseries and garden centers. Grass clippings, compost, and wood chips come free from your yard or garden.

Laying inorganic mulch

Inorganic mulch includes things such as plastic, landscape fabric, and believe it or not, old carpet. I explain how to use all types of inorganic mulches in the following sections.

Plastic

REMEMBER

Plastic is the most-used inorganic mulch for vegetable gardens. Mulching with plastic (see Figure 5-4) works best when you install drip irrigation or a soaker hose underneath the plastic before planting. Otherwise, watering is difficult. (You can place the irrigation on top of the plastic, which enables you to more easily check for clogs, but you have to run individual emitters to each plant.) Plastic doesn't work well with vegetables planted very close together, such as root crops.

FIGURE 5-4:
Planting in black
plastic mulch.

TIP

The color of plastic mulch you use depends on what you're growing. Some vegetables grow better with certain colored plastics. For example:

» **Red:** For growing tomatoes, eggplants, and strawberries

» **Dark green or IRT (infrared transmitting):** For growing melons

» **Silver:** For growing peppers

» **White:** For hot climates where you want to stop weeds from growing but not heat up the soil

» **Black:** For weed control and warming soils, and for growing many vegetables, including cucumbers and squash

To mulch with plastic, follow these steps:

1. **Purchase rolls or sheets of 2- to 4-millimeter plastic (the thicker the better).**

   You can find the thickness of the plastic on its label. Purchase plastic at garden centers or hardware stores, or check the appendix for sources of various colored mulches.

2. **If you're using irrigation under the plastic, lay down your drip irrigation and turn it on for several hours.**

   Note where the wet spots are in the soil. Adjust the drip hose so water doesn't pool in certain areas, but is evenly distributed. See the earlier section on drip irrigation for more details on installing this type of watering system.

3. **A week or two before planting, water the entire area with a hose or sprinkler so it's wet to 6 inches deep.**

   Roll out the plastic over the planting area and cover the edges of the plastic with soil.

4. **Cut holes in the plastic where you want to plant your transplants.**

   You can sow seed this way as well; just make sure that the seed can get through the holes in the plastic after it germinates.

5. **Plant your seeds or transplants in the holes.**

   Make sure you plant in wet spots; otherwise, the plants may not get enough water.

TIP

If you live in a climate that gets very hot in the summer (Texas, for example), after the weather starts to warm, you may want to cover black plastic with an organic mulch to prevent the soil from getting too warm. Or consider using white plastic instead.

Unless you have a problem with the irrigation system, you usually don't have to remove the plastic until the end of the season.

Other inorganic mulches

Beside plastics, you also can use the following inorganic mulches in your vegetable garden:

>> **Cardboard:** Even though it's biodegradable, cardboard takes so long to decompose that I treat it as an inorganic mulch. You can cut cardboard boxes to fit in pathways. If you don't like their look, cover them with hay or straw.

>> **Landscape fabric:** This inorganic mulch doesn't warm the soil as much as black plastic, but it's permeable, enabling you to water through it. It also does a good job of keeping down weeds. You can find landscape fabric at your local nursery. You apply landscape fabric the same way that you do plastic (see the preceding section).

>> **Rug strips:** Roll out 3-foot rug strips and place them nap side down, leaving about 6 inches of open soil between strips for irrigation and planting. Even though rug strips look pretty weird in a garden, they keep the weeds down and make a nice path.

Deciding which mulch to use

Choosing a mulch and deciding when to use it in your vegetable garden depends on the type of vegetables that you grow and when you plant them. Check out these mulching tips for different types of vegetables:

>> **Cool-season vegetables planted in early spring:** You want the sun to warm your soil in the spring because lots of sun helps young plants get off to a fast start. Here are a few mulching pointers for these vegetables:

- Lay down organic mulch when the soil starts to warm and when the plants need regular water. If you mulch too early, the soil stays too cold and wet for proper root growth.

- In areas with short growing seasons, you can plant broccoli, cauliflower, and cool-season plants through plastic. Cover the plastic with organic matter when the weather warms to keep the soil cool.

» **Cool-season vegetables planted in late summer or early fall:** With these vegetables, you want the cooling effect, so put down an organic mulch right after planting. Here are a few other things to keep in mind:

- When the weather starts to cool, rake off or remove the organic mulch so the soil warms.

- You can plant through plastic late in the year, but you should cover it with an organic mulch immediately so the soil doesn't get too hot. Then remove the organic mulch when the weather cools and let the plastic warm the soil through harvest.

- Many root crops can be stored in the ground well into winter if you cover them with a thick organic mulch such as straw. Applied before the ground freezes, the mulch keeps the soil loose and unfrozen so you can dig the vegetables later into winter.

» **Warm-season vegetables planted in spring:** With these vegetables, keep the ground clear if you're planting really early — the more heat the better. Planting through plastic works in early spring. In hot climates, apply an organic mulch when the weather starts to get really warm in summer.

Surveying Some Cool Farmer Techniques

Over the years, farmers, and even gardeners for that matter, have tried almost anything to get better, bigger, and earlier harvests. Some of these techniques, such as planting according to the cycles of the moon, are rooted more in mysticism than in hard science. Others, such as using cover crops and succession planting, are commonsense approaches to farming that are now established practices in modern agriculture. They may also be useful (or just fun) techniques for homesteaders.

Adding nutrients and stability with cover crops and green manures

A *cover crop* is a general term for any plant grown to prevent erosion, improve soil structure, and maintain soil fertility. Sometimes, you'll hear cover crops referred to as *green manures*. Green manures are cover crops that are used primarily to add nutrients to the soil and are tilled into the soil when they're still green. Green manures are the most useful cover crop for vegetable gardeners.

The advantages of using cover crops are impressive:

>> **They add organic matter to the soil.** By adding this matter to the soil, you improve water retention, aeration, and drainage.

>> **They prevent erosion.** Cover crops prevent erosion by holding soil in place in windy or wet areas.

>> **They loosen compacted soils.** Certain cover crops, such as oilseed radish and bell beans, have aggressive *taproots* (roots that grow deeply into the soil), sometimes reaching 3 feet deep, that help break up compacted soils.

>> **They add nutrients to the soil.** Legume cover crops, such as hairy vetch and crimson clover, through a symbiotic relationship (I scratch your back, you scratch mine) with rhizobium bacteria on their roots, convert atmospheric nitrogen into a type that they can use to grow. The process is called *nitrogen fixing*. When the cover crop is tilled into the soil, the nitrogen is released for the next crop. Also, taprooted cover crops bring minerals to the surface from deep below the soil.

>> **They help control weeds.** Cover crops control weeds by shading the weed seeds so they can't grow or by just being more aggressive than the weeds. Some crops, such as buckwheat, actually exude chemicals that inhibit weed growth.

>> **They attract beneficial insects.** Many cover crops attract good bugs that prey on garden pests, reducing insect problems on your vegetables.

If you want a healthier, more productive garden, and you have room, include cover crops each year in different parts of your veggie garden. The following sections focus on how to select and plant the best cover crops for your garden.

Choosing cover crops

Cover crops can be *annual* (they die after flowering or overwinter) or *perennial* (they regrow each year). For home gardeners, the best crops to sow are annual cover crops. These are easy to maintain and won't turn your vegetable garden into a cover crop garden.

The most useful annual cover crops for home gardeners are listed here. All but the grasses and buckwheat are nitrogen fixing:

>> **Annual ryegrass,** *Lolium multiflorum,* is a fast-growing, easy-to-establish grass that grows 2 to 3 feet high. It's hardy to –20 degrees Fahrenheit but can become weedy. Sow ½ to 2 pounds of seed per 1,000 square feet.

>> **Berseem clover,** *Trifolium alexandrinum,* grows 1 to 2 feet high and is easy to mow and till under. It's hardy to 20 degrees. Sow 2 pounds of seed per 1,000 square feet. Crimson clover, *T. incarnatum,* is closely related, grows 18 inches high, and is hardy to 10 degrees. It has pretty red flowers that attract bees.

>> **Buckwheat,** *Fagopyrum esculentum,* is fast growing, reaching 3 to 4 feet tall in about 40 days from seeding. It provides lots of organic matter, smothers weeds with its large leaves by shading them out, and exudes chemicals to prevent weeds from germinating. It breaks down quickly in the soil after tilling. Sow 3 pounds of seed per 1,000 square feet. Buckwheat doesn't fix nitrogen and is frost sensitive, so grow it in summer when the temperatures are warm.

>> **Fava beans,** *Vicia faba,* grow 3 to 8 feet high and are hardy to 15 degrees. Bell beans are a shorter (3 feet) relative. Edible varieties include 'Sweet Loraine' and 'Windsor'. Sow 2 to 5 pounds of seed per 1,000 square feet.

>> **Field peas,** *Pisum arvense* or *P. sativus,* come in several varieties that range in height from 6 inches to 5 feet high. They're hardy to 10 to 20 degrees. Sow 2 to 4 pounds of seed per 1,000 square feet.

>> **Hairy vetch,** *Vicia villosa,* is the hardiest annual legume (–15 degrees) and grows about 2 feet high. Sow 1 to 2 pounds of seed per 1,000 square feet.

>> **Winter rye,** *Secale cereale,* is a very hardy grass (–30 degrees) that grows 4 to 5 feet high. It's the best grass for cold areas with poor, acidic soils and produces lots of organic matter. Sow 2 to 3 pounds of seed per 1,000 square feet.

Planting cover crops

The best time to plant cover crops is late summer to early fall. What happens next depends on the climate where you live:

>> **In mild-winter areas,** the plants will grow throughout winter and can be turned into the soil in spring.

>> **In cold-winter climates,** plant hardy types that will grow for a while in fall, go dormant, and then grow again in spring before eventually dying. Some less hardy types, such as annual ryegrass, will die back in winter and be easier to till under in spring. You can work them into the ground in late spring or early summer and plant vegetables soon after.

An early spring planting of cover crops also works in cold-winter climates, but you won't be able to work the plants in until later in the summer.

Because beds planted with cover crops won't be available for planting vegetables until you turn them under, you have to plan ahead to use your garden efficiently. If you're short on space, consider alternating vegetables and cover crops so that each bed gets a cover crop every two or three years instead of each year.

If you plant cover crops in fall after your vegetables are done, you won't miss a beat and can plant vegetables again in spring. If you plant cover crops during the spring or summer, you'll have to sacrifice some space in your veggie garden. Opt for this route only if your soil is very poor and you need to build it up while growing vegetables at the same time. Just rotate where you plant the cover crops in your garden, and after a few years, your whole garden will get a cover cropping.

Plant cover crops by broadcasting seed. To make sure the proper bacteria are present for nitrogen fixing in legume cover crops, use an inoculate. Most suppliers sell an inoculate that you mix with the seed. Till the soil, sow the seeds, and lightly cover the seeds with soil. If the weather is dry, water the seedbed to get the plants off to an early start and then keep the soil moist until it rains.

If you grow cover crops up to planting time (spring or fall) in your garden, the best time to work the cover crops into the ground is just before they start to bloom. With taller types, you may have to cut or mow the plants down before turning or tilling them in. After you work them in, wait about two weeks before planting vegetables.

Making your garden work double time with intercropping

Intercropping is a space-saving technique in which you grow fast-maturing, smaller crops among slower-growing, larger vegetables. By the time the bigger plants start to take over, you have already harvested the crops in between. Intercropping makes one bed as productive as two.

The best crops for intercropping include beets, carrots, lettuce, onions, radishes, spinach, and turnips. Use these examples to help you decide how to do it:

>> Plant lettuce, carrots, or radishes among young tomatoes and broccoli. For that matter, plant carrots and radishes wherever you have open space.

>> Plant turnips and other root crops among your cabbage.

>> Plant spinach or lettuce under your bean trellis. As the weather warms, the beans will shade the spinach and keep it cool.

>> Plant green onions between rows of corn.

Succession planting for an extended harvest

Succession planting is a method of extending the harvest of vegetables, such as radishes and corn, that ripen all at once and lose quality if left in the garden instead of being harvested. Farmers use the technique to ensure a constant supply of vegetables to take to market; you can use it to produce a consistent supply of vegetables to take to your table. To succession plant, you simply make smaller plantings separated by two to three weeks instead of planting everything at once. Some great crops to succession plant are lettuce and greens, bush beans, beets, carrots, onions, radish, spinach, and sweet corn.

REMEMBER

If you want to experiment with succession planting, use these steps:

1. **Figure out how much of a certain vegetable your family needs for a two- to three-week period and how much room it will take to grow it.**

   Figure 5-5 shows a sample garden plan for succession planting. Check out Chapter 1 of this minibook for additional information on how to plan your garden.

2. **Break your planting beds into three or four appropriate-sized sections to grow your two- to three-week supply of the vegetable.**

3. **At the start of the planting season, plant the first bed; wait about two weeks and plant the second bed, and then plant the third bed about two weeks later.**

   Just about the time you finish harvesting the first bed, the second bed will be ready to harvest.

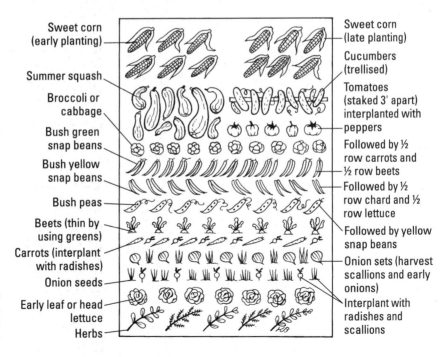

FIGURE 5-5:
A sample plan of succession plantings.

The length of your planting season will determine how many successive plantings you can make and how successful the later plantings are. Depending on the weather, some of your later plantings may not yield well, but that's another reason to plant a number of plantings through the season: you're sure to get some of every type of veggie.

Another way to use succession planting is to replace a crop that's finished producing with a new one in the same place. With this method, you can grow more and a wider variety of vegetables in a small space. Just make sure you're planting a cool-season veggie for spring or fall and a warm-season veggie for summer. Table 5-3 lists some good succession planting combinations to try. You can choose one veggie from each column to plant in succession.

TABLE 5-3

Succession Planting for Different Seasons

Spring	Summer	Fall
Spinach	Bush beans	Kale
Mesclun greens	Cucumber	Lettuce
Peas	Sweet corn	Collards
Radish	Eggplant	Chinese cabbage

Yet another way to ensure a constant harvest of vegetables is to plant using the *square foot method.* This method is for the mathematically inclined (even though you don't need an A in calculus to use it). You select a 4-foot-by-4-foot section of your garden and divide it into 16 squares (each section is 1 square foot). Each square will have a different number of plants, depending on what you're growing:

>> **1 plant per square:** Tomatoes, peppers, broccoli, cabbage, cauliflower, eggplant, corn, melon, squash

>> **4 plants per square:** Lettuce, garlic, Swiss chard

>> **8 plants per square:** Pole beans, peas, spinach

>> **16 plants per square:** Beets, carrots, radishes, onions

By planting so few plants, you'll have many small harvests, and you can easily make more succession plantings and rotate plantings each year. (Crop rotation is described in Chapter 6 of this minibook.)

Planting by the phases of the moon

Planting by the phases of the moon isn't just a New Age technique. It has been used for eons by many ancient farmers and gardeners. They noticed that certain vegetables perform better when planted during different moon phases. The planting seasons don't really change, but planting dates during those seasons become very important.

Here's how moon gardening works: If you divide the 28-day moon cycle (from the new moon to the full moon and back to the new moon) into quarters, as any calendar does, certain quarters are thought to be better than others for planting specific vegetables. The following list gives you an idea of what to plant when, according to the moon cycle:

» **The first quarter,** when the moon goes from new moon (invisible) to a quarter visible, is thought to be best for planting asparagus, lettuce, broccoli, cabbage, cauliflower, and other vegetables that produce their seeds on parts of the plant that aren't eaten.

» **The second quarter,** when the moon goes from half to full, is best for planting vegetables in which the seeds are eaten, such as beans, tomatoes, peppers, and squash.

» **The third quarter,** as the moon moves from full back to half again, is best for planting root crops such as beets, carrots, potatoes, radishes, and turnips.

» **The last quarter,** when the moon goes from half to invisible, is not thought of as a good planting time. Instead, it's a time to prepare the soil and rid the garden of pests and weeds.

Knowing When to Harvest

You should harvest most vegetables when they're young and tender, which often means harvesting the plants, roots, or fruits before they reach full size. A 15-inch zucchini is impressive, but it tastes better at 6 to 8 inches. Similarly, carrots and beets get *woody* (tough textured) and bland the longer they stay in the ground. Table 5-4 provides specific information on when to harvest a variety of veggies.

Other plants are continuously harvested to keep them productive. If you keep harvesting vegetables such as snap beans, summer squash, snow and snap peas, broccoli, okra, spinach, and lettuce, they'll continue to produce pods, shoots, or leaves.

TABLE 5-4

Harvesting Fresh Vegetables

Vegetable	When to Harvest
Asparagus	When spears are 6 to 9 inches long
Beans, snap	Start about two to three weeks after bloom, before seeds mature
Beans, dried	When the pods are dry and crack open easily
Beets	When 1 to 3 inches wide
Broccoli	When flower heads are tight and green
Brussels sprouts	When sprouts reach 1 inch wide
Cabbage	When heads are compact and firm
Carrots	When tops are 1 inch wide
Cauliflower	While heads are still white but not *ricey* (the florets are splitting apart)
Celery	When stalks are large enough to eat
Corn	When silks are dry and brown; kernels should be milky when cut
Cucumbers	When 6 inches long for slicing; when at least 2 inches long for picklers
Eggplant	Before color dulls; flesh should bounce back when pressed lightly
Garlic	Pull up stalks when the bottom leaves yellow
Kohlrabi	When 2 to 3 inches wide
Leeks	When the stalks are at least 1½ inches in diameter
Lettuce and other greens	While leaves are tender
Muskmelons	When fruit slips off vine easily; while *netting* (raised area on skin) is even; when fruit is firm
Okra	When pods are soft and 2 to 3 inches long
Onions	When necks are tight and scales are dry
Parsnips	When roots reach desired size, possibly after light frost
Peanuts	When leaves turn yellow
Peas	While pods are still tender
Peppers	When fruits reach desired size and color
Potatoes	When vines die back
Pumpkins	When shells harden, before frost
Radishes	When roots are up to 1¼ inches wide

Vegetable	When to Harvest
Rhubarb	When it shows red streaks on the stalks
Rutabagas	When roots reach desired size
Shallots	When tops wither and turn brown
Spinach	When leaves are still tender
Squash, summer	When 6 to 8 inches long
Squash, winter	When shells harden, before frost
Sweet potatoes	When they reach adequate size
Tomatoes	When uniformly colored
Turnips	When 2 to 3 inches wide
Watermelons	When undersides turn yellow and produce a dull sound when thumped

TIP

A good rule for many of your early crops is to start harvesting when you have enough of a vegetable for a one-meal serving. Spinach, Swiss chard, scallions, radishes, lettuce, and members of the cabbage family certainly fit the bill here. These veggies don't grow as well in warm weather, so pick these crops in the spring when temperatures are cooler.

After you start harvesting, visit your garden and pick something daily. Take along a good sharp knife and a few containers to hold your produce, such as paper bags, buckets, or baskets. Wire or wood buckets work well because you can easily wash vegetables in them.

TIP

The harvesting information in Table 5-4 is based on picking mature or slightly immature vegetables. But many vegetables can be picked smaller and still have excellent flavor. Pick baby vegetables whenever they reach the size that you want. The following vegetables can be picked small: beets, broccoli, carrots, cauliflower, cucumbers, lettuce and other greens, onions, peas, potatoes, radishes, snap beans, summer squash, Swiss chard, and turnips. In addition, some small varieties of corn and tomatoes fit the baby-vegetable mold.

WARNING

Be sure to avoid harvesting at the following times:

>> **When plants, especially beans, are wet.** Many fungal diseases spread in moist conditions, and if you brush your tools or pant legs against diseased plants, you can transfer disease organisms to other plants down the row.

» **In the heat of the day, because the vegetable's texture may be limp.** For the freshest produce, harvest early in the day when vegetables' moisture levels inside the vegetables are highest and the vegetables are at peak flavor. After harvesting, refrigerate the produce and prepare it later in the day.

In the fall, wait as long as you can to dig up root crops, such as carrots, rutabagas, and beets, if you intend to store them in a root cellar or cold storage room. However, remember that while root crops can withstand frosts, you should harvest them before the ground freezes. They'll come out of the ground easiest if the soil is still slightly moist. Also, don't wash crops that are going to the root cellar; instead, just gently brush away soil crumbs. Use any blemished or cut vegetables within a few days.

Chapter **6**

Dealing with Weeds and Pests

Y ou put a lot of work *into* your garden. But a sizable portion of any gardener's workload involves taking certain things *out*. You've created a healthy and productive environment intended to support life, and now life is literally bursting forth in your garden beds: not only in the form of your fruits and vegetables and herbs but also with the unwanted plants and predatory insects that inevitably follow.

Weeds and pests are two unfortunate facts of life that every gardener must face. They can devour valuable resources — water, soil nutrients, blossoming plants, and your time, money, and energy — that would otherwise be furthering the things you want your garden to produce. But don't let the unpleasant reality of weeds and pests discourage your homesteading efforts. After all, they're just part of the arrangement you've signed up for by working with Mother Nature.

This chapter spells out techniques and tactics for dealing with weeds and pests, including knowing which bugs you should be inviting into your garden.

Fighting Weed Wars

A *weed* is any plant that's growing where you don't want it to. Some weeds are worse than others, but in general, you don't want any weeds in your vegetable garden because they compete with vegetables for light, water, and nutrients. If you have a lot of weeds, you'll have weaker plants and a less substantial harvest. Besides, weeds look terrible.

The key to battling weeds is to get to them early before they're firmly established. When they're young, weeds are easier to pull, easier to till under, and less likely to produce seeds that cause problems down the road.

Making a preemptive strike on weeds

You can reduce weeds in your vegetable beds many different ways. Here are some things that you can do before planting your garden:

>> **Presprout weed seeds.** *Presprouting* — forcing weed seeds to germinate before you plant so you can kill them early — really cuts down on the number of weeds in your beds. Follow these steps:

  1. **Prepare your planting bed several weeks before you're ready to plant.**

     Refer to Chapters 2 and 3 of this minibook for details on planning and preparing your beds for planting.

  2. **Water the soil well and wait a few days.**

     Presto, young weeds begin popping up.

  3. **Kill the weeds.**

     You can choose to kill the weeds one of two ways: pull them out by hand, or rake the bed lightly to uproot the seedlings and then let them dry out to die.

     However you get rid of the young weeds, disturb the soil as little as possible when you do it; otherwise, you'll bring more seeds to the surface.

REMEMBER

>> **Plan for easy weeding.** Leave enough room between rows so you can weed the soil easily.

>> **Solarize the soil.** When you *solarize* the soil, you use the power of the sun to kill weeds. This technique works best in the middle of summer in hot climates such as Arizona and Florida. The only downside to solarizing is that it takes a while. Follow these steps to solarize your soil:

  1. **Prepare your bed for planting and water it well.**

  2. **Dig a 6-to-12-inch-deep trench around the perimeter of the bed.**

3. **Cover the entire bed with thick clear plastic (4 millimeters) and place the edges of the plastic in the trenches and fill the trenches with soil. Then wait.**

   The temperature gets so hot underneath the plastic that it kills insects, disease organisms, and weeds. It usually takes a few months of solarizing to get a beneficial effect.

» **Plant your vegetables at the proper time of year.** That way, they get off to a fast start, and weeds have a harder time catching up with them. See Chapter 4 of this minibook for details.

Battling weeds after planting

If (or when) you come across weeds after you plant your crops, you have several choices for eliminating them:

» **Mulch your beds.** Applying a layer of thick organic mulch is one of the best ways to battle weeds. Even if mulch doesn't smother the weeds and their seeds, the weeds that do come up are easy to pull. Planting through plastic is also an effective way to keep weeds from becoming a problem. See Chapter 5 in this minibook for more information.

» **Pull the weeds by hand.** While they're young, weeds come out of the ground easily. Get 'em roots and all, whenever you see them. If you can't pull out the roots by hand, use a trowel.

» **Cultivate the soil.** Simply hoeing or lightly turning the soil between vegetables exposes the weeds' roots and kills many of them. Cultivating is most effective when you do it often (a few times a week in the first month or so of gardening) and early, when the weeds are small.

» **Keep garden paths clean.** Try to keep your garden paths as weed free as possible; otherwise, weeds will creep into your planting beds. Try covering the paths with a thick mulch to keep weeds from becoming established.

» **Make sure the areas around the garden are weed free.** If you're growing vegetables near a field or weedy woodland edge, try to mow a wide strip between your garden and the field so the weed seeds can't blow in as easily. It won't stop all of them, but every little bit helps.

Using herbicides smartly

When all else fails, gardeners can turn to herbicides to kill the weeds. Generally speaking, homesteaders growing food for their family and raising animals are loathe to introduce toxic chemicals in their garden, for obvious reasons. But the word *chemical* doesn't have to refer to a harmful poison that kills your prized crops right along with the weeds being targeted. As with any chemical treatment — organic or synthetic — use the most powerful ones only as a last resort.

Herbicides work in several ways that depend on a particular plant's life stage or characteristics to be effective:

>> **Pre-emergent herbicide:** Sprouting seeds send out roots first, followed by the stem and first leaves. This vulnerable time is the best and easiest stage to knock them out. Pre-emergent herbicides kill these tiny seedlings as they sprout and are especially useful on lawns and in other places where mature weeds are difficult to remove.

TIP

One relatively new organic pre-emergent herbicide is corn gluten meal, a highly concentrated corn protein extract. It can control weeds for up to six weeks if applied in early spring and again in late summer. As a bonus, it's high in nitrogen.

>> **Herbicidal soap:** Plants have a waxy coating on their leaves that prevents moisture loss. Herbicidal soap damages the waxy layer, allowing the plant to dry out and die. This type of herbicide works best on young, tender, actively growing weeds in hot, dry weather. It's less effective on mature plants and perennial weeds.

Plants are sensitive to changes in pH. Some products use acetic acid (derived from vinegar) or pelargonic acid (derived from fruit) as their active ingredient. These acids damage the plants' protective waxy coating, killing the sprayed plant parts in a matter of hours.

WARNING

Regular kitchen vinegar is only 5 percent acetic acid; though it may kill weed seedlings, it has little effect on mature plants. Commercial formulations of up to 20 percent acetic acid are available. Although these substances are more potent weed-killers, they're also more hazardous to use. Follow label directions, wear gloves and goggles when applying, and store them as you would any other garden chemicals.

These products are acceptable for spot treatments but shouldn't be used extensively because they also kill beneficial organisms and lower soil pH. New formulations made from a combination of vinegar, citrus, cinnamon, or clove oils have been introduced recently.

Keeping Good Bugs Nearby

Most gardens are populated by a huge number of insects, most of which are neither good nor bad. They're just hanging out in your garden at no expense to your plants. But some insects are beneficial, waged in a constant battle with the bugs that are harming your plants.

For most gardeners, the goal is to have a maximum diversity of bugs in the garden. To get the good insects to stick around, follow these tips:

» **Avoid indiscriminately using broad-spectrum chemical or organic pesticides, which kill everything, the good bugs and the bad.** If you do spray, use a spray that specifically targets the pest that you want to eliminate and that has minimal effect on beneficial insects; the label on the spray usually gives you this information. (I discuss safe sprays in detail later in this chapter.)

» **Plant a diverse garden with many kinds and sizes of plants, including flowers and herbs.** Doing so gives the beneficials (beneficial insects) places to hide and reproduce. A garden with a variety of plants also can provide an alternative food source, because many beneficials like to eat pollen and flower nectar, too. Some plants that attract beneficials include Queen Anne's lace, parsley (especially if you let the flower develop), sweet alyssum, dill, fennel, and yarrow.

» **Provide a diverse habitat for beneficial insects.** Have a small bird bath and evergreen and deciduous shrubs to hide in nearby. These elements provide water and shelter for beneficial insects, making it more likely they'll hang around to munch on some insect pests.

Battling Bad Bugs

Despite what you may think, having some bad bugs around is important. Aphids are like hors d'oeuvres for some helpful insects, so it's okay to have a few in your garden. Otherwise, what will the good bugs eat? But accepting the bad bugs also means that you have to accept a little damage once in a while. So just try to manage the pests, not nuke them off the face of the earth. You want to keep them at acceptable levels without letting them get out of control.

It helps to know your enemy, and insect pests command the largest army of invaders. The following sections list the most common insect pests that are likely to infest your vegetables as well as the best ways to control them.

Aphids

Aphids are tiny, pear-shaped pests that come in many colors, including black, green, and red (see Figure 6-1). They congregate on new growth and flower buds, sucking plant sap through their needlelike noses. Heavy infestations can cause distorted growth and may weaken your plants. Aphids leave behind a sticky sap that may turn black with sooty mold and may carry diseases, such as viruses, that infect your plants. Many vegetables can be infested with this pest, including cabbage, cucumbers, and broccoli.

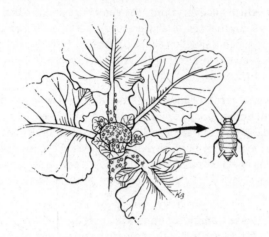

FIGURE 6-1: Control aphids with insecticidal soap, neem oil, or hot pepper spray.

Aphids are easy to control. A strong jet of water from a hose can knock them off sturdy plants (they rarely climb back onto the plant to feed), or you can use insecticidal soap or neem oil. Insecticidal soap also helps wash off the sooty mold. But if you have only a few aphids, wait a week for beneficial insects, especially lady beetles, to move into your garden; they usually take matters into their own hands before serious damage occurs.

Caterpillars and worms

Caterpillars and worms, moth and butterfly larvae, are avid eaters and can cause a lot of damage to a variety of plants. Some are hairy caterpillars; others are smooth skinned and more wormlike. Caterpillars include tomato hornworms and cabbageworms (see Figure 6-2). You can handpick caterpillars and worms to reduce numbers, or you can release trichogramma wasps. But the most effective way to get rid of them is to spray with biological controls, such as Bt (*Bacillus* thuringiensis) or spinosad.

TIP

Sometimes these little guys can blend in quite effectively among your tomato plant's stems and leaves and be hard to spot. Be on the lookout for *frass* — the caterpillar's droppings — on lower stems and leaves. You'll know it when you see it: small black pebbles that may be clumped in barrel-shaped clusters. When you find frass, just search up from there.

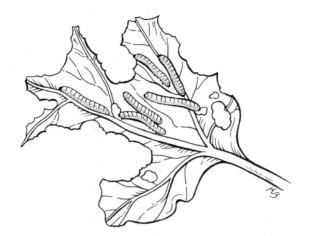

Corn earworms

Corn earworms are a common pest wherever corn is grown. These 1½-inch-long caterpillars with alternating light and dark stripes may be green, pink, or brown. In spring, night-flying moths lay yellow eggs on the undersides of leaves. The resulting first-generation caterpillars feed on the leaves. The eggs of later generations can be found on corn silks; the emerging caterpillars feed on the silks and the kernels at the tips of the corn ears, just inside the husks. The earworms, also called fruitworms, attack a variety of plants including tomatoes, beans, peas, peppers, potatoes, and squash.

The easiest way to deal with corn earworms on your corn plants is to just cut off the tip of the ear before you cook it. Or to prevent worms, you can spray Bt before the caterpillars enter the ears or fruit, but that doesn't always work. To prevent the worms from entering the ears, you also can place a few drops of mineral oil on the silks of each ear just as the silks wilt and start to turn from white or yellow to brown. (Don't do it too early or you'll interfere with pollination, but don't wait until the silks are all brown and shriveled either; you have about a week in which to work.)

Cutworms

Cutworms are ½-inch-long, grayish caterpillars. They emerge on spring and early summer nights to eat the stems of young seedlings, causing the seedlings to fall over like small timbers. Cutworms also climb up to older plants and feed on leaves and flowers.

To protect seedlings, surround their stems with barriers that prevent the cut-worms from crawling close and feeding. These devices can be as simple as empty cardboard toilet paper rolls, Styrofoam cups with the bottoms cut out, or collars made from aluminum foil. Whatever you use, just make sure that the barriers encircle the stem completely and are set 1 inch deep in the soil. You also can trap cutworms by leaving boards around your garden; the worms hide under the boards during the day, enabling you to collect them. Parasitic nematodes also are effective against cutworms.

Flea beetles

Flea beetles are tiny $\frac{1}{16}$-inch beetles that feed on vegetable leaves, riddling them with small holes. These beetles jump rapidly when disturbed, like fleas — hence their name. Various species feed on just about any plant in a garden, including eggplant, tomatoes, broccoli, cabbage, corn, potatoes, spinach, peppers, and sweet potatoes. Adult beetles can spread diseases — wilt in sweet corn, for example — and larvae feed on roots. Adults overwinter in the soil and on garden debris, emerging in early spring. Keep a close watch because these beetles can destroy young plants quickly.

To control flea beetles, make sure you clean up garden debris in the winter and till the soil. Use a floating row cover to exclude adults (I describe these covers later in this chapter), and release parasitic nematodes to attack the larvae. Pyrethrins and insecticidal soap also provide some control.

Japanese beetles

Japanese beetles can really be troublesome in many areas. These ½-inch-long beetles have coppery bodies and metallic green heads. They feed on the foliage of many vegetables, including corn, beans, and tomatoes.

WARNING

Controlling Japanese beetles can be tough. Treating your lawn and garden soil with parasitic nematodes or with *milky spore* (a biological spray) may reduce the white C-shaped larvae, but more adults will probably fly in from your neighbor's yard. Floral-scented traps that attract adult beetles are available, but the traps may attract more beetles than you had before. If you try the traps, keep them at least 100 feet from your vegetables and encourage your neighbors to use them, too, to control the beetles community-wide.

Insecticidal soap and neem oil are effective against adult beetles. You also can handpick the beetles off your vegetables and stomp on them. Picking in early morning or evening is easiest because the beetles are sleepy then and tend not to fly away.

Nematodes

Nematodes are microscopic wormlike pests that can infect soil, especially in warm climates. They feed on the roots of plants and attack many vegetables, including carrots, tomatoes, and potatoes. Nematodes thrive in sandy, moist soil and can quickly stunt plants and cause roots to look hairy and knotted. Your best defense is to plant nematode-resistant varieties and to rotate your crops (see Chapter 5 in this minibook) to prevent a population from building.

Snails and slugs

Snails and *slugs* are soft-bodied mollusks that feed on tender leaves and flowers during the cool of night or during rainy weather. Snails have shells; slugs don't. Snails and slugs proliferate in damp areas, hiding under raised containers, boards, or garden debris.

To control these pests, roam through your garden at night with a flashlight and play pick-and-stomp, or trap them with saucers of beer, setting the rims at ground level. They'll jump in to drink the beer, not be able to climb out, and drown. Refill the saucers regularly. Snails and slugs won't cross copper, so you can also surround raised beds or individual containers with a thin copper stripping, which is sold at most nurseries. In California, you can release decollate snails, which prey on pest snails; ask your Cooperative Extension Service office for information.

If all else fails, you can spread snail and slug bait containing iron phosphate. Sold as Sluggo and Escar-Go! this safe bait attracts and kills slugs and snails without being harmful to wildlife, pets, and kids.

Spider mites

Spider mites are tiny, spiderlike arachnids that you can barely see without a magnifying glass. If the population gets big enough, you can see their fine webbing beneath the leaves of your plants. As they suck a plant's juices, the leaves become yellowish with silvery *stippling* (small yellow dots on the leaves) or sheen. If things get really bad, the plant may start dropping leaves. Mites are most common in hot, dry summer climates and on plants with dusty (sooty) leaves. Tomatoes and beans are commonly infested.

A daily bath with a strong jet of water from a hose helps keep infestations down. You can control spider mites with insecticidal soap, which also helps clean off the plants' leaves. Applying summer oil or neem oil and releasing predatory mites also are effective.

Thrips

Thrips are almost-invisible troublemakers. They feed on leaves, giving them a stippled look and deforming them. You can distinguish thrips from spider mites by looking for the small fecal pellets that thrips leave behind. Thrips often pass on diseases as they feed. Beans, cabbage, onions, and eggplants are commonly infested. Many beneficials feed on thrips, especially lacewings. Insecticidal soaps and pyrethrins also are effective.

Whiteflies

Whiteflies look like small white gnats, but they suck plant juices and can proliferate in warm climates and greenhouses. They tend to congregate on the undersides of leaves, especially on tomatoes and beans. You can trap whiteflies with yellow sticky traps, which are sold in nurseries. In greenhouses, release Encarsia wasps, which prey on greenhouse whiteflies. Insecticidal soaps, summer oil, and neem oil are effective sprays.

More Methods of Attack

If the controls mentioned in the previous sections aren't cutting it and you need to take further action, start with the first line of defense against pest outbreaks: physical barriers that keep the bugs away from your plants. The next step is to apply pesticides that are effective against a certain pest, are pretty safe to use, and have a mild effect on the rest of your garden's life-forms. In general, these products are short-lived after you use them in your garden — that's what makes them so good.

Physical controls

You can physically prevent pests from damaging your vegetables a number of ways. One of the best ways is to grab bugs by their tails, body slam them to the ground, and stomp on them. *Handpicking*, as it's usually called, works best with large bugs such as tomato hornworms, Japanese beetles, snails, and slugs. The best time to handpick slugs is at night, using the light of a flashlight. If you have problems squashing bugs, drop them in a jar of soapy water instead.

Here are some other physical controls to try:

>> **A strong jet of water** often dislodges insects such as aphids and spider mites from the leaves of vegetables, and they rarely climb back onto the plant. This method also keeps the foliage clean.

>> **Barriers** keep pests from reaching your vegetables. For example, place a small copper strip around the outside of raised beds or containers to keep snails from reaching your plants (snails won't cross the copper stripping). *Floating row covers*, those lightweight, blanketlike materials described in more detail in Chapter 6 of this minibook, also keep pests away from plants. And if you have problems with cutworms, push a small cardboard collar (a paper cup with the bottom pushed out works well) into the ground around seedlings to keep bugs from reaching the stems.

>> **Trapping** pests before they reach your vegetables is another way to reduce problems. Trapping works best with night feeders — such as slugs and earwigs — that seek shelter during the day and are attracted to dark, moist environments. You can trap snails and slugs under a slightly raised board at night, and then dispose of the board in the morning. Earwigs will collect in rolled-up newspapers.

Safe pesticides

Here are some recommended safe spray methods of controlling harmful bugs:

>> **Biological controls:** Using *biological controls* involves pitting one living thing against another. Releasing beneficial insects is one example of biological control, but you also can use bacteria that, while harmless to humans, makes insect pests very sick and eventually very dead. The most common and useful biological controls are forms of *Bacillus thuringiensis,* or Bt, which kill the larvae of moths and butterflies (that is, caterpillars). Another variety of Bt, *B.t. tenebrionis* or *B.t. San Diego,* kills the larvae of Colorado potato beetles. *Bacillus popilliae* (milky spore disease) is an effective control of Japanese beetle grubs.

Spinosad is a new biological control agent that has many uses. This soil-dwelling bacteria was discovered in Jamaica as a byproduct in the rum-making industry. It kills a broad range of insects, including caterpillars, thrips, spider mites, and leaf miners, but it isn't harmful to beneficial insects, animals, or pets. However, it is toxic to honey bees so spray it on cloudy days or late in the evening when the bees are less active. As with Bt, the insect must eat the toxin for it to work.

>> **Botanical insecticides:** *Botanical insecticides* are derived from plants. The most useful insecticides against vegetable pests are *pyrethrins,* which are derived from the painted daisy, *Chrysanthemum cinerariifolium.* They're broad-spectrum insecticides, which means they kill a wide range of insects. Unfortunately, that means some of the good guys are killed, too. So to avoid killing bees, for example, spray pyrethrins late in the evening. Use this pesticide as a last resort. The advantage to using pyrethrins is that it kills pests such as aphids and beetles quickly, and has low toxicity to mammals. However, always follow the label and never apply more than is recommended.

The terminology can be confusing. *Pyrethrum* is the ground-up flower of this type of daisy. *Pyrethrins* are the insecticide components of the flower. You also may see insecticides called *pyrethroids,* however. Pyrethroids, such as permethrin and resmethrin, are synthetic compounds that resemble pyrethrins but are more toxic and persistent. They shouldn't be used in organic gardens.

» **Home remedies:** Not all pesticides are exotic. Many gardeners have had great success using common household products to control insects in their gardens. One favorite home remedy is adding a clove or two of garlic and a few teaspoons of cayenne to a quart of water and then blending it all in a mixer. You then strain the solution to remove the chunks, and using a hand-held sprayer, spray your plants to control insects, such as aphids and whiteflies, and repel animals, such as rabbits and deer. Of course, after it rains, you have to reapply the mix. Commercial insecticide products, such as Hot Pepper Wax and Garlic Barrier, which are based on the common foods, also are available. Either type of product is effective, simple, safe, and fun to try.

» **Insecticidal soaps:** Derived from the salts of fatty acids, *insecticidal soaps* kill mostly soft-bodied pests such as aphids, spider mites, and whiteflies. They also can be effective against Japanese beetles. They work fast, break down quickly, and are nontoxic to humans. Insecticidal soaps are most effective when mixed with soft water because soaps can sometimes burn tender foliage.

» **Neem oil:** *Neem oil* is extracted from the seed of the tropical neem tree. It has been used for centuries in India as an insecticide, to kill parasites in cattle, and even as a toothpaste for humans. Needless to say, it's very safe (except to unlucky pests). Home gardeners can purchase neem oil to repel and kill insects including aphids, whiteflies, leaf miners, caterpillars, and many others.

» **Summer or horticultural oil:** When sprayed on a plant, this highly refined oil smothers insect pests and their eggs. The words "highly refined" mean that the sulfur and other components of the oil that damage the plant are removed. This oil is relatively nontoxic and short lived. Use it to control aphids, mites, thrips, and certain caterpillars.

Make sure that you don't confuse summer oil with dormant oil. Dormant oil should be applied to leafless trees and shrubs during the winter. It isn't meant to be used on vegetables.

Double-check the oil's product label to make sure that you can use the oil on plants during the growing season. Then follow the mixing instructions carefully. Water your plants before and after applying the oil. But don't apply the oil if temperatures are likely to rise above 85 degrees Fahrenheit. When it's that hot, the oil can damage plant leaves.

ANSWERING FAQS ON IPM

A fancy buzzword term you'll hear a lot when talking about garden pests is IPM, or integrated pest management. Largely thought of as strictly an organic approach, *IPM* simply outlines logical steps for dealing with garden pests that don't include chemical warfare (pesticides). But IPM isn't just for organic gardeners; many tenets of IPM are just sound gardening strategies that have been covered elsewhere in this book and practiced long before organic was hip.

Putting the right plant in the right place is one IPM tip, because a weakened plant struggling in a bad location is more susceptible to pests. But other IPM techniques can include starting with pest-resistant plant varieties, scattering a crop throughout your homestead rather than in one huge patch, and encouraging beneficial animals such as spiders, birds, toads, bats, lizards, and "good" insects to take up residence near your garden. Often, these beneficial predators are purposely released into the garden to hunt to their hearts' content.

When pests are encountered, IPM first dictates determining whether control is even necessary. If the damage is merely cosmetic, limited to just a plant or two, or unique to a crop that will be harvested imminently, control measures may not be warranted. The pest may be allowed to stay. This process is called *establishing damage thresholds*. Control methods, when needed for unacceptable damage, often include tactics described earlier: physical barriers, handpicking, hosing off with plain water, or trapping. Least-toxic tactics first, more-toxic methods only if necessary, chemical pesticides are not part of the equation.

Integrated pest management may have a mysterious-sounding acronym, but homesteaders who use common sense and nontoxic methods to grow healthy vegetables are already practicing IPM.

REMEMBER

Always follow the instructions on the product label exactly; in fact, not following these instructions is against the law. Also, wear gloves when mixing and spraying pesticides, and spray when the wind is calm. Store the chemicals in properly labeled containers well out of the reach of children (a locked cabinet is best). Dispose of empty containers as described on the label, or contact your local waste disposal company for appropriate disposal sites.

Giving your plants some friends: companion planting

A *companion plant* is one that provides some sort of benefit to other plants growing nearby. It's sort of like how a good friend makes life easier for you. Well, plants have good friends, too. For example, the cover crops mentioned in Chapter 5 of this minibook can be considered companion plants.

Some plants are grown together because they seem to increase each other's yields. But other companion plants repel pests. Is that really possible? Well, no clear-cut evidence says companion planting works against pests. But some people swear by it. It is true, however, that a variety of plants, herbs, and flowers provides a diverse ecosystem so that predatory insects are more likely to hang around and take care of the bad guys. Besides, trying some of these combinations certainly won't hurt your garden.

These plants are thought to repel specific pests; plant them near crops where these pests are a common problem:

>> **Anise** planted among members of the cabbage family (cabbage, broccoli, cauliflower, kale, and so on) is said to repel imported cabbage worms.

>> **Basil** is said to repel whiteflies, aphids, and spider mites; it's a good companion to tomatoes because these are insects that feed on tomato plants.

>> **Catnip** is said to repel some types of aphids, flea beetles, squash bugs, and cucumber beetles.

>> **Garlic** may repel nematodes and other soil insects.

>> **Leeks** are thought to repel carrot flies.

>> **Marigolds** planted around vegetables are said to repel root nematodes, Mexican bean beetles, and Colorado potato beetles.

>> **Mustard greens** are supposed to repel aphids.

>> **Nasturtiums** are said to repel Colorado potato beetles.

>> **Radishes** may repel striped cucumber beetles.

>> **Ryegrass** may repel root-knot nematodes.

>> **Southernwood** may repel moths and flea beetles.

>> **Tansy** is supposed to repel some aphids, squash bugs, and Colorado potato beetles as well as ants.

>> **White clover** may repel cabbage root flies.

>> **Wormwood** may repel flea beetles.

Many herbs, such as rosemary, oregano, and coriander, also are said to repel pests. Smaller companion plants, such as marigolds, can be interplanted with vegetables. Taller or more vigorous plants, such as ryegrass or wormwood, should be planted nearby — but not among — vegetables. You don't want them to overwhelm your veggie plants.

The research on companion planting may be thin, but hey, give it a try to see if it works!

Rotating crops

WARNING

If you plant the same vegetables in the same spot year after year, you're going to cause a number of problems, including these:

>> Insects and diseases that spend part of their life cycle in the soil will build up there and be more difficult to control.

>> Specific nutrients that the vegetables need will consistently be depleted and will be harder to replace.

The way around these problems is to rotate your crops from season to season. In other words, plant them in different beds, as far away as possible from where they were planted before. Crop rotation is easy if you keep a journal and make note of what was planted where. And if you keep things out of the same beds for three years, you'll probably be in good shape.

REMEMBER

It's important to do more than rotate individual crops. You should rotate families of crops as well. A disease or insect that attacks one plant in a family is likely to attack others. Blight on tomatoes and potatoes is an example. When rotating crops, make sure you don't plant a family member in the same spot three years in a row. For example, in one bed, plant beans (legume family), the next year plant potatoes (tomato family), and the third year plant cucumbers (squash family). After that, you can start over with another legume–family vegetable or start another rotation series. Keep the families apart for three years, and you'll have fewer problems in the veggie patch. Table 6-1 shows a few possible rotation schedules.

TABLE 6-1 ## Crop Rotation Ideas

First-Year Crop	Second-Year Crop	Third-Year Crop
Peas	Corn	Cover crop (grasses, legumes, or grains)
Tomato	Radish	Cabbage
Green beans	Squash	Lettuce

The more crop families you have represented in your garden, the more involved the rotation schedule may become. (Here's an instance where keeping a garden journal or crop diary from year to year has saved many gardeners!) The following section offers a rundown of some of the most popular crops in each botanical family:

>> **Amaranthaceae:** Members of the goosefoot family you may recognize are beets, spinach, and chard.

>> **Apiaceae:** Crops in the umbel family include carrots, celery, parsnips, fennel, cilantro, dill, and parsley.

>> **Asteraceae:** In the aster family you'll find lettuce, artichokes, radicchio, and endive. Other members include garden beauties such as sunflowers, cosmos, marigolds, chamomile, and Echinacea.

>> **Brassicaceae:** The cool-season cole crop family includes broccoli, cauliflower, cabbage, kale, radishes, turnips, Brussels sprouts, and collard greens.

>> **Curcurbitaceae:** The gourd family is made up of vining plants. Cucumbers, zucchini, squash, melons, and pumpkins are members of this family.

>> **Fabaceae:** Peas, beans, and peanuts are part of this, the legume family. Be aware that some common cover crops such as clover and alfalfa are also legumes, so they need to be rotated as well.

>> **Lamiaceae:** The mint family features popular herbs such as basil, rosemary, thyme, oregano, sage, lavender, and mints. Homesteaders growing these plants should rotate them just as they do vegetables.

>> **Liliaceae:** Onions, garlic, shallots, leeks, and chives are members of the allium family. So is asparagus, but that must be left to grow in the same bed for several years; when it rotates, it must move to a bed that hasn't seen any of these other family members for several years.

>> **Solanaceae:** The nightshade family includes tomatoes, peppers, eggplants, and potatoes other than sweet potatoes. (Sweet potatoes are in a separate family, along with morning glories.) Okra is sometimes included here, although it is, scientifically speaking, a member of the Malvaceae family, the same as cotton.

If you have only one sunny spot to garden, consider using containers as a way to rotate crops. For example, plant your tomatoes in a container one year and in the garden the next.

Chapter **7**

Extending Your Season

I n most parts of the country, the traditional growing season is straightforward. Prepare the soil in spring, sow in April or May, harvest in summer and fall. Mild winter areas such as Florida, Texas, and southern California have more planting in fall and winter and less in summer, with harvests year-round depending on the vegetable. However, by just planting once or twice a year, vegetable gardeners are missing out on opportunities to extend the harvest season and grow more in less space.

After you start vegetable gardening, you may get hooked on having fresh vegetables from your garden year-round. Unless you live in a mild climate, such as zone 9 or 10 (see Chapter 1 of this minibook for more on zones), the best way to get the most vegetables from your garden is to use season-extending devices and techniques. These methods protect your vegetables from deadly frosts in fall and enable you to get an earlier start in spring. Of course, selecting the right vegetables to grow also is vital to your success.

In general, greens, root crops, and cool-season cole crops are the best vegetables to grow in cold weather. However, you can extend the length of time that you harvest warm-season crops — such as melons, tomatoes, and peppers — by using the season-extending methods in this chapter. Whatever plants you grow, these techniques enable you to harvest fresh vegetables for most of the year.

Covering Your Rows

Floating row covers (see Figure 7-1) are among the best things ever to happen to veggie gardeners. The material, which is like cheesecloth, is lightweight and lets air, sunlight, and water pass through it. Also, when row covers are used on newly sown plants in the spring, they keep the air and soil a little warmer, thereby helping seeds germinate faster and young plants grow more quickly.

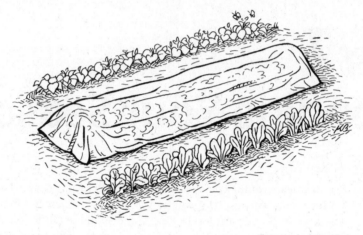

FIGURE 7-1:
Floating
row cover.

Illustration by Kathryn Born

Row cover is available in different thicknesses, depending on how you intend to use it. Some are meant merely to keep out insect pests, while others are for winter use. The delicate material may not seem like much, but it's thick enough to protect plants down into the mid-20 degrees F. Lay the floating row cover over young seedlings, loosely fastening it to the ground with boards or stones, and the plants will literally lift it up as they grow.

You may choose to use floating row covers on peppers, for example, in spring to ensure an early harvest of fruits, because pepper flowers need warm air temperatures. But then the row covers help at the other end of the season, too, by holding in heat and moderating the cool autumn-night temperatures. You can grow greens, root crops, and cole crops to maturity under a floating row cover.

Floating row covers can also keep plants relatively safe from insect pests — such as cabbageworms, cucumber beetles, and squash bugs. They also help keep critters such as rabbits away. But be sure to spread them over your plants early enough in the season. If you wait too long before covering your plants, the insects will have a chance to set up housekeeping in the garden, and they'll thrive under the protective covering.

Get covers in place when plants are young and make sure the edges are secured to the ground so pests can't slip under. And check periodically under the row cover for any insects that might have sneaked inside.

REMEMBER

For vegetables that require pollination by insects, such as pumpkins and squash, remove row covers as soon as you see the first flowers. For crops that don't need pollination by bees, such as lettuce and broccoli, you can leave the row cover on throughout the growing season — as long as it doesn't hold in too much heat. The row cover prevents cabbage moths, aphids, and other pests from getting to your vegetables.

Alternatively, you can use a clear plastic cover draped over half-circle wire or pipe hoops to create a tunnel effect (see Figure 7-2). Clear plastic heats up your crops faster and warmer than floating row cover material, but it needs venting to keep the plants from overheating.

REMEMBER

In parts of the country where snow load is a concern, sturdier pipe should be used to create the hoops for your row covers. Electrical conduit with lumber reinforcement boards running atop the arches for the length of the bed will help keep your tunnel from collapsing due to heavy snow. Home improvement centers sell conduit as well as the required bending tool. Many garden supply sources sell clips that make fastening your cover material to the metal conduit easy.

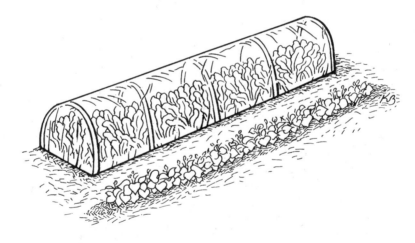

FIGURE 7-2:
A clear plastic grow tunnel.

Using Cold Frames

A clever way to start your growing season earlier in the spring and keep it going long into the frosty fall is to make or buy a cold frame, as seen in Figure 7-3. *Cold frames* are bottomless, insulated boxes made of wood, hay bales, metal, or plastic; they work like miniature greenhouses. The lid of the box is angled slightly to increase its exposure to the sun; its plastic or glass top keeps the inside much warmer than the outside air temperature.

FIGURE 7-3: Cold frames are a good way to extend the growing season in spring and fall.

Illustration by Kathryn Born

Even in the coldest climates, you can use a cold frame to harvest food year-round. Some professional gardeners as far north as zone 5, where winter temperatures can dip down to −20 degrees Fahrenheit, can harvest vegetables every month of the year by planting cold-weather-tolerant crops in cold frames.

In the spring, grow a crop of lettuce in a cold frame, and get your other warm-season crops off to an early start. In the fall and winter, try cold-tolerant spinach, kale, and leeks.

You can make your cold frame large enough to fit over a raised bed in the garden, or keep it small and portable to move around as needed. Cold frames are also handy for hardening off seedlings before transplanting them to the garden.

REMEMBER

Although the purpose of a cold frame is to trap heat, on sunny days, even in winter, a cold frame can get so hot that it burns the tender plants inside. Even on very cool but sunny spring or autumn days, the interior of the box really heats up, much like a car with its windows rolled up. The key to using cold frames is ventilating them as needed. Check your cold frame once a day on sunny days, opening or venting the top slightly to allow hot air to escape. Automatic vent openers, available from greenhouse suppliers, raise and lower the top automatically without electricity, depending on the air temperature.

You can purchase a premade cold frame for $100 to $200, or you can create your own, using materials you may already have lying around. Refer to Chapter 5, Book 1 for the steps to this easy building project that pays big dividends on the homestead.

Going with Greenhouses

Having a greenhouse is a great way to extend the growing season, which is really important in areas where winters are long and summers are short. You can grow plants inside the controlled atmosphere of the greenhouse during times when there's no way they'd grow outside. You can also start seeds in a greenhouse so the plants are already hardy when it's time to put them outside. (You'll find more on starting seeds indoors in Chapter 4 of this miniboook.)

Traditionally, the greenhouse is a separate building (as seen in Figure 7-4), with walls of glass or plastic that let the sun come in and nourish the growing plants, but you can choose from many designs. You can even build a lean-to on the south side of your house or use an entire floor or room in the house as long as it gets good southern exposure.

FIGURE 7-4:
A typical glass greenhouse.

CATCHING SOME RAYS (AND PUTTING THEM TO WORK)

On any given day, 35,000 times the total amount of energy that humans use falls onto the face of the Earth from the sun. If people could just tap into a tiny fraction of what the sun is providing each day, society would be set. Backyard homesteaders, in particular, are keen on harnessing some of the sun's awesome (and free) power to be more self-sufficient in a variety of ways that go beyond greenhouse growing.

Solar-powered landscape lighting can make your garden easier to navigate. A solar fountain is an easy add-on to a pond. Rig up a solar portable shower (like backpackers and campers use) to get a quick and warm rinse-off after a dirty day gardening. Use basic photovoltaic (PV) cells to power electric fences, run lights in your chicken coop, or keep your flock's watering dish from freezing.

Some homesteaders keep stepping up their solar efforts to include an array of panels on the roof of their home to go off the grid and manufacture their own electricity! And to toast all of your new solar-powered energy-producing efforts, you can always make yourself a big batch of sun tea.

Greenhouse gardening can be involved — it's container gardening and vegetable growing at their highest levels in an enclosed, heated, controlled-atmosphere room. You need to pay attention to many more conditions in a greenhouse, such as temperatures that are too hot and too cool, fertility, pests (once they get started, they're tough to stop in a greenhouse), pollination for crops such as cucumbers and melons, and so on. You have to be dedicated; the easiest time to grow good crops in a greenhouse is in the spring and fall to extend the season. Winter and summer are generally the toughest times to grow plants in a greenhouse because of the extremes in temperature and available light.

Gather the materials yourself or go for a kit with everything already cut and sized and ready to put together. Here are some basic components of a greenhouse:

>> **Frame:** Materials for the frames vary widely. You can go with a wood frame, a hoop design using PVC or metal conduit, fiberglass, or molded plastic.

>> **Walls:** The walls can be glass, plastic, or polycarbonate panels (see-through rigid plastic). Glass is expensive, so plastic can be a good alternative. Try a double layer of plastic film to add an insulation buffer. Glass is a poor

insulator, so unless you want to heat the greenhouse during a cold winter, you typically use a glass greenhouse only in warmer months.

» **Heat source:** You can go with the simple form — just letting the sun do its thing during the day — or you can install solar-powered heating. Another heating option is to put a large compost heap inside the greenhouse. Compost generates heat as it decomposes, which can heat the interior.

» **Floor:** A greenhouse floor needs to be able to withstand water leaks and mud spillage. A gravel floor provides hassle-free drainage, but its dark, rough surface also acts as an *absorber* that captures the energy of the sunlight penetrating the space and transforms it into heat.

» **Water system:** Whether you simply use a hose or set up an automatic sprinkling system, you need some way to get water to the plants.

» **Ventilation:** You have to keep the temperature inside within the optimal growing range, not only in cooler seasons. Temperatures in a hot summer area can go over 120 degrees inside. To be sure the heat doesn't kill the plants, you need to ventilate. The air should contain enough moisture to grow plants but not so much that rot and mildew form.

TIP

For the busy homesteader, an automatic vent opener — a compact, mechanical, heat-activated device — can open windows, skylights, greenhouse vents, and so on at a temperature you select. Because they don't use electricity, you can mount them anywhere. For heavy windows and vents, simply use multiple units.

Well-designed greenhouses in cold climates can support the growth of plants all winter long, even in freezing conditions. In fact, greenhouses often need cooling means such as vents or radiant barriers to keep from getting too hot. On the other hand, greenhouses need to be sealed in order to maximize warming in the winter, so the interior air can get stagnant or too humid for comfort. The bottom line is that greenhouses need constant management and manipulation of air movement and sun exposure, not to mention the work needed to grow healthy, vigorous plants. Greenhouses are also prone to getting very dirty, so they're more commonly separated from the house.

TIP

You don't even have to have a glass structure for a greenhouse. You can use plastic hoop houses instead. They're easy to build, inexpensive, and a great way to get into this method of gardening. Like supersized versions of the grow tunnel described earlier in this chapter, walk-through hoop houses (see Figure 7-5) have become popular because of their low cost and ease of use. They have a metal semicircular shell with clear plastic pulled over it and a door on one end (or even at both ends).

They keep the air warmer than a cold frame, but they're not as warm as a conventional greenhouse. Plus, they're relatively inexpensive, starting at under $200. You can add options such as automatic vents, roll-up sides, automatic watering systems, blinds and reflectors, and so on.

For instructions on building your own walk-through hoop house, flip ahead to Book 5, Chapter 1, where you'll find a step-by-step guide.

FIGURE 7-5:
A hoop house is an inexpensive alternative to a greenhouse.

Getting Your Feet Wet with Hydroponics, Aquaponics, and Aeroponics

Some gardening techniques allow the homesteader to not only maximize their conventional growing space but also extend the season by creatively moving some crops to spots where the growing conditions can be carefully controlled. These methods may seem space-age (and are in some cases) because they don't use traditional garden beds — or even dirt!

Urban gardeners have popularized them because of their small space requirements, but many homesteaders may also find value in adding hydroponics, aquaponics, and aeroponics to their repertoire.

Hydroponics

Hydroponics, in its simplest form, is growing plants without soil. All the necessary nutrients that would come from the plants' water supply is instead supplied by a nutrient solution rather than through the soil. Growing plants hydroponically helps gardeners and farmers grow more food more rapidly in smaller areas (greenhouses, living rooms, classrooms, and rooftops, for instance) and to produce food in parts of the world where space, good soil, and/or water are limited.

You may have bought hydroponic tomatoes at the grocery store, or you may have seen the amazing hydroponic lettuce at Disney World. But even for the homesteader, it's possible to grow crops (usually in very small quantities) indoors hydroponically when conditions outside aren't conducive or ideal.

For the plants to grow successfully, the nutrient solution must contain several elements, including nitrogen, potassium, phosphorus, iron, manganese, and sulfur.

Hydroponics is an emerging niche of gardening, with entire retail stores dedicated to it. You do need special equipment and growing techniques, but you can grow any plant this way.

Aquaponics

In *aquaponics*, the nutrient solution is water containing fish excrement. Aquaponics is the integration of hydroponics and aquaculture (the cultivation of the natural produce — such as fish or shellfish — of water). Live fish are raised in a traditional fish tank. The fish excrete their waste into the surrounding water, which is used to supply nutrients to the growing plants positioned above the tank. Bacteria living in the water and on the growth medium eat the fish wastes and unlock nutrients for the plants. The plants absorb the nutrients, and the filtered water is returned to the fish tank. (For more on which kinds of fish may work best for your homestead, go to Book 4, Chapter 5.)

Aeroponics

Aeroponics refers to growing plants in an environment of mostly air. There's no soil, and the water that feeds the plants comes in the form of a mist, usually released automatically at regular intervals. A tower-oriented garden planting system (as shown in Figure 7-6) is one example of a state-of-the-art vertical aeroponic growing system.

Because of its unique technology and vertical design, the Tower Garden uses less than 10 percent of the water and land required by traditional, soil-based agriculture. The Tower is easy to assemble and maintain, and it can be placed in any relatively sunny place outside (or inside if you use grow lights). There's no soil, no weeds, and no ground pests to worry about with these systems. For more on this product, visit www.towergarden.com.

FIGURE 7-6:
A vertical
aeroponics
system.

2

Preserving the Harvest

Contents at a Glance

Chapter **1**

Canning Basics

O ver the years, thanks to busy lifestyles and the convenience of refrigeration and supermarkets, the art of canning food has declined. Other than jams and jellies, many people started thinking of canning as sort of a novelty hobby. But today, many people have a renewed interest in learning this art; they are finding that canning and preserving foods is an inexpensive and easy way to have a full pantry. For the backyard homesteader, canning is an essential skill and the very best way to make the most of what comes out of the garden.

If you're new to canning, don't be overwhelmed or scared off by the rules. This chapter walks you through easy, step-by-step instructions for the two most popular techniques, the only two approved by the United States Department of Agriculture (USDA). After you understand the basic procedures for each method, it's just a matter of concentrating on preparing your recipe.

Starting Successful Canning

Canning is the most popular preserving method used today. Don't let anyone tell you that home-canning is complicated and unsafe. It's simply not true. *Canning* is the process of applying heat to food that's sealed in a jar in order to destroy any microorganisms that can cause food spoilage. All foods contain these microorganisms. Proper canning techniques stop this spoilage by heating the food for a specific period of time and killing these unwanted microorganisms. Also, during the canning process, air is driven from the jar and a vacuum is formed as the jar cools and seals. This prevents microorganisms from entering and re-contaminating the food.

Becoming a successful canner takes time, effort, and knowledge of the rules. Follow these tips for achieving great results:

>> **Start with the freshest, best products available.** Preserving doesn't improve food quality. If you put garbage in, you get garbage out.

>> **Know the rules and techniques for your canning or preserving method before you start your work.** Don't try to learn a technique after you've started your processing.

>> **Work in short sessions to prevent fatigue and potential mistakes.** Process no more than two items in one day, and work with only one canning method at a time.

>> **Stay up to date on new or revised guidelines for your preserving method.** Beyond what you read in this chapter, you can also go to websites such as www.freshpreserving.com, created by the makers of Ball canning supplies. Here you can find tips and directions for canning just about anything.

>> **Use the correct processing method and processing time to destroy microorganisms.** The recipe will tell you what method to use, but it helps if you understand the difference between high- and low-acid foods and how the canning methods for each differ.

>> **Know the elevation you're working at.** Adjust your processing time or pressure when you're at an altitude over 1,000 feet above sea level.

>> **Put together a plan before you start your preserving session.** Read your recipe (more than once). Have the proper equipment and correct ingredients on hand to prevent last-minute shortages and inconvenient breaks (make a list of what you need and check off items as you gather them).

>> **Test your equipment.** If you're using a pressure canner or an electric dehydrator, test out the equipment to ensure everything's working properly. And always check the seals on your jars.

REMEMBER

>> **Use recipes from reliable sources or ones that you've made successfully before.** Follow your recipe to the letter. Don't substitute ingredients, adjust quantities, or make up your own food combinations. Improvisation and safe food preservation aren't compatible. This also means you can't double your recipe. If you require more than what the recipe yields, make another batch. Always use the size jars that are recommended in the recipe as well. Trying to use a larger or smaller jar may throw off the yield and final result.

Gathering Your Canning Gear

The tools that make canning and preserving easier are many of the very same tools that are in most well-stocked kitchens. When a recipe recommends a tool for canning, there's a practical reason for doing so. Using the proper tool for the job decreases the chance of a jar failing to seal or being able to harbor bacteria. It can also reduce the chance of mishaps and injuries.

But the equipment in this section is especially designed for canning, which means you'll use it during canning season but not much otherwise. Make sure you store these items in a safe, clean location. And be sure to look over every piece each time you use it to check for wear and tear.

Canning vessels

The kind of food you'll be canning determines the type of vessel you'll be using: a water-bath canner or a pressure canner.

Water-bath canner

A *water-bath canner*, also referred to as a *boiling-water canner*, is a kettle used for processing high-acid foods (primarily fruits, jams, jellies, condiments, and pickled foods). The canner consists of a large enamelware or stainless-steel pot with a tight-fitting lid and a jar rack. You'll learn how to use this piece of gear in Chapter 2 of this minibook.

Pressure canner

A *pressure canner*, sometimes referred to as a *steam-pressure canner*, is used for canning low-acid foods (primarily vegetables, meats, fish, and poultry) in an airtight container at a specific pressure. A weighted gauge or a dial gauge measures steam pressure in the canner. This ensures that the high temperature of 240 degrees is attained to safely process your food. Dive deeper into pressure canning in Chapter 3 of this minibook.

Canning tools

The tools in this section are must-haves for water-bath or pressure canning. Safety in the kitchen is number one, and the right tools for handling hot, filled jars and other large canning equipment are indispensable.

Canning Basics

Jar lifter

A *jar lifter* is one tool you don't want to be without. It's the best tool available for transferring hot canning jars into and out of your canning kettle or pressure canner. This odd-looking, rubberized, tonglike item (check out Figure 1-1) grabs the jar around the *neck* (the area just below the threaded portion at the top of the jar) without disturbing the screw band.

FIGURE 1-1:
Jar lifters.

Foam skimmer

A *foam skimmer*, shown in Figure 1-2, makes removing foam from the top of hot jelly, jam, or marmalade easy while leaving any pieces of fruit or rind in the hot liquid. (The openings in slotted spoons are too large to achieve quick and efficient foam removal.)

FIGURE 1-2:
A foam skimmer.

Home-canning jars

Over the years, many types of jars with many varieties of seals have been used for home-canning. The most commonly used jars bear the names of Ball and Kerr and are commonly referred to as Mason jars. They use a two-piece cap to produce a vacuum seal in the jar after heat processing.

REMEMBER

To ensure safe home-canning today, use only jars approved for home-canning and made from tempered glass. *Tempering* is a treatment process for glass that allows the jars to withstand the high heat (212 degrees) of a water-bath canner, as well as the high temperature (240 degrees) of a pressure canner, without breaking.

Home-canning jars come in many sizes: 4-ounce, half-pint, 12-ounce, 1-pint, and 1-quart (see Figure 1-3). They offer two widths of openings: regular-mouth (about 2½ inches in diameter) and wide-mouth (about 3⅛ inches in diameter). Regular-mouth jars are used more frequently for jelly, jam, relish, or any other cooked food. Wide-mouth jars are mainly used for canning vegetables and pickles and meats, because it's easier to get the large pieces into the wide opening.

FIGURE 1-3:
Varieties of canning jars: wide-mouth, regular-mouth, and jelly jars.

Two-piece caps

Two-piece caps consist of a lid and a metal screw band (see Figure 1-4). They're made specifically for use with modern-day home-canning jars.

>> **Lids:** The underside edge of the lid has a rubberlike sealing compound that softens when it's heated. This compound adheres to a clean jar rim and creates an airtight seal after the heat-processing period. Traditional lids aren't reusable, but some modern styles are. Check out the Tattler brand at https://reusablecanninglids.com/

>> **Screw bands:** The screw band holds the lid in place during the processing period and secures it in place when storing an opened jar in the refrigerator. After verifying that your cooled jars have successfully sealed, you remove the screw band before you store the canned food. The screw bands may be used many times as long as there are no signs of corrosion or rust and they aren't bent or dented.

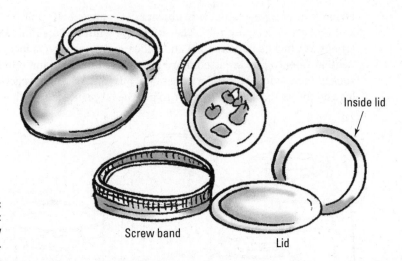

Inside lid

FIGURE 1-4:
Two-piece caps: lids and screw bands.

Screw band

Lid

MASON JARS

If the most commonly used glass home-canning jars bear the names of Ball and Kerr, why do we call them Mason jars? The Mason jar is named for its creator, James Landis Mason. He designed and patented a unique glass jar that uses a screw-top lid to create an airtight seal for food. This easy-to-seal jar replaced the large stoneware vessels that had previously been used for food storage.

The tapered jars we use today were introduced after World War II. They use a two-piece cap consisting of a lid and a metal screw band that fits the threaded jar top. Today, all home-canning jars are generically referred to as Mason jars. Thank you, Mr. Mason, for making the task of home-canning easy with the use of screw-top closures.

Lid wand

A *lid wand* (see Figure 1-5) has a magnet on one end of a heat-resistant stick. With it, you can take a lid from hot water and place it on the filled-jar rim without touching the lid or disturbing the sealing compound.

TIP

Place your lids top to top and underside to underside to prevent them from sticking together in your pan of hot water. If they do stick together, dip them into a bowl of cold water to release the suction. Reheat them in the hot water for a few seconds before using them. Also offset the lids as you place them in the water. This keeps them fanned out and easier to pick up singly.

FIGURE 1-5:
A lid wand.

Thin plastic spatula

A thin, flexible plastic spatula is the right tool for releasing air bubbles between pieces of food in your filled jars (check out Figure 1-6). Buy a package of chopsticks for an inexpensive alternative.

FIGURE 1-6:
A thin plastic
spatula for
releasing air
bubbles.

WARNING

Don't use a metal item or a larger object for this job because it may damage your food and crack or break your hot jar.

Canning Basics

Wide-mouth canning funnel

A *wide-mouth funnel* (see Figure 1-7) fits into the inside edge of a regular-mouth or a wide-mouth canning jar and lets you quickly and neatly fill your jars. This is an essential tool for canning.

Jelly bag or strainer

A *jelly bag* is made for extracting juice from cooked fruit for making jelly. These bags aren't expensive, but if you'd rather not purchase one, make your own using a metal strainer lined with cheesecloth. Use a strainer that hangs on the edge of your pot or mixing bowl and doesn't touch the liquid. Go to the end of this chapter for instructions on making jelly.

Stoneware crocks

Stoneware crocks are available in sizes from 1 gallon to 5 gallons, usually without lids. They're nonreactive and are used for making pickles and olives. Make sure you use only crocks that are glazed on the interior and certified free of lead and *cadmium*, a form of zinc ore used in pigments or dyes.

WARNING

Be wary of using secondhand stoneware crocks. These crocks were often made with leaded glaze that will leach into your foodstuff. Because you do not often know the history of used items, this is an item that is best purchased new and not secondhand.

Putting Safety First

Preventing food spoilage is the key to safe canning. Over the years, home-canning has become safer and better. Scientists have standardized processing methods, and home-canners know more about using these methods. When you follow up-to-date guidelines exactly, you'll experience little concern about the quality and safety of your home-canned and -preserved foods. Here are a few things to keep in mind as you begin your canning career.

Packing your jars with care

How you fill the canning jars is important:

>> **Don't overpack foods.** Trying to cram too much food into a jar may result in under-processing because the heat can't evenly penetrate the food.

>> **Make sure your jars have the proper headspace.** *Headspace* is the air space between the inside of the lid and the top of your food or liquid in your jar or container (see Figure 1-8). Proper headspace is important to the safety of your preserved food because of the expansion that occurs as your jars are processed or your food freezes.

>> **Make sure you release the air bubbles from the jar before sealing the lid.** No matter how carefully you pack and fill your jars, you'll always have some hidden bubbles.

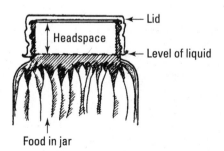

FIGURE 1-8: Headspace.

The all-important headspace

When you're canning food, too little headspace in your canning jars restricts your food from expanding as it boils. Inadequate space for the expanding food may force some of it out of the jar and under the lid, leaving particles of food between the seal and the jar rim. If this occurs, your jar won't produce a vacuum seal.

Leaving too much headspace may cause discoloration in the top portion of your food. Excess headspace can keep your jar from producing a vacuum seal if the processing time isn't long enough to exhaust the excess air in the jar.

Always use the headspace stated in your recipe. If your recipe doesn't give you a headspace allowance, use these guidelines:

>> For juice, jam, jelly, pickles, relish, chutney, sauces, and condiments, leave headspace of ¼ inch.

>> For high-acid foods (fruits and tomatoes), leave headspace of ½ inch.

>> For low-acid foods (vegetables, meats, fish, and poultry), leave headspace of 1 inch.

REMEMBER

Headspace is also important when you're freezing food because frozen food expands during the freezing process. If you fail to leave the proper headspace in your freezer container, the lid may be forced off the container, or the container may crack or break. When your frozen food comes in direct contact with the air in your freezer, the quality of your food deteriorates and the food develops freezer burn (go to Chapter 5 of this minibook for more on freezing food). On the other hand, too much air space allows excess air in your container. Even though your food doesn't come in direct contact with the air in the freezer, the excess space in the top of the container develops ice crystals. When your food thaws, the excess liquid reduces the food's quality.

TIP

If you don't trust yourself to eyeball the headspace, use a small plastic ruler (about 6 inches long) to measure the correct headspace in the jar.

Releasing air bubbles from your jars

The most important thing to do when you're filling your jars is to release trapped air bubbles between the food pieces. This may seem unimportant, but air bubbles can play havoc with your final product:

>> **Jar seals:** Too much air in the jar from trapped air bubbles produces excessive pressure in the jar during processing. The pressure in the jar is greater than the pressure outside the jar during cooling. This imbalance interferes with the sealing process.

>> **Liquid levels:** Air bubbles take up space. When there's trapped air between your food pieces before sealing the jars, the liquid level in the jar drops when the food is heated. (For releasing air bubbles, see Figure 1-9.) In addition, floating and discolored food results from packing your food without the proper amount of liquid in the jars. Snuggly packed food eliminates air and allows enough liquid to completely cover the food with proper headspace (refer to Figure 1-8).

REMEMBER

Never skip the step of releasing air bubbles.

Use a nonmetallic spatula to press back gently on the contents. Go all the way around the jar.

FIGURE 1-9:
Releasing air bubbles from your filled jars.

Knowing the acidity level of your food

Knowing the acidity level of the food you're processing is important because the *pH*, the measure of acidity, determines which canning method you use: water–bath or pressure canning. For canning purposes, food is divided into two categories based on the amount of acid the food registers:

>> **High-acid** foods include fruits and pickled foods. Foods in this group have a pH of 4.6 or lower. Processing them in a water-bath canner destroys harmful microorganisms.

Tomatoes are considered a low-high acid food. With all of the new varieties of tomatoes, it is now recommended that the home canner add an acid to the canning process, to ensure that the proper acidity is reached every time.

» **Low-acid** foods, primarily vegetables, meat, poultry, and fish, contain little natural acid. Their pH level is higher than 4.6. Process these foods in a pressure canner, which superheats your food and destroys the more heat-resistant bacteria, such as botulism.

TIP

If you want to feel as though you're back in science class all over again, you can buy litmus paper at teacher- or scientific-supply stores and test the acidity level of your food yourself. Also referred to as pH paper, litmus paper is an acid-sensitive paper that measures the acid in food. When you insert a strip of pH paper into your prepared food, the paper changes color. You then compare the wet strip to the pH chart of colors that accompanies the litmus paper.

Adjusting your altitude

Properly processing your home-canned foods destroys microorganisms. Knowing your altitude is important because the boiling point of water and pressure in a pressure canner changes at altitudes over 1,000 feet above sea level. This occurs because the air is thinner at higher elevations. With less air resistance, water boils at a temperature below 212 degrees.

To produce food free from microorganisms at higher elevations, adjust your processing time and pressure to compensate for your altitude. Use the altitude adjustment charts in the sections for water–bath canning and pressure canning. These adjustments ensure that your food is heated to the correct temperature for destroying microorganisms.

Detecting spoiled foods

No one can't promise you that your home-canned foods will always be free from spoilage, but you can rest assured that your chances for spoiled food are greatly reduced when you follow the precise guidelines for each preserving method. If you suspect, for any reason, that your food is spoiled or just isn't right, don't taste it. Also, just because your food doesn't look spoiled, doesn't mean that it's not.

The best way to detect food spoilage is by visually examining your jars. Review the following checklist. If you can answer "true" for each of the following statements, your food should be safe for eating:

» The food in the jar is covered with liquid, is fully packed, and has maintained the proper headspace.

» The food in the jar is free from moving air bubbles.

» The jars have good, tight seals.

» The food has maintained a uniform color.

» The food isn't broken or mushy.

» The liquid in the jar is clear, not cloudy, and free of sediment.

After your food has passed the previous checklist, examine your jars more closely. If you discover any spoilage during any step of this process, don't continue your search, but properly dispose of your product.

1. **Hold the jar at eye level.**

2. **Turn and rotate the jar, looking for any seepage or oozing from under the lid that indicates a broken seal.**

3. **Examine the food surface for any streaks of dried food originating at the top of the jar.**

4. **Check the contents for any rising air bubbles or unnatural color.**

   The food and liquid should be clear, not cloudy.

5. **Open the jar.**

   There shouldn't be any spurting liquid.

6. **Smell the contents of the jar.**

   Take note of any unnatural or unusual odors.

7. **Look for any cottonlike growth, usually white, blue, black, or green, on the top of your food surface or on the underside of the lid.**

As mentioned, there are two different methods for canning food, with equipment specific to each. The method you use will depend on the type of food you're preserving. See Chapters 2 and 3 of this minibook to learn the ins and outs of water-bath canning and pressure canning, respectively.

Chapter **2**

Water-Bath Canning

With water-bath canning, you essentially use a special kettle to boil filled jars for a certain amount of time. Common foods for water-bath canning include fruits and tomatoes, as well as jams, jellies, marmalades, chutneys, relishes, pickled vegetables, and other condiments.

You're probably wondering whether water-bath canning is safe for canning food at home. Rest assured: The answer is a most definite "Yes!" — provided that you follow the instructions and guidelines for safe canning.

In this chapter, you discover which foods are safely processed in a water-bath canner and get step-by-step instructions for completing the canning process. In no time, you'll be turning out sparkling jars full of homemade delicacies to dazzle and satisfy your family and friends. A sampling of recipes in included as well to get you started on your water-bath canning adventures.

Water-Bath Canning in a Nutshell

Water-bath canning, sometimes referred to as the *boiling-water method,* is the simplest and easiest method for preserving high-acid food. That means most fruit, as well as tomatoes, pickled vegetables, condiments, and sauces.

To water-bath can, you place your prepared jars in a *water-bath canner* (a kettle especially designed for this canning), bring the water to a boil, and then maintain that boil for a certain number of minutes as determined by the type of food and the size of the jar. Keeping the water boiling in your jar-filled kettle throughout the processing period maintains a water temperature of 212 degrees. This constant temperature is critical for destroying mold, yeast, enzymes, and bacteria that occur in high-acid foods.

WARNING

Water-bath canning and pressure-canning methods aren't interchangeable because the temperature of a water bath reaches only 212 degrees while the temperature of a pressure canner reaches 240 degrees, the temperature necessary to safely process low-acid foods. For more on pressure canning, go to Chapter 3 of this minibook.

Gearing Up for Water-Bath Canning

Just as you wouldn't alter the ingredients in a recipe or skip a step in the canning process, you don't want to use the wrong equipment when you're home-canning. This equipment allows you to handle and process your filled jars safely.

Water-bath canning kettles cost anywhere from $25 to $45. In some instances, you may purchase a "starter kit" that includes the canning kettle, the jar rack, a jar lifter, a wide-mouth funnel, and jars for about $50 to $60.

Following is a list of the equipment you must have on hand, no exceptions or substitutions, for safe and successful water-bath canning:

>> **A water-bath canner:** The water-bath canner consists of a large kettle, usually made of porcelain-coated steel or aluminum, that holds a maximum of 21 to 22 quarts of water, has a fitted lid, and uses a rack (see the next item) to hold the jars (see Figure 2-1). Do not substitute a large stock pot for a water-bath canner. It is important for the jars to be sitting off the bottom of the canner, and racks that fit this purpose are included in your canner kit.

TECHNICAL STUFF

Although aluminum is a *reactive metal* (a metal that transfers flavor to food coming in direct contact with it), it's permitted for a water-bath canner because your sealed jar protects the food from directly touching the aluminum.

>> **A jar rack:** The jar rack for a water-bath canner is usually made of stainless steel and rests on the bottom of your canning kettle. It keeps your jars from touching the bottom of the kettle, or each other, while holding the filled jars upright during the water-bath processing period. The rack has lifting handles for hanging it on the inside edge of your canning kettle (refer to Figure 2-1), allowing you to safely transfer your filled jars into and out of your kettle.

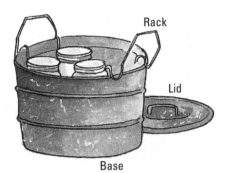

FIGURE 2-1:
A water-bath canning kettle with the rack hanging on the edge of the kettle.

Labels on figure: Rack, Lid, Base

>> **Canning jars:** Canning jars are the only jars recommended for home-canning. Use the jar size recommended in your recipe. For more on canning jars, refer to Chapter 1 of this minibook.

>> **Two-piece caps (lids and screw bands):** These lids and screw bands, explained in Chapter 1 of this minibook, create a vacuum seal after the water-bath processing period, preserving the contents of the jar for use at a later time. This seal protects your food from the reentry of microorganisms.

WARNING

The older-style rubber rings are no longer recommended. Although they are sometimes still available secondhand, the seal is no longer dependable enough to result in a safe product. You can find these rubber rings in some specialty canning stores; however, due to their novelty, they are expensive and sold in small quantities. Reserve this type of canning jar and kitschy design for your fun food gifts, not canning for a family's pantry.

STEAM CANNING: THE HOT NEW THING

A relatively new wrinkle to food preserving is the acceptance of *steam canning* as a safe variant of the water-bath method. In steam canning, filled jars are processed in an enclosed pot (specifically designed for the purpose) with just a bit of boiling water, using steam alone to create an environment that reaches 212 degrees. Steam canners are inexpensive and use far less water than traditional water-bath canners, meaning they're also faster. Only high-acid foods approved for water-bath canning can be processed using the steam method, and any food that requires more than 45 minutes to process should be saved for a conventional water-bath canner. This guideline ensures that the water does not boil off completely, although some steam canner models can run longer than that without going dry. If you are interested in steam canning, buy a good quality steam canner (Victorio makes several popular models), follow all of the manufacturer's directions, and use water-bath recipes from trusted sources.

CAN I WATER-BATH CAN IN MY INSTANT POT?

The programmable pressure cooker (like the ubiquitous Instant Pot) has become an indispensable fixture on kitchen countertops everywhere. It cooks quickly, it can sear and sauté foods, it can operate as a slow cooker, it steams rice, it can keep foods warm, it even has a one-button setting for making porridge (for those families of bears in a rush to leave their just-right houses, presumably).

But can the Instant Pot be used for water-bath canning? Well. . . maybe. Some manufacturers say it can be done, but with a few key caveats. For one, you must use a trivet to elevate the jars off the bottom of the pot insert to reduce the risk of breakage. This then limits the size of jars you can use, since the tops cannot touch the underside of the Instant Pot lid. Remember, too, that your water must stay at a rolling boil for the entire operation, and the Instant Pot's lid prevents you from seeing into it while the lid is on. You can set it for a certain amount of time and hope that the water inside is boiling, but is it? And if you leave the lid off, you might as well just use a regular pot on the stove.

Long story short, although plenty of bloggers add water-bath canning to the long list of ways they love to use their IP, you may decide the smarter move is to play it safe and stick with more proven methods and time-tested equipment.

Water-Bath Canning Step-by-Step

The following section guides you through the step-by-step process for creating delicious, high-quality, homemade treats for your family and friends.

REMEMBER

Always practice proper kitchen sanitation and cleanliness, carefully handle your food, and follow your recipe to the letter. Don't alter your recipe or skip any processing step.

Step 1: Getting your equipment ready

The first thing you do when canning is to inspect your equipment and get everything ready so that when you're done preparing the food (Step 2 in the canning process), you can fill your jars immediately.

Inspect your jars, lids, and screw bands

Always review the manufacturer's instructions for readying your jars, lids, and screw bands. Then inspect your jars, lids, and screw bands for any defects as follows:

>> **Jars:** Check the jar edges for any nicks, chips, or cracks in the glass, discarding any jars with these defects. If you're reusing jars, clean any stains or food residue from them and then recheck them for any defects.

>> **Screw bands:** Make sure the bands aren't warped, corroded, or rusted. Test the roundness of the band by screwing it onto a jar. If it tightens down smoothly without resistance, it's useable. Discard any bands that are defective or *out of round* (bent or not completely round).

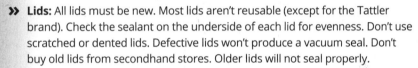

You can reuse screw bands over and over, as long as they're in good condition. And because you remove them after your jars have cooled, you don't need as many bands as jars.

>> **Lids:** All lids must be new. Most lids aren't reusable (except for the Tattler brand). Check the sealant on the underside of each lid for evenness. Don't use scratched or dented lids. Defective lids won't produce a vacuum seal. Don't buy old lids from secondhand stores. Older lids will not seal properly.

REMEMBER

Wash your jars, lids, and screw bands

After examining the jars for nicks or chips, the screw bands for proper fit and corrosion, and the new lids for imperfections and scratches, wash everything in warm, soapy water, rinsing the items well and removing any soap residue. Discard any damaged or imperfect items.

Get the kettle water warming

Fill your canning kettle one-half to two-thirds full of water and begin heating the water to simmering. Remember that the water level will rise considerably as you add the filled jars. Be sure to not overfill at this point.

Heat extra water in a teakettle or saucepan as a reserve. You want to make sure that the jars are covered with at least 1 to 2 inches of water. By adding preheated water, you don't have to wait for the entire canner to reheat before continuing.

TIP

Keep your equipment and jars hot while you wait to fill them

While you're waiting to fill your jars, submerge the jars and lids in hot, not boiling, water, and keep your screw bands clean and handy as follows:

- » **Jars:** Submerge them in hot water in your kettle for a minimum of 10 minutes. Keep them there until you're ready to fill them.

- » **Lids:** Submerge them in hot, not boiling, water in a saucepan. Keeping them separate from your jars protects the lid sealant.

- » **Screw bands:** These don't need to be kept hot, but they do need to be clean. Place them where you'll be filling your jars.

Step 2: Readying your food

Always use food of the highest quality when you're canning. If you settle for less than the best, your final product won't have the quality you're looking for. Carefully sort through your food, discarding any bruised pieces or pieces you wouldn't eat in the raw state.

Follow the instructions in your recipe for preparing your food, such as removing the skin or peel or cutting it into pieces.

Similarly, prepare your food exactly as instructed in your recipe. Don't make any adjustments in ingredients or quantities of ingredients. Any alteration may change the acidity of the product, requiring pressure canning (see the next section) instead of water-bath canning to kill microorganisms.

REMEMBER

If your recipe doesn't tell you which processing method (water-bath canning or pressure canning) is appropriate for your food, don't guess. Instead, use litmus paper to test the pH level of your food (see the previous section). If your food has a pH of 4.6 or lower, use the water-bath canning method; if it has a pH of 4.7 or higher, use the pressure-canning method. Most fruits are naturally high in acid; pickled vegetables also fall into this category, making them safe for water-bath canning. You may change the acid level in low-acid foods by adding an acid, such as vinegar, lemon juice, or *citric acid,* a white powder extracted from the juice of acidic fruits such as lemons, limes, or pineapples. Some examples of altered low-acid foods are pickles made from cucumbers, relish made from zucchini or summer squash, and green beans flavored with dill. Today, tomatoes tend to fall into this category. They can be water-bath canned, but for safety's sake you add a form of acid to them.

REMEMBER

If your recipe states something specifically, it's there for a reason. If you don't follow the recipe instructions to the letter, your final results won't be what the recipe intended.

Step 3: Filling your jars

Add your prepared food (cooked or raw) and hot liquid to your prepared jars as soon as they're ready. Follow these steps:

1. **Transfer your prepared food into the hot jars, adding hot liquid or syrup if your recipe calls for it, and being sure to leave the proper headspace.**

   Use a wide-mouth funnel and a ladle for quickly filling your jars. You'll eliminate a lot of spilling and have less to clean from your jar rims. It also helps cleanup and prevents slipping if you place your jars on a clean kitchen towel before filling.

2. **Release any air bubbles with a nonmetallic spatula or a tool to free air bubbles. Add more prepared food or liquid to the jar after releasing the air bubbles to maintain the recommended headspace.**

   REMEMBER

   Before applying the two-piece caps, always release air bubbles and leave the headspace specified in your recipe. These steps are critical for creating a vacuum seal and preserving your food.

3. **Wipe the jar rims with a clean, damp cloth.**

   If there's one speck of food on the jar rim, the sealant on the lid edge won't make contact with the jar rim and your jar won't seal.

4. **Place a hot lid onto each jar rim, sealant side touching the jar rim, and hand-tighten the screw band.**

   Don't overtighten because air needs to escape during the sealing process.

Step 4: Processing your filled jars

With your jars filled, you're ready to begin processing. Follow these steps:

1. **Place the jar rack in your canning kettle, suspending it with the handles on the inside edge of the kettle.**

2. **Place the filled jars in the jar rack, making sure they're standing upright and not touching each other.**

   Although the size of your kettle seems large, don't be tempted to pack your canner with jars. Place only as many jars as will comfortably fit yet still allow water to move freely between them. And always process jars in a single layer in the jar rack.

Never process half-pint or pint jars with quart jars because the larger amount of food in quart jars requires a longer processing time to kill any bacteria and microorganisms. If your recipe calls for the same processing times for half-pint and pint jars, you may process those two sizes together.

3. **Unhook the jar rack from the edge of the kettle, carefully lowering it into the hot water, and add water if necessary.**

Air bubbles coming from the jars are normal. If your jars aren't covered by at least 1 inch of water, add boiling water from your reserve. Be careful to pour this hot water between the jars, instead of directly on top of them, to prevent splashing yourself with hot water.

Make sure the tops of the submerged jars are covered with 1 to 2 inches of hot water. Add additional water from your reserve teakettle or saucepan to achieve this level.

4. **Cover the kettle and heat the water to a full, rolling boil, reducing the heat and maintaining a gentle, rolling boil for the amount of time indicated in the recipe.**

Start your processing time after the water boils. Maintain a boil for the entire processing period.

If you live at an altitude above 1,000 feet above sea level, you need to adjust your processing time. Check out "Adjusting Your Processing Times at High Altitudes" at the end of this section for details.

Step 5: Removing your filled jars and testing the seals

After you complete the processing time, immediately remove your jars from the boiling water with a jar lifter and place them on clean, dry, kitchen or paper towels away from drafts, with 1 or 2 inches of space between the jars — don't attempt to adjust the bands or check the seals — and allow them to cool completely. The cooling period may take 12 to 24 hours. Do not try to hurry this process by cooling the jars in any way. This may result in unsealed jars or cracked glass.

After your jars have completely cooled, test your seals by pushing on the center of the lid (see Figure 2-2). If the lid feels solid and doesn't indent, you have a successful vacuum seal. If the lid depresses in the center and makes a popping noise when you apply pressure, the jar isn't sealed. Immediately refrigerate unsealed jars, using the contents within two weeks or as stated in your recipe.

Test the seal by depressing the center of the lid of the completely cooled jar

FIGURE 2-2:
Testing your jar seal.

REPROCESSING UNSEALED JARS

Jars may not seal for several reasons: You may have miscalculated the processing time, pieces of food may not have been cleaned from the jar rim, you may have left an improper amount of headspace, or the sealant on the lids may have been defective. The safest and easiest method for treating processed jars that didn't seal is to refrigerate the jar immediately and use the product within two weeks.

If you want to reprocess jars that didn't seal, you can do that. But keep in mind that reprocessing your food takes almost as much time as making the recipe from the beginning. The only time to consider reprocessing jars is if every jar in the kettle doesn't seal.

To reprocess unsealed jars, follow these steps:

1. Remove the lid and discard it.

2. Check the edge of the jar for damage.

   If the jar is damaged, discard the food in case a broken piece of glass fell into the food.

3. Discard any damaged jars.

4. Reheat the food.

5. Follow the step-by-step instructions in this chapter for filling your jars, releasing air bubbles, and processing your sterilized, filled jars.

6. Reprocess the filled jars for the recommended time for your recipe.

7. Check the seal after your jars have completely cooled.

Step 6: Storing your canned food

After you've tested the seal and know that it's good (see the preceding section), it's time to store your canned food. To do that, follow these steps:

1. **Remove the screw bands from your sealed jars.**

2. **Wash the sealed jars and the screw bands in hot, soapy water.**

   This removes any residue from the jars and screw bands.

3. **Label your filled jars, including the date processed.**

4. **Store your jars, without the screw bands, in a cool, dark, dry place.**

Adjusting Your Processing Times at High Altitudes

When you're canning at an altitude higher than 1,000 feet above sea level, you need to adjust your processing time (see Table 2-1). Because the air is thinner at higher altitudes, water boils below 212 degrees. As a result, you need to process your food for a longer period of time to kill any microorganisms that can make your food unsafe.

If you live higher than 1,000 feet above sea level, follow these guidelines:

>> **For processing times of less than 20 minutes:** Add 1 additional minute for each additional 1,000 feet of altitude.

>> **For processing times of more than 20 minutes:** Add 2 additional minutes for each 1,000 feet of altitude.

TIP

If you don't know the elevation of your city, check with your city offices, your public library, or your state or county cooperative extension service listed in your local telephone directory. Or check out http://national4-hheadquarters.gov/extension/index.html. Just enter your city and state in the box at the bottom of the page, click Submit, and scroll down to find the elevation of your city.

TABLE 2-1

High-Altitude Processing Times for Water-Bath Canning

Altitude (in feet)	For Processing Times Less Than 20 Minutes	For Processing Times Greater Than 20 Minutes, Add This
1,001–1,999	Add 1 minute	Add 2 minutes
2,000–2,999	Add 2 minutes	Add 4 minutes
3,000–3,999	Add 3 minutes	Add 6 minutes
4,000–4,999	Add 4 minutes	Add 8 minutes
5,000–5,999	Add 5 minutes	Add 10 minutes
6,000–6,999	Add 6 minutes	Add 12 minutes
7,000–7,999	Add 7 minutes	Add 14 minutes
8,000–8,999	Add 8 minutes	Add 16 minutes
9,000–9,999	Add 9 minutes	Add 18 minutes
Over 10,000	Add 10 minutes	Add 20 minutes

Water-Bath Canning

Canning Fresh Fruit (Yes, That Includes Tomatoes)

Canning fresh fruit is a great way to preserve large quantities of ripe fruit in a short period of time. When selecting your fruit, think fresh, fresh, fresh! The best fruit for canning is freshly picked, ripe fruit. If you don't grow your own fruit, maybe you have a homesteading friend who would share hers with you or trade for something you grow. Some growers offer a "pick your own" option in their growing area for a fee.

Fruit from your supermarket isn't the best choice because it's often picked before it's fully ripened in order to compensate for the time it takes to get the fruit from the field to the store shelf. Don't boycott your supermarket, just be finicky when selecting your fruit for canning.

The sooner you process your picked fruit, the better the texture and flavor of your final product. Your fruit can wait a few hours or overnight before you process it, but be sure to refrigerate it until you're ready.

REMEMBER

Almost all fresh fruits can well with these exceptions: bananas, lemons, limes, melons, persimmons, and strawberries.

Identifying the proper degree of ripeness

How do you know if your fruit is ripe? *Ripe* fruit is defined as being fully developed, or mature, and ready for eating. If you grow your own fruit, you can check its development and maturity daily.

To check the fruit's ripeness

» **Hold the fruit in the palm of your hand and apply gentle pressure with your thumb and fingers.** The fruit should be firm to the touch. If there's an impression in the fruit that doesn't bounce back, the fruit is overripe. If it's hard as a rock, it's underripe. Neither should be canned. If you're picking your fruit for canning, you can perform the same test, with a slight difference: Do it while the fruit's still attached to the tree.

» **Smell the fruit.** Ripe fruit has a rich, full fruit aroma. A peach should smell like a peach; an apple should smell like an apple. The fragrance should be strong enough to entice you to devour the fruit on the spot.

REMEMBER

Always use fruit picked directly from the bush or tree. Fruit collected from the ground (referred to as *dropped fruit* or *ground fruit*) is an indication that the fruit is overripe. Don't use it for canning.

Deterring discoloration

There's probably nothing more unattractive than a piece of perfectly ripe cut fruit that's *oxidized* or *discolored*, dark or brown. Discoloration primarily occurs in apples, apricots, nectarines, peaches, and pears but may occur in other fruits.

You can protect your fruit from oxidation by slicing it directly into one of the following *antioxidant solutions*, a liquid to keep your fruit from darkening:

» **An ascorbic acid or citric solution:** Make a solution with 1 teaspoon of lemon or lime juice in 1 cup of cold water, or use a commercial product, such as Ever-Fresh or Fruit-Fresh, available in most supermarkets. When using one of these products, follow the instructions on the container.

Ascorbic acid or citric acid is simply vitamin C. It doesn't change the fruit flavor. It's sold in powder form and is usually found in drugstores.

» **Vinegar, salt, and water:** Make this solution with 2 tablespoons of vinegar (5 percent acidity), 2 tablespoons of salt (pickling or kosher), and 1 gallon of cold water. Don't leave your fruit in this solution longer than 20 minutes because the solution extracts nutrients from your fruit and changes its flavor.

After its dip in your antioxidant solution, you just rinse and drain your fruit before packing it into your prepared jars.

Raw pack and hot pack

Raw pack and *hot pack* refer to two methods of getting the product into the jars. Generally, both methods can be used for either water-bath canning or pressure canning (covered in Chapter 3 of this minibook). Whether you use one or the other is determined by the texture of the food and its tendency (or not) to not fall apart from a lot of cooking. Whether you raw-pack or hot-pack also affects the processing times of the foods. With a few exceptions, most fresh fruits may be packed raw or hot. Always start with clean, ripe fruit and follow your recipe instructions.

» **Raw pack:** A raw pack is the preferred method for fruits that become delicate after cooking, such as peaches and nectarines. This method is what it says: packing raw fruit into hot jars.

» **Hot pack:** Hot packing heats your fruit in a hot liquid before packing it into your prepared jars. The advantages of hot packing over raw packing include fitting more fruit into the jars because the fruit's softer and more pliable, using fewer jars because you can fit more fruit into the jars, and spending less time waiting for the water in your kettle to boil because the filled jars are hot in the middle.

Lining your jars with liquid

You always add liquid when canning fresh fruit. Your options are boiling water, sugar syrup, or fruit juice. Determining which liquid you use is up to you, but consider the final use for your canned fruit. For instance, if you're using your canned berries in a fruit cobbler, boiling water may be the better choice because you'll add sugar to the cobbler. If you'll be eating your canned fruit out of the jar, use a sugar syrup or fruit juice.

REMEMBER

After adding the hot liquid to your filled jars, you release any trapped air bubbles in the jar. If the headspace drops after releasing the air bubbles, add more liquid to maintain the proper headspace (refer to Chapter 1 of this minibook for information about headspace). If the fruit level drops, you need to add fruit.

Sugar syrups

Sugar syrup is simply a mixture of sugar and water. It adds flavor to your canned fruit, preserves its color, and produces a smooth, firm texture. Other sweeteners, such as honey, may be added in addition to or without the sugar.

SUGAR SYRUP RECIPE ALTERNATIVES

Although syrup of sugar and water is the most common liquid used when canning fresh fruit, you may use honey in place of or in addition to granulated sugar. Use a mild-flavored honey that won't detract from the natural flavor of your fruit. Here are some suggestions:

Type of Syrup	Sugar	Honey	Water	Syrup Yield
Light	1 cup	1 cup	4 cups	5½ cups
Light	None	1 cup	3 cups	4 cups
Medium	2 cups	1 cup	4 cups	6 cups
Medium	None	2 cups	2 cups	4 cups

Combine the syrup ingredients in a saucepan over medium heat, stirring the syrup to dissolve the sugar and/or the honey. After the liquid boils, keep it hot or refrigerate it up to two days. If you refrigerate your syrup, reheat it to a boil before adding it to your filled jars.

Remember: Honey and canned goods made with honey should never be fed to children under one year of age due to the danger of infant botulism.

Use these guidelines for making your sugar–syrup choice:

>> **Super-light syrup:** This syrup adds the least number of calories. The sweetness level is the closest to the natural sugar level in most fruits.

>> **Extra-light syrup:** Use this syrup for a sweet fruit, such as figs.

>> **Light syrup:** This is best with sweet apples and berries.

>> **Medium syrup:** This syrup complements tart apples, apricots, nectarines, peaches, and pears.

>> **Heavy syrup:** Use this with sour fruit, such as grapefruit.

Table 2-2 offers you five concentrations of sugar syrup. Allow ½ to ¾ cup of liquid for each filled pint jar and 1½ cups of liquid for each filled quart jar of fruit. Bring your syrup ingredients to a boil in a saucepan over high heat; stir to dissolve the sugar.

TIP

Always prepare your hot liquid before you prepare your fruit. The liquid should be waiting for you; you shouldn't be waiting for your liquid to boil.

TABLE 2-2

Sugar Syrup Concentrations

Syrup Strength	Granulated Sugar	Water	Approximate Yield
Super-light	¼ cup	5¾ cups	6 cups
Extra-light	1¼ cups	5½ cups	6 cups
Light	2¼ cups	5¼ cups	6½ cups
Medium	3¼ cups	5 cups	7 cups
Heavy	4¼ cups	4¼ cups	7 cups

Water or fruit juice

Packing fresh fruit in boiling water or fruit juice produces fruit with a soft texture. Two good choices for fruit juices are unsweetened pineapple juice or white grape juice. Use water you like to drink, without minerals and not the sparkling variety.

REMEMBER

Always use the hot-pack method (see the "Raw pack and hot pack" section, earlier in this chapter) when using water or unsweetened fruit juice for your canning liquid.

Fresh Fruit Canning Recipes

This section features foods that are commonly grown in home gardens. The quantity guide for each fruit fills a 1-quart jar. If you're using pint jars, cut the quantity in half.

The recipes use the water-bath canning method. For detailed instructions on water-bath canning, filling and processing your jars, and releasing air bubbles, refer to the step-by-step guidelines earlier in this chapter. And for a more extensive list of fruits, download the *Complete Guide to Home Canning and Preserving*, Revised 2015, by the United States Department of Agriculture at www.healthycanning.com/wp-content/uploads/USDA-Complete-Guide-to-Home-Canning-2015-revision.pdf.

Apples

Choose apples suitable for eating or making pies. Prep is easy: Just peel and core the apples and then cut them into slices or quarters. To prevent discoloration, treat the fruit with an antioxidant (refer to "Deterring discoloration," earlier in this chapter).

Apricots, nectarines, and peaches

Peaches are a wonderful fruit, and by canning them yourself you can save a lot of money. Use a light syrup so that you can enjoy the full flavor of the peach. Trust us: Home-canned peaches are much nicer than the heavy sweetness you find in store-canned varieties.

Nectarines and apricots are just as tasty as peaches and have the benefit of not needing to be peeled, making them even easier to can. For a quick guide to peeling fruit, see Figure 2-3.

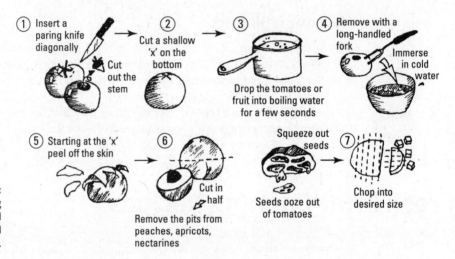

① Insert a paring knife diagonally Cut out the stem

② Cut a shallow 'x' on the bottom

③ Drop the tomatoes or fruit into boiling water for a few seconds

④ Remove with a long-handled fork Immerse in cold water

⑤ Starting at the 'x' peel off the skin

⑥ Cut in half Remove the pits from peaches, apricots, nectarines

Squeeze out seeds Seeds ooze out of tomatoes

⑦ Chop into desired size

FIGURE 2-3: Peeling soft-skinned fruit and tomatoes.

TIP

Apricots make a sunny-flavored addition to the winter meals. They make a great substitute for apples in an apple crisp recipe, too — you'll love the results!

Berries (except strawberries)

Canned berries have so many uses! You can use them to make smoothies or pies and as a sweet addition to your oatmeal. If your pantry is like ours, your berries will be the first things used up.

For canning, you want perfect, not soft or mushy, berries. Leave them whole. Wash and drain the berries (handling them as little as possible); remove any stems or hulls.

REMEMBER

Strawberries don't can well. During the processing, they turn mushy and lose their taste and red color. They do, however, freeze very well. See Chapter 5 of this minibook for complete instructions.

Depending on the type of berry, you'll use either the raw or hot pack method:

» **Raw pack:** Raw packing is best for soft berries, such as blackberries, boysenberries, and raspberries.

» **Hot pack**: Use this method for firmer berries, such as blueberries, cranberries, and huckleberries.

Tomatoes

Tomatoes are misunderstood. Are they a fruit or a vegetable? By definition, a *fruit* is a sweet, edible plant containing seeds inside a juicy pulp — which defines tomatoes perfectly. Each tomato variety has its own color, flavor, and texture. Roma or paste tomatoes and slicing varieties are all used for canning. Paste varieties simply have less juice and, therefore, require less cooking to remove excess water for paste and thick sauces. You can use both interchangeably, but cooking times will vary.

REMEMBER

Not all tomato varieties are suitable for canning due to their lack of taste and mass-production genetics. Stick with those that boast good canning results on the plant's tag or use a proven Heirloom variety. Some varieties that work well include Ace, Amish paste, Homestead 24, and Rutgers.

As always, choose nice, ripe, unblemished tomatoes. And to ensure the proper acidity level for your variety (4.6 or lower), add an acid, such as bottled lemon juice or powdered citric acid: Add 2 tablespoons lemon juice per quart jar or 1 tablespoon lemon juice per pint. If you're using citric acid, add ½ teaspoon per quart and ¼ teaspoon per pint.

THE BEST THING YOU'RE NOT DOING WITH TOMATOES: HOMEMADE PASTE

Tomato paste is packed with flavor, and if you're overrun with tomatoes, the Tomato Paste recipe in this chapter is the answer because it uses *a lot* of fruit! You can use this thick paste as-is for pizza (it's only slightly less thick than store bought but just as rich and fabulous); simply add your seasonings right on top. Your family will love the extra tomato taste. You can also add this paste to soups for amazing flavor and extra vitamins. Use paste or plum tomatoes, which have much less extra water to cook off.

Canned Apples

PREP: 15 MIN	PROCESSING: 20 MIN	YIELD: 8 PINTS OR 4 QUARTS

INGREDIENTS

12 pounds apples

Sugar syrup, light

1 Prepare your canning jars and two-piece caps (lids and screw bands) according to the manufacturer's instructions. Keep the jars and lids hot. (For detailed instructions on preparing your jars, see the step-by-step directions earlier in this chapter.)

2 Wash, core, and peel your apples; then slice them into ¼-inch pieces or cut them into even chunks. Meanwhile, bring the sugar syrup to a boil.

3 Pack apples firmly into hot jars and pour boiling hot sugar syrup over the apples, leaving ½-inch headspace. Wipe the jar rims; seal the jars with the two-piece caps, hand-tightening the bands.

4 Process the filled jars in a water-bath canner for 20 minutes for pints and quarts from the point of boiling.

5 Remove the jars from the canner with a jar lifter. Place them on a clean kitchen towel away from drafts. After the jars cool completely, test the seals (see the step-by-step directions earlier in this chapter). If you find jars that haven't sealed, refrigerate them and use them within two weeks.

PER ½-CUP SERVING: *Calories 137 (From fat 4); Fat 0g (Saturated 0g); Cholesterol 0mg; Sodium 0mg; Carbohydrates 36g (Dietary fiber 3g); Protein 0g*

NOTE: Canned apples are wonderful for apple crisp, breads, and other recipes calling for slices or chunks of fruit.

NOTE: Use any crisp, tart apple that ripens in the fall. Summer-ripened apples tend to be softer and won't hold up well to canning.

VARY IT! For a sweeter canned apple, try a medium syrup instead.

Apple Pie Filling

PREP: 15 MIN	COOKING: 45 MIN	PROCESSING: 25 MIN	YIELD: 6 PINTS

INGREDIENTS

6 pounds apples

2 cups sugar

2 teaspoons cinnamon

½ teaspoon nutmeg

2 tablespoons lemon juice

1 Peel and slice or cube the apples. Place the apples and the other ingredients into a heavy pan. Allow the mixture to stand about 30 minutes or until it becomes juicy.

2 While the apples are standing, prepare your canning jars and two-piece caps (lids and screw bands) according to the manufacturer's instructions. Keep the jars and lids hot. (For detailed instructions on preparing your jars, see the step-by-step directions earlier in this chapter.)

3 Cook the apple mixture over medium heat until the apples are softened, about 7 minutes.

4 Ladle the pie filling into the pint jars, leaving ¼-inch headspace. Release any air bubbles with a nonreactive utensil (refer to Chapter 1 of this minibook). Wipe the jar rims; seal the jars with the two-piece caps, hand-tightening the bands.

5 Process the filled jars in a water-bath canner for 25 minutes from the point of boiling.

6 Remove the jars from the canner with a jar lifter. Place them on a clean kitchen towel away from drafts. After the jars cool completely, test the seals (see the step-by-step directions earlier in this chapter). If you find jars that haven't sealed, refrigerate them and use them within two weeks.

NOTE: To thicken this filling to just the right consistency for a pie, add 1 tablespoon of flour to the filled pie before adding the top crust.

VARY IT! Substitute or add to the spices listed to create the pie your family likes.

PER ½-CUP SERVING: *Calories 121 (From fat 3); Fat 0g (Saturated 0g); Cholesterol 0mg; Sodium 0mg; Carbohydrates 31g (Dietary fiber 2g); Protein 0g*

Applesauce

PREP: 15 MIN	COOKING: 1 HR	PROCESSING: 20 MIN	YIELD: 4 QUARTS

INGREDIENTS

10 pounds apples, cut in half

2½ cups sugar

1 Prepare your canning jars and two-piece caps (lids and screw bands) according to the manufacturer's instructions. Keep the jars and lids hot. (For detailed instructions on preparing your jars, see the step-by-step directions earlier in this chapter.)

2 Cut the apples in half (don't peel or core them) and place them in a 12-quart pot. Add enough water to cover the bottom of the pot and to keep the apples from scorching. Cook the apples over medium heat until they're soft, about 20 minutes. Press the softened apples through a food mill or sieve to remove the skins and seeds.

3 Return the apple purée to the pot and add the sugar. Bring the mixture to a boil, stirring often to prevent scorching.

4 Ladle the hot applesauce into your prepared jars, leaving ½-inch headspace. Release any air bubbles with a nonreactive utensil (refer to Chapter 1 of this minibook). Wipe the jar rims; seal the jars with the two-piece caps, hand-tightening the bands.

5 Process the filled jars in a water-bath canner for 20 minutes from the point of boiling.

6 Remove the jars from the canner with a jar lifter. Place them on a clean kitchen towel. After the jars cool completely, test the seals (see the step-by-step directions earlier in this chapter). If you find jars that haven't sealed, refrigerate them and use them within two weeks.

TIP: For a richer flavor, use a variety of apples.

TIP: To help prevent scorching, use a stovetop heat diffuser under the pot.

VARY IT! Try adding cinnamon and cloves for a spicy version.

PER ½-CUP SERVING: *Calories 129 (From fat 3); Fat 0g (Saturated 0g); Cholesterol 0mg; Sodium 0mg; Carbohydrates 34g (Dietary fiber 2g); Protein 0g*

Canned Apricots, Nectarines, and Peaches

PREP: 15 MIN	PROCESSING: PINTS, 25 MIN; QUARTS, 30 MIN	YIELD: 8 PINTS OR 4 QUARTS

INGREDIENTS

10 pounds apricots, 10 pounds nectarines, or 12 pounds peaches

Sugar syrup, light

1 Prepare your canning jars and two-piece caps (lids and screw bands) according to the manufacturer's instructions. Keep the jars and lids hot. (For detailed instructions on preparing your jars, see the step-by-step directions earlier in this chapter.)

2 Wash your fruit. To prepare peaches, peel them; then cut them in half and remove the pits (see Figure 2-3). To prepare nectarines or apricots, simply cut them in half and remove the pits. Meanwhile, bring the sugar syrup to a boil.

3 Pack the fruit firmly into hot jars and pour boiling hot sugar syrup over fruit, leaving ½-inch headspace. Release any air bubbles with a nonreactive utensil (refer to Chapter 1 of this minibook). Wipe the jar rims; seal the jars with the two-piece caps, hand-tightening the bands.

4 Process the filled jars in a water-bath canner for 25 minutes (pints) or 30 minutes (quarts) from the point of boiling.

5 Remove the jars from the canner with a jar lifter. Place them on a clean kitchen towel away from drafts. After the jars cool completely, test the seals (see the step-by-step directions earlier in this chapter). If you find jars that haven't sealed, refrigerate them and use them within two weeks.

(continued)

VARY IT! To make a sweeter canned fruit, use a medium syrup.

TIP: To make peaches easy to peel, blanch them to loosen the skin: Dip them in boiling water for 30 seconds and then dip them in cold water.

PER ½-CUP SERVING APRICOTS: *Calories 118 (From fat 5); Fat 1g (Saturated 0g); Cholesterol 0mg; Sodium 2mg; Carbohydrates 29g (Dietary fiber 3g); Protein 2g*

PER ½-CUP SERVING NECTARINES: *Calories 118 (From fat 5); Fat 1g (Saturated 0g); Cholesterol 0mg; Sodium 0mg; Carbohydrates 29g (Dietary fiber 2g); Protein 1g*

PER ½-CUP SERVING PEACHES: *Calories 88 (From fat 1); Fat 0g (Saturated 0g); Cholesterol 0mg; Sodium 4mg; Carbohydrates 23g (Dietary fiber 2g); Protein 1g*

Canned Raspberries

PREP: 15 MIN	PROCESSING: PINTS, 15 MIN; QUARTS, 20 MIN	YIELD: 8 PINTS OR 4 QUARTS

INGREDIENTS

12 pounds raspberries

Sugar syrup, light

1 Prepare your canning jars and two-piece caps (lids and screw bands) according to the manufacturer's instructions. Keep the jars and lids hot. (For detailed instructions on preparing your jars, see the step-by-step directions earlier in this chapter.)

2 Wash the berries gently in cold water to firm them and remove any stems or hulls. Meanwhile, bring the sugar syrup to a boil.

3 Pack berries loosely into your prepared jars and pour boiling hot sugar syrup over them, leaving ½-inch headspace. Release any air bubbles with a nonreactive utensil (refer to Chapter 1 of this minibook), adding more sugar syrup as necessary to maintain the proper headspace. Wipe the jar rims; seal the jars with the two-piece caps, hand-tightening the bands.

4 Process the filled jars in a water-bath canner for 15 minutes (pints) or 20 minutes (quarts) from the point of boiling.

5 Remove the jars from the canner with a jar lifter. Place them on a clean kitchen towel away from drafts. After the jars cool completely, test the seals (see the step-by-step directions earlier in this chapter). If you find jars that haven't sealed, refrigerate them and use them within two weeks.

NOTE: Use this recipe to can any other soft berry, such as boysenberries or blackberries.

VARY IT! For sweeter canned berries, use medium syrup.

PER ½-CUP SERVING: *Calories 138 (From fat 8); Fat 1g (Saturated 0g); Cholesterol 0mg; Sodium 0mg; Carbohydrates 34g (Dietary fiber 12g); Protein 2g*

Canned Blueberries

PREP: 20 MIN	PROCESSING: PINTS, 15 MIN; QUARTS, 20 MIN	YIELD: 8 PINTS OR 4 QUARTS

INGREDIENTS

10 pounds blueberries

Sugar syrup, light

Boiling water

1   Prepare your canning jars and two-piece caps (lids and screw bands) according to the manufacturer's instructions. Keep the jars and lids hot. (For detailed instructions on preparing your jars, see the step-by-step directions earlier in this chapter.)

2   Wash the berries gently in cold water to firm them and remove any stems or hulls.

3   Measure the berries into a saucepan and add ½ cup sugar for each quart of berries. Bring the mixture to a boil over medium-high heat and stir occasionally to prevent sticking. In a large pot, bring water for your reserve to a boil.

4   Ladle the hot berries and liquid into your prepared jars, adding boiling water if there isn't enough liquid to fill the jars, leaving ½-inch headspace. Release any air bubbles with a nonreactive utensil (refer to Chapter 1 of this minibook), adding more berries and water as necessary to maintain the proper headspace. Wipe the jar rims; seal the jars with the two-piece caps, hand-tightening the bands.

5   Process the filled jars in a water-bath canner for 15 minutes (pints) or 20 minutes (quarts) from the point of boiling.

6   Remove the jars from the canner with a jar lifter. Place them on a clean kitchen towel away from drafts. After the jars cool completely, test the seals (see the step-by-step directions earlier in this chapter). If you find jars that haven't sealed, refrigerate them and use them within two weeks.

NOTE: Follow the same directions for any other type of hard berry.

VARY IT! For sweeter canned berries, use medium syrup.

PER ½-CUP SERVING: *Calories 124 (From fat 3); Fat 0g (Saturated 0g); Cholesterol 0mg; Sodium 2mg; Carbohydrates 32g (Dietary fiber 6g); Protein 1g*

Canned Tomatoes

PREP: 15 MIN	PROCESSING: PINTS, 35 MIN; QUARTS, 45 MIN	YIELD: 6 PINTS OR 4 QUARTS

INGREDIENTS

12 pounds whole tomatoes

Bottled lemon juice or citric acid

Canning salt (optional)

Boiling water

1 Prepare your canning jars and two-piece caps (lids and screw bands) according to the manufacturer's instructions. Keep the jars and lids hot. (For detailed instructions on preparing your jars, see the step-by-step directions earlier in this chapter.)

2 Wash and peel the tomatoes. (To make peeling tomatoes easier, blanch them first to loosen the skins: Dip them in boiling water for 30 seconds and then into cold water.) After peeling, cut the larger tomatoes into halves or quarters.

3 Place the tomatoes into your prepared canning jars, pressing them to release their juice. (Use a canning funnel to keep the rims clean.) To each pint jar, add 1 tablespoon lemon juice or ¼ teaspoon citric acid and, if desired, ½ teaspoon salt. To each quart jar, add 2 tablespoons lemon juice or ½ teaspoon citric acid and, if desired, 1 teaspoon salt. If there's not enough juice to cover the tomatoes, add boiling water to the jars, leaving ½-inch headspace. Release any air bubbles with a nonreactive utensil (refer to Chapter 1 of this minibook), adding more tomatoes as necessary to maintain the proper headspace. Wipe the jar rims; seal the jars with the two-piece caps, hand-tightening the bands.

4 Process the filled jars in a water-bath canner for 35 minutes (pints) or 45 minutes (quarts) from the point of boiling.

5 Remove the jars from the canner with a jar lifter. Place them on a clean kitchen towel away from drafts. After the jars cool completely, test the seals (see the step-by-step directions earlier in this chapter). If you find jars that haven't sealed, refrigerate them and use them within two weeks.

TIP: Use wide-mouth pints or quart jars for ease in filling. Although not necessary, they will make the entire process go faster and with less mess.

PER ½-CUP SERVING: *Calories 44 (From fat 6); Fat 1g (Saturated 0g); Cholesterol 0mg; Sodium 19mg; Carbohydrates 10g (Dietary fiber 2g); Protein 2g*

Tomato Paste

PREP: 15 MIN	COOKING: 1 HR, PLUS 3 HR	PROCESSING: 30 MIN	YIELD: 16 HALF-PINTS

INGREDIENTS

16 pounds plum or paste tomatoes, cubed

3 cups sweet pepper, chopped

2 bay leaves

2 tablespoons salt

3 cloves garlic

Bottled lemon juice or citric acid

1   Combine all ingredients in a 6-quart pot and cook slowly over medium heat for 1 hour, stirring frequently to prevent sticking. Remove the bay leaves and press the mixture through a food mill or sieve. Return the mixture to the pot and continue to cook for another 3 hours over medium-low heat, stirring often.

2   Prepare your canning jars and two-piece caps (lids and screw bands) according to the manufacturer's instructions. Keep the jars and lids hot. (For detailed instructions on preparing your jars, see the step-by-step directions earlier in this chapter.)

3   Pour the hot mixture into your canning jars, leaving ¼-inch headspace. Add ½ tablespoon lemon juice or ⅛ teaspoon citric acid to each half-pint jar. Release any air bubbles with a non-reactive utensil (refer to Chapter 1 of this minibook), adding more of the mixture as necessary to maintain the proper headspace. Wipe the jar rims; seal the jars with the two-piece caps, hand-tightening the bands.

4   Process the filled half-pint jars in a water-bath canner for 30 minutes from the point of boiling.

5   Remove the jars from the canner with a jar lifter. Place them on a clean kitchen towel away from drafts. After the jars cool completely, test the seals (see the step-by-step directions earlier in this chapter). If you find jars that haven't sealed, refrigerate them and use them within two weeks.

TIP: To check for sauce thickness, put a spoonful of sauce onto the center of a plate. Wait for 60 seconds and see if water seeps from it. If so, cook for 30 minutes more and recheck.

PER ½-CUP SERVING: Calories 48 (From fat 6); Fat 1g (Saturated 0g); Cholesterol 0mg; Sodium 455mg; Carbohydrates 11g (Dietary fiber 2g); Protein 2g

Jam, Chutney, Relish, and Salsa Recipes

For many, a batch of homemade jam is their first tentative step into the world of water-bath canning. From there, it's just a short hop, skip, and jump to versatile fruit accompaniments such as chutneys, relishes, and salsas that can be preserved and used many months later to dress up your favorite foods at any meal. The following section gets your creative juices flowing and then follows up with recipes for great ways to enjoy fresh fruit all year long.

Jamming out

Making sweet spreads like jams, jellies, and marmalades is basic chemistry, using exact proportions of fruit and sugar, cooking the two, and sometimes adding acid or pectin.

Pectin is a natural, water-based substance that's present in ripe fruit. It's essential for thickening jams, jellies, and other types of preserves. Some recipes add commercial fruit pectin when more than the naturally occurring amount of pectin is needed (like when you want to thicken a fruit juice into a jelly). If your recipe does include such an ingredient, you'll see the kind of pectin (powdered or liquid) listed.

WARNING

Never alter the amount of sugar your recipe calls for or use sugar substitutes. Exact amounts of sugar, fruit, and pectin are a must for a good *set* — that is, a consistency that isn't too thick to spread or too runny. Any alteration or adjustment to the recipe upsets the perfect chemical balance and adversely affects your spread by producing inferior results. If you want more of the same recipe, make it twice. If you would like to use less sugar, find another recipe that uses your desired amount.

Pectin is available in two forms: liquid and powdered (dry). Although both products are made from fruit, they're not interchangeable. Be sure to use the correct type and amount of pectin your recipe calls for.

Using liquid fruit pectin

Liquid pectin is usually made from apples. Today, a box contains two 3-ounce pouches. The most common brand is Certo.

TECHNICAL STUFF

Liquid fruit pectin was originally sold in 6-ounce bottles. Older recipes may call for "one-half of a bottle." If you read a pouch of liquid pectin today, it states, "1 pouch equals ½ bottle."

Because you have to add your liquid pectin at the specified time and temperature, have it at the ready: Cut off the top of the pouch and stand it in a measuring cup or other container to keep it from spilling (see Figure 2-4). Then, when it's time to add the liquid pectin, add it all at the same time, squeezing the pouch with your fingers like you do to get the last bit of toothpaste out of the tube.

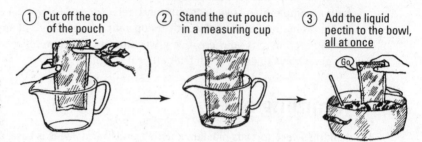

① Cut off the top of the pouch ② Stand the cut pouch in a measuring cup ③ Add the liquid pectin to the bowl, all at once

FIGURE 2-4: Getting a pouch of liquid pectin ready.

Using powdered (dry) fruit pectin

Powdered pectin is made from citrus fruits or apples. It comes in a box similar to a gelatin- or pudding-mix box and contains 1¾ ounces (the most commonly used size) or 2 ounces. Use the size stated in your recipe ingredients, and add it before you heat the fruit mixture.

In addition to different sizes, powdered pectin comes in two varieties: fruit pectin for homemade jams and jellies, and fruit pectin for lower-sugar recipes. Use the variety your recipe calls for; they're not interchangeable.

Making great accompaniments

Condiments and accompaniments are to food what accessories are to clothing. They're not necessary, but they enhance what's there. They cover a wide range of flavors including savory, spicy, salty, sweet, or a combination. Think of them as the bright spot on an otherwise dull winter plate. And they're a great way to incorporate more of the fruits, veggies, and herbs from your homestead into your everyday meal prep!

The Green Tomato Chutney recipe is a great way to use your green tomatoes. It produces a super-thick chutney that makes a great gift and looks lovely on the shelf. Although you'll be eager to try the chutney as soon as it's done, let it sit for one month before you use it, longer if you can to help develop the fine flavor. This recipe uses half-pint jars — the perfect size for a picnic basket!

Relish wears many hats and complements a wide variety of foods, from hamburgers and hot dogs, to meat and poultry. Relish is a cooked mixture of fruit or vegetables preserved with vinegar. Flavor can be sweet to savory and hot to mild with textures ranging from smooth to finely chopped or chunky. Including an overnight soak, this unique relish takes two days to make.

Strawberry–Rhubarb Jam

PREP: 45 MIN	PROCESSING: 20 MIN	YIELD: 3 PINTS

INGREDIENTS

4 cups strawberries, crushed

2½ cups chopped rhubarb

¼ cup lemon juice

One 1.75-ounce package pectin powder

6 cups sugar

1 Prepare your canning jars and two-piece caps (lids and screw bands) according to the manufacturer's instructions. Keep the jars and lids hot. (For detailed instructions on preparing your jars, see the step-by-step directions earlier in this chapter.)

2 Hull and crush the strawberries. Clean the rhubarb; trim the ends and remove the leaves. Cut the rhubarb into ½-inch pieces.

3 Combine the strawberries, rhubarb, lemon juice, and pectin powder in a large saucepan. Bring the mixture to a boil over medium-high heat. Add the sugar, stirring to dissolve. Return the mixture to a full, rolling boil and boil hard for 1 minute. Remove the saucepan from the heat. Skim any foam from the surface with a foam skimmer, if necessary.

4 Ladle the boiling-hot jam into your hot jars, leaving ¼-inch headspace. Release any air bubbles with a nonreactive utensil (refer to Chapter 1 of this minibook), adding more jam as necessary to maintain the proper headspace. Wipe the jar rims; seal the jars with the two-piece caps, hand-tightening the bands.

5 Process the filled pint jars in a water-bath canner for 20 minutes from the point of boiling. (Note: It doesn't matter if you have a less-than-full canner. Simply arrange the jars so that they're evenly spaced, if possible.)

6 Remove the jars from the canner with a jar lifter. Place them on a clean kitchen towel away from drafts. After the jars cool completely, test the seals (see the step-by-step directions earlier in this chapter). If you find jars that haven't sealed, refrigerate them and use them within two weeks.

PER 1-TABLESPOON SERVING: *Calories 53 (From fat 0); Fat 0g (Saturated 0g); Cholesterol 0mg; Sodium 1mg; Carbohydrates 14g (Dietary fiber 0g); Protein 0g*

Green Tomato Chutney

PREP: 1 HOUR 15 MIN | PROCESSING: 10 MIN | YIELD: 8 HALF-PINTS

INGREDIENTS

4 pounds green tomatoes, chopped

2 medium onions, chopped

1½ green apples, peeled, cored, and chopped

1 cup golden raisins

1 teaspoon salt

½ teaspoon ground red pepper

1 teaspoon allspice

1 teaspoon curry, or to taste

1 cup brown sugar

2 cups cider vinegar

1 Prepare your canning jars and two-piece caps (lids and screw bands) according to the manufacturer's instructions. Keep the jars and lids hot. (For detailed instructions on preparing your jars, see the step-by-step directions earlier in this chapter.)

2 Place all the ingredients in a 6-quart pot, and simmer on medium heat until the mixture is thick and rich, the consistency of very thick, chunky applesauce, about 45 minutes. Stir often to prevent scorching.

3 Ladle the mixture into the prepared jars. Leave ¼-inch headspace. Release any air bubbles with a nonreactive utensil (refer to Chapter 1 of this minibook), adding more mixture as necessary to maintain the proper headspace. Wipe the jar rims; seal the jars with the two-piece caps, hand-tightening the bands.

4 Process the filled half-pint jars in a water-bath canner for 10 minutes from the point of boiling.

5 Remove the jars from the canner with a jar lifter. Place them on a clean kitchen towel away from drafts. After the jars cool completely, test the seals (see the step-by-step directions earlier in this chapter). If you find jars that haven't sealed, refrigerate them and use them within two weeks.

NOTE: Although you'll be eager to try the chutney as soon as it's done, let it sit for one month or longer before you use it, to help develop the fine flavor.

PER 1-TABLESPOON SERVING: *Calories 16 (From fat 0); Fat 0g (Saturated 0g); Cholesterol 0mg; Sodium 21mg; Carbohydrates 4g (Dietary fiber 0g); Protein 0g*

Summer Squash Relish

| PREP: 45 MIN | SOAKING: 12 HR | PROCESSING: 15 MIN | YIELD: 6 PINTS |

INGREDIENTS

5 pounds (about 10 to 12) medium zucchini

6 large onions

½ cup kosher or pickling salt

Cold water to cover the vegetables (about 4 to 5 quarts)

2 cups white wine vinegar

1 cup granulated sugar

Two 4-ounce jars pimientos, undrained

2 teaspoons celery seed

1 teaspoon powdered mustard

½ teaspoon ground cinnamon

½ teaspoon ground nutmeg

½ teaspoon freshly ground black pepper

1 On the first day, finely chop the zucchini and onions. (If you're using a food processor, chop them in three batches.) Place the vegetables in a 5- to 6-quart mixing bowl and sprinkle them with the salt. Add water to cover them, place a cover on the bowl, and refrigerate overnight or at least 12 hours.

2 On the second day, drain the vegetables in a colander. Rinse well with running water; drain. Transfer the vegetables to a 5- to 6-quart pot. Add the vinegar, sugar, pimientos, celery seed, mustard, cinnamon, nutmeg, and pepper. Stir to combine.

3 Bring the vegetables to a boil over medium-high heat, stirring occasionally. Reduce the heat and simmer, uncovered, until the mixture reduces to 3 quarts, about 30 to 40 minutes. Stir the vegetables every 10 minutes to prevent sticking. The zucchini color turns a dull shade of green.

4 While your relish is cooking, prepare your canning jars and two-piece caps (lids and screw bands) according to the manufacturer's instructions. Keep the jars and lids hot. (For detailed instructions on preparing your jars, see the step-by-step directions earlier in this chapter.)

5 Spoon the hot relish into your prepared jars, leaving ¼-inch headspace. Compact the relish with a spoon to release any air bubbles. Add more relish as necessary to maintain the proper headspace. Wipe the jar rims; seal the jars with the two-piece caps, hand-tightening the bands.

6 Process your filled jars in a water-bath canner for 15 minutes from the point of boiling.

(continued)

7 Remove the jars from the boiling water with a jar lifter. Place them on a clean kitchen towel away from drafts. After the jars cool completely, test the seals (see the step-by-step directions earlier in this chapter). If you find jars that haven't sealed, refrigerate them and use them within 2 months.

VARY IT! Use 3 pounds of zucchini and 2 pounds of patty pan or yellow crookneck squash.

PER 2-TABLESPOON SERVING: *Calories 16 (From fat 1); Fat 0g (Saturated 0g); Cholesterol 0mg; Sodium 14mg; Carbohydrates 4g (Dietary fiber 1g); Protein 0g*

Jalapeño Salsa

PREP: 30 MIN	PROCESSING: 15 MIN	YIELD: 3 PINTS

INGREDIENTS

2 pounds tomatoes, peeled and chopped, to measure 3 cups

7-ounce can diced jalapeño chilies or 12 fresh jalapeño chilies, finely chopped, seeds removed

1 onion, peeled and chopped

6 garlic cloves, minced

2 tablespoons finely chopped fresh cilantro

2 teaspoons ground oregano

1½ teaspoons kosher or pickling salt

½ teaspoon ground cumin

1 cup cider vinegar

1 Prepare your canning jars and two-piece caps (lids and screw bands) according to the manufacturer's instructions. Keep the jars and lids hot. (For detailed instructions on preparing your jars, see the step-by-step directions earlier in this chapter.)

2 Place all the ingredients in a 5- to 6- quart pot. Bring the mixture to a boil over high heat, stirring to combine. Reduce the heat to low; simmer, uncovered, for 10 minutes.

3 Ladle your hot salsa into the prepared jars; leaving ¼-inch headspace. Release any air bubbles with a nonreactive utensil (refer to Chapter 1 of this minibook), adding more salsa as necessary to maintain the proper headspace. Wipe the jar rims; seal the jars with the two-piece caps, hand-tightening the bands.

4 Process the filled jars in a water-bath canner for 15 minutes from the point of boiling.

5 Remove the jars from the boiling water with a jar lifter. Place them on a clean kitchen towel away from drafts. After the jars cool completely, test the seals (see the step-by-step directions earlier in this chapter). If you find jars that haven't sealed, refrigerate them and use them within 2 months.

PER 2-TABLESPOON SERVING: *Calories 6 (From fat 0); Fat 0g (Saturated 0g); Cholesterol 0mg; Sodium 99mg; Carbohydrates 2g (Dietary fiber 0g); Protein 0g*

Chapter **3**

Pressure Canning

ressure canning is a process for preserving food with a low-acid content by exposing the food to a high temperature (240 degrees) under a specific pressure for a specific period of time in a specific type of pot: the pressure canner.

People who hear someone talking about pressure canning often ask, "Is it safe?" or "Won't the pressure canner explode?" These concerns are certainly valid ones, but rest assured, when you know the right way to use a pressure canner, you can safely process a variety of low-acid foods. While pressure cookers and canners of the past may have once exploded if not closed properly, the new generation of canners and cookers are much lighter in weight and have built-in safety features that release steam if the pressure gets too high. None of your grandparents' pressure cooking equipment had this.

This chapter leads you step by step through the pressure-canning process, including an explanation of pressure canning, what to look for when purchasing a pressure canner, and how to fill your canner and safely process your filled jars. You also discover recipes for making those homegrown veggies last well beyond the harvest.

Understanding the Fuss about Low-Acid Foods

Low-acid foods contain little natural acid and require more care during the canning process than other types of foods. (If you're a techie, note that low-acid foods are foods with a *pH factor* — that's a measure of acidity in food — higher than 4.6.) Foods in this category include vegetables, meats, poultry, seafood, and combination foods (such as soups, meat sauces, and salsas) that contain low-acid and high-acid ingredients. Exceptions to these low-acid foods sometimes include tomatoes, which are really a fruit and can be water-bath canned (although for safety's sake, you still add acid to tomatoes) and vegetables converted to high-acid foods such as sauerkraut, pickles, or pickled vegetables (discussed in Chapter 4 of this minibook).

WARNING

Low-acid foods require pressure canning to kill microorganisms that are harmful if not destroyed before ingesting the food. Pressure canning at 240 degrees kills the botulism bacteria. If this temperature isn't achieved and the bacteria isn't destroyed, one taste of this spoiled food can kill you. And to make matters worse, these botulism-causing bacteria are odorless, have no taste, and actually thrive in low-acid foods that are in a moist environment and not in contact with air — the exact condition provided in a jar of canned food. Simply boiling food on the stovetop will not kill any botulism and should not be considered a safety step.

REMEMBER

In a water-bath canner, the temperature of boiling water never increases above 212 degrees (the boiling point for water). While 212 degrees is fine for water-bath canning high-acid foods, it's *not* sufficient to safely can low-acid foods. For that, you need to superheat your filled jars to a temperature of 240 degrees, which only a pressure canner can achieve. Be sure to use a pressure canner that's approved for pressure canning by the United States Department of Agriculture (USDA).

Choosing a Pressure Canner

A *pressure canner*, shown in Figure 3-1, is a heavy kettle made for processing home-canned food. It includes a locking, tight-fitting cover that makes the kettle airtight. The purpose of pressure canning is to sterilize the food by destroying hard-to-kill microorganisms, especially the bacteria that cause botulism.

For the home canner, a pressure canner with a capacity of 16 to 22 quarts is generally adequate. This size holds seven 1-quart jars and permits good air circulation during processing. The cost of a pressure canner may vary from $100 on the low end to upward of $600, depending on size, features, and reputation of the manufacturer.

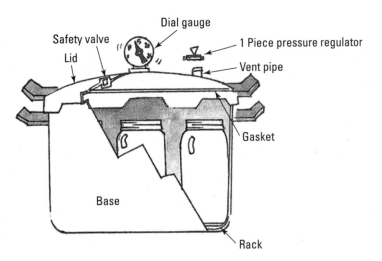

FIGURE 3-1:
A pressure
canner.

Dial gauge

Safety valve

1 Piece pressure regulator

Lid

Vent pipe

Gasket

Base

Rack

Don't confuse pressure canners with pressure cookers; they are *not* interchangeable. A pressure canner is used to process and sterilize home-canned, low-acid foods. The purpose of a pressure cooker is to cook food fast. Pressure cookers are not large enough to hold the jars and the amount of water necessary to can properly. They also do not have pressure gauges that allow you to maintain the constant pressure required.

WARNING

Attention Instant Pot fanatics! At the time of this writing, instant pressure cookers (like the Instant Pot) have *not* been approved by the USDA for pressure canning. This type of cooker is regulated by a pressure sensor, not a thermometer, so there is no way to ensure that the interior is getting hot enough to safely pressure-can food. But beware: some models boast a "canning" feature and even have a "canning" button on their control panels. (Water-bath canning of foods such as pickles and jams is technically possible, but comes with challenges. See the sidebar "Can I water-bath can in my Instant Pot?" in Chapter 2 of this minibook.) The technology in these machines is evolving rapidly to meet consumers' demands, so future models may one day make great pressure canners. But for now, follow the guidelines laid out here for pressure canning, and save your Instant Pot for weeknight dinner prep.

The following section highlights different features of various pressure canners so that you can determine which ones you prefer. The type of pressure canner you choose doesn't matter as long as the model is made and approved for processing home-canned foods.

REMEMBER

No matter which type or size of pressure canner you choose, the goal is always the same: to superheat and process low-acid food at a high temperature (240 degrees) that destroys microorganisms.

Covers

You can find two types of covers for pressure canners: a lock-on cover and a metal-to-metal cover that's attached with wing nuts. The difference is that one has a rubber gasket to ensure an airtight seal; the other one doesn't. For a beginner, a lock-on cover is the easiest and most fail-proof to use.

Lock-on cover

A *lock-on cover* (see Figure 3-2) usually has a rubber gasket between the cover and the base unit to ensure to the airtight seal. To securely fasten the cover to the pressure canner, rotate the cover on the base to the locked position (matching up the handles or matching arrows or other markings on the unit) or with a type of clamping handle. To ensure that the pressure canner is properly closed, refer to your owner's manual for precise instructions.

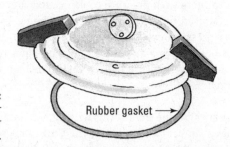

FIGURE 3-2:
A lock-on cover and rubber gasket.

Rubber gasket →

WARNING

Over time, the rubber gasket may stretch out of shape or begin to rot and deteriorate (indicated by cracking or splitting). If your gasket is in this condition, don't use your pressure canner until you've replaced the gasket. A gasket in poor condition may prevent the canner from reaching the pressure required to superheat the food and kill microorganisms.

TIP

After each use, carefully remove the gasket from the cover. Thoroughly wash the gasket in hot, soapy water and dry it well. After the gasket is completely dry, put it back on the cover so that your pressure canner is always ready for use. Some manufacturers suggest lightly coating the gasket with cooking oil, but check your owner's manual before doing this.

Metal-to-metal cover with wing nuts

A *metal-to-metal cover* (see Figure 3-3) doesn't require a gasket to create a tight seal; instead, this pressure canner uses wing nuts. To secure a cover with wing nuts, tighten two wing nuts on opposite sides of the canner at the same time by hand (don't use a tool and don't tighten one side at a time). Repeat this process for the remaining wing nuts.

FIGURE 3-3:
A metal-to-metal cover with wing nuts.

Wing nut on metal-to-metal cover

REMEMBER

Never tighten one nut at a time because uneven results will occur. If your wing nuts aren't tightened properly, as soon as the pressure starts to rise, water leaks out. You then have to carefully remove the canner from the heat and wait for the pressure to subside before untightening and retightening all over again.

Every year, check for nicks and dents in the rim of both the lid and the canner itself. These imperfections will prevent the canner from making a seal.

Gauges

Gauges are located on the top of the pressure canner cover and regulate pressure within the canner. Two types of gauges are available: a weighted gauge and a dial gauge (see Figure 3-4). A dial gauge indicates the pressure of the canner, while a weighted gauge indicates and regulates the pressure of the contents. If you're a beginner, go with the weighted gauge.

Dial gauge

Weighted gauge

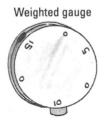

FIGURE 3-4:
Pressure canner gauges.

Weighted gauge

A *weighted gauge* is simple and accurate. It's sometimes referred to as an *automatic pressure control* or a *pressure regulator weight*. This gauge allows you to cook without looking: The weighted gauge automatically controls the pressure by jiggling as the canner reaches the correct pressure. When the pressure in the canner is too high, the weighted gauge jiggles faster, and may hiss, as it releases excess steam from the canner.

A weighted gauge has a preset control that needs no service or testing to ensure an accurate pressure measurement. The pressure settings are indicated by three numbers marked on the gauge (refer to Figure 3-4): 5, 10, and 15. The numbers represent the pounds per square inch (psi) of pressure created by the trapped steam from the boiling water in the pressure canner.

REMEMBER

The most common pressure used in pressure canning is 10 pounds, but never guess — always refer to your recipe.

Dial or steam pressure gauge

A *dial* or *steam pressure gauge* (refer to Figure 3-4) is a numbered instrument that indicates the pressure in the canner. You have to watch dial gauges carefully to be sure they don't rise too high, and you have to turn the heat up or down to keep the pressure in the right area.

Unlike the weighted gauge that requires no service, you must check this control for accuracy each season or at least once every year of use. To obtain service, refer to your owner's manual for service locations, check with the store where you purchased the canner, or contact your local cooperative extension services.

WARNING

If your annual service shows that your dial gauge is off by 5 or more pounds, replace the gauge. An inaccurate reading may not produce the temperature required to kill all microorganisms. You can have your canner checked for a nominal fee, if not free, at your local hardware store or county extension office.

Vent tube, pipe vent, or petcock

Whatever the name of this feature — *vent tube, pipe vent,* or *petcock* — the function is the same (see Figure 3-5). These terms refer to an opening in the pressure-canner cover for emitting steam. Sometimes the weighted gauge sits on the vent tube.

REMEMBER

To work properly, the vent tube opening cannot be obstructed with food or other matter. Obstructions restrict the optimum pressure and temperature required for your recipe. To check the vent for obstructions, hold it up to the light. If the vent appears to be clogged, insert a piece of wire (or other item suggested in your owner's manual) into the tube. Rinse the vent with hot water. Repeat the procedure if you still see an obstruction.

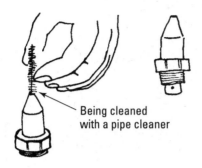

Being cleaned with a pipe cleaner

FIGURE 3-5:
A vent tube.

Overpressure plug

An *overpressure plug* (see Figure 3-6) releases (pops up) if too much pressure exists in your pressure canner due to a blocked vent tube. The overpressure plug is a safety feature that's solely for your protection. If you follow the instruction manual for your pressure-canner operation, chances are this plug will never be used.

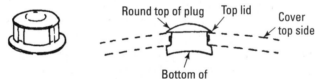

Round top of plug   Top lid   Cover top side

Bottom of plug is indented

FIGURE 3-6:
An overpressure plug.

Rack

Your pressure canner should come with a rack. (If the rack is missing, contact the store where you made your purchase.) The perfect rack lies flat in the bottom of your canner and has lots of holes and openings that allow steam to circulate around your filled jars. Figure 3-7 is an example of a canner rack.

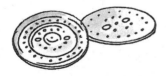

TIP

Make sure your rack is stable when you place it in the bottom of the canner. A stable rack holds jars in place, thus preventing the jars from tipping, touching other jars, or touching the sides of the canner.

Pressure Canning Step-by-Step

To ensure a processed product of high quality, free from microorganisms, be sure to follow each step in this section. Don't omit or modify any part. You may spend a bit more time canning low-acid foods with a pressure canner than you would canning high-acid foods in a water-bath canner, but the end result is worth the extra effort.

TIP

If you've never used a pressure canner before, do a trial run with no jars: Heat up the canner and go through the steps of pressurizing and depressurizing to famil-iarize yourself with the sounds the pressure canner makes as it builds and then releases pressure. You'll hear the steam escaping, the weight gauge shaking, and the ticking of the canner as it heats and cools; if you don't know what to expect, you could misinterpret these noises as scary or wrong.

Step 1: Gearing up

At least a couple of weeks before you want to use it, check your pressure canner and replace any gasket or missing part, have a dial gauge checked professionally, and replace a missing manual. Also count your jars and two-piece caps and exam-ine the jars for nicks or chips, the screw bands for proper fit and corrosion, and the new lids for imperfections and scratches. It's also a good idea to select your recipe, and inventory your pantry for any nonperishable ingredients, adding any needed items to your shopping list. Your goal is to have all the supplies you need and your pressure canner in good working order on the day you're ready to can.

REMEMBER

Preparing your pressure canner before the actual canning season means you will not find the store out of supplies and the extension agent too busy to check your gauge in time to begin canning when the produce is ripe.

On the actual canning day, get your tools ready by following these steps:

1. **Assemble your prechecked equipment and utensils.**

   In addition to your pressure canner and the standard canning supplies (jars with two-piece lids), other items can make your canning easier: a food scale, extra pans for cooking your veggies and keeping a water reserve on hand, a wide-mouth funnel, and so on.

2. **Wash your jars and screw bands in warm, soapy water, rinsing well to remove any soap residue.**

   Double-check for nicks and dents and discard any damaged items.

3. **Place your clean jars and lids in a kettle of hot — not boiling — water until you're ready to fill them.**

WARNING

   Never boil the lids because the sealant material may be damaged and won't produce a safe vacuum seal.

4. **Ready your canner by filling it with 2 to 3 inches of water and heating the water.**

Step 2: Preparing your food

Always start with food of the highest, freshest quality. Food that's spoiled or bruised doesn't improve in quality during the pressure–canning process! To prepare your food for pressure canning, follow these steps:

1. **Wash all food prior to packing it in the jars or precooking it.**

2. **Thoroughly cut away all evidence of spoilage or discard any inferior products.**

3. **Prepare the food by precisely following your recipe.**

   Some recipes call for you to fill your jars with raw food; others may want you to precook the food. If you're precooking your low-acid food before filling your jars, don't discard the cooking liquid; use this liquid for filling your jars.

REMEMBER

Work in manageable batches. To determine just what a "manageable batch" is, consider how much food fills one canner load at a time. Most recipes are geared for manageable batches, but if you're in doubt, check the yield for the recipe.

Step 3: Filling your jars

Always place your product into hot jars (you keep them hot by leaving them in a kettle of hot water, as explained in "Step 1: Gearing up.") To fill your jars, follow these steps:

1. **Remove a jar from the kettle and pack the food into the jar so that the food is snug, yet loose enough for liquid to circulate into the open spaces.**

TIP

2. **Ladle boiling water (or the liquid from precooking the vegetables) into the jars, leaving the amount of headspace stated in your recipe.**

   If you're adding cooking liquid, divide the cooking liquid evenly among the jars and finish filling the jars with boiling water, if necessary. That way, if you run short of the cooking liquid, you won't have one jar filled with only boiling water.

3. **Release any air bubbles with a nonmetallic spatula or a tool to free bubbles.**

   If the headspace drops, add additional food and liquid to the jar.

4. **Wipe the jar rims with a clean, damp cloth.**

   Have a few rags handy to be sure you're using a clean one every time.

5. **Place a lid on the jar (seal side down) and secure the lid in place with a screw band.**

   Hand-tighten the band without overtightening it.

REMEMBER

Always work quickly, stopping for nothing. Time is of the essence! Your hot foods need to remain hot, your lids seal best if placed on the jars while hot, and your food needs to be processed as quickly as possible to preserve the most flavor and quality.

Step 4: Placing the jars in the canner

Place your filled and closed jars carefully on the rack in the pressure canner, making sure you have the recommended amount of simmering water in the bottom of the canner. Don't crowd the jars or place more jars in the canner than is recommended for your size of pressure canner. Place them so that they're stable, won't tip, and don't touch each other or the side of the canner.

REMEMBER

If your recipe makes more jars than your canner can hold, fill only enough jars for one canner load and do the rest in the next batch. Do not fill all the jars and leave a few waiting for the next canner load.

TIP

Unlike water-bath canning, you can process a second layer of pint or half-pint jars at the same time as long as your canner accommodates the height of the two layers. To build the second layer, place a second rack on top of the first layer of jars. Stagger the second layer of jars so they aren't directly above the bottom layer. This permits proper air circulation for achieving the proper pressure and temperature. After you have a few simple canning sessions successfully under your belt, try this technique to save a little time.

Step 5: Closing and locking the canner

For optimum performance, steam must be allowed to steadily escape from the canner for a specified period. This process is called *exhaustion*. Properly closing and locking your pressure canner ensure that exhaustion can take place. Closely follow your owner's manual when closing and locking the pressure canner. (If not sealed properly, the canner won't build pressure or hot water will spit out or both.)

Step 6: Processing your filled jars

Once your canner lid is locked on, you're ready to beginning processing your filled jars. Follow these steps:

1. **Allow a steady stream of steam to escape from the pressure canner for 10 minutes or the time recommended in your manual.**

2. **Close the vent, bringing the pressure to the amount specified in your recipe.**

If you live in higher altitudes, see the section "Pressure Canning at Higher Altitudes" for information on how to adjust the pounds of pressure used during processing.

REMEMBER

Processing time starts when your canner reaches the required pressure. The pressure must remain constant for the entire processing time. If your pressure drops at any time during processing, so will your temperature. To remedy this problem, return the pressure to the specified amount by increasing the heat. After your pressure has been regained, start your processing time from the beginning.

3. **After the processing time has passed, turn the heat off and allow the pressure to return to 0.**

Allowing the pressure to return to 0 may take as long as 30 minutes. Don't disturb the canner; jars that are upset may not seal properly.

Step 7: Releasing the pressure after processing

Approximately 10 minutes after the pressure returns to 0, or at the time stated in the manual, remove the lid, opening the cover away from you and allowing the steam to flow away from you.

Don't underestimate the importance of following the instructions in your owner's manual, step by step, for releasing the pressure in the canner after your processing time is concluded. There's no quick-release method for a pressure canner as there is for a pressure cooker. Don't confuse the two!

WARNING

Running water over your pressure canner to reduce the pressure is a definite no-no. The sudden change in temperature can cause the jars to burst.

Step 8: Removing and cooling the jars

Ten minutes after you release the pressure (Step 7), remove the jars from the pressure canner with a jar lifter. Place them on a clean towel, away from drafts with 1 to 2 inches of space around the jars.

The jars may take as long as 24 hours to completely cool. Don't be tempted to play with the lids or adjust the bands.

REMEMBER

As your jars cool, you'll hear a popping noise coming from them, indicating a vacuum seal. You will soon learn to look forward to these tiny pings and dings. This canning music means you have successfully saved your summer bounty.

Step 9: Testing the seal and storing your bounty

The final pressure-canning step is to test the seals on your completely cooled jars: Push on the center of the lid. If the lid feels solid and doesn't indent, you've produced a successful seal. If the lid depresses when applying pressure, this jar isn't sealed. Refrigerate any unsealed jars immediately, using the contents within two weeks or the period stated in your recipe.

To store jars, do the following:

1. **Remove the screw bands of the sealed jars.**

2. **Remove any residue by washing the jars, lids, and bands in hot, soapy water; then dry them.**

3. **Label your jars with the content and date of processing.**

4. **Store the jars without the screw bands, in a cool, dark, dry place.**

WARNING

Although you may follow all the steps and procedures for pressure canning low-acid foods, you still have a chance for spoilage. Botulism poisoning can be fatal. Because botulism spores have no odor and can't be seen, you can't always tell which jars are tainted. If you suspect that a jar of food is spoiled, never, never, never taste it. Instead, dispose of the food responsibly.

Pressure Canning at Higher Altitudes

If you're canning at an elevation higher than 1,000 feet above sea level, adjust the pounds of pressure used during processing, according to Table 3-1. Your pressure-canner processing time will remain the same.

TIP

If you don't know your altitude level, you can get this information by contacting your public library, a local college, or the cooperative extension service in your county or state. Or go to http://national4-hheadquarters.gov/Extension/index.html. Click on your state on the map and follow the instructions on your state's website.

TABLE 3-1

High-Altitude Processing Times for Pressure Canning

Altitude	Process at This Pressure
2,000–3,000	11½ pounds
3,000–4,000	12 pounds
4,000–5,000	12½ pounds
5,000–6,000	13 pounds
6,000–7,000	13½ pounds
7,000–8,000	14 pounds
8,000–9,000	14½ pounds
9,000–10,000	15 pounds

Canning Vegetables

Early in the growing season, your garden produces enough each day for one or two meals, and then the explosion starts. Tomatoes, zucchini, and beans, to name a few, abound. You wonder, "How can just a few plants produce so many vegetables?" You're proud to share your bounty with friends, neighbors, and coworkers, but there's a limit to how much you can give away!

Now, reality sets in. You have to do something with this harvest or it will go to waste! It's time to get out your pressure canner, check your equipment, and get busy pressure canning. You must act quickly if you plan to preserve these vegetables for use in the winter and spring.

Picking the perfect produce

Whether harvesting your vegetables from the garden or shopping at a farmer's market or your local supermarket, select vegetables that are free of bruises and imperfections. These marks could encourage the growth of bacteria in your food. Follow this basic rule for evaluating damage on vegetables for canning: If you won't eat that portion of the vegetable, don't buy it and can it.

The key to keeping all this wonderful, perfect freshness? Process the vegetables the day of harvesting or purchasing — the sooner the better. If you need to wait a day, store the items in your refrigerator to preserve the quality and prevent deterioration of your food. Don't make your vegetables wait longer than one day!

Vegetables not recommended for pressure canning

Some vegetables shouldn't be preserved by pressure canning because the food may discolor, produce a stronger flavor when canned, or just lose its look (meaning it disintegrates or falls apart when placed under high heat and high pressure). Other methods, such as pickling (see Chapter 4 of this minibook) or freezing (see Chapter 5 of this minibook), may be better preserving choices for these foods. Table 3-2 lists some vegetables you may be tempted to pressure-can but that will preserve better in other ways.

TABLE 3-2

Vegetables Not Recommended for Pressure Canning

Vegetable	Suggested Preservation Method
Broccoli	Freezing
Brussels sprouts	Freezing
Cabbage	Pickling (to make sauerkraut)
Cauliflower	Pickling
Cucumbers	Pickling
Eggplant	Pickling
Mushrooms (For safety, use ones that are commercially grown; don't go out and pick some yourself.)	Pickling
Parsnips	Pickling
Rutabagas	Pickling
Turnips	Pickling

Cleaning your vegetables

Properly cleaning your vegetables is important to your finished. The method and amount of cleaning required is determined by where the vegetables were grown: above the ground (such as beans or squash) or in the ground (such as carrots or beets).

>> **Vegetables growing above the ground:** These vegetables usually have a thinner, more tender skin than vegetables grown in the ground. Remove any stems and leaves. Run water over them, gently rub the skin with your fingers and remove any dirt. Shake off the excess water and place your food on clean kitchen or paper towels.

>> **Vegetables growing in the ground:** Root vegetables, such as carrots and beets, may require soaking to loosen any clinging soil. After first rinsing the vegetables, immerse them in a basin of cool water. Using a stiff brush (a new toothbrush works well), scrub the surface of the vegetables, removing any clinging soil. Rinse thoroughly with running water, placing the vegetables on clean kitchen or paper towels to drain.

Raw packing versus hot packing

Raw packing and hot packing foods refers to the way the food is treated before it is placed in the jars. In raw packing, you don't cook the food prior to processing. In hot packing, you do. The following section goes into more details on which method is preferable when you're canning vegetables.

REMEMBER

Packing food raw or hot doesn't change your processing time. Reaching the required pressure in your canner, usually 10 pounds, takes the same amount of time, regardless of the temperature of your raw- or hot-packed jars.

Raw (cold packing)

The *raw packing* (also called cold packing) method uses raw, unheated vegetables for filling your prepared jars. Filling the jars with raw vegetables keeps them firm without being crushed during processing. Refer to your recipe instructions to decide whether to remove the skin or cut the vegetables into pieces.

Disadvantages of using raw vegetables include the following:

>> **Floating food:** During the pressure-canning process, air is removed from the vegetable fiber, causing the food to shrink. With more room in the jars, the vegetables have room to float toward the top of the jar (this is called *floating food*). Floating food doesn't affect the quality of your final product, but it may be unattractive.

>> **Discoloring:** *Discoloring* occurs when the food comes in contact with air in the jar, causing a color change in your food after two or three months of storage. The flavor of your product is not affected, but the change in color in a portion of the food may appear odd.

To fill your jars using a raw packing method, follow these instructions:

1. **Wash your vegetables.**

2. **Prepare the hot liquid (refer to your recipe) for filling your jars.**

3. **Fill the hot, prepared jars with your raw vegetables.**

4. **Add the hot liquid and canning salt, if required.**

5. **Release any air bubbles with a nonreactive tool (refer to Chapter 1 in this minibook).**

   If the headspace in your jar drops, add additional food and liquid to maintain the headspace stated in your recipe.

6. **Wipe the jar rims; add the two-piece caps, and process the filled jars in a pressure canner.**

Hot packing

When you *hot pack*, you precook or heat your vegetables prior to placing them in your prepared canning jars. It's the preferred method for the majority of vegetables, particularly firm ones, such as carrots and beets. Using precooked vegetables improves the shelf life of the processed food by increasing the vacuum created in the jar during the pressure-canning period.

Precooking your vegetables in a boiling liquid, usually water, preshrinks the food and makes it more pliable, which allows you to pack more food into your jars. This results in using fewer jars. The method is a simple one:

1. **Wash your vegetables.**

2. **Heat your liquid to a boil in a large pot and add the vegetables, precooking them as directed in your recipe.**

3. **Immediately fill your prepared jars with the hot vegetables, followed with the hot cooking liquid.**

4. **Release any air bubbles with a nonreactive tool.**

   If the headspace in your jar drops, add additional food and liquid to maintain the headspace stated in your recipe.

5. **Wipe the jar rims, add the two-piece caps, and process the filled jars in a pressure canner.**

Vegetable Canning Recipes

This section offers instructions and guidelines for pressure canning some of the more common fresh vegetables. Included are tips for selecting your vegetables, determining the approximate amounts of fresh vegetables for yielding 1 quart of a finished product, and which method is preferred.

Asparagus

Select firm, bright-green stalks with tightly closed tips. Stalks with small diameters indicate a young, tender vegetable. Cut stalks into 1-inch pieces or can them whole, placing the tips of the stalks toward the top of the jar (be sure to trim them from the bottom to maintain the headspace indicated in the recipe).

Canning asparagus is a great way to preserve this delicate vegetable. With only one short season, it is usually a special treat or pricy delicacy during the rest of the year. Keeping plenty on hand will ensure that your family can enjoy this treat any time it wants. In Chapter 4 of this minibook, you can find a recipe for Pickled Asparagus.

Beans

When you can green, string, Italian, or wax beans, select ones that are tender and small. Remove the ends and strings from the beans, as shown in Figure 3-8. Can them whole or cut them into 1- to 2-inch pieces.

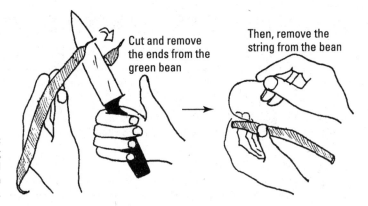

Cut and remove the ends from the green bean

Then, remove the string from the bean

FIGURE 3-8: Removing the ends and strings from green beans.

Beets

Select beets with a deep red color. A beet with a diameter of 1 to 2 inches is the most desirable size for pressure canning. Larger-size beets are best pickled (head to Chapter 4 of this minibook for information on pickling and a Spiced Pickled Beets recipe). Figure 3-9 details how to prepare a beet.

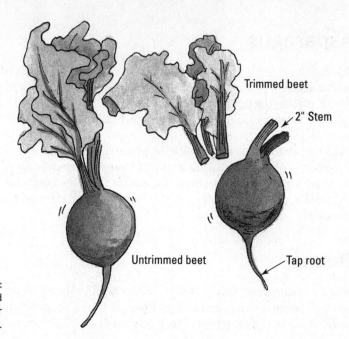

FIGURE 3-9:
A trimmed
beet ready for
precooking.

Trimmed beet

2" Stem

Untrimmed beet

Tap root

Bell peppers (green, red, orange, yellow)

Sweet, firm bell peppers produce the best results. With so many beautiful colored peppers available, a jar of canned bell peppers could turn into a lovely gift.

REMEMBER

Because of the extremely low acid level in this vegetable, you must adjust the acidity level of the bell peppers by adding bottled lemon juice. Use only pint or half-pint jars for this extremely low-acid vegetable.

To peel peppers easily, heat them in a 400-degree oven for 6 to 8 minutes, or until the skin blisters. Then cover them with a damp cloth and let them cool. Voilà! You can now easily remove skins with a knife or simply by rubbing them with your hands as you run cool water over the pepper.

Carrots

For canning, choose carrots with a diameter of 1 to 1½ inches. Canned carrots make a favorite side dish even faster. Once reheated, add brown sugar and butter for a sweet treat.

Carrots are an inexpensive vegetable at farmer's markets during their season, and canning is an excellent way to preserve them. They keep all of their sweet flavor and the texture remains very nice.

Corn

Starting with corn that has the husks on and the silk attached allows you to assess the freshness of the corn. Choose ears with brightly colored husks that are free of spots and moisture; silks should be golden, not matted or brown.

Creamed corn doesn't contain cream. Its creaminess comes from the naturally sweet juice, or *milk*, of the kernel. To obtain the creaminess, simply cut off the kernels and run your knife against the cob a second time, even closer to release the milk. Creamed corn is a great base for soups and makes a classic comfort food.

TIP

Here's a surefire way to select corn that is sure to be juicy and tender: Peel back the husk slightly to check for any pests. If all is clear (no bugs or mold), use your thumbnail to depress a kernel about an inch below the top of the corn. If the ear has adequate moisture, liquid will squirt out. Buy this ear! If no spitting occurs, select another ear and repeat the test.

Onions

Onions are a staple ingredient in many recipes. Their savory flavor often is the finishing touch to your favorite meal. Canning onions leave them soft but flavorful. Keep these onions in your pantry as an important ingredient for your favorite recipe.

Peas

There is nothing like the taste of garden fresh peas. If your kids have decided they don't like cooked peas, convince them that your own canned peas are worth a try.

Potatoes

The only potatoes recommended for pressure canning are sweet potatoes, yams, and white, or Irish, potatoes. Using any other potatoes yields inferior results because of their chemical makeup (texture and composition).

>> **White or Irish:** These potatoes are round and white with a thin skin. Peel the potatoes prior to precooking. Small potatoes (2 to 3 inches in diameter) may be left whole; cut larger potatoes into quarters before precooking.

>> **Sweet potatoes and yams:** Sweet potatoes are roots and yams are tubers — so they're actually from two different plant species. Even though sweet potatoes and yams are unrelated, they're suitable for the same uses. Sweet potatoes have skin colors ranging from light yellow to dark orange and flesh colors ranging from pale yellow to medium orange and are sweeter than

yams. Yams contain more natural sugar and have a higher moisture content than sweet potatoes; they're white to deep red in flesh color with skin colors ranging from creamy white to deep red. Small potatoes may be left whole; cut larger ones into quarters before removing the skins.

Try draining canned potatoes to use in homemade hash in the winter. They are hearty breakfast fare after a cold morning on the homestead.

Sweet potatoes can complement a meal with their rich, naturally sweet flavor. The bright orange color makes a dish pop, and many who think they don't like any veggies are pleasantly surprised at the delicious taste of the sweet potato. The recipe in this chapter produces a firmer finished product with much more flavor — a definite improvement over store-bought sweet potatoes from a can.

Summer squash

Summer squash include crookneck, zucchini, and patty pan, to name a few. The skins are thin and edible, eliminating the need to peel them.

Canned Asparagus

PREP: 15 MIN	PROCESSING: PINTS, 30 MIN; QUARTS, 40 MIN	PRESSURE: 10 POUNDS	YIELD: 14 PINTS OR 7 QUARTS

INGREDIENTS

24 pounds fresh, young asparagus

Boiling water

Canning salt

1 Prepare your canning jars and two-piece caps (lids and screw bands) according to the manufacturer's instructions. Keep the jars and lids hot. (For detailed instructions on preparing your jars, see the step-by-step directions earlier in this chapter.)

2 Wash the asparagus spears. Cut them into 1-inch pieces. In a 12-quart pot, bring water to a boil. Heat the asparagus pieces in the boiling water for 2 to 3 minutes, until the spears are bright green but still firm inside. Do not drain.

3 Loosely pack the cut spears into jars (don't press them down). Pour the boiling cooking liquid over the pieces, leaving 1-inch headspace. Add ½ teaspoon salt to each pint jar or 1 teaspoon salt to each quart jar. Release any air bubbles with a nonreactive utensil, adding more liquid as necessary to maintain the proper headspace (refer to Chapter 1 of this minibook). Wipe the jar rims; seal the jars with the two-piece caps, hand-tightening the bands.

4 Process the filled jars in a pressure canner at 10 pounds pressure for 30 minutes (pints) or 40 minutes (quarts). When the processing time is done, allow the pressure to return to 0, wait an additional 10 minutes, and then carefully open the canner lid.

5 Remove the jars from the canner with a jar lifter. Place them on a clean kitchen towel away from drafts. After the jars cool completely, test the seals (refer to the step-by-step directions earlier in this chapter). If you find jars that haven't sealed, refrigerate them and use them within two weeks. Before eating or tasting, boil the food for 15 minutes.

PER ½-CUP SERVING: *Calories 23 (From fat 3); Fat 0g (Saturated0); Cholesterol 0mg; Sodium 301mg; Carbohydrates 4g (Dietary fiber 2g); Protein 3g*

Pressure Canning

Canned Fresh Green Beans

PREP: 15 MIN	PROCESSING: PINTS, 20 MIN; QUARTS, 25 MIN	PRESSURE: 10 POUNDS	YIELD: 16 PINTS OR 8 QUARTS

INGREDIENTS

4 pounds fresh green beans

Boiling water

Canning salt

1 Prepare your canning jars and two-piece caps (lids and screw bands) according to the manufacturer's instructions. Keep the jars and lids hot. (For information on preparing your jars, see the step-by-step directions earlier in this chapter.)

2 In an 8-quart pot, bring 2 quarts of water to a boil. While water is boiling, trim off the ends of the beans and cut them into 2-inch pieces.

3 Tightly pack the cut beans into the prepared jars. Pour the boiling water over the beans, leaving 1-inch headspace. Add ½ teaspoon salt to each pint jar or 1 teaspoon salt to each quart jar. Release any air bubbles with a nonreactive utensil, adding more water as necessary to maintain the proper headspace (refer to Chapter 1 of this minibook). Wipe the jar rims; seal the jars with the two-piece caps, hand-tightening the bands.

4 Process the filled jars in a pressure canner at 10 pounds pressure for 20 minutes (pints) or 25 minutes (quarts). Allow the pressure to return to 0, wait an additional 10 minutes, and then carefully open the canner lid.

5 Remove the jars from the canner with a jar lifter. Place them on a clean kitchen towel away from drafts. After the jars cool completely, test the seals (refer to the step-by-step directions earlier in this chapter). If you find jars that haven't sealed, refrigerate them and use them within two weeks. Prior to eating or tasting, boil the food for 15 minutes.

PER ½-CUP SERVING: *Calories 10 (From fat 1); Fat 0g (Saturated 0g); Cholesterol 0mg; Sodium 292mg; Carbohydrates 2g (Dietary fiber 1g); Protein 1g*

Canned Beets

PREP: 15 MIN	PROCESSING: PINTS, 30 MIN; QUARTS, 35 MIN	PRESSURE: 10 POUNDS	YIELD: 14 PINTS OR 7 QUARTS

INGREDIENTS

21 pounds beets without tops

Canning salt

1 Prepare your canning jars and two-piece caps (lids and screw bands) according to the manufacturer's instructions. Keep the jars and lids hot. (For information on preparing your jars, see the step-by-step directions earlier in this chapter.)

2 Scrub your beets clean of dirt and remove the tap roots (see Figure 3-9). Place the cleaned beets in a 12-quart pot and cover them with water. Boil the beets for 15 to 20 minutes. When beets are cool enough to handle, the skins will peel off easily. Remove them from the water and peel. Trim the remaining root and stem. Leave small beets whole, and cut larger beets in half for a better fit in the jar. Reserve the cooking liquid.

3 Pack the beets into your prepared jars. Pour the cooking liquid over the beets, leaving 1-inch headspace. Add ½ teaspoon salt to each pint jar or 1 teaspoon salt to each quart jar. Release any air bubbles with a nonreactive utensil, adding more liquid as necessary to maintain the proper headspace (see Chapter 1 of this minibook). Wipe the jar rims; seal the jars with the two-piece caps, hand-tightening the bands.

4 Process the filled jars in a pressure canner at 10 pounds pressure for 30 minutes (pints) or 35 minutes (quarts). Allow the pressure to return to 0, wait an additional 10 minutes, and then carefully open the canner lid.

(continued)

Pressure Canning

5 Remove the jars from the canner with a jar lifter. Place them on a clean kitchen towel away from drafts. After the jars cool completely, test the seals (refer to the step-by-step directions earlier in this chapter). If you find jars that haven't sealed, refrigerate them and use them within two weeks. Prior to eating or tasting, boil the food for 15 minutes.

NOTE: To preserve the bright, red color of the beet, add 1 tablespoon of vinegar (with an acidity of 5 percent) to each quart of liquid before sealing the jars.

PER ½-CUP SERVING: *Calories 72 (From fat 3); Fat 0g (Saturated 0g); Cholesterol 0mg; Sodium 416mg; Carbohydrates 0g (Dietary fiber 0g); Protein 0g*

Canned Bell Peppers

PREP: 15 MIN	PROCESSING: HALF-PINTS, 35 MIN; PINTS, 40 MIN	PRESSURE: 10 POUNDS	YIELD: 10 HALF-PINTS OR 5 PINTS

INGREDIENTS

5 pounds sweet peppers

Boiling water

Canning salt

Lemon juice

1 Prepare your canning jars and two-piece caps (lids and screw bands) according to the manufacturer's instructions. Keep the jars and lids hot. (For information on preparing your jars, see the step-by-step directions earlier in this chapter.)

2 Wash the peppers and cut them into quarters and remove the stem and seeds. Meanwhile bring 2 quarts of water to a boil.

3 Pack flattened peppers firmly into jars. Pour the boiling water over the peppers, leaving 1-inch headspace. Add ½ tablespoon lemon juice and ¼ teaspoon salt to each half-pint jar or 1 tablespoon lemon juice and ½ teaspoon salt to each pint jar. Release any air bubbles with a nonreactive utensil, adding more water as necessary to maintain the proper headspace (see Chapter 1 of this minibook). Wipe the jar rims; seal the jars with the two-piece caps, hand-tightening the bands.

4 Process the filled jars in a pressure canner at 10 pounds pressure for 35 minutes (half-pints) or 40 minutes (pints). Allow the pressure to return to 0, wait an additional 10 minutes, and then carefully open the canner lid.

5 Remove the jars from the canner with a jar lifter. Place them on a clean kitchen towel away from drafts. After the jars cool completely, test the seals (refer to the step-by-step directions earlier in this chapter). If you find jars that haven't sealed, refrigerate them and use them within two weeks. Before eating or tasting, boil the food for 15 minutes.

PER ½-CUP SERVING: *Calories 32 (From fat 2); Fat 0g (Saturated 0g); Cholesterol 0mg; Sodium 584mg; Carbohydrates 8g (Dietary fiber 2g); Protein 1g*

Pressure Canning

Canned Carrots

PREP: 15 MIN	PROCESSING: PINTS, 25 MIN; QUARTS, 35 MIN	PRESSURE: 10 POUNDS	YIELD: 6 PINTS OR 3 QUARTS

INGREDIENTS

12 pounds of carrots, peeled and without tops

Canning salt

1 Prepare your canning jars and two-piece caps (lids and screw bands) according to the manufacturer's instructions. Keep the jars and lids hot. (For information on preparing your jars, see the step-by-step directions earlier in this chapter.)

2 Rinse and scrub the carrots with a brush to remove any dirt. Alternatively, remove the skin with a vegetable peeler. Remove the carrot tops. Cut the carrots into ¼-inch slices or dice the carrots, being sure that all the diced pieces are approximately the same size.

3 Place the sliced or diced carrots in a 12-quart pot and cover them with water. Bring them to a boil. Reduce heat to medium and allow the carrots to simmer for 5 minutes, or until they're still slightly firm in the center but tender on the outside. Do not drain.

4 Pack the hot carrots into your prepared jars. Pour the cooking liquid over them, leaving 1-inch headspace. Add ½ teaspoon salt to each pint jar or 1 teaspoon salt to each quart jar. Release any air bubbles with a nonreactive utensil, adding more liquid as necessary to maintain the proper headspace (see Chapter 1 of this minibook). Wipe the jar rims; seal the jars with the two-piece caps, hand-tightening the bands.

5 Process the filled jars in a pressure canner at 10 pounds pressure for 25 minutes (pints) or 35 minutes (quarts). Allow the pressure to return to 0, wait an additional 10 minutes, and then carefully open the canner lid.

6 Remove the jars from the canner with a jar lifter. Place them on a clean kitchen towel away from drafts. After the jars cool completely, test the seals (refer to the step-by-step directions earlier in this chapter). If you find jars that haven't sealed, refrigerate them and use them within two weeks. Prior to eating or tasting, boil the food for 10 minutes.

PER ½-CUP SERVING: *Calories 94 (From fat 3); Fat 0g (Saturated 0g); Cholesterol 0mg; Sodium 424mg; Carbohydrates 22g (Dietary fiber 7g); Protein 2g*

Pressure Canning

Canned Corn

PREP: 15 MIN	PROCESSING: PINTS, 55 MIN; QUARTS, 85 MIN	PRESSURE: 10 POUNDS	YIELD: 12 PINTS OR 6 QUARTS

INGREDIENTS

24 pounds fresh corn on the cob

Boiling water

Canning salt

1 Prepare your canning jars and two-piece caps (lids and screw bands) according to the manufacturer's instructions. Keep the jars and lids hot. (For information on preparing your jars, see the step-by-step directions earlier in this chapter.)

2 Remove the husk and silk from the corn. Using a sharp knife, slice the corn from the cob, measuring the corn as you go so that you know how many total pints or quarts of corn kernels you have. Meanwhile, bring 1 gallon of water to a boil in an 8-quart pot (you'll use this as a reserve).

3 Place the corn in a 12-quart pot. For each pint of corn, add 1 cup of boiling water; for each quart of corn, add 2 cups of boiling water. Place the pot over medium-high heat and bring to a simmer. Then reduce heat to medium and allow the corn to simmer for 5 minutes.

4 Ladle the corn into your prepared jars and pour additional boiling water over it if necessary, leaving 1-inch headspace. Add 1 teaspoon salt to each quart jar or ½ teaspoon salt to each pint jar. Release any air bubbles with a nonreactive utensil, adding more water as necessary to maintain the proper headspace (see Chapter 1 of this minibook). Wipe the jar rims; seal the jars with the two-piece caps, hand-tightening the bands.

5 Process the filled jars in a pressure canner at 10 pounds pressure for 55 minutes (pints) or 1 hour 25 minutes (quarts). Allow the pressure to return to 0, wait an additional 10 minutes, and then carefully open the canner lid.

6 Remove the jars from the canner with a jar lifter. Place them on a clean kitchen towel away from drafts. After the jars cool completely, test the seals (refer to the step-by-step directions earlier in this chapter). If you find jars that haven't sealed, refrigerate them and use them within two weeks. Prior to eating or tasting, boil the food for 15 minutes.

PER ½-UP SERVING: *Calories 136 (From fat 15); Fat 2g (Saturated 0g); Cholesterol 0mg; Sodium 312mg; Carbohydrates 32g (Dietary fiber 3g); Protein 4g*

Pressure Canning

Canned Creamed Corn

PREP: 20 MIN	PROCESSING: PINTS, 95 MIN	PRESSURE: 10 POUNDS	YIELD: 9 PINTS

INGREDIENTS

20 pounds corn

Boiling water

Canning salt

1 Prepare your canning jars and two-piece caps (lids and screw bands) according to the manufacturer's instructions. Keep the jars and lids hot. (For information on preparing your jars, see the step-by-step directions earlier in this chapter.)

2 In a 12-quart pot, bring 2 gallons of water to a boil. Remove the husk and silk from the corn. Blanch the corn on the cob for 4 minutes in the boiling water. Allow the corn to cool enough to handle. Slice the corn kernels from cob with a sharp knife. Then run the knife blade along the ear again to remove the extra juice or milk. Measure the corn as you go so that you know how many pints of corn and corn milk you have.

3 Place the corn and corn milk in a 12-quart pot. For each pint of corn and corn milk, add 2 cups of water. Heat the corn to boiling.

4 Using a canning funnel, pour the corn and corn milk mixture into your prepared jars, leaving 1-inch headspace. Add ½ teaspoon salt to each jar. If necessary to attain the required headspace, add boiling water to the jars. Release any air bubbles with a nonreactive utensil, adding more water as necessary to maintain the proper headspace (see Chapter 1 of this minibook). Wipe the jar rims; seal the jars with the two-piece caps, hand-tightening the bands.

5 Process the filled pint jars in a pressure canner at 10 pounds pressure for 1 hour 35 minutes. Allow the pressure to return to 0, wait an additional 10 minutes, and then carefully open the canner lid.

6 Remove the jars from the canner with a jar lifter. Place them on a clean kitchen towel or paper towels away from drafts. After the jars cool completely, test the seals (refer to the step-by-step directions earlier in this chapter). If you find jars that haven't sealed, refrigerate them and use them within two weeks. Prior to eating or tasting, boil the food for 10 minutes.

NOTE: This recipe uses pints (quarts aren't recommended).

PER ½-CUP SERVING: *Calories 151 (From fat 16); Fat 2g (Saturated 0g); Cholesterol 0mg; Sodium 605mg; Carbohydrates 35g (Dietary fiber 4g); Protein 5g*

Canned Onions

PREP: 20 MIN	PROCESSING: PINTS AND QUARTS, 40 MIN	PRESSURE: 10 POUNDS	YIELD: 20 PINTS OR 10 QUARTS

INGREDIENTS

20 pounds fresh onions

Canning salt

1. Prepare your canning jars and two-piece caps (lids and screw bands) according to the manufacturer's instructions. Keep the jars and lids hot. (For information on preparing your jars, see the step-by-step directions earlier in this chapter.)

2. Peel and wash the onions. If you're using large onions, chop them or slice them into ½-inch pieces.

3. Place the onions in a 12-quart pot, cover them with water, and bring them to a boil over medium high heat. Boil them for 5 minutes, or until they're translucent.

4. Using a slotted spoon, remove the onions from cooking liquid (reserve the liquid for filling the jars) and firmly pack them into the prepared jars. Add ½ teaspoon salt to each pint jar or 1 teaspoon salt to each quart jar. Pour the hot cooking liquid over the onions, leaving 1-inch headspace. Release any air bubbles with a nonreactive utensil, adding liquid as necessary to maintain the proper headspace (refer to Chapter 1 of this minibook). Wipe the jar rims; seal the jars with the two-piece caps, hand-tightening the bands.

5. Process the filled jars in a pressure canner at 10 pounds pressure for 40 minutes (pints or quarts). Allow the pressure to return to 0, wait an additional 10 minutes, and then carefully open the canner lid away.

6 Remove the jars from the canner with a jar lifter. Place them on a clean kitchen towel away from drafts. After the jars cool completely, test the seals (refer to the step-by-step directions earlier in this chapter). If you find jars that haven't sealed, refrigerate them and use them within two weeks. Before eating or tasting, boil the food for 15 minutes.

PER ½-CUP SERVING: *Calories 42 (From fat 2); Fat 0g (Saturated 0g); Cholesterol 0mg; Sodium 294mg; Carbohydrates 10g (Dietary fiber 1g); Protein 1g*

Canned Peas

PREP: 15 MIN	PROCESSING: PINTS AND QUARTS, 40 MIN	PRESSURE: 10 POUNDS	YIELD: 14 PINTS OR 7 QUARTS

INGREDIENTS

28 to 30 pounds fresh, young peas in the pod

Canning salt

1 Prepare your canning jars and two-piece caps (lids and screw bands) according to the manufacturer's instructions. Keep the jars and lids hot. (For information on preparing your jars, see the step-by-step directions earlier in this chapter.)

2 Wash and remove the pods. Place the peas in an 8-quart pot, cover them with water, and bring to a boil over high heat. Allow the peas to boil for 3 to 5 minutes, or until they're bright green but not fully cooked.

3 Remove the peas from the cooking liquid (reserve the liquid for filling jars) and loosely pack the peas into the prepared jars. Pour hot cooking water over them, leaving 1-inch headspace Add ½ teaspoon salt to each pint jar or 1 teaspoon salt to each quart jar. Release any air bubbles with a nonreactive utensil, adding liquid as necessary to maintain the proper headspace (refer to Chapter 1 of this minibook). Wipe the jar rims; seal the jars with the two-piece caps, hand-tightening the bands.

4 Process the filled jars in a pressure canner at 10 pounds pressure for 40 minutes (pints or quarts). Allow the pressure to return to 0, wait an additional 10 minutes, and then carefully open the canner lid.

5 Remove the jars from the canner with a jar lifter. Place them on a clean kitchen towel away from drafts. After the jars cool completely, test the seals (refer to the step-by-step directions earlier in this chapter). If you find jars that haven't sealed, refrigerate them and use them within two weeks. Before eating or tasting, boil the food for 15 minutes.

PER ½-CUP SERVING: Calories 70 (From fat 3); Fat 0g (Saturated 0g); Cholesterol 0mg; Sodium 295mg; Carbohydrates 13g (Dietary fiber 4g); Protein 5g

Canned White Potatoes

PREP: 15 MIN	PROCESSING: PINTS, 35 MIN; QUARTS, 40 MIN	PRESSURE: 10 POUNDS	YIELD: 14 PINTS OR 7 QUARTS

INGREDIENTS

7 pounds fresh, young potatoes

Canning salt

Pressure Canning

1 Prepare your canning jars and two-piece caps (lids and screw bands) according to the manufacturer's instructions. Keep the jars and lids hot. (For information on preparing your jars, see the step-by-step directions earlier in this chapter.)

2 In a 12-quart pot, bring 2 gallons of water to boil. Wash and peel your potatoes. Cube the potatoes into ½-inch pieces. Carefully place the potatoes in the boiling water and cook for 2 minutes or until potatoes are partially cooked but still firm.

3 Pack the hot potatoes into the prepared jars (reserve the liquid you cooked them in). Add ½ teaspoon salt to each pint jar or 1 teaspoon salt to each quart jar. Pour the cooking liquid over the potatoes, leaving 1-inch headspace. Release any air bubbles with a nonreactive utensil, adding liquid as necessary to maintain the proper headspace (refer to Chapter 1 of this minibook). Wipe the jar rims; seal the jars with the two-piece caps, hand-tightening the bands.

4 Process the filled jars in a pressure canner at 10 pounds pressure for 35 minutes (pints) or 40 minutes (quarts). Allow the pressure to return to 0, wait an additional 10 minutes, and then carefully open the canner lid.

5 Remove the jars from the canner with a jar lifter. Place them on a clean kitchen towel away from drafts. After the jars cool completely, test the seals (refer to the step-by-step directions earlier in this chapter). If you find jars that haven't sealed, refrigerate them and use them within two weeks. Prior to eating or tasting, boil the food for 15 minutes.

PER ½-CUP SERVING: *Calories 36 (From fat 1); Fat 0g (Saturated 0g); Cholesterol 0mg; Sodium 292mg; Carbohydrates 7g (Dietary fiber 1g); Protein 1g*

Canned Sweet Potatoes

PREP: 15 MIN	PROCESSING: PINTS, 65 MIN; QUARTS, 90 MIN	PRESSURE: 10 POUNDS	YIELD: 14 PINTS OR 7 QUARTS

INGREDIENTS

21 pounds sweet potatoes

Canning salt

1 Prepare your canning jars and two-piece caps (lids and screw bands) according to the manufacturer's instructions. Keep the jars and lids hot. (For information on preparing your jars, see the step-by-step directions earlier in this chapter.)

2 In a 12-quart pot, bring 2 gallons of water to boil. Wash and peel the sweet potatoes. Cube them into ½-inch pieces. Carefully place the sweet potatoes into the boiling water and cook for 10 minutes, or until the potatoes are partially cooked but still firm. Reserve the cooking liquid.

3 Pack the hot sweet potatoes into the prepared jars. Add ½ teaspoon salt to each pint jar or 1 teaspoon salt to each quart jar. Pour the cooking liquid over the sweet potatoes, leaving 1-inch headspace. Release any air bubbles with a non-reactive utensil, adding liquid as necessary to maintain the proper headspace (refer to Chapter 1 of this minibook). Wipe the jar rims; seal the jars with the two-piece caps, hand-tightening the bands.

4 Process the filled jars in a pressure canner at 10 pounds pressure for 1 hour 5 minutes (pints) or 1 hour 30 minutes (quarts). Allow the pressure to return to 0, wait an additional 10 minutes, and then carefully open the canner lid.

5 Remove the jars from the canner with a jar lifter. Place them on a clean kitchen towel away from drafts. After the jars cool completely, test the seals (refer to the step-by-step directions earlier in this chapter). If you find jars that haven't sealed, refrigerate them and use them within two weeks. Prior to eating or tasting, boil the food for 15 minutes.

PER ½-CUP SERVING: *Calories 139 (From fat 4); Fat 0g (Saturated 0g); Cholesterol 0mg; Sodium 308mg; Carbohydrates 32g (Dietary fiber 2g); Protein 2g*

Canned Summer Squash

PREP: 15 MIN	PROCESSING: PINTS, 30 MIN; QUARTS, 40 MIN	PRESSURE: 10 POUNDS	YIELD: 14 PINTS OR 7 QUARTS

INGREDIENTS

8 to 20 pounds summer squash

Canning salt

1 Prepare your canning jars and two-piece caps (lids and screw bands) according to the manufacturer's instructions. Keep the jars and lids hot. (For information on preparing your jars, see the step-by-step directions earlier in this chapter.)

2 In a 12-quart pot, bring 2 gallons of water to boil. Wash and cut the summer squash into ¼-inch slices or 1-inch cubes. Carefully place the cubed or sliced squash into your boiling water and return to a boil for 5 minutes, or until slightly softened. Reserve the cooking liquid.

3 Using a canning funnel, loosely pack the squash into the prepared jars. Pour the hot cooking liquid over the squash, leaving ½-inch headspace. Add ½ teaspoon salt to each pint jar or 1 teaspoon salt to each quart jar. Release any air bubbles with a nonreactive utensil, adding liquid as necessary to maintain the proper headspace (refer to Chapter 1 of this minibook). Wipe the jar rims; seal the jars with the two-piece caps, hand-tightening the bands.

4 Process the filled jars in a pressure canner at 10 pounds pressure for 30 minutes (pints) or 40 minutes (quarts). Allow the pressure to return to 0, wait an additional 10 minutes, and then carefully open the canner lid.

5 Remove the jars from the canner with a jar lifter. Place them on a clean kitchen towel away from drafts. After the jars cool completely, test the seals (refer to the step-by-step directions earlier in this chapter). If you find jars that haven't sealed, refrigerate them and use them within two weeks. Prior to eating or tasting, boil the food for 10 minutes.

PER ½-CUP SERVING: *Calories 28 (From Fat 3); Fat 0g (Saturated 0g); Cholesterol 0mg; Sodium 294mg; Carbohydrate 6g (Dietary Fiber 3g); Protein 2g*

Pressure Canning

Chapter **4**

Pickling

Pickling is used for a wide range of foods, including fruits and vegetables. Although pickling isn't practiced much today, don't overlook this rewarding process.

This chapter gives you an overview of pickling, describing the ingredients, the utensils, and the methods used. In no time, you'll be making easy-to- prepare pickled food and condiments that will wow your taste buds and let you enjoy that bumper crop of cukes (and other veggies) all year long.

Perusing Pickling Ingredients

Pickling preserves food in a *brine solution,* a strong mixture of water, salt, vinegar, and sometimes sugar or another sweetener, such as corn syrup. Brining is what gives the vegetables the pickled texture and flavor you're going for.

Some recipes (usually older ones) include a brining step before the actual canning. Other pickling recipes add the brine solution to the raw vegetable and the brining happens in the sterile canning jar as it sits on your shelf. These recipes generally have a recommendation for how many weeks to wait for best flavor.

The four basic ingredients for pickling are salt, vinegar, water, and herbs and spices. Use high-quality ingredients for the best results.

The perfect balance of salt, vinegar, water, and herbs and spices safely preserves your pickled food. You can achieve this balance by precisely measuring your ingredients and following each step in your recipe.

Salt

Salt is used as a preservative. It adds flavor and crispness to your food, especially pickles. Use a pure, additive-free, granulated salt. Acceptable salts are *pickling and canning salt* (a fine-grained salt containing no additives), most kosher salt, and *sea salt,* salt produced from evaporated seawater.

Not all kosher salts are the same. The two most popular brands, Diamond and Morton, are quite different in many respects, including (believe it or not) their saltiness! Add the same measurement of each brand to two recipes that are otherwise identical; the difference will not only astound you, it can even ruin some pickling recipes. Without getting into the technical nuts and bolts of how each company makes their salt (which accounts for the disparity), the part you need to know is this: Morton's kosher salt tastes almost twice as salty as Diamond's product. When using Morton kosher salt in recipes, it is suggested that you use the prescribed amount, knowing you may need to add a pinch more than the table or pickling salt measurement. If you have Diamond kosher salt on hand, double the prescribed amount to keep the finished flavor in check.

Additives in salt cause cloudy liquid. Always read the ingredient label on your salt container to ensure it's additive-free. Salts *not* suitable for brining and pickling solutions are

>> **Table salt and iodized salt:** These contain *anti-caking agents,* additives that keep the salt from sticking together. These cloud your liquid. Iodine darkens food.

>> **Rock salt:** Rock salt keeps roads free of ice and isn't made for use with food. It's okay in an ice-cream freezer because it never touches the food.

>> **Salt substitutes:** These products contain little or no sodium.

Vinegar

Vinegar is a tart liquid that prevents the growth of bacteria. For pickling, you must use a vinegar with an acidity level of 5 percent. If the level of acidity isn't on the label, don't use the vinegar — the strength of the acid may not be adequate for safe food preservation.

The preferred vinegar for pickling is distilled white vinegar, which has a sharp, tart flavor, maintains the color of your food, and is relatively inexpensive. For a milder flavor, you can substitute apple cider vinegar. Keep in mind, though, that using cider vinegar will change the overall color of your finished foods, not always for the better. You may get unappetizing gray or brown results from using the wrong type of vinegar.

To avoid cloudy pickles, use a vinegar that's clear from sediment. Cider and wine vinegars often have sediment, and you may even be able to see things floating around. What causes the sediment? Vinegars that still contain the *mother*, a harmless bacterium that creates the vinegar but also causes sediment to form on the bottom of the bottle.

WARNING

Never dilute or reduce the amount of vinegar in a recipe. To ensure a safe product, the brine must have the right acidity level. Never use a vinegar with less than 5 percent acidity.

TIP

If the flavor's too tart, add ¼ cup granulated sugar for every 4 cups of vinegar. Treating flavors in this manner won't upset the balance of your vinegar. If you don't like the flavor when you make the recipe, try another recipe. Don't forget to jot down your changes on your recipe card!

Water

Soft water is the best water for your brine solution. Too much iron in your water can cause discoloration of the finished product. *Distilled water,* water with all minerals and other impurities removed, is also a good choice. If you use tap water, make sure it's of drinking quality; if it doesn't taste good to you, it won't taste better in your food. Also, avoid using sparkling water.

Herbs and spices

Use the exact amount of herbs or spices called for in your recipe. If your recipe calls for a fresh herb, use the fresh herb. If your recipe calls for a dried spice, use one with a strong aroma. (For more information on drying herbs and spices, check out Chapter 6 of this minibook.)

Pickling spices are blends of many spices including allspice, bay leaves, cardamom, cinnamon, cloves, coriander, ginger, mustard seed, and peppercorns. They're mixed by the manufacturer and vary in flavor. Although these spices are generally whole and therefore good keepers, it is best to buy fresh, new spices each year, before you start canning.

Brining Education

The brining process is a key part of the pickling process because it does these important things:

>> Chemically, it draws out the natural juices and replaces them with salty/vinegar solution, giving your veggies that familiar pickled flavor and texture.

>> It extracts juice and sugar from your food, forming *lactic acid,* a bitter-tasting tart acid. This lactic acid serves as the preservative in your pickled food.

>> Because the brining solution typically includes vinegar (an acid), it safely converts your low-acid foods (those with a pH level over 4.6) to high-acid foods (with a pH level of 4.6 or less), making it safe for water-bath canning. (This is why you must prepare your recipe as it's written and *not* modify the amounts.)

As mentioned previously, sometimes you brine your vegetables before canning; other times, you add the brine solution to the raw vegetables and let the brining occur in the canning jar. The following sections explain how to prepare your veggies for each.

Fresh (or raw) packing: Adding brine to the raw veggies

In this method, you place fresh raw vegetables in prepared jars and then cover them with hot flavored liquid, usually a spicy vinegar, and process the filled jars in your water–bath canner. To ensure the pickling process can occur uniformly, make sure your vegetables are completely submerged in the brining solution. Most of the recipes in this chapter require raw packing.

Complete precooking

In this method, you cook your food completely before filling your jars. The following relish recipe is precooked before canning. The taste of the relish is present before you add it to the jars, and it's ready to eat once it is cooked.

Brining before canning

When brining your vegetables beforehand, how long you let your vegetables soak can vary anywhere from a few hours to several weeks. Your recipe provides the details. Here's what you need to know about these long or short brines:

>> **Long brine:** This process is primarily used for making pickles from cucumbers. The veggies stay in the brine anywhere from five days to six weeks. The brine solution is quite heavy with salt and may contain some vinegar and spices. None of the recipes in this chapter require a long brine.

>> **Short brine:** The soaking period for this method is 24 hours or less. Follow your recipe for the correct proportions in your brine solution. You use a short brine for the Sweet Pickle Relish and Zucchini Bread and Butter Pickles.

In both cases, you submerge the food in the brine solution, where it *ferments* (stays in the solution) for the recommended period of time. (Your recipe gives you the details.) After fermenting, follow your recipe and make a fresh brine solution for filling your jars. (And for much more on fermenting, see Book 3, Chapter 2.)

PICKLING VERSUS FERMENTING

Pickles are generally associated with the traditional cucumber in brine, but you can pickle all kinds of things, from fruit and vegetables to meat, fish, and eggs. In India, some of the most popular pickles are made from mango and lime. In Europe, you'll find pickled herring, olives, and beets. From Asia to Europe, the world of pickling is vast and varied.

Pickling is the process of preserving food using a brine (saltwater) solution. The salt in pickling acts on the food by drawing out the water from its cells and kills any bad bacteria that may spoil the food. Pickles are often added to a meal to help aid with digestion, giving your body that extra bit of *Lactobacillus acidophilus* it needs to restore some healthy gut and intestinal flora.

So, what's the difference between pickling and fermenting? Fermenting and pickling can seem very similar, but they're not the same thing. The process that occurs inside the brine is called fermentation, but the act of making brine and placing food into the saltwater solution is called pickling. Pickling also usually requires added heat through a canning process, whereas fermented goods can sit out on your shelf and don't require heat. Fermented foods thrive in anaerobic conditions and make use of naturally occurring "good" bacteria submerged under the saltwater. Fermented foods have a bit of a tangy flavor, while pickled goods taste salty or vinegary all the way through.

The role of salt in fermentation is to help draw out water from foods and make a salty living environment so bad bacteria have little chance of survival. A brine is created in fermented recipes to preserve fruits and vegetables or other food products. Making brine can be a bit of an experiment, and the salt measurements sometimes depend on your personal preference. Remember that a little salt goes a long way! Some brine even contains a bit of sugar to balance out the salty flavor.

Pickling

TIP

Be sure to keep your food completely submerged in the brine solution, whether it's for a few hours or longer. To do this, place a sealed, water-filled glass jar on top of your food. The jar applies pressure to keep the foods submerged when you cover your brining container.

Stoneware crocks are excellent choices for brining food. You can find them at specialty cookware stores or where canning supplies are sold. But there's an important caveat: Don't use a crock that you've gotten from a thrift store or other secondhand store. Without the original packaging, you have no way of knowing whether it's lead-free and suitable for brining.

TIP

Old-time canning recipes may instruct you to "soak your pickles in salt brine strong enough to float an egg." This equates to a 10-percent brine mixture of 1 pound (about 1½ cups) of salt dissolved in 1 gallon of water.

Adding Crunch to Your Food

The best method for maintaining crispness, crunch, and firmness in your vegetables during the soaking period is to add ice, preferably crushed ice, to your soaking solution. This works best for short brine soaking.

After the soaking period, drain your vegetables in a colander, following your recipe instructions for any rinsing. Some recipes instruct you to roll the drained food in clean kitchen towels to dry it. This works well for larger pieces of food (it isn't for finely chopped relishes).

Note: In older pickling recipes, you may see the addition of alum or pickling (slaked) lime. The recipes in this chapter don't add either of these products because they aren't necessary when you're using modern canning methods.

TIP

For the best tasting pickles, follow these four tips:

>> Pick produce that is blemish free and pickle your produce within 24 hours of harvesting. Never use vegetables that you have to trim off spoiled or moldy parts.

>> To ensure that every piece is pickled at the same time, always pack your jars with uniformly sized vegetables.

>> Scrub the vegetables well to get rid of any dirt, which contains bacteria, and trim ⅛ inch from the blossom and stem ends of cucumbers. These ends may have enzymes that will spoil or soften your pickles.

>> Pack your jars tightly. Because pickling causes vegetables to shrink slightly, having them tightly filled helps prevent them from floating.

Pickling Equipment and Utensils

In addition to the basic equipment for water-bath canning (refer to Chapter 2 of this minibook), you need nonreactive utensils and equipment for handling, cooking, and brining your food. *Nonreactive* items are made of stainless steel, nonstick-surfaced items (without a damaged nonstick surface), enamelware, or glass.

WARNING

Don't use enamelware with chips or cracks or equipment or utensils made from or containing copper, iron, or brass. These items react with the acids and salt during the pickling process, altering the color of your food and giving the finished product a bad taste. *Definitely* don't use galvanized products, which contain zinc. These produce a poison when the acid and the salt touch the zinc, which is transferred to your food causing serious illness (or worse).

Pickled Vegetable Recipes

Many homesteaders start out making a basic batch of homemade pickles. But few homesteaders stop there. That's because once you see how simple pickling is, you'll no doubt want to try your hand at pickling all sorts of vegetables (and even other foods such as eggs, meats, and fruits).

The following sections will help get you started in pickling with some basic and versatile recipes.

Pickled toppers

Relish is a staple in many kitchens. Use this pickled treat anytime you'd use a relish, on a hamburger or hot dog, in tuna salad, or anytime you want to add flavor to a sandwich.

One advantage of homemade relish is mixing flavors you don't find in commercially produced relishes. Make more than you believe your family will consume in a year because this relish has a way of disappearing. Try it in homemade Thousand Island dressing.

Pickles

So what's so important about what kind of cucumber you use for pickles? After all, a cucumber is a cucumber, right? This is definitely not the case. The common salad cucumber has a thick, dark-green, waxy skin. Don't use this cucumber for making pickles because the brine solution won't penetrate the waxy coating. Use this cucumber when your recipe doesn't specify "pickling cucumbers."

REMEMBER

A pickling cucumber is the only cucumber to use for making pickles. The skin of a pickling cucumber is thin, not waxy, and is left on the cucumber. Pickling cucumbers are about 4 inches in length, smaller than salad cucumbers. Don't eat pickling cucumbers raw; their flavor can be extremely bitter. Some varieties are now sold for both pickling and slicing. These are fine to use. For pickling, use the smaller size of this variety; for slicing, use the larger size. Always look for cucumbers that are recommended for pickling, such as Kirby or Boston Pickling.

The Speedy Dill Pickles recipe in this chapter makes an old-fashioned dill pickle in almost the blink of an eye. It's an excellent confidence-builder for the beginning canner. Try it!

The Zucchini Bread and Butter Pickles recipe is the perfect solution when you're overrun with zucchini. Pick your vegetables when they are cucumber sized, and use that day for the best texture. As a bonus, these pickles are ready to eat as soon as they cool.

Pickled vegetables

Pickled vegetables are delicious additions to green salads or a relish plate. Enjoy these treats for a change of pace from plain, raw vegetables. They still retain their crisp texture, but with an extra added bite from the brine.

WARNING

Avoid long boiling periods for your vinegar solution. Lengthy boiling reduces the acetic-acid level in vinegar, changing the pH level of the food. This change may compromise the safety of your pickled food.

Asparagus

Asparagus is one of those foods that you either wish for or have too much of. Pickling the young asparagus spears provides a great way to add a new dimension to this early spring vegetable. Put these up in pints, as part of their charm is the look of the straight spears packed like soldiers inside.

Beans

Serve the beans from the Dilly Beans recipe in a Bloody Mary in place of a piece of celery. For a variation, use a combination of green and yellow string beans.

Beets

Use beets that are small and tender, not larger than 2 inches in diameter. Purchase beets with the top leaves attached. If the leaves are wilted and quite dark, the beets aren't fresh; continue your search for fresher beets. Once canned, beets are ready for eating.

Brussels sprouts

Brussels sprouts are an unusual treat when pickled and canned. In fact, you can eat them as a condiment.

TROUBLESHOOTING PICKLE PROBLEMS

Occasionally, pickling cucumbers develop hollow interiors as they grow or if they wait too long between harvesting and pickling. You can't fix hollow pickles, but you can identify them because they float when they're put in a sink of water. (Don't throw out the hollow pickles; use them for making relish.)

If your pickles are shriveled, too much salt, sugar, or vinegar was added at once to the cucumbers. Start with a weaker solution and gradually add the full amount of ingredients called for in your recipe.

Discolored pickles may be from using hard water with minerals in it. Use soft water for your brine solution as well as for the liquid for filling your jars. Reactive metals such as brass, iron, copper, aluminum, or zinc in pots and utensils cause darkening as well. Use nonreactive equipment such as enamelware with no chips or cracks, glass, stainless steel, or stoneware. Finally, your pickles may have absorbed ground spices. Prevent this by using whole spices rather than ground ones. These problems don't indicate spoilage, but your pickle flavor may be altered slightly.

Mushy or slippery pickles indicate spoilage. Discard the pickles without tasting them. Prevent these problems by accurately measuring your salt, using a vinegar with 5 percent acidity, and completely covering your pickles with liquid during the brining process and in your filled jars.

Remove the scum from your brining solution daily, use a modern-day recipe, follow your recipe to the letter, and use a heating period long enough to destroy any microorganisms.

Soft pickles in a jar with white sediment indicate spoilage. Don't taste these; simply discard them. But if the pickles are firm, they're safe to eat. The sediment is a harmless lactic acid or yeast that develops in the jar and settles to the bottom.

Sweet Pickle Relish

PREP: 55 MIN	SOAKING: 2 HR	PROCESSING: 10 MIN	YIELD: 7 HALF-PINTS OR 3 PINTS

INGREDIENTS

5 to 6 medium cucumbers

3 to 4 green and/or red bell peppers

3 to 4 medium onions

¼ cup kosher or pickling salt

Cold water, about 4 to 6 quarts

3 cups granulated sugar

2 cups cider vinegar

2½ teaspoons celery seeds

2½ teaspoons mustard seed

½ teaspoon turmeric

1 Peel the cucumbers, cut them in half lengthwise, and remove the seeds (see Figure 4-1). Finely chop the cucumbers in a food processor fitted with a metal blade, to measure 6 cups. Remove the stems and seeds from the bell peppers. Finely chop them in a food processor fitted with a metal blade, to measure 3 cups. Remove the skin of the onions. Finely chop them in a food processor fitted with a metal blade, to measure 3 cups.

2 Combine the vegetables in a 5- to 6-quart bowl. Sprinkle them with salt and add cold water to cover them. Cover the bowl; let the veggies stand at room temperature for 2 hours. Rinse the vegetables with running water in batches in a colander. Drain well.

3 Combine the sugar, vinegar, celery seeds, mustard seeds, and turmeric in a 5- to 6-quart pot. Bring the liquid to a boil over high heat, stirring occasionally to dissolve the sugar. Add the drained vegetables and return the mixture to a boil. Reduce the heat to medium-high and simmer, uncovered, stirring occasionally, for 20 to 30 minutes or until most of the excess liquid has evaporated.

4 While your relish is cooking, prepare your canning jars and two-piece caps (lids and screw bands) according to the manufacturer's instructions. Keep the jars and lids hot. (For information on preparing your jars, see Chapter 1 of this minibook.)

5 Spoon and lightly compact the hot relish into the prepared jars. Release any air bubbles with a nonreactive utensil, adding more relish and liquid as necessary to maintain the proper headspace. Wipe the jar rims; seal the jars with the two-piece caps, hand-tightening the bands.

6 Process your filled jars in a water-bath canner for 10 minutes from the point of boiling.

7 Remove the jars from the boiling water with a jar lifter. Place them on a clean kitchen towel away from drafts. After the jars cool completely, test the seals (as explained in Chapter 1 of this minibook). If you find jars that haven't sealed, refrigerate them and use them within two months.

TIP: This recipe is ready to eat as soon as you're done precooking it. So save one jar to cool for dinner the night you make it.

PER 2-TABLESPOON SERVING: *Calories 51 (From fat 1); Fat 0g (Saturated 0g); Cholesterol 0mg; Sodium 499mg; Carbohydrates 13g (Dietary fiber 0g); Protein 0g*

FIGURE 4-1:
Seeding a cucumber with ease.

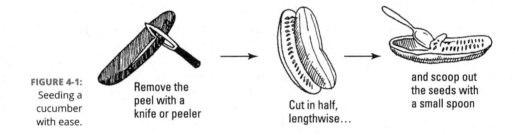

Remove the peel with a knife or peeler

Cut in half, lengthwise...

and scoop out the seeds with a small spoon

Speedy Dill Pickles

PREP: 35 MIN	PROCESSING: PINTS, 10 MIN; QUARTS, 15 MIN	YIELD: 6 PINTS OR 3 QUARTS

INGREDIENTS

4 pounds pickling cucumbers

6 tablespoons kosher or pickling salt

3 cups distilled white vinegar

3 cups water

1 tablespoon whole mixed pickling spices

18 black peppercorns

3 tablespoons dill seed

Fresh dill springs (optional)

1 Wash your cucumbers. Leave them whole if they're smaller than 4 inches in diameter. For larger cucumbers, cut them into slices or lengthwise, in halves or quarters.

2 Prepare your canning jars and two-piece caps (lids and screw bands) according to the manufacturer's instructions. Keep the jars and lids hot. (For information on preparing your jars, see Chapter 2 of this minibook.)

3 Combine the salt, water, and vinegar in a 3- to 4-quart saucepan. Bring the liquid to a boil over high heat, stirring occasionally to dissolve the salt. Keep the liquid hot over medium heat.

4 Snuggly pack the cucumbers into your prepared jars. To each pint jar, add ½ teaspoon of pickling spices, 3 peppercorns, and 1½ teaspoons of dill seed. To each quart jar, add 1 teaspoon of pickling spices, 6 peppercorns, and 1 tablespoon of dill seed. If you're using fresh dill, add a sprig or two to each pint or quart jar in between the inside edge of the jar and the cucumbers.

5 Ladle the hot liquid into your filled jars, leaving ¼-inch headspace in the pint jars and ½-inch headspace in the quart jars. Completely submerge the cucumbers in the liquid. If they protrude from the jar, adjust them until you have the proper headspace, because the lids may not properly seal from the internal pressure. Release any air bubbles with a nonreactive tool, adding more liquid as necessary to maintain the proper headspace. Wipe the jar rims; seal the jars with the two-piece caps, hand-tightening the bands.

6   Process your filled jars in a water-bath canner for 10 minutes (pints) or 15 minutes (quarts) from the point of boiling.

7   Remove the jars with a jar lifter. Place them on a clean kitchen towel away from drafts. After the jars cool completely, test the seals (as explained in Chapter 2 of this minibook). If you find jars that haven't sealed, refrigerate and use them within two months.

8   Keep the pickles on the pantry shelf for at least two weeks for the taste to develop.

VARY IT! For kosher-style dill pickles, add 2 cloves of peeled, halved garlic to each jar of pickles.

PER 2-OUNCE SERVING: *Calories 11 (From fat 1); Fat 0g (Saturated 0g); Cholesterol 0mg; Sodium 1,308mg; Carbohydrates 2g (Dietary fiber 1g); Protein 1g*

Zucchini Bread and Butter Pickles

PREP: 40 MIN	SOAKING: 3 HR	PROCESSING: 10 MIN	YIELD: 12 PINTS

INGREDIENTS

6 pounds thinly sliced zucchini

2 cups thinly sliced onions

½ cup kosher or pickling salt

2 cups sugar

2 quarts ice water

2 quarts distilled white vinegar

¼ cup whole mustard seed

¼ cup celery seed

1 teaspoon turmeric

1 Slice the zucchini into ¼-inch thick rounds. Peel the onions and cut them in half lengthwise from the tip to the bottom core. Lay them on a cutting board, cut side down; then slice them, starting at the top of the onion, to a thickness of ¼ inch.

2 Place the zucchini and onion slices in a 12-quart nonreactive stock pot. Sprinkle them with salt. Add ice water to cover the vegetables. Stir them once; then cover the bowl and let the veggies stand at room temperature for 3 hours. Transfer the veggies to a colander and rinse them thoroughly with running water (you may need to do this in more than one batch). Drain well. Roll the pieces in a clean, dry kitchen towel to partially dry them.

3 Prepare your canning jars and two-piece caps (lids and screw bands) according to the manufacturer's instructions. Keep the jars and lids hot. (For information on preparing your jars, see Chapter 2 of this minibook.)

4 In the nonreactive pot, combine the sugar, vinegar, mustard, celery seed, and turmeric. Bring the liquid to a boil over high heat, stirring occasionally to dissolve the sugar and mix the spices. Add the vegetables and return the mixture to a boil.

5 Pack the boiling hot pickles into the prepared jars and add the hot liquid, leaving ½-inch headspace. Release any air bubbles with a nonreactive tool, adding more pickles and liquid as necessary to maintain the proper headspace. Wipe the jar rims; seal the jars with the two-piece caps, hand-tightening the bands.

6 Process your filled jars in a water-bath canner for 10 minutes from the point of boiling.

7 Remove the jars with a jar lifter. Place them on a clean kitchen towel away from drafts. After the jars cool completely, test the seals (as explained in Chapter 2 of this minibook). If you find jars that haven't sealed, refrigerate and use them within two months.

TIP: Pick your vegetables when they are cucumber sized, and use that day for the best texture.

NOTE: These pickles are ready to eat as soon as they cool.

PER 2-OUNCE SERVING: *Calories 22 (From fat 0); Fat 0g (Saturated 0g); Cholesterol 0mg; Sodium 116mg; Carbohydrates 6g (Dietary fiber 1g); Protein 0g.*

Pickling

Pickled Asparagus

| PREP: 10 MIN | PROCESSING: 10 MIN | YIELD: 8 PINTS |

INGREDIENTS

12 pounds young asparagus spears

8 small dried peppers (optional)

4 tablespoons dill seed

4 teaspoons whole mustard seed

8 cloves garlic

5 cups distilled vinegar

5 cups water

½ cup canning salt

1 Prepare your canning jars and two-piece caps (lids and screw bands) according to the manufacturer's instructions. Keep the jars and lids hot. (For information on preparing your jars, see Chapter 2 of this minibook.)

2 Wash the asparagus thoroughly and cut it into lengths to fit your pint jars.

3 Place 1 hot pepper, ½ teaspoon dill, ½ teaspoon mustard seed, and 1 clove of garlic in each jar.

4 Firmly pack the asparagus spears vertically into the jars, but don't force them. If necessary, trim the spears to leave ½-inch headspace.

5 In an 8-quart nonreactive pot, combine the vinegar, water, and salt and heat to boiling. Pour the boiling hot solution over the asparagus spears, leaving ½-inch headspace. Release any air bubbles with a nonreactive utensil, adding more liquid as necessary to maintain the proper headspace. Wipe the jar rims; seal the jars with the two-piece caps, hand-tightening the bands.

6 Process the filled jars in a water-bath canner for 10 minutes from the point of boiling.

7 Remove the jars from the boiling water with a jar lifter. Place them on a clean kitchen towel away from drafts. After the jars cool completely, test the seals (as explained in Chapter 2 of this minibook). If you find jars that haven't sealed, refrigerate them and use them within two weeks.

8 Let these beautiful spears sit for two weeks on the pantry shelf for the flavors to develop.

PER ¼-CUP SERVING: *Calories 26 (From fat 5); Fat 1g (Saturated 0g); Cholesterol 0mg; Sodium 358mg; Carbohydrates 4g (Dietary fiber 2g); Protein 2g*

Dilly Beans

INGREDIENTS

2½ cups distilled white vinegar

2½ cups water

¼ cup coarse kosher or pickling salt

2½ pounds fresh green beans, washed, with the ends and strings removed

4 stalks fresh dill, washed and drained

4 cloves garlic, peeled

4 dried whole red chile peppers

1 teaspoon cayenne pepper

1 teaspoon dill seed

1 Prepare your canning jars and two-piece caps (lids and screw bands) according to the manufacturer's instructions. Keep the jars and lids hot. (For information on preparing your jars, see Chapter 2 of this minibook.)

2 Combine the vinegar, water, and salt in a 6- to 8-quart pot. Bring the liquid to a boil over high heat; boil for 1 minute, stirring to dissolve the salt. Reduce the heat to low and keep the mixture hot.

3 Pack the beans into the prepared jars (see Figure 4-2), leaving ¼-inch headspace (trim the tops of the beans, if necessary). Add the following to each jar: a sprig of dill, 1 garlic clove, 1 dried red chile pepper, ¼ teaspoon cayenne pepper, and ¼ teaspoon dill seed.

4 Ladle the hot liquid over the beans, leaving ¼-inch headspace, covering the tops of the beans. Release any air bubbles with a nonreactive tool, adding more liquid as necessary to maintain the proper headspace. Wipe the jar rims; seal the jars with the two-piece caps, hand-tightening the bands.

5 Process your filled jars in a water-bath canner for 10 minutes from the point of boiling.

6 Remove the jars from the boiling water with a jar lifter. Place them on a clean kitchen towel away from drafts. After the jars cool completely, test the seals (as explained in Chapter 2 of this minibook). If you find jars that haven't sealed, refrigerate them and use them within two months.

(continued)

Pickling

7 Let the beans sit for two weeks on your pantry shelf for the flavors to fully develop.

VARY IT! Use a combination of green and yellow string beans.

PER ½-CUP SERVING: *Calories 40 (From fat 2); Fat 0g (Saturated 0g); Cholesterol 0mg; Sodium 167mg; Carbohydrates 10g (Dietary fiber 2g); Protein 1g*

FIGURE 4-2: Packing raw beans into a jar.

Pack raw beans into a jar by holding the jar at an angle on its side

Spiced Pickled Beets

PREP: 95 MIN | PROCESSING: 30 MIN | YIELD: 4 TO 5 PINTS

INGREDIENTS

4 pounds beets

3 cups thinly sliced white or yellow onions (about 3 medium)

2½ cups cider vinegar

1½ cups water

2 cups granulated sugar

1 teaspoon kosher or pickling salt

1 tablespoon mustard seed

1 teaspoon whole allspice

1 teaspoon whole cloves

3 cinnamon sticks, broken into pieces

1 Trim your beets, leaving the taproots and 2 inches of the stems. Wash and drain the beets, using a stiff brush to remove any clinging soil. Cover the beets with water in a 5- to 6-quart pot. Bring the water to a boil over high heat and cook the beets until they pierce easily with a fork, about 20 to 30 minutes. Drain the beets. Run cold water over them and remove the skin. Remove the stem and taproot. Slice the beets into ¼-inch-thick slices. Place the beets in a bowl; set them aside.

2 Prepare your canning jars and two-piece caps (lids and screw bands) according to the manufacturer's instructions. Keep the jars and lids hot. (For information on preparing your jars, see Chapter 2 of this minibook.)

3 Place the onions, vinegar, water, sugar, salt, mustard seed, allspice, cloves, and cinnamon sticks in the pot. Bring the mixture to a boil over high heat; reduce the heat and simmer for 5 minutes. Add your beet slices and simmer the mixture to heat the beets, about 3 to 5 minutes. Remove the cinnamon stick pieces.

4 Pack the hot beets and onions into the hot jars and ladle the hot liquid over the beets, leaving ¼-inch headspace. Release any air bubbles, adding more beets and liquid as necessary to maintain the proper headspace. Wipe the jar rims; seal the jars with the two-piece caps, hand-tightening the bands.

5 Process your jars in a water-bath canner for 30 minutes from the point of boiling.

(continued)

Pickling

6 Remove the jars with a jar lifter. Place them on a clean kitchen towel away from drafts. After the jars cool completely, test the seals (as explained in Chapter 2 of this minibook). If you find jars that haven't sealed, refrigerate them and use them within two months.

TIP: Use beets that are small and tender, not larger than 2 inches in diameter.

TIP: Purchase beets with the top leaves attached. If the leaves are wilted and quite dark, the beets aren't fresh; continue your search for fresher beets.

NOTE: Once canned, these beets are ready for eating.

PER ¼-CUP SERVING: *Calories 71 (From fat 2); Fat 0g (Saturated 0g); Cholesterol 0mg; Sodium 107mg; Carbohydrates 17g (Dietary fiber 1g); Protein 1g*

Pickled Brussels Sprouts

PREP: 15 MIN	PROCESSING: 10 MIN	YIELD: 6 PINTS

INGREDIENTS

12 to 14 cups young Brussels sprouts

½ cup canning salt

2 cups distilled vinegar

3 tablespoons dill weed

1 Prepare your canning jars and two-piece caps (lids and screw bands) according to the manufacturer's instructions. Keep the jars and lids hot. (For information on preparing your jars, see Chapter 2 of this minibook.)

2 Wash the Brussels sprouts and remove any outer leaves that have insect damage or brown edges. Cook the sprouts for 5 minutes in boiling water and then dip them immediately into cold water. Drain.

3 Pack the sprouts into your hot pint jars, leaving ½-inch headspace. To each jar, add 1½ teaspoons dill weed. Combine the vinegar and salt and pour this solution over the sprouts, leaving ½-inch headspace. Release any air bubbles with a nonreactive utensil, adding more liquid as necessary to maintain the proper headspace. Wipe the jar rims; seal the jars with the two-piece caps, hand-tightening the bands.

4 Process the filled jars in a water-bath canner for 10 minutes from the point of boiling.

5 Remove the jars from the boiling water with a jar lifter. Place them on a clean kitchen towel away from drafts. After the jars cool completely, test the seals (as explained in Chapter 2 of this minibook). If you find jars that haven't sealed, refrigerate them and use them within two weeks.

6 Let your pickled Brussels sprouts sit for two weeks so that the flavors can develop.

PER ¼-CUP SERVING: *Calories 26 (From fat 2); Fat 0g (Saturated 0g); Cholesterol 0mg; Sodium 475mg; Carbohydrates 6g (Dietary fiber 1g); Protein 1g*

Pickling

Chapter **5**

Freezing

Welcome to freezing, the simplest and least time-consuming method for preserving food. Freezing works well for almost any food. With a minimum of planning and equipment (you may already have most of it), proper storage containers, and basic freezing techniques, keeping food from spoiling and tasting fresh from the garden is easy, convenient, and relatively inexpensive. The results produced from freezing food are superior to canning or drying.

This chapter gives you the basics as well as detailed instructions on freezing some of the fruits and veggies most popular with backyard homesteaders.

Focusing on Freezing

When food is properly prepared, packaged, and quickly frozen, there's no better method for retaining its natural color, flavor, and nutritive value. The process of freezing lowers the temperature of the food to 0 degrees or colder. This low temperature halts microorganism activity by slowing the growth of enzymes. Freezing doesn't sterilize food or destroy the microorganisms; it only stops the negative changes in the quality of your frozen food. The goal with freezing is to preserve the fresh quality of your food.

Temperature: the cold, hard facts

Whether you use your kitchen refrigerator's freezer compartment, an upright standalone model, or a commercial freezer chest, it's critical to keep your freezer at 0 degrees or colder. Frozen food stored at 15 to 20 degrees may appear as solid as food stored at 0 degrees or colder, but the quality of your thawed food stored at the warmer temperature is lower than food stored at 0 degrees or colder.

Packaging foods for freezing

Proper packaging is important for preserving the quality of your frozen food both during the freezing process and after it's thawed. Any excess air in your container may compromise the quality of your thawed food. Remove as much air as possible in bags and wraps, and allow the recommended headspace in rigid freezer containers.

Protecting foods during the storage period requires containers that are easy to seal, suitable for low temperatures, and, most importantly, moisture and vapor proof. For fruits and vegetables, two types of packaging materials meet the criteria for proper freezing: rigid containers and freezer bags. (Freezer paper and wrap is a great choice for meat, but seldom used for the kinds of produce coming out of your garden.)

Rigid containers

Rigid containers are the perfect solution for freezing any soft or liquid food, such as casseroles and soups, and they're reusable. The most desirable material for rigid containers is plastic, although some glass jars are made for freezing. Container sizes range from ¼ of a cup to 1 quart with a variety of sizes in between. Purchase container sizes that fit your freezing needs.

TIP

Choose square- or rectangular-shaped containers. They save space and fit better in your freezer than round containers.

REMEMBER

Rigid containers approved for freezing prevent the spoilers from attacking your food as well as stopping moisture and vapors from penetrating your food. When you use them, be sure to allow the proper headspace so that your food or liquid can expand without forcing the top off (you can find a table listing headspace guidelines later in this chapter). A good rule: Allow ½ inch of headspace for shallow containers and 1 inch for tall containers. For freezing in freezer bags, always press all the air possible out of the bag.

Freezer bags

Freezer bags are readily available, reasonably inexpensive, require a minimum amount of storage space, and come in a variety of sizes. When using freezer bags (we prefer the locking zipper variety), purchase bags labeled for freezing, because the thickness is moisture proof and protects the flavor of your food.

TIP

After placing your food in the bag, force out as much air as possible by folding the filled part of the bag against the nonfilled portion of the bag, pressing the air out while sealing the bag.

TIP

You can use a drinking straw to remove air. Insert one partway into the bag (but away from the food), and then close the bag as much as the straw allows. Suck on the straw to remove the remaining air, quickly slide out the straw, and finish sealing the bag.

VACUUM-SEALING MACHINES

A vacuum-sealing machine is a handy appliance that's great for packaging foods for the freezer. Air is almost completely removed from the package through a suction process, the trademark of this appliance. Most vacuum-sealing machines use materials that are freezer safe or even microwavable and boil-proof. (This is handy for single-serving meals for home or at work.)

Consider these additional items when you're purchasing a vacuum-sealing machine:

- **Cost:** Electric plug-in types range from under $50 for small household models to several hundred dollars for commercial-grade machines. Battery or hand-powered vacuum sealers are available for as little as $10.

- **Replacement bags:** Most machines include bags to get you started. Consider the cost of replacement bags and the reputation of the manufacturer. Investing in a vacuum sealer that is limited by a certain make of bags may limit use of your machine in years to come.

- **Storage requirements:** Depending on the size of your kitchen, storing a vacuum-sealing machine may or may not be an issue. The ideal location for a vacuum sealer is usually on a counter, where you can use it at a moment's notice.

To extend the life of your vacuum-sealing bags, cut them larger than necessary and reseal them each time you remove some of the food inside. This works well for dry products. You can also refill and reseal the bags if the item inside was dry and fresh. This technique is not recommended for juicy foods or meats.

Freezing

Warming up to thawing out

Following the guidelines for freezing won't guarantee a great product without practicing proper thawing methods. So what's the big deal about thawing? Freezing only halts the growth of microorganisms. After thawing, bacteria and enzymes in your food are free to multiply as if they hadn't been frozen. Keep this growth at a standstill by thawing your food at a low temperature, preferably in a refrigerator, in its freezer container or packaging.

Thaw only what you need, using your food immediately upon thawing. If your food tastes funny or smells odd, harmful microorganisms may be present. Don't hesitate to dispose of any questionable food.

TIP

You don't need to thaw vegetables before adding them to a dish you're cooking. Instead, you can add them directly to the dish in the last 10 minutes of cooking. You can also place frozen unbaked goods directly into the oven to bake. Many previously prepared foods can be placed directly into the oven to reheat and bake as well.

Heat makes the spoilers grow faster, so the lower the temperature during the thawing period, the better for you and the quality of your food. Here are your best options for safely thawing and maintaining the quality of your food:

>> **Thawing in your refrigerator:** This is the best and safest process for thawing your food because of the low temperature. Plan your meal the night before and place your choice in your refrigerator to thaw.

>> **Thawing at room temperature:** Leave your frozen food at room temperature for 2 hours; then immediately place it in the refrigerator for the remainder of the thawing process. This option is a great alternative if you forgot to take your food out of the freezer the night before.

>> **Thawing in the microwave:** Use this method only if your microwave has a defrost cycle. This is important because you want the food to defrost evenly, not be cooked in one portion and frozen in another part.

>> **Thawing in water:** Immerse your packaged food in cold water, never hot or warm water. By maintaining the lowest temperature possible when thawing your food, you'll inhibit bacteria and enzyme activity.

REMEMBER

Proper freezing preserves your food for a long time but not indefinitely. You can safely keep all vegetables and most fruits frozen at 0 degrees for as long as 12 months. Citrus fruits have a freezer lifespan of just 3 to 4 months.

WARNING

Certain fruits and veggies with a high water content break down when frozen and become mushy beyond recognition when thawed. Some examples are lettuce, watermelon, citrus fruit, and cucumbers. Tomatoes are an exception to this if you're using them in cooked dishes, such as stews (where the soft, watery texture is desired). Cut fresh tomatoes into quarters and package them in one-cup portions for quick freezing and easy measuring. Don't freeze potatoes; they become watery and grey when thawed, and rendered so mealy that they are rarely suitable even in a cooked dish.

Rethinking refreezing

From time to time, even the best-laid plans change and your defrosted food doesn't get used when you planned. If your food is only partially defrosted, indicated by the presence of ice crystals, it may be refrozen.

Refreezing food shouldn't be a regular practice, but if you're considering it for any reason, keep these things in mind:

>> Don't refreeze completely defrosted low-acid foods, such as vegetables or meat sauces, after they reach room temperature. These foods may not be safe to eat.

>> You may refreeze high-acid foods and most fruits and fruit products if they're still cold.

>> You may safely refreeze partially thawed foods containing ice crystals if the food was thawing in your refrigerator.

REMEMBER

Refrozen foods have a shorter shelf life than when first frozen. They may also taste different. If you refreeze an item, make a note on the package including the refreezing date. Use refrozen food as soon as possible. Follow this simple rule when evaluating refrozen, thawed food: When in doubt, throw it out! Eating spoiled food can be quite dangerous.

Giving Fruit the Freeze

The key to a great frozen product starts with perfect, ripe fruit. Choose only perfect fruit, free of bruises and not overly ripe. Be prepared to process your fruit the day it's picked or immediately after bringing it home from the market.

At the end of this section, you'll find several recipes that will help ensure the freezing success of your favorite fruits.

Preparing your fruit

Fresh fruits require a minimum of preparation before packaging them for the freezer. First you need to wash them and then choose a packing method.

Fruits may be frozen raw, with added sugar, or with added syrup (a mixture of sugar and water). Although adding sugar to your fruit isn't necessary, it's preferred. Occasionally, you'll add an *antioxidant* (an anti-darkening agent) to the liquid to keep your fruit from discoloring.

Following are your packing choices:

>> **Dry or unsweetened pack:** When you'll be eating the fruit or using it for pies, jams, or jellies, use this method. No sugar or liquid is added. There may be minor changes in the color, flavor, or texture of your fruit.

>> **Dry sugar pack:** This is preferred for most berries unless you're making pies, jams, or jellies (see the preceding bullet). Place your washed fruit on a shallow tray or a baking sheet. Evenly sift granulated sugar over the fruit (a mesh strainer works well). Then transfer the berries to a bowl or a rigid freezer container and allow them to sit. The longer the berries sit, the more juice is drawn out. (It's not necessary for the sugar to dissolve as in the wet-pack-with sugar method, below.) When your berries are as juicy as you want them, transfer the berries, including the juice, to a rigid freezer container, allowing the recommended headspace (refer to Table 5-2).

>> **Wet pack with sugar:** Place your fruit in a bowl and sprinkle it with granulated sugar. Allow the fruit to stand until the natural fruit juices drain from the fruit and the sugar dissolves. Transfer your fruit and the juice to a rigid freezer container, allowing the recommended headspace (refer to Table 5-2).

>> **Wet pack with syrup:** Place your fruit in a rigid freezer container, adding syrup (see Table 5-1 for a variety of syrup concentrations) to completely cover the fruit and allowing the recommended headspace (listed in Table 5-2). Your fruit needs to be fully submerged in the syrup before sealing the containers.

TIP

To solve the problem of *floating fruit,* fruit rising to the top of the liquid in the jar, wad a piece of moisture-proof paper (foil works well) into a ball. Place it on top of the fruit to force the fruit to stay completely submerged when the container is sealed. Remove the paper after thawing your fruit.

REMEMBER

Not all packing methods are suitable for all fruits. Only methods recommended for each fruit are supplied in the recipes in this chapter.

Syrup concentrations at a glance

As mentioned previously, syrup is a sugar-and-water combination. Table 5-1 lists the different types of syrups. To make the syrup, you simply dissolve the appropriate amount of sugar into water. You can use either cold or hot water. If using hot water, let the sugar syrup cool to room temperature before adding it to fruit.

TABLE 5-1

Syrup for Freezing Fruit

Type of Syrup	Sugar Concentration	Sugar	Water	Syrup Yield
Extra-light	20	1¼ cups	5½ cups	6 cups
Light	30	2¼ cups	5¼ cups	6½ cups
Medium	40	3¼ cups	5 cups	7 cups
Heavy	50	4¼ cups	4¼ cups	7 cups

REMEMBER

The concentration of sugar syrup is up to you, but usually a thin syrup is used to prevent a loss of flavor, especially if the fruit is naturally sweet or mild flavored. A medium to heavy syrup is used for sour fruits, such as sour cherries or grapes. Different recipes may call the syrup concentrations different things. Simply follow the concentrations as specified in the recipe you are using.

TIP

Use these syrup estimates for planning the amount of syrup to make for filling your storage containers:

>> **Sliced fruit or berries:** ⅓ to ½ cup of syrup for 1½ cups of fruit in a 1-pint container

>> **Halved fruit:** ¾ to 1 cup of syrup for 1½ cups of fruit in a 1-pint container

Headspace guidelines

Headspace is very important when freezing foods. Food expands when frozen, and you need the extra space to allow for this. In addition, if you're using glass jars and don't have enough headspace to accommodate the expanding food, the jars can break. To avoid this problem, use the headspace recommendation for the size containers you have (see Table 5-2).

TABLE 5-2

Headspace Guidelines for a Dry or Wet Pack

Packing Method	Container Opening Size	Pints	Quarts
Dry pack	Narrow mouth	½ inch	½ inch
Dry pack	Wide mouth	½ inch	½ inch
Wet pack	Narrow mouth	¾ inch	1½ inches
Wet pack	Wide mouth	½ inch	1 inch

Freezing

Frozen Fruit Recipes

Whether you're freezing fruits to use later in baking recipes, as tasty toppings, or for healthy smoothies, the hardest part may be finding enough freezer space to keep all of your favorites on hand throughout the year.

Here's what you need to know about freezing fruits, plus a handful of recipes that will help you produce the best results.

Apples

When freezing apples, use crisp apples with a firm texture such as Pippin or Golden Delicious. Because apples tend to get a little mushy when you defrost them, frozen apples are ideal for use in baked goods.

Berries

Jams, jellies, and preserves made with frozen berries produce a product superior in color, flavor, and texture to one made with fresh berries. The recipe in this chapter uses blueberries, but you can use any type of berry (except strawberries); they all freeze well with this method. (The best way to freeze strawberries is to pack them in sugar, as explained in the later Frozen Strawberries Packed in Sugar recipe.) Whatever berries you choose, make sure they're firm.

Peaches, nectarines, and apricots

In addition to freezing peaches with the recipe in this chapter, you can also freeze nectarines and apricots the same way — all varieties of these fruits freeze well. Use fully ripe fruit without any bruised areas.

Strawberries

Strawberries are put in a category of their own for freezing. Cut them and treat them with sugar or pack them in syrup.

Frozen Apples Packed in Sugar

PREP: 20 MIN | YIELD: 1 PINT

INGREDIENTS

1¼ to 1½ pounds apples

1½ tablespoons lemon juice

8 cups of water

½ cup granulated sugar

1 Peel, core, and slice your apples into 12 or 16 pieces, dropping the slices into 1½ tablespoons of lemon juice to 8 cups of water to keep them from turning brown as you finish them all. (If you prefer, you can use an ascorbic or citric acid solution instead of the lemon juice and water.)

2 Remove the apples from the antioxidant solution and place them in a shallow dish or on a baking sheet. Sprinkle the apple slices with granulated sugar, one part sugar to four parts apples. Let your apples be the guide here: Taste a slice with sugar to see if it is to your liking.

3 Fill your container and allow the proper headspace (refer to Table 5-2) and freeze.

NOTE: Use crisp apples with a firm texture such as Pippin or Golden Delicious. Because apples tend to get a little mushy when you defrost them, these are ideal for use in baked goods.

VARY IT! You can also pack your apples in syrup. To do so, place your drained apple slices in rigid freezer containers, filling them with a cold heavy syrup (refer to Table 5-1), adding ½ teaspoon of an antioxidant solution to each container and allowing the proper headspace (refer to Table 5-2).

PER ½-CUP SERVING: *Calories 168 (From fat 3); Fat 0g (Saturated 0g); Cholesterol 0mg; Sodium 0mg; Carbohydrates 44g (Dietary fiber 2g); Protein 0g*

Freezing

Quick-Frozen Blueberries

PREP: 15 MIN	YIELD: 1 PINT

INGREDIENTS

1 to 1½ pounds blueberries

1 Gently wash the berries, removing any stems. Spread the washed berries onto a towel-lined cookie sheet and allow them to air dry (about 15 to 20 minutes) to prevent them from sticking together while freezing.

2 Spread your washed berries on a baking sheet, placing it in your freezer. (This process is known as *quick-freezing* or *flash-freezing*.) When the berries are frozen, transfer them to freezer bags or rigid freezer containers.

NOTE: This recipe uses blueberries, but you can use any type of berry (except strawberries). (The best way to freeze strawberries is to pack them in sugar, as explained in the Frozen Strawberries Packed in Sugar recipe.) Whatever berries you choose, make sure they're firm.

VARY IT! To pack your berries in syrup, place the berries into rigid freezer containers, covering them with cold medium syrup (refer to Table 5-1), allowing the proper headspace (refer to Table 5-2). If the berries float, add a ball of moisture-proof paper to keep the berries submerged.

PER ½-CUP SERVING: *Calories 64 (From fat 4); Fat 0g (Saturated 0g); Cholesterol 0mg; Sodium 7mg; Carbohydrates 16g (Dietary fiber 3g); Protein 1g*

Frozen Peaches Packed in Syrup

PREP: 30 MIN | **YIELD: 1 PINT**

INGREDIENTS

1 to 1½ pounds peaches

½ cup medium syrup

¼ teaspoon antioxidant

1 Blanch the peaches to remove the skin (don't leave the fruit in the boiling water for more than 1 minute).

2 Place ½ cup of cold medium syrup (refer to Table 5-1) and an antioxidant into each rigid freezer container. Slice or halve the fruit directly into the pint container, discarding the fruit pits.

3 Fill the container with additional syrup, allowing the proper headspace (refer to Table 5-2) and freeze.

TIP: Use freestone peaches to make removing the pit much easier.

NOTE: Use fully ripe fruit without any bruised areas.

NOTE: In addition to freezing peaches with this recipe, you can also freeze nectarines and apricots the same way — all varieties of these fruits freeze well.

PER ½-CUP SERVING: *Calories 65 (From fat 1); Fat 0g (Saturated 0g); Cholesterol 0mg; Sodium 0mg; Carbohydrates 17g (Dietary fiber 2g); Protein 1g*

Frozen Strawberries Packed in Sugar

PREP: 20 MIN   YIELD: 1 PINT

INGREDIENTS

¾ to 1½ pounds fresh
strawberries

½ cup sugar

1 Wash your strawberries in water, being careful to not bruise them. Remove the hulls (stems).

2 Slice the strawberries lengthwise into a bowl. Add ¾ cup granulated sugar for each quart of strawberries, stirring the berries to dissolve the sugar. Let the strawberries and sugar sit for 30 minutes for the juice to develop.

3 Transfer your strawberries to rigid freezer containers, allowing the proper headspace (refer to Table 5-2).

VARY IT! To pack your strawberries in syrup, place the sliced strawberries into rigid freezer containers. Fill the containers with a cold medium syrup (refer to Table 5-1), allowing the proper headspace (refer to Table 5-2).

PER ½-CUP SERVING: *Calories 121 (From fat 3); Fat 0g (Saturated 0g); Cholesterol 0mg; Sodium 1mg; Carbohydrates 31g (Dietary fiber 2g); Protein 1g*

Blanching Perfect Vegetables

Like fresh fruit, fresh vegetables are quick and easy to freeze. The key to great frozen vegetables is a process called blanching. *Blanching* scalds the vegetables in boiling water, slows down the enzymes and the spoiling process, and preserves the color, flavor, texture, and nutritive value.

This section spells out how to blanch your favorite vegetables to prepare them for freezing, and then offers detailed recipes to help make the fruits (or veggies, in this case) of your labor last well beyond the harvest.

TIP

Blanching isn't necessary when you're using your frozen vegetables, such as onions, in foods where you're concerned with only flavor and not color.

Blanching requires 100 percent of your attention. Vegetables blanched for too short of a time won't stop the enzymes in the vegetables, and microorganisms start where they were stopped after the vegetables thaw. Vegetables left in the boiling water too long start cooking and may become limp.

Follow these steps for successful blanching:

1. **Wash and drain your vegetables; then remove any peel or skin, if needed. If you're not freezing your vegetables whole, cut them now.**

2. **Bring a 5- to 6-quart pot of water to a boil and fill a large mixing bowl with ice water.**

   Add ice cubes to the mixing bowl because the hot vegetables increase the temperature of the ice bath. Cold stops the cooking process.

3. **Add your prepared vegetables to the boiling water for the amount of time specified in the recipe.**

   Begin timing your vegetables as soon as they're in the boiling water; don't wait for the water to return to a boil.

TIP

   Blanch your vegetables in batches, no more than 1 pound of vegetables in 1 gallon of water.

4. **Remove your vegetables from the boiling water and plunge them into the ice-water bath, stirring the vegetables and circulating the ice water to stop the cooking process as quickly as possible.**

   Don't leave your vegetables in the ice-water bath longer than they were in the boiling water.

Freezing

5. After the vegetables are chilled all the way through, remove them from the ice-water bath and drain them in a colander. If you're dry- packing them, roll them in or lay them on clean, dry kitchen towels to remove excess moisture.

Frozen Vegetable Recipes

Frozen veggies are a huge time-saver in the kitchen. And freezing your own home-grown crops preserves all the nutritional value of your healthy garden favorites at a fraction of the price of store-bought.

Follow these guidelines when getting your veggies ready for the deep-freeze, and use the recipes later in this section to help achieve perfect results.

Beans

Freezing beans is a great way to have them on hand for quick soups and stews. You can add the frozen beans directly to the dish 10 minutes before it is finished cooking. You can use the following recipe for many types of common beans: Green, string, Italian, or wax all work equally well.

Bell peppers

For the recipe in this chapter, you can use green, red, orange, or yellow peppers. Peppers really make an otherwise boring meal sparkle. Try freezing multiple-colored peppers in the same package. Because bell peppers become a little mushy when you defrost them, they're perfect for use in any cooked recipe.

Broccoli

Broccoli is such an undervalued vegetable. Use the perfectly prepared spears in the Frozen Broccoli recipe in all your soups and casseroles.

Brussels sprouts

Brussels sprouts can be a delicious treat — if they're picked at their freshest and processed right away. Try adding these to your roasted vegetable mix, with browned butter and garlic, or doused with balsamic vinegar for a new twist on this tasty vegetable.

Cauliflower

Cauliflower is great for adding to all your winter dishes. Frozen cauliflower also roasts well; just add with your potatoes and onions to the roasting pan. Don't let this delicious vegetable go unused!

Corn

You can never have enough corn in the pantry. An easy way to keep plenty on hand (and put the prefrozen, store-bought bags to shame) is to freeze your own. Add frozen corn to a soup or stew during the last 5 minutes of cooking. Make sure your corn is sweet when you buy it. It won't taste any sweeter after freezing.

Greens

Greens are easy to grow, inexpensive to buy in the farmer's markets, and really pack a nutritional punch. Try keeping plenty on hand to add some extra flavor to your egg dishes, casseroles, and soups, when fresh vegetables are not available.

Peas

Nothing compares to a fresh garden pea. To preserve their sweet flavor, add them to the dish during the last 5 minutes of cooking. Delicious!

Summer squash

Summer squash includes crookneck, patty pan, and zucchini squash. Are all unbelievably tasty vegetables. Once frozen, they lose their attractive look, but still hold onto that summer-fresh flavor. They are suitable for casseroles and egg dishes, soups and stews, and other dishes that benefit from their great taste.

Winter squash

Winter squash includes banana, butternut, and Hubbard. Winter squashes are known for their creamy smooth flavor. They are usually cooked with brown sugar or honey and are a gorgeous bright orange or yellow color from the high vitamin A content. You can add them interchangeably to any bread, cake, stew, or pancake recipe calling for pumpkin.

Frozen Wax Beans

PREP: 20 MIN	YIELD: 1 PINT

INGREDIENTS

⅔ to 1 pound fresh wax beans

1 Wash and drain the beans. Remove the ends and strings, and cut them into 1-inch pieces.

2 Blanch the beans for 2 to 3 minutes; cool immediately in an ice bath. (See the earlier section "Blanching perfect vegetables" for complete blanching instructions.) Spread beans on a dry kitchen towel to dry thoroughly before freezing.

3 Place the cooled beans in quart-sized freezer bags, removing all excess air before sealing and placing the bag in the freezer.

NOTE: You can use this recipe for many types of common beans: Green, string, Italian, or wax all work equally well.

PER ½-CUP SERVING: *Calories 26 (From fat 0); Fat 0g (Saturated 0g); Cholesterol 0mg; Sodium 8mg; Carbohydrates 6g (Dietary fiber 3g); Protein 1g*

Frozen Bell Peppers

PREP: 15 MIN	YIELD: 2 PINTS

INGREDIENTS

1 to 3 pounds fresh peppers

1 Wash and drain the peppers. Remove the stems and seeds and slice the peppers into uniform pieces. (*Note:* You do not blanch peppers before freezing.)

2 Place the bell peppers into a rigid container, leaving the appropriate amount of headspace (refer to Table 5-2). Seal and freeze.

TIP: Bell peppers become a little mushy when you defrost them, so they're best used in a cooked recipe.

PER ½-CUP SERVING: *Calories 15 (From fat 1); Fat 0g (Saturated 0g); Cholesterol 0mg; Sodium 1mg; Carbohydrates 4g (Dietary fiber 1g); Protein 1g*

Frozen Broccoli

PREP: 20 MIN	YIELD: 1 PINT

INGREDIENTS

1 pound fresh broccoli

1 Wash and drain the broccoli, removing leaves and damaged spots. Cut the broccoli spears into ½-inch pieces.

2 Blanch the broccoli for 3 to 4 minutes; cool immediately in an ice bath. (See the earlier section "Blanching perfect vegetables" for complete blanching instructions.)

3 Place the cooled broccoli pieces in freezer bags, removing all excess air before sealing the bag and placing it in the freezer.

PER ½-CUP SERVING: Calories 30 (From fat 0); Fat 0g (Saturated 0g); Cholesterol 0mg; Sodium 29mg; Carbohydrates 6g (Dietary fiber 3g); Protein 3g

Frozen Brussels Sprouts

PREP: 20 MIN   **YIELD: 1½ PINT**

INGREDIENTS

1 pound fresh Brussels sprouts

1 Wash and drain the Brussels sprouts, removing the leaves and sorting by size for blanching (the smaller-sized sprouts use the shorter blanching time).

2 Blanch the smaller Brussels sprouts for 3 minutes, the larger for 5 minutes; cool immediately in an ice bath. (See the earlier section "Blanching perfect vegetables" for complete blanching instructions.) Spread the blanched Brussels sprouts on a clean kitchen towel to remove all of the excess moisture before freezing.

3 Place the cooled Brussels sprouts in freezer bags, removing all excess air before sealing the bag and placing it in the freezer.

PER ½-CUP SERVING: *Calories 32 (From fat 4); Fat 0g (Saturated 0g); Cholesterol 0mg; Sodium 17mg; Carbohydrates 7g (Dietary fiber 2g); Protein 2g*

Frozen Cauliflower

PREP: 20 MIN	YIELD: 1 QUART

INGREDIENTS

1¼ pounds cauliflower

Water

White vinegar

1 Wash and drain the cauliflower, removing the leaves and core and breaking the flesh into 1-inch pieces (do not cut).

2 Blanch the cauliflower in a water-vinegar mixture (1 tablespoon of vinegar to 1 gallon of water) for 3 minutes; cool immediately in an ice bath. (See the earlier section "Blanching perfect vegetables" for complete blanching instructions.)

3 Place the cauliflower pieces in freezer bags, removing all excess air before sealing the bag and placing it in the freezer.

PER ½-CUP SERVING: Calories 7 (From fat 1); Fat 0g (Saturated 0g); Cholesterol 0mg; Sodium 8mg; Carbohydrates 2g (Dietary fiber 1g); Protein 1g

Frozen Corn

INGREDIENTS

4 pounds corn (about 12 ears)

1 Remove the husks and the silk from the corn. Wash the ears.

2 Blanch the ears whole for 4 minutes; cool immediately in an ice bath. (See the earlier section "Blanching perfect vegetables" for complete blanching instructions.) Cut the kernels from the corn after cooling.

3 Place the corn in freezer bags, removing all excess air before sealing the bag and placing it in the freezer.

NOTE: Make sure your corn is sweet when you buy it. It won't taste any sweeter after freezing.

PER ½-CUP SERVING: *Calories 47 (From fat 6); Fat 1g (Saturated 0g); Cholesterol 0mg; Sodium 8mg; Carbohydrates 10g (Dietary fiber 2g); Protein 2g*

Frozen Greens

INGREDIENTS

1 to 1½ pounds greens (beet, spinach, or Swiss chard)

1 Wash the greens well, removing any thick stems.

2 Blanch the greens for 1½ minutes, stirring constantly to separate the leaves; cool immediately in an ice bath. (See the earlier section "Blanching perfect vegetables" for complete blanching instructions.)

3 Place the cooled greens in freezer bags, removing all excess air before sealing the bag and placing it in the freezer.

NOTE:YOUR actual yield will vary depending on the type of greens you use. Spinach, for example, wilts much more than kale does and produces a smaller yield.

PER ½ CUP SERVING:_Calories 36 (From fat 2); Fat 0g (Saturated 0g); Cholesterol 0mg; Sodium 320mg; Carbohydrates 7g (Dietary fiber 4g); Protein 3g_

Frozen Shelled Peas

PREP: 20 MIN	YIELD: 1 QUART

INGREDIENTS

2 to 4 cups shelled peas

1 Rinse the peas in cold running water.

2 Blanch the loose peas for 1½ minutes; cool immediately in an ice bath. (See the earlier section "Blanching perfect vegetables" for complete blanching instructions.)

3 Place the cooled peas in freezer bags, removing all excess air before sealing the bag and placing it in the freezer.

PER ½-CUP SERVING: *Calories 29 (From fat 1); Fat 0g (Saturated 0g); Cholesterol 0mg; Sodium 1mg; Carbohydrates 5g (Dietary fiber 2g); Protein 2g*

Frozen Summer Squash

PREP: 20 MIN	YIELD: 1 PINT

INGREDIENTS

1 to 1¼ pounds summer squash

1 Wash the squash, remove the stems, and slice it into ½-inch pieces.

2 Blanch the squash for 3 minutes; cool it immediately in an ice bath. (See the earlier section "Blanching perfect vegetables" for complete blanching instructions.)

3 Place the cooled squash in a rigid container, leaving the appropriate amount of headspace. Seal and freeze.

PER ½-CUP SERVING: *Calories 22 (From fat 0); Fat 0g (Saturated 0g); Cholesterol 0mg; Sodium 2mg; Carbohydrates 5g (Dietary fiber 2g); Protein 1g*

Frozen Winter Squash

PREP: 30 MIN	YIELD: 1 PINT

INGREDIENTS

1 to 1½ pounds winter squash

1 Peel the outer skin of the winter squash, scrape out the seeds, and cut the flesh into chunks.

2 Place the squash in a 3-quart saucepan and add enough water to cover the bottom of the pan. Cook the squash over medium-low heat until the flesh is soft, about 10 to 30 minutes. or until a chunk slides off a fork. Remove the squash from the pan and mash it until smooth.

3 Place the mashed squash in a rigid container, leaving the appropriate amount of headspace (refer to Table 5-2). Seal and freeze.

TIP: You can add winter squash to any bread, cake, stew, or pancake recipe calling for pumpkin.

NOTE: Follow this same recipe to freeze pumpkin.

PER ½-CUP SERVING: *Calories 43 (From fat 1); Fat 0g (Saturated 0g); Cholesterol 0mg; Sodium 3mg; Carbohydrates 11g (Dietary fiber 3g); Protein 1g*

Freezing

Freezing Fresh Herbs

The flavors fresh herbs impart in just about any dish are truly a gift from nature. Frozen herbs are a great compromise when fresh herbs aren't available.

REMEMBER

Thawed herbs are great in cooked dishes, but they aren't suitable as a garnish because they're limp after freezing and thawing. If you grow your own herbs, harvest them early in the day before the sun wilts the leaves. Some herbs that freeze well include basil, chervil, chives, cilantro, comfrey, dill, lovage, mint, parsley, savory, sweet fennel, and thyme.

To prepare fresh herbs for the freezer, follow these steps (see Figure 5-1):

1. **Clean the herbs.**

   Hold the bottom of the stems (don't remove the leaves from the stems) and swish the herbs in a bowl of cool water.

2. **Drain and dry the herbs, gently shaking off any excess water.**

3. **Lay the herb sprigs flat, not touching each other, on a piece of wax paper.**

4. **Starting at one end, roll the wax paper snuggly over the herbs.**

   This keeps the herbs separate and easy to use one sprig at a time.

5. **Place the rolled herbs in a freezer bag, label the package, and freeze.**

   There's no need to thaw the herbs before using them.

TIP

Some herbs, such as basil, mint, parsley and cilantro, turn black if you freeze the leaves directly. For these herbs, purée them in just enough olive oil to make a paste and then freeze them in ice cube trays. They keep their fresh flavor and color.

TIP

If you're still stumped for more ways you can freeze fresh herbs, try the following:

>> **Herb cubes:** After washing the herbs, remove the leaves from the stem and cut them into pieces. Place 1 teaspoon to 1 tablespoon of herbs in each opening of an ice-cube tray. Pour boiling water into the tray and freeze the herb cubes. After the cubes are frozen solid (usually 24 hours) pop them out of the tray and into a plastic freezer bag. When your recipe calls for 1 teaspoon or 1 tablespoon of an herb, add the ice cube to the dish and continue cooking!

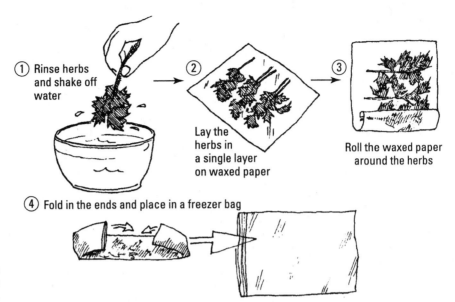

① Rinse herbs and shake off water

② Lay the herbs in a single layer on waxed paper

③ Roll the waxed paper around the herbs

④ Fold in the ends and place in a freezer bag

FIGURE 5-1: Wrapping herbs for freezing.

» **Herbed butter:** Add chopped fresh herbs to one cube of softened, unsalted butter. For a mild herb flavor, start with ¼ cup of herbs, adjusting the amount to your personal taste. Transfer the flavored butter to an ice-cube tray sprayed with no-stick cooking spray and freeze the butter. After the butter is frozen (about 24 hours), remove the butter cubes, placing them in a labeled freezer bag. Serve the flavored butter with bread or add one to a casserole.

» **Herbed butter logs:** Flavor the butter as stated in the previous paragraph. Form the flavored butter into a log in a sheet of wax or parchment paper. Twist the ends, place the log in a freezer bag, and freeze it. Slice off what you need and return the log to the freezer.

Chapter **6**

Drying

n the world of food preservation, sun-drying is the oldest method known. Although canning and freezing require exact applications of processing procedures, drying food isn't exact or precise. Don't be surprised if you find yourself working by trial and error when it comes to knowing how long it takes for your food to reach its degree of doneness. Just follow the general guidelines provided and make adjustments.

In this chapter, you can find basic techniques for drying food, the best drying methods, and recipes for drying your own fruits, veggies, and herbs. Drying is simple and easy to do in your home. Most of the equipment and tools you need, except an electric dehydrator, are probably already in your kitchen.

Opening the Door to Successful Food Drying

Drying food is also referred to as *dehydrating*. The goal is to remove moisture from your food. Achieving a successfully dried product requires removing 80 to 95 percent of the food's moisture. Removing moisture inactivates the growth of bacteria and other microorganisms but doesn't kill them.

The following factors affect your finished product:

>> **Heat:** The correct temperature is important in drying food. It must be high enough to force out moisture but not so high that it cooks the food. If your temperature is too high, your food exterior cooks or hardens before the interior of the food dries, trapping moisture in your food — known as *case hardening*. If your temperature is too low or the humidity too high, your food dries too slowly. Both of these dilemmas may cause your food to spoil before you consume it.

REMEMBER

The temperature guidelines for drying food are as follows: 125 degrees for vegetables and 135 degrees for fruit. Always follow the instructions for the correct drying temperature for your food in your recipe or the owner's manual for your dehydrator.

>> **Dry air:** Dry air absorbs moisture leaving the food in the drying process. The higher the humidity, the longer foods takes to dry because of the additional moisture in the air.

>> **Air circulation:** Circulating air carries away moisture absorbed by dry air. This keeps the humidity level constant in the drying chamber.

>> **Uniform size:** Pieces of food uniform in size and thickness contain about the same amount of moisture and therefore dry in the same general time, preventing some pieces from not being completely dried and spoiling the entire batch when stored.

Choosing a Drying Method

The three approved methods for drying food are using an electric dehydrator, using a conventional oven, and drying in the sun. All methods work well when you follow basic food-drying procedures, use high-quality fresh food, and practice good sanitation for food preparation.

An electric dehydrator

If you dry a lot of food, an electric dehydrator is a great investment (see Figure 6-1). It's the most reliable method for achieving the most consistent results each time you dry food. This method dries your food evenly and quickly, doesn't tie up your oven, and produces great results in any weather.

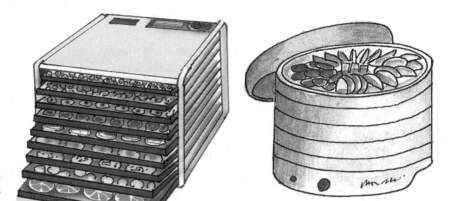

FIGURE 6-1:
Two examples
of electric
dehydrators.

An electric dehydrator dries your food by heating the air inside the chamber to a low temperature and circulating the warm air through the chamber with a fan, passing the heat evenly over your food for the entire drying process. After you place your food in your dehydrator, it needs little or no attention.

To use an electric dehydrator, follow these steps:

1. **Prepare your food according to the recipe and arrange it carefully on the drying trays.**

2. **Following the instructions for using your dehydrator, allow the food to dry for the specified period of time.**

   Turn the pieces of food and rotate the trays from bottom to top to ensure even drying of all the food in the dehydrator.

3. **Test your food for doneness and then label and store it in an airtight container.**

If you're purchasing a dehydrator, carefully assess your needs. Then consider the following factors when making your final decision:

» **Overall construction:** Purchase a unit that's approved for safe home use by the Underwriters Laboratory (UL). If the unit isn't UL approved, don't buy it — it may not be safe for use in your home. Choose one with insulated walls that's easy to clean and drying trays that you can move easily in and out of the dehydrator without disturbing the food.

>> **Capacity:** Purchase a dehydrator big enough to hold the amount of food you'll dry at one time. Typically, the most common-sized food dehydrator has four trays. Each tray holds about ¾ to 1 square foot of food. Some dehydrators expand to utilize 30 trays at one time. Snack-size dehydrators with two trays are also available.

>> **Heat source:** Select one with an enclosed heating element. Wattage needs to accommodate about 70 watts for each tray the unit holds.

>> **Fan:** The fan circulates the heated air around your food. Purchase a dehydrator with a quiet fan, because it runs for long periods of time. If your unit isn't equipped with a fan, you need to rearrange the trays more often during the drying period for an even drying.

TIP

When buying a dehydrator secondhand, always plug it in to hear how it sounds when running. The level of noise is not an indicator of quality, but a loud dehydrator needs an out-of-the-way place to run, or it'll be too inconvenient to use.

>> **Thermostat:** Purchase a dehydrator with an adjustable thermostat. Your temperature options need to range from 85 to 160 degrees.

>> **Drying trays:** Check for trays that are sturdy and lightweight; made from a food-safe product such as stainless steel, nylon, or plastic; and easy to clean. Some manufacturers offer dehydrator accessories such as extra drying trays and trays for drying fruit leather and herbs.

>> **Cost:** Dehydrator prices may start as low as $65 and reach $200 or more.

>> **Warranty:** Check out the warranty term (one year is a good average) and any restrictions the manufacturer has for your dehydrator.

A conventional oven

If you have an oven — gas or electric — that maintains a temperature between 130 and 150 degrees with the door propped open, you can use your oven to dry food.

REMEMBER

Your oven must maintain a temperature of 130 to 150 degrees for 1 hour to safely dry food; maintaining these acceptable temperatures is difficult unless your oven can be set at less than the standard 200 degrees as the lowest temp. The problem with higher temperatures is that they cook — they don't dry — the food. To test your oven's temperature, put an oven thermometer in the center of your oven with the door propped open.

Oven-drying takes longer than using a dehydrator and costs more because the oven uses a greater amount of electricity than an electric dehydrator does. In addition, if you use your oven for drying, it isn't available for any other use during that time.

To dry food in a conventional oven, follow these steps:

1. **Preheat your oven to the temperature setting in your recipe.**

   Use a separate oven thermometer to check for accuracy. Check the oven frequently to be sure food isn't over- or underdried.

2. **Wash and prepare your food as directed in your recipe.**

3. **Place your filled trays in the oven and leave the door propped open to allow moisture to escape during the specified drying time.**

   If you use baking sheets or other trays without holes or openings in the bottom, you must turn your fruit to achieve an evenly dried product. After the first side of the fruit has absorbed all the liquid on the top of the food, turn it over and repeat this for the other side. After this has been done on both sides, turn the food occasionally until it's done.

4. **Test your food for doneness and then label and store it in an airtight container.**

The sun

Sun-drying is the oldest and least expensive of the three methods and it lets you dry large quantities of food at one time. But — and these are big buts — it's dependent on perfect conditions to produce a safely dried product and it can take days compared to hours in a dehydrator or a conventional oven.

REMEMBER

Weather conditions must be perfect for sun-drying, making only a few climates suitable for this method. The ideal temperature for sun-drying fruit is 85 degrees or hotter for many consecutive days, with the humidity level low to moderate. If your temperature drops more than 20 degrees below your highest temperature during the drying period, your conditions are *not* suitable for this method. You also need good air circulation, a minimum of air pollution, and insect control around the food. Sun drying is even less attractive for drying vegetables because the temperature needs to be at 100 degrees or above for a number of days with the lowest evening temperature never dropping below 80 degrees (even at night) *and* the humidity level needs to be low.

If you're willing to deal with the variances in weather conditions and the lengthy drying time, follow these step-by-step instructions:

1. **Wash and prepare your food as specified in your recipe.**

2. **Line your drying trays or racks with a double layer of cheesecloth or nylon netting.**

3. **Place your food on the tray and cover your trays with a single layer of cheesecloth or nylon netting to protect your food from insects and dust.**

   Stretch the cover tightly over the trays, but don't let it touch the food.

4. **Place your filled trays on benches or tables in full sunlight and check regularly.**

   Check your trays at different times of the day, keeping them in full sun at all times. If your nighttime temperature varies more than 20 degrees from the temperature at the hottest part of the day, move your trays to a warmer area (indoors or an enclosed patio area) for the evening, returning them outside when they can be in full sunlight. Relocate the trays if it rains, regardless of the temperature.

   If you use baking sheets or other trays without holes or openings in the bottom, you must turn your fruit to achieve an evenly dried product. After the first side of the fruit has absorbed all the liquid on the top of the food, turn it over and repeat this for the other side. After this has been done on both sides, turn the food daily until it's done.

5. **Check your fruit daily for evidence of mold.**

6. **Test your food for doneness and then label and store it in an airtight container.**

REMEMBER

If one day is hot and sunny, yet the next is cloudy, you have a problem because mold can develop on partially dried foods before the weather turns back to hot and sunny again. In this situation, you need to use an alternative to sun-drying to finish the foods.

Protecting the Life of Your Dried Food

You'll receive many months of rewarding flavor from your dried foods when they're protected from air, moisture, light, and insects. Generally speaking, food dried and stored properly can be kept from six months to one year.

Cooler air provides a longer shelf life for your food. The best storage temperature is 60 degrees or colder. This will hold your food for at least one year. Temperatures between 80 and 90 degrees preserve the quality of your dried food for only about three to four months.

REMEMBER

Check your unused dried food from time to time for any visible moisture or spoilage. If the food has signs of moisture, such as droplets of liquid in the containers, your food isn't completely dried. Use it immediately or repeat the dehydrating process and repackage it.

Suitable storage containers include the following:

>> **Glass**: Home-canning jars with two-piece caps (see Chapter 1 of this minibook) are a perfect choice for storing dried food. Wash them with hot soapy water and rinse them well or wash them in a dishwasher. Dry and cool your jars completely before filling them and adding the two-piece caps. Reusing glass jars with lids also works well. Remove the cardboard liner that sometimes lines the underside of the plastic lid before washing and filling with herbs.

>> **Plastic:** Heavy-duty (freezer) plastic bags with locking zipper-style seals work well. After placing your dried food in the bag, roll the bag to remove any extra air and press the seal together, making the bag airtight.

>> **Metal:** If you buy coffee in cans, line the inside of a clean can with heavy plastic wrap, place your food inside, and add the tight-fitting lid.

>> **Vacuum sealers:** If you own one of these units, now's the time to use it. Check your owner's manual for operating instructions and start packaging your dried food.

Always label your container with the type of food it contains, the date of processing, and, if you measure your food before placing it into the storage container or bag, list the amount.

TIP

Because some pieces of fruit contain more moisture than others, be sure all your fruit is dried the same for storage. Try this tip from the Oregon State Extension Office: Fill a plastic or glass container with cooled, dried fruit about ⅔ full. Cover or seal tightly. Shake the container daily for two to four days. Excess moisture in some of the fruit will be absorbed by drier pieces. Vegetables dry almost completely; you don't have to do this with them.

Snacking on the Run: Drying Fruit

Dried fruit has many uses — from snacks to sauces, dessert toppings to baked-good fillings. Using the best, perfectly ripe fruit for drying is important for a dried fruit that's worthy of high marks and rave reviews. Most fruit is suited for this process with a few exceptions. Fruits *not* recommended for drying include avocados, citrus fruits (except for the peel), crab apples, guavas, melons, olives, pomegranates, and quinces.

Cutting it down

Drying time is determined by the moisture in your fruit, the size of your fruit pieces, the moisture in the air (even if you're using a dehydrator or an oven), and the pretreating method you choose. Larger pieces of fruit take longer to dry than smaller pieces of the same fruit. So the smaller you cut your peaches or the thinner you slice your bananas, the less time you need to produce a safely preserved dried product.

REMEMBER

Fruit contains a lot of water, and you may be surprised at just how much volume you lose when you dry it. So don't be put off by the amount of fruit you start with, wondering where you're going to store it all. Four pounds of fresh blueberries, for example, makes 1¼ cup dried blueberries. And the best news? All the taste and nutrition is still there. All that's missing is the water.

Pretreating your fruit

Pretreating makes your fruit look good by preventing *oxidation* and *discoloration*, the darkening of the fruit flesh after it's exposed to air. This process retards the enzyme activity in the fruit that causes it to ripen.

REMEMBER

Pretreating only slows down the ripening process in fruit; it doesn't stop it.

Using a pretreating method before drying your fruit isn't as important as when you're canning fresh fruit. In fact, it's not necessary at all, but it does assist you with the drying process by shortening the drying time.

The following section explains your pretreating choices.

WARNING

At one time, sulfuring fruit was popular for preserving fruit color and vitamins in dried fruit. Sulfur is unsafe for any drying method other than sun-drying because the sulfur produces dangerous fumes of sulfur dioxide when it's heated, which occurs when you dry fruit in an oven or a dehydrator. People with asthma or other allergies should avoid this product.

Water blanching

Water blanching is the best for maintaining the bright fruit color. Immerse the fruit in boiling water for a short period of time and then immediately plunge it into ice water to stop the cooking process started from the boiling water. Drain the fruit well.

Steam blanching

Steam blanching is the most common method used for fruit. The steam quickly heats the fruit, shortens the drying and rehydrating times, sets the color and flavor, and slows down the enzyme activity, in some cases killing microorganisms. In fact, fruit retains more of its water-soluble vitamins and minerals from steam blanching than water blanching.

To steam blanch, hang a colander on the inside edge of a pot of boiling water, making sure the colander doesn't touch the water. Place your fruit in the colander and heat it as directed in your recipe. Cool your fruit quickly in a bowl of ice water. Drain the fruit well.

Dipping in a solution

With this method, you immerse your fruit into a liquid or a solution to control darkening. Dipping the fruit helps it retain vitamins A and C that are lost during the oxidation process. You can use any of the following liquids:

- » **Lemon or lime juice:** Fresh citrus juice is the most natural of the dipping solutions. Mix 1 cup of juice with 1 quart of water. Soak the fruit no longer than 10 minutes; drain thoroughly before drying.

- » **Ascorbic acid:** This white, powdery substance is available in drugstores. Its common name is vitamin C. Dissolve 1 tablespoon of powder in 1 quart of water. Don't soak your fruit longer than 1 hour; drain it well before drying.

- » **Commercial antioxidants:** These products are found in supermarkets or where canning supplies are sold. Some common brand names are Fruit-Fresh and Ever-Fresh. Follow the directions on the product package for making your solution and determining the soaking time.

Enjoying the labors of your drying

Most dried fruit is used just as it's stored after the drying process. It's great added to hot or cold cereal or baking batters. It's perfect if you're always on the go: It travels well and can be eaten right out of the container. For a fun twist to your teas, add a few dried berries to your teapot before steeping. The berries will lightly infuse the pot of tea with sweetness.

If you prefer your dried fruit a bit chewier, soften or rehydrate it. *Rehydrating* is the process of adding moisture back to the fruit. Use rehydrated fruit right away because it's not dry enough to go back on the shelf without spoiling.

Your rehydrating options are

>> **Boiling water:** Place the desired amount of fruit in a bowl. Cover the fruit with boiling water, allowing it to stand for 5 to 10 minutes to plump, or add moisture, to your fruit. Use this method when adding fruit to jams, chutney, or baked goods. Substitute fruit juice or wine for water.

>> **Steaming:** Place your fruit in a steamer or a colander over a pot of boiling water (refer to steam blanching earlier in this chapter). Steam your fruit for 3 to 5 minutes or until the fruit plumps.

>> **Sprinkling:** Put your fruit in a shallow bowl. Sprinkle the fruit with water or fruit juice. Allow it to soak in the moisture. Repeat the process until the fruit reaches the level of moistness you desire.

Dried Fruit Recipes

Dried fruit is ideal for dropping into baked goods, as a healthy addition to kids' lunchboxes, as a healthy and satisfying snack, or for grabbing on the go.

This section gives you a few things to keep in mind when choosing fruit to be dried, and then presents easy recipes that you and your family will love.

Apples

Apples with tart flavors and firm texture dry best. Some good choices are Pippin, Granny Smith, Jonathan, and Rome Beauty.

Apricots

Even though apricots are one of the most naturally sweet-tasting fruits right off the tree, dehydrating makes them taste even better!

Blueberries

Blueberries will make a nice surprise for your family. Use them in place of raisins and listen to them rave! Use plump berries that aren't bruised.

Cherries

Drying cherries only enhances their rich taste. They taste great out of hand or in your next muffin recipe. Any sweet or sour cherries work well.

Citrus

Dried citrus peel make a great addition to your tea. It gives a fruity zip to desserts and sweetbread recipes. Try citrus peel in muffins and cakes. Use grapefruit, lemon, lime, oranges, or tangerines with unblemished skin. Don't use fruit with color added.

Pineapple

If you have never tasted a dried pineapple, you're in for a huge surprise! Drying creates a chewy morsel that is packed with sweet flavor. Use fully ripe fruit.

Puréed fruit

Fruit leather is dried puréed fruit rolled up in plastic. The result is a chewy, fruity, taffylike treat. Some good choices for fruit leathers are apples, apricots, berries, cherries, nectarines, peaches, pears, pineapple, and plums. If you try drying nothing else, fruit leather is a *must* have. It is so delicious that your family will never guess how nutritious it is.

Dried Apples

PREP: 20 MIN	DRYING: 6 TO 8 HR	WATER CONTENT: 84%	YIELD: 1½ CUPS

INGREDIENTS

4 pounds firm apples

1 Wash, peel, and core your apples. Slice the apples into ¼- to ½-inch thick rings (see Figure 6-2). Dip the apple slices in your choice of dipping solution (refer to "Pretreating your fruit" in this chapter for your options and detailed instructions).

2 Arrange the apple slices on your trays and dry in a conventional oven or dehydrator for 6 to 8 hours at 130 to 135 degrees, rotating the trays occasionally to facilitate even drying. (Sun-dry for 2 to 3 days.)

3 Test for doneness: The apples should be soft, pliable, and leathery.

NOTE: Apples with tart flavors and firm texture dry best. Some good choices are Pippin, Granny Smith, Jonathan, and Rome Beauty.

PER ¼-CUP SERVING: *Calories 147 (From fat 7); Fat 1g (Saturated 0g); Cholesterol 0mg; Sodium 0mg; Carbohydrates 38g (Dietary fiber 5g); Protein 0g*

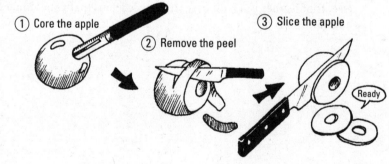

① Core the apple
② Remove the peel
③ Slice the apple
Ready

FIGURE 6-2:
Cutting apple rings.

Dried Apricots

PREP: 20 MIN	DRYING: 18 TO 20 HR	WATER CONTENT: 85%	YIELD: 2 CUPS

INGREDIENTS

6 pounds fresh apricots

1 Wash the apricots and then them cut in half, discarding the pits. Dip the apricot halves in your choice of dipping solution (refer to "Pretreating your fruit" in this chapter for your options and detailed instructions).

2 Arrange the apricot halves on your trays, skin side down, cut side up. Dry them in a conventional oven or dehydrator for 18 to 20 hours at 130 to 135 degrees, rotating the trays occasionally to facilitate even drying. (Sun-dry for 2 to 3 days.)

3 Test for doneness: The apricots should be pliable and leathery with no moisture pockets.

PER ¼-CUP SERVING: *Calories 152 (From fat 11); Fat 1g (Saturated 0g); Cholesterol 0mg; Sodium 3mg; Carbohydrates 35g (Dietary fiber 8g); Protein 4g*

Dried Blueberries

PREP: 20 MIN	DRYING: 24 HR	WATER CONTENT: 83%	YIELD: 1¼ CUPS

INGREDIENTS

4 pounds fresh blueberries

1 Drop the blueberries into boiling water for 30 seconds. Remove them from the water and drain. Place the drained berries on paper towels to remove any excess water.

2 Place the blueberries on your trays and dry in a conventional oven or dehydrator for about 24 hours at 130 to 135 degrees, rotating the trays occasionally to facilitate even drying. (Sun-dry for 2 to 4 days.)

3 Test for doneness: The blueberries should be leathery and hard, but shriveled like raisins.

PER ¼-CUP SERVING: *Calories 203 (From fat 12); Fat 1g (Saturated 0g); Cholesterol 0mg; Sodium 22mg; Carbohydrates 51g (Dietary fiber 10g); Protein 2g*

Dried Cherries

PREP: 20 MIN	DRYING: 14 TO 28 HR	WATER CONTENT: SWEET CHERRIES, 80%; SOUR CHERRIES, 84%	YIELD: 2 CUPS

INGREDIENTS

6 to 8 pounds fresh sweet or sour cherries

1 Wash the cherries in cold water. Then cut them in half and remove the pits.

2 Place the cherry halves on your trays skin side down, cut side up. Dry them in a conventional oven or dehydrator for 2 to 3 hours at 165 degrees, or until there is a slightly leathery appearance to the skin and cut surface. Then reduce the heat to 135 degrees and dry for an additional 12 to 25 hours. (Sun-dry for 2 to 4 days.). Rotate the trays occasionally to facilitate even drying.

3 Test for doneness: The cherries should be leathery, hard, and slightly sticky.

PER ¼-CUP SERVING: *Calories 220 (From fat 27); Fat 3g (Saturated 1g); Cholesterol 0mg; Sodium 0mg; Carbohydrates 51g (Dietary fiber 7g); Protein 4g.*

Dried Citrus Peel

PREP: 20 MIN	DRYING: 1 TO 2 HR	WATER CONTENT: 86%	YIELD: ⅛ CUP

INGREDIENTS

1 pound fresh oranges

1 Wash the citrus fruit and remove a thin layer of peel with a vegetable peeler. Be careful not to get any of the white, bitter pith. If you do, don't use that part of the peel.

2 Arrange the peel on your trays and dry in a conventional oven or dehydrator for 1 to 2 hours at 135 degrees, rotating the trays occasionally to facilitate even drying. (Sun-drying is not recommended.)

3 Test for doneness: The peels should be crisp, but not brittle.

NOTE: You can also use grapefruit, lemon, lime, or tangerines with unblemished skin. Don't use fruit with color added.

PER 1-TEASPOON SERVING: *Calories 2 (From fat 0); Fat 0g (Saturated 0g); Cholesterol 0mg; Sodium 0mg; Carbohydrates 1g (Dietary fiber 0g); Protein 0g*

Dried Pineapple

PREP: 20 MIN	DRYING: 12 TO 18 HR	WATER CONTENT: 86%	YIELD: 1½ CUPS

INGREDIENTS

6 pounds fresh pineapple

1 Cut away the peel and the eyes from the pineapple and remove the core. Cut the flesh into ¼-inch-thick rings.

2 Arrange the pineapple rings on your trays and dry in a conventional oven or dehydrator for 12 to 18 hours at 130 to 135 degrees, rotating the trays occasionally to facilitate even drying. (Sun-dry for 4 to 5 days.)

3 Test for doneness: The pineapple rings should be leathery and not sticky.

TIP: Use fully ripe pineapple.

PER ¼-CUP SERVING: *Calories 116 (From fat 9); Fat 1g (Saturated 0g); Cholesterol 0mg; Sodium 2mg; Carbohydrates 29g (Dietary fiber 3g); Protein 1g.*

Fruit Leather

PREP: 20 MIN OR LONGER	DRYING: 6 TO 18 HR	YIELD: 4 CUPS OF FRUIT PURÉE MAKES 8 TO 12 SERVINGS

INGREDIENTS

One of any of the following fresh fruits:

2 to 3 pounds apples (about 8 to 12)

3 to 4 pound apricots (about 24)

3 to 4 pound peaches (about 8 to 12)

4 pints strawberries

Water or fruit juice (optional)

Corn syrup or honey (optional)

⅛ teaspoon ground spices (optional): choose from allspice, cinnamon, cloves, ginger, mace, nutmeg, or pumpkin pie spice

¼ to ½ teaspoon pure extract flavors (optional): choose from almond, lemon, orange, or vanilla

1 Cover your drying trays or baking sheets with a heavy-duty, food-grade plastic wrap. If your dehydrator comes with special sheets for your trays, use those. For this recipe, 2½ cups of puree covers an area, ¼-inch thick.

2 Wash your fruit and remove any blemishes. Prepare your fruit as directed in the guidelines for preparing fruit in this chapter.

3 Purée the fruit in a blender until smooth. Strain out any small seeds, if desired, with a mesh strainer or a food mill. If your purée is too thick, add water or fruit juice, 1 tablespoon or less at a time. If your purée is too tart, add corn syrup or honey, 1 teaspoon at a time. If you're adding spices or other flavorings, add them now.

4 Spread the purée onto the prepared trays to a thickness of ⅛-inch in the center and ¼-inch-thick around the edges (you want the edges thicker than the center because the edges dry faster). See Figure 6-3. If you use cooked fruit, it must be completely cool before spreading it on the trays.

5 Dry your fruit leather at a temperature of 135 degrees in a dehydrator or 140 degrees in a conventional oven. Dry the fruit until it's pliable and leatherlike with no stickiness in the center. The amount of time will depend on the amount of moisture in the fruit; about 6-8 hours in an electric dehydrator, or up to 18 hours in a conventional oven.

6 Roll the warm fruit leather, still attached to the plastic, into a roll. Leave the rolls whole, or cut them into pieces with scissors. Store the rolls in a plastic bag or an airtight container.

NOTE: Some other good choices for fruit leathers are cherries, nectarines, pears, pineapple, and plums.

NOTE: The spice flavoring will intensify as this dries. Use a light hand, and no more than⅛ of a teaspoon total in each batch.

PER ½-CUP SERVING OF APPLE PURÉE: *Calories 55 (From fat 3); Fat 0g (Saturated 0g); Cholesterol 0mg; Sodium 0mg; Carbohydrates 14g (Dietary fiber 2g); Protein 0g*

PER ½-CUP SERVING OF APRICOT PURÉE: *Calories 76 (From fat 6); Fat 1g (Saturated 0g); Cholesterol 0mg; Sodium 2mg; Carbohydrates 18g (Dietary fiber 4g); Protein 2g*

PER ½-CUP SERVING OF PEACH PURÉE: *Calories 64 (From fat 1); Fat 0g (Saturated 0g); Cholesterol 0mg; Sodium 0mg; Carbohydrates 16g (Dietary fiber 3g); Protein 1g*

PER ½-CUP SERVING OF STRAWBERRY PURÉE: *Calories 43 (From fat 5); Fat 1g (Saturated 0g); Cholesterol 0mg; Sodium 1mg; Carbohydrates 10g (Dietary fiber 3g); Protein 1g*

① After you remove the peel, stems, and cores, blend the fruit to a smooth paste.

② Spread the purée evenly on a lined baking sheet with turned up sides.

③ Dry the purée until it feels leather-like and pliable. Remove it from the tray while it's still warm. Roll it!

④ Cut each roll into 4 to 6 pieces. Wrap each piece in plastic wrap or wrap each whole roll in plastic wrap.

FIGURE 6-3: Preparing and rolling fruit leather.

Drying Vegetables for Snacks and Storage

Drying foods is a super way to store a large amount of food in a surprisingly small space. If you are short on pantry space or lack more than a small freezer in the kitchen, drying may be the perfect storage solution for you. It's easy to mix and match your family's favorite vegetables and create easy to store and use vegetables for your pantry.

As discussed earlier, there are different methods you can use for drying food. For vegetables, a food dehydrator is your best bet because a controlled, clean heat combined with constantly moving air results in a completely dried vegetable. To use a dehydrator, you simply layer your vegetables onto stacked trays and turn on the unit. Some dehydrators have fans that blow the warmed air over the drying food. Other units have a heating element at the bottom, and as the warm air rises, it filters through all the trays, drying the produce in the process.

Drying know-how

Although drying seems pretty, well, cut and dried (pick the freshest vegetables you can find, prepare them as necessary, and put them in a food dehydrator for the required time and temperature), you can ensure that you'll end up with a tasty, edible veggie by following some basic rules:

TIP

>> Not all vegetables need to be peeled before drying. Leaving on clean, washed skin increases the final nutritional content. Peels often contain fiber and other nutrients that only add to the overall benefit of the vegetable. You can find the best prep method in the drying instructions.

>> While your vegetables are drying, switch the trays around to ensure they all get even heat. For best results, be sure to cut all the food into evenly sized pieces and spread the pieces in a thin layer on the drying trays.

WARNING

>> Some vegetables dry faster than others due to the water content of the vegetable while fresh. When setting up your trays, don't mix juicy vegetables with those that are drier.

Vegetables with different water content can have much different drying times. If you dry them all together, you can end up with mildew because some may not get completely dehydrated.

>> Make sure the vegetables are completely dried before sealing. To know that, you need to know what a properly dried vegetable looks and feels like. Not all are crispy when dried. Often, a vegetable is dried properly and yet remains pliable. (You can find out how to tell whether a vegetable is properly dried in the vegetable-specific sections that appear later in the chapter.)

REMEMBER

The drying process involves many factors: moisture in the food that is being dried, the accuracy of the thermostat in the dehydrator, how full the trays are, and the humidity on the day you are drying. You may have to experiment a bit to figure out what works best. The drying process is not as accurate as other methods in this book, such as canning and freezing. The final goal is to remove enough moisture so that organisms that spoil food cannot grow.

Storing and using your dried produce

When you take the vegetables from the dehydrator, they're ready to be stored in an airtight container in a cool, dry place out of direct sunlight.

TIP

For best results, store batches of vegetables together, but keep them in separate containers. For example, keep all dried tomatoes in a gallon jar, but inside the jar, divide them into separate storage bags, with each bag holding tomatoes dried on different days. This way, if something isn't quite right about a particular batch of vegetables, your entire season's storage isn't ruined.

You can store dried vegetables for up to a year as long as they are kept dry and out of sunlight.

Dried vegetables can be used for snacking and adding to soups and stews in the last few minutes of cooking. To rehydrate your dried vegetables add 1½ cups boiling water to 1 cup of dried vegetables. Let them stand for 20 to 30 minutes to absorb the water. If all the water is absorbed and they're not as plump as you'd like, add about 2 cups additional water and let them stand until most of the water is absorbed. Use the vegetables as you would raw ones; cook them or add them to a soup or stew. A good rule of thumb is 1 cup of dried vegetables equals two cups of reconstituted vegetables.

TIP

Avoid pouring or sprinkling vegetables over a steaming pot, straight from the storage container. Doing so can cause the moisture from the steam to condense in the container and promote mold. Always pour dried vegetables into a separate dish or your hand before adding to your recipe.

Dried Vegetable Recipes

Dried veggies make for a fun snack and are also a superb pantry item that can quickly bolster soups and stews and many other recipes at a moment's notice.

The tips that start this section and the recipes that follow will help you dehydrate your favorite vegetables with great results.

Shell beans

Dried shell beans take up little room on the pantry shelf. Store yours in quart-sized jars because they look so pretty and are easy to pour from.

Beets

For drying beets, choose young, firm beets. Avoid large ones that can be fibrous. To use dried slices, eat them as-is or boil for 30 minutes in plain water, until soft once again.

Carrots

The best carrots for drying are young and tender. You can add dried, shredded carrots as-is to sweetbreads and cakes for added fiber and natural sweetness; they'll absorb moisture and become delicious during the cooking process. You can also add dried slices to any soup or stew and simmer until tender, about 30 minutes. Or try sprinkling shredded carrot directly into eggs when making omelets. They'll cook as the eggs do and add a colorful look to the dish.

Greens

Select young, fresh greens for drying. To use, crumble dried greens into broth, tomato-based sauces, stews, and any other dish that you want to add some nutritional punch to.

Peas

Choose young green peas when they are at their peak of flavor. They shrivel up quite a bit when dried but plump up nicely when added back to water or broth. Add dried peas to broth or stew and simmer for 30 minutes.

Potatoes

Select young, unblemished potatoes for drying. Because they have such a long drying time, plan on drying potatoes overnight. To use dried potatoes, cover them with water and bring to a simmer until soft again — about 45 minutes. Dried sweet potatoes make a great snack as-is.

Zucchini

Young zucchini usually have no seeds to deal with, and the skin may be soft enough to leave on before slicing, cubing, or grating in advance of drying. If you're working with mature zucchini, remove the seeds and surrounding pulp and peel off the hard skin.

Dried Shell Beans

PREP: 10 MIN	DRYING: 6 TO 8 HR	YIELD: 1½ CUPS

INGREDIENTS

1 pound of shell beans of your choice

1 Remove the pods and collect the beans. Place the beans on the dehydrator tray(s) in a single layer, adding enough to fill, but be sure that the beans are in a single layer on the trays.

2 Set your dehydrator temperature to 120 degrees and dry the beans for 6 to 8 hours, or until you can break a bean in half by hitting it with a hammer or other heavy object. Rotate the trays occasionally to facilitate even drying.

3 Remove your dried beans from the trays, place them in a tightly sealed container, and freeze them overnight to kill any tiny bug eggs that may be hiding in them.

4 Store your dried beans for up to one year.

PER ½-CUP SERVING: *Calories 129 (From fat 10); Fat 1g (Saturated 0g); Cholesterol 0mg; Sodium 37mg; Carbohydrates 26g (Dietary fiber 6g); Protein 12g*

Dried Beets

INGREDIENTS

2 pounds of beets

1 Cut off the leaf and root ends of your beets and cook the beets in boiling water just long enough to slip the skins off easily (this may take from 5 to 15 minutes). Thinly slice the beats and arrange them in a single layer on your dehydrator trays.

2 Set your dehydrator temperature to 120 degrees and dry the beets for 8 to 10 hours, or until the slices are hard. Rotate the trays occasionally to facilitate even drying.

3 Place the dried beets in an airtight container and store for six months in a cool dry place, out of direct sunlight.

TIP: An easy way to get the skin off a beet is to drop each boiled beet into ice water for a few seconds before pulling off the skins.

PER ½-CUP SERVING: *Calories 65 (From fat 2); Fat 0g (Saturated 0g); Cholesterol 0mg; Sodium 119mg; Carbohydrates 15g (Dietary fiber 4g); Protein 2g*

Drying

Dried Carrots

INGREDIENTS

1 pound fresh carrots

1 Scrub the carrot skin with a vegetable brush to remove any trace of dirt. Cut off the tops and about ¼ inch of the carrot itself to remove any of the green, bitter part of the carrot. Then cut the carrots into ⅛-inch slices or shred finely. Blanch the slices or shreds for 2 minutes in boiling water and then cool immediately in ice water. Drain well. Layer carrot slices or shreds in a single layer on your dehydrator trays.

2 Set the temperature on your dehydrator to 120 degrees and dry the carrots for 8 to 10 hours, or until they're tough and leathery, stirring at least once to ensure that the pieces don't stick and rotating the trays periodically to facilitate even drying.

3 Store the dried carrots for up to one year in a tightly sealed container.

TIP: To remove as much water as possible from the blanched carrots, especially for shreds, use paper towels.

PER ½-CUP SERVING: *Calories 102 (From fat 0); Fat 0g (Saturated 0g); Cholesterol 0mg; Sodium 116mg; Carbohydrates 23g (Dietary fiber 6g); Protein 3g*

Dried Greens

INGREDIENTS

1 pound fresh greens

1 Trim and wash the greens thoroughly to remove any fine grit. Blanch the greens until they are limp, about 2 minutes. Spread them in a thin layer onto your drying trays.

2 Set the temperature on your dehydrator to 120 degrees and dry the greens for 4 to 6 hours, or until the greens are crispy, stirring once to keep them from sticking together and rotating the trays occasionally to facilitate even drying.

3 Store your dried greens for up to one year in a tightly sealed container.

NOTE: Check drying greens carefully to ensure they are layered loosely enough to fully dry. Greens that are stuck together may hold moisture and develop mold.

VARY IT! You can create a powder to add as-is to any sauce or baked good. Simply pulverize the dried greens in a food processor and then dry them in your dehydrator for at least 4 hours.

PER ¼-CUP SERVING: *Calories 227 (From fat 29); Fat 3g (Saturated 0g); Cholesterol 0mg; Sodium 195mg; Carbohydrates 45g (Dietary fiber 9g); Protein 15g*

Drying

Dried Peas

INGREDIENTS

1 pound fresh peas

1 Shell and blanch your peas for 2 minutes in boiling water; then chill in ice water and drain. Arrange the peas in a thin layer on your drying trays.

2 Set the temperature on your dehydrator to 120 degrees and dry until the peas are shriveled and hard, about 9 to 12 hours, stirring at least once to prevent sticking and rotating the trays periodically to facilitate even drying.

3 Store your dried peas for up to one year in a tightly sealed container.

PER ¼-CUP SERVING: *Calories 367 (From fat 16); Fat 2g (Saturated 0g); Cholesterol 0mg; Sodium 23mg; Carbohydrates 66g (Dietary fiber 23g); Protein 25g*

Dried Potatoes

PREP: 10 MIN	DRYING: 10 TO 12 HR	YIELD: ¾ CUP

INGREDIENTS

1 pound potatoes (about 4 to 5 medium)

1 Wash and peel the potatoes. Cut them into ½-inch strips for shoestring potatoes, or ⅛-inch slices, making sure all pieces are of uniform size for even drying. Blanch the potatoes for 5 minutes and drain. Arrange them in a single layer on your drying trays.

2 Set the temperature on your dehydrator to 120 degrees and dry the potatoes until they're hard and brittle, at least 10 to 12 hours, stirring after the first 4 hours to prevent sticking. Rotate the trays occasionally to facilitate even drying.

3 Store the dried potatoes for up to one year in a tightly sealed container or in plastic freezer bags.

TIP: To prevent your potatoes from turning brown during drying, dip them in a mixture of 2 tablespoons lemon juice to 1 quart of water prior to drying.

PER ¼-CUP SERVING: *Calories 108 (From fat 1); Fat 0g (Saturated 0g); Cholesterol 0mg; Sodium 6mg; Carbohydrates 25g (Dietary fiber 2g); Protein 2g.*

Sweet Potato Crunch Sticks

PREP: 10 MIN	DRYING: 12 HR	YIELD: 8 SERVINGS

INGREDIENTS

1 pound sweet potatoes, washed, peeled and sliced into shoestrings

1 tablespoon olive oil

½ teaspoon sea salt

1 Blanch the shoestring sweet potatoes in boiling water for 5 minutes and dip in ice cold water. Drain well. Dry the potatoes on paper towels to remove any outside moisture.

2 Place the sweet potatoes in an 8-quart bowl and add olive oil. Toss well to coat. Spread the shoestring pieces in a single layer on your drying trays. Sprinkle with salt.

3 Set the temperature on your dehydrator to 120 degrees and dehydrate the shoestring potatoes until they're crispy, at least 12 hours. Rotate the trays occasionally to facilitate even drying.

4 Store (if you can!) in a cool, dry place.

VARY IT! For a slightly different flavor, add an additional seasoning you like at Step 2.

PER SERVING: *Calories 50 (From fat 16); Fat 2g (Saturated 0g); Cholesterol 0mg; Sodium 291mg; Carbohydrates 8g (Dietary fiber 1g); Protein 1g*

Zucchini Chips

PREP: 10 MIN	MARINATING: 15 MIN	DRYING: 12 HR	YIELD: 4 SERVINGS

INGREDIENTS

1 pound zucchini (about 3 medium)

¼ cup Italian-style salad dressing

1 Wash and slice the zucchini into ⅛-inch thin slices. Place the slices in a large bowl or gallon-size plastic, sealable storage bag. Pour the Italian-style dressing over the slices and toss to coat. Marinate the zucchini in the dressing for 15 minutes. Place marinated slices in a single layer on your drying trays.

2 Set the temperature on your dehydrator to 120 degrees and dry the zucchini slices for 12 hours (or until crisp), turning at least once. Rotate the trays occasionally to facilitate even drying.

3 Store the zucchini chips for up to three months in a 1-gallon, sealable plastic storage bag.

NOTE: After you open the bag, use the chips as quickly as possible, before they absorb moisture and become soft.

PER SERVING: *Calories 91 (From fat 66); Fat 7g (Saturated 1g); Cholesterol 0mg; Sodium 118mg; Carbohydrates 6g (Dietary fiber 2g); Protein 11g.*

DIYing the Drying of Herbs

Drying herbs is a wonderful way to be sure you have the freshest seasoning possible for your cooking. Because you pick herbs throughout the growing season, you can collect the finest herbs again and again, drying them as you go. Drying herbs is also an easy way to create your own signature blends for cooking and herbal tea. You will always have your favorites on hand if you dry them yourself.

The best herbs for drying are those that are *resinous,* or contain the most oils. The oils are where the scents and flavor come from. Herbs that have very juicy stems and overly thick leaves don't dry well.

Harvest your herbs just after the morning dew has dried, but before the hot, noonday sun has hit them. The heat from the sun drives the fragrant oils out of the leaves and blossoms, so the herbs have less flavor.

TIP

If you find that your herb of choice seems to become tasteless or dries to a black mess, try freezing that herb instead. Two herbs that are commonly used in cooking but do not dry well are chives and basil. Some have luck drying basil at a low temperature, but we don't recommend it for those just starting out. Blend in a little olive oil with these too fussy herbs and freeze instead (go to Chapter 5 of this minibook for details).

TIP

You can use either an oven or a dehydrator set between 115 and 125 degrees. This temperature is just high enough to heat but not cook the herbs. Don't set the temperature any lower than 115 degrees though, because it takes too long and sometimes allows mildew.

Store your dried herbs in small containers. Glass jars with tight-fitting lids work best. For your herbs to maintain the best flavor during storage, keep them away from heat, light, and your refrigerator.

The following sections outline several herbs that are easy to dry. When selecting your herbs, choose those that you're familiar with first.

Chamomile

Chamomile is a delicate flower that is as lovely as it is useful. Harvesting chamomile, however, is difficult in a major scale, making it loved by home gardeners but expensive as an herb farm crop.

TIP

Chamomile has a lightly fruity taste. Because the taste differs slightly from variety to variety, tasting is the best way to find the right chamomile for your garden.

AIR-DRYING FRESH HERBS

An electric dehydrator and oven aren't your only options when it comes to drying herbs. Air-drying them is an easy alternative. Follow these steps to air-dry herbs and check out the figure as well:

1. If you're harvesting herbs from a garden, cut the stems, don't pick them, leaving an extra inch or two for tying them in bunches.

   Harvest the herbs in the morning after any moisture on the leaves has dried.

2. Rinse your herbs quickly by dipping them in a bowl of cool water and shaking off the excess water.

   Pat them dry with a paper towel, making sure they're completely dry to prevent mildew.

3. Tie the herb stalks near the cut part of the stem in small bunches (no more than five or six stems) with cotton string or thread.

   Don't mix your herb bunches because flavors transfer during the drying process.

4. Either hang the herbs upside down in a warm room (the kitchen works well) near a south-facing window and out of direct sunlight or place the tied herb bundle in a paper bag with holes or slits cut in it for air circulation before hanging the bag in a warm room. Place the herb bundle upside down in the bag with the stems toward the top opening of the bag. Tie the top of the bag closed. The bag protects the herbs from light and catches any loose seeds for replanting your herbs.

   Your herbs will dry in two to three weeks with good air circulation.

Herbs are dry when they crumble easily. Remove the leaves from the stems. Crush soft leaves (such as basil, sage, and oregano) by hand. Store harder leaves (such as rosemary, tarragon, and thyme) whole, crushing them with a rolling pin before using them.

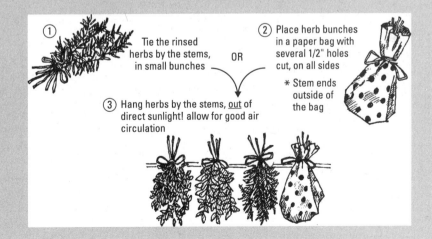

① Tie the rinsed herbs by the stems, in small bunches   OR   ② Place herb bunches in a paper bag with several 1/2" holes cut, on all sides

* Stem ends outside of the bag

③ Hang herbs by the stems, <u>out</u> of direct sunlight! allow for good air circulation

To harvest chamomile for drying, pick the individual chamomile flowers as they bloom and just after the dew has dried in the morning. This is very important because chamomile's delicate scent is easily lost if you're not careful. Some leaves are fine to include because they also have some chamomile flavor.

To dry chamomile, follow these steps:

1. **Lay the flowers in a single layer on trays.**

2. **Set your oven or dehydrator temperature to between 115 and 125 degrees and dry for 3 to 5 hours, checking carefully after 4 hours and rotating the trays periodically to facilitate even drying.**

    You don't want to overdry them. Flowers are fully dry when the tiny petals curl inward, and the center of the blossom is totally dry.

3. **Store in an airtight container, out of sunlight.**

To use your dried chamomile, pour 1 cup of boiling water over 1 tablespoon dried flowers; then cover and steep for 3 minutes. (Don't steep chamomile too long; it can produce a bitter taste.)

Dill

Dill, an herb that grows anywhere, has tiny leaves and a large, flowering seed head. Harvest the leaves any time you want. Use dill leaves in dressings and pickle mixes. It makes a refreshing dip for vegetables and tastes great added to your summer salads.

TIP

Dill can quickly become an invasive plant. Once the plant goes to seed, it starts popping up everywhere. Be sure to keep it in check by trimming off the flowers and seeds before the plant makes itself a permanent member of your garden.

Drying dill is super easy. Follow these steps:

1. **Lay the dill leaves in a single, loose layer on trays.**

2. **Set your oven or dehydrator temperature to between 100 and 115 degrees and dry 3 to 5 hours, rotating the trays periodically to facilitate even drying.**

    Properly dried dill leaves are crispy.

3. **Store dried dill in airtight containers, out of light.**

    This herb loses its delicate flavor quickly if left in sunlight for too long.

TIP

Chewing a few dill seeds can help with indigestion. Historically, dill was an ingredient in gripe water for colicky infants.

Mint

Mint is arguably the herb most people are familiar with and also the easiest herb to grow. It requires only sunlight and water to thrive. Yes, you can grow mint on a counter in a glass of water — forever!

Mint comes in dozens of flavors, with more being created all the time. From citrus to chocolate, mints are available for any palate. Grow as many varieties as you want, but keep them contained! And harvest them often, throughout the growing season, for drying.

TIP

Mint is a highly invasive herb and will overtake a garden within one growing season if left to spread on its own. Plant mint in a container to keep from having it go wild (literally). If you grow more than one variety of mint, plant them at least 10 feet apart to avoid cross-pollination. Although you will still get mint, it will no longer be true to the original scent you planted, if cross-pollinated.

To dry mint, follow these steps:

1. **Cut the stems that seem to want to straggle, and lay them on a drying tray.**

2. **Set your dehydrator or oven temperature to between 115 and 125 degrees and dry for 3 to 5 hours, rotating the trays periodically to facilitate even drying.**

   Properly dried mint leaves easily crumble in your hand.

3. **Store mint in airtight containers.**

TIP

Try making it into tea or adding a few leaves, crumbled, to boiled potatoes.

Oregano

Oregano is another easy-to-dry herb. Used in any tomato-based dish, oregano adds a distinct flavor to your meals. By drying oregano, you ensure that you have plenty of this popular flavoring available throughout the winter months. Use only young leaves, as older oregano has a tendency to taste bitter.

To dry oregano, pick the young leaves once the dew has dried in the morning and then follow these steps:

1. **Remove any leaves that have insect damage or have been crushed while harvesting.**

   These sometimes turn an unappealing black when drying.

2. **Arrange in a single layer on trays, but don't fill them too full. You want air to flow around them.**

3. **Set the temperature on your dehydrator to between 115 and 125 degrees and dry the oregano for 3 to 5 hours, rotating the trays periodically to facilitate even drying.**

   Properly dried oregano is dry and crumbly.

4. **Store dried oregano in its whole form until ready to use.**

To use dried oregano, crush the leaves in your hand just before adding to the dish. Add oregano to the dish in the last 10 minutes of cooking to preserve the flavor.

Rosemary

Rosemary is a centerpiece to any herb garden. Its scent is recognizable by nearly everyone, and its lovely bluish flowers are truly special. Rosemary can be harvested throughout the season. To dry, cut the smaller, side stems where they branch off from the main stem and then follow these steps:

1. **Lay the whole stems onto the drying trays.**

2. **Dry the herb for 6 to 8 hours at a temperature between 110 and 115 degrees, rotating the trays periodically to facilitate even drying.**

   They're done when the leaves slightly shrivel and release from the stem easily.

3. **Remove the leaves by holding the stem over a dish or container and running your fingers along the stem.**

   The leaves come off with a gentle touch and you are left with a clean stem.

4. **Store rosemary leaves whole, and break them up right before adding to your recipe.**

   This keeps most of the flavor inside until needed.

TIP

Save the dried rosemary stems for making kabobs. They contain plenty of the rosemary flavor, and make a unique presentation. Use the stems as you would skewers.

Sage

Sage is an easy-to-grow herb that is available as seeds or plants that quickly grow into small, lovely bushes. You can use any variety of garden sage for drying. Some offer a stronger flavor than others, so be sure to taste it before purchasing to find your favorite. To dry sage leaves, harvest them as they become large enough (½ inch or more in length) and then follow these steps:

1. **Lay out your sage leaves in a single layer on your drying trays.**

   Be sure to leave room between the leaves for even drying.

2. **Dry the herb for 6 to 8 hours at a temperature between 115 and 125 degrees, rotating the trays periodically to facilitate even drying.**

   It's dry enough if a leaf crumbles in your fingers.

   Be careful to dry these leaves thoroughly; they are slightly thicker than many other herbs and require careful attention.

REMEMBER

3. **Store the dried leaves in their whole form until needed.**

   If you find that you use rubbed sage often, dry the whole leaves and rub them through a mesh strainer to create a fluffy sage powder perfect for cooking.

TIP

Thyme

Thyme has many uses: It tastes great mixed with other herbs for flavoring Italian dishes and it can hold its own when paired with poultry. Thyme comes in many varieties, but the drying technique is the same. Follow these steps:

1. **Snip off stems as soon as your plants are large enough for drying and lay them whole, in a single layer, on your drying tray.**

2. **Set your oven or dehydrator temperature to between 110 to 115 degrees and dry the thyme for 4 to 6 hours, rotating the trays periodically to facilitate even drying.**

   Properly dried thyme leaves are dry and crisp.

3. **Store dried thyme, stems and all, in a cool, dry place away from sunlight.**

   Thyme loses its flavor quickly when left in sunlight.

When it comes time to use your dried thyme, crush the tiny stems right along with the leaves. If stems are too woody, strip leaves off, right before use.

The next time you have a cough or cold, make a tea out of dried thyme leaves. Thyme tea tastes very soothing when you are congested.

TIP

Chapter **7**

Root Cellaring and Storage

A n often overlooked storage idea is underground storage. The traditional root cellar is an efficient way to keep many foods fresh throughout the winter months. Keeping your harvest at its best through cold storage is easier than you think! If you're not lucky enough to have a place for a root cellar, you can keep food at the proper temperature in all sorts of other creative ways.

In this chapter, you discover creative ways to store your produce and find out how to select the best foods to keep in cold storage.

Finding the Perfect Place for Cold Storage

Before refrigeration and artificial preservatives, cold storage was the way to go if you needed to store produce over the winter. The basic idea behind cold storage is that you can prolong the shelf life of both fresh and canned produce by keeping them in a cool, dark place under just the right conditions.

By combining the perfect mix of temperature and humidity, you can expand your storage to a large variety of foods. Temperature and humidity aren't the only considerations, however. An area used for cold storage also needs to have proper ventilation to keep the food as fresh as possible. And ease of access is vital, too.

» **Temperature:** Cold storage temperatures range from 32 to 60 degrees. The right temperature for any given food is one that slows the enzymes responsible for decay. Different foods require different storage temperatures. Beets, for example, need temps just above freezing; pumpkins and squashes, on the other hand, need temps in the 50- to 60- degree range.

» **Humidity:** Depending on the foods you want to store, your root cellar or alternative cold storage area needs a humidity range from 60 to 95 percent. Foods such as carrots, parsnips, and turnips store best at 90 to 95 percent humidity. Sweet potatoes and onions, on the other hand, do much better at a humidity of no more than 70 percent.

If you plan to store foods that require very different humidity and temperature levels, you need to use more than one storage area. It's not uncommon to have a dry cold storage area with lower humidity (like you'd get in an area that has a cement floor) and a higher humidity area (which you get in an area with a dirt or gravel floor).

To keep track of temperature and humidity level in the air, buy a simple thermometer unit, called a *hydrometer* (see Figure 7-1).

» **Ventilation:** No matter what type of storage area you choose, it must be able to let warm air out and cool air in.

» **Ease of access:** Because you have to regularly check your stored food, you need a place that is easy to get into and that allows you to easily move things around.

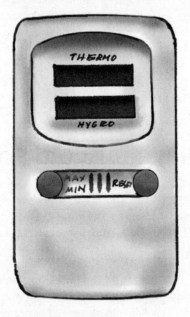

FIGURE 7-1:
A hydrometer for checking temperature and humidity.

Read on to find out what your cold-storage options are, and head to the section "Preparing Foods for Cold Storage" to discover the optimum humidity levels and temperatures required for specific foods.

Tried and true: The traditional root cellar

Root cellars have had a long and important place in the history of food storage. Root cellars were most often the actual cellar of old homes and farmhouses. These older houses had cellars with dirt floors, perfect for keeping foods cool and the humidity higher than average.

If you're lucky enough to have a dirt-floor root cellar, you just need to provide sturdy shelving and rodent-proof the area by covering any holes or potential rodent-friendly entryways with wire mesh. You can also place rodent bait in out-of-the-way areas and check often for rodent activity.

TIP

A preexisting root cellar usually contains some sort of air vent or pipe located at the top of the area to allow warm air to rise and escape. If you don't have a pre-existing air vent, periodically open a window or door to the outside to allow warm air out and fresh air in.

REMEMBER

In modern homes, cellars (or basements) often have concrete floors and are generally too warm and dry for food storage. Carefully measure your temperature and moisture content before placing your produce in a cellar that may not have optimum conditions.

DIY storage spaces

If you don't have a cellar with a dirt floor, there are alternatives. Take a look at your cellar layout and consider the areas suggested in the following sections.

Stairwells

Does a stairwell lead from your basement to the outside? If so, add an insulated door to separate the stairwell from the main room, and voilá, you have a cold storage space that has built-in shelves: the stairs! Just place bins of produce on each step and pans of water under the stairs for moisture, and you have an efficient storage area, as shown in Figure 7-2.

FIGURE 7-2:
A stairwell
converted into a
cold storage area.

REMEMBER

A stairwell is particularly good because the stairs create areas with varying temperatures, allowing for a wide array of conditions that can benefit many different kinds of foods.

Be sure to place a hydrometer in this area, as well as a few, inexpensive thermometers on different steps, to gauge the best conditions for your stored foods. There will be quite a variation in temperature as you go up the stairs.

Storm shelters

Do you have a storm shelter (also called a storm cellar)? In the Midwest, storm shelters are often underground cellars separate from the house or basement. (Think of Dorothy in *The Wizard of Oz*, when she runs through the yard to get to the storm cellar during the tornado.) These shelters are perfect for adding some shelves and neat bins of produce. They're below the frost line, have adequate ventilation, and are weatherproof. Whether your home had a storm shelter when you moved in or you decided to build one yourself, be certain to block any ventilation pipes with fine screen to keep out rodent activity.

TIP

Your stored foods will be used up long before the storm season approaches. Even so, keep your cold storage organized and neat.

Straw-bale storage

If you have a small area in your yard, you can construct a simple straw-bale storage area (see Figure 7-3) to hold your root crops, such as potatoes, rutabagas, turnips, and parsnips.

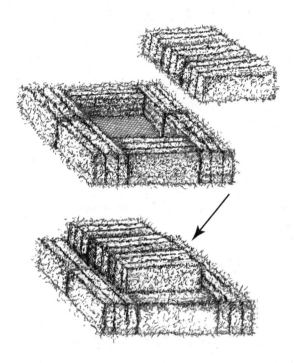

FIGURE 7-3: Straw-bale storage.

The best location for straw-bale storage is one that tends to stay dry. Don't place these storage areas in high moisture areas (where you generally have a buildup of snowdrift, for example, or where water tends to puddle after storms). Also, don't build one close to buildings that protect the area from winter temperatures. You want the straw bales to be able to stay freezing cold on the outside and yet insulate the produce inside.

After you've found a suitable location, follow these steps to build your storage area:

1. **Place two bales of straw in a line, with the ends touching. About 16 inches away, place two more bales parallel to the first two.**

    The spacing is adequate for the bales that are laid on top to cover the open space completely.

2. **Place one straw bale on each of the remaining ends to enclose a box shape in the center.**

   You've just made a large square in the center.

3. **Cover the ground in the center of the square with a screen.**

   You don't have use the screen, but doing so helps keep your produce protected from critters that may be inclined to dig under the whole thing.

4. **Layer some soft straw on the bottom of the square to cushion the produce.**

   If you put a screen in the center, place the straw over the screen.

5. **Layer your root crops, very gently, into the bin.**

   Take care to not dump or toss your vegetables. Bruised food quickly turns to spoiled food.

REMEMBER

6. **When the bin is full, layer another couple of inches of straw onto the food.**

7. **Place bales of straw across the top of the now-filled bin.**

   Your food is now protected from winter in a breathable storage bin.

To check on or access the food inside, simply remove the top two bales. Replace the bales carefully and evenly to cover the hole each time. In the late spring, or when the straw-bale storage area is empty, simply take the bin apart, and use the straw as mulch for your garden.

WARNING

Some people use hay bales for these storage bins, but we don't recommend it. Hay molds rather quickly, sometimes spoiling the produce inside. Hay bales also seem to absorb more moisture than straw bales. If you use hay, check periodically for moisture damage, and remove the offending produce immediately.

Rubber trash cans

You can bury these up to their rims in the ground, place your produce inside, put on the lid, and then cover the whole thing with a thick layer of straw for a simple cold storage arrangement. These bins are easy to wash and the tight lids keep the foods fresh and sanitary and keep rodents out.

Following Simple Storage Rules

Underground storage is the fastest and possibly easiest way to store foods. There are, however, some rules to follow, no matter what variety of food you want to keep over the winter:

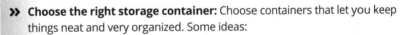

» **Be careful about the quality of the food you store:** Foods must be in perfect condition — not too ripe or picked too early. Overly ripe fruit is extremely fragile and in the last stage before naturally decaying. Food that's too green doesn't do particularly well, either. These foods may change color or become agreeably soft in storage, but they won't truly ripen and develop their best flavor in these conditions.

Make sure you pick your food at just the right ripeness, as fresh as possible, and store it immediately. *Don't* allow it to sit at room temperature while you decide what you are going to do with it.

» **Be careful about how you pair foods:** Some foods produce gases that make other foods spoil. For instance, apples produce a gas that makes potatoes start to sprout. Put these two together, and you'll end up with potatoes that are soft and inedible. Cabbage is a very strongly scented food that is better stored in an outside area, away from more delicately flavored items.

» **You must care for the foods, even while in storage:** Weekly checking for bruising, decay, dryness, and mold is essential. The old adage about a rotten apple spoiling the barrel definitely applies here. As the winter progresses, remove any produce that has blemishes. Your remaining foods will continue to last longer.

TIP

Rearrange your produce carefully. You may discover that you've used enough of your stored produce to enable you to bring the bottom layer up to the top. Be careful of excess handling though; gently place each food back in place to avoid bruising.

» **Choose the right storage container:** Choose containers that let you keep things neat and very organized. Some ideas:

- **Rubbermaid-style tubs:** These can be stacked when not in use, their covers fit tightly, and they can easily be filled with damp sand for foods needing increased humidity. Use clear bins to avoid colors leaching into foods and so that you can easily see all the produce inside.

- **Wooden bins or boxes:** Recycle these from thrift stores and some grocery stores. Even if you have to pay a few dollars each, they will give years of service and allow for neat, tidy stacking. If stacking wooden boxes, place the first row in a line, place a couple of sticks across the boxes for air circulation, and then place the next boxes. You want to let the moisture and gases escape, which allows the food to last longer.

- **Five-gallon pails:** You can find these for next to nothing from bakers and other restaurants. You don't need to include the lid; in fact, for cold storage, it is best not to. Fill the clean, dry bucket with produce, layer a damp cloth on the top and you can stack these buckets in a pyramid shape, allowing plenty of airflow between.

- **Old dressers:** You can arrange these unconventional pieces against a wall and use the drawers to keep your produce in a dry and safe place. Line the drawers with newspaper for easy cleaning. Keep them slightly ajar for proper air circulation.

Preparing Foods for Cold Storage

Foods that store well are generally the less juicy and delicate things, such as root vegetables and firm fruits. The following sections list several fruits and vegetables that keep very well in cold storage. They are foods that many families enjoy; they provide a fresh taste when bland winter fare abounds; and they extend your food pantry to include fresh, tasty choices. (*Note:* You may be able to extend the life of more tender foods, such as eggplant or broccoli, but don't count on them lasting for months as the other foods will. You can keep these treats in storage about two weeks, but no longer.)

TIP

As a general rule, harvest root crops as late as you can in the season and don't wash the dirt from the roots. Simply use your hand or a rag to remove some of the loose soil.

Apples

Apples store very well. Choose a variety that is known for storage. Kept well, apples can last throughout the entire winter — four to six months! Toward the end of that time, a perfectly good apple may become slightly shriveled. This is simply from the loss of moisture, not nutrition.

Choose apples that are unblemished and firm (they shouldn't give at all when pressed). Check in bright light for dents and soft spots.

To store, layer the apples carefully in very cold temperatures (between 30 and 35 degrees), with a high humidity between 80 and 90 percent. (Place a pan of water in the area where they're stored.)

TIP

Try covering your bin of apples with a damp (not dripping) cloth, which remains damp for at least a day. And make it a habit to replace the cloth every couple of days when you check other stored produce.

Beets

Beets are prolific and inexpensive to grow, meaning you'll end up with plenty for storage if you plant a few rows. Harvest beets late in the season, after the nights become freezing cold. If you're buying beets at a farmer's market, look for fresh, crisp tops. This is the best indication that the beets are just picked.

To prepare the beets for storage, cut off the tops, leaving the beet itself intact (don't wash them). Then place the beets in your coldest storage, temperatures just above freezing, 32 to 40 degrees, with 90 to 95 percent humidity. To increase humidity naturally, place the beets on moist sand.

Some gardeners recommend leaving beets in the ground, covered with a thick layer of straw. They say beets and other root crops can be harvested directly from the ground into the coldest part of the winter. Be aware, though, that rodents may destroy root crops before you get a chance to harvest them. So before you follow the advice of the "leave 'em in the ground" crowd, make sure you — and not rodents — will be the benefactors.

Cabbage

Cabbage adds bulk and crunch to many winter dishes. Keeping cabbage in storage requires a few extra precautions, however, to ensure that it remains useable throughout the winter and doesn't ruin other food nearby.

First, cabbage gives off a strong odor while in storage, which is normal (don't confuse this smell with spoilage). The problem with the smell is that apples and other fruits can absorb the flavor of cabbage. The key is to make sure you don't store cabbage too closely to these other types of foods. If you must store cabbage close to other foods, wrap individual heads with newspaper to contain the odor.

TIP

The longer cabbage remains in storage, the stronger the taste when it's cooked. If your family does not like the stronger taste, plan on using up cabbage early in the storage season.

Second, cabbage needs to be stored in a damp area. If you store cabbage in a place that's too dry, the heads dry out, and the dry, wilted leaves are wasted. Fortunately, you can take care of this tendency with a simple pan of water.

To prepare cabbage for storage, choose unblemished cabbage that has not been picked for long. Remove the tough outer leaves. Wrap each head in newspaper and store it where temperatures are just above freezing, 32 to 40 degrees, and the humidity levels are between 80 to 90 percent. Place a pan of water near the cabbage to provide enough moisture during storage.

Carrots

Carrots are another root vegetable that stores well and tastes sweet and crisp throughout the winter months. Just as you do with beets, pick carrots as late as possible in the season. Avoid any that have grown too large and pithy, however, because these carrots have used up their natural sweetness and will taste bitter.

To prepare carrots for storage, trim off the tops, leaving the carrot itself intact. Don't wash them; simply brush off excess soil if you want to. Place carrots with beets in coldest storage of 32 to 40 degrees with high humidity of 90 to 95 percent. Carrots do especially well in moist sand.

Garlic

You can never have enough garlic, especially since garlic is so easy to store. If you're growing your own garlic, simply pull the bulbs after the tops have dried and fallen over. Allow the garlic bulbs to dry thoroughly out of direct sunlight until the outside of the bulbs has become dry and papery. Purchased garlic bulbs have already been dried. Look for the papery outer layer that you always see on a store-bought bulb.

Dry bulbs on newspaper outside during the warm summer days, but bring them in during the cool nights to prevent condensation. Repeat this process for a few days, until the garlic is completely dry.

When the garlic is thoroughly dry, tie bunches of tops together, braid in attractive garlic braids. Alternatively, you can trim tops from bulbs and place them in women's stockings, tying a knot between bulbs. You can hang this long chain of bulbs on a nail in a cool and slightly damp area. You may have luck placing garlic in a cool coat room, instead of an actual root cellar. They are in a convenient location for cooking, and let's face it, they make quite a conversation piece! If you do keep them in cold storage, place them in 30 to 45 degrees with a humidity level of 60 to 70 percent.

Onions

Most onions keep very well in cold storage. Some varieties, such as the extra sweet onions, however, don't last long. When planting, choose varieties that say they work well for storage (you'll see the term *good keeper*). These onions last throughout the storage season.

Harvest onions the same as garlic. Pull them when the tops turn brown and fall over. They must then be cured, like garlic: Place them on newspaper to dry during the warm days, bringing them in during the cool night hours to avoid condensation buildup. When storing purchased onions, you don't have to worry about this step. They are already dried for you.

To store, gently place onions in a crate, loose mesh bag, or ladies' stockings, tying a knot between each onion. To prevent mildew on onion skins, air circulation is vital, so make sure your cold storage has adequate ventilation (see the earlier section "Finding the Perfect Place for Cold Storage"). The ideal storage conditions are temperatures of 35 to 40 degrees and humidity of 60 to 70 percent. If, throughout the season, you find onions with some mildew on them, simply use those onions first. Generally the mildew is on the outer layers, leaving the inside onions fresh.

Pears

Pears store very well and make a nice change from apples. In years when apples are affected by blight or scald and are too expensive, pears can be more available.

Pick pears you plan to store when they're just ripened. (Don't choose pears that are too ripe, or soft; simply leaning against each other can cause them to bruise.) To help protect the fruit, wrap each pear in a sheet of newspaper before storing. Keep temperatures cold, 30 to 35 degrees, with high humidity (80 to 90 percent). Pears can keep for several months in this manner.

Potatoes

Potatoes are the easiest of all fruits and vegetables to store. To prepare for storage, harvest late in the season. Don't wash the potatoes; instead remove excess soil with your hand or a soft rag. Inspect them carefully for bruising or nicks in the skin (fresh potatoes have a more delicate skin than those that have been harvested for a few days). If you find any bruising or nicks, keep these potatoes out of storage and use them within a few days.

Store potatoes in complete darkness at 32 to 40 degrees and 80 to 90 percent humidity. Every week, check them for damage. At least once a month, turn and rearrange them. Finally, don't let them freeze. A frozen potato is a ruined potato; it can't be saved.

REMEMBER

The most important rule for storing potatoes is to store them in complete darkness. First, the darkness signals dormancy for the potato, and it won't sprout. Second, potatoes subjected to light become bitter over time. Other than perfect darkness, potatoes really do well in almost all storage conditions.

Turnips

Turnips are an underappreciated root crop. They are easy to grow: You simply plant them early in the season, weed them a few times, and harvest them late in the season, after the nights become freezing cold, sometime in November.

To prepare turnips for storage, don't wash them. Simply brush off any excess soil with your hand or a rag, and trim off the turnip tops.

Store them in your coldest storage area; just above freezing is ideal (temperatures of 30 to 40 degrees). The humidity should be high; between 90 to 95 percent is optimal. Turnips are another food that stores well in damp sand.

TIP

Consider turnips a crop that provides two separate foods: the greens and the root. So, after you trim the tops to prepare the root for cold storage, don't throw away the greens. You can dry them for use later. To see how to keep turnip tops, head to Chapter 6 of this minibook for info on drying greens.

Tomatoes

You may be surprised to see tomatoes, which are both fragile and juicy, in this list of good cold-storage vegetables. Tomatoes can, however, be kept for a limited period of time in cold storage.

When you store tomatoes, you store the whole plant, not just the individual tomatoes. So at the end of the growing season, select any tomato plants that have fruit with the slightest hint of ripening (any color change, from slight yellow to orange) and follow these steps:

1. **Remove any fruits from the plant that are still fully green or too small to ever ripen.**

2. **Pull the entire plant out of the ground and hang it upside down in temperatures between 55 and 70 degrees, with moderate humidity of 60 to 70 percent.**

   An unheated garage or cellar stairwell works great for this.

The tomatoes will ripen slowly over time, right on the vine. You will be amazed at the vine-fresh flavor.

3

Making
Your Own

Contents at a Glance

Chapter **1**

Brewing Beer

As a homesteader, you're already eating the fruits of your labor that come out of your garden. Why not bring that same do-it-yourself mentality to something you enjoy out of a glass, too? Homebrewed beer can be every bit as good as — if not better than — a lot of commercial beer, with more flavor and character than most. In fact, avoiding mass-market beer was the original inspiration for homebrewing. Since homebrewing became legal almost 30 years ago, the interest in hand-crafted beer has blossomed.

But forget any preconceived notions you may have about shiny copper kettles and coils taking up your whole kitchen and huge wooden vats bubbling and churning in the cellar — those notions are the product of vivid imaginations and vintage Hollywood movies. Human civilization is well into the stainless-steel and plastic age, where everything is smaller, more durable, and lighter.

You can brew your own beer with minimal equipment — readily available in simple kit form — and a short time commitment. A batch of beer is about a three-week process (on the short end), but that includes only four to six hours of work; the rest is waiting as you let the beer do its thing.

Adding some homebrewing efforts to your homestead will be pretty painless — and with a tasty, frothy reward waiting for you at the end!

Setting Up Shop to Brew

To the first-timer, the vast quantities of equipment and ingredient choices related to homebrewing can be somewhat intimidating. Homebrewing equipment varies, as shown in Figure 1-1, but any homebrew supply shop worth its salt can get you what you need to get started. If you don't have a local homebrew supply retailer in your area, mail order is the next best option. Many mail-order shops have toll-free phone numbers or websites for ordering, and most offer free catalogs.

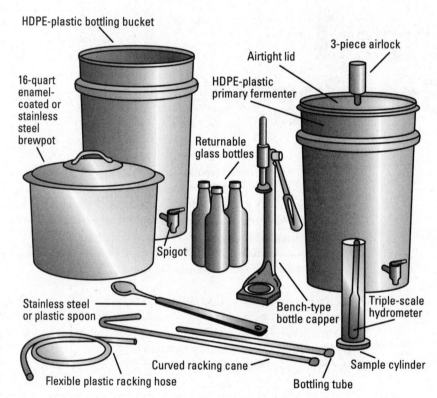

FIGURE 1-1: Many homebrew shops sell this basic equipment as a start-up kit.

At the beginner level, the minimum amount of equipment you need to brew beer correctly will cost about $70. This setup is relatively bare-bones, but it's enough to get you up and running. As you become more familiar and comfortable with the processes and procedures, you'll want to acquire additional and better equipment.

To help you get the wheels turning, Table 1-1 provides a starter list of necessary items and their approximate costs.

TABLE 1-1   ## Beginner Brewing Equipment and Its Cost

Equipment	Approximate Cost
Brew pot, 16 qt. minimum	$40/20 qt., $80/30 qt.
Brew spoon (HDPE plastic)	$4 or less
Primary fermenter (HDPE plastic) with spigot, lid	$20 or less
Airlock	$2 or less
Drilled rubber stopper for airlock	$2 or less
3 to 4 feet of food-grade plastic hose, ½ inch in diameter	$3
Bottling or "priming" bucket (HDPE plastic) with spigot	$15 or less
Bottles (must be the reusable type that don't use twist-off caps)	$20–$30 for one batch of beer (5 gallons); the exact number of bottles depends on their size: 12 oz., 16 oz., 22 oz., or 1 qt.
Bottle rinser	$12
Bottle brush	$3
Bottling tube (HDPE plastic) with spring valve	$4 or less
Bottle capper	$35 (bench-type) or $15 (two-handed)
Hydrometer (triple scale) with cylinder	$10 ($5 or less for the cylinder)

HOW MUCH DOES A HOMEBREWED BATCH COST?

The average batch of homebrewed beer is 5 gallons, or 53.3 12-ounce bottles of beer. At the beginner level, the ingredients for a typical batch run about $30 to $35. The amount you pay fluctuates because of many factors, including where you shop for your ingredients (don't forget shipping charges for mail order), whether you buy top- or bottom-of-the-line ingredients, and the style of beer you like to brew. Big-bodied, alcoholic beers require more fermentable ingredients than do light-bodied, watery beers. (Barley wines can cost as much as 100 percent more to make than pale ales, for example.)

Getting to Know Your Ingredients

Brewing uses grain (mostly malted barley), hops, yeast, and water. Thanks to many stores and Internet sites that specialize in brew supplies, homebrewers today have access to most of the same ingredients used by corporate brewhouses everywhere. Of course, these shops don't just provide the everyday ingredients for the average beer; different hop varieties and yeast strains from around the world are now available in the homebrewing market.

Grain

Of the four main ingredients used to make beer (barley, hops, yeast, and water), barley — really, grain in general — makes the biggest contribution. It's responsible for giving beer its color, underlying flavor, sweetness, body, head of foam, and *mouthfeel* (the textural qualities of beer on your palate and in your throat — *viscosity*, or thickness, carbonation, alcohol warmth, and so on). Grains also contribute the natural sugars that feed the yeast, which in turn converts the sugars into alcohol and carbon dioxide during fermentation.

Before you can brew with barley, it must undergo a process known as malting. The *malting process*, simply put, simulates the grain's natural germination cycle. Only after the barley has undergone the malting process does it become *malt*, or *barley malt*.

Hops

If malts represent the sugar in beer, hops surely represent the spice. In fact, you use hops in beer in much the same way that you use spices in cooking. The divine mission of hops is to accent the flavor of beer and, most importantly, contrast the sweetness of the malt.

Hops contribute bitterness (to offset the sweet flavor of malt), a zesty flavoring (to accent the malt character), a pungent floral or herbal aroma, bacterial inhibitors, and natural clarifying agents.

The hop cones used in the brewing process grow on vines that may reach 25 feet on commercial hop farms. Hop plants are hardy perennial plants that are prolific under ideal conditions, and each may produce up to 2 pounds of dried hop cones per season.

Traditionally, brewers handpicked hops from the vine and air-dried them in bulk before tossing them whole into the brew kettle. Today, however, hops are processed and sold in four forms: small processed pellets, larger compressed plugs, whole-leaf hops (see Figure 1-2), and concentrated liquid hop extract.

Hop pellets Hop plug Whole-leaf hops

FIGURE 1-2:
Some of the
different ways
that brewers
process hops.

Yeast

Although yeast is an ingredient that the average beer consumer rarely contemplates, brewers often consider it the most important ingredient. Yeast can have a greater influence and effect on the finished beer than any other single ingredient.

Yeast is a member of the fungus family. It's a living single-celled organism and one of the simplest forms of life. Because it has cell-splitting capabilities, it's also self-reproducing. Yeast is the one ingredient responsible for carrying out the *fermentation* process in brewing: simply put, the natural conversion of sugar to alcohol. (For much more on fermentation in other homesteading applications, check out Book 3, Chapter 2.)

Brewers categorize and classify beer styles by the type of yeast used to ferment them. Therefore, they choose a yeast according to the style of beer they want to make: ale or lager.

A WORD ABOUT ALCOHOL CONTENT

You can brew beer at home without caring one whit about its alcohol content, but you'd likely be in the small minority. Most homebrewers are keenly interested in knowing how much alcohol is in their brew, whether it's on the high side or the low side. And most make a concentrated effort to target specific alcohol levels in their beer.

That's where a hydrometer comes in. A standard and readily-accessible piece of homebrewing equipment, a *hydrometer* registers alcohol by volume, referred to as ABV in the beer world.

Brewers who want to produce a nonalcoholic beer at home may be disappointed; it's not as easy as just not adding yeast. Unfermented beer is thick, sweet, and not at all thirst-quenching. It takes a lot of specialized equipment and technology to produce and necessitates extra steps that are generally not worth the effort on a small scale. All things considered, it's cheaper and easier to simply buy nonalcoholic beer at the store.

Ale yeast is a *top-fermenting* strain, meaning it floats on the top of the beer. Virtually all ale yeast works best in fairly warm temperatures (60 to 70 degrees Fahrenheit). *Lager yeast* is a *bottom-fermenting* strain (meaning it sinks to the bottom of the fermentation vessel at the end of fermentation) and works best between 38 to 50 degrees Fahrenheit.

Yeast for the homebrewer comes in both a dry form and a liquid form. Because of its convenience, dry yeast — granulated and contained in a small packet — is recommended for beginners. The packets that come with malt extract kits are sufficient to ferment a 5-gallon batch of homebrew. Dry yeast is freeze-dried, so it should last a long time (but refrigerate all yeast to maintain optimum freshness).

TIP

For the best results with dry yeast, always rehydrate the dormant cells by pouring them into a cup of warm water. This gentle wake-up call prepares the yeast for the upcoming fermentation. Be sure to sanitize the vessel in which you rehydrate the yeast.

Water

Considering that it constitutes up to 95 percent of a beer's total ingredient profile, water can have a tremendous influence on the finished product. The various minerals and salts found in water used for brewing can accentuate beer flavors or contribute undesirable flavor components. In many cases, water chemistry is key in the flavor profile of a classic beer style.

That said, you can still make good beer with average tap water. Thousands of homebrewers are proving it every day. A general rule says, "If your water tastes good, so will your beer".

REMEMBER

At any skill level, make sure that you keep the following things in mind:

>> If your water is from a private underground well, it may be high in iron and other minerals that may affect your beer's taste.

>> If your water is softened, it may be high in sodium.

>> If your water is supplied by a municipal water department, it may have a high chlorine content. Other than chlorine, the *filtering* (the primary method of removing elements and impurities from water) performed at municipal water sources usually produces water that is sufficiently pure for brewing.

High iron, sodium, and chlorine contents in your brewing water are not desirable. If these minerals are present in your brewing water, you may want to consider buying bottled water for your brewing needs.

WARNING

If you choose to buy your water, you may be tempted to buy *distilled* water because it's the purest form available. But distilled water is also devoid of some of the important natural elements beneficial to beer.

Brewing Your First Batch

Enough of the preliminary stuff. It's time to get brewing! This section walks you through the step–by–step process of brewing at home. Just follow along and you can make great beer in no time.

The following numbered list covers 24 steps that walk you all the way through the brewing process. Twenty-four steps may sound intense, but rest assured they're easy, quick, and painless (unless you consider turning on a burner to be exhausting work). Besides, when you're done, you've brewed your first beer!

1. **Fill your brew pot about ⅔ full with clean tap water or bottled water and then place it on the largest burner of your stove.**

   Use bottled water if your home's water source is loaded with chlorine, iron, or high concentrations of other trace metals.

TIP

   The exact volume of water isn't terribly important during this step, because you add cold water to the fermenter later to bring the total to 5 gallons.

2. **Set the burner on medium-high.**

3. **Remove the plastic lids from the kits and set the yeast packets aside.**

4. **Strip the paper labels off the two cans of extract and place the cans in a smaller pot or saucepan filled halfway with tap water. Place the pot or saucepan on another burner near the brew pot.**

   The water's purity isn't important here because you don't use this water in the beer.

5. **Set the second burner on medium.**

6. **Using hot pads, flip the cans in the warming water every couple of minutes.**

7. **As the water in the brew pot begins to boil, turn off the burner under the smaller pot (containing the cans), remove the cans from the water, and remove the lids from the cans.**

8. **Using a long-handled spoon or rubber spatula, scrape as much of the warmed extract as possible from the cans into the water in the brew pot.**

9. **Immediately stir the extract/water solution and continue to stir until the extract completely dissolves in the water.**

   This malt extract/water mixture is now officially called *wort* in brewer-speak.

WARNING

   If you don't stir the wort immediately, you risk scorching the extract on the bottom of the brew pot.

10. **Top off the brew pot with more clean tap or bottled water, keeping your water level a reasonable distance — about 2 inches — from the top of the pot to avoid boil overs.**

11. **Bring the wort to a boil (turn up the burner if necessary).**

12. **Boil the wort for about an hour, stirring the pot every couple of minutes to avoid scorching and boil overs.**

Never put the lid on the brew pot during the boiling phase! Stove-top boil overs occur regularly when a brew pot's lid is on. Boil overs are not only a sticky, gooey mess but also a waste of good beer!

13. **Turn off the burner and place the lid on the brew pot.**

14. **Put a stopper in the nearest sink drain, put the covered brew pot in the sink, and fill the sink with very cold water.**

Fill the sink completely (or up to the liquid level in the brew pot if the sink is deeper than the brew pot).

15. **After 5 minutes, drain the sink and refill it with very cold water — repeat as many times as needed until the brew pot is cool to the touch.**

16. **While the brew pot is cooling in the sink, draw at least 6 ounces of lukewarm tap water into a sanitized cup or bowl.**

17. **Open the yeast packets and pour the dried yeast into the cup or bowl of water.**

Called *proofing,* this process is a gentle but effective way to wake up the dormant yeast and ready it for the fermentation to follow.

18. **When the brew pot is relatively cool to the touch, remove the brew pot lid and carefully pour the wort into the fermentation bucket.**

Make sure the spigot is closed!

19. **Top off the fermenter to the 5-gallon mark with cold, clean water, pouring it vigorously into the bucket.**

This splashing not only mixes the wort with the additional water but also aerates the wort well.

The yeast needs oxygen to get off to a good healthy start in the fermentation phase. Because boiled water is virtually devoid of oxygen, you need to put some oxygen back in by aerating the wort. Failure to aerate may result in sluggish and sometimes incomplete fermentations.

20. **Take a hydrometer reading.**

See the section "Brewing day reading" in this chapter for specific information about this process.

21. **After you take the hydrometer reading and remove the hydrometer, pour the hydrated yeast from the cup or bowl into the fermenter and give it a good brisk stir with your brew spoon.**

22. **Cover the fermenter with its lid and thoroughly seal it.**

Brewing Beer

23. Put the fermenter in a cool, dark location, such as a basement, a crawl space, or an interior closet.

Don't put the fermenter in direct sunlight or where there's a daily fluctuation in temperatures, such as your garage. This temperature fluctuation can mess with your beer's fermentation cycle.

24. After the fermenter is in a good place, fill the airlock halfway with water and replace the cap; attach the rubber stopper and position it snugly in the fermenter lid.

Check to make sure that the fermenter and airlock are sealed airtight by pushing down gently on the fermenter lid. This gentle pressure causes the float piece in the airlock to rise; if it doesn't, you have a breach in the seal. Recheck the lid and airlock for leaks.

Fermentation should begin within the first 24 hours and last anywhere from 7 to 10 days. This wait can be nerve-wracking for first-timers, but patience is rewarded with great beer.

How quickly the beer begins to ferment and how long the fermentation lasts depends on the amount of yeast, the health of the yeast, the temperature at which the beer is fermenting, and whether or not the wort was properly aerated. Healthy yeast, mild temperatures (65 to 70 degrees Fahrenheit), and an abundance of oxygen in the wort make for a good, quick ferment. Old, dormant yeast, cold temperatures, and under-oxygenated wort cause fermentations to start slowly, go on interminably, or even quit altogether.

After your beer has been in the fermenter for about a week or so, check the bubbling action in the airlock. If visible fermentation is still taking place (as evidenced by the escaping bubbles), continue to check the bubbling on a daily basis. When the float piece within the airlock appears to be still and the time between bubbles is a minute or more, your beer is ready for bottling. Before you begin the bottling procedures, however, you need to take a second gravity reading to make sure that the fermentation is complete (see the section "Prebottling reading" in this chapter for specifics on how to do this).

Bottling beer before it's finished fermenting may result in exploding bottles.

Taking Hydrometer Readings

A *hydrometer* is a fragile glass measuring device used to calculate the density of your beer in two separate scales: the specific gravity scale and the Bailing scale. (Both scales measure liquid density but in different increments, similar to measuring temperature in Fahrenheit and Celsius.) Most homebrewers use the specific gravity scale.

A hydrometer also measures the amount of alcohol that the yeast has produced in your homebrew. Using a hydrometer and understanding its readings can also call attention to possible fermentation problems. (See Figure 1-3 for a look at a hydrometer in action.)

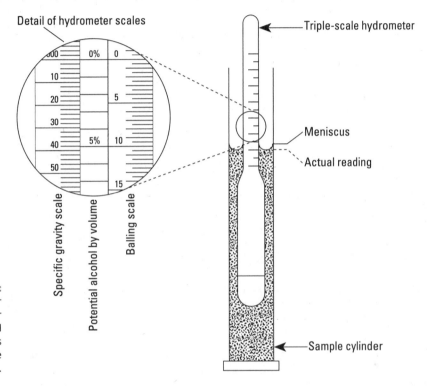

FIGURE 1-3:
A hydrometer displays your brew's liquid density and helps you calculate the alcohol content.

Some people argue that a hydrometer isn't a necessary piece of equipment at the beginner level. But the truth is, a hydrometer isn't expensive, it's easy to use, and anyone who wants to progress in the world of homebrewing needs to learn how to use one. It's the only way to fully know what it is you've just made with your homebrewing endeavor.

The following information shows you how to take hydrometer readings on brewing and bottling days.

Brewing day reading

You want to take the first hydrometer reading on brewing day (see Step 20 in the "Brewing Your First Batch" section of this chapter). To take a good reading, do the following:

1. **Sanitize the hydrometer.**

2. **Lower the hydrometer directly into the cooled and diluted wort inside the fermenter.**

TIP

As you lower the hydrometer into the wort in the fermenter, give the hydrometer a quick spin with your thumb and index finger. This movement dislodges any bubbles clinging to the hydrometer that may cause you to get an incorrect reading.

3. **Record the numbers at the liquid surface on the hydrometer scales.**

You need this information on bottling day to decide whether fermentation is complete and to figure out the alcohol content in your beer. The gravity of your malt extract and water mixture will determine the numbers you see on the scales. Typically, 6 or so pounds of malt extract diluted in 5 gallons of water appear on the hydrometer's O.G. scale as 1.048, and the alcohol potential (as noted on the hydrometer's alcohol potential scale) is around 6 percent.

Prebottling reading

When you think your beer is ready for bottling (based on the bubbling action in the airlock), it's time to take another hydrometer reading. This reading helps you decide whether or not your beer is ready to be bottled:

1. **With your hydrometer test cylinder in hand, take a sample of beer from the spigot of the fermenter.**

Be sure to fill the cylinder to within 1 inch of the opening, leaving room for liquid displacement of the immersed hydrometer.

2. **Immerse the hydrometer in the beer, record the numbers at the liquid surface of the hydrometer, and compare with those numbers recorded on brewing day.**

The average healthy yeast consumes at least 65 percent of the available sugars in the wort. If the final gravity reading on your fermented beer isn't 35 percent or less of the original gravity, too much natural sugar may be left in your beer.

Here's a sample equation: If your beer has an original gravity of 1.048, subtract 1 so that you have 0.048; then multiply .048 by 0.35, which results in 0.017. Now add the 1 back in. If the final gravity of your beer is higher than 1.017, you want to delay bottling a few more days.

Bottling Your Brew

Bottling homebrew isn't a difficult procedure, but many brewers often deride it as one that's tedious at worst and boring at best. But for millions of people who brew their beer at home, bottling represents the only option for packaging their finished brew, making it a mandatory step in the homebrewing process.

The American brewing industry continues to package beer — albeit in limited markets — in a variety of 7-, 12-, 16-, and 22-ounce and quart-size returnable bottles; check with your local beer retailer. You can easily purchase brand-new 12- and 22-ounce bottles through homebrew supply shops, but the cost is sometimes prohibitive, mostly due to the cost of shipping.

Using larger bottles is a way to expedite the bottling process as well as free you from its drudgery. The more beer the bottles can hold, the fewer bottles you need. For instance, to bottle an entire 5-gallon batch of beer in 7-ounce nip bottles, you need to clean, fill, and cap more than 90 of them. If you use 22-ounce bottles, on the other hand, you need only 30 of them.

Now, here are the steps for the bottling brigade:

1. **Fill your utility tub or other designated sanitizing basin with enough cold water to cover your submerged bottles, adding bleach or another sanitizing agent according to the manufacturer's directions.**

2. **Submerge as many bottles as you need to contain your full batch of 5 gallons of beer.**

REMEMBER

Make sure your bottles are scum-free before dunking them in the sanitizing solution. Any bottle with dried or living crud in the bottom needs to be scrubbed separately with a cleanser such as trisodium phosphate (TSP) before you sanitize it.

TIP

You can fill and submerge the bottles in less than half the time if you place a drinking straw in the bottles; the straw enables the air in the bottle to escape through the straw instead of slowly bubbling through the opening (your bottling tube with the valve detached suffices here).

3. **Allow your bottles to soak for at least half an hour (or the time necessary according to the package's directions).**

4. **While the bottles soak, dissolve ¾ cup of dextrose in a pint or so of water in one of the saucepans, cover the solution, and place it on a burner over low heat.**

5. **Put your bottle caps into your other saucepan, fill the pan with enough water to cover all the caps, and place the pan on another burner over low heat.**

TIP

Put enough bottle caps for as many bottles as you have soaking plus a few extra; having too many sterilized caps ready for bottling is better than not having enough.

6. **Allow both pans to come to a boil, remove them from the heat, and allow them to cool.**

7. **After the bottles soak for half an hour, connect the bottle rinser to the faucet over the sanitizing tub.**

8. **With one hand over the opening (so that you don't get squirted), turn on the hot water.**

After the initial spray, the bottle washer holds back the water pressure until a bottle is lowered over the stem and pushed down.

9. **Start cleaning the bottles one-by-one with the bottle brush, and then drain the sanitizer, rinse your bottles with the bottle rinser, and allow them to air dry.**

Continue this step until all bottles are clean.

Visually check each bottle for cleanliness rather than just assume that they're all clean.

TIP

Four dozen free-standing bottles make one heck of a breakable domino effect. Always put your cleaned bottles back into six-pack holders or cardboard cases to avoid an aggravating and easily avoidable accident.

10. **Drain the utility tub of the bottle-cleaning water.**

WARNING

11. **Place the bottling bucket in the tub and fill it with water and the sanitizing agent of your choice.**

12. **Place the bottling hose, bottling tube, and hydrometer cylinder into the bottling bucket and allow them to soak for half an hour (or according to sanitizing agent directions).**

13. **While the bottling equipment soaks, retrieve the still-covered fermenter from its resting place and place it on a sturdy table, counter, or work surface about 3 or 4 feet off the ground.**

    At this point, you need to set up your bottling station, making sure that you have the priming sugar mixture (still in the saucepan), bottle caps, bottle capper, bottles, and hydrometer with cylinder on hand.

    If you're bottling your brew directly from the primary fermenter, you want to have already taken a hydrometer reading to confirm completion of fermentation. If you're bottling from your secondary fermenter (glass carboy), incomplete fermentation isn't a concern, and you can take a hydrometer reading (to determine final gravity and alcohol content) as the beer drains into the bottling bucket.

14. **After half an hour, drain the sanitizing solution from the bottling bucket through the spigot on the bottom. After the bucket is empty, thoroughly rinse the remaining pieces of equipment (hose, bottling tube), along with the bottles and caps, and bring them to your bottling station.**

15. **Place the bottling bucket on the floor directly below the fermenter and connect the plastic hosing to the spigot on the fermenter, allowing the other end of the hosing to hang inside the bottling bucket.**

    If you're initiating the bottling procedures from your glass carboy, you can't rely on the convenience of a spigot to drain out the beer. You need to use your racking cane and siphon the brew.

16. **Pour the dextrose and water mixture into the bottling bucket.**

    The dissolved corn sugar mixes with the beer as the beer drains from the fermenter into the bottling bucket. After you've bottled the beer, this sugar becomes another source of food for the few yeast cells still remaining in the liquid. As the yeast consumes the sugar, it produces the beer's carbonation within the bottle. Eventually, the yeast again falls dormant and creates a thin layer of sediment on the bottom of each bottle.

WARNING

If, by chance, you bottle a batch of beer that isn't fully fermented or you somehow add too much dextrose at bottling time, you may find out first-hand what a mess exploding bottles can make. Excess sugar (whether added corn sugar or leftover maltose from an unfinished fermentation) overfeeds the yeast in an enclosed bottle. With nowhere for the pressure to go, the glass gives before the bottle cap. Kaboom! Mess! Do not over-prime. (Use no more than ¾ cup of dextrose in 5 gallons of beer.)

17. **Open the spigot on the fermenter and allow all the beer to run into the bottling bucket.**

Don't try to salvage every last drop from the fermenter by tilting it as the beer drains down the spigot. The spigot is purposely positioned about an inch above the bottom of the fermenter so that all the spent yeast and miscellaneous fallout remains behind.

18. **After the last of the beer drains, close the spigot, remove the hose, and rinse it.**

TIP

Avoid splashing or aerating your beer as you bottle it. Any oxidation that the beer picks up now can be tasted later. Yuck.

19. **Carefully place the bottling bucket up where the fermenter was, connect the rinsed hose to the spigot on the bottling bucket, and attach the bottling tube to the other end of the hose.**

20. **Arrange all your bottles on the floor directly below the bottling bucket (keeping them all in cardboard carriers or cases to avoid breakage and spillage).**

21. **Open the spigot on the bottling bucket and begin to fill all the bottles.**

Gently push the bottling tube down on the bottom of each bottle to start the flow of beer. The bottle may take a short while to fill, but the process always seems to accelerate as the beer nears the top. Usually, a bit of foam rushes to the top of the bottle; don't worry! As soon as you withdraw the bottling tube, the liquid level in the bottle falls.

22. **Remove the tube from each bottle after foam or liquid reaches the top of the bottle.**

Figure 1-4 shows you how full you want your bottles to be.

TECHNICAL
STUFF

After you remove the bottling tube from the bottle, the level of the beer falls to about an inch or so below the opening. Homebrewers have differing opinions as to how much airspace (or *ullage*) is necessary. Some say the smaller the airspace, the less oxidation that can occur. Others claim that if you don't have correct ullage, the beer can't carbonate properly. Basically, if it looks like the space in bottles of beer from commercial breweries, go with it!

23. **After you completely drain the bottling bucket, close the spigot, remove the hose, toss it inside the bottling bucket, and set everything aside to be cleaned after all the bottling procedures are complete.**

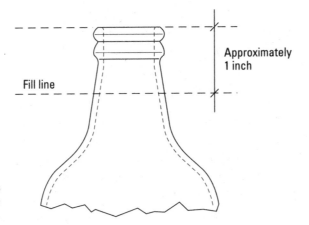

Approximately
1 inch

Fill line

FIGURE 1-4:
Correct bottle
fill level.

24. **Place all the bottles on your tabletop or work surface. Place a cap on each bottle, position your bottles in the capper (one at a time), and pull down on the capper handle or levers slowly and evenly.**

You may want to do this task as soon as each bottle is full as insurance against everything that can go wrong when full bottles of your precious brew are sitting around open. A *bench capper*, as seen in Figure 1-5, is free-standing and can be attached to a work surface (permanently, if you like), which leaves one hand free to hold the bottle steady.

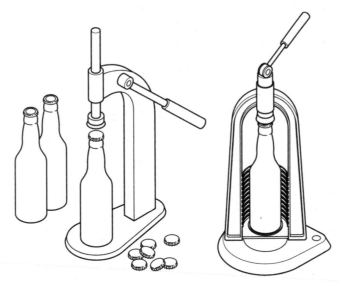

FIGURE 1-5:
You can attach
a bench-type
bottle capper to
a work surface
for easy use.

TIP

Both bench- or two-handle-style cappers come with small magnets in the capper head designed to hold and align the cap as you start crimping. Many homebrewers don't trust the magnet to hold the caps in alignment and prefer to seat them on the bottles by hand.

Occasionally, a cap may crimp incorrectly. If you suspect that a cap didn't seal right, tilt the bottle sideways and check for leakage. If you find you have a leaker, yank the cap and replace it. (You boiled extras — right?)

25. **Your homebrew needs to undergo a two-week conditioning phase, so store your liquid lucre in a cool, dark location (such as the same place that you kept the fermenter).**

This phase is where the remaining yeast cells chow down on the dextrose and carbonate your beer.

WARNING

Putting your brew in the fridge isn't a good idea — at least for the first two weeks — because the cold temperatures stunt the yeast's carbonating activity. Aim for fifty degrees Fahrenheit.

26. **Thoroughly rinse your brewing equipment in hot water and store it in a place that's relatively dust- and mildew-free. You may even want to go that extra step and seal all your equipment inside a large-capacity garbage bag.**

After two weeks pass, check to see whether the bottles have clarified (the yeasty cloudiness has settled out). Chill a bottle or two for taste–testing. Like any commercial beer, you need to decant homebrew before drinking, not only to release the carbonation and the beer's aromatics but also to pour a clear beer. Drinking homebrew out of the bottle stirs up the sediment, creating a hazy beer.

Chapter **2**

Fermenting

You may not realize it, but you're likely already a consumer of one or more fermented food products. Have you had any sourdough bread, soy sauce, tofu, yogurt, cheese, or a glass of cider or wine lately? Does your sandwich come with a salty pickle or some sauerkraut on the side? You can thank the process of fermentation for these items.

Although fermentation is technically a method of preserving food (like the techniques covered in Book 2), the chemical process changes that food into something different. In the modern kitchen, fermentation is a natural and fun way to discover new flavors and recipes and go on a mind-bending adventure through a history of food that has existed for centuries around the world. If you're lucky, fermentation can even act as a tool for self-discovery and a vehicle for self-exploration in health and healing.

This chapter gets you started on that path with a little behind-the-science of fermentation and a lot about making your own fermented foods.

Getting Familiar with Fermentation

Fermentation turns sugars to alcohol or other acids using yeast and bacteria. The chemical change often involves increasing the acidic environment and develops in places without oxygen (*anaerobic* conditions).

Fermenting is a glamorous term for decaying your food in a controlled method. Yes, you're allowing your food to decay. Your food is decaying from the moment you pick it. If you ferment correctly, you create the perfect environment of temperature, liquid, and oxygen (or lack thereof) to change your food into a delectable, sometimes healthier food. After a food has been fermented, it not only tastes different but also *is* different on a molecular level.

Fermented foods have existed for centuries as populations around the globe learned how to capture the slow decomposition process of organic materials and preserve them by adding salts, sugars, or yeasts. They controlled mold and promoted good bacteria with the intention of maximizing the shelf life of their foods, enhancing flavors, or gaining health benefits.

Fermenting releases some nutrients that would otherwise be unavailable for digestion and creates an environment for *probiotic,* or beneficial, bacteria to thrive. These bacteria already live in a healthy digestive tract and help break down food properly. Antibiotics and digestive illnesses can reduce the number of good bacteria, making you susceptible to illness. Your immune system includes your digestive tract, and improving digestion can only help overall health.

If you've never fermented, don't worry. The piquant taste is something that's enjoyable for most people and unforgettable to anyone who tries it. Fermenting is a technique that you can try without a lot of financial investment in equipment and specialty supplies. It has always been a simple way of preserving foods, easy enough to do in the homesteading kitchen.

REMEMBER

Fermenting is decaying with style. There's a fine line between going bad and fermenting, so the rules of a good fermenting system are stringent. These rules become easier to adhere to as you become proficient, and the benefits are worth it.

Fermenting Essentials

The fundamental things you need to ferment foods are often the same, but the many variations of those ingredients can change your results:

>> **Fermenting containers:** Fermented foods must be made without the presence of oxygen or spoilage will occur. A good fermenting container is essential to your success. Use a sturdy container that's large enough to hold your fermented goods. Containers are best made from glass, such as Mason jars, or nonreactive materials, such as a crockpot made from ceramic or a well-cleaned plastic bucket. The key to fermentation is creating an anaerobic, or oxygen-free, environment by sealing out any outside air.

Look for fermentation jars with an airlock seal that allows gas to escape but no air to get inside, though in some recipes a weighted lid will do the trick.

Sometimes people use a weighted object to cover their food as it ferments. Whether you use one depends on the fermenting container you're using. Keeping your food submerged under the wet brine is most important. A weight, something as simple as a heavy plate or a plate with a stone on top, helps to put pressure on the top of your container and pack down your food.

>> **Lactobacilli:** These naturally occurring bacteria are essential to the fermentation process. These good bacteria have been proven to fight intestinal inflammation and help create a healthy gut. They also enhance the flavors and digestibility of fermented foods — they're the invisible workers that make your food ferment!

>> **Salt:** Salt can kill any bacteria that may cause illness. It does this by removing water from the plant cells, creating a less inhabitable environment. Salt also helps enhance the flavors of food. It can reduce sweetness or bitterness in foods, a desirable thing for your recipes!

The common table salt most folks have on hand has iodine added, as well as some chemicals to keep it from clumping, and it isn't the best salt for fermenting. But most stores sell kosher, canning, and sea salt, and all those are fine for your fermenting projects.

>> **Spices and herbs:** You add herbs and spices to your fermented foods to create unique recipes. Think of adding ginger to your kombucha, cranberries to your sauerkraut, or caraway seeds to your pickled goods!

>> **A starter or a culture:** Many fermented recipes require a starter or a culture. No, we're not looking for you to adopt a new way of life; this type of culture is one full of existing microbial life. A fermentation starter can come in the form of a dried powder, yeast, or a wet substance and is essentially used to boost the food's flavor and the digestion process. You can get good results using a kick-start from a previous batch to accelerate the fermentation process. You can purchase starters or, depending on the product, reuse them from other food products such as sourdough or yogurt.

>> **Sugar:** Almost all fermenting recipes call for some sweetener, usually sugar. Sugar helps feed the good microbes as they get started fermenting your food. When a recipe calls for sugar, you can use organic raw sugar or regular table sugar. You also use sugar to help preserve foods when salt would be undesirable. (Imagine making jam or kombucha with salt. Yuck!) Most commonly used in wet brine, sugar can include cane sugar, honey, or maple syrup.

Don't use sugar substitutes or half sugar-half substitute products in a fermenting recipe. These don't feed the good microbes and may also contribute to an off flavor in food. After food is through fermenting, if you feel it needs additional sweetener to taste good, you can add a sugar substitute.

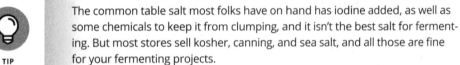

Fermenting

>> **Time:** Every good fermented food product needs time. The tiny microbes will work to turn those starches into sugars and alcohol and will slow down only if you place them in cooler temperatures. Depending on the end product, you'll leave your ferments anywhere from two to seven days, or longer! Check your recipe and taste your food according to the flavors you desire.

Cleaning, Sanitizing, and Sterilizing

When fermenting, having a clean work space and tools ensures that your good bacteria outnumber the bad. This means your chances of creating a delicious fermented food are much greater. In short, cleaning your work area and equipment is essential to the final product:

>> Cleaning means washing containers and equipment with hot water and soap. You can do it in a dishwasher or by hand. You should remove all visible particles of food or dirt. Always clean things before sanitizing or sterilizing them.

>> Sanitizing is done with chemicals. The easiest thing to use is chlorine bleach — bleach without scent or color added. Add 1 tablespoon of bleach to each quart of warm water and soak your containers and utensils in it for five minutes. Everything must be submerged in the water. You can use a clean sink or large tub for sanitizing. If you can't submerge an item, soak a clean cloth in bleach solution and wipe the item. Use a different cloth for each item.

Alternatively, brewing shops and stores that cater to commercial restaurants carry other chemical sanitizing agents. Follow the label directions for their use, and always rinse your containers and utensils with clean water after sanitizing.

TIP

You don't need to sanitize your containers and equipment if you're going to sterilize them.

>> **Sterilizing** means boiling your equipment and supplies in water for three minutes. Your equipment and containers must be able to stand up to this temperature without melting. In some cases, you pour boiling water into larger containers and allow them to sit for a few minutes, but this isn't perfect sterilization. Some dishwashers actually have a sterilize setting that you can use.

Fermenting Vegetables (including Sauerkraut and Kimchi)

Naturally crisp and crunchy vegetables make satisfying ferments. You'll notice that many of the recipes in this section feature vegetables that come into season toward the end of summer and into fall. This allows you to create ferments that will last you well into the colder months.

Sauerkraut, which is simply cabbage (and salt), and its Korean cousin kimchi are perhaps the best-known fermented vegetables.

Vegetables contain all the lactic acid they need to trigger fermentation, so technically, you don't need to add a starter. In practical terms, though, salt is almost always used for flavor and to slow fermentation. It also offers these benefits:

>> Salt pulls water out of vegetables, which helps submerge them in liquid, inhibiting bacterial growth.

>> Salt promotes lactic acid bacteria (the "good guys") so they can crowd out other bacteria.

The key to fermenting vegetables is to ensure that they're covered with a liquid. This creates an oxygen-deprived environment where "bad" bacteria is unable to grow.

Fermenting vegetables is an easy process that involves only a few steps and a bit of time.

Preparing your vegetables

You can chop, shred, or leave your veggies whole, depending on the vegetable you're using and the end result you want to achieve. Sauerkraut is most often shredded, whereas cabbage for kimchi is traditionally chopped in larger pieces. Root vegetables can be cubed or sliced thin for a different texture. Cucumbers can be sliced into coins, halved, or left whole.

Salting

The two basic approaches to salting vegetables for fermentation follow:

>> **Brine:** Dissolve salt in water. Add to your fermentation vessel with the vegetables, making sure that they are completely covered. Some recipes call for soaking vegetables in a brine for a few hours to soften them before draining and packing as usual.

>> **Dry salt:** Sprinkle salt on your prepared vegetables, then massage and pound them (with a spoon or even your hands) until they release enough juice to cover them in your chosen fermentation vessel.

TIP

You can make a basic brine by dissolving 3 tablespoons of sea salt in 1 quart of water. Use this ratio to make whatever quantity of brine you need. Then just pour over your veggies and let the fermentation begin!

Packing the jars

After your vegetables have been chopped and salted, it's time to pack them up. Add them to your jar or crock and press down to submerge the vegetables in their juices and release any air bubbles. This could take some time, so keep trying if at first it doesn't seem like there's enough juice to cover them. If the vegetables still aren't covered, you can add some filtered water.

Waiting and tasting (and waiting some more!)

How quickly your vegetables ferment will depend on a few factors, including how much salt was used in the preparation and how warm the location is. More salt will result in a slower ferment. A warmer room will speed it up.

Your vegetables will start to ferment after a few days, but the process will continue for much longer. Traditionally, fermented vegetables were prepared to preserve the harvest through winter, so keep that in mind when deciding when your batches are ready. The flavors will change and grow as days and weeks go by.

After your ferment has reached its peak (according to your own tastes), move it to the fridge. It will still continue to ferment, but at a much slower pace. And it will probably be eaten before too long!

Sauerkraut

PREP: 30 MIN | **FERMENT: 3–4 WEEKS** | **YIELD: 4 QUARTS**

INGREDIENTS

5 pounds cabbage

3 tablespoons canning salt

1 Peel off damaged outer leaves of cabbage. Quarter the cabbage and remove the hard core. Finely shred the cabbage by hand or use a food processor.

2 Scald a glass gallon jar with boiling water. Add a 1-inch layer of the cabbage mixture to the jar. Sprinkle with salt. Tamp firmly with a wooden utensil to remove any hidden air pockets and bruise the cabbage, making it release juice. Repeat Step 2 until all ingredients are used up.

3 Cover the jar with a coffee filter and leave for two hours to allow time for the salt to draw out water from the cabbage. Every 30 minutes, tamp down the cabbage to help draw out brine and force it to be submerged.

4 After 2 hours, if you still don't have enough natural brine, mix 1 teaspoon canning salt to 1 cup water and pour over mixture. When the cabbage is fully submerged, remove the coffee filter and place a small saucer that fits just inside the top of the jar so it rests directly on the submerged cabbage. Add a weight, such as a water-filled quart jar, to keep the saucer and product under the brine.

5 Cover with a clean dishcloth to keep out dust and insects. Place the jar out of the way, at room temperature. Check the jar daily, for three to four weeks. Skim off any scum that may build up on the top. Replace the clean dishcloth with another each time you remove scum buildup.

Spinach Sauerkraut

PREP: 30 MIN | FERMENT: 3-4 WEEKS | YIELD: 4 QUARTS

INGREDIENTS

1 cup chopped spinach

5 pounds cabbage

3 tablespoons canning salt

1 Wash spinach in plenty of water, rinse well, and chop it into thin shreds.

2 Peel off damaged outer leaves of cabbage. Quarter the cabbage and remove the hard core. Finely shred the cabbage by hand or use a food processor. Add spinach and mix together so they are evenly incorporated.

3 Scald a glass gallon jar with boiling water. Add a 1-inch layer of the cabbage and spinach mixture to the jar. Sprinkle with salt. Tamp firmly with a wooden utensil to remove any hidden air pockets and bruise the cabbage, making it release juice. Repeat Step 2 until all ingredients are used up.

4 Cover the jar with a coffee filter and leave for two hours to allow time for the salt to draw out water from the ingredients. Every 30 minutes, tamp down the ingredients to help draw out brine and force the cabbage mixture to be submerged.

5 After two hours, if you still don't have enough natural brine, mix 1 teaspoon canning salt to 1 cup water and pour over mixture. When the mixture is fully submerged, remove the coffee filter and place a small saucer that fits just inside the top of the jar so it rests directly on the submerged cabbage. Add a weight, such as a water-filled quart jar, to keep the saucer and product under the brine.

6 Cover with a clean dishcloth to keep out dust and insects. Place the jar out of the way, at room temperature. Check the jar daily, for three to four weeks. Skim off any scum that may build up on the top. Replace the clean dishcloth with another each time you remove scum buildup.

Fermenting

Kimchi

| PREP: 20 MIN, PLUS STANDING | FERMENT: 2–3 DAYS | YIELD: 1–2 QUARTS |

INGREDIENTS

1 medium Napa cabbage

1 to 2 inches fresh ginger

1 medium onion

1 head garlic

½ cup salt

3 tablespoons soy sauce or tamari

1 Wash, core, and chop the cabbage into ½- to 1-inch pieces. Peel and shred the ginger and onion. Peel garlic, but leave the cloves whole.

2 Place a layer of cabbage in a glass gallon jar. Sprinkle the salt over the cabbage. Repeat until all cabbage is used. Allow the cabbage and salt to sit at room temperature for 6 hours. Rinse the salt off the cabbage and place the cabbage in a large mixing bowl.

3 Mix the ginger, onion, garlic, and soy sauce with the cabbage. Place the mixture in a glass gallon jar. Cover the filled jar with cheesecloth.

4 Allow to ferment at room temperature for two to three days. Place the jar in the refrigerator to ferment for another week, or until the desired taste has developed.

Fermented Garden Vegetables

INGREDIENTS

1 green pepper

1 red pepper

1 yellow pepper

1 head garlic

2 medium onions

1 head broccoli

1 head cauliflower

2½ tablespoons sea salt

2 quarts water

1   Scald a glass gallon jar with boiling water. Remove the seeds from all the peppers and thinly slice them into rings.

2   Peel the garlic cloves. Peel and thinly slice the onions. Cut the broccoli and cauliflower into florets.

3   In a large pot, combine the salt and water. Place all the vegetables in a gallon jar and pour the saltwater brine over all. Place a saucer that fits inside the jar directly onto the vegetables to hold them under the brine.

4   Cover the jar with a muslin cloth and place it in an out of the way place at room temperature. Check the jar daily, removing any scum, washing and replacing the saucer and recovering the jar with a clean cloth.

5   After the fourth day, taste for a desired flavor. After one week, place the jar in the refrigerator for up to a month.

TIP: Consider changing up your veggies by trying this with carrots, beets, green beans, or red cabbage.

Garlic Dilly Beans

PREP: 10 MIN	FERMENT: 7 DAYS	YIELD: 1 QUART

INGREDIENTS

1 cup fresh green beans

3 cloves garlic

1 teaspoon dill seed or 2 fresh dill heads

Basic brine

1 Soak the green beans in cool water to get firm and crisp.

2 Pack all the ingredients in a 1-quart size jar.

3 Pour over brine to cover all the beans.

4 Leave a 1-inch space at the top of jar, put on lid and band, and screw tightly.

5 Allow to ferment at room temperature for three to seven days.

6 Transfer to the fridge when ready; they will keep for several months.

TIP: This recipe is the perfect way to make your tender sweet summer green beans last longer. They stay crisp in the brine and taste delicious next to some quinoa or in a salad.

Starting Sourdough

When you begin exploring the world of fermentations, you'll hear people talking about sourdough, sourdough starters, and wild yeasts. A sourdough starter is really just another name for any fermented grain. It's a grain that starts to predigest during the fermentation process, which ultimately makes the flavor sourer.

Here are just a few great reasons to make your very own sourdough:

>> Sourdough is delicious.

>> Sourdough helps improve your digestion.

>> Sourdough predigests gluten and phytic acid.

>> Sourdough saves you the cost of buying commercial yeasts.

>> Making the sourdough starter and keeping it alive is fun.

You can use anything from spelt flour to whole wheat to kamut to other ancient grains to experiment with sourdough. You'll be surprised just how many recipes you can make, from muffins to pancakes to breads . . . anything goes!

TIP

Kamut is a type of ancient grain that's 20 to 40 percent higher in protein than wheat and is richer in several vitamins and minerals. Unlike some grains, kamut has a low oxidation level and retains most of its nutritional value after grinding and processing. It can be purchased at many high-end markets, health food retailers, and a growing number of grocery stores.

Feeding your sourdough starter with tender loving care

If you care about your sourdough starter, you'll feed it. Just like your body, sourdough requires food. The fermentation process feeds off of the sugars and carbohydrates in the flour. To keep the sourdough alive, consistent and regular feeding of flour is required. As long as you keep feeding your sourdough and store it in a good environment, it will stay alive, and you can keep making more recipes with it.

Sometimes you'll even hear people call the sourdough starter the *mother* because it creates other sourdough babies. Sourdough starter is very different from commercial yeasts, which require you to continue buying them and have a strong need for a stable environment. Sourdough is unique because it predigests the gluten and phytic acids in the grain.

Fermenting

Choosing the type of sourdough starter to use

All sourdoughs require a sourdough starter, the essential life force that makes your amazing breads and other recipes. The interesting thing about these starters is that they take on the flavor of the naturally occurring yeast and bacteria in your environment and the flour you use. From one batch to the next, each sourdough is a bit unique and different from the last!

You can purchase dry sourdough starters or find a friend who has a wet sourdough starter. But making your own starter is easy. It does take up to a week, but it's a pretty hands-off process that lets you take full credit for your sourdough from start to finish. You're a homesteader: Why spend money to buy something you can make instead?

A dry sourdough starter may come as a dehydrated formula that contains sourdough yeast. A wet sourdough starter is a more traditional culture that has been started from scratch, fed continuously with flour, and is now bubbling and alive. It's wet and sticky. When such a wet starter is fully thriving, it should be fed with water and flour at least once a week. See the upcoming recipes for a sourdough starter recipe, along with recipes for breads, muffins, and more.

Sourdough Starter

INGREDIENTS

2 cups flour of your choice
(except white flour)

2 cups filtered water

1 packet dry yeast

1 Place ¼ cup of water into a wide-mouth jar. Then add ⅜ cup of your chosen flour and mix well.

2 Stir the flour and water well. This brings in air and helps oxygenate your starter. Make sure you scrape all the sides and get all the flour into the starter.

3 Cover the jar with a cloth napkin or paper towel and secure with a rubber band.

4 Let the starter sit in a relatively warm place for 12 to 24 hours. Room temperature is ideal; you don't want to exceed 85 degrees.

5 By now you may see some bubbles in your mixture. Every 12 to 24 hours, discard half the starter and mix another ¼ cup of water and ⅜ cup of flour in the same jar as your starter. As it begins to expand over the next several days, your starter will start to get bubbly and fluffy and have a slight sour smell.

6 If you don't see any bubbles yet, your starter may need help to make room for good bacteria. Try removing about half of the starter from the jar and adding another ¼ cup of water and ⅜ cup of flour. Let the starter sit for another 12 hours until bubbles occur and you see it grow in size.

7 Reserved starter should be kept in a crock or jar and stored in the refrigerator. (If using a screw-top jar, keep the lid loose instead of airtight to allow the starter to continue its natural expansion.) Feed stored starter once a week with the same water-and-flour mix to keep it wet and thriving.

NOTE: If you're using a dehydrated starter, simply open the package, empty the contents into the jar, and follow the same steps.

NOTE: The starter will get bigger the more you feed it. You may need to discard some of it or transfer it to larger containers along the way. Also, the presence of liquid (which you can stir in) and a sour smell are normal.

NOTE: You can end up discarding a lot of starter as you're nursing it along. Share some with a homesteading friend, or search online for recipes that call for *discarded starter*. Put it to delicious use by turning it into pizza crust, pretzels, waffles, even chocolate cake!

Fermenting

Traditional Sourdough Bread

PREP: 10 MIN	COOK: 45 MIN	YIELD: 1 LARGE LOAF

INGREDIENTS

2 cups kamut sourdough starter

1 tablespoon coconut sugar

4 cups kamut flour

2 teaspoons salt

1   In a large mixing bowl combine the starter, coconut sugar, and salt. Adding 1 cup of flour at a time, stir in as much as you can with a wooden spoon.

2   When the dough is firm enough to knead by hand, roll it on a lightly floured surface until the dough is no longer sticky. Knead it by hand so it is moist and flexible!

3   Wash the mixing bowl with some hot water, dry it, and place the dough in the warm bowl. Cover the bowl with a dishcloth and let the dough rise in a warm place until it has doubled.

4   Now for the fun part: Punch down the dough! Form it into one round loaf and let it rise a second time on a lightly greased cookie sheet.

5   Bake the loaf in a preheated oven at 350 degrees for 40 to 50 minutes or until the crust is brown. The bread should feel hollow when you give it a tap!

6   It's hard to resist, but let your bread cool before you slice and serve it!

NOTE: If your kitchen isn't warm enough for your bread to rise, try putting it in a cold oven with the oven light on. The light bulb may raise the temperature inside just enough to do the trick, but remember not to preheat the oven for other baking!

Mooving On to Dairy

Fermenting dairy provides not only delicious food but also improved nutritional value. Many people who have assorted digestive issues see improvement with regular consumption of fermented dairy.

In fact, fermenting dairy can make it tolerable and even healthful to someone who's lactose intolerant. Through the fermentation process, the beneficial bacteria consume the lactose and turn it into lactic acid. There's also evidence that eating fermented foods on a regular basis helps reestablish a healthy level of beneficial bacteria in the gut, improving all digestion.

Making lactose tolerable by fermenting

Many dairy products that are familiar on the store shelf can be naturally fermented and well tolerated by those who are lactose intolerant. The following list is by no means exhaustive, but does include some of the more common forms of fermented dairy:

>> **Buttermilk:** True cultured buttermilk isn't a grocery store item. It's fermented with a variety of *lacto* bacteria that gives it the tang and health benefits of a fermented product.

>> **Cheese:** The largest class of fermented milk products, cheese is created by using specific bacteria and molds developed for specific flavors and textures.

>> **Cultured butter:** You create this product by adding some cultured buttermilk to the cream you churn. Allow it to ripen and then make your butter.

>> **Kefir:** Kefir is created with bacterial grains that resemble cauliflower. These gelatinous grains are removed and reused again. They eventually grow in size and can be divided to share.

>> **Koumiss:** This fermented, carbonated dairy drink was traditionally made from mares' milk in central Asia. Koumiss has been used medicinally in various times. Depending on the level of fermentation, it can contain varying degrees of alcohol. The recipe for the version in this chapter uses yeast to start the fermentation.

>> **Sour cream:** Cultured sour cream is different from the product found on most grocery shelves. The fermenting process results in a deliciously acidic food, using *Lactococcus lactis,* a bacterium that's also used in the making of buttermilk and many cheeses.

>> **Yogurt:** Yogurt is usually made from dairy milk and beneficial bacteria such as *Lactobacillus bulgaricus* and *Streptococcus thermophilus.* You can use a small scoop of finished yogurt to start a new batch, in an endless cycle.

Fermenting

Choosing pasteurized or raw milk

Many fermented food enthusiasts recommend using only raw milk products to make fermented dairy. Does this mean that any dairy you use must be raw? What is *raw*, anyway? Read on for an explanation of the different processes that milk undergoes before you purchase it:

REMEMBER

>> **Raw:** This means that the milk has gone through a filtering process and nothing else. No heat has been applied to the milk, and it will separate into a layer of cream and a layer of milk if left undisturbed. Raw milk still contains the enzymes that are naturally present, and instead of going sour over time like store milk, it simply clabbers, or ferments. Raw milk isn't legal to sell in all states, so check your local laws before buying it.

The argument against raw milk is that it may contain harmful bacteria and may transfer disease to the people who drink it. Although this is true in theory, raw milk farmers go through the same rigorous hygienic standards as farmers who pasteurize their products. In fact, some are held to even higher standards for bacterial counts than their pasteurizing neighbors. Advocates of raw milk believe that drinking raw milk with the natural enzymes and good bacteria still in it is healthier than drinking a sterilized milk product.

>> **Pasteurized:** This is the process of heating milk to kill certain types of bad bacteria, such as *E. coli* or *listeria.* Milk is heated to 145 degrees for a period of time and then rapidly cooled.

>> **Homogenized:** For this process, milk is agitated and filtered to break the naturally occurring fat into small enough particles that it no longer separates into a layer of cream and milk.

>> **Ultra-pasteurized:** This type of milk is more common in Europe, although it has become more popular in the United States in recent years. In ultra-pasteurization, milk is heated to 280 degrees for 2 seconds and then rapidly cooled. Ultra-pasteurization makes the milk shelf-stable for up to 70 days from the day of processing, when it's packaged in sterile containers.

Some recipes require the separation of cream and milk, and if that's how a recipe is listed, following the recipe is best. You can separate some milk by allowing it to sit without movement for a few hours or overnight. Cow's milk is like this. The next morning, you have a thick layer of cream atop the lower-fat milk underneath. This lower-fat milk is still not the nonfat variety sold in stores, but it is lighter tasting.

WARNING

However, you shouldn't leave goat milk to separate. The naturally occurring caprylic acid increases over the life of the milk, and you end up with a goaty-tasting product. (Sorry, but that's the best way to describe it.) Avoid this by using a cream separator turned to the lowest setting to remove the cream from goat's milk.

REMEMBER

Not all milks are created equal. They're all nutritious, but the flavor and texture of the finished product can be wildly different. As you start fermenting your own dairy products, remember that they won't be the same as store-bought examples. They won't contain thickeners and sweeteners like the products on the grocery shelves usually do.

If you find that the flavor of your fermented dairy is not to your liking, you can change the type of milk and see whether that helps, or you can ferment for a shorter period of time. The longer you leave a food to ferment, the tarter it becomes.

Sourcing your starter cultures

After choosing your milk, your next step is to find out where to buy the specific cultures needed to make your own fermented dairy products.

If you're trying to start your home-fermented products by using store-bought varieties, check that the beneficial bacteria are present. You need a living food to use as a starter for the next batch of living food. If you're shopping at a health-food store, tell the clerk you're looking for live cultured products. These products may have to be processed according to your state's food laws.

Another option is to buy a fermented food culture from someone who's also fermenting. The nice thing about fermented foods is that, after you have a batch going, you then have the future starter to make more indefinitely. Saving a bit from one batch to the next also creates a specific culture that loves where you're keeping it!

Keep in mind that starters are living bacteria. They're best kept at the proper temperature and fed regularly.

Serving and storing fermented dairy products

Fermented dairy products are cultured at room temperature or above. After they reach the desired fermentation, you chill them to slow the fermentation. For fermented dairy recipes, follow the recipe to the letter, taste it, and decide whether to stick with the same storage time based on how well you like the flavor. Though properly fermented food doesn't go bad, it does eventually become too sour-tasting to enjoy eating.

Serve fermented dairy products at their optimal flavor, especially when you're introducing someone to the idea of home-fermented items. For someone who's new to the taste, the tanginess may be off-putting if the product is overripe.

TIP

When serving things such as yogurt and kefir, many people expect a highly sweetened taste. To retrain their palate, many add a bit of fruit or natural sweeteners such as honey, maple syrup, or organic sugar to the recipe. They can slowly cut back as their taste develops for the unsweetened product.

Trying your hand at cheese

Cheese making is fermenting, although cheese isn't often put in the same category as other fermented dairy products such as kefir. The idea behind creating a cheese through fermenting is the same: You introduce the proper bacteria (or culture) to the milk, and eventually the proper fermenting happens, and you have a fairly predictable flavor.

Despite how technical modern cheese making has become, it all comes down to a few basic steps:

1. **Bring the milk up to temperature (to simulate the animal's body temperature, which activates the starter culture) and add the starter culture.**

   You can make cheese from virtually any milk, but most modern-day recipes recommend the type of milk to use and also what alternate milks can be used. The ingredient that's not always interchangeable is the added amount of cream. When a cheese recipe asks for both a measure of milk and cream, you must add both.

2. **Add a coagulant, such as rennet.**

   Rennet is the magic that makes cheese happen. Rennet is an enzyme in the stomach of ruminants that have yet to start grazing or chewing their own cud. It's sold in stores in liquid and tablet form, and your recipe will recommend one or the other.

   When purchasing rennet, look for it in the refrigerated section of the store. It's usually in the dairy section, although some stores keep it in the meat department.

TIP

Many times, the rennet is interchangeable, but breaking off a fraction of a tablet, instead of measuring out the equivalent in drops of liquid, may be difficult.

3. Form and mold the curd, and drain the whey.

Instead of discarding the whey, you can use it as a vitamin and protein booster in smoothies, as a cooking liquid for potatoes or pasta, as animal feed, on your hair and skin, or as a compost pile addition! An online search will lead you to plenty of creative ways to reuse whey.

4. Salt the cheese.

Salt slows down enzymatic activity, enhances flavor, and keeps unwanted organisms away, such as bacteria that can ruin the cheese or sour the taste. Salt also draws out moisture and helps form the rind, or the outside of the cheese.

5. Age the cheese (during which rind develops, with the exception of fresh cheeses).

This stage needs to be done in a controlled environment because, just like the regular rules of fermenting, you're trying to grow the bacteria you want and avoid giving the unwanted bacteria a chance. Every style of cheese requires a different treatment.

Some recipes omit one or more of these steps, but all cheese requires the milk to at least be brought up to temperature so it can coagulate. This is where the proteins clump together to form curds.

Fermenting

Homemade Yogurt

PREP: 20 MIN	FERMENT: 7 HR	YIELD: 1 QUART

INGREDIENTS

2 quarts cow or goat milk

2 tablespoons yogurt that contains active cultures

1 In a 6-quart pot, heat the milk to 185 degrees. Don't allow the milk to boil. Cool the milk to 110 degrees by placing the entire pot into an ice-filled sink and swirling it around.

2 Add the yogurt to the cooled milk, stirring well. Pour the yogurt into the container that you'll be storing it in and place it in a dehydrator with an accurate thermometer gauge. Keep the yogurt at 110 degrees for seven hours, or until it thickens and is as tangy as you like.

3 Refrigerate the finished yogurt until ready to eat. Store it for up to two weeks in the refrigerator. Keep 2 tablespoons of this yogurt as the starter for the next batch.

NOTE: Goat's milk yogurt is naturally looser than cow's milk yogurt. This is normal.

NOTE: If you don't have a dehydrator or yours is too small to hold your containers, many people have success using a turned-off oven with the light on or a picnic cooler with a hot water bottle or heating pad inside. Many programmable pressure cookers now have a yogurt-making setting, and fully dedicated yogurt-making machines are available, too.

VARY IT! Flavor your yogurt by adding ¼ to ½ tsp of vanilla or lemon extract and ⅛ to ¼ cup of sugar per quart.

Kefir

INGREDIENTS

4 tablespoons kefir grains

1 quart milk

1 Place the grains in the bottom of a quart canning jar. Pour the milk over the grains, leaving ½-inch head space.

2 Cover the jar with a coffee filter and place an elastic band around the filter, if desired. Place the jar in an out-of-the-way place at room temperature.

3 After 24 hours, the kefir is ready. Strain out grains for the next batch and refrigerate the finished kefir. Store the kefir in the refrigerator for up to one week.

TIP: You can find kefir grains by doing a search online. A huge community of kefir drinkers willingly shares grains through the mail.

NOTE: Kefir is carbonated at first. Be aware that it can bubble over if agitated too much after it's finished. Never use metal utensils in any part of kefir making.

Fermenting

Koumiss

PREP: 30 MIN	COOK: 30 MIN	FERMENT: 2 DAYS	YIELD: ABOUT 1 GALLON

INGREDIENTS

1 gallon goat milk

2 tablespoons honey

⅛ teaspoon champagne yeast

¼ cup warm water

1 Heat the goat milk to 180 degrees in a stainless-steel pot and remove any film that forms. Add the honey and allow the mixture to cool to 70 degrees.

2 Dissolve the champagne yeast in 115 degree water and let it stand for ten minutes. Stir the yeast mixture into the milk. Cover it with a clean cloth and allow it to stand at room temperature until it foams (about 24 hours).

3 Pour the koumiss into sanitized beer bottles that can withstand carbonation pressure. Fill only to 1 inch below the bottom of the neck of the bottle.

4 Store the koumiss at room temperature for 24 hours and then refrigerate. Shake the bottles gently every few days but not just before opening.

TIP: You can buy the champagne yeast at a beer maker's shop.

TIP: Koumiss keeps for six to eight weeks but then becomes increasingly acidic. You can add honey to hide the acidic taste.

Cottage Cheese

PREP: 30 MIN, PLUS STANDING AND STORING	COOK: 45 MIN	FERMENT: 15–20 HR	YIELD: ABOUT 4 CUPS

INGREDIENTS

1 gallon pasteurized whole cow's milk

½ teaspoon mesophilic direct-set starter culture

4 tablespoons heavy cream

¼ teaspoon fine salt

1 In a double boiler, slowly heat the milk to 72 degrees.

2 Remove from heat and stir in the mesophilic starter culture.

3 Cover and place in an out-of-the-way place, wrapped in a towel to help keep the pot at 70 to 72 degrees.

4 Allow the curds to sit for 15 to 20 hours. They'll become firm during this time.

5 With a long, stainless-steel knife, cut the curds into 3/8- to ½-inch cubes and allow them to settle for 30 minutes.

6 In a double boiler, slowly heat the curds over 45 minutes, stirring every 5 minutes to prevent them from sticking together. Your goal is to raise the temperature to 110 degrees during this time.

7 Keep the curds at 110 degrees, and gently stir for 25 to 35 minutes more. The curds will start to firm up during this time.

8 Remove the pot from the heat and allow the curds to settle for 10 minutes.

9 Line a colander with cheesecloth and place it in a clean pot to drain for 10 minutes.

10 Tie the ends of the cheesecloth together and dip the curds into clean water three times to rinse and firm them.

11 Drain the cottage cheese again in the colander for 15 minutes more.

12 Place the drained curds into a clean bowl and gently stir in the cream and salt.

13 Refrigerate for two hours before serving.

Chevre (Goat Cheese)

COOK: 10 MIN	FERMENT: 60 HR	YIELD: 4 SMALL ROUNDS

INGREDIENTS

½ gallon pasteurized or raw goat milk (not ultra-pasteurized)

⅛ teaspoon MA4001 or similar freeze-dried, direct-set mesophilic culture

¼ teaspoon liquid calcium chloride mixed with 1 tablespoon water

⅛ teaspoon liquid rennet mixed with 1 tablespoon water

Flaked or kosher salt

1 Add the milk to a 3-quart, stainless-steel pot and slowly bring it to 86 degrees. Remove the warmed milk from the heat.

2 Sprinkle in the culture, wait 5 minutes, and then stir with 20 gentle strokes.

3 Add the calcium chloride–water mixture and stir gently.

4 Add the rennet mixture, stir, and cover. Let the mixture stand at about 72 degrees for at least 12 hours. Don't agitate or stir the mixture while the curd sets.

5 Place a draining rack inside the drain pan and place the forms onto the draining rack. Ladle the curd, which looks like thickened yogurt, into the forms. Allow the curd to drain for 24 hours at room temperature, pouring off the whey from the drain pan as needed to keep the cheeses above the liquid.

6 Remove the cheeses from the forms and place directly on the draining rack. Sprinkle on all sides with salt. Let the cheeses dry for another 24 hours at room temperature or refrigerate if it is especially warm weather, turning once or twice.

7 If desired, roll the cheeses in herbs before wrapping in wax paper, then wrap in plastic wrap. Refrigerate for up to several weeks.

NOTE: Direct set culture can be found at any cheesemaking supply store.

Mozzarella

PREP: 25 MIN   COOK: 30–40 MIN   YIELD: 2 POUNDS

INGREDIENTS

2 gallons whole raw or pasteurized milk (not ultra-pasteurized)

1 tablespoon citric acid, dissolved in ¼ cup water

½ teaspoon liquid rennet, mixed in ¼ cup water

½ teaspoon lipase powder, dissolved in ¼ cup water, and set aside for 10 to 20 minutes

Kosher salt

1. Using a double boiler, warm the milk to 55 degrees. Gently stir in the dissolved citric acid. Then stir in the dissolved lipase.

2. Slowly heat the milk to 88 degrees over low to medium heat. The milk will begin to curdle.

3. Stir in the rennet as you raise the temperature of the milk to 100 to 105 degrees. Within a few minutes, you'll begin to see more curds forming. After you reach the appropriate temperature, turn off the heat and remove the pan from the stove. When the whey is relatively clear, the curds are ready.

4. Remove the curds from the whey by either pouring them out through a strainer or ladling the curds into a bowl. Whichever method you choose, reserve the whey in a separate stock pot.

5. Begin the kneading process that will make the mozzarella nice and elastic. To do so, heat the reserved whey to 170 to 180 degrees. Wearing gloves, shape the curd into a ball, set the ball on the ladle, and submerge the ladle into the whey, dipping it as needed (you want the curd to be smooth and elastic in texture). Knead the curd again and re-submerge into the hot whey. Continue kneading and re-dipping the curd until it reaches 145 degrees, the temperature at which the curd will stretch.

6. When the curd is the right temperature (145 degrees), it's ready to be stretched. Sprinkle a small amount of kosher salt on the cheese (as you would seasoning food to flavor it) and then fold the salt into the cheese. Continue to knead and pull the cheese until it's smooth and elastic. When the cheese pulls with the consistency of taffy, it's done.

7. Shape the mozzarella into small or large balls. You can eat it while it's still warm, or you can place the balls in ice water for about five minutes to quickly bring the inside temperature of the cheese down. Hot or cold, the cheese is best served fresh. For storage, place the balls in a freezer bag with a few tablespoons of milk and keep refrigerated. Eat within a few days.

NOTE: Real mozzarella must come from buffalo milk. But this home version is fun to make and tastes wonderful.

Fermenting

Raising a Glass to Fermented Beverages

You can drink your fermented creations, too! Some are healthful creations full of probiotics and others are fun for the whole family to make and enjoy.

The dairy drink *kefir* is covered in the previous section of this chapter with other dairy ferments. Chapter 1 of this minibook is devoted to brewing your own beer, which also depends on the science of fermentation. This section gets you started with making other fermented beverages: ginger soda, root beer, and kombucha.

Here are some things each of your fermented drink recipes all have in common:

>> Fermented drinks naturally become carbonated and fizzy.

>> Fermented drinks are naturally full of living probiotics.

>> Fermented drinks use starters such as yeast or kefir grains.

>> Fermented drinks produce trace amounts of alcohol.

>> The longer your drink ferments and sits out, the more sour, sweet, or vinegary its taste will become.

>> Sweeten all your fermented drinks as you desire using honey or an alternative sugar.

>> Be sure when bottling to leave some head space in the top or it could explode from fizzy-pressure.

>> You can vary your recipes using different fruits or herbs.

Starting with starters

Starter cultures are the microorganisms that inoculate your fermented foods to help get the desired changes. The greatest role of the starter culture is its ability to speed up the fermentation process and get guaranteed results. Any culture starter will give your recipe added enzymes and flavors, change its texture, and add health benefits.

REMEMBER

Not all fermented foods require a starter culture. Be sure to check your recipe and see which ones do and do not.

For some recipes, you might use fermented grains, a yeast (plenty more on yeast in Chapter 1 of this minibook), or bacteria. No matter what starter culture you decide to use, starter cultures are easy to make. Starter cultures take time to grow, but you can save some time by purchasing starters pre-made from friends, at health food shops, or online. The beauty is that once you master making them, you can keep them for a long time and continue to use them to make more of your favorite fermented cultured foods.

Getting fizzy with it: carbonated drinks

It's hard to beat the satisfaction of making homemade carbonated drinks! You'll learn to love the fresh flavors and sodalike qualities. Making natural carbonated drinks at home is simple and easy to do, with the bonus of being healthy. You can control the amount of sugar you put in, and plus, they're far less expensive than store-bought sodas!

Ginger soda

Nothing beats a fresh bubbly ginger brew to wake up your senses! Ginger soda has several different steps but it's definitely worth the wait.

Root beer

Did you know that traditionally root beer was made using a tree called Sassafras? Today, many people use wintergreen and licorice root. Homemade root beer will give you a taste for the good ol' days and is full of herbal infusions.

Kefir

Kefir is said to originate in Eastern Europe and was a drink that originally began as a way to preserve milk. (See the previous section for a basic milk kefir recipe.) But there are non-dairy kefir alternatives, too. The sugar and bacteria in these liquids will create a bubbly and refreshing drink that is a bit sour, but great for the gut.

Kombucha

Kombucha has its roots in ancient Asian tradition but has become highly popular due to the health properties that captured the hearts and health of many.

Kombucha has a tangy, slight vinegary taste, but its base relies on unrefined sugar, water, and tea bags. It is said to have many detoxifying qualities and to give vitality; sometimes it is known as the *immortality elixir*. However, note that the base of this drink is unrefined sugar, which regardless of the other health benefits can still be bad in large quantities. But in small doses kombucha is said to increase digestibility, energy, and gut flora.

To make kombucha, you need a *SCOBY*, which stands for the symbiotic colony of bacteria and yeast. It is essential for kombucha making! Sometimes you will hear people use funny names for it, such as *the mother* because it is the source of life for kombucha, or *a mushroom* because it turns into a big, gelatinous, bacterial component that can resemble a fungus.

A healthy SCOBY can take on a range of appearances. It may be smooth or bumpy and lumpy. It may have holes in it or stringy remains from the culture. It may be ragged and misshapen. It can sink to the bottom of the brewing solution, float on top, or hover in the middle. All can be perfectly normal.

WARNING

The main thing to look out for is any mold. Mold is rare but dangerous. If you see any signs of blue or black mold on your SCOBY, throw away the SCOBY and the kombucha. You can use the same container again, but just ensure that you clean it out well!

Here are some tips to keep in mind when making kombucha:

>> Plain white, black, or green tea work for kombucha.

>> Use a fresh SCOBY to get your best results.

>> Choose a wide-mouth jar. Your SCOBY will grow big and form to your jar! With every new batch you make, you will see your SCOBY reproduce and get thicker. It will make SCOBY babies.

>> Avoid brewing your kombucha for too long, but leave it long enough so it turns from too sweet to just sour enough.

>> Although refined white sugar is the best for kombucha to digest, try to use cane sugar or unrefined for better health.

>> Avoid plastic or metal objects to make it! Kombucha needs glass and wood as it becomes highly acidic.

Ginger Soda

PREP: 5 MIN	FERMENT: 48–72 HR	YIELD: 1 GALLON

INGREDIENTS

Filtered water

Ginger root

Unrefined sugar such as cane or Sucanat

⅓ cup lemon juice

1 **Make the starter for your soda:** Fill a 4-cup jar with water, about two-thirds of the way full.

2 Grate the ginger, enough for 1 heaping tablespoon. Do not remove the skin. You will also need ⅓ cup of ginger later for the wort; feel free to grate that now. Place the 1 tablespoon of grated ginger into the jar of water.

3 Stir in 1 large tablespoon of sugar and lemon juice until it is dissolved.

4 Place cheesecloth and a rubber band on your jar — you want to allow some breathing room out but prevent bacteria or dust from coming in.

5 Place the jar in a warm place. The ideal temperature is 75 to 85 degrees for the jar to ferment. Insulate and cover the jar. (You can use cloth towels to surround and cover it.) Allow the jar to rest and work its fermentation magic!

6 Stir your starter once a day for three to seven days. Taste and add ginger and sugar as desired to taste! Once you begin to see bubbling, the starter is nearing its finish.

1 **Make the wort, or pre-fermented liquid:** Fill a gallon jar with approximately 10 cups of water, or two thirds of the way full.

2 Add ⅓ cup of grated ginger and 1½ cups sugar to the jar of water. Stir well!

3 Take 1 cup from your starter recipe and stir it into the jar.

4 Stir in the remaining ⅓ cup of lemon juice. Stir again until all the sugar is dissolved.

(continued)

Fermenting

5 Cover the jar with cheesecloth and a rubber band. Let the jar sit in a warm location, or cover with towels in room temperature. Let your wort rest.

6 Stir once or twice a day for three to seven days. Once you achieve the soda taste you desire, bottle or store your homemade soda in the fridge!

TIP: Taste your wort once in a while. Is it sweet and gingery as you desire? Add water, sugar, or ginger as desired. Is your soda fizzing? Add more starter if you need to!

TIP: Always buy fresh ingredients where you can. Ginger root fresh from the market will give you the best flavors for this soda recipe.

Root Beer

PREP: 25 MIN	FERMENT: 48–72 HR	COOK: 30–40 MIN	YIELD: APPROX. 18 CUPS

INGREDIENTS

8 cups water

20 inches sassafras root

1 piece vanilla bean, 3 inches long

1¾ cup brown sugar or Sucanat

⅛ teaspoon ale yeast

¼ cup lukewarm water

1 Bring 8 cups of water to a boil and stir in the sassafras and vanilla bean. Let the pot stay uncovered.

2 Reduce the heat to simmer the roots for 15 to 20 minutes. You will notice the water begin to turn red in color. It should also smell delicious! Smell and color not strong enough? Add more roots!

3 Stir in the unrefined sugar until it dissolves.

4 Let the liquid cool to room temperature.

5 Drain the roots and vanilla bean through a cheesecloth or thin-meshed strainer, placing the infused liquid into a large jar or pitcher.

6 In a separate cup, combine the yeast and ¼ cup of lukewarm water. Let it sit about five minutes.

7 Add the yeas -liquid to the jar. Close the jar and shake it around to get the yeast going throughout the liquid.

8 Bottle your root beer! (Best to use flip-top bottles.)

9 Store at room temperature, or in a cool dark room.

10 Watch your homemade root beer bubble and fizz over two to three days.

11 After you have enough carbonation in your drink and are satisfied, refrigerate!

VARY IT! Try adding other interesting roots and herbs in your root beer recipe for added flavors. Some people like to try licorice root, ginger root, and juniper berry, some wintergreen for some minty freshness, or even wild cherry!

Fermenting

Vanilla Cinnamon Coconut Kefir

PREP: 15 MIN	FERMENT: 48–72 HRS	YIELD: 2 CUPS

INGREDIENTS

2 cups coconut kefir

½ teaspoon fresh vanilla bean powder

1 tablespoon honey or maple syrup

¼ teaspoon cinnamon

1 Mix all of your ingredients together into a jar.

2 Cover your glass jar with lid, a towel or cloth napkin and let the magic work from 12 to 36 hours.

3 Be sure to check the coconut kefir every few hours and remember to always remove the kefir grains as soon as it reaches the texture and taste you desire.

4 Close your glass jar with the lid and place your delicious kefir in the fridge.

Green Tea Kombucha

PREP: 20 MIN | FERMENT: 5–10 DAYS | YIELD: 12 CUPS

INGREDIENTS

6 green tea bags

1 cup sweetener of choice, preferably unrefined sugar

3 or 4 liters water

A kombucha SCOBY

1-2 cups of raw apple cider vinegar or leftover kombucha

1. In a large pot, combine the tea bags, sugar, and 2 to 3 cups of water.

2. Bring to a simmer and remove from heat.

3. Cover and let the green tea bags steep for 10 to 15 minutes.

4. Add 2 cups of cool water to bring the tea temperature down.

5. Place the SCOBY and finished kombucha or raw apple cider vinegar in your large gallon jar.

6. Add cooled-down tea to the jar.

7. Use a wooden spoon (do not use metal) to help the SCOBY float at the top. It's okay if it is sinking, but it should rise during fermentation.

8. Cover the jar with a paper towel or cheesecloth, and secure with a rubber band.

9. Let the liquid ferment at room temperature for 5 to 10 days.

10. Taste to see if it is not too sweet and if it is fizzy enough. Sweeten as desired to your taste!

11. When the kombucha is well carbonated and has a slight vinegary smell, pour the kombucha through a strainer into a clean jar or jug.

12. Be sure to leave the SCOBY and approximately 1 or 2 cups of finished kombucha behind. This is your starter for a second batch of tea!

13. Refrigerate it to prevent it from souring any more or if needed, keep it at room temperature for a few days to build up more carbonation.

TIP: Don't let your kombucha build up carbonation too long or it could explode when bottled. Also, the longer kombucha sits out, the more sour and vinegary its taste will become.

Fermenting

Honey Kombucha

PREP: 20 MIN	FERMENT: 5–10 DAYS	YIELD: 12 SERVINGS

INGREDIENTS

6 green or black tea bags

12 cups water

1 cup raw honey or unrefined sugar such as Sucanat

Kombucha SCOBY

1–2 cups raw apple cider vinegar or leftover kombucha

1 Combine the tea bags and a few cups of water in a large pot.

2 Bring the water to a simmer, and remove from heat.

3 Stir in the honey until it is dissolved.

4 Cover and let the green tea bags steep for 10 to 15 minutes.

5 Add 8 cups of cool water to the pot to cool down the tea.

6 Place the SCOBY and raw apple cider vinegar in your large gallon jar.

7 Add your now cooled-down tea to the jar.

8 Use a wooden spoon (metal will harm your bacteria) to help the SCOBY float at the top. If it does not rise, it should rise during fermentation!

9 Cover the jar with cheesecloth or a paper towel, and secure with a rubber band. Let ferment at room temperature for 5 to 10 days.

10 Check on it and taste it! Is it tangy, sweet, and fizzy enough?

11 Pour the kombucha through a strainer into a clean large jar or several bottles. (In this case, leave the SCOBY and 1 to 2 cups of finished kombucha behind for your next batch!)

12 When you have the taste you desire, refrigerate!

VARY IT! Want some new flavors in your kombucha? Kombucha can be made with a wide range of added flavors! Try adding a slice of ginger, or throw a few juniper berries into your next batch!

Chapter **3**
Baking Bread

Many people get nervous about baking bread from scratch, thinking that you have to have some secret talent to make it rise or come out tasting good. And because bread is so readily available and such a staple for many people, picking up a loaf at a local grocery store or bakery is much easier than making your own from scratch.

Although no one is suggesting that you'll *never* pick up another store-bought loaf, in this chapter you discover that making your own bread is deeply satisfying yet simple. From the relaxing repetition of kneading the dough to the slow, quiet rise to the shaping of the loaves and the heavenly smell of it baking in the oven . . . nothing is quite like it.

And for homesteaders trying to become more self-sufficient, baking bread at home is a skill that saves money and delights family and friends. In addition, homemade bread is a wonderful way to use some of the fruits and veggies you've grown as well as honey straight from your backyard bees!

Understanding Yeast Breads

Entire books have been dedicated to the art of breadmaking, and there are hundreds of different techniques and doughs that you can bake. Instead of overwhelming you with too much information, we'll cover just the basics, to lay a good solid foundation upon which you can build your bread-baking knowledge. When you feel comfortable with the mixing, kneading, and rising of basic bread doughs, you can move on to fancier types of loaves and rolls. First, you need to know how all the ingredients work together, in order to have a better understanding about the making of bread.

Yeast

Yeast is the ingredient that makes bread rise. It's a live plant, which, when dissolved in warm water (no more than 110 degrees) and given something to eat, becomes active. Yeast needs food to stay alive. Generally, the sweetener (usually sugar or honey) added to the dough is the yeast's initial food. When the bread is kneaded, more sugar is made in the starch from the flour, which sustains the yeast until it finally dies when it's baked in the oven.

You'll see different types of yeast when shopping, including bread machine yeast, compressed cake yeast, and brewer's yeast. For our purposes, we stick with active dry yeast.

Active dry yeast has a longer shelf life and is easier to store than fresh compressed cake yeast. It's available in foil packs or jars coded with an expiration date. One package of active dry yeast contains 1 scant tablespoon (*scant* means "barely"), so if you don't have yeast in the premeasured packages, measure out 1 level tablespoon and gently shake back just a little.

REMEMBER

To ensure that your yeast stays fresh for as long as possible, store it in the refrigerator until you're ready to use it.

Yeast likes to be snug and warm, but not hot. The most common mistake that first-time breadmakers make is to kill the yeast by overheating it. One of the first steps in breadmaking is to dissolve the yeast in warm water- sometimes a temperature is given (not over 110 degrees). How can you tell if the water temperature is correct? The most accurate way is to use a thermometer. If you don't have one, you can measure the temperature almost as accurately by feel. Your body temperature is about 98.6 degrees, so run the hot water until it's just slightly warm to the touch, but not uncomfortable.

Flour

Flour is the main ingredient in bread. Flours made from wheat contain proteins that, when liquids are added and the dough is kneaded, form gluten. This gluten gives the dough its elasticity, allows the dough to stretch as it traps the gases released by the yeast, and causes the bread to rise. The different varieties of flour that are made from wheat have different amounts of gluten-making proteins, so it's good to know a little about your choices for breadmaking.

>> **All-purpose enriched white flour:** A mix of hard and soft wheats, this flour is the most common. Because it is *all-purpose,* it's a good flour to have around if you want to make a cake, bread, or cookies, but the results may not be as good as if you chose a flour specifically intended for each purpose (cake flour for cakes and bread flour for bread).

>> **Bread flour:** Bread flour is protein-rich white flour made from hard wheat. It's a good choice for breadmaking because it's a gluten-rich flour that makes a good, elastic dough and gives good volume when your bread rises. Loaves made with bread flour are likely to be a bit tastier, lighter, and better risen than those made with all-purpose flour.

WARNING

Bread flour absorbs more liquid than all-purpose flour, so you may need less flour if your recipe calls for all-purpose flour and you're using bread flour instead.

>> **Self-rising flour:** This flour is all-purpose flour with salt and baking soda mixed in it. It is not recommended for yeast breads.

>> **Unbleached white flour:** Unbleached flour is a mixture of hard and soft wheats and has not been chemically whitened (such as all-purpose). It has a slightly higher protein content and contains more nutrients though, making it a good choice for baking bread.

>> **Whole-wheat flour:** Commercial whole-wheat flour is milled to include the flour, bran, and germ of the wheat. If a recipe calls for white flour and you want to use whole wheat, try substituting whole-wheat flour for half the amount of white flour.

WARNING

Whole-wheat flour produces a much denser loaf of bread and absorbs more liquid than white flour, so if you're substituting whole-wheat flour for white flour, add the minimum amount of flour called for in the recipe and then continue to add more slowly to make sure that you don't toughen the dough.

Sweeteners

The usual sweeteners you find in breadmaking are sugar and honey. Although the sweetener typically doesn't make the bread sweet like a cake, it does add some flavor and feed the yeast. When the yeast eats the sugar, it begins a fermentation process, which produces the gases that cause the bread to rise. The sweetener also browns during baking, which helps produce a bread with a nice texture and golden-brown crust.

Salt

Salt is quite important in baking bread. It adds flavor, controls yeast growth, and prevents overrising. Don't overdo it, though, or the salt will inhibit the proper growth of the yeast. Just use the amount called for in the recipe.

Fat

Fat in bread recipes adds to the tenderness and texture of the bread. Fats are also flavor carriers and act as natural preservatives, helping your loaf retain its moisture and stay mold free. Butter adds a bit of color, but you can substitute shortening or lard for butter measure for measure. Some recipes also use vegetable or olive oil.

Eggs

Eggs are not essential to breadmaking, but some recipes call for them. The addition of eggs produces a richer dough and gives the dough a lovely pale-yellow color. And you have plenty of eggs from your backyard flock, right?

Liquids

The liquid in a bread recipe moistens the flour, which activates the gluten. It also can feed the yeast. Typical liquids found in bread recipes are water, milk, and buttermilk. Water gives bread a brown, crisp crust. Milk gives a velvety, creamy texture to the bread. Buttermilk adds a nice tangy flavor. Yeast dissolves a bit more slowly in milk than in water.

TIP

If you use milk or buttermilk, warm it slightly (so that it's warm to the touch) to remove the chill of the refrigerator before dissolving the yeast in it.

Mixing and Kneading Breads

Typically, a recipe calls for you to dissolve the yeast in a liquid and then add several other ingredients (butter, salt, and sugar) to the yeast. Then you add the flour.

You can mix doughs in two ways: with a mixer with a dough hook or by hand. Either way, adding the flour slowly is important. The first 2 to 3 cups will be absorbed quickly into the dough, making a wet, loose batter. Then you start adding the flour in ½-cup intervals and continue mixing until the dough starts to come away from the sides of the bowl.

If you have a sturdy mixer with a good motor, using it is the easy way to mix bread dough. If you're using a mixer with a dough hook attachment, knead the dough for about five minutes on medium speed. Remove the dough from the bowl and finish kneading by hand on a lightly floured surface.

Mixing bread dough by hand is a little more work, but it has its rewards. When the dough comes away from the sides of the bowl, turn the dough out onto a lightly floured surface. A large wooden cutting board, a clean countertop, or a large slab of marble makes a good kneading surface. Just make sure that it's dry, and then lightly dust it with flour. Also, rub your hands with a little flour to keep the dough from sticking to them.

Follow these simple steps to knead dough by hand like a pro:

1. **Turn the dough onto a lightly floured surface.**

2. **Dust the top of the dough with flour.**

   Don't use more than a tablespoon or two of flour for each dusting.

3. **Press the heels of your hands into the top of the dough.**

   You need to use some arm strength, so lean into the dough and push the dough hard into the kneading surface. Linking you fingers together, one hand on top of the other, may increase your kneading strength.

4. **Fold the dough in half toward you and press down again with the heels of your hands.**

5. **Give the dough a quarter turn, fold it again, and continue the pushing and kneading with the heels of your hands, always turning the dough and folding it so that all the dough gets worked.**

6. **Continue to lightly dust the dough if it sticks to the board or your hands.**

   Keep up the kneading process for about ten minutes (three to five minutes if you've used a mixer). If you're kneading by hand, it's unlikely that you'll overwork the dough.

Kneading is an important step in good breadmaking, so don't cut corners. If you get tired and need to rest, that's okay. Just cover the dough with a clean dish towel and rest for five minutes. The dough will be glad to rest, too. You'll know you're done when your dough is smooth, elastic, and a bit satiny. If you press into the dough and it springs back, you've done the job correctly. Figure 3-1 shows kneading in action.

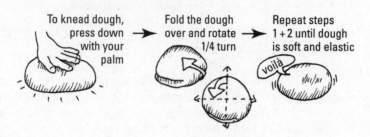

FIGURE 3-1:
Kneading bread dough by hand.

Encouraging Bread to Rise

After you've finished kneading, it's time to set the bread aside to rise. Ceramic bowls are good insulators. Metal or glass bowls may fluctuate with the exterior temperature, but you can use them if you want. Yeast rises best when it's cozy warm, so preheat your bowl by rinsing it out with warm water and drying it thoroughly. Then generously grease the inside of the bowl with softened butter, margarine, or even shortening (just don't use oil).

To increase the chances of your bread dough rising sufficiently, follow these steps:

1. **Form the dough into a ball and place it in the bowl.**

2. **Turn the dough once around the bowl to grease the dough itself.**

3. **Dampen a clean dish towel with warm water and drape it over the top of the bowl.**

The purpose of the cover is to keep the dough draft-free and prevent anything from entering the dough as it rises, but the dough also needs to breathe, so you don't want to seal it off from air.

TIP

Many cooks agree that the best place to let dough rise is in a gas oven, turned off. The heat that the pilot light gives off creates the perfect cozy spot for bread to rise, and the oven itself should be draft-free. The microwave oven, if it's large enough, is also a good, draft-free choice. Of course, the kitchen countertop is fine, too.

REMEMBER

The dough needs to double in size, which usually takes 1 to 1½ hours. Always check it after the minimum amount of time. If you're using rapid-rise yeast, check it after 30 to 40 minutes.

You'll know that your bread has finished rising when you can poke your finger about ½ inch into the dough and the indentation stays. If it springs back, continue letting it rise. Don't allow the dough to more than double in size. If a recipe calls for a second rising, literally punch down the dough, give it a few quick turns in the bowl, re-cover the bowl, and allow the dough to rise again.

If you're going to shape the dough into loaves, punch down the dough and turn it out onto a lightly floured board. Knead the dough again for two to three minutes. Then divide the dough, if necessary, into the portions you need, letting the dough rest for about five minutes before shaping the loaves.

Shaping and Baking the Loaves

If you're making two loaves of bread from one batch of dough, pat or roll the dough out into a rectangle slightly shorter than the loaf pans. Fold the dough in thirds like a letter or roll it up like a jelly roll. Tuck the ends under and place it seam side down into the prepared loaf pan, as shown in Figure 3-2. Cover and allow the bread to rise until it just comes up to the side of the pan.

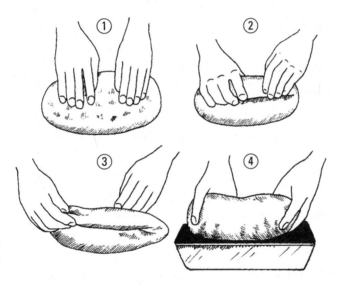

FIGURE 3-2:
Preparing dough
for a loaf pan.

In the first 15 or so minutes of baking, you'll discover that your bread has a growth spurt during which the yeast gets really active and pushes up the bread before the crust begins to set. Always account for this sudden growth spurt by not allowing your bread to rise over the top of the pan during the second rising time. When the dough gets pretty close to the top of the pan — but not over — it's time to get your loaf in the oven.

Always bake your bread in a preheated oven. Usually, the baking time given for a recipe is accurate, but if you're unsure, give a thump on the bread (watch out, it will be hot!). If it sounds hollow, it's finished. If you still aren't sure whether it's done, you can go ahead and insert a long wooden skewer into the middle of the loaf. If it comes out clean, your bread is finished. Don't judge doneness by the color of the loaf. If you find that your bread is browning too quickly, cover it with aluminum foil for the last 15 or 20 minutes of baking.

Turn the bread out of the pans onto cooling racks when you remove them from the oven. They should slip out easily. If you want a soft crust, you can brush the top with melted butter.

Let the bread cool for at least 30 minutes before you slice it; otherwise, you run the risk of ruining the bread you've worked so hard to make. If you cut it too soon, the center will be gummy, and the bread will not be set enough to cut and can taste doughy.

Yeast Bread, Quick Bread, Muffin, and Biscuit Recipes

Yeast breads are some of the most satisfying foods you can bake. Few things are as welcoming as a home filled with the aroma of freshly baked bread. Quick breads are quite popular because they're a snap to put together and can satisfy either a sweet or a savory desire. Because they're leavened with baking soda or baking powder, they don't require the rising time yeast breads do, which means they're fast and easy to make.

This section features recipes for several yeast breads as well as a few quick bread options. From full loaves to individual servings and from savory to sweet, there's something here that will complement most any meal.

Basic White Buttermilk Bread

PREP: 25 MIN	RISING: 90 MIN	BAKING: 35 MIN	YIELD: 2 LOAVES (ABOUT 24 SERVINGS)

INGREDIENTS

¼ cup warm water (not above 115 degrees)

1 package active dry yeast

2 tablespoons sugar

¼ cup (½ stick) butter, melted and cooled to lukewarm

2 cups buttermilk, at room temperature

5 to 6 cups bread flour

1 teaspoon salt

¼ teaspoon baking soda

1 In a large mixing bowl, combine the water, yeast, and sugar. Stir with a whisk to dissolve the yeast. Add the melted butter to the buttermilk and mix it into the yeast mixture.

2 In a separate bowl, mix together 5 cups of the flour, the salt, and the baking soda; mix it into the yeast mixture to form a dough (add up to 1 cup additional flour, if necessary).

3 Knead the dough on a lightly floured surface until smooth and elastic, about 10 minutes.

4 Place the dough in a buttered bowl, cover, and set it in a warm place to rise until doubled, about 1 hour

5 Grease two 9-x-5-inch loaf pans. Punch down the dough and knead it again for about 1 minute. Divide the dough in half and shape it into two loaves. Place them in the prepared pans, cover, and let rise in a warm place until the dough just barely reaches the edge of the pan, about 30 minutes.

6 Preheat the oven to 350 degrees. Bake the bread until it's browned and crusty, about 35 minutes. Cool the bread on wire racks.

TIP: If you don't have buttermilk on hand, you can substitute whole milk.

TIP: This bread is excellent toasted or fried as French toast.

PER SERVING: *Calories 100 (From Fat 17); Fat 2g (Saturated 1g); Cholesterol 4mg; Sodium 99mg; Carbohydrate 17g (Dietary Fiber 1g); Protein 3g*

Honey-Oatmeal Bread

PREP: 45 MIN	RISING: 90 MIN	BAKING: 35 MIN	YIELD: 2 LOAVES (ABOUT 24 SERVINGS)

INGREDIENTS

2 cups simmering water

1 cup quick-cooking oatmeal (not instant)

2 tablespoons butter

1 package active dry yeast

½ cup warm water (not above 115 degrees)

¾ cup honey or maple syrup

5 to 7 cups flour

2 teaspoons salt

1 Combine the water, oatmeal, and butter in a small bowl and let stand until it's cool to the touch, about 30 minutes.

2 In a small bowl, combine the yeast, warm water, and honey or maple syrup. Stir to dissolve and let stand for about 5 minutes (the water should be foamy).

3 Measure 5 cups of the flour and the salt into a mixing bowl. Add the oatmeal and yeast mixture and stir, adding more flour if necessary, until the mixture forms a kneadable dough (add up to 2 cups additional flour, if necessary).

4 Knead the dough on a lightly floured surface, adding more flour if the dough gets sticky, until the dough is smooth and elastic and springs back when you touch it, about 10 minutes.

5 Place the dough in a buttered bowl, cover, and set in a warm place to rise until doubled, about 1 hour.

6 Grease two 9-x-5-inch loaf pans. Punch down the dough and knead it again for about 1 minute. Divide the dough in half and shape into two loaves. Place them in the prepared pans, cover, and let rise until the dough barely reaches the edges of the pans, about 30 minutes.

7 Preheat the oven to 375 degrees. Bake the bread until it's browned and crusty, about 35 minutes. Cool the bread on wire racks.

TIP: Whenever you serve oatmeal for breakfast, it's easy to have a lot left over. Don't waste it: Incorporate it into a loaf of bread!

PER SERVING: *Calories 112 (From Fat 10); Fat 1g (Saturated 1g); Cholesterol 2mg; Sodium 146mg; Carbohydrate 23g (Dietary Fiber 1g); Protein 3g*

Jeff's Potato Bread

PREP: 35 MIN	RISING: 90 MIN	BAKING: 35 TO 45 MIN	YIELD: 2 LOAVES (ABOUT 24 SERVINGS)

INGREDIENTS

1 package active dry yeast

½ cup lukewarm water (not above 115 degrees)

½ cup plus 1 teaspoon sugar

1 cup milk, warmed (not above 115 degrees)

1 cup warm mashed potatoes (instant is okay)

½ cup shortening, melted and cooled

2 eggs, beaten

2 teaspoons salt

6 to 7 cups bread flour

1 Dissolve the yeast in the warm water with 1 teaspoon of the sugar and let stand for about 10 minutes.

2 In a large mixing bowl, combine the warm milk with the mashed potatoes and shortening. Add the beaten eggs to the potato mixture. Add the yeast mixture and stir to combine. Add the ½ cup sugar and the salt to the mixture. Mix in enough flour to make a kneadable dough.

3 Knead the dough on a lightly floured surface until it is smooth and elastic, adding additional flour if the dough gets sticky, about 10 minutes. Place the dough in a buttered bowl, cover, and set it in a warm place to rise until doubled, about 1 hour.

4 Grease two 9-x-5-inch loaf pans. Punch down the dough and knead it again for about 1 minute on a lightly floured surface. Divide the dough in half and shape it into two loaves. Place the loaves in the prepared pans, cover, and let rise until the dough barely reaches the tops of the pans, about 30 minutes.

5 Preheat the oven to 350 degrees. Bake the bread until it's browned and crusty, 35 to 45 minutes. Remove the loaves from the pans and cool on wire racks.

PER SERVING: *Calories 150 (From Fat 39); Fat 4g (Saturated 1g); Cholesterol 15mg; Sodium 171mg; Carbohydrate 24g (Dietary Fiber 1g); Protein 4g*

Fluffy Dinner Rolls

PREP: 30 MIN	RISING: 90 MIN	BAKING: 30 TO 40 MIN	YIELD: ABOUT 2 DOZEN

INGREDIENTS

6 to 7 cups flour

6 tablespoons sugar

1¼ teaspoons salt

1 package active dry yeast

2¼ cups warm water (not above 115 degrees)

3 tablespoons vegetable oil

1 In a large mixing bowl, combine 6 cups of the flour, 5 table-spoons of the sugar, and the salt.

2 In a medium-sized mixing bowl, dissolve the yeast and the remaining 1 tablespoon sugar in the warm water. Let stand for about 5 minutes until the top gets a bit foamy. Stir in the vegetable oil. Slowly add the yeast mixture to the flour mixture and mix until it's thoroughly incorporated.

3 Remove the dough from the bowl and knead, adding the remaining cup of flour if the dough gets sticky, and kneading until the dough is smooth and satiny and springs back when you touch it, about 10 minutes.

4 Place the dough in a large buttered bowl. Cover and let rise in a warm place until the dough has doubled in bulk, about 1 hour.

5 Punch down the dough and knead it for about 1 more minute. Pinch off enough dough to make a 1½-inch ball. Roll the dough into a ball and place it in a greased 13-x-9-inch baking pan. Repeat with the remaining dough until you have about 24 balls. They can touch each other in the pan and fit snugly against the sides. Cover and let rise until doubled in bulk, about 30 minutes.

6 Preheat the oven to 350 degrees. Bake the rolls for about 30 to 40 minutes, until golden brown and fluffy.

NOTE: The water you use should be only slightly warmer than your body temperature.

TIP: Brush the tops of the rolls with melted butter before baking them for a tender crust.

PER SERVING: Calories 143 (From Fat 18); Fat 2g (Saturated 0g); Cholesterol 0mg; Sodium 122mg; Carbohydrate 27g (Dietary Fiber 1g); Protein 4g

Amish Applesauce Bread

PREP: 15 MIN	BAKING: 50 TO 60 MIN	YIELD: 12 TO 14 SERVINGS

INGREDIENTS

2 cups all-purpose flour

1 teaspoon baking powder

1 teaspoon salt

1 teaspoon baking soda

1 teaspoon ground cinnamon

½ teaspoon ground nutmeg

½ cup (1 stick) butter, softened

¾ cup sugar

2 eggs

1 teaspoon vanilla extract

1 cup applesauce

½ cup walnuts, chopped (optional)

1 Preheat the oven to 350 degrees. Grease a 9-x-5-inch loaf pan.

2 In a medium bowl, sift together the flour, baking powder, salt, baking soda, cinnamon, and nutmeg.

3 In a separate mixing bowl, cream together the butter and sugar. Beat in the eggs and vanilla.

4 Gradually add the dry ingredients to the creamed butter. Stir in the applesauce and, if desired, the walnuts, mixing just enough to blend all the ingredients.

5 Pour the batter into the prepared pan. Bake for 50 minutes to 1 hour, until a toothpick inserted into the center comes out clean. Cool the loaf on a wire rack for 10 minutes before removing from the pan to finish cooling.

PER SERVING: *Calories 215 (From Fat 79); Fat 9g (Saturated 5g); Cholesterol 56mg; Sodium 343mg; Carbohydrate 31g; (Dietary Fiber 1g); Protein 3g*

Southern Corn Bread

PREP: 10 MIN	BAKING: 20 MIN	YIELD: ONE 8- OR 9-INCH CORN BREAD

INGREDIENTS

2 tablespoons butter or vegetable oil

2 cups finely ground cornmeal

4 teaspoons baking powder

1½ teaspoons salt

1½ cups buttermilk

1 egg, lightly beaten

1 Preheat the oven to 450 degrees. Place the butter or vegetable oil in the bottom of an 8- or 9-inch square baking pan (or a 10-inch cast iron skillet) and place it in the oven while it heats for about 3 minutes (if you're using butter, keep an eye on it to make sure it doesn't burn).

2 In a large bowl, combine the cornmeal, baking powder, and salt.

3 In a separate bowl, mix together the buttermilk and egg and add it to the cornmeal mixture. Stir just to combine; do not overmix.

4 Pour the batter into the preheated skillet or pan and bake for about 20 minutes, until a knife inserted into the center comes out clean. Cool the corn bread in the skillet for 20 minutes before serving.

PER SERVING: *Calories 120 (From Fat 27); Fat 3g (Saturated 2g); Cholesterol 24mg; Sodium 456mg; Carbohydrate 19g (Dietary Fiber 2g); Protein 4g*

Blueberry Muffins

PREP: 15 MIN	BAKING: 20 MIN	YIELD: 24 MUFFINS

INGREDIENTS

2 cups all-purpose flour

2 teaspoons baking powder

1 cup sugar

½ cup (1 stick) butter, melted

½ cup milk

1 teaspoon vanilla extract

2 eggs, lightly beaten

2½ cups blueberries, fresh or frozen (not packed in syrup)

1 Preheat the oven to 400 degrees. Grease or line two 12-cup muffin cups.

2 In a small bowl, combine the flour and baking powder; set aside.

3 In a large mixing bowl, combine the sugar, butter, milk, vanilla, and eggs. Mix to combine.

4 Slowly add the flour mixture to the sugar mixture and stir just to moisten the dry ingredients. Fold in the blueberries just to combine. Don't overmix.

5 Fill the muffin cups three-quarters full of batter. Bake (both pans side by side is okay) for 20 minutes or until golden brown. A wooden toothpick inserted into the center of the muffins will come out clean when the muffins are done. Let the muffins rest for 5 minutes on the cooling rack before removing them from the pan.

NOTE: The secret to bumpy, rounded muffin tops and a moist interior is to avoid overmixing the dough and to use only a bowl and a spoon for mixing. Don't use a handheld or stand mixer. When you combine the flour mixture with the liquids, just give it a few (no more than five) good turns with a sturdy wooden spoon. A tiny bit of unmixed flour should remain in your batter, and that's okay. The batter will finish mixing in the oven, and the unmixed flour will not be present in the muffin.

TIP: If you don't user liners, grease only the bottoms of the muffin cups (the sides of the cup should be left ungreased). Not greasing the sides gives you a better-shaped muffin.

PER SERVING: *Calories 122 (From Fat 41); Fat 5g (Saturated 3g); Cholesterol 29mg; Sodium 41mg; Carbohydrate 19g (Dietary Fiber 1g); Protein 2g*

Buttermilk Biscuits

PREP: 15 MIN	BAKING: 10 TO 12 MIN	YIELD: 16 BISCUITS

INGREDIENTS

2 cups White Lily brand soft white flour or cake or all-purpose flour

¼ teaspoon baking soda

1 teaspoon baking powder

1 teaspoon salt

Pinch of sugar

6 tablespoons cold butter, cut into 6 pieces

¾ cup buttermilk

1 Preheat the oven to 425 degrees.

2 Add the buttermilk and mix until just moistened.

3 Pat out the dough onto a lightly floured surface until it is about ½-inch thick. Cut the dough into 2-inch circles (use a drinking glass or cookie cutter). Gather up the scraps and pat them out again. Place biscuits on an ungreased baking sheet.

4 Bake until just light brown, for 10 to 12 minutes. Serve hot.

NOTE: Biscuits are a lot like pie pastry in that too much handling will toughen the dough, and the biscuit won't be as delicate. Because you don't want to overmix your biscuit dough, working efficiently when making biscuits is important.

NOTE: Steam is a powerful leavener for biscuits, so it's okay if your biscuits are a bit moist when you roll them out. Don't over-flour the dough to make it easier to handle. Just pat out the dough, cut it with a cookie cutter, and then place the biscuits on a baking sheet.

TIP: If you want biscuits with soft sides, place them in the pan so their sides are touching. If you want them to have crusty sides, place them about an inch apart on the baking sheet.

PER SERVING: *Calories 100 (From Fat 41); Fat 5g (Saturated 3g); Cholesterol 12mg; Sodium 249mg; Carbohydrate 13g (Dietary Fiber 0g); Protein 2g*

Chapter **4**

Making Candles and Soap

For many homesteaders, the drive to become increasingly more self-sufficient is strong. And it predictably leads to adding new skills and embarking on new experiments to see whether just a little bit more can be produced independently, to find the next thing that doesn't have to be bought conventionally.

Let's say you're growing your own vegetables, creating rich compost for the garden, getting fresh eggs from chickens you're raising yourself, and harvesting honey from your own colony of backyard bees. Perhaps you're canning and pickling some of that produce, trying your hand at techniques such as fermenting and dehydrating. Maybe you've even started brewing your own beer, making your own wine, and baking bread from scratch.

From there, it's just a short hop to making your own candles and soap. And when many homesteaders feel the urge to branch out to "the next thing," this is often one of the things they land on.

This chapter ushers you in to the hobby of making your own candles and soap as a way to save money, be more self-sufficient, or just create useful and beautiful homemade items that you'll use often.

Igniting Your Candlemaking Hobby

Making candles can be a relaxing and rewarding hobby. Nothing quite compares to the feelings of pride and pleasure that come from looking at a beautiful, burning candle and knowing that you created it with your own two hands. And because candlemaking isn't an expensive hobby, you can decorate your home with candles, as well as give them as gifts.

Waxing about the types of waxes

Without wax, your candle won't burn. But certain waxes are more appropriate for certain types of candles.

Paraffin wax: The winner and still champion

Paraffin wax is a petroleum-based wax and the most popular wax for making candles. If you're new to candlemaking, paraffin wax makes a great starting point. Paraffin wax is inexpensive, easy to color, and available practically anywhere. It has a colorless and odorless nature that enables you to easily add and reliably predict your end colors and aromas. Paraffin wax is commonly available in chunks and large slabs.

WARNING

Don't be tempted to do one-stop shopping and buy your paraffin wax at the grocery store. This wax isn't the type you use in candlemaking; instead, it's used for sealing food that you've jarred.

Beeswax: No stings attached

A popular choice, *beeswax* is an all-natural product that has a pleasant honey aroma when burned. In addition to its natural golden shade, beeswax is available in white and other colors. You can buy beeswax in honeycomb sheets, blocks, or beads. If you have your own backyard colony of bees, you can harvest the honeycombs right out of your hive.

Beeswax's low melting point (approximately 140°F) and strength (if you drop it, it dents but doesn't shatter) makes beeswax a great wax to use when you're making container candles with children.

Gel wax: Feels like jelly

A newer product on the market, *gel wax* is basically mineral oil combined with resin to create a mixture that's the consistency of jelly. Gel wax is also called (surprise!) *jelly wax* and looks like a clear gel. You can find gel wax at most craft stores, usually in a round, bucketlike container.

If you've ever purchased a gel candle, you're aware that gel wax doesn't set hard. Because gel wax is clear, it's popular for embedding nonflammable objects, such as shells or decorative glass objects.

Vegetable-based wax: Straight from the earth

Believe it or not, waxes made from items such as soybeans, palm wax, and other vegetable bases are available. Fans of these waxes say they burn cleanly and are longer lasting than other chemical-based waxes, such as paraffin. But the main reason to opt for this type of wax is if you're a vegan.

REMEMBER

If the package doesn't specifically say that the wax is all vegetable, it probably isn't.

Finding the right wick

Any wick you choose should cause your candle to burn. But a well-chosen wick consumes all the melted wax at just the right pace, so that the wax doesn't drip off the candle and so that there's enough wax to keep the flame going.

Table 4-1 lists wick types and for which candles they're most appropriate.

TABLE 4-1

Types of Wicks and Their Uses

Type of Wick	Best Use
Flat braided	Tapers
Square braided	Beeswax candles, pillars, and other large candles
Metal cored	Any type of candle, but especially container candles, gel candles, votives, and tealights
Paper cored	Votives, tealights, and container candles (but don't use in gel candles)

After you decide on the type of wick, you need to figure out what size of wick you need. That decision depends mainly on your candle's diameter. If you're not sure what the diameter is, simply measure the width of your candle at its widest point. Table 4-2 gives you a general guide for choosing your wicks.

TABLE 4-2

Sizing Your Wick

Candle diameter	Suggested wick size
0–1 inch	Extra small, 20 ply
1–2 inches	Small, 24 ply
2–3 inches	Medium, 30 ply
3–4 inches	Large, 36 ply
4 inches or more	Extra-large, 40-plus ply

Rolling Beeswax Candles

This may just be the perfect first candle for beginners. You don't need to melt any wax or use a lot of fancy equipment. You simply roll sheets of beeswax into a round candle. No hot wax, no mess.

And if your homesteading efforts include beekeeping, your annual harvest doesn't have to begin and end with the honey; you can use your colony's own honeycombs!

Beeswax candles are desirable; unlike paraffin, they don't drip, don't sputter, and don't smoke, but they do burn a long time. Buy them in a gift store, and they're fantastically expensive. But not when you make them yourself!

The only downside is that beeswax is sticky at any temperature, and it gets even stickier when it's warm. But stickiness can work in your favor because the bees-wax sheets adhere to each other as you roll them.

TIP

When you roll your candle, you want your beeswax sheet to be at room temperature. Ideally, it's been at this temperature for at least a few days.

To roll a beeswax candle, you need two sheets of beeswax and a primed wick. Here's what you want to do:

1. **Cut your primed wick so that it's ¾ inch longer than the height of your finished candle.**

    If you're using a normal beeswax sheet, which measures 8 inches x 16 inches, your candle will be about 8 inches tall, so you want your wick to be approximately 8¾ inches. If you want to make two 8-inch tapers instead, just cut the sheet in half long ways and roll two candles.

2. **Lay your beeswax sheet on a hard surface and place your wick along the edge, as shown in Figure 4-1.**

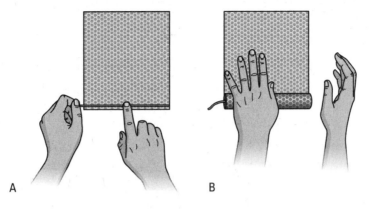

FIGURE 4-1:
Making a
beeswax candle
is as simple as
adding a wick and
gently, but tightly,
rolling it into
a candle.

A   B

3. **Apply pressure, smoothly but firmly rolling the edge of the sheet around the wick and continue rolling the beeswax into a cylinder shape.**

   You want to make sure that you're rolling straight; otherwise, your edges won't align. You also want to roll tightly enough so that you don't trap air between the layers, which can affect how well your candle burns.

TIP

   If you want to make a square candle, just flatten each side with a hard object as you roll. If you want to make a shorter candle, cut the short side of the beeswax sheet in half prior to rolling it.

4. **When you reach the end of the first sheet, attach your second sheet of beeswax by firmly pinching the edges of each sheet together and then continue rolling.**

   For a larger candle, you can use as many sheets of beeswax consecutively until you reach your desired diameter.

5. **Trim your wick.**

   Wait at least a day, preferably longer, before lighting.

REMEMBER

You want your beeswax to be at least room temperature or warmer, or it will break. If you're having trouble, try using a hairdryer to heat the sheets. But don't go too warm, or the wax may begin to melt and become a sticky mess.

Making Molded Candles

The type of candle you'll probably make the most is a basic molded candle. You can use this one basic technique to make many different types of candles. The type of mold you use doesn't matter; the steps are pretty much the same.

After you choose your mold, you need to figure out how much wax you need to melt. Pour water into your mold and measure the amount you used. For every 3.5 fluid ounces of water, you need 3 ounces of unmelted wax.

1. **Melt your wax to the package's specified temperature.**

   Place the wax in the top part of a double boiler. Bring the water in the bottom section to a rolling boil over medium heat until melted. Use a wax or candy thermometer to monitor the temperature.

   WARNING

   Don't use a microwave to melt your wax because the temperature is too hard to control, and you can easily overheat the wax.

   Unlike food, wax doesn't look done, and you can't test it with a fork. You need to constantly check your wax's temperature. As a rule, if you're registering temperatures in the 200°F range, you want to be careful. Most waxes combust if they're 400°F or more, and wax heats up quickly. Each wax's *flashpoint* — the temperature at which it combusts — is listed on its packaging.

2. **Spray your mold with a mold release, such as silicone or vegetable spray.**

   Using a releasing agent helps you remove the candle from the mold.

   TIP

   If you make candles regularly, you may want to use commercial grade release spray instead of vegetable oil because the vegetable oil can leave a film on your mold over time. However, if you make candles only on occasion, the vegetable oil spray works just fine.

3. **Cut your wick so that it's 2 inches longer than your finished candle's height and then insert it into your mold.**

4. **When your wax reaches the required temperature, add any additives, color, or scent.**

   Unless you're using a flexible mold, add stearin in proportion to 10 percent of your wax. Stearin has many benefits, but one in particular that is beneficial here is that it shrinks the wax, which makes your candle easier to remove from the mold.

   When you add ingredients, your wax's temperature will probably drop, so continue heating your wax a little longer until it reaches the proper temperature again.

5. **Remove your wax from the heat and slowly and smoothly pour it into your mold.**

   Be careful not to get any water into your wax. Remember that the container is hot, so you want to use potholders and get a firm grip on the container's handle. Pour your wax into the mold until it's almost full. Stop about ½ inch before you reach the top of the mold. Pouring smoothly is key. Don't constantly change directions; you can wiggle the mold later to get it to set perfectly.

6. **Wait a few minutes and then gently tap the side of your mold to remove any air bubbles.**

7. **As your wax cools, poke holes in the wax around the wick to release tension.**

   If you don't, the wax pulls the wick off center and may create a concave section on the outside of the candle.

8. **After your wax has cooled quite a while, reheat the extra wax you saved and pour it into any holes that have occurred as the wax cools.**

   This step is called a *repour*.

9. **Let your wax cool almost completely and then do a second repour.**

WARNING

   Don't rush this step. If you repour the wax while the candle is still hot and liquid, you're just adding more hot wax that has to shrink.

   After your candle has completely cooled, you're ready to remove it from the mold. You simply remove any mold sealer that you used, which should release the candle.

REMEMBER

When you remove your candle from the mold, remember that the bottom of the mold now becomes the top of the candle.

If your candle isn't coming out of your mold, you may not have let it cool long enough. Wait a few hours and try again later.

After some practice, you'll almost certainly want to add color or scent or both to your candles. You can add solid wax dye disks or liquid dyes to your wax during the melting process. To make a scented candle, use fragrances designed for candles and add it to the wax at the last possible moment before pouring. You can try essential oils, but they rarely work well in candles.

Taking a Dip with Tapers

Dipping candles is a fairly easy process. You basically melt the wax, dip both ends of a wick in it, let it cool, and repeat 20 to 30 times or more until your candle is the desired width. (Most tapers are usually ½ inch in diameter, but don't feel like you need to follow the crowd. Just remember that if you make the candle too thick, you're creating a funny-looking pillar instead of a slim taper!) Fortunately, you don't have to do anything special to create the tapered look; it just naturally happens.

Here's how the process works:

1. **Figure out how tall you want each taper, add a couple of extra inches so that your wick protrudes, double that amount, and then add 4 inches for space.**

   When you make tapers, you usually dip in pairs, but you use only one wick. If you want to create a 6-inch taper, for example, then you take 6 inches plus 2 inches to get 8 inches. You multiply that number by 2 to get 16 inches (enough wick for two candles) and then add 4 inches to the total so that you have space in between the candle. (You don't want the ends of your wick to touch each other when you dip.) So to make two 6-inch tapers, you need to cut your wick to 20 inches.

2. **Tie a weight to each end of the wick so that it stays submerged and straight while you dip.**

   Rocks work just fine as weights. You remove these weights later when the wick is strong enough to stay straight.

TIP

3. **Melt your wax.**

   When you dip candles, you usually use paraffin wax or a mixture of beeswax and paraffin. Either way, you probably need to add the usual 10 percent stearin. Melt twice the wax you think you need. You need to have plenty left over so that you have enough wax to dip in.

   Dipping works best when your wax is approximately 160°F to 170°F.

4. **Fill your dipping can with wax.**

   You need to make sure that your dipping can is tall enough to accommodate the size of the candle you want to make. Also fill the dipping can fairly full so that you can dip almost all the way up the wick. You have to keep adding wax to the dipping can throughout the process to keep it full.

5. **Dip your wick into your melted wax, allow it to cool, and then re-dip your wick repeatedly until you reach your desired diameter, as shown in Figure 4-2.**

   You want to dip your wick deep enough so that you have only a few inches of undipped wick remaining. Don't linger too long on this dip, though. You want your wick in the wax only for a second. Plunge it in and then remove it smoothly so that the wax doesn't blob.

   - If your taper looks bumpy, your wax isn't warm enough.

   - If your wax isn't building up on your wick, your wax is too hot.

   - If the wax isn't firming up enough between dips, you need to let it cool longer in between dips.

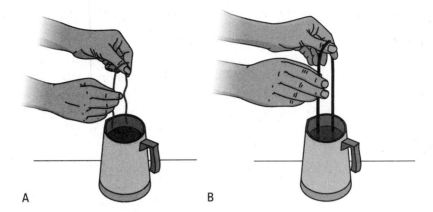

FIGURE 4-2:
Dipping a taper.

A   B

WARNING

Make sure that the ends of your wick don't touch each other, or you'll end up with a wax glob. You can use your hands to keep the ends apart, or you may want to use a straw, dowel rod, or piece of cardboard.

6. **Place your wicks over a rack or dowel rod until they cool.**

The cooling process takes approximately 3 minutes. Basically, the wax should feel cool to your touch.

7. **Repeat Steps 5 and 6 until your candle is the diameter you want.**

You may have to dip your candles 20 or 30 times or even more. Every time you dip, more wax builds up on your wick. Eventually, your wick becomes two tapers.

TIP

If you want your surface to be glossy, then dip it immediately into cool water after your last dip.

8. **Let your tapers cool a few hours before handling them and trimming your wick to ¼ inch.**

In general, taper candles are 7/8 inch in diameter at the bottom so that they can fit into most candleholders. If you're not using a mold, you probably need to cut the base of the candle down to that size.

Of course, if you already know which candle holders you'll be using, you can cut your candle's base down to that particular holder's size. To do so, use a craft knife to score around the base of your cooled candle. Then simply remove the strips of wax until your taper fits perfectly into the holder.

Cleaning Up with Homemade Soap

The technique you use to make your own soaps determines the amount of time you invest in your hobby. This book covers two basic soapmaking techniques: hand milling and melting and pouring. (You can also make soap from scratch by using lye, but the process is more complex and requires care in handling sodium hydroxide, which is a caustic substance. So we don't cover it here.)

Making hand-milled soap

If you don't like the idea of working with chemicals, you may want to try making hand-milled soap. All you do is take an existing bar of commercial soap, grate it, and then remelt it with water. You can then color, scent, and mold it as you please.

Many diehard soapmakers scoff at this technique. They say that you're technically not making the soap because you're using commercial soap, which *may* be soap but more than likely is a synthetic detergent bar. (If you have a preference for "real" soap, be sure to read the label and buy soap that has ingredients such as sodium cocoate, sodium palmate, sodium olivate, and so on.) But if you want to exercise a little creativity, you can still do so when you hand-mill soap. You can craft soap that looks and smells the way you want it to- something you can't always find at the store.

TIP

If you plan to scent your soap, make sure that you start with an unscented bar of commercial soap.

If you think you want to make soap, why not try hand-milling soap that you already have? The only special tool that you really need is a hand grater.

Here are the basic steps.

1. **Grate your soap, as shown in Figure 4-3.**

   The smaller you grate your pieces, the quicker the melting time.

2. **Melt your pieces in water in the top pot of a double boiler or in a microwave.**

   Use approximately 1 cup of water for every 2 cups of soap gratings. If using the microwave, heat the shavings and water in short bursts and check often, stirring as needed. Some people set their microwaves at 50 percent power when melting clear glycerin soap base or shavings. Experiment with what works best for you and your microwave.

3. **Stir your soap as it melts.**

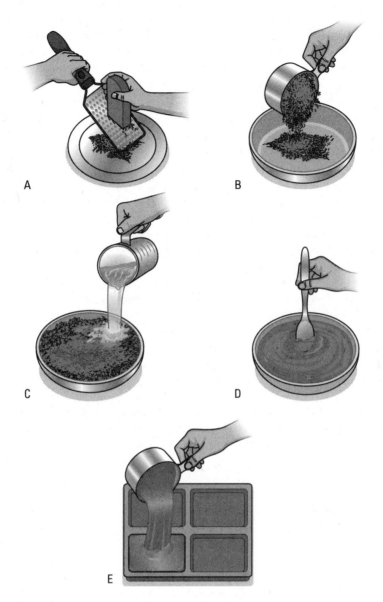

FIGURE 4-3:
Hand-milling
soap.

4. After the soap has melted, stir in your color.

5. Continue stirring until the soap is thick and creamy and then remove it from the heat.

6. Add any other additives, such as essential oils.

7. Pour your soap into the mold.

8. Let the soap cool overnight before removing it from the mold.

REMEMBER

Your soap isn't finished just because it's out of the mold. Allow it to solidify for three to seven days.

Making melt-and-pour soap

If making hand-milled soap sounds like cheating to you, then making melt-and-pour soap may be right up your alley. Instead of using commercial soap, you use a melt-and-pour soap base that you purchase in a craft store. The base comes in blocks, chunks, or nuggets, and you simply melt the amount you need and then mold it.

Probably more than any other soapmaking technique, melt-and-pour soapmaking resembles the steps involved in making candles. Like candlemaking, you use premade material, melt it, and mold it. If you love to make candles, chances are you'll enjoy making melt-and-pour soaps.

Here's how melt-and-pour soapmaking works:

1. **Melt your soap chunks in a double boiler over medium heat or melt them in a heat-resistant bowl in the microwave (see Figure 4-4).**

   You can also cut 1- or 2-inch chunks off a large 1-pound or 5-pound block of soap if you're not using precut chunks.

   If you're melting your soap in the microwave, melt your soap at 50 percent heat for approximately 1 minute. Stir your soap. Continue melting it at 20-second intervals until the soap is completely melted.

2. **Remove your melted soap from the heat and stir in any additives, such as color.**

3. **Pour your melted soap into the mold.**

   Most melt-and-pour soaps shrink as they set, so you probably don't need to spray your mold with a releasing agent.

4. **Allow your soap to cool for approximately 1 hour.**

Although melt-and-pour soap is immediately safe for the skin, let it dry out and harden for a few days before use, so that it will last longer.

Enhancing your soap with additives

Additives are generally anything you add to your soap base to enhance its color, scent, texture, skin-care benefits, or overall aesthetic value.

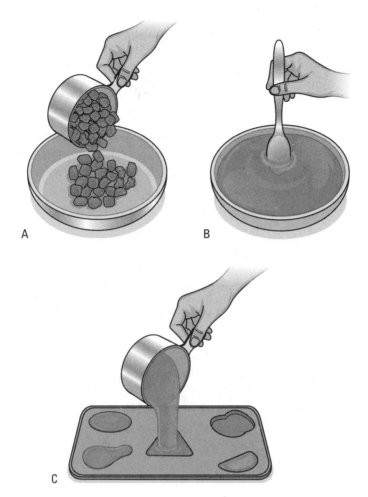

FIGURE 4-4:
You can use a microwave to melt your soap chunks. Then you just need to pour your melted soap into a mold.

A

B

C

You stir in the additives as the last step before pouring your soap into the mold and after the soap has been melted.

TIP

If you're adding a solid additive to melt-and-pour soap, be aware that it may *separate,* or sink to the bottom of your mold. To avoid this problem, let your soap cool more than you usually would, stirring the additive into the soap the entire time. You want the soap mixture to thicken in your bowl before you pour it into the mold, much like thickening gelatin. Waiting longer than usual can help the solid additive stay suspended in the soap.

Table 4-3 describes popular additives.

You can add color to your soap by using a melt-and-pour soap base or soap dyes. To add a scent, use your favorite essential oils, manufactured fragrance oils, or even spices and extracts from the kitchen or herbs straight from the garden!

TABLE 4-3   Common Soapmaking Additives

Additive	Description
Almond oil	Soothes irritated, itchy skin. Also used as base. Has slight odor.
Aloe vera	Relieves dry and burned skin. Can use in plant or gel form.
Apricot	Softens skin. A popular bath additive. To use, place dried apricots in water for several hours and then liquefy.
Apricot kernel oil	Softens skin. Especially good for sensitive skin.
Beeswax	Hardens soap and contributes scent. Need to melt before adding to soap. Don't use more than 1 ounce per pound of soap.
Clay	Helps dry out oily skin. Choose finely powdered French clay.
Cocoa butter	Hardens soap and moisturizes. Looks and smells like white chocolate, but can be purchased in a deodorized form if you want its qualities without the chocolate smell.
Cucumber	Acts as astringent. Use grated skin or liquefied.
Glycerin	Moisturizes skin.
Herbs	Contribute texture and color.
Honey	Moisturizes skin and makes soap softer.
Lanolin	Hardens soap. Moisturizes and softens skin. Can cloud soap. Don't use if allergic to wool.
Lemon	Adds texture and speckling, as well as antibacterial qualities. Use grated peel.
Oatmeal	Softens and exfoliates skin. Adds texture. Use ground rolled oats. Limit to a maximum of ½ cup rolled or ¼ cup ground or pulverized oats per pound of soap. A blender works well for making oat flour.
Pumice	Removes tough dirt, but can be harsh. Adds texture.
Vitamin E oil	Use as a preservative when you add fresh fruit or other additive at risk of spoiling.
Wheat germ	Exfoliates skin, as well as adding bulk and texture. Shows up in soap as light speckling. Use no more than 3 tablespoons per pound of soap.

4
Raising Animals

Contents at a Glance

Chapter **1**

Introducing Beekeeping

For many homesteaders just starting out, incorporating a colony of bees into their backyard is a box they're eager to check. And although the first motivator might be honey, that sweet reward is by no means the only reason folks are attracted to beekeeping. Since the 18th century, agriculture has recognized the value of pollination by bees. Without the bees' help, many commercial crops would suffer serious consequences. More on that later.

Even backyard beekeepers witness dramatic improvements in their garden: more and larger fruits, flowers, and vegetables. A hive or two in the garden makes a big difference in your success as a gardener and a homesteader.

This chapter helps you understand a bit more about beekeeping and the commitment involved, to help you decide whether bees would "bee" (just once — had to) a worthy addition to your homestead. From there, you can take a closer look at the different types of hives for housing your colony, and the pros and cons of each. Finally, you'll need some specialized stuff for your new beekeeping endeavor; the last section gets you geared up properly.

If you're looking for more hands-on info on caring for your colony throughout the year, troubleshooting potential problems, and harvesting honey, skip ahead to Chapter 2 of this minibook.

Breaking into Backyard Beekeeping

How do you know whether you'd make a good beekeeper? Is beekeeping the right hobby for you? Here are a few things worth considering as you ponder these issues.

Environmental considerations

Bees are remarkable creatures that do just fine in a wide range of climates. Bee-keepers can be found in areas with long, cold winters; in tropical rain forests; and in nearly every geographic region in between. If flowers bloom in your part of the world, you can keep bees.

How about space requirements? You don't need much. There are even beekeepers in the heart of Manhattan! They have a hive or two on their rooftops or terraces. Keep in mind that bees travel one to two miles from the hive to gather pollen and nectar. They'll forage an area as large as 6,000 acres, doing their thing. So the only space that you need is enough to accommodate the hive itself.

Honey bees are amazingly adaptable, but you'll get optimum results and a more rewarding honey harvest if you follow some basic guidelines (see Figure 1-1). Basically, you're looking for easy access (so you can tend to your hives), good drainage (so the bees don't get wet), a nearby water source for the bees, dappled sunlight, and minimal wind. Keep in mind that fulfilling all these criteria may not be possible.

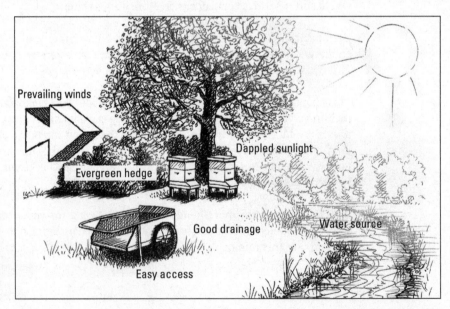

FIGURE 1-1:
The picture-perfect bee yard. Not always possible, but an admirable objective.

Courtesy of Howland Blackiston

Do the best you can by

>> Facing your hive to the southeast. That way your bees get an early morning wake-up call and start foraging early.

>> Positioning your hive so it is easily accessible come honey harvest time. You don't want to be hauling hundreds of pounds of honey up a hill on a hot August day.

>> Providing a windbreak at the rear of the hive.

>> Putting the hive in dappled sunlight. Ideally, avoid full sun or deep, dark shade.

>> Making sure the hive has good ventilation. Avoid placing it in a gully where the air is still and damp. Also, avoid putting it at the peak of a hill, should you live in a region where the bees will be subjected to winter's fury.

>> Placing the hive absolutely level from side to side, and with the front of the hive just slightly lower than the rear (a difference of an inch or less is fine) so rainwater drains out of the hive (and not into it).

TIP

Mulching around the hive prevents grass and weeds from blocking its entrances.

>> Locating your hive on firm, dry land.

Zoning and legal restrictions

Most communities are quite tolerant of beekeepers, but some have local ordinances that prohibit beekeeping or restrict the number of hives you can have. Some communities let you keep bees but ask that you register your hives with the local government. Check with local bee clubs, your town hall, your local zoning board, or your state's Department of Agriculture (bee/pollinating insects division) to find out about what's okay in your neighborhood. You want to practice a good-neighbor policy so that folks in your community don't feel threatened by your new hobby.

Costs and equipment

What does it cost to become a beekeeper? All in all, beekeeping isn't a very expensive hobby. You can figure on investing about $300 to $400 for a start-up hive kit, equipment, and tools — less if you build your own hive from scratch. You'll spend around $100 or more for a package of bees and queen. For the most part, these are one-time expenses. Keep in mind, however, the potential for a return on this investment. Your hive can give you 60 to 90 pounds of honey every year. At around $8 per pound (a fair going price for all-natural, raw honey), that should give you an income of $480 to $720 per hive!

How many hives do you need?

Most beekeepers start out with one hive, which is probably a good way to start your first season. But in short order, most beekeepers wind up getting a second hive. Why? For one, it's twice as much fun! Another more practical reason for having a second hive is that recognizing normal and abnormal situations is easier when you have two colonies to compare. In addition, a second hive enables you to borrow frames from a stronger, larger colony to supplement one that needs a little help. You may choose to start with one hive until you get the hang of things and then consider expanding in your second season.

What kind of honey bees should you raise?

The honey bee most frequently raised by beekeepers in the United States today is European in origin and has the scientific name *Apis mellifera.*

Of this species, the most popular variety is the so-called Italian honey bee. These bees are docile, hearty, and good honey producers. They are a good choice for the new beekeeper. Both Carniolans and Russians are also gentle, productive, and do well in many different climates. Italians, Carniolans, Russians: all are great bees for beginning beekeepers. Look no further than these three in your first year.

Time and commitment

Beekeeping isn't labor intensive. Sure, you'll spend part of a weekend putting together your new equipment. And there should be time spent reading up on your new hobby. But the time that you absolutely *must* spend with your bees is surprisingly modest. Other than your first year (when you should inspect the hive frequently to find out more about your bees), you need to make only five to eight visits to your hives every year. Add to that the time you spend harvesting honey, repairing equipment, and putting things away for the season, and you'll probably devote 35 to 40 hours a year to your hobby (more if you make a business out of it).

Stings and allergies

If you're going to become a beekeeper, you can expect to get stung once in a while. It's a fact of life. But when you adopt good habits as a beekeeper, you can minimize or even eliminate the chances that you'll be stung.

All bee stings can hurt a little, but not for long. It's natural to experience some swelling, itching, and redness. These are *normal* (not allergic) reactions. Some folks are mildly allergic to bee stings, and the swelling and discomfort may be more severe. And yet, the most severe and life-threatening reactions to bee stings occur in less than 1 percent of the population. So the chances that you're dangerously allergic to honey bee venom are remote. If you're uncertain, check with an allergist, who can determine whether you're among the relatively few who should steer clear altogether of beekeeping.

TIP

Some beekeepers actually look forward to getting stung a few times early each season. They claim that occasional stings produce a kind of tolerance to the swelling and itching that follow, until the side effects of being stung disappear entirely for some. (The sting itself still smarts, though.) However, medical research shows that true allergic reactions worsen with each sting suffered over time. The takeaway? Having an EpiPen on hand isn't a bad idea, just in case you or someone else does experience a severe reaction.

Dealing with nervous neighbors

Bees living near people can cause anxiety, especially in the close quarters of city living or in a suburban environment. Education is, of course, one of the best remedies for making neighbors more comfortable. And so is a tasty bribe. Give a jar of honey to your neighbors to sweeten their view of bees and beekeeping. Promise them that there's more where that came from!

TIP

If your hive has not yet produced honey, don't wait until it does. Just buy someone else's honey and present it to nervous neighbors as a preview of the sweet treat that awaits them in the future.

With the gift jar, include a thoughtfully worded letter that explains what you are planning to do. Let them know it's perfectly legal (assuming it *is* legal in your area). Explain the wonder of honey bees. Exude the virtues of pollination. Share the magic of how local honey fends off pollen allergies. Reassure them that bees rarely sting unless threatened. Give your neighbors time to get past the fear factor; let them digest what they've read and appreciate what they've tasted.

Choosing the Right Hive

Beehives come in many different styles, sizes, and shapes. This section helps you understand the differences among the most popular hives for homesteading purposes and allows you to select a hive style that best meets your needs and objectives. Each has some benefits and drawbacks, but any one of these is functional and fun for your adventure in beekeeping.

Langstroth hive

Hands down, the *Langstroth hive* is the most popular and widely used hive today. Invented in 1852 by Reverend Lorenzo Langstroth, the basic design has remained mostly unchanged, which is a testament to its practicality. See Figure 1-2.

FIGURE 1-2: This is a ten-frame Langstroth hive, showing a bottom board, two deep-hive bodies, and a cover.

The big advantage of this hive is that the bees build honeycomb into frames, which can be removed, inspected, and moved about with ease. Some other advantages to consider regarding the Langstroth hive include the following:

>> **Capacity:** Because this design consists of modular, interchangeable hive parts, you can add extra medium or shallow honey supers as the colony grows and honey production increases. Capacity for bees and honey is virtually unlimited.

>> **Frames:** There are both eight- and ten-frame versions of the Langstroth hive available (the eight-frame version being a slightly smaller and lighter hive in weight than its ten-frame cousin). Both versions use a Langstroth-style of self-centering frame with beeswax foundation inserts.

>> **Universality:** Because the Langstroth hive is so widely used around the world, you can easily find replacement parts, gadgets, and add-ons for this popular hive. They are widely available from many beekeeping supply stores (search the web and you will find many such suppliers).

Kenyan top bar hive

In recent years, interest has increased in the *Kenyan top bar hive,* with its elegantly simple, practical design, particularly because more and more backyard beekeepers are seeking natural and environmentally sustainable options. Top bar hives are used extensively throughout Africa and in other developing countries where building materials are scarce. This particular design (shown in Figure 1-3) is referred to as a Kenyan top bar hive because of its sloped sides, which tend to result in stronger, more balanced combs. In addition, the sloped sides discourage the bees from attaching the comb to the bottom and sides of the hive.

FIGURE 1-3:
The Kenyan top bar hive is likely one of the oldest beehive designs, going back centuries.

Courtesy of Bee Thinking

A Kenyan top bar hive has many design variations. Basically they all consist of a long, horizontal hive body with sloped sides, top bars (not frames), and a roof. It's a practical and functional hive.

Here are some of the basics to consider:

>> **Capacity:** You can't add supers or additional hive bodies. The space is fixed and thus limited to the size of the hive and the top bars it accommodates.

>> **Frames:** There are no frames. This design uses top bars. There are no side bars, no bottom bar, and no full sheets of beeswax foundation to deal with (nor the costs associated with these elements). The bees attach their comb

naturally onto each of the top bars placed in the hive. The top bar hive can be made any length, but it's typically between 3 and 4 feet long, containing approximately 28 top bars in all.

>> **Universality:** The dimensions for top bar hives are not standardized, and thus the gadgets and add-ons that are easy to find for Langstroth hives (for example, feeders, screened bottom boards, honey-extracting equipment) are usually not commercially available for top bar hives. Often beekeeper must custom build their own accessories.

If you plan to also have Langstroth hives, none of the equipment is interchangeable between top bar and Langstroth hives.

However, there are also some cons:

>> There tends to be lower honey production from this type of hive.

>> Combs are much more fragile than comb built in a Langstroth-style frame (with the support of side bars and a bottom rail). Care needs to be taken when removing and handling combs of a top bar hive.

>> Some feel this horizontal design may not be the best option for those keeping bees in areas with long and harsh winters.

>> This hive has the largest footprint of the hives mentioned in this chapter. That may be an issue for beekeepers with limited real estate to work with (such as urban beekeepers).

Warré (people's) hive

The *Warré hive* (shown in Figure 1-4) was developed in France during the early 20th century by Abbé Émile Warré, an ordained priest and an avid beekeeper. His vision was to develop an easy-to-build and easy-to-manage beehive with which everyone could have success (thus, it is often referred to as *the people's hive*). This simple, cost-effective, and efficient design has been gaining renewed popularity among DIY beekeepers.

Here are some of the reasons that the Warré hive has gained such popularity among hobbyists:

>> **Capacity:** The tall, vertical design provides ample room for the colony to naturally grow throughout the season. The beekeeper does not need to anticipate the colony's growth and add hive bodies during the season. All the space that's needed is provided from the get-go.

FIGURE 1-4:
The Warré hive is a top bar hive without foundation that allows the bees to build comb as they would in nature.

Courtesy of Bee Thinking

>> **Frames:** This design does not use frames or foundation. It uses top bars, upon which the bees draw out their own natural comb. There are no side bars, no bottom bar, and no full sheets of beeswax foundation to deal with (nor the costs associated with these elements). The bees build their comb without restriction onto each of the top bars placed in the hive (see Figure 1-5).

>> **Universality:** All the gadgets and add-ons that you might use with a conventional Langstroth hive (feeders, queen excluders, foundation, and honey-extracting equipment) are irrelevant to the Warré. Its design is virtually all-inclusive and requires no extras. However, if you need a new roof, there are an increasing number of beekeeping supply stores offering pre-built Warré components.

The Warré hive provides more natural conditions to the bees, offering a living arrangement that is similar to how bees live in the wild (within the hollow of a tree). As a result, the bees tend to be less stressed and thus less prone to disease.

On the downside, harvesting of honey requires destroying the comb, since it must be crushed to extract the honey. And due to the hive's construction, making artificial swarms, splits, reversals, and other manipulations, such as feeding sugar syrup or administering medications, are difficult or even impossible. But the whole idea of this design is to provide as natural an environment as possible for your bees. Frequent manipulations are contrary to the all-natural objective.

FIGURE 1-5:
The Warré hive
is a top bar
hive without
foundation that
enables bees to
build comb as
they would in
nature.

Courtesy of Bee Thinking

Five-frame nuc hive

The design of the *five-frame nuc (nucleus) hive* is similar to the Langstroth hive, only in miniature (see Figure 1-6). Although the nuc hive may not be your only hive in the yard, it's mighty handy to have one or two of these "mini-me" hives nearby: as a nursery for raising new queens, to house a captured swarm, as a supplementary source of brood, pollen, and nectar, or just to help with pollination.

FIGURE 1-6:
A nuc hive is a
small hive with
a few frames
of bees.

Courtesy of Bee-Commerce

They say that good things come in small packages. See what you think as you review the basic statistics for the five-frame nuc:

- >> **Capacity:** Because this design consists of only five frames, there is no room for expansion as the colony grows in population, so the capacity for bees is limited. Theoretically, you could build additional nuc hive bodies and stack them one on top of the other to allow the colony to grow. That's not really the purpose of a nuc hive, though.

- >> **Frames:** This nuc hive uses a Langstroth-style of self-centering deep frame with deep beeswax foundation inserts. A total of five frames are used with the nuc hive.

- >> **Universality:** Because the nuc uses Langstroth-style frames, you can easily purchase the right size foundation for this hive. Virtually all suppliers sell nuc hives and their associated parts.

A disadvantage of a nuc hive is that it doesn't overwinter well in colder climate zones. It *can* be done, but it takes effort and talent on the part of the beekeeper. Another disadvantage is that these small hives are more fragile and difficult to manage than larger hives. They get overcrowded and swarm frequently, and the population is too small to deal with environmental ups and downs.

Gearing Up for Beekeeping

Beekeepers use all kinds of fantastic tools, gadgets, and equipment. Quite frankly, part of the fun of beekeeping is putting your hive together and using the paraphernalia that goes with it.

Bee-proof clothing

At minimum, new beekeepers should wear a long-sleeved shirt when visiting the hive. Light colors are best — bees don't like dark colors (black, navy, and so on). Wear long pants and slip-on boots. Tuck your pant legs into the boots. Alternatively, use Velcro or elastic strips (even rubber bands) to secure your pant legs closed. You don't want a curious bee exploring up your leg! Better yet, order a bee suit (coveralls) or a bee jacket from your beekeeping supplier. You should also invest in veils and gloves, which are discussed in this section.

Veils

Don't ever visit your hive without wearing a veil. Although your new colony of bees is likely to be super gentle (especially during the first few weeks of the season), it defies common sense to put yourself at risk around upwards of 60,000 bees.

Veils come in many different models (see Figure 1-7) and price ranges. Some are simple veils that slip over your head; others are integral to a pullover jacket or even a full coverall. Choose the style that appeals most to you. If your colony tends to be more aggressive, more protection is advised. But remember, the more that you wear, the hotter you'll be during summer inspections.

FIGURE 1-7: This beekeeper uses a veil-and-jacket combination, leather gloves, and high boots to keep him bee-tight.

Courtesy of Howland Blackiston

TIP

Keep an extra veil or two on hand for visitors who want to watch while you inspect your bees.

Gloves

New beekeepers understandably like the idea of using gloves (see Figure 1-8), but it's best not to use them for installing your bees or for routine inspections.

You don't need them at those times, especially with a new colony or early in the season. Gloves only make you clumsier. They inhibit your sense of touch, which can result in your inadvertently injuring bees. That's counterproductive and only makes them more defensive when they see you coming.

FIGURE 1-8:
Although not needed for routine inspections, it's a good idea to have a pair of protective gloves.

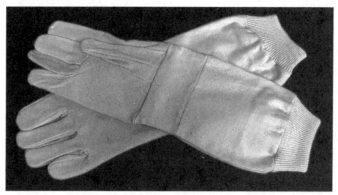

Courtesy of Howland Blackiston

The only times that you really need to use gloves are

» Late in the season (when your colony is at its strongest)

» During honey harvest season (when your bees are protective of their honey)

» When moving hive bodies (when you have a great deal of heavy work to do in a short period of time)

Other times leave the gloves at home. If you must, you can use heavy gardening gloves, or special beekeeping gloves with long sleeves (available from beekeeping supply vendors).

Fundamental tools

Two tools — the smoker and the hive tool — are musts for the beekeeper. They're used every time you visit any kind of hive and are indispensable.

Smoker

The smoker will become your best friend. Smoke changes the bees' behavior and enables you to safely inspect your hive. Quite simply, the smoker is a fire chamber with bellows designed to produce lots of cool smoke. Figure out how to light it so it stays lit, and never overdo the smoking process. A little smoke goes a long way.

TIP

To watch an online video on how to light and properly use a smoker, just go to www.dummies.com/go/beekeepingfd4e.

Smokers come in all shapes, sizes, and price ranges. Two models are shown in Figure 1-9. The style that you choose doesn't really matter. The key to a good smoker is the quality of the bellows. Consider one fabricated from stainless steel to avoid rusting.

FIGURE 1-9: Two styles of smokers.

Courtesy of Howland Blackiston

Hive tool and frame lifter

The versatility of the simple hive tool is impressive. Don't visit your hives without one! Use it to scrape wax and *propolis* (a sticky, resinous material that bees collect from trees and plants and use to seal up cracks and strengthen comb; think "bee glue") off woodenware. Use it to loosen hive parts, open the hive, and manipulate frames. In addition, a frame lifter is used by many beekeepers to firmly grip a frame and remove the frame from the hive. Bee suppliers offer a wide range of styles and designs to choose from. The ones pictured in Figure 1-10 are among the most commonly used.

Elevated hive stand

Elevated hive stands are something you're more likely to build than purchase. Alternatively, you can fashion an elevated stand from a few cinderblocks or a simple post, or you can purchase a commercial-grade stand that's waterproof and comes with a built-in frame rest (see Figure 1-11). In any case, having the hive off the ground means less bending over during inspections and makes the hive far easier to work with.

FIGURE 1-10:
A frame lifter
(top) and a hive
tool (bottom).

Courtesy of Howland Blackiston

FIGURE 1-11:
This commercially
available
hive stand is
weatherproof
and includes a
built-in
frame rest.

Courtesy of Beesmart.com

TIP

To help prevent ants from invading your hive and nesting under your top cover, the legs of the stand can rest in a container of liquid large enough to act as a moat. This will prevent ants from crawling up the legs. Raising the entrance using an elevated hive stand also is a natural way to deter skunks from snacking on your bees.

Frame rest

For users of a Langstroth hive, a frame rest is a super-helpful device. This gadget hangs on the side of the hive, providing a convenient and secure place to rest frames during routine inspections (see Figure 1-12). It holds up to three frames, giving you plenty of room in the hive to manipulate other frames without crushing bees.

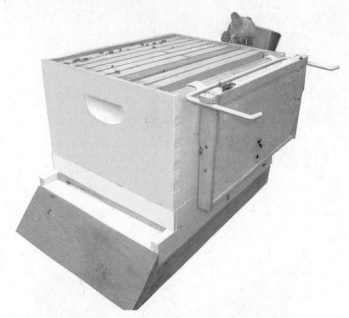

FIGURE 1-12:
A frame rest is
a handy device
for holding
frames during
inspections.

Courtesy of Howland Blackiston

Bee brush

The long, super-soft bristles of a bee brush enable you to remove bees from frames and clothing without hurting them (see Figure 1-13). Some beekeepers use a goose feather for this purpose. Keep that in mind in the event you have an extra goose around the house.

FIGURE 1-13:
Use a soft bee
brush to gently
remove bees
from frames and
clothing.

Courtesy of Howland Blackiston

Chapter **2**

Caring for Your Bee Colony

Although beekeeping doesn't require a huge time commitment for the backyard homesteader, some regular maintenance is involved. Luckily, it's spread out throughout the calendar year, and can be easily incorporated into your normal workflow of planting and composting and weeding and watering and harvesting and canning and feeding chickens and gathering eggs and making jam and fixing the gate and building a tool shed and figuring out what's eating your tomatoes and deciding whether goats are a good idea and coming up with a better way to collect all the rainwater that's just being wasted when it falls on the driveway. (Homesteading is fun, right?)

This chapter lays out a year's worth of what you should be doing for your colony of backyard bees, season by season. It also gets to the sweet and sticky reason why you got into bees to begin with: honey. You learn how to harvest every last drop, whether you're keeping it all for yourself, treating friends and family at gift-giving season, or bottling it for sale as a side business. Finally, every beekeeper needs to be on the lookout for certain problems and diseases that could threaten your hive. This chapter gets you started on keeping your colony healthy and happy.

Busying Yourself with Bee Activity

The seasonal calendar of events in Maine obviously looks different than one in Southern California. But different climates mean different schedules and activities for the hive and beekeeper. Regardless of their precise location, honey bees are impacted by the general change of seasons. Knowing what major activities are taking place within the hive and what's expected of you during these seasons is useful. For a good beekeeper, *anticipation* is the key to success.

This section contains a suggested schedule of seasonal activities for the beekeeper. However, you must note that geography, weather, climate, neighborhood, and even the type of bees influence the timing of these activities. The checklist is written from the viewpoint of a beekeeper experiencing a distinct change in seasons and climate (spring, summer, autumn, winter).

Lazy, hazy, crazy days of summer

Nectar flow usually reaches its peak during summer. That's also when the population of the colony usually reaches its peak. When that's the case, your colonies are quite self-sufficient, boiling with worker bees tirelessly collecting pollen, gathering nectar to convert into honey, and building beeswax comb to store both. Note, however, that the queen's rate of egg laying drops during the late summer. And on hot and humid nights, you may see a huge curtain of bees hanging on the exterior of the hive. Don't worry; they're not running away. They're simply cooling off on the front porch. It's called *bearding* (see Figure 2-1).

Late in summer the colony's growth begins to diminish. Drones are still around, but outside activity begins slowing down when the nectar flow slows. Bees seem to be restless and become protective of their honey.

TIP

A top bar hive colony will sometimes build honeycomb on both sides of the brood nest. This behavior can lead to the colony becoming "honey bound" with no place for the queen to lay. As you inspect your top bar hive colony and notice this behavior, you can simply move the honeycombs toward the rear and insert a few blank bars. This will allow the brood to continue to expand and also help control the urge to swarm.

Your summer time commitment: You can't do all that much until the end of the summer and the honey harvest because your bees are doing it all! Figure on spending about eight to ten hours with your bees during the summer months. Most of this time involves harvesting and bottling honey.

On a summer evening, the bees are cooling off on the exterior of a hive.

Courtesy of Howland Blackiston

Harvest your honey crop at the end of the nectar flow. Remember that in zones experiencing cold winters, the colony requires at least 60 pounds of honey for use during winter.

Falling leaves point to autumn chores

Most nectar and pollen sources become scarce as days become shorter and weather cools in autumn. All in all, as the season slows down, so do the activities within your hive: The queen's egg-laying is dramatically reduced, drones begin to disappear from the hive, and hive populations drop significantly.

Your bees begin bringing in propolis, using it to chink up cracks in the hive that may leak the winter's cold wind. The colony is hunkering down for the winter, so you must help your bees get ready.

Feed your colony. They'll accept a 2-to-1 sugar-syrup feeding (see the "Autumn syrup recipe") until colder weather contracts them into a tight cluster. At that point, temperatures are too cold for them to leave the cluster, so they are likely to ignore your offering.

Keep feeding your bees until they stop taking the syrup, or until the temperature drops, and they form the winter cluster. A hive-top feeder works best. If you are medicating, the first 2 gallons should be medicated with Fumigilin-B — subsequent feedings are not medicated.

If you're in a climate where the winter gets below freezing for more than several weeks, wrap the hive in black tar paper (the kind used by roofers). Make sure you don't cover the entrance or any upper ventilation holes. The black tar paper absorbs heat from the winter sun and helps the colony better regulate temperatures during cold spells. It also acts as a windbreak. This kind of wrap can be done on either a Langstroth hive or a top bar hive.

Place a rock on top, as shown in Figure 2-2, to keep the paper from blowing off. The metal mouse guard keeps unwanted visitors out, and the hole in the upper deep aids ventilation.

Courtesy of Howland Blackiston

Your autumn time commitment: Figure on spending three to five hours total to get your bees fed and bedded down for the winter months ahead.

Clustering in a winter wonderland

A lot goes on inside the hive during the winter. The queen is surrounded by thousands of her workers — kept warm in the midst of the winter cluster. The winter cluster starts in the brood chamber when ambient temperatures reach 54 to 57 degrees (12 to 14 degrees Celsius). When cold weather comes, the cluster forms in the center of the two hive bodies. It covers the *top* bars of the frames in the lower chamber and extends over and beyond the *bottom* bars of the frames in the food chamber (see Figure 2-3).

AUTUMN SYRUP RECIPE

Use a special heavy syrup for feeding bees that are about to go into the winter months. A thicker-consistency recipe makes it easier for bees to convert the syrup into the capped honey they'll store for the winter.

Boil 2½ quarts of water on the stove. When it comes to a rolling boil, turn off the heat and add 10 pounds of white granulated sugar. Be sure you turn off the stove. If you continue boiling the sugar, it may caramelize, and that makes the bees sick. Stir until the sugar dissolves completely. The syrup must cool to room temperature before you can add medication. Note that this is a recipe for thicker syrup than that used for feeding bees in the spring.

If you see clear evidence of nosema (you'll notice mustard brown drips on the hive and at the entrance), you may want to medicate your syrup. A colony with nosema will have a hard time surviving the winter. To medicate the syrup, mix 1 teaspoon of Fumigilin-B in approximately a half cup of lukewarm water (the medication won't dissolve in the syrup). Add the medication to the syrup and stir. Only the first two gallons you feed your bees need to be medicated. Subsequent batches do not need to be medicated.

FIGURE 2-3:
This cutaway illustration shows the winter cluster's position.

Courtesy of Howland Blackiston

Although the temperature outside may be freezing, the center of the winter cluster remains between 90 and 93 degrees (32 and 34 degrees Celsius). The bees generate heat by "shivering" their wing muscles.

No drones are in the hive during winter, but some worker brood begin appearing late in the winter. Meanwhile, the bees consume about 50 to 60 pounds of honey in the hive during winter months. They eat while they are in the cluster, moving around as a group whenever the temperature gets above 40 to 45 degrees (4 to 7 degrees Celsius). They can move to a new area of honey only when the weather is warm enough for them to break cluster.

Bees won't defecate in the hive. Instead, they hold off until they can leave the hive on a nice, mild day when the temperature reaches 45 to 50 degrees (7 to 10 degrees Celsius) to take *cleansing flights.*

Make sure the bees have enough food! The late winter and early spring are especially hazardous because during this time colonies can die of starvation.

Late in the winter, on a nice, mild day when there is no wind and bees are flying, take a quick peek inside your hive. It's best not to remove any frames. Just have a look-see under the cover. Do you see bees? They still should be in a cluster in the upper deep. Are they okay?

REMEMBER

If you don't notice any sealed honey in the top frames, you may need to begin some emergency feeding. But remember that once you start feeding, you *cannot* stop until the bees are bringing in their own pollen and nectar.

Your winter time commitment: During this time, the bees are in their winter cluster, warm inside the hive. Figure on spending two to three hours repairing stored equipment.

Spring is in the air

Spring is one of the busiest times of the year for bees (and beekeepers). It's the season when new colonies are started and established colonies come back to life.

Days are getting longer and milder, and the established hive comes alive, exploding in population. The queen steadily lays more and more eggs, ultimately reaching her greatest rate of egg-laying. The drones begin reappearing, and hive activity starts hopping. The nectar and pollen begin coming into the hive thick and fast. The hive boils with activity.

Conduct an early-bird inspection. Colonies should be given a quick inspection as early in the spring as possible. The exact timing depends on your location (earlier in warmer zones, later in colder zones).

You don't need to wait until bees are flying freely every day nor until the signs of spring are visible (the appearance of buds and flowers). Do your first spring inspection on a sunny, mild day with *no wind* and a temperature close to 50 degrees (10 degrees Celsius).

TIP

A rule of thumb: If the weather is cold enough that you need a heavy overcoat, it's too cold to inspect the bees.

Determine that your bees made it through the winter. Do you see the cluster? The clustered bees should be fairly high in the upper deep hive body. If you don't see them, can you hear the cluster? Tap the side of the hive, put your ear against it, and listen for a hum or buzzing.

If it appears that you've lost your bees, take the hive apart and clean out any dead bees. Reassemble it and order a package of bees as soon as possible. Don't give up. All beekeepers lose their bees at one time or another.

Check to make sure you have a queen. If your hive has a live colony, look down between some of the frames. Do you see any brood? That's a good sign that the queen is present. To get a better look, you may need to carefully remove a frame from the center of the top deep. Can you see any brood? Do you spot any eggs?

WARNING

This inspection must be done quickly because you don't want to leave the frame open to chilly air. If you don't see any brood or eggs, your hive may be without a queen, and you should order a new queen as soon as possible, assuming, that is, the hive population is sufficient to incubate brood once the new queen arrives. What's sufficient? The cluster of bees needs to be *at least* the size of a large grapefruit (hopefully larger). If you have fewer bees than that, you should plan to order a new package of bees (with queen).

Check to ensure the bees still have food. Looking down between the frames, see if you spot any honey. Honey is capped with white cappings (tan cappings are the brood). If you see honey, that's great. If not, you must begin emergency feeding your bees.

Feed the colony. A few weeks before the first blossoms appear, you need to begin feeding your bees (regardless of whether they still have honey).

Reverse your hive bodies. See the upcoming "Reversing hive bodies" section.

Your spring time commitment: Spring is just about the busiest time for the beekeeper. You can anticipate spending 8 to 12 hours tending to your bees.

Caring for Your
Bee Colony

Reversing hive bodies

Bees normally move upward in the Langstroth hive during the winter. In early spring, the upper deep is full of bees, new brood, and food. But the lower deep hive body is mostly empty. You can help colony expansion by reversing the top and bottom deep hive bodies (see Figure 2-4). Doing so also gives you an opportunity to clean the bottom board.

FIGURE 2-4: Reversing hive bodies in the spring helps to better distribute brood and food.

Illustration by Howland Blackiston

Follow these steps:

1. **When a mild day comes along (50 degrees [10 degrees Celsius]) with little or no wind and bright, clear sunlight, open your hive using your smoker in the usual way.**

2. **Place the upturned outer cover on the ground and then remove the upper deep hive body with the inner cover in place.**

3. **Place the deep across the edges of the outer cover so there are only four points of contact (you'll squeeze fewer bees that way).**

4. **Close the oval hole in the middle of the inner cover with a piece of wood shingle or tape.**

    Now you can see down into the lower deep that still rests on the bottom board.

5. **The lower deep is probably empty, but even if some inhabitants are found, lift the it off the bottom board and place it crossways on the inner cover that is covering the deep you previously removed.**

6. **Scrape and clean the bottom board.**

   Note: This is a good opportunity to add a slatted rack. Slatted racks help with the hive's ventilation and can promote superior brood patterns. They also encourage the queen to lay eggs all the way to the front of the hive because of improved ventilation and draft control.

7. **Now stand the deep body — which had been the relatively empty bottom one — on one end, placing it on the ground.**

8. **Place the full hive body (the one that had been on top) onto the clean bottom board (or on the slatted rack, if you added one).**

9. **Smoke the bees and remove the inner cover so you can place the empty deep (the box that had been the lowest) on top.**

10. **Replace the inner and outer covers.**

This reversing procedure enables the bees to better distribute brood, honey, pollen, fresh nectar, and water. Reversing gives them more room to move upward, which is the direction they always want to move.

Repeat this reversal in about three to four weeks, restoring the hive to its original configuration. At that time you can add one or more honey supers above the two brood boxes — assuming the bees are now bringing in their own food and you have ceased feeding.

Expanding the brood nest

Springtime is all about colony expansion. Your top bar hive will begin to build out brood in the direction of the entrance. With incoming nectar and pollen, your job will be to ensure that the brood nest has plenty of room to expand by supplying new bars as needed or by moving the follower board so you always have two to three empty top bars waiting for bee expansion. Observe what your colony is doing and insert either blank bars or more drawn comb from the previous season. If the colony feels it has run out of room to raise brood, it may decide to initiate a swarm.

Holding Out for Honey

It all comes down to honey. That's why most people keep bees. For eons honey has been highly regarded as a valuable commodity. And why not? No purer food exists in the world. It's easily digestible, a powerful source of energy, and simply delicious. In many countries, honey even is used for its medicinal properties. The honey bee is the only insect that manufactures a food we eat. And we eat a lot of it — more than 1 million tons are consumed worldwide each year.

What a thrill it is to bottle your first harvest! You'll swear that you've never had honey that tastes as good as your own. And you're probably right. Commercial honey can't compare to homegrown. Most supermarket honey has been cooked and ultra-filtered; these processes make the product more visually attractive for commercial sale. And alas, some commercial honey isn't even pure honey, having been blended with less-expensive sweeteners to increase profits. Yours will be just the way the bees made it — pure, natural, and packed with aroma and flavor.

Having realistic expectations

In your first year, don't expect too much of a honey harvest from your Langstroth hive. Sorry, but a newly established colony doesn't have the benefit of a full season of foraging. Nor has it had an opportunity to build its maximum population. That's disappointing new, but be patient. Next year will be a bonanza!

Table 2-1 gives you a rough calculation for determining how much honey is in your hive.

TABLE 2-1   **Estimating Honey Yields**

Type of Honeycomb	Estimated Honey Capacity (Per Comb)
Langstroth deep frame	6 pounds
Langstroth medium frame	4 pounds
Langstroth shallow frame	3 pounds
Warré top bar	3 to 4 pounds*
Kenyan top bar	4 to 6 pounds*

Estimating honey yield in top bar hives is difficult because they vary in length and the free-form construction of the honeycomb can vary considerably.

Beekeeping is like farming. The actual yield depends on the weather. Many warm, sunny days with ample rain result in more flowers and greater nectar flows. When gardens flourish, so do bees. If Mother Nature works in your favor, a hive can produce 60 and even up to 100 pounds of surplus honey (that's the honey you can take from the bees). If you live in a warm climate (such as Florida or Southern California), you can expect multiple harvests each year. But remember that your bees need you to leave some honey for their own use. In cold climates, leave them 60 pounds; in climates with no winter, leave 20 to 30 pounds.

Assembling the essential extracting equipment

You need to get the appropriate kind of equipment. This section discusses the various types that you need to extract honey. *Extracted honey* refers to honey that is removed from wax comb. The honey is bottled in a liquid form, as opposed to harvesting comb or chunk honey where the honey isn't removed from the wax comb before it's packaged.

REMEMBER

Harvesting *extracted* honey is easier for you and the bees, and you're far more likely to get a substantial crop than if you were trying to produce *comb* honey. Comb honey requires picture-perfect conditions to realize a successful harvest (large hive population, hard-working and productive bees, ideal weather conditions, and excellent nectar flows).

Honey extractors

An extractor spins honey from the comb using centrifugal force (see Figure 2-5). Extractors come in different sizes and styles to meet virtually every need and budget. Hand-crank models or ones with electric motors are available. Small ones for the hobbyist with a few hives, huge ones for the bee baron with many hives, and everything in between can be found. Budget extractors are made entirely of plastic, while rugged ones are fabricated from food-grade stainless steel.

FIGURE 2-5:
This hand-crank stainless-steel extractor can extract up to six shallow frames at a time.

Courtesy of Howland Blackiston

Uncapping knife

The wax cappings on the honeycomb form an airtight seal on the cells containing honey — like a lid on a jar. Before honey can be extracted, the lids must be removed. The easiest way is by using an electrically heated uncapping knife. These heated knives slice quickly and cleanly through the cappings (see Figure 2-6).

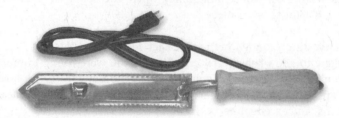

Courtesy of Howland Blackiston

Honey strainer

The extracted honey needs to be strained before you bottle it. This step removes the little bits of wax, wood, and the occasional sticky bee. Any kind of conventional kitchen strainer or fine-sieved colander will suffice. Nice stainless-steel honey strainers (see Figure 2-7) are made just for this purpose and are available from your beekeeping supplier.

Courtesy of Howland Blackiston

TIP

Or you can use a disposable cloth paint strainer (available at your local paint supply store). It does the trick just fine and fits nicely over a five-gallon, food-grade plastic bucket.

Harvesting Your Honey

The day you've anticipated all year is finally here, and it's time to reap the rewards of all your efforts (actually the bees did most of the work, but go ahead and take the credit anyway). It's time for the honey harvest!

Knowing when to harvest

In general, beekeepers harvest their honey at the conclusion of a substantial nectar flow and when the hive is filled with cured and capped honey (see Figure 2-8). Note that the Langstroth frame (top figure) supports the sides and bottom, but the top bar hive (bottom figure) has no such support for its delicate comb.

FIGURE 2-8:
A frame of comb from a Langstroth hive (top) and honeycomb from a top bar hive (bottom).

Courtesy of Howland Blackiston with Jasmine and Zack Cecelic, www.wildhoodfarm.com

Take a peek under the hive cover every couple of weeks during summer. Check in the honey supers that you placed on the hive earlier in the season. Note what kind of progress your bees are making and find out how many of the frames are filled with capped honey.

When a frame contains 80 percent or more of sealed, capped honey, you're welcome to remove and harvest this frame. Or you can practice patience — leave your frames on and wait until one of the following is true:

>> The bees have filled all the frames with capped honey.

>> The last major nectar flow of the season is complete.

WARNING
Don't leave the honey supers on the hive too long! After the last major nectar flow, with winter looming on the distant horizon, the bees will start to eat much of the honey you'd hoped to harvest. Or they will start moving it to open cells in the lower deep hive bodies. Either way, you've lost the honey that should have been yours. And if the weather turns too cold, the honey will thicken or even granulate and become impossible to extract from the comb.

Planning your extracted honey harvest setup

Giving some thought to where you plan to extract and bottle your honey is important. You can use your basement, garage, tool shed, or even your kitchen. You don't need a big area. The guidelines in the following list will help you choose the best location:

>> The space you choose must be absolutely bee-tight. That is to say, you don't want any bees getting into the space where you're working. The smell of all that honey will attract them, and the last thing you want is hundreds (or thousands) of ravenous bees flying all about.

WARNING
>> Never, ever attempt to harvest your honey outdoors. If you do, disaster is imminent! In short order you'll be engulfed by thousands of bees, drawn by the honey's sweet smell.

>> Set up everything in advance, and arrange your equipment in a way that complements the sequential order of the extraction process (see Figure 2-9).

>> Have a bucket of warm water — better yet, hot and cold running water — and a towel at the ready. Life gets sticky when you're harvesting honey, and the water is a welcome means for rinsing off your hands and uncapping knife.

Uncapping tank

Honey extractor

Bottling setup

FIGURE 2-9:
Here's a typical setup, left to right, for extracting honey.

Courtesy of Howland Blackiston

>> If you're using an electric uncapping knife, you'll need an electrical outlet. But remember that water and electricity don't mix well, so be careful!

>> Place newspapers or a painter's drop cloth on the floor. This little step saves time during cleanup. If your floor is washable, that really makes life easy!

Getting the bees out of the honey supers

Regardless what kind of hive you have (frames or top bars), you must remove the bees from the honeycomb before you can extract or remove the honey.

Removing bees from honeycomb can be accomplished in many different ways. Before attempting any of these methods, be sure to smoke your bees the way you normally would when opening the hive for inspection.

WARNING

The bees are protective of their honey during this season. Besides donning your veil, now's the time to wear your gloves. If you have somebody helping you, be sure he is also adequately protected.

Shakin' 'em out

This bee-removal method involves removing frames (one by one) from honey supers and then shaking the bees off in front of the hive's entrance (see Figure 2-10). The cleared frames are put into an empty super. Be sure that you cover the super with a towel or board to prevent bees from robbing you of honey. You can use a bee brush to gently coax any remaining bees off the frames.

FIGURE 2-10:
Shaking bees off a Langstroth frame.

WARNING

Don't try to shake bees off top bar comb because the wax comb is not secured with a wooden frame (unlike a Langstroth frame). The unsupported comb on a top bar is very delicate. The shaking method will likely break the comb apart, so it's best to use the bee brush method to remove bees from the comb.

Shaking and brushing bees off frames aren't the best options for the new beekeeper because they can be quite time-consuming, particularly when you have a lot of supers to clear. Besides, the action can get pretty intense around the hive during this procedure. The bees are desperate to get back into those honey frames, and, because of their frenzy, you can become engulfed in a fury of bees. Don't worry — just continue to do your thing. The bees can't really hurt you, provided you're wearing protective gear.

Blowin' 'em out

One fast way to remove bees from Langstroth supers (not recommended for top bar hives) is by blowing them out. Rest assured, they don't like it much. Honey supers are removed from the hive (bees and all) and stood on end. By using a special bee blower (or a conventional leaf blower), the bees are blasted from the frames at 200 miles an hour. Although it works, to be sure, the bees wind up disoriented and *very* irritated. So again, this method is not recommended for the novice beekeeper.

Fume board and bee repellent

A *fume board* looks like an outer cover with a flannel lining. A liquid bee repellent is applied to the flannel lining and the fume board is placed on top of the honey supers (in place of the inner and outer covers). Within five minutes, the bees are repelled out of the honey supers and down into the brood chamber. Instant success! The honey supers can then be safely removed and taken to your harvesting area.

TIP

This approach can be used for Langstroth- and Warré-style hives. It will not work with a Kenyan top bar hive.

TIP

Keep in mind that a shallow super full of capped honey and frames can weigh 40 pounds. You'll have a heavy load to move from the beeyard to wherever you'll be extracting honey. So be sure to save your back and take a wheelbarrow or hand truck with you when removing honey supers from the hive. Figure 2-11 shows a hive carrier.

FIGURE 2-11: If you have a friend to help, a hive carrier like this makes carrying heavy supers and hive bodies much easier.

Courtesy of Howland Blackiston

Honey extraction from a Langstroth frame

After the bees are out of the honey supers, prepare to process your honey as soon as possible (within a few days). Doing so minimizes the chance of a wax moth infestation. Besides, extracting honey is easier to do when the honey is still warm from the hive because it flows much more freely.

Harvesting honey using an extractor

Follow this procedure when extracting honey from your Langstroth-style frames:

1. **One by one, remove each frame of capped honey from the super.**

Hold the frame vertically over the double uncapping tank and tip it slightly forward. This helps the cappings fall away from the comb as you slice them.

2. Use your electric uncapping knife to remove the wax cappings and expose the cells of honey.

A gentle side-to-side slicing motion works best, like slicing bread. Start a quarter of the way from the bottom of the comb, slicing upward (see Figure 2-12). Keep your fingers out of harm's way in the event the knife slips. Complete the job with a downward thrust of the knife to uncap the cells on the lower 25 percent of the frame.

FIGURE 2-12:
Remove wax cappings using an electric uncapping knife.

3. **Use an uncapping fork (also called a cappings scratcher) to get any cells missed by the knife.**

   Flip the frame over, and use the same technique to do the opposite side.

4. **When the frame is uncapped, place it vertically in your extractor (see Figure 2-13).**

   An extractor is a device that spins the honey from the cells and into a holding tank.

   After you've uncapped enough frames to fill your extractor, put the lid on and start cranking. Start spinning slowly at first, building some speed as you progress. Build speed gradually, without initially spinning the frames as fast as you can because extreme centrifugal force may damage the delicate wax comb. After spinning for five to six minutes, turn all the frames to expose the opposite sides to the outer wall of the extractor. After another five to six minutes of spinning, the comb will be empty. The frames can be returned to the shallow super.

5. **As the extractor fills with honey, it becomes increasingly difficult to turn the crank (the rising level of honey prevents the frames from spinning freely), so you need to drain off some of the harvest.**

   Open the valve at the bottom of the extractor and allow the honey to filter through a honey strainer and into your bottling bucket.

6. **Wait about an hour before bottling.**

   This resting period allows any remaining wax pieces and air bubbles to rise to the top.

Cleaning frames after extracting

Never store extracted frames while they're wet with honey. You'll wind up with moldy frames that have to be destroyed and replaced next year. You have to clean up the sticky residue on the extracted frames. How? Let the bees do it!

At dusk, place the supers with the empty frames on top of your hive (sandwiched between the top deep and the inner and outer covers). Leave the supers on the hive for a few days and then remove them (you may have to coax any remaining bees from the supers by shaking them off the frames, or by using a bee escape or fume board). The bees will lick up every last drop of honey, making the frames bone dry and ready to store until next honey season.

Caring for Your
Bee Colony

FIGURE 2-13:
Place the uncapped frame vertically in the extractor.

Harvesting honey from your top bar hive

Before you can harvest honey from your top bar hive, you must determine whether your colony made excess honey and where it is in the hive.

REMEMBER

A top bar hive has honey stored in bands above the brood area on each comb. That honey is *not* part of the harvest and should be left for the bees' winter stores.

The honey you can harvest comes from those combs completely filled with honey and capped. Remember that these same capped honey stores can also be critical for the survival of the colony in winter. You must approach the harvest in a conservative way, always leaving enough to see the bees through the winter months.

Selecting the comb to harvest

The pure honeycombs are likely to be found farthest from the entrance. In the case of a front-entrance colony, that would be toward the back.

You may notice that some of the honeycombs are capped on top, but the bottom still has some open cells. Those cells will have a higher moisture content and are not suitable to be included in the harvest. If a significant amount of your comb is uncapped, your honey is not ready and should be left in the colony until it's capped.

If just a few rows at the bottom of a comb are not capped, you can harvest those combs and discard the uncapped cells or, better yet, eat them on the spot.

After you've identified what honeycombs you will take, the issue of handling the removed combs comes next. Top Bar combs filled with honey are very heavy and very fragile. The comb can break off the bar when mishandled. It is not recommended that you harvest on very hot days because the likelihood of breakage increases with higher temperatures. Build some kind of covered box or container that will allow you to transport the comb in a protected way to head off a robbing frenzy (see Figure 2-14).

FIGURE 2-14: This box makes it easy to protect and transport comb.

Courtesy of William Hesbach

Harvesting using the crush-and-strain method

If you have just a few combs to harvest, your best option is to crush and strain them. The process is simple but decidedly messy. Slice or break a small section of comb off the top bar and squeeze it to release the honey. Use a clean pair of kitchen gloves to keep your hands from getting sticky. Keep squeezing until all the honey is out. At this point the comb will harden into a ball. Break the ball apart and leave it in the strainer. Continue until all your combs are crushed. Leave them to strain until no honey is dripping through the paint strainer. Once all your honey is strained, it's ready for you to jar or enjoy.

REMEMBER

Regardless of whether you use the crush-and-strain method or a honey press (see the following section) to extract your honey, the comb is destroyed and the bees will have to build new comb before they can store more honey. That's both a disadvantage and an advantage of top bar honey harvesting. The disadvantage is the time and resources that the bees have to expend to draw more comb. The advantage is that you will have fresh, new comb that ensures the purity of your honey products (pesticide buildup can occur on old comb used year after year, as can happen when spinning frames and extracting honey).

Harvesting honey using a honey press

The crush-and-strain method (see the preceding section) of gathering honey from your top bar hive is a sticky, messy job. If you have multiple top bar–style hives, such as Warré or Kenyan hives, and need to process lots of full honeycombs, the honey press procedure is quite simple:

1. **One by one, slice the comb off each top bar using a serrated bread knife or an electric uncapping knife.**

   Allow the entire comb (wax and capped honey) to drop into the honey press's container. Depending upon the size and style of your press, you are likely to get several entire combs into the hopper.

2. **When the hopper is filled, put the lid and screw mechanism in place.**

   Following the manufacturer's instructions (each brand is slightly different), apply pressure (using the screw mechanism; see Figure 2-15) to squeeze and crush the honey from the wax combs. The extracted honey will ooze through the metal or cloth filter, and you can capture it in a clean honey bucket.

3. **Remove the crushed wax, clean the filter, and repeat the process until all the combs have been processed.**

   This method for harvesting honey also harvests a lot of beeswax, so be sure to save and process the crushed wax. Check out Book 3, Chapter 4 for details on creating homemade candles from that beeswax.

FIGURE 2-15:
This is one style of honey press that is used for extracting honey from top bar hives.

Courtesy of Swienty Beekeeping

4. Return the now-empty top bars to their hive.

   The bees will need to rebuild new comb on these bars before they use them again next season.

Honey presses are not that easy to find, and they can be expensive. You are more likely to find honey presses from suppliers in Europe, where they are more commonly used. But if you are clever at building things, the Internet will turn up an array of plans for making your own.

ANTICIPATING BEE PROBLEMS

Despite the best intentions and the most careful planning, things occasionally go wrong. It happens. The bees swarm. The queen is nowhere to be found. The whole colony dies or flies away. That's nothing to be ashamed of. It's part of the process.

The key lesson is to *anticipate*. Discipline yourself to plan ahead and look out for potential problems *before* they happen. You can head off 80 to 90 percent of potential problems if you anticipate trouble and take steps to avoid it.

Swarming and Absconding

Sometimes bees disappear. They simply get up and go. Poof! In one common scenario, called *swarming*, about 50 percent of the colony packs up with the queen and takes flight. In the other scenario, called *absconding*, 100 percent of the colony hits the road, leaving not a soul behind. Neither scenario is something you want to happen.

Swarming

A swarm of honey bees is a familiar sight in the spring and early summer. It's one of the most fascinating phenomena in nature and an instinctive way that honey bees manage the colony's growth and survival. To witness a swarm pouring out of a hive is simply thrilling — though the pleasure may be less so if the swarm of bees is yours!

Starting about a week before swarming, the bees that intend to leave the colony gorge themselves with honey (like packing a box lunch before a long trip). Then, all at once, like someone flipped a switch, tens of thousands of bees exit the hive.

There's no telling where a swarm might land. It could land on any convenient resting place: a bush, a tree branch, a lamppost, or perhaps a piece of patio furniture. In any case, the swarming bees won't stay there long. As soon as scout bees find a more suitable and protected home, the swarm will be up, up, and away.

In its temporary resting place, the swarm is a bundle of bees clustered together for protection and warmth. Their queen is in the center of it all. Depending on the size of the hive that swarmed, the cluster may be as small as a grapefruit or as large as a watermelon. The bees will remain in this manner for a few hours or even a few days while scout bees look for a new home. When they return with news of a suitable spot, off they all go to take up residence in a hollow tree, within the walls of an old barn, or in some other cozy cavity.

If you're a first-year beekeeper, rest assured that a new colony is unlikely to swarm during its first season. But older and more crowded colonies are likely candidates for swarming behavior. Remember, swarming is a natural and normal instinct for bees. At one point or another, your bees will want to swarm. It's only natural. It's nature's way of reproduction. But discouraging them from doing so is a skill every beekeeper should have because a swarm means fewer bees to make honey for you.

The two primary reasons why bees swarm are congestion of the brood area and poor ventilation.

Avoiding congestion

Reverse your hive bodies in the early spring to better distribute the fast-growing population, and add a queen excluder and honey supers *before* the first nectar flow in the early spring to help prevent congestion.

Make sure to anticipate your bees' needs and provide them with more room *before* they need it. If you wait until it's obvious that the brood area is crowded, you're too late! The colony is likely to swarm, and there is little you can do to prevent them from swarming once they've set their minds to it.

Providing adequate ventilation

If your inner cover has a notched ventilation hole in the front of the inner cover, make sure it's open.

Use a short screw or piece of wood to create a spacer in each of the four corners of the inner cover. By doing so, you create a thin gap between the inner cover and the hive and improve airflow into and out of the hive.

Drill wine cork–sized holes in your upper deep (below the hand hold) and in all your honey supers, as shown in Figure 2-16. Doing so not only provides extra ventilation but also provides the bees with additional entrances.

FIGURE 2-16:
A useful way to provide a colony with ventilation is to drill wine-cork–sized holes in the hive bodies and supers.

Courtesy of Howland Blackiston

Caring for Your
Bee Colony

A week after your colony swarms, inspect the hive to determine whether it has a new queen. After the swarm, it will take one to seven days for the queen cell to open and a new virgin queen to emerge. Then allow a week or more for her to be ready to mate with drones. After mating, it will be another two days before she starts laying eggs. That's when you should start looking for eggs.

Do you see eggs? If so, you have a queen, and your colony is off and running. Close things up and celebrate. If there's still no sign of a queen or her eggs, wait a few days and check again. Still no eggs? Order a new queen from your bee supplier. Hive the replacement queen as soon as she arrives

If you don't follow up after a swarm, the colony can easily become queenless without you ever being aware of it. No queen, no brood. No brood, no good.

Absconding

Absconding is a cruel blow when it happens. One day, you go to the hive and find no one home. Every last bee (or nearly every bee) has packed up and left town. Unlike a swarm, which leaves a portion of the colony behind, absconding leaves you with no bees at all.

Typical causes are lack of food, loss of the queen, a hive that's too hot or too wet, an insect infestation, an ongoing wildlife problem, mites and disease, or even colony collapse disorder, which will be discussed later in this chapter.

Playing Doctor: Fighting Disease

Nothing is more devastating than losing a colony to disease. But let's get real. Honey bees, like any other living creatures, are susceptible to illness. Although some of these diseases aren't too serious, some can be devastating.

But none of the health problems that affect bees have any effect on human health. These diseases are 100 percent unique to your bees. They're not harmful or contagious in any way to you or your family.

Medicating or not?

Should you put medication in your hive or not? Wouldn't keeping everything natural and avoiding the use of any chemicals, medications, or antibiotics be better? Maybe you can even save a few dollars. Or should you just take on the attitude of going for the "survival of the fittest"?

Well, do you avoid taking your dog to the vet for distemper shots and heartworm pills? Would you withhold antibiotics if your child came down with bronchitis? Probably not. Bees are no different. Without some help from you, they will eventually have a problem. You may even run the risk of losing your hive entirely. It need not be that way.

Follow a sensible health-check regime and look carefully for signs of trouble every time you inspect your colony. If things get serious, be prepared to judiciously apply remedies to prevent losing your colonies.

TIP

Here's the real key . . . be thoughtful regarding medicating. Unknowingly, many beekeepers have overdone it when it comes to bee health, administering medications "just in case" they might get sick. Don't do it. This kind of prophylactic regime has contributed to an increasing ineffectiveness of meds, antibiotics, and insecticides over recent years. If you choose to medicate, do so only when really necessary.

WARNING

Remember that you should never, ever medicate your bees when you have honey on the hive that is intended for human consumption.

Knowing the big six bee diseases

You should be on the lookout for six honey-bee diseases. Others are out there, but these six are the most common you may face.

Nosema

Nosema is the most widespread of adult honey-bee diseases and contributes increasingly to the weakening or demise of colonies. It was recently determined that there are *two* kinds of nosema, and they are quite different from each other.

Nosema apis is caused by a small, single-cell parasite but is classified as a fungus. nosema apis affects the intestinal tracks of adult bees — similar to dysentery in humans. It can weaken a hive and reduce honey production by between 40 and 50 percent. It can even wipe out a colony of bees. It's most common in spring after bees have been confined to the hive during the winter.

Symptoms include a slow-building colony in the spring, bees that shiver and crawl aimlessly around the front of the hive, and mustard-brown spotting and streaking of feces in and on the hive. The problem is that by the time these symptoms are visible, it has gone too far and is difficult or impossible to treat.

You can discourage nosema apis by selecting hive sites that have good airflow and a nearby source of fresh, clean water. Avoid damp, cold conditions that can encourage the fungus. Provide your hives with full or dappled sunlight. Creating

Caring for Your
Bee Colony

an upper entrance for the bees during winter improves ventilation and discourages nosema apis. Purchase your bees and queens from reputable suppliers.

Nosema ceranae is also caused by a single-cell parasite, and it is also classified as a fungus. But the symptoms of nosema ceranae are not clear, which makes it difficult to identify just by observation. For example, no feces-spotting occurs in the hive. Only a microscopic analysis in the lab can confirm its presence of nosema ceranae. But the devastation on the colony is significant.

Nosema ceranae is relatively new and treatment protocols are still evolving. Beekeepers may want to subscribe to a bee journal and keep yourself informed regarding the latest news on nosema.

Chalkbrood

Chalkbrood is a common fungal disease that affects bee larvae. Chalkbrood pops up most frequently during damp conditions in early spring. It is rather common and usually not that serious. Infected larvae turn a chalky white color, become hard, and may occasionally turn black. You may not even know that your bees have it until you spot the chalky carcasses on the hive's "front porch." Worker bees on "undertaker duty" attempt to remove the chalkbrood as quickly as possible, often dropping their heavy loads at the entrance or on the ground in front of the hive.

No medical treatment is necessary for chalkbrood; your colony should recover okay on its own. But you can help your bees out by removing mummified carcasses from the hive's entrance and from the ground around the hive. Also, usually just one frame will have most of the chalkbrood cells.

Sacbrood

Sacbrood is a viral disease of brood similar to a common cold. It isn't considered a serious threat to the colony. Infected larvae turn yellow and eventually dark brown. They're easily removed from their cells, because they appear to be in a water-filled sack.

No recommended medical treatment exists for sacbrood. But you can shorten the duration of this condition by removing the sacs with a pair of tweezers. Other than that intervention, let the bees slug it out for themselves.

Stonebrood

Stonebrood is a fungal disease that affects larvae and pupae. It is rare and doesn't often show up. Stonebrood causes the mummification of brood. Mummies are hard and solid (not spongelike and chalky as with chalkbrood). Some brood may become covered with a powdery green fungus.

No medical treatment is needed for stonebrood. In most instances worker bees remove dead brood, and the colony recovers on its own. You can help things along by cleaning up mummies at the entrance and around the hive, and removing heavily infested frames.

American foulbrood (AFB)

American foulbrood (AFB) is a nasty bacterial disease that attacks larvae and pupae. This serious threat is highly contagious to bees and, left unchecked, is certain to kill your entire colony. It's the most terrible of the bee diseases.

Be on the lookout for larvae that has changed color from a healthy pearly white to tan or dark brown and die *after* they're capped. Check for cappings of dead brood that appear concave and possibly perforated, or have a wet and greasy appearance. And be aware of a capped brood pattern that is no longer compact, but spotty and random.

If you see these conditions, confirm that it's AFB by thrusting a toothpick or matchstick into the dead brood, mixing it around, and then *slowly* withdrawing the toothpick. Observe the material that is being drawn out of the cell as you withdraw the toothpick. Brood killed by AFB will be stringy and will *rope out* about ¼ inch (like pulling taffy) and then snap back like a rubber band. That test can confirm the presence of AFB.

If you suspect that your bees *have* AFB, immediately ask your state bee inspector or a seasoned local beekeeper to check your diagnosis. Treatment for AFB is subject to state law in the United States. If AFB is rampant, it is likely that your hives and equipment will have to be burned and destroyed. Why such drastic measures? Sleeping spores of AFB can remain active (even on old, unused equipment) for up to 70 years.

WARNING

Be wary of purchasing old, used equipment, no matter how tempting the offer may be or no matter how well you know the seller. If the bees that once lived in that hive ever had AFB, the disease-causing spores will remain in the equipment for decades. No amount of scrubbing, washing, sanding, or cleaning can remedy the situation. Start your new adventure in beekeeping by purchasing new and hygienic equipment.

European foulbrood (EFB)

Larvae infected with the bacterial disease *European foulbrood (EFB)* die *before* they're capped. It's not as horrific as AFB, but it's a problem that should be dealt with if you see signs of it.

Watch for a very spotty brood pattern (many empty cells scattered among the capped brood), sometimes referred to as a shotgun pattern. Capped cells may be sunken in and perforated, but the toothpick test won't result in the telltale ropy trail as described previously for AFB.

Infected larvae are twisted in their cells like an inverted corkscrew. The larvae are either a light tan or brown color and have a smooth, melted appearance as opposed to the glistening, bright white color of normal, healthy larvae.

Because EFB bacteria don't form persistent spores, this disease isn't as dangerous as AFB. Colonies with EFB sometimes recover by themselves after a good nectar flow begins. Although serious, EFB is *not* as devastating as AFB. There's no medical treatment for curing EFB once it has infected a colony, although there are products on the market (such as Tera Bee) that are sold as a preventative of EFB.

If you've detected EFB, re-queen your colony to break the brood cycle and allow the colony time to remove infected larvae. You can even help the bees by removing as many of the infected larvae as you can using a pair of tweezers.

Battling Varroa Mites

Somehow the little pest known as *Varroa destructor*, shown in Figure 2-17, has made its way from Asia to all parts of the world. Varroa has been a problem since the late 1980s (and maybe longer) and has created quite a problem for beekeepers. Resembling a small tick, this mite is about the size of a pinhead and is visible to the naked eye. And like a tick, the adult female mite attaches herself to a bee and feeds on its blood.

Mites attached to foraging worker bees enable the infestation to spread from one hive to another. They reproduce at a fantastic rate and cause a great deal of stress to the colony. The health of the colony can weaken to a point that bees become highly susceptible to viruses. Within a few seasons, the entire colony can be wiped out.

Symptoms of a varroa mite infestation include brown or reddish spots on the white larvae or a batch of newly emerged bees that appear badly deformed. If you actually *see* Varroa on adult bees (usually behind the head or nestled between the bee's abdominal segments), you already have a problem.

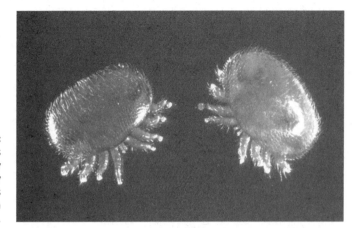

FIGURE 2-17: Varroa mites can seriously weaken a hive by attaching to bees and feeding on their blood.

Testing for varroa mites

If you suspect a Varroa mite problem, confirm your diagnosis with this simple test. The powdered–sugar–shake technique for detecting Varroa is effective, natural, and nondestructive (no bees are killed in the process). You can use this process in the early spring or later fall (when no honey supers are on the hives) as well as in summer (when supers are in place). Follow these steps:

1. **Obtain a 1-pint, wide-mouthed glass jar and modify the lid so it has a coarse screen insert. Just cut out the center of the lid and tape or glue a wire screen over the opening (see Figure 2-18).**

   Size #8 hardware cloth (eight wires to the inch) works well. Now you have something resembling a jumbo saltshaker.

2. **Scoop up about half a cup of live bees (about 200 to 300) from the brood nest and place them in the jar.**

   WARNING

   Don't scoop up the queen!

3. **Put 3 to 4 tablespoons of powdered sugar (confectioners' sugar) into the jar and then screw on the perforated lid.**

   Alternatively, you can use granulated sugar.

4. **Cover the screened lid with one hand (to keep the sugar from spilling out) and shake the jar vigorously for 30 to 60 seconds (like a bartender making a martini . . . shaken, not stirred).**

   TIP

   Shake your sugar cocktail authoritatively. Doing so dislodges any mites that are on the bees.

   This action doesn't really harm the bees, but it sure wakes them up!

Caring for Your Bee Colony

5. **Place the jar in a sunny spot for about a minute to allow the mites to drop off the bees; then give the jar another shake like before.**

6. **Shake all the sugar through the screened top and onto a white sheet of paper.**

7. **Open the top and deposit the bees onto the entry area of the colony (they are too covered with sugar to fly home). You may want to stand to the side because they will be rather unhappy. Shake any remaining sugar onto the paper.**

8. **Count the mites, which are easy to spot because they contrast with the white paper and white powdered sugar.**

If you count ten or more mites, you should proceed with the recommended treatment (see the next section, "Controlling Varroa mites"). Seeing many dozens of mites means the infestation has become significant. Take remedial action fast!

WARNING

Bees can be returned unharmed to the hive using this technique. Although they may be coated with sugar, their sisters will have a grand time licking them clean. Just wait 10 to 15 minutes to let them calm down before releasing them. All that jostling can make them understandably irritable — and revengeful.

Controlling varroa mites

Several techniques and products are available that help reduce or even eliminate Varroa mite populations:

» **Use drone comb to capture Varroa mites.** Bee suppliers sell a special drone foundation that has larger hexagons imprinted in the sheet. The bees will build drone comb only on these sheets. That's useful because Varroa mites prefer drone brood over worker brood. By placing a frame of drone comb in each of your hives, you can capture and remove many mites.

After the drone cells are capped, remove the frame and place it overnight in your freezer. This kills the drone brood and the mites that have invaded the cells. Then uncap the cells and place the frame (with the dead drone brood and dead mites) back in the hive. The bees will clean it out, removing the dead drone brood and mites. The cells will get filled again, and you repeat the process.

» **Powdered-sugar dusting to control Varroa mites.** This technique involves dusting the bees with powdered sugar. The powdered sugar knocks many of the mites off the bees, and the mites fall down through the screened bottom board and perish in the grass below the hive (assuming you are using an elevated hive stand and a screened bottom board with the insert removed). Use this method continually during the season to help keep the mite populations below harmful levels.

Here's the process:

1. **On a day with low humidity, sift a pound of powdered sugar using a baking flour sifter.**

   Do this twice to ensure no lumps.

2. **Put the sifted sugar into an empty (and cleaned) baby-powder container (or something similar).**

3. **Smoke and open the hive. Then place a frame on the rest and do your dusting thing.**

   Remove frames one by one, and dust the bees with the sugar. Aim for light clouds of sugar dust — don't shake the sugar directly on the bees.

4. **Avoid dusting any open cells.**

   You just want to dust the backs of the bees.

5. **Put the dusted frame back into the hive and repeat this process with each frame.**

6. **When you're finished, put a little extra dusting along all the top bars.**

Repeat this process once a week for two to three weeks.

Caring for Your Bee Colony

Both methods fall under the category of Integrated Pest Management (IPM), the practice of controlling pests with minimal chemicals. For more on IPM in the garden, check out Book 1, Chapter 4.)

A few effective and approved *synthetic miticide chemicals* (chemicals that kill mites) are available. One is fluvalinate, which is sold under the brand name *Apistan* and is available from your beekeeping supplier. Another is amitraz, sold under the brand name *Apivar,* and yet another is coumaphos (marketed as *CheckMite+*). Formic acid is also used as a treatment for tracheal mites (sold in plastic strips under the brand name *Mite Away Quick Strips*). In addition, there are "soft" (safer) chemicals such as thymol (marketed as *Apiguard*). Also consider oxalic acid (which sounds scary but is derived from plants). When using one of these treatments, be sure to carefully follow the directions on the package.

Varroa mites aren't the only pest that can threaten your colony. Tracheal mites are another nasty parasite you may encounter. The bad news is that the only way to identify an infestation is by dissecting an adult bee and examining its trachea (breathing tube) under magnification. The good news is that a tracheal mite infestation is a problem, not a hopeless fate.

Other pests that beekeepers need to be mindful of include wax moths, which can destroy wax comb; small hive beetles, which eat pollen, honey, bee brood, and eggs; ants, which can overrun a colony and force the bees to abscond; mice seeking warmth in the hive; and racoons and skunks, who love to eat bees. And believe it or not, bears are a genuine nuisance in more places than you might imagine.

Colony Collapse Disorder

Unless you have been living in a remote cabin on the side of a forgotten hill, you have likely noted that the media has been abuzz with news about "the vanishing bees".

In the autumn of 2006, a beekeeper in Florida filed the first report of a sudden and unexplained disappearance of his bees. They didn't die. They just packed up and left. More reports of heavy losses (mostly from commercial migratory beekeepers) quickly followed. In subsequent years, beekeepers have reported losing anywhere from 30 percent to 90 percent of their hives. Like a firestorm, this tragedy has swept across nearly all of the United States as well as some countries overseas. It has affected both commercial beekeepers and hobbyists. It is a far-reaching problem that has serious consequences.

Colony collapse disorder (CCD) is characterized by the sudden and unexplained disappearance of all adult honey bees in the hive, usually in the fall. In one scenario, a few young bees and perhaps the queen may remain behind while the adults disappear. Or in another scenario, there may be no bees left in the hive. Honey and pollen are usually present, and there is often evidence of recent brood rearing. This abrupt evacuation is ordinarily highly unusual because bees are not inclined to leave a hive if there is brood present.

Colonies that experience CCD have the following characteristics:

>> All or nearly all of the bees pack up and leave within a two- to four-week time period. But there are no dead adult bodies.

>> In some instances the queen and a small number of young-aged survivor bees are present in the brood nest. No bees or very few dead bees are in the hive or at the hive entrances.

>> Capped brood is left behind.

>> There is stored pollen and capped honey.

>> Empty hives are *not* quickly invaded by opportunists (robbing bees, wax moths, small hive beetles, and so on).

Why is CCD making headlines? Well, a world without bees would be a vastly different world. Did you know that honey bees account for 30 percent of everything you eat? Commercial beekeepers provide honey bees to farmers all around the country to pollinate the crops that wind up in our supermarkets. If these pollinating mavericks were all to disappear, there would be reduced crop variety and most likely higher prices in your grocery store. No question about it. Honey bees are critical for agricultural pollination — adding more than $15 billion in value to about 130 crops — especially crops such as berries, nuts, fruits, and vegetables. The unexplained disappearance of so many colonies is not a matter to take lightly.

If you think your hives have fallen to CCD, don't panic. As a new beekeeper, you may be jumping to unwarranted conclusions. To date, CCD has been far more prevalent among commercial beekeepers, although losses among hobbyists like us happen sometimes.

TIP

If you believe you may have a problem, call your state's department of agriculture and ask to speak with the head bee inspector. He or she is likely to provide you with some helpful information. If you have records of the number of mites in your hive prior to the collapse, it will be helpful for the inspector to know.

Caring for Your Bee Colony

No one knows for certain what's causing CCD, at least not at the time of this writing. But researchers have managed to dismiss some "wild" theories and are now focusing on other, more probable causes. In all likelihood, CCD is not due to a single factor.

In a nutshell, several potential causes are being studied by scientists around the world: parasites (such as mites), pathogens (disease), environmental stresses (which include pesticides), and management stresses (including nutrition problems).

Don't let all this gloomy news hinder your enjoyment of beekeeping. Although CCD is a serious concern for our honey bees, researchers are working on potential remedies. As mentioned earlier, becoming a backyard beekeeper is the single best thing you can do to help our honey bees. Embrace and enjoy this glorious hobby, and feel good about helping the honey bee get back on its feet. All six of them.

Chapter **3**

Introducing Backyard Chickens

Chickens make colorful, moving lawn ornaments, and they can even furnish your breakfast. But they do take some attention, expense, and good information to care for properly.

For many, adding a flock of chickens is what truly turns a gardener into a homesteader. You're suddenly caring for a group of animals on your property and, in turn, feeding your family with what they produce. You're practically a farmer! While raising a flock of backyard chickens is one of the most enjoyable parts of homesteading for many, it's not a commitment to be taken lightly. There's plenty for you to consider beforehand to make sure that chicken-keeping is a fit for your family homestead.

This chapter helps you decide if a backyard flock is right or even feasible for you and then goes over various breeds to choose from. Lastly, special consideration is given to what you'll need to provide your flock in terms of housing — all the basics your chickens will expect in a coop.

Thinking Through Chickenkeeping

Before you become a chicken owner, you need to make some important decisions. Caring for a flock is different from bringing home a puppy or taking in a stray kitten, and quite frankly, it ends up not being right for everyone who tries it. A little planning goes a long way toward a good first attempt at raising chickens. Before you start compiling your favorite Sunday brunch recipes for all those fresh eggs you're envisioning, take some time to carefully consider if you and a flock of chickens will be a good match.

Dealing with legal issues

To know whether you can legally keep chickens, first you need to know the zoning of your property. Next, ask your government officials about any laws regarding keeping animals and erecting sheds or other kinds of animal housing in your zone. You need to be concerned about two types of laws and ordinances before you begin to raise chickens:

>> **Laws concerning the ownership of animals at your home location:** Restrictions may cover the number of birds, the sex of the birds, and where on the property chicken coops can be located. In some areas, the amount of property you have and your closeness to neighbors may determine whether you can keep birds and, if so, how many. Your neighbor may own 5 acres and be allowed to keep chickens, but on your 2-acre lot, poultry may be prohibited. Or you may be allowed to keep so many pets per acre, including chickens. Or you may need to get written permission from neighbors. Many other rules can apply.

>> **Laws that restrict the types of housing or pens you can construct:** Do you need a permit to build a chicken coop? Does it need to be inspected?

REMEMBER

Don't take the word of neighbors, your aunt, or other people not connected to local government that it's okay to raise chickens at your home. If you're in the midst of buying a home, don't even take the word of real estate agents about being able to keep chickens or even about the property zoning. You never know whether the information you're getting is legitimate when it comes from a secondary source, so it's best to go straight to the primary source of legal info.

Assessing your capabilities: basic chicken care and requirements

Chickens can take as much time and money as you care to spend, but you need to recognize the *minimum* commitments required to keep chickens. In the next sections, we give you an idea of what those minimums are.

Time

When we speak about time here, we're referring to daily caretaking chores. Count on a minimum of 15 minutes in the morning and in the evening to care for chickens in a small flock, if you don't spend a lot of time just observing their antics. Even if you install automatic feeders and waterers, a good chicken-keeper should check on the flock twice a day. If you have laying hens, collect the eggs once a day, which shouldn't take long.

Try to attend to your chickens' needs before they go to bed for the night and after they're up in the morning. Ideally, chickens need 14 hours of light and 10 hours of darkness. In the winter, you can adjust artificial lighting so that it accommodates your schedule. Turning on lights to do chores after chickens are sleeping is stressful for them.

You will need additional time once a week for basic cleaning chores. If you have just a few chickens, these chores may be less than an hour. The routine will include removing manure, adding clean litter, scrubbing water containers, and refilling feed bins. Depending on your chicken-keeping methods, you may need additional time every few months for more intensive cleaning.

Space

We devote an entire section of this minibook to the all-important chicken coop, and then provide step-by-step plans for building your own (in Book 5, Chapter 3). For now, here are some basic space requirements for your birds.

Each full-size adult chicken needs at least 2 square feet of floor space for shelter and another 3 square feet in outside run space if it isn't going to be running loose much. So a chicken shelter for four hens needs to be about 2 feet by 4 feet, and the outside pen needs to be another 2 feet by 6 feet, to make your total space used 2 feet by 10 feet (these dimensions don't have to be exact). For more chickens, you need more space, and you need a little space to store feed and maybe a place to store the used litter and manure. Of course, more space for the chickens is always better.

As far as height goes, the chicken coop doesn't have to be more than 3 feet high. But you may want your coop to be tall enough that you can walk upright inside it.

Besides the size of the space, you need to think about location, location, location. You probably want your space somewhere other than the front yard, and you probably want the chicken coop to be as far from your neighbors as possible, to lessen the chance that they complain.

Money

Unless you plan on purchasing rare breeds that are in high demand, the cost of purchasing chickens won't break most budgets. Adult hens that are good layers cost less than $10 each. Chicks of most breeds cost a few dollars each. Sometimes you can even get free chickens! The cost of adult fancy breeds kept for pets ranges from a few dollars to much, much more, depending on the breed.

Housing costs are extremely variable, but they are one-time costs. If you have a corner of a barn or an old shed to convert to housing and your chickens will be free-ranging most of the time, your housing start-up costs will be low — maybe less than $50. If you want to build a fancy chicken shed with a large outside run, your cost could be hundreds of dollars. If you want to buy a pre-built structure for a few chickens, count on a couple hundred dollars.

You may have a few other one-time costs for coop furnishings, including feeders, waterers, and nest boxes. For four hens, clever shopping should get you these items for less than $50.

TIP

Bargain hunters can often find used equipment online. Check websites such as Craigslist or eBay, or ask on neighborhood social networks (the modern-day "classifieds"). Lots of people go gung-ho raising chickens and then call it quits after just a year or two; you may be able to score a good bit of gently-used gear at a bargain price!

Commercial chicken feed is reasonably priced, generally comparable to common brands of dry dog and cat food. How many chickens you have determines how much you use: Count on about a third to a half pound of feed per adult, full-sized bird per day. We estimate the cost of feed for three to four layers to be less than $20 per month.

Focusing your intentions: specific considerations

You may be nostalgic for the chickens scratching around in Grandma's yard. You may have heard that chickens control flies and ticks and turn the compost pile. You may have children who want to raise chickens for a 4-H project. Maybe you want to produce your own quality eggs or organic meat. Or maybe you want to provoke the neighbors. People raise chickens for dozens of reasons. But if you aren't sure, it helps to decide in advance just why you want to keep chickens.

Egg layers, meat birds, and pet/show chickens have slightly different housing and care requirements. Having a purpose in mind as you select breeds and develop housing will keep you from making expensive mistakes and will make your chicken-keeping experience more enjoyable.

It's okay to keep chickens for several different purposes — some for eggs and others as show birds, for example — but thinking about your intentions in advance makes good sense.

Want eggs (and, therefore, layers)?

The egg that we enjoy with breakfast was meant to be food for a developing chick. Luckily for us, a hen continues to deposit eggs regardless of whether they have been fertilized to begin an embryo.

If you want layers, you need housing that includes nest boxes for them to lay their eggs in and a way to easily collect those eggs. Layers appreciate some outdoor space; if you have room for them to do a little roaming around the yard, your eggs will have darker yolks and you will need less feed.

Thinking about home-grown meat?

Don't expect to save lots of money raising your own chickens for meat unless you regularly pay a premium price for organic free-range chickens at the store. Most homeowners raising chickens for home use wind up paying as much per pound as they would buying chicken on sale at the local big-chain store. But that's not why you want to raise them.

You want to raise your own chickens because you can control what they eat and how they are treated. You want to take responsibility for the way some of your food is produced and take pride in knowing how to do it.

You need enough space to raise at least 10 to 25 birds to make meat production worthwhile. If you live in an urban area that allows only a few chickens, producing meat probably isn't for you.

Average people who have the space and enough time can successfully raise all the chicken they want to eat in a year. And with modern meat-type chickens, you can be eating fried homegrown chicken 10 weeks after you get the chicks — or even sooner.

Raising chickens to eat isn't going to be easy, especially at first. But it isn't so hard that you can't master it. For most people, the hardest part is the butchering, but the good news is that you can usually find folks who will do that job for you for a fee.

You can raise chickens that taste just like the chickens you buy in the store, but if you intend to raise free-range or pastured meat chickens, expect to get used to a new flavor. The meat has more muscle, or dark meat, and a different flavor. For most people, it's a *better* flavor, but it may take some getting used to.

Considering neighbors

Neighbors are any people who are in sight, sound, and smelling distance of your chickens. Even if it's legal in your urban or suburban area to keep chickens, the law may require your neighbors' approval and continued tolerance. And it pays to keep your neighbors happy anyway. If neighbors don't even know the chickens exist, they won't complain. If they know about them but get free eggs, they probably won't complain, either.

A constant battle with neighbors who don't like your chickens may lead to the municipality banning your chickens — or even banning everyone's chickens. Regardless of your situation, the following list gives you some ideas to keep you in your neighbors' good graces:

» **Try to hide housing or blend it into the landscape.** If you can disguise the chicken quarters in the garden or hide them behind the garage, so much the better. Don't locate your chickens close to the property line, if at all possible.

» **Keep your chicken housing neat and clean.** Your chicken shelter should be neat and immaculately clean.

» **Store or dispose of manure and other wastes properly.** Consider where you're going to store or dispose of manure and other waste. You can't use poultry manure in the garden without some time to age because it burns plants. It makes good compost, but a pile of pure chicken manure composting may offend some neighbors. You may need to bury waste or haul it away. Or if you're already composting in the garden like a good homesteader, consider adding your chicken manure to your pile. It may help mask the smell of the manure and enrich your overall mix. (Plenty more on composting in Book 1, Chapter 4.)

» **Even if roosters are legal, consider doing without them.** You may love the sound of a rooster greeting the day, but the noise can be annoying to some people. Roosters can and do crow at all times of the day — and even at night. Roosters aren't necessary for full egg production anyway; they're needed only for producing fertile eggs for hatching.

» **Keep your chicken population low.** If you have close neighbors, try to restrain your impulses to have more chickens than you really need. We suggest two hens for each family member for egg production. The more chickens you keep, the more likely you'll have objections to noise or smells.

» **Confine chickens to your property.** Foraging chickens can roam a good distance. Chickens can easily destroy a newly planted vegetable garden, uproot young perennials, and pick the blossoms off annuals. They can make walking barefoot across the lawn or patio a sticky situation. Mean roosters can scare or even harm small children and pets. And if your neighbor comes out one morning and finds your chickens roosting on the top of his new car, he's not going to be happy.

You can fence your property if you want to and if it's legal to do so, but remember that lightweight hens and bantams can easily fly up on and go over a 4-foot fence. Some heavier birds may also learn to hop the fence. Chickens are also great at wriggling through small holes if the grass looks greener on the other side.

>> **Be aggressive about controlling pests.** In urban and suburban areas, you must have an aggressive plan to control pest animals such as rats and mice. If your chickens are seen as the source of these pests, neighbors may complain.

>> **Share the chicken benefits.** Bring some eggs to your neighbors or allow their kids to feed the chickens. A gardening neighbor may like to have your manure and soiled bedding for compost. Just do what you can to make chickens seem like a mutually beneficial endeavor.

>> **Never butcher a chicken in view of the neighbors.** Neighbors may go along with you having chickens as pets or for eggs, but they may have strong feelings about raising them for meat. If you butcher at home, you need a way to dispose of blood, feathers, and other waste. This waste smells and attracts flies and other pests. We strongly advise those of you who raise meat birds and have close neighbors to send your birds out to be butchered.

Finally, don't assume that because you and your neighbors are good friends, they won't care or complain about any chickens kept illegally.

Getting the right number

No matter how many chickens you intend to have eventually, if you're new to chicken-keeping, it pays to start off small. Get some experience caring for the birds and see whether you really want to have more. Even if you have some experience, you may want to go to larger numbers of birds in steps, making sure you have proper housing and enough time to care for the birds at each step.

Because chickens are social and don't do well alone, you need to start with at least two birds: two hens or a rooster and a hen. (Two roosters will fight!) Beyond two birds, the number of birds you choose to raise depends on your needs and situation:

>> **Layers:** You can figure that one young hen of an egg-laying strain will lay about six eggs a week, two will lay a dozen eggs, and so on. If the birds aren't from an egg-laying strain but you still want eggs, count on three or four hens for a dozen eggs a week. So figure out how many hens you need based on how many eggs your family uses in a week — just don't forget to figure on more hens if you don't get them from an egg-laying strain.

>> **Meat birds:** It really doesn't pay to raise just a few chickens for meat, but if your goal is to produce meat and space is limited, you can raise meat birds in batches of 10 to 25 birds, with each batch of broiler strains taking about six to nine weeks to grow to butchering size. If space and time to care for the birds aren't problems, determine how many chickens your family eats in a week and base your number of meat birds on that.

If it takes six to nine weeks to raise chickens to butchering age and your family wants two chickens a week, you probably want to buy your meat chickens in batches of 25 and start another group as soon as you butcher the first. Or if you want a rest between batches, raise 50 to 60 meat chicks at a time and start the second batch about three months after the first. Remember that frozen chicken retains good quality for about 6 months.

>> **Pet and show birds:** When you're acquiring chickens for pet and show purposes, you're limited only by your housing size and the time and resources you have to care for them. Full-size birds need about 2 square feet of shelter space per bird; bantam breeds need somewhat less. Don't overcrowd your housing.

If you're going to breed chickens to preserve a breed or produce show stock, plan on at least two hens for each rooster, but not more than ten. In some large breeds with low fertility, you may need a ratio of five or six hens per rooster.

Chicken Breeds

A *chicken breed* is a group of chickens that look similar, have similar genetics, and, when bred together, produce more chickens similar to them. Breeds don't just emphasize visual differences, however. Like most domesticated animals, chickens have been selected over time for their capability to fit certain needs that humans have for them. Some chickens are better as meat birds, some are better at laying eggs, and some are just better looking.

To make choosing the breeds you want to raise easier, chickens are grouped into the following categories:

>> **Dual-purpose breeds:** Dual-purpose breeds are the kind many people keep around the homestead. They lay reasonably well, are calm and friendly, and have enough meat on their bones that excess birds can be used for eating.

>> **Egg layers:** The laying breeds won't sit on their own eggs. In the first year of production, they may lay 290 to 300 eggs and only slightly less for the next two years. They don't make good meat birds, although they can be eaten.

>> **Meat breeds:** Meat birds were developed to have deeper, larger breasts, a
larger frame, and fast growth. Most of the chickens we call meat breeds are
hybrids, although some purebreds, such as the Cornish, are considered great
meat birds. Meat-type birds generally don't lay well.

>> **Show breeds:** Some chickens are kept for purely ornamental reasons. They
generally don't lay a lot of eggs, although their eggs are certainly edible. Most
ornamental-type birds don't make good meals, either, although any chicken can
be eaten. These birds are kept for their beautiful colors or unusual feathers.

>> **Bantam breeds:** Bantams are miniature versions of bigger chicken breeds or
small chickens that never had a larger version. If there's no large version,
they're called true bantams. These birds range from two to about five pounds.

If you want it all: dual-purpose breeds

Home flock owners often want chickens that will give them a decent amount of
eggs and also be meaty enough so that they can use excess birds as meat birds.
The eggs taste the same; you just don't get as many as you do from laying breeds.
The meat tastes the same if you raise the dual-purpose birds like you raise
meat birds, but their breasts are smaller and the birds grow much more slowly.
Figure 3-1 illustrates common dual-purpose breeds, including these breeds:

FIGURE 3-1:
Common
dual-purpose
breeds — Barred
Plymouth Rock
(left) and Wyan-
dotte (right).

>> **Barnevelder:** The Barnevelder is an old breed that's making a comeback
because of its dark brown eggs. Barnevelders are fair layers and are heavy
enough to make a good meat bird, although they're slow growing. They come
in black, white, and blue-laced, as well as other colors. These calm, docile birds
are fluffy looking and soft feathered.

>> **Brahma:** The Brahma is a large, fluffy-looking bird that lays brown eggs.
Brahmas are good sitters and mothers and, as such, are often used to hatch

other breeds' eggs. They're good meat birds, but they mature slowly. Their feet are feathered, and they come in several colors and color combos. They withstand cold weather well, and they're calm and easy to handle.

» **Orpington:** Orpingtons deserve their popularity as a farm breed. They're large, meaty birds, and they're pretty good layers of brown eggs. They'll also sit on eggs and they're good mothers. Buff or golden-colored Orpingtons are the most popular, but they also come in blue, black, and white. These birds are calm and gentle. They can forage pretty well but don't mind confinement.

» **Plymouth Rocks:** These birds are an excellent old American breed, good for both eggs and meat. White Plymouth Rocks are used for hybrid meat crosses, but several other color varieties of the breed, including buff, blue, and the popular striped black-and-white birds called Barred Rocks, make good dual-purpose birds. They are pretty good layers of medium-size brown eggs, will sit on eggs, and are excellent home meat birds. They're usually calm, gentle birds, good for free-range or pastured production.

» **Wyandotte:** These large, fluffy-looking birds are excellent as farm flocks. They're pretty good layers of brown eggs (some will sit on eggs), and they make excellent meat birds. They come in several colors, with Silver Laced and Columbian being the most popular. Wyandottes are fairly quick to mature, compared to other dual-purpose breeds. Most are docile, friendly birds.

» **Turken/Transylvanian Naked Neck:** With an odd name like this, you may think this breed was crossed with a turkey — but it isn't. This breed comes in many colors, but the distinguishing feature is a lack of feathers on the neck. The genes that make the neck bare also contribute to a good-sized, meaty breast area in the chicken and make it easier to pluck. These birds are fairly good layers of medium to large light brown eggs. Although they may look ugly, Turkens are calm and friendly birds.

For egg lovers: laying breeds

If you want hens that lay a certain color of eggs, you can read breed descriptions or you can look at the color of the skin patch around the ear. Hens with white skin around the ear generally lay white eggs. Red skin around the ears generally means brown eggs, in any number of shades. (There's no way to tell what shade of brown from looking at the ear patch.) The breeds that lay greenish–blue eggs usually have red ear–skin patches.

REMEMBER

It's important to remember that all colors of eggs have the same nutritional qualities and taste.

White-egg layers

The white-egg layers in the following list (see Figure 3-2 for an illustration) are the most productive, although many others also exist. Although there are individual exceptions, white-egg layers tend to be more nervous and harder to tame than brown-egg layers. That may be why many home flocks consist of the latter. But if you want a lot of white eggs, the following birds are the best breeds to choose from:

>> **White or Pearl Leghorn:** This bird accounts for at least 90 percent of the world's white-egg production. It's lightweight and has a large, red, single comb. Leghorns also come in other colors that don't lay as many eggs but are fine for home flocks. Leghorns tend to be nervous and don't do as well in free-range or pastured situations as other breeds. California Whites are a hybrid of Leghorns and a Barred breed that are quieter than Pearl Leghorns. Other hybrids are also available.

FIGURE 3-2: Common breeds that lay white eggs — Minorca (far left), white Leghorn (middle), and Hamburg (right).

Illustration by Barbara Frake

>> **Ancona:** Anconas lay large white eggs. They're black feathered, and some feathers have a white tip that gives the bird a dotted appearance. They're similar in shape to the Leghorn. Anconas are flighty and wild acting. Originally from Italy, they're becoming rare and harder to find.

>> **Andulusian:** The Andulusian chicken has enjoyed an upswing in popularity in recent years. Originally developed in Spain, the bird is known for its beautiful blue-gray shade; the edges of the feathers are outlined in a darker gray. These chickens are good layers of medium to large white eggs. They are lightweight birds and like to fly, which can be a problem when confining them. Andulusians are a purebred breed of chicken, but the blue color doesn't breed true: Offspring can be black or white with gray spots, called a splash. These colors are equally fine as layers — they just can't be shown.

» **Hamburg:** One of the oldest egg-laying breeds, Hamburgs are prolific layers of white eggs. They come in spangled and penciled gold or silver, or solid white or black. Hamburgs of all colors have slate-blue leg shanks and rose combs. They're active birds and good foragers, but they're not especially tame.

» **Minorca:** Minorcas are large birds that lay lots of large to extra-large white eggs. They come in black, white, or buff (golden) colors. Minorcas can have single or rose combs. They're active and good foragers, but they're not easy to tame. The Minorca is another bird that's becoming hard to find.

Brown-egg layers

For home flocks, brown–egg layers are popular (see Figure 3-3). The brown eggs these birds lay can vary from light tan to deep chocolate brown, sometimes even within the same breed. As hens get older, their eggs tend to be lighter in color.

FIGURE 3-3: Common brown-egg layer breeds — Australorp (left) and Rhode Island Red (right).

Illustration by Barbara Frake

Some of the best brown–egg layers follow:

» **Isa Brown:** This hybrid makes up the world's largest population of brown-egg layers. Isa Browns are a genetically patented hybrid chicken. Only a few hatcheries can legally produce and sell the chicks, which means chicks hatched at someone's home or at a hatchery other than a licensed one aren't selling real Isa Browns. Isas are a combination of Rhode Island Red and Rhode Island White chickens — which are considered to be separate breeds, not colors — and possibly other breeds.

Isa Brown hens are red-brown in color, with some white under-feathering and occasional white tail feathers; the roosters are white. The hens lay large to extra-large brown eggs that range in color from light to chocolate brown. These calm and gentle birds are easy to work with and are also good foragers.

They may be production birds, but they have great personalities and are people-friendly. The disadvantages are that they can't be kept for breeding (they don't breed true), and the roosters don't make good meat birds.

» **Amber Link:** This breed is a close relative to the Isa Brown, with a slightly darker brown egg that tends to be medium to large in size. Amber Links are white with some gold-brown feathers in the tail and wing area. They're productive and hardy, and are also calm, gentle birds. You'll probably be able to find them only at hatcheries that sell Isa Browns.

» **Red Star, Black Star, Cherry Egger, and Golden Comet:** All these are variations of the same breeding that produced Isa Browns. Some were developed from New Hampshires or other heavy breeds other than Rhode Island Reds. They're prolific layers of brown eggs, but they won't sit on eggs. They also don't make good meat birds because of their light frames. They're usually calm and friendly birds. If you're not going to breed birds and you just want good egg production, any of these chickens will fill the need.

» **Australorp:** A true breed rather than a hybrid, Australorps lay a lot of medium-size, light-brown eggs. Before Isa Browns, they were the brown-egg-laying champions. Both the hens and the roosters are solid black birds with single combs. They're calm, they mature early, and some will sit on eggs. They were developed in Australia from meat birds, and the roosters make moderately good eating.

» **New Hampshire Red:** New Hampshire Reds are similar to Rhode Island Reds, and the two are often confused with one another. True New Hampshire Reds are lighter red, they have black tail feathers and the neck feathers are lightly marked with black. They're more likely to brood eggs than Rhode Island Reds. New Hampshire Reds are usually calm and friendly but active. The breed has two strains: Some are good brown-egg layers, whereas others don't lay as well but are better meat birds.

» **Rhode Island Red:** Rhode Island Reds were developed in the United States from primarily meat birds, with an eye toward making them productive egg layers as well. They lay a lot of large brown eggs. Both sexes are a deep red-brown color and can have a single or rose comb. They're hardy, active birds that generally aren't too wild, but the roosters tend to be aggressive.

» **Rhode Island White:** Rhode Island Whites were developed from a slightly different background than Rhode Island Reds, which is why they're considered separate breeds and can be hybridized. They lay brown eggs. They birds are white with single or rose combs, and they're calm and hardy.

» **Maran:** These birds aren't recognized as a pure breed in all poultry associations. They are sometimes referred to as Cuckoo Marans — *cuckoo* refers to a color type (irregular bands of darker color on a lighter background). The breed has several color variations, including silver, golden, black, white, wheat, and copper. Marans were once rare, but they're now popular for their very dark brown eggs. (Remember, though, eggs of different colors taste the same!) Not every Maran lays equally dark eggs. The eggs vary in size from medium to large. Most Marans are good layers, but they're not as good as some of the previously noted breeds. The various strains exhibit a lot of variation in the breed in terms of temperament and whether they will brood.

>> **Welsummer:** Welsummers are also popular for their very dark brown eggs, which are medium to large in size. The hens are partridge colored (dark feathers with a gold edge), whereas the roosters are black with a red neck and red wing feathers. As members of an old, established breed, Welsummers are friendly, calm birds. They're good at foraging, and some will sit on eggs.

Colored-egg layers

Like the brown-egg layers, the colored-egg layers are also popular with home flock owners (Figure 3-4 illustrates two). Colored-egg layers are a novelty. Despite catalogs that show eggs in a rainbow of colors, their eggs are shades of blue and blue-green. Sometimes brown-egg layers whose eggs are a creamy light brown are said to lay yellow eggs. Pink, red, and purple eggs are said to exist, but these colors are generally caused by odd pigment mistakes and often aren't repeated. Some colors also are in the eye of the beholder (or the camera exposure), and what you call pink we may call light reddish-brown.

FIGURE 3-4:
Common colored-egg layer breed — Araucana.

Looking to add some pops of color to your egg collection basket? Check out these chicken breeds:

>> **Ameraucana:** The origin of the Ameraucana is debatable: Some say it developed from the Araucana (see the next bullet), whereas others say it developed from other South American breeds that lay blue eggs. Ameraucanas come in many colors. They have puffs of feathers or muffs at the side of the head, and

some have beards. They have tails, which help distinguish them from Araucanas. Their temperament varies; however, many will sit on eggs. The eggs are blue or blue-green.

>> **Araucana:** This breed of chicken is seldom seen in its purebred form. Many chickens sold as Araucana are actually mixes, so buyer beware. Purebred Araucanas have no tail feathers. They either have tuffs (small puffs of feathers at the ears) instead of large muff clumps or are clean faced. They don't have beards, and they have pea combs. Most have willow (gray-green) legs. The breed has many color variations. Araucanas lay small blue to blue-green eggs and are not terribly prolific layers. They're calm and make good brooders.

>> **Easter Egger:** These birds are the mutts in the world of chickens because no one is quite sure of their background. They're usually a combination of the previous breeds and maybe some other South American blue-egg layers or other layers. They can be a bit more prolific in egg laying, but the egg color and temperament of the birds, as well as their adult body color, range greatly. They lay shades of blue, blue-green, and olive eggs.

Best breeds for the table

In the not-so-distant past, most meat chickens were young males that were the excess offspring from laying or show birds. They were kept just long enough to make a good meal — and that usually meant about five to six months of feeding and caring for the young roosters. The excess males in most heavy, generally brown-egg-laying breeds of chickens were used as meat. And in your great-grandparents' day, any hen that quit laying was also used for meat.

About 50 years ago, breeders began to create hybridized strains of chickens specifically for meat (see Figure 3-5). They grew fast and gained weight quickly on less feed than other chickens. They had more breast meat, something consumers seem to want. Over the years, these hybrids — particularly one hybrid, a cross between White Rocks and White Cornish breed chickens — have dominated the commercial meat market. In fact, almost every chicken you can buy in a grocery store is a strain of the previously mentioned cross.

Most meat birds stem from one hybrid, but home flock owners can consider other good meat breeds as well. Many backyard breeders are trying to develop meat breeds that grow quickly and have good meat yield, but are hardy and active enough to do well in pasture or free-range situations.

The meat of these other meat breeds may taste slightly different if the birds are raised on pasture and take longer to grow. The meat is a little firmer, and there's less breast meat. The taste is described by some as old-fashioned chicken flavor, which is hard to describe unless you've eaten both types. If the chickens eat commercial feed and aren't allowed to get too old before butchering, the older type meat birds taste much like hybrid meat birds. The advantage of hybrids is that they grow about twice as quickly and, on less feed, than conventional meat breeds.

FIGURE 3-5: Common meat breeds — Jersey Giant (left) and Cornish X Rock (right).

If you're raising chickens for meat, here are some breeds to consider:

» **Cornish X Rock hybrids:** Almost all chickens sold for meat today are a hybrid of White Cornish and White Rock chickens. They've been tinkered with until we now have an extremely fast-growing bird with huge breasts. They're often ready to butcher at 10 weeks, and they do a remarkable job of converting feed into meat. They have soft, tender-textured, bland-flavored meat and lots of white breast meat. Both sexes make good eating and grow at nearly the same rate. If you have eaten only store-purchased chicken, you certainly know how they taste.

Different strains exist, even some where feather color has been introduced. Basically, however, commercial meat birds are Cornish-Rock crosses. These birds have special nutritional needs and aren't good for free-range or pastured poultry. They're excellent if you want quick, plump meat birds, but they're not good for anything else.

These breeds gave up some features to achieve these meat goals. They're closely related genetically, with three or so large firms controlling the production of parent stock. They have to be managed carefully and fed a high-protein diet to avoid problems with their legs and hearts. Basically, they're basketballs with feathers, they're inactive, and they spend most of their time eating. They can't reproduce normally.

» **Cornish:** The Cornish is an old breed known for its wide stance and big breasts. Several colors other than the white ones used to make meat hybrids exist, including red, buff, and laced patterns. They have a rose comb, and their feathers are tight and sleek. These birds are poor layers of small white eggs; some will brood. They can be aggressive with each other, but they're fairly tame with keepers. Cornish chickens are only fair foragers and are better raised in pens.

>> **Jersey Giants:** This American breed comprises the world's largest chickens. They come in black or white. They're meaty birds, but they grow slowly. Jersey Giants are fairly good layers of medium-size brown eggs. They're calm, they're good at foraging, and they make good brooders.

>> **Freedom Rangers/Red Rangers:** These birds were developed to be good pasture-fed meat birds, primarily for the organic meat market. They thrive on lower-protein feed and are better foragers than Cornish-Rock crosses. Most are red in color, with a few barred or black spotted feathers; gray and bronze colors are also seen. These birds take a few weeks longer than the Cornish-cross broilers to be ready to butcher, but many people think they taste better. They're also less likely to suffer from leg problems or die of heart failure than the Cornish-cross broilers. Rangers can be hard to find, and the breed still has a lot of variability: Some birds mature faster and have more meat than others.

Analyzing the Anatomy of a Coop

If you plan on keeping chickens, you'll need somewhere for them to live. A dedicated chicken coop is a must for anyone getting into the hobby, and something you'll need to figure out fairly early in the process. And it won't take much shopping around for you to realize that you will have a lot of options when it comes to housing your flock.

Whether you buy a pre-built coop or build your own housing (Book 5, Chapter 3 has detailed construction plans for a basic coop), you can go as simple or as fancy as you want.

Although the aesthetics may mean a great deal to you and your family as you embark on your coop-building adventure, the chickens, quite frankly, couldn't give a cluck. To your birds, a new chicken coop needs only to have a few select things going for it. Here's a quick list of what you need to consider before you start building a coop or settle on a specific design.

Providing the basics

Whether the coop you have pictured in your mind is a basic box cobbled together from some scrap wood or an enormous architectural masterpiece with its own ZIP code, a coop must provide the following:

>> **Shelter:** Even wild chickens take cover when the weather turns nasty. If you're going to keep chickens in your suburban backyard, you have to give them a place where they can find shelter from rain, wind, heat, and cold.

>> **Protection:** Humans aren't the only carnivores who enjoy a finger-lickin' good chicken dinner every now and again. A primary requirement of any coop is that it effectively offers protection from predators.

>> **Space:** Regardless of your property's space constraints, here's a golden rule to always keep in mind: Your coop should provide 2 to 4 square feet of floor space for each bird you keep.

>> **Lighting:** Chickens need around 14 hours of sunlight every day. They aren't always able to get all of it outdoors. Whether it's via a window, a door, or a skylight, your coop needs to allow some light inside.

>> **Ventilation:** Chickens poop. Often. Wherever they happen to be when nature calls. The coop will get stinky. You can't prevent that, but you must exhaust that ammonia-saturated air for the health of you and your birds.

>> **Cleanliness:** Once again, chickens poop. The coop will get messy. You need to think through how you, their caretaker, will take care of that dirty job on a regular basis.

REMEMBER

Just because a neighbor in your area has chickens or a mighty fine backyard coop or both does *not* automatically mean that everything is cool for you to do the same. His property's zoning may be different from yours. He may have started raising chickens before some change in local laws or the advent of the neighborhood's covenants. He may have gone through proper channels to obtain a zoning variance. Or it may just be that he's in violation of the law himself and keeping chickens illegally.

Do your homework and know what's acceptable before investing your time, effort, and money in a backyard flock or a built-from-scratch chicken coop. Be sure to check with local government officials about zoning restrictions and whether building permits are needed for constructing a coop on your property. This may mean a trip to your city or township hall, the community planning board, the county clerk's office, or even animal control! And even if *they* all give you the green light, make sure your neighborhood or subdivision doesn't have a rule against a backyard chicken coop.

Figuring out features

Even though coops come in a myriad of shapes and sizes, with special amenities and added quirks as varied as the chicken-owners who build them, there are a few basic features that every chicken shelter should have. Think of the following items as furniture for your coop, the physical things that take an empty structure and turn it into a chicken's home:

>> **Roosts:** A *roost* is where your chicken will sleep. True free-range chickens in the wild find a tree branch to perch on each night to sleep. This offers them protection from non-climbing predators, and a branch under the canopy of a tree can provide cover from hungry owls and nasty weather. In your coop, a horizontally-oriented pole or board that's elevated off the floor serves the same function, as seen in Figure 3-6.

REMEMBER

Aim for giving each bird at least 12 inches of roost. Your roost (or roosts) should be as high as possible inside the coop while still allowing your chickens to sit fully upright on it. (But because chickens aren't big flyers, they may need some help reaching the roost, especially as they get older. A ramp or series of horizontal "steps" to the roost bar can be used as needed.) Also, realize that the area directly under the roost will collect the greatest concentration of droppings, so plan accordingly.

FIGURE 3-6:
A simple roost
is a chicken's
master bedroom.

>> **Nest boxes:** If you're keeping chickens for their eggs, nest boxes are a necessity (even though many owners of particularly-finicky chickens will tell you that their nest boxes go unused more often than not). A *nest box* (see Figure 3-7) is exactly that: a safe, comfortable, and secluded spot where your hens can lay their eggs.

REMEMBER

- Hens will share nest boxes, so having one nest box for every two (or even three) birds is sufficient.

- Each box should be a minimum of 12 inches square, or big enough so a chicken can comfortably walk in, turn around in a circle, and then stand fully upright when she's done laying.

- A nest box should be in a dimly lit and warm area of the coop, no more than 3 or 4 feet off the floor.

- If you have more than one box, bunch them together to allow the birds to socialize with one another as they do their business.

FIGURE 3-7:
Nest boxes are critical if you're encouraging egg production from your flock.

» **Runs:** A *run* is the yard for your chicken coop, giving your flock access to fresh air and sunshine. It's an open-air space, usually wrapped in some sort of fencing material and may even be fully covered by a roof. A run should allow each bird to have 3 to 6 square feet, but more is better. For most backyard chicken owners, a coop that incorporates the run into one structure is generally easiest to build and maintain, but folks with enough land may prefer to have a large fenced run that encompasses the chickens' shelter, or even allow the birds to roam free-range with no fencing at all.

» **Ramps:** Chickens are birds, but that doesn't mean they soar through the air like eagles. Many coops are built with a sizable (for a chicken) drop from the shelter down to the ground. Your chickens will be much happier if they don't have to flutter and flop their way in and out of the coop on a regular basis. Look at constructing a simple ramp that lets your flock strut up and down in style. It usually requires no more than a few pieces of scrap wood, but it'll make all the difference in the world to your birds.

Building your own chicken coop is a great way to save some money and a low-pressure way to work on your carpentry skills. No matter your tool prowess, your flock will be forgiving when it comes to the craftsmanship of their coop, and you'll be just a little more self-sufficient for having done it yourself. Check out Book 5, Chapter 3 for step-by-step instructions for a basic coop that checks all the boxes.

Chapter **4**

Raising Your Chicken Flock

So you've decided to get chickens. Now what? Bringing your birds home and introducing them to your yard is just the beginning of this new adventure. And making your flock an integral contributing part of your backyard homestead? Well, that will require a little bit of effort on your part.

This chapter covers feeding your chickens, explains the ins and outs of raising baby chicks, lays out the threats presented by pests and predators, and cracks open what you need to know about the reason why you're considering chickens in the first places: eggs. All the information in this chapter will help ensure that you're not just — ahem — "winging it" when it comes to raising chickens.

Feeding Your Flock

Probably more controversy swirls over feeding chickens than any other part of chicken raising — *everybody* has an opinion. Some believe you don't need to feed chickens at all; just turn the birds loose to find their own feed. Others devise elaborate diets that chickens love but that really aren't necessary. Chickens aren't fussy eaters; they'll eat just about anything. However, they're like small children: When faced with an abundance of choices, they don't always make the wise ones.

Chickens aren't vegetarians by nature. They're *omnivorous*, meaning that they eat both animal protein and plant-produced foods such as seeds, fruits, and leaves. Wild chickens get their protein in two ways:

>> **They actively hunt for it.** They chase butterflies and grasshoppers and gobble up tiny frogs and baby mice.

>> **They scavenge it.** They have no qualms about picking apart a dead carcass, including the body of another chicken.

In a domesticated setting, chickens still love to roam the grounds looking for food, but the places we choose to keep them don't always support their nutritional needs. Most chickens need to be fed by you, the chicken-keeper.

Nutritional needs

Chickens need 16 to 24 percent protein in their diet, depending on their age and intended use. Laying hens need good-quality protein in their diet to produce quality eggs for long periods of time. If broiler-type birds don't get enough protein, their legs and wings may become deformed, and they may become unable to walk. They then need to be disposed of because they won't eat well.

Chickens don't require a lot of fat. High-energy broiler feeds need 6 to 7 percent fat, and laying feed and chick starter need about 3.5 to 4 percent fat. Hens do need some fat for the production of egg yolk, but carbohydrates should furnish the bulk of the diet, and a commercial diet based on grain easily supplies them. Carbs are burned in the bodies of all animals as fuel for all life processes, such as breathing and growth. Diets based on pasture or vegetation need grain supplements to provide enough carbohydrates.

Chickens require all the vitamins and minerals we do except vitamin C, which their bodies can make. Chickens get these vitamins and minerals from a properly formulated feed. Some types of chickens may need more of some nutrients. Layers, for example, need more calcium than other birds to continue laying well. This variation is why having the expertise of chicken nutrition specialists to formulate rations is so valuable.

WARNING

Some people have an abundance of homegrown grain or other products available to them and want to use those ingredients and their own recipe to supply to a feed mill. Despite what most people assume, the homemade recipe approach has more drawbacks than positives. For starters, homemade feed *isn't* cheaper than store-bought. Moreover, making your own recipes requires a complex understanding of chicken nutrition. And beyond those two negatives, most mills won't even custom-mix less than 1,000 pounds of feed.

Choosing the right commercial feed

As with other animals' feeds, chicken feed runs the gamut from top-quality name-brand feeds to poor-quality cheap feed. If a feed is labeled "complete and balanced," it must contain the recommended amounts of nutrients set by the National Research Council for poultry of the listed type and age.

When choosing commercial feed, first look for feed that suits your chickens' age and type, such as meat bird starter, layer, or all adult poultry. Most feed stores also sell a general-purpose poultry feed that you can give to birds not intended to be meat birds or layers, as well as a few specialized feeds.

Starter rations (for chicks)

The ration for layer-breed chicks should be 20 percent protein. It's usually just called "starter feed." From the time they start eating, meat chicks need a high-protein feed of about 22 to 24 percent protein for the first six weeks. It's called "meat bird starter" or "broiler starter."

If you've just received some baby chicks that you intend to be laying hens in the future, look for "chick starter." Buy the same feed for pet or show birds. But if you have meat-type chicks, buy "meat bird or broiler starter."

TIP

If you have different types of birds in a brooder, it's better to feed the higher-protein meat bird feed to all the chicks than use a lower-protein feed. However, separating your future layers from meat birds when they leave the brooder is strongly recommended. Meat birds need a protein level of about 22 to 24 percent until they're butchered, which is too high for layers.

Layer rations

When chickens that are being raised to be laying hens leave the brooder, or at six weeks, you need to change from a starter ration to the next level of feed. Taking care to feed young laying chickens correctly results in healthy birds that give you optimum egg production. Because they're around longer than meat birds, you should take an additional feeding step when raising them from chicks.

Here are the types of rations you should use:

>> **Grower pullet ration:** The ration for growing pullets, from leaving the brooder at 6 weeks to about 14 weeks, should be about 18 percent protein. You want them to grow slowly enough to develop good strong bones and to reach a normal body weight before they begin producing eggs. High-protein diets tend to hurry the birds into production before their bodies are ready.

Finding a feed labelled "grower" with this level of protein may be hard. If you can't find the 18 percent grower feed, use the 16 percent finishing ration listed in the next bullet. These feeds are usually called "grower-finisher" feeds.

>> **"Developer or finishing" pullet ration:** From 15 weeks to 22 weeks, it's ideal to lower the protein level of the feed to 16 percent. The object is to get pullets well grown without too much fat.

Your feed should have normal levels of calcium and other vitamins until the birds start laying. Feeding an adult layer diet high in calcium and phosphorus to birds that aren't laying yet can damage their kidneys. If young hens start laying early, switch them right over to a laying ration.

>> **Adult layer rations:** After the hens reach the age of 22 weeks or begin laying, and throughout their laying careers, they need a protein level of 16 to 18 percent. The calcium and minerals should be formulated for laying hens. A rooster housed with a laying flock will be fine consuming laying rations. These feeds are appropriately called "layer feed."

WARNING

Don't force extra calcium and minerals on hens by adding things to a properly formulated feed. Too much calcium can cause kidney failure. If you're getting a lot of thin eggshells or soft-shelled eggs, give your hens some calcium in the form of crushed oyster shells in a feeder where they can choose the amount.

Broiler rations

Home flock owners may encounter two types of meat birds: the Cornish X Rock crosses that grow extremely quickly and require precise diets, and the excess males from heavy breeds of chickens, which require slightly different management. Here are the details:

>> **Cornish X Rock broiler hybrids:** After the first six weeks, you can lower the protein percentage for these birds to 18 to 20 percent until they're butchered. "Meat bird" or "broiler grower-finisher" is generally used on the label for these feeds aimed at meat birds in their last weeks. Many people feed starter rations for broilers right up to butchering — that strategy is fine, although grower rations are generally cheaper. (Check the label, if the starter feed is medicated, to see if you need to stop feeding that brand a few days before butchering.) A slightly lower protein percentage in the last few weeks of these broiler hybrids' lives may keep them from sudden death syndrome, a condition in which rapidly growing birds flip over on their backs and die, and prevent them from getting weak legs.

>> **Heritage birds, dual-purpose males, and free-range meat birds:** These types of meat birds grow more slowly and add less muscle meat than the

broiler hybrids. They take longer to reach a satisfactory butchering rate. After the first six weeks, you can lower the protein to 18 to 20 percent for the next six weeks; after that, protein content can be 16 percent.

Whole-grain mixtures or scratch feed

Chickens do love whole-grain mixes, but they're almost impossible to accurately mix to provide all the nutrients a chicken needs. Many cheaper mixes are filled with pieces of corn cob and seeds that chickens don't seem to care for, such as milo. Scratch and whole-grain mixtures are best used to supplement the diets of chickens that have good free-range or pasture conditions or to relieve boredom in confined birds.

Selecting a form of feed

Most chicken feed is ground, mixed, cooked, or steam-treated and then turned into mash, crumbles, or pellets. When products are mixed and bound together, each piece contains a balanced proportion of the mix. The vitamins and minerals don't sift out to the bottom, and chickens aren't able to pick out favorite pieces and waste others.

Feed comes in three forms:

>> **Crumbles:** In research done on feeding chickens, the birds seemed to prefer medium-size pieces of feed, commonly known as *crumbles,* and they seemed to grow better and lay eggs better on this type of feed. Crumbles are broken-up pellets. Finisher rations for pullets or meat birds are commonly crumbles, but adult feeds also can be crumbles.

>> **Pellets:** Pellets are the second-best method of feeding and the second most popular form of feed with chickens. *Pellets* are long, narrow, cylinder-shaped pieces of compressed feed. They're usually used for adult birds.

>> **Mash:** Mash is the least preferred form of feed. *Mash* is finely ground feed; the texture is like cornmeal. Starter feeds for chicks are usually mash texture and are best for small chicks.

If mash is the only type of feed available to you for older chickens, you can add a little warm water to the feed just before serving it, which gives it the consistency of thick oatmeal. Water from cooking potatoes or other vegetables or milk also can be used. Serving mash is a good way to use up the fine pieces of crumbles or pellets left in the bottom of a bag or the feed dish. However, don't let this wet mixture sit too long because it will spoil and become moldy, which may harm the chickens.

Supplementing diets with grit

Because they have no teeth, chickens need grit in their *gizzard*, a muscular pouch that's part of the digestive system, to help break down food particles. In nature, chickens pick up small rocks, pieces of bone, and shells and store them in the gizzard to help digest food.

If you're feeding any kind of homemade diet, if you're giving whole grains, or if you have your birds on pasture, you need to supply them with some kind of grit. If you're feeding only a commercial mash, crumble, or pellet, your chickens won't require additional grit because these feeds are already quite easy for chickens to digest. Birds that range freely part of the day will pick up enough grit. However, some chicken owners feel that chickens are happier when they have grit — even if they don't need it because of the diet they're on.

You can purchase grit in feed stores. It consists of crushed limestone and granite. Different sizes are available for chicks and adult birds. If you have just a few chickens, you can purchase canary or parakeet grit in pet stores. It's finely ground but is fine for chicks or, in a pinch, for older birds.

Deciding when to put out feed

Most people fill their chickens' feed dishes so food is available much of the day, or they use feeders that hold several days' worth of feed. You can use this feeding method for all types of chickens. It's the way chickens eat in nature; they eat small amounts frequently.

Other folks still feed their chickens at certain times of the day, generally morning and evening. That way, they can control the amount of feed that may attract pests. And if the chickens are too heavy, it restricts the amount they can eat. Usually, however, it's just a matter of preference; some people like to observe and tend to their chickens more often than others. This method works well for all but meat birds.

Chickens that are given free range may be more inclined to come to the coop to lay if they're fed there in the early morning. And if you need to lock the chickens up every night to protect them from predators, feeding them in the coop in the evening entices them there.

Because of their heavy rate of growth, the meat-type broiler chickens need to have food available to them for longer periods of time. Remember, chickens don't eat in the dark, so the lights must be on for them to eat. For the Rock-Cornish crosses, the lights need to be on 18 to 22 hours a day, and feed should be in the feed pans for those hours.

Determining how much to feed

Determining how much feed your chickens are going to eat per day or week is difficult because so many variables are involved. The type of chickens, whether they're growing or laying, and how active they are, affect the amount of feed each bird needs. How neat you are, the type of feeders you have, and the number of free-loading pests you support also change the amount of feed you need. The weather is a factor, too: Chickens eat more in cold weather and less in hot weather.

Our modern, high-production egg breeds convert feed to eggs very efficiently, especially if they're fed a ration formulated for laying hens. After they're laying well, it takes about 4 pounds of a quality feed of 16 to 18 percent protein to produce a dozen eggs. The breeds kept for dual purposes (eggs and meat) generally have heavier body masses to support and need more feed to produce a dozen eggs than a lighter-production breed.

About 2 pounds of feed are needed to produce 1 pound of body weight on a growing meat-type bird. So if a broiler weighs about 6 pounds at 10 weeks, it will have eaten about 12 pounds of feed. Remember that it ate less when it was small, and the amount of feed consumed increased each week. A medium-weight laying hen will eat about ¼ pound of feed per day when she begins producing. These figures are rough estimates, but they give you some idea of what to expect.

REMEMBER

When you pick up your birds, they should feel well fleshed but without rolls of fat. If the breastbone feels very sharp and prominent, they're probably too thin. Chickens that don't get enough feed will stop laying. The thinner birds in the flock and the ones in which vitamin and mineral deficiencies show up first are the ones that are lowest in the pecking order; dominant birds tend to eat first and eat the best of what's available.

Hydrating your hens (and roosters)

Having a source of clean water is vitally important to your chickens. Chickens whose water intake is restricted don't eat as well as chickens with unrestricted access, and they don't grow as fast or lay as well, either. People often don't realize how important water is to their chickens until they go from pouring water in a dish once a day to a system that allows birds to always have fresh water available. The birds with unrestricted access to clean water grow better, are healthier, and lay more eggs.

In moderate weather, a hen may drink a pint of water a day. In hot weather, that amount nearly doubles. Broilers may drink even more as their metabolism works much harder, producing more heat and using more water. Birds roaming freely may drink more or less than confined birds, depending on the moisture content of the food they consume and how active they are.

In hot weather, providing an unlimited quantity of cool, clean water may mean the difference between life and death for your birds. In winter, if temps are below freezing, offer water at least twice a day in sufficient quantity that all birds can drink until they're full. Alternately, use a heated water container.

WARNING

Any time birds stop eating as much as usual, check the water supply. Be sure to manually check nipple systems frequently to make sure they're working. There are plenty of horror stories of nipple valve systems becoming clogged by mineral deposits or other materials and failing to work. These devices freeze up easily in cold weather, too. If the chicken caretaker fails to notice that the chickens can't get water, the birds die of thirst.

Raising Baby Chicks

Many people start with chicks because they fall in love with some at the farm store or someone gives their kids chicks for Easter. Beginning your chicken-raising experience with baby chicks is probably the most economical and practical way to start, for the following reasons:

» You can choose from a wide assortment of breeds.

» Chicks are less likely to carry disease and parasites than older birds, especially if you buy them from a well-run hatchery.

» You don't have to guess how old the birds are.

» Most hatcheries will sex the chicks for you, so you don't have to guess at sex.

» Chicks usually cost less than older birds.

Many mail-order hatcheries operate across the United States. You can order chicks by catalog or from online sites. Some have dozens of breeds available; others specialize in one or two breeds. Baby chicks survive the trip through the mail pretty well.

TIP

When you mail-order baby chicks, you're usually required to order at least a minimum number of chicks. Usually this is 25 chicks, which may be 20 more chicks than you need or want. If you live near a hatchery and can pick up the chicks, you may be able to purchase fewer. You may also have local chicken breeders in your area who will sell you just a few chicks. The local feed store may also sell chicks, or at least be able to tell you who does.

Chicks are cute, but for many people, they may not be the best way to begin keeping chickens. Baby chicks do have their drawbacks:

- >> **They need TLC.** All baby animals take extra time and effort to care for.

- >> **They're fragile.** Small children and pets can easily damage or kill them.

- >> **They require special brooding equipment.** They need to be kept warm and protected.

- >> **Their quality is hard to judge.** Judging the quality of a chick is difficult, so if you want to show chickens, you need to keep a lot of chicks until they're adults so you can then pick the best of the bunch.

- >> **They need time to mature.** If you want chickens for eggs, know that pullet (female) chicks need at least five months to mature and begin to lay eggs. Some breeds need several months longer.

- >> **Their sex is hard to determine.** Although hatcheries can do a pretty good job of sexing chicks, you may not end up with as many hens as you expect, and then you'll have extra roosters to deal with, too. If you buy your chicks from a private breeder, his or her skills at sexing chicks may be poor, and you may not get any hens at all.

- >> **They need extra protection.** If you just want chickens for living lawn ornaments, it's going to be several months before they can be allowed to roam safely. You may want to consider adult birds if you're the impatient type.

The basics of brooders

Baby chicks need to be kept quite warm their first few weeks of life. Without the proper warmth, they won't eat or drink and will soon die. In natural conditions, they snuggle under their mama's breast and belly.

Chicks raised without their mama need a source of warmth, too, and that's where you come in. Unless you have the money and means to heat an entire room to 95 degrees Fahrenheit, you need to provide a brooder for your chicks. A *brooder* is an enclosed area that allows chicks to find that perfect warm spot but also gives them a little space where the air is cooler. A brooder also protects the chicks in the absence of a mother hen.

Many types of brooders are on the market. Most use a heat lamp, but some use gas or propane to heat the unit. Alternatively, you can make your own brooder. Fashioning one from materials found around the home or from local stores is relatively easy to do.

Knowing when chicks need a brooder

Chicks need to go right from an incubator to a brooder. If you're getting your chicks from another source, put them into the brooder as soon as you get them. Set up the brooder a few days in advance of putting chicks in it so you can see how it operates and adjust the temperature as necessary to keep it around 95 degrees Fahrenheit.

Your chicks need a brooder for at least a month, depending on the weather and where they're housed. If you're raising chicks at a very cold time of the year, they may need to be kept warm even longer, especially at night.

If the weather is very hot (above 90 degrees Fahrenheit), take special care to see that the brooder doesn't get above 100 degrees. Older chicks may be uncomfortable at temperatures above 90 degrees, especially if the humidity is high. In this case, you need to provide some ventilation or other cooling to lower the temperature. The chicks may still need the brooder to confine them and keep them safe, however.

Choosing the brooder size and shape

Average-size chicks need about 36 square inches per chick for the first month. This space looks like a lot of room at first, but chicks grow rapidly, and it won't look like too much room when they're a month old. Some brooders are designed to be expandable so they can grow as the chicks grow.

Brooders need to be at least 18 inches deep, especially if the source of heat is overhead, as is the case with heat lamps. If your brooder uses heat lamps, be sure to adjust them upward as the chicks grow so their heads can't touch them. A deeper brooder can help prevent older chicks from jumping out, and the brooder should have some sort of cover to prevent the chicks from escaping.

Chicks need to be able to move from an area of optimal warmth to a cooler area within the brooder, if possible, so they can find just the right temperature that makes them comfortable. Rectangular brooders allow the heat source to be at one end, with progressively cooler temperatures toward the opposite end of the brooder. With square or round brooders, the heat source needs to be in the center.

Getting the temperature just right

For the first week, baby chicks need a temperature of 95 degrees Fahrenheit. Measure the temperature at the height of a chick's back, about 2 inches or so from the floor. Every week, lower the temperature by 5 degrees until you reach about 70 degrees. If temperatures fall below 50 degrees at night, you may want to turn on the heat at night for a few more weeks.

After you gain a little experience, you won't need a thermometer to tell you whether the temperature in a brooder is right. The actions and sounds of the chicks will let you know if it's too hot or cold. Watch the chicks for a few minutes with these tips in mind:

>> If the chicks are casually and quietly walking around, eating and drinking, and some of them are peacefully snoozing near the heat source, the temperature is probably fine.

>> If the chicks are huddled in a pile near the heat source or in a corner of a propane or gas unit, cheeping shrilly, they're cold. Cold chicks also eat less and are less active.

>> If the chicks are spread along the edges of the brooder far from the heat source and have their beaks open, panting, they're too warm. Hot chicks drink more, eat less, and aren't very active.

Choosing brooder bedding

Chicks need some bedding in the brooder to absorb moisture, dry droppings, and reduce odor. You can use many materials for bedding, but pine shavings are easy to find and seem to be the best choice for many people. Clean sand and coarse sawdust are other good options.

Don't use paper (newspaper or any other kind), cardboard, or plastic on the bottom of brooders. These materials get slippery when wet, and the chicks can develop *spraddle legs*, which can lead to permanent disfigurement. Other materials not to use include kitty litter (which is often treated with dyes and scents and may swell if ingested), soil, vermiculite, perlite, cedar shavings (which sometimes irritate eyes and lungs), cotton batting, hay, leaves, and straw.

Hay, leaves, and straw, in particular, may contain harmful substances, may get slippery and moldy when wet, and aren't absorbent. Also avoid shavings made from unknown wood or from hardwoods. When moist and warm, hardwood shavings can develop a harmful mold. Anytime you notice mold on bedding, remove the bedding at once.

How often you need to change the bedding in a brooder varies with the type of litter, the age and number of chicks, the type of brooder, and many other factors. In general, if the bedding is damp and smelly, you need to change it completely. If it appears dry and fluffy but dirty, just add a fresh layer on top. After a while, the litter gets either wet or too deep for the brooder and needs to be changed.

You usually need to remove the chicks to change the litter. Place them in a large box where they'll be safe as you work. Unless it's really cold, they'll be warm enough for a short time without a heat source. If you wash the brooder with disinfectants or strong soaps, make sure you rinse the brooder well and dry it before adding bedding and chicks.

Always scrub a brooder between batches of chicks. Use a good disinfectant, such as common bleach (1 part bleach to 4 parts water), rinse it well, and let it air dry.

Helping a hen provide warmth and protection

If mother hen is present when the chicks hatch, she'll take care of their warmth. She needs just a little help from you to protect the chicks. If they're penned up, you need to separate the mom and her chicks from other chickens. In a coop, make sure the babies aren't able to get out and be harmed by other chickens. Roosters seldom bother chicks, but not all hens are motherly types, and they may hurt chicks.

In a free-range situation, if a hen hides and hatches eggs somewhere, the other chickens probably won't bother her — but her babies will be at risk from predators. Mama hen will try to protect them, but often she's no match for sneaky or overpowering predators. Mother hens may also steal babies from other hens if the babies are about the same age. A hen does have a limit to how many she can care for, and if chicks end up with surrogate moms, you may never know who's related to whom.

To save as many chicks as possible, enclose mama hen and chicks in a cage or pen that the chicks can't squeeze out of, at least until the chicks are about half grown and well feathered — about three months old. If the chicks do manage to get out and the mom can't, she has no way to protect them.

In pens or cages where baby chicks are present, make sure the chicks can reach water, but also ensure that the dish is too shallow for them to drown in. Chicks need finely ground starter feed instead of adult feed. The water and feed issues are another reason why separating chicks from older birds is a good idea. If they're free-ranging, they may find enough to eat in nature, but it doesn't hurt to offer some chick feed in a shallow dish.

Feeding and watering chicks

REMEMBER

Baby chicks don't *need* to eat or drink right away. The remains of the egg yolk in their abdomen will sustain them for a couple days — that's how they can be shipped in the mail to you. However, if you hatch them at home or get them soon after hatching from a local source, it's a good idea to offer feed and water as soon as the fluff has dried and the chicks are moving around.

Nature built in a little time before the chicks have to be fed, to give other eggs more time to hatch. In nature, a few chicks often hatch before the rest. The hen stays on the nest waiting for more eggs to hatch, and the hatched chicks usually stay under her. After a day or so, the hen leaves the eggs that didn't hatch and leads her young ones out to forage.

Feeding facts

Baby chicks need chick starter feed, which is available at farm and pet stores. It's formulated for them and sized right for tiny beaks. Adult chicken feed, feed for other animals, bread crumbs, and so on may keep chicks alive, but they won't grow well with these types of food.

Chicks grow fast. The broiler-type chicks especially need a high-protein starter feed, or they'll quickly start having problems with their legs. The feed is labeled as "broiler feed" or "meat bird feed." You can also use game-bird starter feed. Whatever you use, make sure the protein level is a minimum of 22 percent. If chicks don't get enough protein to sustain their rapid growth, their legs can become weak and twisted, and their wings may also grow distorted.

If you have only pet and layer-type chicks, you can use regular chick starter feed. When you have a mixture of meat and layer birds, use meat bird starter. It doesn't hurt the others, although you want to switch the layer chicks to a lower-protein feed when you separate them and move them from the brooder around five weeks. Regular starter feed needs a protein level of 20 percent.

Another choice to consider is whether to buy medicated or unmedicated feed. To get baby chicks off to a good start, medicated feeds include antibiotics and medications to control parasites and bacterial diseases. We strongly recommend medicated feed for the first month of a chick's life, especially if you don't vaccinate chicks. But we also know some chicken-keepers worry about raising animals on antibiotics and other medications. If you choose to use unmedicated feed you may lose more baby chicks and your chicks may not grow as well as those on medicated feeds, but it's a personal choice.

Place the feed in fairly shallow containers or dishes at first. Use dishes that are long and narrow or that have a slotted cover to prevent chicks from walking in the feed or scratching it out. As chicks grow, so must their feed containers. Have several feed containers or one large enough that all the chicks can eat at one time. You may need to add feeders in addition to switching to bigger ones as chicks grow. Many chick feeders and water containers are colored red, which is thought to attract chicks, but they'll learn to eat and drink from containers of any color. Figure 4-1 shows some common feed and water containers.

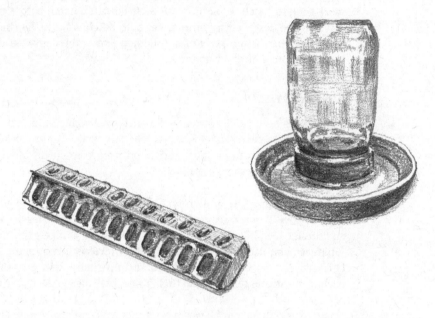

Illustration by Barbara Frake

FIGURE 4-1: Examples of typical chick feed and water containers.

Meat-type chicks need to have feed before them for at least 16 hours a day. But a few hours without feed, usually achieved by darkening the brooder so they can't eat, makes the broiler chicks grow a bit more slowly, which makes them healthier. For other chicks, a dish that's empty for a few hours is okay, as is feed available all the time. But if your chicks act ravenous and swarm the feeder when you add feed, you're not giving them enough.

Wondering about watering

Always have water available for your chicks. A special waterer for baby chicks with a shallow, narrow opening is best. You can buy inexpensive rings that screw onto a wide-mouth jar or purchase larger, more elaborate water holders.

Baby chicks will drown in deep water containers, so don't use anything more than a couple inches deep.

If you use open containers, such as saucers, lids, and so on, add marbles or small stones so that there's little open surface. You want to prevent chicks from walking through water or perching on top of water containers. Keep the watering station clean. The area around the dish generally becomes wet and messy, and water dishes often get shavings or other bedding kicked into them. Scrub out any algae or scum that develops in containers. Then disinfect with a bleach solution of nine parts water and one part bleach, and then dry. If you want to inhibit mold growth without harming the chicks, use four to six drops of unscented household bleach per gallon of drinking water.

Place your water as far from the heat source as you can. Chicks don't like to drink really warm water, and water splashed on a hot bulb can break it.

Chicks and children

Children love fuzzy baby chicks, and young children often think of them as toys. But of course, they're not toys, and the decision to buy chicks for children should never be made on a whim. If your children are begging for the baby chicks they see in the farm store, don't buy them that day (unless that was your secret intention).

Tiny chicks are fragile, and even the loving squeeze of a small child can prove deadly. If the chest and rib cage of chicks are held so tightly that the chest can't move, the chick will suffocate even if the mouth and nostrils are clear. Children don't mean to squeeze, but they're often afraid of having the chick get out of their hands. So teach them: No squeezing.

Other problems result when chicks fall from the hands of children and are injured, or when they're picked up by their legs or necks. Adults should pick up chicks by scooping them up from underneath and carefully transferring them to a small child who, preferably, is sitting down. The child should be taught to cup both hands to hold the chick and not to hold it with one hand.

Even children who are old enough to properly pick up and handle chicks shouldn't be allowed to play with them too often. Taking the chick out of the brooder is stressful to it, and if chicks are too frequently handled, they may not grow as well and may become more susceptible to disease.

Everyone needs to thoroughly wash their hands in hot, soapy water after handling chicks or chickens, their food or water dishes, soiled bedding, roosts — anything to do with chickens. Children are more likely to eat or touch their mouths or eyes without washing their hands and, therefore, are more likely to become ill from handling chicks. When toddlers are around chicken coops, prevent them from putting anything in their mouth that may have been contaminated. After handling chicks or adult chickens, children especially need to thoroughly wash their hands before doing anything else.

Pests and Predators

Most chicken owners have to deal with pests or predators at some point in their chicken-rearing. Having to endure losses from predators can be extremely frustrating and heartbreaking. As a keeper of domestic animals, one of your responsibilities is to guard your chickens and keep them safe. A predator in the hen house can ruin your day and end your chickens' days, so it's important to understand how to deal with the predators that roam your area.

Pests may not kill chickens and are usually more of a problem to the chicken-keeper than the chickens. They can spread disease however, and they often cost you a lot of money and time. Knowing how to manage pests is an important part of chicken keeping.

Preventing pests

Pests are creatures that don't directly kill and eat chickens or feed off them like parasites. Instead, they eat chicken feed or eggs. Preventing pests is always better than dealing with an established population. Be diligent, clean, and tidy, and pest problems may never bother you or your birds. The following list shows you several actions you can take to prevent pest problems:

>> **Store feed properly.** Part of dealing with pest problems is storing feed products correctly. Be sure to store feed in insect- and mouse-proof containers. Metal trash cans with tight-fitting lids work best. Insects destroy the nutritional value of feed, and mice can eat through the bottom of a feed bag in seconds. After people discover how to store feed correctly and keep freeloaders from eating it, they're often amazed at how little their chickens actually eat.

>> **Keep feeding areas clean and dry.** Clean up any spilled feed. Wet areas are most likely to support maggot growth, so keep the place dry as well.

>> **Don't give rodents a place to hide.** Keep trash picked up, and remove piles of junk that can shelter rats and mice. Keep grass and weeds trimmed around buildings. Rats are more likely than mice to come from a neighbor's buildings or yard and to go from feeding at your place to sleeping at theirs, so you may have to enlist the help of the neighbor to control these pests.

>> **Cover what you can.** Covering feeding stations and water containers outside can prevent wild bird droppings from getting into them. You also may need to cover your pasture pens with fine bird netting (like that used to protect fruit from birds).

>> **Don't allow wild birds to nest inside buildings where you keep chickens.** This advice applies for all types of birds, from sparrows to swallows. Besides disease, wild birds can bring parasites such as lice to your chickens. Excluding the birds from the building and removing any nests you find promptly are the best ways to handle this.

Common culprits

The most common pests are insects and rodents. They occur in both rural and urban areas. Clean conditions, proper storage of feed, and an action plan (for when you start seeing signs of pests) are your best defenses.

>> **Mice:** Chickens actually eat mice, so mice seldom set up housekeeping right in the chickens' home. Instead they work on the fringe, getting into stored feed, chewing up building insulation and wires, and running under your feet when you least expect them. Mice don't eat eggs, but they can eat and soil a lot of feed, cause allergy problems for some people, and spread certain diseases. It's best to try to get rid of them or at least control their numbers.

Mice are controlled fairly easily with poison bait. However, place the bait where children, pets, and curious chickens can't get to it. If you're kindhearted and choose a trap that catches mice alive, you then have to do something with them. Don't just take them outside the door and turn them loose; they'll be back inside before you know it. The best bet is to take them to the woods or a field far from other homes where they can feed some animal you're trying to keep away from your chickens.

>> **Rats:** Rats are larger, meaner, and more secretive than mice. They can eat eggs, and they've been known to eat baby chicks and even feed on larger birds as they sit on roosts or nests in the dark. Chickens and even most cats leave rats alone. Rats eat a lot of feed and destroy more by soiling it. They also do considerable damage by chewing on the structure and its parts, such as wiring and plastic pipes.

Rats are suspicious of new things, so it may take days to get them to eat poison bait or fall victim to a trap. Traps must be placed close to pathways that rats habitually use. Traps aren't as effective at controlling rat populations as poison, however. Buy a poison specifically for rats, and change the type of poison you use from time to time so resistant populations don't build up.

Read the label to find out if the bait works with one feeding or multiple feedings. Remember to use bait stations to protect pets, children, and chickens, or place the bait where they can't find it.

>> **Weevils, grain moths, meal worms, other insects:** Weevils, grain moths, meal worms, and other insects attack stored feed. They may provide a little extra protein for the chickens, but their feeding strips the nutritional value of the feed, leaving only husks behind. You know you've got grain pests if you notice fine webbing or tiny worms in your feed. Buy only the amount of feed you can use in about two months. Keep your feed in tightly closed containers, not open bags.

TIP

If you have a way to freeze feed for a few days, doing so will effectively kill most grain pests. In the winter, just leave the feed in your car for a few days when the temperature is below freezing. If you still have insects in the feed, use that feed promptly if it isn't too badly infested, or discard it if it is. Then thoroughly clean the feed container with hot, soapy water and allow it to dry in the sun. Metal and plastic containers are better to use than wood because they don't absorb moisture and insects and other pests can't chew through them as easily. Be sure to clean up any spilled feed, and empty and clean the feed dishes.

Protecting from predators

A predator in the hen house can be a huge frustration — and worse for the chickens it kills. *Predators* are animals that eat other animals or kill them just for fun. Chickens are high on the preferred food list for many predators. Some predators destroy all the birds they can when they gain access to a coop; others take one every so often when they're hungry.

Most chickens do little else but squawk and run to defend themselves, so knowing how to deal with predators is important. Case in point: it takes one loose dog just a few minutes to completely destroy a prized flock of chickens.

Predators are more likely to begin attacking poultry when the birds are raising young in the late spring or early summer, or in winter when food is scarce. And when predators find a good source of food, they often return. Remember that predators live in both urban and rural areas. In fact, some urban areas may have higher numbers of predators than rural areas.

The following tips can help you further protect your chickens from predators:

>> **Be careful about letting your chickens roam.** Chickens that range freely may disappear without a trace. In areas with heavy predator presence, letting chickens roam freely may be impractical. Keeping chickens penned until later in the morning and bringing them in early in the evening can help.

>> **Prevent nighttime attacks.** Good, predator-proof shelters can be closed up at night. A light left in the coop at night further ensures the safety of your chickens.

>> **Cover coop windows.** Put strong wire over open shelter windows.

>> **Keep an eye out for dogs.** Keep your own dogs from chasing chickens, even in play. If neighbors let their dogs run loose all the time, your chickens are probably going to need to be penned up.

>> **Fence your chickens in.** Pens of sturdy wire are the best protection your chickens can have. If raccoons are around, you need strong, welded wire to keep them out. To keep out larger predators, a foot of heavy wire bent outward at the bottom of the run fencing and either buried or weighted down with large rocks is advisable.

Electric fencing is effective at keeping raccoons, foxes, dogs, and coyotes out of chicken pens. A single strand of electric wire near the top of outside runs and near the bottom of any flexible fencing should keep them out. (For more on keeping critters out of certain areas of your homestead, refer to Book 1, Chapter 1. And to learn about installing certain types of fencing, such as electric fencing, go to Book 1, Chapter 3.)

>> **Steer clear of trees.** Make sure predators can't jump off nearby trees into the pen or get on the roof of the coop from nearby trees.

>> **Beware of aerial attacks.** If you let your chickens roam, choose dark-colored birds, which are harder for birds of prey to spot. White birds are easy pickings if they roost outside at night, so make sure they roost inside. If hawks and owls take chickens out of fenced runs, you may need to cover them with nylon netting or fencing.

Tracking the transgressor

The most common predator of chickens is the dog; this animal may be man's best friend, but it certainly isn't a chicken's. However, many other predators occur in both urban and rural areas as well.

Determining which predator killed or injured your chickens can sometimes be difficult. If a chicken simply disappears, it's probably impossible to find out what happened, but in some cases, you may find clues. examine the victims and chicken housing closely and consider the following questions:

>> Can you see an obvious way the predator entered, such as through a large hole in the fence?

>> Has more than one bird been killed?

>> Were the birds eaten or just killed?

>> What part of the body did the animal feed on, and where are the wounds?

>> Were eggs smashed or carefully cracked? If cracked, how were they opened?

>> Do you see animal tracks in snow or mud?

>> Do you live in an urban or rural area and/or by water?

Table 4-1 can help you answer these questions.

TABLE 4-1 **Figuring Out Whodunit**

Predator	What It Hunts	Hunting Hours	Signs
Dog	Chickens	Day or night	Chickens killed but not eaten; survivors may have deep puncture wounds or large pieces of skin pulled off; scattered blood and feathers
Opossum	Usually eggs; occasionally chickens	Night	Droppings look somewhat like cat droppings; tracks similar to tiny human handprints, with five toes and one toe pointing off to the side or backward on the back feet; one chicken killed at a time and partly consumed; eggs usually cracked and eaten in the nest
Raccoon	Baby birds and eggs but also capable of killing adult birds	Night	Several or all birds killed; heads bitten off; flesh torn from breast area; pieces of flesh and blood around water container; feed bags and bins trashed
Fox	Chickens	Early morning and late evening	Chickens free-ranging or pastured away from humans in a rural area; may find partially buried carcass of a bird
Coyote	Chickens and sometimes eggs; seldom enter chicken housing	Mostly night; may hunt during day in cold weather if there's little human activity	Several birds missing at once
Hawk, eagle, or owl	Baby chicks or adults; large hawks, eagles, and large owls can kill adult chickens	Hawks and eagles during day; owls mostly nights, though sometimes days during winter	Hawks, eagles: Birds carried away or picked apart on the spot where killed Owls: Birds plucked from roost and carried outside; in coop, heads may be pulled off, with a single bite taken out of each breast
Mink or weasel	Chickens, eggs, and rats	Day or night, but they shy away from human activity	Chickens kept in rural areas near water sources; heads bitten off; small amounts of flesh eaten; birds may be piled up

Expecting Eggs (for Eating)

Getting hens to lay well and keeping them laying takes a little more care than many people think, but something about producing some of their own food makes many people want to try. Our focus is on producing eggs to eat rather than incubating them to produce more chicks; here we discuss hen management and problems you may encounter with egg laying. The only thing breeders of eggs for hatching need to do differently is add a rooster!

Because it takes more than 24 hours for an egg to work its way from being released from the ovary to being laid, a hen can't lay an egg 365 days a year. Some high-producing hens have been known to lay 300 eggs the first year, but your home-raised hens will probably lay between 200 and 250 eggs their first year of laying if they're a breed developed for egg production.

If you have production egg layer breeds, such as Isa Browns, Pearl Leghorns, or Cherry Eggers, and they're well managed and healthy, they'll probably produce five to six eggs a week in their first year. Other breeds, such as Orpingtons, Plymouth Rocks, and so on, will probably produce four to five eggs per week. Some fancy breeds, such as Polish, Modern Games, Houdans, and so on, produce fewer eggs in a more seasonable pattern — higher in spring and summer, and lower or absent in fall and winter. If you have mixed-breed birds, your egg production will vary widely.

A family that's keeping four hens from a good egg-laying breed can expect to collect about 18 eggs a week, at least in the first year. You may get lucky and collect up to two dozen eggs. Remember, some eggs you collect may be cracked or otherwise unusable.

Providing encouragement

Hens begin laying anywhere from 18 weeks to one year of age, depending on breed and what time of year it is when they mature. In breeds bred for egg production, laying usually begins around the 22nd week.

Pullets (young hens) like to play house as their hormones begin to prepare them for laying. If they have the proper nest boxes available, they'll try them out by sitting in them, arranging nesting material, and practicing crooning lullabies. Dark, comfortable, secluded nest boxes attract them. Try to have nest boxes in place by the 18th week.

You can keep adult hens laying more reliably when you use artificial lighting to supplement natural light. The length of the day and the intensity of light stimulate the hormones of hens and prompt egg-laying. In the winter, hens that get only natural light may stop laying, but if you add artificial light, you can keep your hens laying. Fourteen to 16 hours of bright light followed by 8 to 10 hours of dim light or darkness is the ideal lighting ratio to keep hens laying. Many people buy a timer for the coop lighting so that they don't need to get up early or go out late to turn lights on and off.

Just as most animals are at their best in calm, comfortable surroundings, your hens lay better in those kinds of situations. Make sure your hens have everything they need to be comfortable — good feed; clean water; dry, clean surroundings; nest boxes; roosts; and maybe a sandbox to bathe in.

Don't disturb hens too much in the morning before laying. It's not the time to bring in visitors, catch birds, or clean the coop. You can do your normal feeding and watering, but you may want to avoid providing extra treats that cause every-one to come running.

Getting your eggs in one basket

Get yourself one nice basket, pan, or bowl to handle your largest egg collection, and faithfully collect your eggs each morning. If you have free-range hens and you can't confine them until after they lay in the morning, get used to checking several locations each day where the hens are known to lay. With hens that lay in nest boxes, collecting the eggs is easy. If you have free-range hens, you may find eggs popping up in all kinds of unexpected places.

Hens lay most eggs within a few hours after sunrise, which, of course, varies with the season. If your coop is lighted for egg production, your hens will lay most eggs before 10 a.m. Try to collect eggs soon after your hens have finished laying. This keeps them from being broken, which keeps hens from learning that they're good to eat. It also gives other animals less time to raid nests. If you can't pick up the eggs soon after they're laid, at least pick them up once a day. If you have a lot of hens, you may want to schedule morning and evening collection times.

TIP

If you find eggs and you're not sure how old they are, you can try one trick. Fill a large bowl with water and gently put the eggs in it. Eggs that sink on their side are probably fresh. Eggs that stand upright or that float are probably old and need to be discarded. As an egg ages, it loses moisture and the air space gets bigger, which causes the egg to float.

The color of eggshells ranges from chalk white to deep chocolate brown. Some chicken eggs are green, blue, olive, or khaki colored. Light brown eggs may have a rosy tint, but you won't find any red, orange, or pink eggs unless the Easter Bunny leaves them.

REMEMBER

The important point to remember about eggshell color is that it has nothing to do with taste or the nutrient content of an egg. It also has nothing to do with the internal yolk color. We think brown eggs have gotten a reputation for tasting better because they're often the eggs produced at home or locally and are therefore fresher.

If you like the look of white eggs or your kids refuse to eat any eggs that aren't white, nothing is wrong with producing white eggs at home. Your home-produced white eggs will taste much better than store eggs and will taste every bit as good as brown eggs.

Cleaning your cache

Some people recommend storing eggs without washing them, but even if you work hard to keep fresh, clean nesting material in your nests, some eggs are going to get dirty. Usually they're dirtied by chicken poop, but sometimes a broken egg, muddy hen feet, or other contaminants will soil them. We think that keeping dirty eggs in the refrigerator is a good way to spread harmful bacteria. Even if they look clean, we recommend washing all eggs before storing them.

Rinse eggs in running, mildly warm water, washing all sides. Don't scrub too hard — sometimes eggs have rough spots or "pimples," and if you scrub these off, you damage the shell and allow the inside to be contaminated. Use a paper towel to scrub eggs; never use abrasive pads. Discard towels after each egg, for best food safety.

TIP

After washing the eggs, dry them with paper towels before placing them in storage. Wet eggs can stick to cartons or other containers, and then when they're picked up, a piece of the shell may come off.

Storing and handling eggs

Always store clean, dry eggs in the refrigerator at about 40 degrees. Fresh eggs remain safe to eat for several days at room temperature, but they lose quality quickly. Always store eggs in covered containers that retain some moisture. Store the eggs with the large end up. Never freeze eggs in the shell. The shells will crack, and bacteria can contaminate the inside of the egg.

The egg carton was designed to keep eggs fresh and safe and home flock owners can use cartons to store eggs too. You can recycle cartons from store-bought eggs or you can purchase cartons from poultry supply catalogs and feed stores. Egg cartons allow you to stack the eggs to save room, and they allow you to easily mark the carton with a date so you know when you collected the eggs. Eggs remain edible for a couple months if properly stored.

TIP

The easiest way for homeowners to store eggs for a long time is to freeze them. Before freezing, crack them into a bowl with a pinch of salt or sugar (discard the shells) and then lightly beat them. You can combine the eggs in twos, threes, or other amounts you find useful and freeze them in baggies or small containers. Frozen in this way, the eggs remain good for about six months. You can use them in cooking or making scrambled eggs after you thaw them.

Always discard eggs that are cracked, soft, or thin-shelled and eggs that look or smell bad. Eggs that are really dirty have a heavy bacterial load and probably should be discarded. After three months in the refrigerator and six in the freezer, discard the eggs.

If you have a lot of excess eggs, you may be able to sell some. The USDA allows people to sell eggs without USDA inspection if they have fewer than 3,000 laying hens, sell less than 30 dozen eggs at a time, and sell only eggs they produce on their farm. However, almost all states add regulations for eggs sold without USDA inspection. Before you sell eggs, check to see what the laws in your state and local area say about home egg sales.

Chapter **5**

Opting for Other Animals

Y ou've probably already shared your home with a dog or cat or two. But a backyard homestead open up opportunities for sharing your farm with other types of animals that you may not have dealt with in the past.

Dogs, of course, are one of the best early warning systems: great foretellers of potential danger and also great lifeguards for when you walk out to the garden late at night to check on something. And cats live to manage your local population of not only rodents, but other critters who can wreak havoc on your gardens, chickens, and vegetables.

But besides the flock of hens you maintain for eggs and maybe meat (as discussed in Chapters 3 and 4 of this minibook) and the bees you keep on-site for honey and pollination purposes (see this minibook's Chapters 1 and 2), you may want to have other animals around as residents of your homestead.

This chapter gives you a few options to consider. But this is by no means an exhaustive list of what you can do on your homestead. Want to have horses? Corral cattle? Parent pigs or chaperone sheep or llove your very own llamas? You can if you have the acreage and the inclination, but you're inching your way toward *farming* rather than *homesteading*.

Four our purposes here, we keep it pretty basic. But feel free to take these ideas as a starting point and use your imagination to come up with something unique that works especially for you.

Raising Rabbits

You've no doubt heard the phrase *tastes like chicken* when someone is describing an unusual meat. Well, that description holds true for the meat of the rabbit, which is low in cholesterol. Rabbits, which eat grass and leafy weeds, are more productive and are cheaper to feed than chickens. A rabbit can produce up to 1,000 percent of her body weight in food per year, which brings new meaning to the phrase *multiplying like a rabbit!* You can skin and butcher about five rabbits in the same amount of time it'd take to do a chicken.

Rabbits also produce a fine, soft fiber. Rabbit fur is very soft, and people have used rabbit pelts for years as fur accents on coats or hats, among many other uses.

The fiber of the Angora rabbit can also be spun into a super soft yarn known simply as *angora.* Rabbits such as the Angora shed their coats a few times a year. (Yes, that means you can get the fiber and still keep the critter.) The rabbits should be brushed regularly to keep the coats free of knots, and the stuff you brush off can be added to the pile that you can later spin. For rabbits who don't shed their coats, you can shear them or you can brush or hand-pull the loose fibers out. (You know it's time to harvest the rabbit's fur when you notice clumps of wool sticking to the cage.)

Here are a few things to consider:

>> Rabbits don't need much space to be happy. They should be kept confined to reduce the threat of predators.

>> Take care when building their enclosures to ensure their safety. Hutches should be well above the ground and out of the way of curious dogs and other smaller critters, such as skunks.

>> Because Angora hair is so long and soft, it has a tendency to mat and shed. (Matted fiber is no good.) Shedding not only means the loss of potential spinning fodder but can also make a mess of the cage and cling to your clothes. Regular brushing is crucial.

Rabbits, like other animals, need protection from predators, and the very dogs that you use to guard other animals may be the same critters that threaten the rabbits. Outdoor rabbit houses, called *hutches,* are typically aboveground, secured shelters, so dogs (and skunks, raccoons, and coyotes) can't even get close to them.

The bottoms of the cages are typically a wire mesh-type material so the frequently produced poop can flow freely out of the cage. The hutches my dad used had chicken wire on three sides and on the bottom, and the other side and the roof were wood. Such wire-and-wood hutches can adequately protect the rabbits from the weather (rain, snow, and so on); for warmth, you can put some straw or other bedding materials inside.

WARNING

Keep the hutches inside fences where predators can't get close. When rabbits get nervous and freak out, they kick. The kicking feet can go down through the wire mesh, damaging the rabbits' feet and legs. They can wear their hocks down to nothing (a *hock* is like an elbow on the back of the leg). This can lead to bone infections that are nasty to deal with and are pretty much fatal.

Getting Your Goats

Goats are fantastic animals that have been domesticated for more than 10,000 years, and they are a great way for the modern homesteader to become more self-sufficient.

Imagine never having to buy milk or cheese again. If you raise dairy goats you can achieve that goal. Your goats need to have kids to give you milk, and then you can milk them throughout the year for up to three years without re-breeding, if you want. Or you can stagger the kidding each year so that you have a milk supply year-round. Just one standard-size dairy goat can give you an average of 6 to 8 pounds (3 to 4 quarts) of milk each day. And, depending on the butterfat content of the milk, you can get up to a pound of cheese for every gallon of milk.

Goat meat has always been popular in the developing world, because goats are much more affordable and use fewer resources than animals such as cows. According to the U.S. Department of Agriculture, the demand for goat meat is expected to continue growing. Goat meat is easily digestible, tasty, and low in fat. If you're in charge of your own source of meat, you know how it was raised and what feed or medications went into it.

If you raise fiber goats, you can spin your own yarn and make hats, blankets, sweaters or other products. You can also sell the fiber to spinners or to companies that make these products, while having the benefit of these friendly creatures.

Goats are also well-known for their ability to wipe out weeds. In fact, some people have made businesses out of renting out their goat herds to cities and other municipalities to clean up areas that are overgrown with weeds or blackberry bushes. But be warned: your goats will treat your vegetable garden like a salad buffet if given access, so keeping your goats contained is key.

Opting for Other Animals

WARNING

Goats tend to be escape artists, so fences need to be strong and sturdy. Chicken wire and a couple of metal posts aren't enough — you need something stronger, such as chain link or metal fence panels.

REMEMBER

Check out ordinances in your area regarding keeping livestock. you may need to buy a license for a goat, just like you do for a dog. In some cities, you can't keep backyard goats. In an urban area, even if goats are allowed, your neighbors may complain, much like they do with a barking dog. Be aware of what your local noise ordinance covers.

Goats need a safe, clean place to hang out, sleep in, or retreat to when the weather is too hot, cold, windy, or rainy. Consider buildings that are already on your property that may be feasible for housing goats. You can remodel a chicken house or other farm building or even use a prefab garden shed for a goat house. Many people house urban goats in a section of garage that opens into the back yard.

Finally, run the numbers! In almost all cases, getting only one goat is a recipe for trouble. Goats are not dogs and do not thrive on human companionship alone. Goats are herd animals and need other goats to keep them healthy and happy. A goat without a friend will cry and can even become depressed. Never get just one goat; always buy at least two goats so they can keep each other company. That said, start slow and don't get the maximum number of goats that your homestead can handle right away. And then think about what you are doing when you start breeding your goats. They grow exponentially, and all of the kids are way too cute!

Figuring Out Fowl: Ducks, Geese, and Turkeys

Many chicken-keepers add other poultry to their backyard flock. In general, ducks, geese, and turkeys get along well with chickens. However, you may need more room than a small backyard to keep them with chickens. All of these birds need to be kept where they have a lot of space to roam and a place to bathe.

Ducks and geese

Ducks are typically raised for their meat, eggs, and down. Their meat is a more exotic one and is often used in gourmet foods in pricey restaurants (*foie gras* is one example). Their eggs are larger and richer than that of a chicken and thus are prized among chefs.

They're a popular animal to have on the farm because they're easy to care for (they're happy with kitchen scraps), they eat bugs, and they're just fun to watch. They can also act as alarms and fend off small predators.

Geese are hardy birds and aren't as susceptible to diseases as some of their poultry cousins. They're easy to care for because they're foragers — by eating their favorite food, they help control your weeds. They even love grass clippings. Their eggs are a delicacy, and their feathers (particularly their down) make for soft and warm insulation material.

WARNING

Be aware that most ducks and geese can be noisy, and neighbors may not welcome them.

You can mix ducklings or goslings (baby geese) with chicks in a brooder without them harming each other. However, you'll need a plan for meals. We usually recommend that chicks start out with medicated feed, but ducklings and goslings shouldn't have medicated starter feed because they're sensitive to the antibiotic used. Since you can't keep them from eating each other's feed, all the babies will need unmedicated feed. This compromise may then lead to more disease problems in the chicks.

We recommend using a higher-protein feed, such as broiler feed, for ducklings — the chicks will be okay with that choice, too. As adults, ducks, geese, and chickens can eat the same feed, although special feed mixes for ducks are available.

Keep in mind that ducks are messy, even when they're ducklings. They'll play in the water, and their droppings are more liquid than chicks, so brooders with ducklings need more frequent cleaning to keep them dry. Ducklings don't need to swim while in the brooder (although they will if they can fit inside the water container), and it's not recommended to let them bathe if you're keeping them with chicks. Goslings aren't quite as messy with water.

Geese can be aggressive, and they go after unfamiliar visitors who come into their territory. And because geese are rather big birds, they're capable of defending themselves and their territory against small to medium predators such as raccoons or weasels. But their biggest guarding benefit is that when they're upset, they don't stop squawking until the danger is gone. As long as you're home, you'll be notified that something is amiss out in the yard and that you should go check it out.

Ducks can be territorial, too, going after and nipping at a critter who doesn't belong, but they're not so big and are no match against larger predators.

You'll need to address one other consideration when keeping ducks with chickens. Don't keep male ducks with chickens without female ducks also being present.

Opting for Other Animals

Ducks are often aggressive sexually. If they're deprived of their own females, they may mate with hens.

Mother hens and ducks sometimes raise each other's babies when allowed to mingle freely. They may lay in each other's nests and sit on each other's eggs. Chicks don't usually follow a stepmama duck into water, but it has happened. Baby ducklings can confuse a hen when they pop into water to swim, but it rarely causes a problem.

Turkeys

Turkeys, of course, are the most popular Thanksgiving meal. Turkeys need to be a bit older than chickens do at slaughter — hens (females) should be 14 to 16 weeks old, and toms (males) should be 19 to 20 weeks.

Most commercial turkeys are bred to have a lot of meat on them, and that means they're unable to fly. That also means you should provide shelter — protection not only from the elements but also from predators, because they can't fly up to the top of the barn if something gets too close.

Turkeys eat grain (with a little higher protein content that what you'd give a chicken) and have a life expectancy of about ten years.

Goin' Fishin'

Fish can be fun to raise because they're rather easy to care for, but what types and even whether or not you can do this depends on your state's laws. The most common types of farm-raised fish are catfish and trout.

If the fish are for your own enjoyment, you have little to do in the way of caring for them. For instance, if you have a natural pond on your property, you don't have to do much besides catch them. With human-made ponds or repurposed pools, you need to take care of feeding them and keeping their homes pest-free.

If you're raising fish (such as tilapia, perch, catfish, or trout) for food, you have more health-related issues to consider, such as being careful about the herbicides you use for controlling aquatic plants and keeping the fish disease free.

Fish raised in captivity have some problems their wild counterparts do not. Their diet is different, so they can have a different taste or color. They also have less room to swim and can be prone to diseases, so you have to consider using antibiotics.

5

Building It Yourself

Contents at a Glance

Chapter **1**

Starting Small with Garden Projects

For some homesteaders, the self-reliant streak that got them started on growing and preserving their own food manifests itself in other ways, too. Just like that bumper crop of tomatoes, why buy from the store what you can produce yourself? It's no surprise, then, that many homesteaders are avid (or at least enthusiastic) do-it-yourselfers.

Building some of what you need in the garden lets you customize things to suit your conditions and needs. Repurposing materials you may already have is a great way to recycle items that might otherwise end up in a landfill. And face it, if you're making it yourself and not paying retail, that's more money you can spend on plants (or seeds or tools or chicken feed or canning jars or any number of other things that homesteaders get excited about).

Even if you don't consider yourself particularly handy, this chapter has some ideas for DIYing some of your own small projects around the garden. You feed your family with food you grew from seed; you can certainly handle the easy builds contained in this chapter.

Making an A-Frame Trellis

Some vegetables have climbing or sprawling habits that require some kind of support as they grow. (Figure 1-1 shows some common techniques.) Twining or clinging plants such as beans and peas grow best when they're supported by some type of string trellis. An A-frame string trellis enables you to grow plants on both sides, but single poles are fine, too.

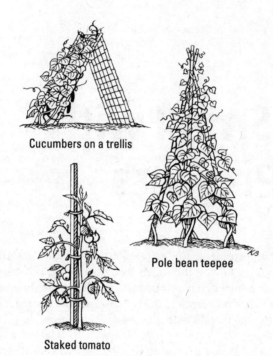

Cucumbers on a trellis

Pole bean teepee

FIGURE 1-1:
Techniques
for supporting
vegetables. Staked tomato

Making an A-frame string trellis is easy; just follow these steps:

1. **Using at least six 2-by-2-inch redwood or cedar stakes, build two 6-by-6-foot squares.**

   Redwood and cedar stakes are naturally rot resistant and good choices.

2. **Secure the corners of the squares with metal corner braces and connect the two squares on one side with sturdy hinges.**

   The hinges enable you to easily move or store the trellis.

3. **Hammer small nails at 2- to 4-inch intervals along the top and bottom of the trellis.**

   Don't pound the nails in all the way; leave about 1 inch sticking out.

4. **Weave some sturdy twine or string up and down the trellis, between the nails.**

   Bingo; you have an A-frame string trellis.

Handmade wooden teepees are a great way to support your beans, and kids love them because they're great places to hide. Here's how to construct your own teepee:

1. **Using four to six 2-by-2-inch redwood or cedar stakes that are 6 to 8 feet long, form a conelike teepee.**

2. **Tie the stakes together with twine at the top of the teepee.**

3. **Run some string or twine around the bottom of the teepee, securing the string or twine at each stake with a small nail.**

4. **Run more string back and forth around the stakes, from the top of the teepee to the bottom, leaving several inches between each run.**

Leave one side of the teepee open so your kids can get inside, and then plant beans around the base of the teepee. In time, the beans will cover the trellis, creating a great fort for your kids.

Crafting the Ultimate Tomato Cage

You've no doubt seen the inexpensive cone-shaped tomato cages at your local gardening center. And if you've ever grown tomatoes, you've probably bought more than your fair share of them. They're easy to come by, sure, but let's be honest: they're flimsy and don't hold up well from season to season, and most of the time, they're not even tall enough to support your tomato plants into late summer!

If you're willing to spend just a little more money and invest a few minutes of your time, here's a way to solve all those issues with strong, sturdy, supersized tomato cages that may be the last ones you'll ever need (see Figure 1-2). The idea comes from Joe Lamp'l, host of the TV series "Growing a Greener World" and the website www.joegardener.com.

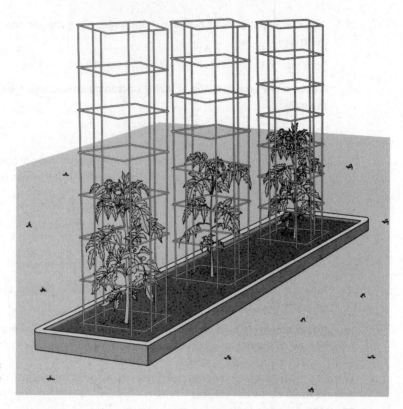

FIGURE 1-2:
The ultimate
tomato cage.

Go to a farm supply store and buy *cattle panels* or *livestock panels*. They're welded grids of galvanized steel rod, with openings about 6 inches square. Think chicken wire or hardware cloth, but much bigger and exponentially stronger. Each panel is 16 feet long and over 4 feet wide, and you'll be able to make one tomato cage per panel. They're somewhat pricey at about $20 apiece, but the cages you make from them will last forever; you'll never have to buy one of those flimsy cones again.

Arm yourself with a pair of heavy bolt cutters and have some strong nylon zip ties ready. That's all you need. Your new tomato cage takes just minutes to make:

1. **Cut the panel lengthwise.**

   Place the panel on a flat work surface such as your driveway. Count down six squares, and cut the length of the panel to make a section that's 16 feet long and just six squares wide.

2. **Divide the new section into two equal pieces.**

   Count down nine squares and cut across the panel just above the horizontal bottom bar of the ninth square. You'll be left with eight full squares and a set of long spiky ends. These ends will be the stakes that anchor the cage in the soil. You can remove one more set of horizontal bars to make extra-long stakes if desired. Repeat this step to make a second matching section.

TIP

Save the scrap pieces! You'll likely find all kinds of uses for them around the homestead, from handy layout guides for even plant spacing to miniature trellises for other garden vines and climbers!

3. **Bend the sections to form 90-degree corners.**

   Working with one section at a time, place a 2 x 4 over the grid, running lengthwise at the halfway point. Stand on the 2 x 4, grab one edge of the wire, and pull. The idea is to bend the wire up against the 2 x 4 to make a long L-shaped corner piece.

4. **Put the bent panels together to create a square-shaped column.**

   Drive the stake ends into the planting bed. Position the two pieces to form a tight square column around the plant. Having two sections means you can assemble the cage around delicate plants instead of trying to carefully lower one of those cone-shaped cages over the top of a maturing plant.

5. **Lash the panel pieces to one another with zip ties.**

   It's easy to cut the ties after the harvest and separate the panel pieces for easy stacking and more compact storage.

Building Raised Garden Beds

Raised beds relieve the tedium of bending over to plant, weed, and care for your vegetables and flowers. They also offer a way to terrace a sloping yard or solve soil problems, such as excess clay or rocks. (More about incorporating raise beds into your overall plan in Book 1, Chapter 1.) You can even gopher-proof your raised beds to control these pesky varmints. Figure 1-3 shows an example.

Although a raised bed is nothing more than a large, bottomless box, some designs include a wide enough edge around the top for sitting or setting things on. Raised beds vary in height from 8 to 18 inches, depending on the material you use. Make the beds no wider than 4 feet, so that you can reach the interior areas. They can be any length you want, although multiples of 4 generally let you take good advantage of standard lumber lengths with little to no waste. Plan 30 inches of space between beds for wheelbarrows and easy access.

FIGURE 1-3:
A raised garden
bed built from
stacked 2 x 8
lumber.

For a lumber bed, use 2-by-boards, such as a single 2 x 12 or a pair of stacked 2 x 8s. For a bed measuring 4 feet wide by 8 feet long, for example, you would need three 8-foot lengths (or two 12-foot lengths) of lumber for each layer. Use heartwood lumber of a durable species. To build a lumber bed, do the following:

1. **Drive 4 x 4 stakes into the ground at the four corner locations and every 4 feet along the long sides.**

   Use stringlines to keep them aligned and a level to keep them plumb.

2. **Cut the side pieces to length and place them around the outside of the 4 x 4s to make a box.**

   After you level each piece, clamp it to the 4 x 4s, drill ⅝-inch diameter holes through the lumber and stakes, and bolt them together with ½-inch carriage bolts.

3. **If you stack boards, overlap the corners log cabin style.**

4. **After you attach all of the side pieces, trim the 4 x 4s flush with the tops of the sides.**

5. **For a seat, install 2 x 8s around the top of the box. If necessary, reinforce the 2 x 8s by attaching a 2 x 4 cap piece around the top of the box.**

   Cut the ends at 45 degrees for miter joints (joints with no end grain showing, like a picture frame).

6. **Position the 2 x 8s on the 4 x 4s and the top edge of the side pieces, and attach them with 3-inch galvanized deck screws.**

TIP

To keep burrowing animals, such as gophers, out of your raised bed, cut metal chicken wire or hardware cloth to fit the bottom of the box. Secure it to the sides with poultry-netting staples before filling the box with soil.

Landscape timbers, also stacked log-cabin-style, make an extra-sturdy, wide-ledged bed that's attractive and easy to build. Stack 6 x 6 timbers two or three high. Check the first course (layer) with a level before adding the second two courses. Drill ½-inch diameter holes through each timber, aligning the holes over each other. Drive ½-inch *rebar* (rod used for concrete reinforcement) into the holes after you stack the timbers to lock them in place.

Constructing a Cold Frame

Cold frames are essentially are mini-greenhouses. They're usually wooden boxes covered with windowpanes or clear plastic (see Figure 1-4). Some professional gardeners as far north as zone 5, where winter temperatures can dip down to −20 degrees Fahrenheit, can harvest vegetables every month of the year by planting cold-weather-tolerant crops in cold frames. You can learn more about extending your growing season with cold frames and greenhouses in Book 1, Chapter 7.)

FIGURE 1-4:
A sample cold frame.

Although anyone with a credit card can purchase a premade cold frame for $100 to $200, you can easily create your own simple cold frame by following these steps:

1. **Build a 3-foot-x-6-foot box from untreated lumber. Cut the box so that the back is 18 inches high, sloping to a front height of 14 inches.**

   This sloping angle enables more sun to reach the plants, and it sheds rain and snow as well.

2. **Hinge an old window sash over the top of the cold frame or make a frame by using tightly stretched clear plastic, which creates a sealed growing environment.**

   You can insulate the cold frame by adding rigid foam insulation around the insides of the cold frame and by weather stripping along the top edge.

3. **Position the cold frame so that it faces south.**

   It's best to put a cold frame next to a structure, such as a house, to protect it from cold winds.

REMEMBER Even though the purpose of a cold frame is to trap heat, on sunny days, even in winter, a cold frame can get so hot that it burns the plants. Check your cold frame once a day on sunny days, opening or venting the top slightly to allow hot air to escape.

Elevating Your Rain Barrel on a Stand

Harvesting rainwater from your gutters into a barrel and using the water to irrigate your planting beds is a wonderful way to make the most of this precious resource that just falls freely from the sky. The easiest way to use that captured water is with a simple garden hose, but you need gravity to help. The barrel must be higher than the hose to get running water when you turn on the spigot. Therefore, every inch off the ground you can situate your rain barrel, the better. That's where a rain barrel stand comes in, as shown in Figure 1-5.

WARNING A gallon of water weighs over 8 pounds. A full rain barrel can easily tip the scales at over 500 pounds! The moral of the story is: If you're going to elevate your rain barrel, don't skimp. Flimsy building materials, using too few fasteners, or inadequate barrel support can make a serious mess or cause physical harm if that rain barrel comes crashing down.

Using just a bit of basic lumber (maybe even scraps you already have), you can construct a simple and sturdy stand that raises your rain barrel to a comfortable height that ensures the water is always flowing freely in your garden.

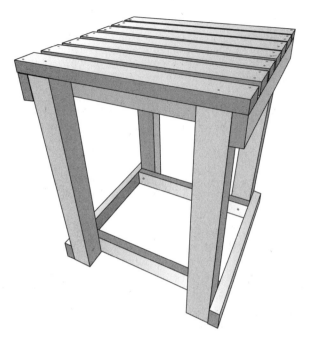

FIGURE 1-5:
A simple rain
barrel stand.

Just follow these steps:

1. **Cut 4 pieces of 4 x 4 lumber to a length of 34½ inches.**

   These are the legs of your rain barrel stand. They'll put your barrel on a surface 36 inches off the ground; cut your legs shorter as needed.

2. **Cut 11 pieces of 2 x 4 lumber to a length of 29 inches (4 supports, 7 top planks) and 4 pieces to a length of 26 inches (stretchers).**

   If you're buying new lumber, 5 8-footers will give you more than enough wood.

3. **Build two sides.**

   Fasten two supports horizontally to a pair of upright 4 x 4 legs. One support should be flush with the tops of the legs; the other should sit flush with the bottoms. The outer edges of the legs should sit 29 inches apart. Make sure the corners are square. Repeat for the second side piece. Build on a level surface so that the stand will be level after it's completed.

   Outdoor-rated 2½-inch deck screws will be sufficient for this project. Drill small pilot holes before driving the screws to prevent the wood from splitting.

   TIP

4. **Join the sides with stretchers.**

   Connect the side pieces to one another with two stretchers at the top and two at the bottom. Fit the stretchers between the top supports and inside the stand, fastening them at both the supports and the 4 x 4 legs. You should end up with the skeleton of a square column, 29 inches by 29 inches.

5. Add the top planks.

Evenly space the 2 x 4 top planks by leaving a gap between the boards. Fasten them with screws driven through the planks and into the supports underneath.

You may choose to finish the rain barrel stand with paint or stain, or to add hardware that allows you to hang your hose directly on the stand.

Organizing Made Easy with a Tool Wall

All of those shovels, rakes, hoes, and other tools you use to keep your homestead running take up space. But for many gardeners, that space isn't conveniently located to the garden they're actually working. That means a lot of wasted time trudging back and forth retrieving and returning tools.

Plenty of gardeners have come up with a nifty way of stashing their tools *in* the garden, so that everything they need is within easy reach at a moment's notice. It's often called a *tool wall*, and it's exactly what it sounds like: a vertical surface where your various homesteading implements live when they're not being used. Check out Figure 1-6 for an example.

FIGURE 1-6: An outdoor tool wall.

Hanging tools on a wall is not a radical idea, but once you start looking around your yard, you may be surprised at the number of places you could put this concept to work with your gardening gear. Any exterior wall of a house, garage, barn, or shed can be used to hang tools. You could turn a section of existing fence into a tool wall. You could even erect a portion of a wall specifically for this purpose, and have it do double-duty as a windbreak or privacy screen. Plus, it can make an eclectic focal point in the yard and add a bit of character to the homestead . . . all while helping you be more organized and efficient.

The best tool walls offer a maximum of flexibility with a lot of square footage that can be used for tools of varying sizes and shapes. Sure, you can place some hooks all in a row on a single board and mount it to a wall, but there's a good chance that some of the tools you'd like to hang won't fit well with others. Some tools hang by their handle, some upside-down by the business end. Some tools are quite tall; others become harder to reach if they hang too high. Some tools might hang well off a bare nail, while others may need a curved hook or a long arm or a double-pronged piece of hardware. It's about making all of your tools fit, not lining them up in perfect rows at a uniform height.

Ideally, you probably want the ability to move tools around as you acquire new ones. Being able to unscrew a hook, move it over 3 inches and down two, and simply screw it back in to the wall at the exact spot that allows your new compost fork to have a home is something you'll appreciate; so much the better if you're not worried about the screw hole left behind in the wall of an old barn or on an expanse of wood that was designed for the purpose.

TIP

An outdoor tool wall is a great place to repurpose leftover wood you've had lying around. Just make sure the wood will hold up to exposure in the elements. Recycled barn wood or old fence pickets make an inexpensive wall surface and add a touch of rustic homestead flair!

Here are step-by-step instructions for building a freestanding tool wall of your own.

1. **Lay out your wall location to establish post spacing.**

   a. Use a string and wooden stakes to determine the wall's placement. The length of the wall should be dictated by the wood you'll use and how big you want your wall to be. Six to eight feet is adequate for many gardeners. Depending on the location in your yard, you may be able to hang tools on both sides of your wall, doubling your storage capacity!

   b. Mark the stakes' location on the ground; this is where you'll sink the end posts.

2. **Dig post holes and anchor the posts in the ground.**

Basic 4 x 4 posts should be sufficient to support your wall. Make sure you use outdoor-approved lumber.

a. Dig holes for each post that are two to three times wider than the posts themselves. Dig to a depth that is ⅓ the post height plus 6 inches. For example, if you want to end up with 6-foot posts (and the same height wall), dig holes that are 30 inches deep and have posts that measure 8½ feet.

b. Fill the bottom 6 inches of the hole with gravel.

c. Set your posts on the gravel and use temporary braces to hold them plumb.

d. Use the string to make sure the fronts of the posts line up. (If the string makes good contact with the faces of the posts, the boards that comprise your wall will, too, for easy installation.)

e. With the posts' orientation set and braces, backfill the holes with concrete.

3. **Fasten wall boards between the posts.**

a. After the concrete has hardened and set, remove the post braces and attach wall boards to the posts. It's usually easiest to start at the bottom and work your way up. Make sure the first board you attach is level, and they should stay level as you add more.

b. Leave a gap at the bottom of the wall (you can't hang anything that low anyway) and don't go higher than you can comfortably reach.

c. Repeat on the other side of the posts if you're building a double-sided tool wall.

4. **Add blocking between the wall surfaces.**

For added support, sandwich a few lengths of lumber between the two wall surfaces and fasten them through both sides of the wall boards. This will increase the wall's strength and keep it from bowing outward once you start hanging tools.

5. **Hang your tools.**

Test-fit tools against the wall to see how each one should best hang. Try different positions, placements, and configurations to maximize space. Use nails, screws, screw-in hooks, or a combination to accommodate all the tools you want to hang.

TIP

Check hardware stores and home improvement centers for a huge array of hooks and hangers. Most often found with garage organization or shelving supplies, you can find hangers specifically designed to safely hold everything from post–hole diggers to wheelbarrows on a wall!

Creating a Compost Bin (or Two)

When it comes to compost, you don't necessarily need to enclose it at all. After all, composting occurs when organic matter is piled in a heap and left to rot (as described in Book 1, Chapter 5), so obviously the decomposer organisms don't care if a high-rise condo surrounds their food supply. However, in the interest of keeping your homestead as tidy as possible, you may decide to organize your composting area with some type of structure.

This section gives you two options for creating your own compost bin.

Using wood shipping pallets

Because composting is all about recycling organic matter, it seems appropriate for composting bins to be made from recycled materials as well. Wood shipping pallets are used as platforms to support consumer goods being transported by forklifts and other equipment. Recycled pallets are a fantastic option for creating easy-to-build and highly effective composting systems, especially when you have a lot of organic matter to process.

They're easy to come by, piled at construction sites or stacked at loading docks behind businesses and warehouses, awaiting recycling or disposal. Explain to the head honcho you'd like to recycle some to make a compost bin. Most places pay to have them hauled away and are happy to oblige.

WARNING

Pallets can be heavy, weighing up to 50 pounds apiece. Make sure you can manage moving them around yourself, or enlist an extra set of hands. And make sure you select pallets that are in sound structural shape. They can get beat up by forklifts and heavy equipment; you'll be able to identify a pallet that's falling apart with just a quick once-over.

One person can assemble a shipping pallet compost bin, although it goes smoother with two: one to hold the pallets upright and steady while the other ties them together. Follow these steps to erect the bin shown in Figure 1-7:

1. **Level the ground where your bin will be.**

2. **Set the pallets upright in a box shape.**

3. **Lash the pallets securely together at the corners with wire or rope ties.**

   The front pallet acts as a hinged door, allowing you to access your compost by undoing the ties on one side and swinging it open. You can also remove the entire pallet to have wider access when adding or turning organic matter.

Starting Small with
Garden Projects

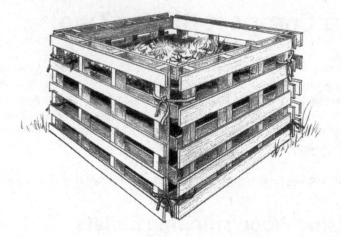

FIGURE 1-7:
Shipping pallet
compost bin.

TIP

Add second and third bins to your first shipping pallet bin using common side walls. You need three pallets for each additional bin.

Wood and wire three-bin composter

A stationary wood and wire three-bin system, shown in Figure 1-8, offers a variety of advantages, including the ability to compost large amounts of yard materials in little time. Wire mesh sides or bottoms or both keep pests out of the bin while allowing the aeration needed for decomposition, and the wood construction blends unobtrusively for a natural appearance in your landscape.

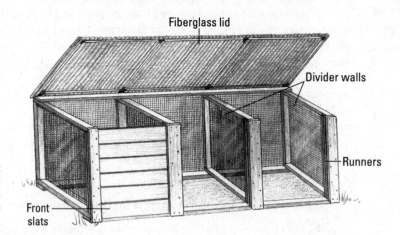

Fiberglass lid

Divider walls

Runners

FIGURE 1-8:
A wood and
wire three-bin
system with a
fiberglass lid.

Front
slats

You can also fabricate pest-proof hinged lids from wood and wire or fiberglass. (A fiberglass lid maintains moisture within the pile or keeps out excessive rain or snow, depending on your conditions.)

WARNING

Building this bin style yourself requires more carpentry skills and tools than other projects in this chapter, and the materials are more expensive than other home-built styles. You can build this unit for approximately $300 to $375.

This bin design and construction project is courtesy of Seattle Public Utilities. The overall outside dimension of the finished project is 9 feet wide x 3 feet deep x 32 inches high; each bin section measures 35½ inches wide x 3 feet deep x 32 inches high. You can downsize the design to a one- or two-bin system if that's all the space you require. For instructions for building other types of composting bins, visit www.seattletilth.org, or use your favorite Internet search engine to find instructions for other designs.

Materials

The list of materials and tools needed to construct the three-bin composter is lengthy, but you should be able to find everything you need at a home improvement store:

Quantity	Item
2	18' lengths of 2"x4" cedar
4	12' lengths (or 8 6' lengths) of 2"x4" cedar
1	9' lengths of 2"x2" pine lumber
2	6' lengths of 2"x2" pine lumber
1	16' length of 2"x6" cedar
9	6' lengths of 1"x6" cedar
22'	½-inch hardware cloth, 36" wide
12	½-inch carriage bolts, 4" long
12	Washers and nuts for bolts
3 lbs	16d galvanized nails
½ lb	8d galvanized casement nails
250	Poultry wire staples or power stapler
12'	Sheet of 4-oz clear corrugated fiberglass
8'	Sheet of 4-oz clear corrugated fiberglass

Quantity	Item
3	8′ lengths of wiggle molding
40	Gasketed aluminum nails
2	3″ zinc-plated hinges
8	Flat 4-corner braces with screws
4	Flat 3″ T-braces with screws

Instructions

The following steps walk you through building the three-bin composter, starting with the dividers and finishing with the fiberglass lid.

1. Cut two 31½-inch and two 36-inch pieces from each 12-foot 2 x 4.

2. Butt end nail the four pieces into a 35-x-36-inch divider section (see Figure 1-9). Check to make sure each divider section is square.

FIGURE 1-9:
Align corners to butt end nail them together.

3. Repeat Step 2 for the other three divider sections.

4. Cut four 37-inch-long sections of hardware cloth and bend back the edges 1 inch. Stretch across each divider frame, check for squareness of the frame, and staple the screen tightly into place every 4 inches around the edge.

5. Set the dividers up parallel to one another 3 feet apart.

6. Measure and mark the centers of the two inside dividers.

7. Cut four 9-foot pieces out of the two 18-foot 2 x 4 boards.

8. Place two 9-foot base boards on top of the dividers and measure the positions for the two inside dividers.

9. Mark a centerline for each divider on the 9-foot 2 x 4. With each divider, line up the centerlines and make the baseboard flush against the outer edge of the divider.

10. Drill a ½-inch hole through each junction centered 1-inch in from the inside edge. Secure baseboards with carriage bolts, but don't tighten them yet.

11. Turn the unit right side up and repeat Steps 9 and 10 for the top 9-foot board.

12. Using the carpenter's square or measuring between opposing corners, make sure the bin is square, and tighten all bolts securely.

13. Fasten a 9-foot-long piece of hardware cloth securely to the backside of the bin with staples every 4 inches around the frame.

14. Cut four 36-inch long 2 x 6s for front slat runners.

15. Cut two of the boards from Step 14 lengthwise to 4¾-inches wide and nail them securely to the front of the two outside dividers and baseboard, making them flush on the top and outside edges.

   Save the remainder of the rip cut boards from this step for use as back runners.

16. Center the remaining 36-inch, full-width 2 x 6 boards on the front of the inside dividers flush with the top edge, and nail securely.

17. To create back runners, cut the remaining 2 x 6 into a 34-inch long piece and then rip cut it into four equal pieces, 1¼ x 2 inches. Nail the back runner parallel to the front runners on the side of each divider, leaving a 1-inch gap for slats.

18. Cut all the 1 x 6-inch cedar boards into slats 31¼ inches long.

19. Use the last 9-foot 2 x 4 for the back of the lid. Cut four 32½-inch 2 x 2s and one 9-foot 2 x 2 from it.

20. Lay the pieces from Step 19 on the ground in a rectangle and make sure they're square. Screw in corner braces and T-braces on the bottom side of the frame.

21. Center the lid frame from Step 20 on the bin structure, brace side down, and attach it to the bin with the hinges.

22. Cut wiggle board to fit the front and back 9-foot sections of the lid frame.

23. Pre-drill the wiggle board with a ⅛-inch drill bit, and nail it to the frame with 8d casement nails.

24. Cut the fiberglass to fit flush with the front and back edges of the frame.

25. Overlay the fiberglass pieces at least one channel wide. Pre-drill the fiberglass and wiggle board for each nail hole.

26. Nail the fiberglass and wiggle board to the lid frame, nailing on top of every third corrugated hump with gasketed nails.

Whipping Up a Walk-In Hoop House

As explained in Book 1, Chapter 7, a hoop house (see Figure 1-10) is a great way to extend your growing season. Although some hoop houses are built just large enough to enclose a row of plants, you can construct a walk-in version that puts several hundred square feet of your garden in a weather-protected, solar-heated environment. And all it takes is some plastic sheeting stretched over a PVC skeleton, and a little homesteader resourcefulness.

FIGURE 1-10:
A walk-in hoop house.

You can scale your hoop house's size as needed, but using 25-foot-wide polyethylene plastic and 20-foot lengths of PVC pipe (both readily available in home improvement stores) creates a hoop house that's 6 feet tall in the center and 12 feet wide — plenty of space for getting veggies off to a great start even in the dead of winter.

White PVC pipe is most commonly found in the plumbing department of your hardware store or home improvement center. Many hoop houses are made from 1½ inch diameter pipe. Smaller diameters may not provide enough strength, while larger diameters cold prove less flexible and harder to build with.

REMEMBER

Plumbing PVC will gradually break down the longer it is exposed to sunlight, though it could take a decade or more to notice any weakness in your hoop house skeleton. Some builders prefer grey electrical PVC conduit, which is usually flared at one end so that sections can be joined together without separate connector pieces. Galvanized steel pipe can be used for a super-sturdy hoop house where extreme winds and heavy snow load are a concern, but bending it is a challenging job some DIYers aren't interested in. You may find that curved lengths of pipe can come in handy on the homestead; look for a specially designed bending tool at home improvement centers or online from vendors such as www.johnnyseeds.com.

Similarly, most backyard hoophouses use ordinary plastic sheeting, sold in rolls of a hundred feet or more. Greenhouse plastic sheeting is available, too: it's specially formulated for UV exposure and is more tear-resistant than the polyethylene sold in your hardware store's paint department. You may choose to start simple with your first hoop house and upgrade materials down the road. But many gardeners consider a hoop house to be something they build on the cheap, meant to last one year. They simply build another one the next year.

Here are the steps for constructing your own walk-in hoop house. You might want to make some modifications to better suit your space or needs:

1. **Start by building a ground frame.**

   A four-sided ground frame made of outdoor-approved lumber gives your hoop house a base to anchor to. Some gardeners choose to build a hoop house over existing raised beds, and use the beds themselves as the frame.

2. **Drive anchors for the hoop pipes.**

   Short lengths of steel rebar (used to reinforce concrete) are a popular choice. Pound one piece into the ground at each corner of the frame, leaving 12 inches exposed above grade. Drive another rebar anchor every three feet along the length of the ground frame.

3. **Erect the PVC ribs of the hoop house.**

   Slide one end of the PVC pipe over one rebar anchor. Bend the pipe and slip the other end over the anchor on the opposing side of the ground frame. Where the PVC meets the ground frame, it's a good idea to use a few screws to fasten the pipe directly to the lumber to lock it in place.

WARNING

Have a helper when working with long pieces of PVC. Both ends of the pipe must be held securely while it's being bent and positioned over the anchors to keep it from snapping back and being a danger.

Starting Small with
Garden Projects

If 20-foot lengths of PVC are not available (or prove to be too cumbersome to transport and work with), you can use shorter lengths of pipe. You'll just need to include the appropriate couplers to connect them to one another to create the desired overall length.

4. Install side supports.

The PVC ribs need extra support to keep the structure rigid. Purlins are horizontal supports that help hold the PVC skeleton together. Basic 2 x 4 lumber works well for this purpose. One purlin should be installed at the top of the arch, one set a few feet off the ground on either side wall, and one more set halfway between. All purlins should run the entire length of the hoop house (on the inside of the pipes) and be fastened directly to the ribs with long screws or bolts, drilling through the PVC and the lumber.

In some parts of the country where wind and snow are not an issue, lightweight purlins made from more PVC are adequate. These PVC purlins can be lashed to the ribs with heavy baling wire or nylon zip ties.

5. Put on the plastic.

With at least one helper (and probably some ladders), unroll the plastic sheeting and slip it over the PVC skeleton. Pull and adjust the plastic as needed, making sure there is excess along the ground frame on each long side.

You can dig a trench and bury the bottom of the plastic to secure it. Some hoop house owners wrap the excess around lumber strips and fasten these strips to the ground frame to keep everything tight. Some use rope to tie the loose ends of the plastic down. Some fasten a second set of purlins on top of the first, sandwiching the plastic in between. This holds the plastic in place but allows the ends to be kept loose, in case you might want to roll up the walls of your hoop house as needed for ventilation and temperature control. In many locations, roll-up sides are a necessity to keep the hoop house interior from overheating.

6. Enclose the ends.

Now you have a tunnel. To make it a hoop house, you need to enclose the ends. Most owners construct a simple lumber frame at one end and anchor it to the ground frame, purlins, and ribs. Then they stretch the plastic over the frame before attaching it permanently.

The other end opening also gets a wood frame that's clad in polyethylene, but don't forget to include a door! You can make the door from scratch using the same 2 x 4 lumber as the frames; make it wide enough for you to get in and out comfortably (presumably while carrying gardening tools or trays of seedlings). Attach it to the frame with door or gate hinges and cover it with its own piece of plastic sheeting.

Chapter **2**

Building a Backyard Beehive

Homesteading beekeepers are an especially self-reliant lot. They're quick to find practical ways to care for their bees and discover innovative, cost-effective solutions to beekeeping problems. Typically, beekeepers are passionate about nature and the well-being of the environment. So it's no wonder that more and more beekeepers are finding out how to build their own beehives and equipment. Sure, you can purchase kits from beekeeping supply vendors, but doing it yourself is very enjoyable and satisfying. You may even save some money!

In today's green world of self-sufficiency, sustainability, and back-to-basics mentality, why not roll up your sleeves and make a beeline for a little side hobby that both you and your bees will appreciate and benefit from?

Whether you're a new beekeeper or a seasoned old-timer, this chapter provides you with a step-by-step approach for building one of the most cost-effective and popular hive styles. And don't fret if you don't know much about carpentry or woodworking — the instructions are simple and straightforward.

Choosing Materials

Beehives, including all the ones in this book, are typically made from wood. You have hundreds of kinds of wood to choose from. But from a practical and financial viewpoint, you should limit your "discovery" to wood that is readily available from most lumberyards and home improvement centers. Some woods are cost-effective (cheap), and some are exotic (expensive). In the following sections, a few options for your lumber are presented.

The best woods for beehives

A handful of woods are used most frequently for making beehives. Sometimes the choice is regional (selecting a wood that's readily available in your area), sometimes the choice is financial (selecting a wood because it's the lowest price), and sometimes the choice is based on durability (selecting a wood because it stands up to the elements better than other woods). What follows are the woods most frequently used by the commercial manufacturers of beekeeping equipment:

>> **Pine:** Hands down, pine is the most widely used choice. It is readily available everywhere, among the least expensive lumber to purchase, and easy to work with. Note that there are different grades of pine. Two are of interest here:

- **Knotty (sometimes referred to as *standard* pine):** The knotty grade of pine is the least expensive and is perfectly sound for building, but it does contain knots and some other cosmetic imperfections. If you can live with a more rustic-looking hive, by all means go for the standard grade and save a few bucks. You may need to order a little more material than stated in the plans, because the knots sometimes fall right where you plan a critical piece of joinery. So having a little extra material allows you to choose an alternate piece of wood without the offending knot.

- **Clear (sometimes referred to as *select* or *premium* pine):** The clear grade is pricier. As the name suggests, this grade is clear of knots and other blemishes. The grain of the wood also tends to be tighter and straighter. It makes for a very nice looking, defect-free hive.

TIP

Pine isn't the most durable wood to weather the elements, so you must protect pine with some coats of outdoor-quality paint, exterior polyurethane, or marine varnish. (See the later section "Protecting Your Hive with Paint and More" for details.)

>> **Cypress:** The cypress tree produces a sap-type oil that preserves the wood and naturally repels insects and mold. So cypress is a terrific wood for making beehives and beekeeping equipment. But with most of the wood coming from

southern states in the United States, it's not readily available all across the country. But if you can get your hands on some cypress, you won't be disappointed in the results. It's a beautiful and naturally durable wood for building beehives.

>> **Cedar:** Cedar is a beautiful wood, and it smells divine. The natural oils make it less prone to warping, less susceptible to bug infiltration, and less likely to rot than other woods. Though you can paint it, you certainly don't have to because of its naturally durable qualities. Left untreated it will weather to a lovely, light gray patina. Many varieties of cedar exist, and depending on where you live, cedar lumber can sometimes be tricky to find. It's also more expensive than pine. Western red cedar is the most widely available type across the United States.

>> **Spruce and fir:** Pine, spruce, and fir trees are all conifer trees. But when it comes to nomenclature in the lumberyard, spruce and fir are typically associated with *stud* lumber (versus *board* lumber). The plans in the book make use of spruce or fir studs (either spruce or fir is fine, as they're interchangeable) that you use for making frames, top bars, and some other applications.

WARNING

You'll likely want to steer clear of pressure-treated wood to avoid exposing your bees to chemicals. Although since 2004, this category of wood product no longer uses toxic copper, chromium, and arsenic (CCA) to protect it from insects and mold. The new recipe is supposed to be safe. But if you're going to the effort to construct your own beehive, why take a chance? Stick to all-natural, untreated wood and rest easy.

Sizing up lumber

Most everyone has heard of a *two-by-four.* It's the lumber used to frame a house. And that's how you'd order it at the lumberyard: "I need a two-by-four." But did you know that it doesn't measure 2 inches by 4 inches? It actually measures 1½ inches by 3½ inches. However, when the board is first rough-sawn from the log, it *is* a true 2x4. By the time it's dried and planed, it becomes the finished 1½ inch by 3½ inch size.

REMEMBER

Nominal dimensions refer to lumber *before* it's dried and planed to size at a lumber mill. You use nominal dimensions when you order wood. *Dimensional lumber* is the product that leaves the mill *after* drying and planing. These are the actual dimensions that you have to work with. For the plans included here, the materials list refer to the nominal dimensions (how you order your materials), and the cut lists refer to the actual dimensional size (what you have to work with).

Table 2-1 lists the nominal and dimensional measurements for various sizes of lumber.

TABLE 2-1 **Nominal Dimensions versus Actual Dimensions**

Nominal Dimensions	Dimensional Lumber Size
⁵⁄₄ x 6 (decking)	1" x 5½"
1 x 3	¾" x 2½"
1 x 4	¾" x 3½"
1 x 5	¾" x 4½"
1 x 6	¾" x 5½"
1 x 8	¾" x 7½"
1 x 10	¾" x 9½"
1 x 12	¾" x 11½"
⁵⁄₄ x 3	1" x 2½"
2 x 3	1½" x 2½"
2 x 4	1½" x 3½"
2 x 6	1½" x 5½"
4 x 4	3½" x 3½"

Getting the scoop on plywood

Many kinds of plywood are available. True plywood is made up of multiple thin layers of laminated wood veneers, each oriented at a 90-degree angle to the previous layer. This results in a product that resists warping and is incredibly strong. But note that any plywood meant for *interior* use won't last long in your bee yard. After a few rains or snowstorms, the layers that make up the plywood quickly peel apart like an onion.

For bottom boards that are exposed to weather, use either ¾ inch or ⅜ inch exterior grade plywood. Exterior plywood uses water-resistant glue to adhere its layers together. Don't use anything other than this for exterior applications.

Rifling through roofing materials

The roof of your hive takes the brunt of abuse from sun, rain, snow, and other climatic challenges. The roof (or outer cover) is a critical component for keeping your hive dry and your bees safe from the elements. You can optimize the roof's effectiveness and maximize its durability by adding some form of weatherproofing (just like the roof on your house). Most of the following options are interchangeable with one another. Pick the roofing material that best meets your needs and preferences.

>> **Aluminum flashing:** Aluminum flashing makes a good roof material. This is the stuff that's used on the roofs of houses as a moisture barrier. It's easy to cut (with tin snips or even a utility knife) and a breeze to bend and shape. It's also readily available from any home improvement store. Aluminum flashing works well for both flat- and peaked-roof hives.

>> **Asphalt roofing shingles:** This option is a little fussier because the application of roofing shingles takes a bit more work than some of these other options. But shingles are very practical and can give your hive a "little house" appearance. Roofing shingles come in a huge selection of colors. They work best on peaked-roof hives. Use a roofing nail that's short enough that it won't go all the way through both the shingles and the wooden hive top (¾ inch should be ample).

>> **Cedar shake shingles:** Now we're talking! This option results in a very elegant cottage look. If you're selling your handiwork, this roof treatment would be very attractive to potential buyers. You won't find this kind of stylishness in your typical beekeeping supply catalogue. Roofing shingles work best on peaked-roof hives. Use a roofing nail that's short enough that it won't go all the way through both the shingles and the wooden hive top (¾ inch should be ample).

>> **Copper flashing:** This is similar to aluminum flashing, but, as the name indicates, it's made of copper. It's pricey, but it can really dress up a hive if such aesthetics are important to you. Copper weathers to a soft green patina (like the Statue of Liberty). If you're building hives to sell, this extra bit of bling can be attractive to buyers and even command premium prices for your hives. Copper flashing tends to be available in a heavier gauge than aluminum flashing, so it's a little more difficult to cut (tin snips work best) and even trickier to bend. Copper flashing works well for both flat- and peaked-roof hives.

>> **Roofing felt paper:** Also called *tar paper,* this material is made of glass fiber infused with tar and asphalt. It makes a very practical but not very elegant roofing material for any beehive. It's easy to cut with heavy duty scissors or a utility knife and can be tacked to the hive's roof using a heavy-duty staple gun (be sure to use stainless steel staples to prevent rusting). It can wear out or tear over time, so you may have to replace it every few years. Felt paper works well for both flat- and peaked-roof hives.

TIP

When purchasing any of these roofing materials, you'll likely wind up with a lot of surplus material (unless you plan to make a number of hives). For example, aluminum flashing is typically sold in a 10-foot roll, and you need only around 2 feet of flashing for the roof of one hive. So rather than purchase more than you need, visit a home construction site and see if the foreman is willing to give you some leftover material to cover the roof on your hive. You don't need that much for one hive. A jar of honey may just be the perfect barter for a couple of feet of flashing or a few dozen roof shingles!

Selecting screening materials

Some hive designs call for screening material designed to keep the bees contained in a given area. But this isn't your ordinary window screening material (that stuff is too fine, and the bees would surely clog it up with propolis). Instead, the screening material of choice for beekeeping is *hardware cloth,* which consists of wire that's woven and welded into a grid.

Specifically, you need hardware cloth with ⅛-inch square openings. It's known as #8 hardware cloth. It typically comes in 3-foot-by-10-foot rolls. If your local hardware store doesn't have #8 hardware cloth (they likely won't), you can easily find it online. Some beekeeping supply stores are now selling it by the foot (see www.bee-commerce.com or www.brushymountainbeefarm.com). You can cut hardware cloth to size using tin snips or even a pair of extra-heavy-duty.

Protecting Your Hive with Paint and More

After you build your masterpiece, you'll want to protect it from the elements. After all, most of this beekeeping stuff is intended to be kept outdoors year-round, where rain, sleet, and the gloom of night can take their toll. It's recommended that you apply some kind of protection to all exterior wooden surfaces. Protecting your woodenware with exterior grade paint, weatherproof polyurethane, or marine varnish not only looks nice but also adds many seasons of life to your wooden beehives and equipment.

Here are some options for protecting the exterior of hives:

>> **Most beekeepers paint their hives using a good quality exterior paint.** Either latex or oil-based paints are fine. Semi-gloss paints are generally easier to keep clean than matte. As to color, it really doesn't matter — it's up to you. White is the most traditional color in the United States, but in other countries, the sky's the limit. Like your house, you'll need to repaint the hive every few years if you want it looking fresh.

WARNING

Keep in mind that really dark colors heat up more than light colors. Dark hives may be fine in the cold winter but can quickly overheat the colony in the dog days of summer. So avoid black, navy blue, and aubergine!

>> **Another approach is to polyurethane your woodenware.** You can even stain the wood first if you want to. This is an attractive, natural-looking alternative to paint. In fact, this approach not only protects the wood but also tends to blend in better with the environment (which can be helpful if you don't want to draw attention to your hives). Be sure to use exterior grade polyurethane; gloss, semigloss, or satin is fine. Oil-based polyurethanes tend to stand up better to the elements. The resulting finish isn't very flexible and may crack over time and require touch-ups.

>> **Alternatively, you can apply several coats of marine-grade (spar) varnish to your woodenware.** Again, you could stain the wood first if you want to. Spar varnish is slower drying but more flexible than polyurethane. Its flexibility means it tends not to crack. However, it must be reapplied periodically as it does tend to chip and flake off over time.

REMEMBER

All the interior parts of the hive are best left *untreated* — no paint, no stain, no polyurethane, and no varnish. Keep the interior (where the bees live) au naturel. Doing so is healthier for the bees, and the bees prefer the natural living conditions because they're more like the inside of a tree, where bees live in nature.

Your hives and accessories undergo a good deal of stress over the seasons from weather conditions and from you frequently opening and closing the hives, moving the hives, swapping hive bodies, harvesting honey, and on and on. The goal is to build strong assemblies that stand the test of time. You can take a little extra step to ensure the wooden parts hold together for a long, long time. Use a good-quality, weatherproof wood glue in addition to nail and screw fasteners. Although gluing isn't absolutely necessary, your joinery will have a better chance of long-term survival if you take the time to apply a thin coat of weatherproof wood glue before screwing or nailing wooden parts together.

Building the Kenya Top Bar Hive

The top bar hive is likely one of the world's oldest beehive designs, going back centuries. In recent years, this simple, practical design has seen a resurgence among backyard beekeepers, particularly because more and more backyard beekeepers are seeking more natural beekeeping options. Top bar hives are used extensively throughout Africa and in other developing countries where building materials are scarce. The design in this chapter is called a Kenya top bar hive; its sloped sides tend to result in stronger combs and to discourage the bees from attaching the comb to the bottom of the hive.

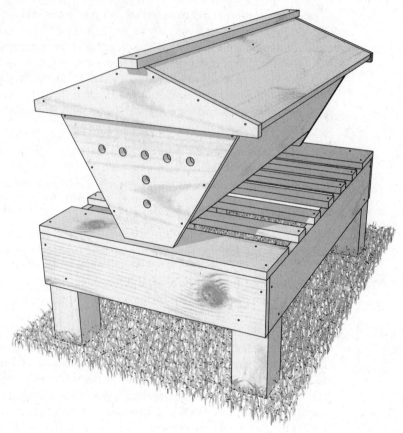

Illustration by Felix Freudzon, Freudzon Design

The Kenya top bar hive has many design variations, but they all consist of a long, horizontal hive body with sloped sides, top bars (instead of frames), and a roof. The design in this chapter was developed by beekeeper Mike Paoletto. It's a very practical and functional hive, but like all top bar hives, it has some pros and cons. First the pros:

» The top bars (which, unlike frames, have no bottom or side rails and use no full sheets of foundation) allow the bees to build their comb freestyle and without restrictions on cell size.

» The design provides a living arrangement that's similar to how bees live in the wild (within the hollow of a tree). As a result, the bees tend to be less stressed and thus less prone to disease.

>> The hive is relatively easy and inexpensive to build.

>> You don't need a honey extractor, as you typically cut the comb from the hive and crush it to extract the honey. Alternatively, you can harvest chunks of natural comb honey.

>> The hive requires less heavy lifting than a conventional, Western-style hive, which requires you to remove and manipulate supers and hive bodies.

>> You don't need to store empty honey supers during the winter months because this design has no supers.

>> The hive yields lots of beeswax because you remove most of the comb during the honey harvest. You can then use the wax for making candles, cosmetics, and furniture polish.

WARNING

However, the Kenya top bar hive also has some cons:

>> To harvest the honey, you must destroy the comb. On the other hand, that means that every year, the colony uses a fresh supply of beeswax comb, so chances of a pesticide buildup are less than in wax that's used over and over.

>> Compared to supermarket honey, the honey you harvest may contain a high percentage of pollen and be cloudy in appearance. But one could argue that this honey is far more natural than the ultra-filtered and pasteurized commercial honey found in many stores. And the pollen content provides the honey with extra protein.

>> Moving the fragile top bars in the hive and doing various beekeeping manipulations are difficult or even impossible compared to what's possible with a hive using Langstroth-style frames (which support the comb on all four sides). But the whole idea of this design is to provide as natural an environment as possible for your bees with fewer interruptions from the beekeeper. Those manipulations are contrary to the all-natural objective.

>> Administering medications to your bees can be difficult (the hive doesn't have a feeder, for example). But hey, a top bar hive is all about a sustainable, more natural approach to beekeeping. So medication and chemicals need not apply. Bees tend to be healthier when under less stress and in a more natural environment, and this simple design provides just that.

>> This type of hive has the potential of lower honey production because it has a fixed number of top bars versus more modern designs, where multiple honey supers and frames can be stacked endlessly, one on top of the other.

>> Combs are much more fragile than those built in a Western-style frame (such as a Langstroth hive; see Book 4, Chapter 1). You need to be very careful when inspecting combs of a top bar hive.

Vital stats

Here's an at-a-glance look at the Kenya top bar hive, to help you decide whether it's the best type for you to build for your backyard:

» **Size:** 38 inches x 24 inches x 31¼ inches.

» **Capacity:** You can't add supers or additional hive bodies. The space is fixed and thus limited.

» **Type of frame:** This design uses a top bar, not a frame. It doesn't have side bars, a bottom bar, or full sheets of beeswax foundation to deal with (nor the costs associated with these elements). The bees build their comb naturally and without restriction onto each of the top bars placed in the hive (28 in all).

» **Universality:** All the gadgets and add-ons that you might use with a conventional Langstroth hive (feeders, queen excluders, frames, foundation, and honey-extracting equipment) are irrelevant to the Kenya top bar hive. Its design is virtually all-inclusive and requires no extras. And with no standardization of design, commercial replacement parts for top bar hives aren't available.

» **Degree of difficulty:** This is likely one of the easiest hives to build. It has no complex joinery and requires no complicated frame building or foundation insertion. That's why this design has remained so popular in Africa and other developing countries.

» **Cost:** Using scrap wood (if you can find some) would keep material costs of this design very minimal, but even if you purchase the recommended knotty pine, hardware, and fasteners, you can likely build this hive (including the top bars and the stand) for around $120.

Materials list

The following table lists what you'll use to build your Kenya hive and the top bars used with it. In most cases, you can make substitutions as needed or desired.

Quantity	Lumber	Hardware	Fasteners
2	8' lengths of 1" x 6" clear pine lumber	Weatherproof wood glue	20 #6 x 2½" deck screws, galvanized, #2 Phillips drive, flat-head with coarse thread and sharp point

Quantity	Lumber	Hardware	Fasteners
1	8' length of 1" x 12" knotty pine lumber	⅛" hardware cloth (you'll need a piece that measures 36½" x 7¾"); #8 hardware cloth typically comes in a 3' x 10' roll, but some commercial beekeeping supply vendors sell it by the foot	80 #6 x 1⅜" galvanized deck screws with coarse thread and sharp point
1	8' length of 1" x 12" knotty pine lumber	½ pound beeswax (to melt and brush on the frames' starter strips)	25⅜" staples for use in a heavy-duty staple gun
2	12" x 36" x ³⁄₃₂" balsa wood sheets	Optional: 2 quarts latex or oil exterior paint (white or any light color), exterior polyurethane, or marine varnish	25⅜" staples for use in a heavy-duty staple gun

TIP

Here are a few notes about the materials for your Kenya top bar hive:

>> Because of its simple butt-joinery, knotty pine is perfectly okay for this hive, and it's about the least expensive board lumber out there. But pine isn't the most durable wood; it benefits from a protective coating of paint, varnish, or polyurethane. Alternatively, consider keeping your hive as all-natural as possible by using cedar or cypress. Although these woods are more expensive than knotty pine, they stand up well to weather without paint or protective chemicals.

>> You can purchase ³⁄₃₂-inch thick sheets of balsa wood online or from a hobby store. Use a utility knife to cut the balsa wood sheets into the 13⅝ inch x ¾ inch starter strips.

Cut list

The following sections break down the Kenya top bar hive into its individual components and provide instructions on how to cut and build those components.

REMEMBER

Lumber in a store is identified by its *nominal* size, which is its rough dimension before it's trimmed and sanded to its finished size at the lumber mill. The actual finished dimensions are always slightly different from the nominal dimensions. For example, what a lumberyard calls *1 inch x 6 inch lumber* is in fact ¾ inch x 5½ inch, and 4 inch x 4 inch posts are actually 3½ inch x 3½ inch. In the following tables, each Material column lists nominal dimensions, and each Dimensions column lists the actual, final measurements.

You make a number of special cuts in this chapter, including rabbet cuts and saw kerfs.

A *rabbet* (called a *rebate* in the UK) is a recess cut into the *edge* of a piece of wood. When viewed in cross-section, a rabbet is two-sided and open along the edge of the wood. Think of a rabbet as the letter *L* (see Figure 2-1). Rabbet cuts are sometimes used to join two pieces of wood together, but they're also used to create shelves or ledges (such as the shelf upon which the frames rest).

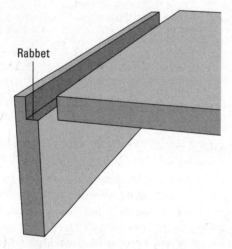

Rabbet

FIGURE 2-1:
A rabbet cut is shaped like an L.

A *saw kerf cut* is the incision made by a saw in a piece of wood. The *kerf* is the miniscule amount of wood that's removed by the width of the blade itself (usually around ⅛ inch). When making a kerf cut, you don't cut all the way through the wood. You simply cut a groove or slot that's ⅛ inch wide by the depth specified in the plans.

You can adjust the height of the elevated hive stand to suit your needs by adjusting the length of the 4-inch-x-4-inch cedar posts. Longer legs result in less bending over during inspections. The 13-inch height of the stand is just right for many beekeepers.

Elevated hive stand

Quantity	Material	Dimensions	Notes
4	4" x 4" cedar posts	12½" x 3½" x 3½"	These are the leg posts of the stand. Rabbet 5½" x ¾" deep along one end of each post (this rabbet accommodates the long sides of the stand).

Quantity	Material	Dimensions	Notes
4	1" x 6" clear pine	24" x 5½" x ¾"	Two of these are the short sides of the stand and the other two are the wide struts for the top.
2	1" x 6" clear pine	36½" x 5½" x ¾"	These are the long sides of the stand.
5	1" x 6" clear pine	24" x 2¼" x ¾"	These are the narrow struts for the top.

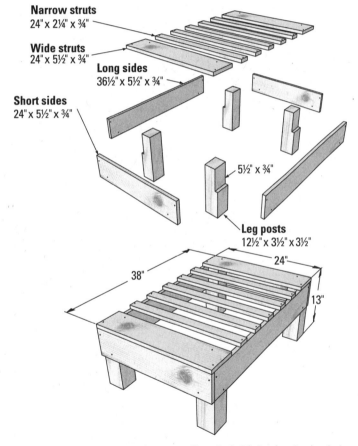

Narrow struts
24" x 2¼" x ¾"

Wide struts
24" x 5½" x ¾"

Long sides
36½" x 5½" x ¾"

Short sides
24" x 5½" x ¾"

5½" x ¾"

Leg posts
12½" x 3½" x 3½"

24"

38"

13"

Illustration by Felix Freudzon, Freudzon Design

Hive body

Quantity	Material	Dimensions	Notes
2	1" x 12" knotty pine	34½" x 10⅜" x ¾"	These are the long sides. Bevel the top long edge so that the outside height measurement of the board is 9" while the inside height measurement remains at 10⅜". This provides the necessary slope to accommodate the inclined roof boards.
2	1" x 12" knotty pine	18" x 11¼" x ¾"	These are the V-shaped end panels. The top edge is 18" and the bottom edge is 5⅛". These dimensions are centered, and they're what determine the V shape of this piece. Drill seven ¾" ventilation/access holes into *one* of the end panels (see the following figures for the approximate placement of the holes).
1	#8 hardware cloth	36½" x 7¾"	This is the screened bottom of the hive. Staple it in place as indicated in the drawing.

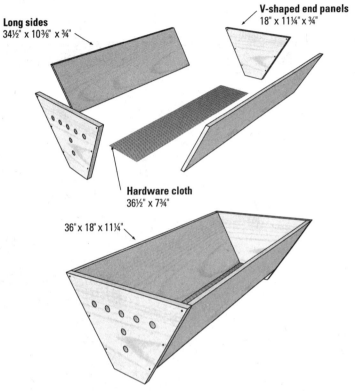

Long sides
34½" x 10⅜" x ¾"

V-shaped end panels
18" x 11¼" x ¾"

Hardware cloth
36½" x 7¾"

36" x 18" x 11¼"

Illustration by Felix Freudzon, Freudzon Design

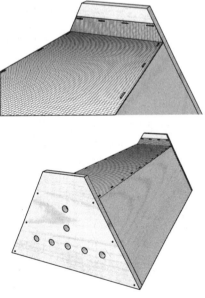

Illustration by Felix Freudzon, Freudzon Design

Top bars

Quantity	Material	Dimensions	Notes
28	1" x 12" knotty pine	19⅛" x 1⁵⁄₁₆" x ¾"	Cut a saw kerf on one side centered along the entire length, ⅛" wide by ¼" deep (you'll glue a starter strip of wood into this groove).
28	³⁄₃₂" balsa wood	13⅝" x ¾" x ³⁄₃₂"	These are the starter strips that you glue into the kerf cut groove.

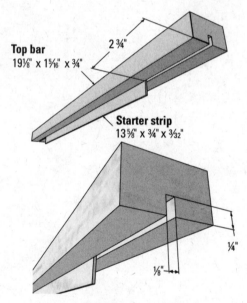

Top bar
19⅛" x 1⁵⁄₁₆" x ¾"

2 ¾"

Starter strip
13⅝" x ¾" x ³⁄₃₂"

¼"

⅛"

Illustration by Felix Freudzon, Freudzon Design

Ventilated roof

Quantity	Material	Dimensions	Notes
2	1" x 12" knotty pine	36½" x 10⅞" x ¾"	These are the inclined roof boards.
2	1" x 12" knotty pine	22" x 4¾" x ¾"	These are the roof gables.
			Cut into a V shape by leaving a 1" rise at the bottom and a 1⅝" flat cap at the top (see the following figures for details).
1	1" x 12" knotty pine	40" x 1¾" x ¾"	This is the roof ridge.
1	1" x 12" knotty pine	6¼" x 2¾" x ¾"	This is the roof support wedge.
			Cut into a V shape by leaving a 1⅝" rise at the bottom (see the figures for details).

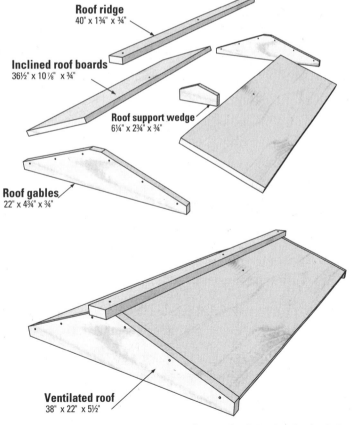

Roof ridge
40" x 1¾" x ¾"

Inclined roof boards
36½" x 10⅞" x ¾"

Roof support wedge
6¼" x 2¾" x ¾"

Roof gables
22" x 4¾" x ¾"

Ventilated roof
38" x 22" x 5½"

Illustration by Felix Freudzon, Freudzon Design

CHAPTER 2 **Building a Backyard Beehive**   597

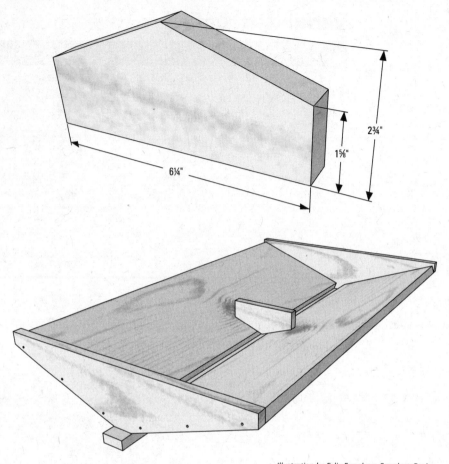

Illustration by Felix Freudzon, Freudzon Design

Dimensions shown: 6¼", 1⅝", 2¾"

Assembling the hive

Now the real fun begins — putting all the pieces together to build your hive! You start at the ground and work your way up and up.

TIP

The screws and nails will go in easier if you first drill a $7/64$-inch hole in each spot you plan to place a screw. The pre-drilling also helps prevent the wood from splitting. Do this for all the components you'll be assembling.

TIP

Consider using weatherproof wood glue in addition to the screws. It helps make all the assemblies as strong as possible. Place a thin coat of glue wherever the wooden parts are joined together.

1. **Assemble the hive stand.**

   a. Fasten the long sides into the rabbet cut of the leg posts and secure to each post using two 2½ inch deck screws per post. The edge of the side rail should be flush with the post. Stagger the placement of the screws (as shown in the earlier figure) to prevent splitting the wood.

   b. Using deck screws, attach the two short sides to the leg posts and the long sides. One screw goes into the leg post, and another goes into the edge of the long side rail. Use two screws for each corner.

   c. Attach the two wide struts to the top of the stand. Position each flush with the front and rear ends of the stand. Secure each end of each strut using two deck screws, as shown in the earlier figure.

   d. Attach the five narrow struts to the top of the stand. By eye, evenly space them between the two wide struts and secure them to the top edge of the long sides (use one deck screw at the end of each strut).

   e. Optional: Paint, varnish, or polyurethane the entire hive stand to protect it from the elements. Use two or three coats, letting each coat dry completely before adding the next coat. If you elect to paint the stand, any color will do — it's up to you.

2. **Assemble the hive body.**

   a. Affix the two V-shaped end panels to the long sides using 1⅜ inch deck screws (as shown in the earlier figure). Use a total of six screws on each end panel. Note that the top edges of the end panels and side boards should be flush with each other.

   b. Now turn the hive body upside down and staple the hardware cloth to cover the opening that runs along the entire length of the hive body. Place one ⅜ inch staple every couple of inches. At each end of the screening, bend the screening at a 90-degree angle and staple to the end panels. Trim excess screening as necessary using tin snips.

   c. Optional: Paint the exposed exterior wood of the hive body with a good quality outdoor paint (latex or oil). This greatly extends the life of your woodenware. You can use any color you want, but a light pastel or white is best. With dark colors, the hive builds up lots of heat in the summer, and your bees spend a lot of energy cooling the hive — energy they could be spending collecting nectar. Alternatively, you can use a few protective coats of polyurethane or marine varnish on the exterior wood.

3. **Assemble the top bars.**

   a. You'll assemble a total of 28 top bars. Assembly simply consists of gluing a thin strip of wood into the kerf cut groove. This is the starter strip that gives the bees a starting point to build honey comb on the top bar. For each top bar, center the starter strip into the kerf cut and glue in place using weatherproof wood glue. Let the glue dry before proceeding.

b. Melt ½ pound of beeswax over low electric heat or in a double boiler. Use a disposable brush to coat the starter strips with a thin coat of beeswax. This further encourages the bees to get started making comb.

Never melt beeswax using an open flame! Beeswax is highly flammable.

c. Now place the bars into the hive body. The bars rest on the top edge of the hive body and are butted side by side, like the wooden bars of a marimba.

Never paint your top bars because that could be toxic to your bees. Leave all interior parts of any hive unpainted, unvarnished, and all-natural.

4. **Assemble the ventilated roof.**

a. Affix the two inclined roof boards to the two peaked gables using 1⅜ inch deck screws. The screws go through the peaked gables and into the edges of the roof boards. Use six evenly spaced screws per gable (see the figure for approximate placement; precise spacing isn't critical). Note that there's a 1⅝-inch-wide ventilation opening at the peak of the roof.

b. Now take the ridge rail and screw it in place using one 1⅜ inch screw at each end. Screws go through the ridge rail and into the flat top of the gable pieces.

c. Center the roof support wedge in the middle of the ventilation opening (underside of the roof) and secure in place with a 1⅜ inch screw driven through the ridge rail and into the support wedge.

d. Optional: Paint the exposed exterior wood of the roof assembly with a good quality outdoor paint (latex or oil). You can use any color you want, but a light pastel or white is best. Alternatively, you can use a few protective coats of polyurethane or marine varnish on the exterior wood.

5. **Stack all the pieces together (see the following figure).**

a. Choose the spot where you want to locate your hive and place the elevated hive stand on the ground. The stand provides the bees with good ventilation, keeps the hive off the damp ground, and raises the colony so it's much easier for you to inspect.

b. Place the hive body centered on top of the stand. The end of the hive with the holes is the entrance, so be sure the hive is facing in the direction you intend for the bees to fly.

c. Fill the hive body with the top bars, all 28 of them. The bees will build their beautiful comb on the underside of each top bar along the waxed starter strips. Here they'll raise their brood and store pollen and honey.

d. Now top everything off with the ventilated roof. It provides your bees with protection from the elements. That's it! You're ready for the bees!

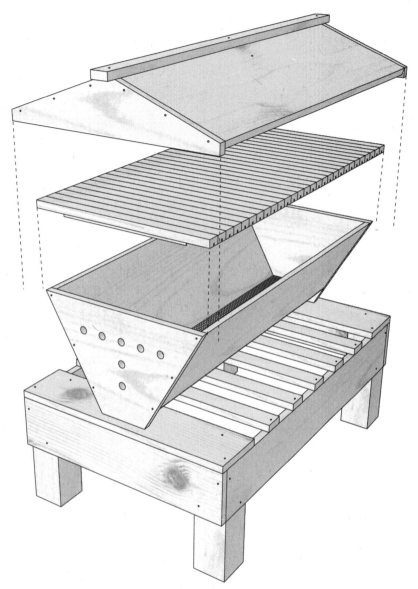

Illustration by Felix Freudzon, Freudzon Design

Chapter **3**

Building a Chicken Coop

Homesteaders are a particularly self-reliant and improvisational bunch. It's about making do and adapting. Those who raise their own chickens (as discussed in Book 4, Chapters 3 and 4) get paid back in eggs — the equivalent of just a few bucks a month — so the vast majority of caretakers go to great lengths to keep chicken-keeping a low-cost hobby. The whole endeavor is meant to make you just a little more self-sufficient; why spend gobs of cash to do it in the first place?

Now, technically speaking, a chicken owner could let a bunch of hens fend for themselves without a coop. It's *possible*, but it's not *practical*. For almost every one of us, no matter where we live, having some sort of housing is a prerequisite to keeping chickens.

Maybe that helps explain why so many chicken folks build their own coops. Sure, you can purchase a pre-built shelter for your birds (and some awfully nice ones at that), but for many, that goes against the whole reason they got into this to begin with. Why pay for something that you can provide for yourself? And if you're clever enough and self-sufficient enough to see the benefits of raising chickens, you can indeed build your own chicken coop.

Choosing Materials

Your brand-new chicken coop is out there right now: full lengths of lumber, unopened boxes of nails, sealed stacks of shingles, uncut sheets of plywood. They're spread out between the hardware store and the lumberyard, hiding in your own basement or toolshed, or maybe even sitting unused at a neighbor's house. These are the raw materials you'll use. Only they don't know it yet. Maybe you don't either.

Remember, you need to meet just a few requirements when housing chickens. Book 4, Chapter 3 looks at the basic anatomy of a coop — what it *must* have as far as the chickens are concerned.

TIP

By their very nature, chicken-owners are wonderful improvisers who love being self-sufficient and able to adapt to most any circumstance. As a result, chicken coops are often elaborate amalgamations of whatever materials are handy at the time of the build.

Have a stack of old deck lumber taking up space in your garage? Leftover pieces of plywood from a previous project? An unopened stack of shingles from when you had your roof replaced last year? You kept these things for a reason, right? Thinking that maybe someday, you'd find a use for them? Well, welcome to someday.

Using recycled materials is a fabulous way to cut costs on a coop build. Anything you don't have to buy is money you can spend on other things, chicken-related or not. Your flock won't care if its coop window is the annoying one from your living room that you replaced because it was old and outdated. It won't matter to them if their coop is painted with the gallon that you meant to use in the bathroom until you got over your "orange-is-making-a-comeback" phase. Got corrugated roofing panels in two different colors? It's all the same to the chicks. As long as the material in question is sound, there's no reason not to use it. We've seen particularly enterprising chicken owners use wooden pallets as walls. One even turned a junked 1970 Morris Traveller into a fantastically funky coop! Whether you're starting from scratch with all-new materials or recycling some items from a previous project, you have plenty of choices to make.

Boards

You'll find many kinds of lumber at your home supply center. Here's a quick rundown to help you choose the best type for your application:

>> **Construction lumber:** Construction lumber is what you'll find the most of at the local lumberyard. It's milled from softwoods (usually meaning pine, fir, or some other evergreen) and has the stereotypical whitish-yellow lumber color.

It's meant for use indoors or where the lumber itself won't be exposed to moisture or weather.

>> **Pressure-treated lumber:** Whereas construction lumber is intended for indoor use, green-tinted, pressure-treated lumber is made for outdoor exposure. But contrary to popular belief, the chemicals used to pressure-treat lumber aren't designed to combat moisture. Pressure-treated lumber is all about making wood that will get wet unattractive to pests, fungus, and bacteria that would otherwise converge on it as if it were a dessert bar. Nevertheless, pressure-treated wood is the way to go for lumber that will be exposed to the elements, because it results in a longer-lasting structure.

Different classifications of pressure-treated lumber exist for boards that will be used above-ground, on-the-ground, or underground. Consult with a sales associate at the lumberyard to make sure you select the lumber that suits your application.

>> **Cedar and redwood:** Cedar and redwood offer chemical-free resistance to rot and insects, thanks to their naturally-occurring tannins and oils. They're beautiful woods, but they can also be quite expensive. You may not find all of the same board sizes at your local home improvement warehouse. Although these woods may be a welcome feature for exposed pieces of the coop, using them for hidden framing members or interior structural supports probably isn't money well spent.

>> **Other board types:** An increasing number of man-made wood substitutes have made their way to market in recent years. Called *composite woods,* these engineered products (whose brand names include Trex, Veranda, and GeoDeck, among others) are made up of mixtures of resins, regular lumber scrap or sawdust, natural plant material and fibers, and even recycled plastics. From a building perspective, working with them is just like working with real wood. These boards need little to no maintenance and come in a variety of colors. The downsides? This stuff is often prohibitively expensive and can be absurdly heavy. And because it's primarily a decking material, composites often aren't available in regular lumber sizes.

Sheet goods

Much of the wood you'll buy for your coop comes not in board form, but rather in large, thin sheets. These sheet goods cover big expanses quickly and cleanly, often serving as the cladding over a lumber framework, as on a subfloor, a roof, or walls.

>> **Plywood:** *Plywood* has become a bit of a catch-all phrase used to describe any type of wood product sold in a flat sheet. But true plywood is made up of several super-thin layers of laminated wood veneer, with new layers added

(usually in odd numbers, to prevent warping) during manufacture until the desired thickness is reached (see Figure 3-1). Each layer is oriented at a 90-degree angle to the layers above and below it, giving plywood incredible strength.

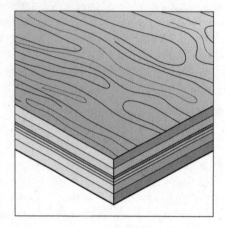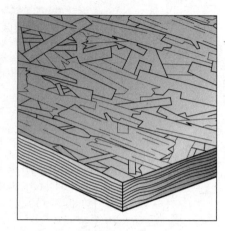

FIGURE 3-1:
Popular sheet
goods for coop
construction
include plywood
and OSB.

REMEMBER

You'll often see references to plywood thicknesses of ¼ inch, ½ inch, and ¾ inch. But these nice, neat sizes don't actually exist. Once you get to the lumberyard, you'll see that plywood is typically stamped with its *exact* thickness. So what you *call* ¾-inch plywood will *in actuality* measure $^{23}/_{32}$ inch. The former is just easier to say, so don't waste your time searching high and low for plywood that actually measures ¾ inch.

Plywood meant for interior use won't last long in the great outdoors. A few good rains or prolonged exposure to high humidity will peel the layers of interior plywood like an onion. Exterior plywood uses water-resistant glue to adhere its layers together and resist rot.

>> **OSB:** Short for *oriented strand board,* this reconstituted product is made of large flakes (or strands) of wood. Like plywood, thin layers are built up and glued together at 90-degree angles to create thickness and provide strength. OSB's low cost when compared to plywood makes it a popular choice as an underlayment or sheathing, where it won't be the finished visible surface. OSB, sometimes also called waferboard, is not considered a good all-weather option for exterior exposure.

REMEMBER

If you're planning to clad the exterior of your coop in some sort of siding, you can afford to be a lot less concerned about whether the sheathing is exterior-grade. Siding (as dealt with later in this chapter) requires some sort of weather barrier between it and the sheathing, so regular plywood or even OSB can be used to cut overall costs.

Particle board and medium-density fiberboard (MDF) are widely available sheet goods but not recommended for coop construction, as any sort of water exposure is detrimental.

Flooring

For the vast majority of coops, the flooring of the housing structure is constructed from basic plywood or some other sheet wood. But the wise coop-owner is already thinking ahead, even at this early planning stage, about long-term use, care, and maintenance. That coop you're about to build will be sparkly, shiny, and new only until the moment you let a chicken inside. And that plywood floor you precisely measured, carefully cut, and meticulously fastened into place will quickly become, well, a toilet. So cleaning that floor will become a major concern. Even though you'll almost certainly want to use some type of loose bedding on the floor of your coop, many people like to make the floor itself as easy to clean as possible.

Here are a few popular choices for flooring:

>> **Linoleum/vinyl flooring:** Although a wooden sheet material is easy to work with, even exterior-grade plywood isn't meant to be repeatedly and thoroughly hosed down on a regular basis. A layer of cheap linoleum or similar flooring product on top of a solid subfloor can work wonders in making cleanup a breeze. (But you'll still want to throw a layer of soft bedding material on top of it to keep it from becoming a chicken Slip 'n' Slide.)

More than a few coop-owners have fallen in love with a product called Glasbord. A fiberglass-reinforced plastic that comes in panels, Glasbord won't mold, mildew, or rot. It's extraordinarily resistant to moisture, staining, and scratching. It's even lightly pebbled, providing a bit of traction under your flock's feet. You may need to do some searching to find a local distributor, but those who have used Glasbord on a coop floor swear by it.

>> **Concrete:** Many people choose to build their coop on an unused corner of a patio and not construct a floor at all. Concrete is a perfectly acceptable floor for a chicken coop. It's easy to clean and can be hosed down without worry.

>> **Wire mesh:** Some very small coops have wire floors. (You can find more detail on wire products later in this chapter.) From a maintenance standpoint, this can be a godsend, as chicken waste falls through the wire mesh and disappears below. But remember that the waste doesn't vanish; it still goes somewhere, and that "somewhere" is usually just under the coop. So now *that* will need to be cleaned up from time to time. Some coops employ some sort of a removable tray under a wire floor, whereby coop cleanup involves pulling the tray out, cleaning it, and replacing it without ever interrupting the chickens.

>> **Dirt:** Plenty of coops are built directly on the ground, using good old Mother Nature as the floor of the shelter. A dirt floor may sound like the ultimate in low-maintenance, but it has its downsides, too. Expect an increase in pests, and possibly even a burrowing predator or two. A dirt-floored coop can also be a nightmare to really clean out well (and there will be times you'll want to do just that).

REMEMBER

Whatever material the floor itself is made out of, practically all coop-owners choose to cover it with some type of loose bedding material. It's perhaps better thought of as *litter*: something that makes the floor of the shelter easier to clean and is topped off or replaced on a regular basis. The ideal bedding is absorbent and acts as an odor combatant (but only to a certain extent!). Most chicken-owners use wood shavings (pine being the most commonly available and the cheapest), but others have had success with sawdust, horse bedding, sand, and even finely-shredded landscape mulch.

Walls

The walls of your chicken coop offer perhaps the greatest amount of flexibility in terms of what material you elect to use. For many utilitarian coops, simple plywood (as discussed earlier in this chapter) will suffice. Other coop-builders may choose something else, either to make the coop look more attractive or in order to utilize a material they happen to already have on-hand. Check out this short list of some of the more widely-used wall materials:

>> **Siding:** Most commonly made of wood, vinyl, or fiber cement (brands such as HardiePlank), siding is easy to install and quite versatile. You typically install horizontal planks over plywood sheathing and a weatherproofing layer of felt paper or housewrap. Using siding can allow you to match your own house or customize your coop with color.

>> **Exterior paneling:** For a rustic look, consider a popular plywood product often referred to by contractors as T1-11 (pronounced "tee one-eleven"). With vertical grooves every 8 inches or so, this exterior-grade plywood is specifically designed for projects where the final look matters. It's sold in 4-x-8-foot sheets, just like regular plywood, with tongue-and-groove edges to allow sheets to fit together cleanly with no visible seam. It's usually unfinished, so whether you paint or stain it after the build is up to you and the chickens.

Roofing

Putting a roof over your flock's heads is practically the whole point of building a chicken coop. But there simply aren't that many materials you'd want to use to roof a coop. Here's the rundown.

Shingles

Most coops are roofed just like a home, using a multi-layered approach (see Figure 3-2) to make the structure weather-tight.

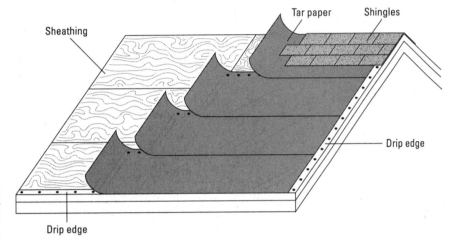

Sheathing

Tar paper

Shingles

Drip edge

FIGURE 3-2: The anatomy of a typical shingled roof.

Drip edge

Here's what you should know about the layers that make up a shingled roof:

>> The overlapping shingles, the outermost layer that's exposed to the elements, are most commonly made of asphalt, but can be found as cedar, metal, or even slate.

>> Underneath the shingles is a layer of roofing paper, also called felt or tar paper. This underlayment serves the critical purpose of acting as a moisture barrier for the shingles. Shingles can become drenched during heavy rains; roofing paper keeps that water out of your chicken coop.

>> The bottom layer of a typical roof is plywood sheathing, the solid surface that provides rigidity to the structure.

Shingles are fairly inexpensive and easy to install, requiring no special tools or hardware other than specialized roofing nails.

Corrugated panels

Corrugated panels, shown in Figure 3-3, are an inexpensive and lightweight alternative to shingles for many outdoor structures such as patios, carports, greenhouses, toolsheds, and — drum roll, please — chicken coops! These sheets, usually made of metal or translucent fiberglass, come in a variety of sizes and colors.

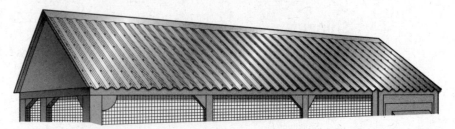

FIGURE 3-3:
Corrugated
roofing panels
are lightweight
and economical,
but do require
special hardware.

The translucent panels let in diffused light, which can aid in your chores and coop maintenance. But corrugated panels can be tough to work with. On a small-scale structure like a coop, you'll almost certainly have to cut the panels to size, which can be a tricky proposition for a DIYer because they're made of either metal or brittle fiberglass. Roof panels have a reputation for being easy to break, a real consideration if your coop will be located under tree limbs.

And finally, you'll have to buy installation accessories. To offer proper weather-proof protection, fiberglass panels must be used with special support pieces called *closure strips* and all panels require specialized fasteners that typically include some sort of rubber grommet to help create a watertight seal at each screw location.

Fencing in a chicken run

Proper living arrangements for your flock should include more than just a structure in which they can sleep protected at night, lay eggs undisturbed, or seek shelter from wind and rain. Most coop-builders also want to incorporate a *run* — an outdoor enclosure that's somewhat confined and protected, yet still exposed to fresh air and sunshine.

Without some kind of fencing material, those chickens are technically free-rangers. Making a smart selection about fencing material usually boils down to two factors: the material's strength and the size of the openings. When considering strength, remember that your fencing has to do more than just keep your flock contained. Even more important, it must keep predators from prying their way in, so stronger is better. Second, look at the openings in the fencing material you're considering. Just because a raccoon can't squeeze all the way through some types of fencing doesn't mean it offers adequate protection for your birds. A predator doesn't have to get all the way into a run to wreak bloody havoc. Nimble predators love to reach in with their arms and wave their razor-sharp claws around, trying to slash at chickens who wander too close.

Here are facts you should know about fencing as you design your run.

>> **Chicken wire:** It seems like a no-brainer that a product actually called *chicken wire* should be the most obvious and best choice for fencing. Yes, it's easy to

find, it's inexpensive, and it's quite malleable and therefore a cinch to work with. But most seasoned chicken-owners will tell you that true chicken wire, with its thin-gauge wire and wide hexagonal openings (see Figure 3-4), is far too lightweight to fend off any serious attack from a would-be chicken-snatcher.

>> **Nylon/plastic:** Nylon and plastic are even more flexible than chicken wire, making them easier on your hands during building. Your options here may be spread all over your home center, from light garden netting all the way up to the heavy-duty orange snow fencing you often see on a highway construction project. Like chicken wire, though, plastic and nylon fencing tends to be great for keeping your chickens in — but not so great for keeping predators out.

TIP

If your neck of the woods is home to birds of prey, you may find garden netting or a similar lightweight material to be a low-cost and not-terribly-unattractive canopy for covering the top of the run, even if the walls of the run are made of something sturdier. Hawks and owls should be adequately deterred, but this type of flimsy material won't offer much defense against raccoons and other varmints that can climb the fence walls and go right through a nylon canopy.

>> **Hardware cloth:** Often stocked right next to the chicken wire at your hardware store is something called *hardware cloth*. Wire stock — usually heavier than that of chicken wire — is woven and welded into a grid (with normally either ¼-inch- or ½-inch-square openings in the mesh), and it's often a sturdier choice for fencing a chicken run.

>> **Welded wire:** Welded wire looks a lot like hardware cloth, but it's usually made with even heavier wire. Although it's stronger than hardware cloth, its openings are generally much larger as well, leaving your chickens more susceptible to the long and nimble arms of a raccoon.

TIP

Many coop-owners like to double up, layering a 1- or 2-foot-tall run of hardware cloth along the bottom of a full fence of welded wire. This two-ply approach takes advantage of the considerable strength of welded wire for the overall structure, but keeps precious chicks on the ground more safely contained behind the hardware cloth's tighter mesh.

Selecting the Right Coop for Your Flock

Based on zoning and neighborhood restrictions, location, utilities, drainage, and desired flock size, you may find that only one style of housing will work for your unique situation, or you may have your pick of the entire roster.

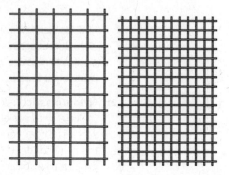

FIGURE 3-4:
Chicken wire is a very lightweight run option. Hardware cloth is stronger.

Here's a quick thumbnail sketch of a few popular types. These aren't the only chicken coop styles out there, but they represent the most commonly seen coops and are all DIY-friendly.

A-frames and hoops

Taking the same concept in two geometrically-different directions, A-frame coops and hoop coops are among the simplest coops you'll typically find. They're great for small yards where space is at a premium and large flocks aren't practical. They're lightweight and easy to move from place to place in the yard.

Because of their small size and basic design, these coop styles require a minimum of materials and know-how to construct. They are, therefore, probably the least expensive coop types to build and great examples of what a low-cost hobby raising chickens can be. Here are a few details on both types:

REMEMBER

>> **A-frames:** An A-frame (see Figure 3-5) is long and triangular in shape. Two sides lean against one another and come to a point, serving as both the walls and the roof of the structure. Most often, a solid, covered shelter portion is connected to a fenced run portion in one long unit. Although the shelter generally has a floor, the run doesn't — it simply rests on the ground. Usually, both the shelter and the run have a door or hatch that's accessible from outside the coop.

You can find full step-by-step plans for constructing an A-frame coop like this one later in this chapter.

>> **Hoops:** A hoop coop (see Figure 3-6) is typically rounded and tunnel-shaped. Flexible piping (such as PVC) often makes up the frame, with some kind of bendable fencing material covering it. A simple tarp or solid fabric can be draped over a portion of the hoop to make a decent shelter. Many chicken owners with larger coops keep a hoop handy to use as temporary housing during the main coop's clean-out day. A small hoop coop can be very lightweight and may need to be anchored to the ground to keep it from tipping over in high winds.

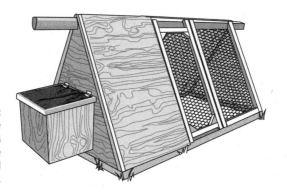

FIGURE 3-5:
An A-frame coop gets an *A* for small-scale simplicity and efficient design.

FIGURE 3-6:
A hoop coop's well-rounded design is a cinch to assemble.

Chicken tractors

A chicken *tractor* (refer to Figure 3-7) is a type of housing that's meant to be moved from place to place. (A-frames and hoops, described in the preceding section, can be considered a subset of the tractor family.)

A tractor coop typically features a roof and four walls, but no bottom (except in the shelter). This allows the chickens to work the soil and fertilize different patches of ground, depending on where the chicken-keeper places the tractor.

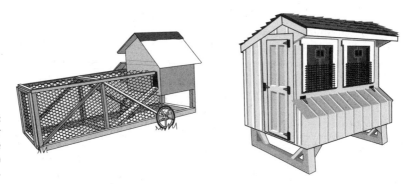

FIGURE 3-7:
A chicken tractor is meant to be moved around on wheels or skids.

To facilitate moving the coop around the property frequently, most tractors are built either with wheels or on heavy lumber skids. Smaller tractors can be dragged by the chicken-owner (or the chicken-owner's oh-so-helpful-and-energetic kids), although larger, heavier tractors may require a real tractor to do the pulling.

All-in-one-coops

Many owners like how A-frames, hoops, and tractors incorporate the shelter and run into one unit, but don't need the coop to be portable and want it to be big enough for them to enter themselves. Welcome to the all-in-one coop.

As shown in Figure 3-8, an *all-in-one* coop usually features a shelter and a run under one tall roof that covers everything and provides human access to the run but not the shelter. This access — for egg-collecting, feeding, cleaning, and chicken-gathering — makes this an attractive coop style where carefree maintenance is a goal.

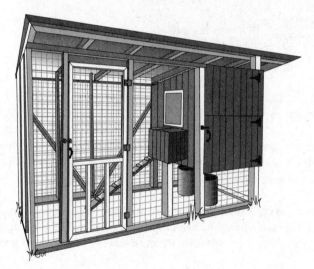

FIGURE 3-8:
An all-in-one coop puts the shelter and run under one roof.

WARNING

All-in-one coops start to get larger than the styles previously outlined, with real stud walls, tall support posts, and an actual roof that includes rafters and such. The all-in-one coop is a big structure, tall enough for a human caretaker to enter, so the materials list can be lengthy. Building this coop style may require a good bit of skill and probably isn't a one-weekend kind of project.

Walk-in coops

If you have the property to pull it off and the skills to slap one together, a walk-in coop (as seen in Figure 3-9) is generally considered the primo option for backyard chicken-keepers. As the name says, a walk-in coop is large enough for you to stand upright in. (Think of it as a full-size toolshed with chickens living in it.) This obviously makes maintenance, cleaning, and all other chicken chores much easier on you, and it gives your flock a lot of room to move about inside their shelter.

FIGURE 3-9:
A walk-in coop is generally considered the "coop de ville" of chicken housing.

REMEMBER

The primary distinguishing feature of a walk-in coop is a heavy floor that allows you, the caretaker, to enter the shelter. The larger size also means you can increase the size of your flock more easily (or just start out with more chickens) than if you had a smaller coop.

But even the gold standard of chicken coops comes with a drawback or two. For starters, a walk-in is big. That means it takes up a lot of space, requires a lot of material, and demands a good deal of skill to build. This kind of coop will almost certainly take several weekends to construct, even for someone who knows what he's doing and invites friends over to help.

WARNING

Walk-in coops seldom factor in a run. The outdoor run is almost always a completely separate entity, to be designed, laid out, and incorporated however you see fit. That makes it like two fairly sizable projects, so keep that in mind as you decide.

TIP

Most backyard chicken-keepers eventually end up with a walk-in coop, even if they start out with a smaller coop style. Don't be afraid to begin your hen hobby with a compact, low-cost A-frame, hoop, or tractor to test the waters. You can always graduate to a walk-in when your time and budget allow, and you'll have the smaller coop to use as a backup, for temporary housing during cleaning, or to quarantine sick birds from the others.

Constructing the Alpine A-Frame Coop

A simple A-frame coop takes up a minimum of yard space yet is ideally scaled for a small starter flock. A-frames often require just a modest list of basic building materials and can usually be built very quickly, even by a novice DIYer.

Because an A-frame is one of the most popular coop styles around, and often the perfect choice for the first-time chicken-keeper, coop-builder, or homesteader, it's the coop we teach you how to build in this chapter.

Vital stats

At a glance, here's how the Alpine A-frame stacks up in several key categories. Use these stats and selling points to determine whether the A-frame is the right coop for your flock as well as your building skills:

>> **Size:** At roughly 4 feet wide and 10 feet long, it occupies just a small footprint in your yard and can easily be tucked into an out-of-the-way corner if needed. At its peak, it stands 46 inches high.

>> **Capacity:** The shelter measures 16 square feet, and the run takes up 24 square feet, making this coop just right for two to four birds.

>> **Access:** One entire side of the A-frame roof acts as a door that can be lifted open for easy cleaning and access, and then latched closed. Chickens have their own door to the run which can also be left open or latched shut.

>> **Nest boxes:** Two nest boxes built into the exterior wall of the shelter share a top-opening (and latchable!) lid for hassle-free egg-gathering.

>> **Run:** A large door positioned in the center of the run allows you to reach in to catch a chicken without having to crawl all the way inside.

>> **Degree of difficulty:** The Alpine is one of the smallest coops featured, and is therefore one of the easiest to construct. Any homeowner with even a basic set of tools and rudimentary skills should be able to build this coop with relatively little trouble.

>> **Cost:** Prices will vary considerably, of course, but assuming that you have all the tools you need, you could easily purchase all of the materials to build this coop from scratch for well under $300.

Materials list

The following is a list of the materials that we used to construct the Alpine. In most cases, substitutions may be made as needed or desired.

Lumber		Hardware		Fasteners	
3	4' x 8' sheets of T1-11	1	4' x 16' panel of 1" x 2" wire mesh	70	2½" wood screws or 12 nails
1	4' x 4' sheet of ⁷⁄₁₆" OSB	1	piece of metal 6" x 49" (bent lengthwise in the middle)	140	1¼" screws or 7d nails
3	4' lengths of 2x4 pressure-treated lumber	1	piece of rubber 8" x 48½"	120	1¼" fencing staples
3	6' lengths of 2x3 pressure-treated lumber	8	5" T-style hinges		
18	6' lengths of 2x3 lumber	3	hook-and-eye latches		
1	4' length of 2x2 lumber	1	gate latch		
2	6' lengths of 1x3 pressure-treated lumber				
2	6' lengths of 1x3 lumber				
1	8' length of 1x2 lumber				

Cut list

This section breaks down how the materials should be cut to create the appropriate-sized pieces you need to assemble the Alpine as shown.

REMEMBER

This coop features several pieces that are cut on an angle. You'll see boards throughout the cut list that specify L.P. or S.P. Here are the details:

» *L.P.* stands for *long point,* where the board's listed length refers to the tip-to-tip measurement at the board's longest point, with the angle making one side shorter.

» *S.P.* is an abbreviation for *short point.* When you see it, know that the board's listed length measures just to the end's shortest point, meaning that the long end of the board will be greater than the cut list's specified length. For example, a 2x4 listed as 36 inches S.P. with a 45-degree angle will actually be almost 39½ inches long at its longest point.

Shelter floor

Quantity	Material	Dimensions
1	OSB	48" x 47"
3	Pressure-treated 2x4s	48" long

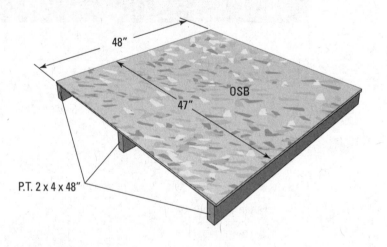

48"

OSB

47"

P.T. 2 x 4 x 48"

Gable 1 (nest box side)

Quantity	Material	Dimensions	Notes
1	Sheet of T1-11	48" wide x 42" high	From top center point, cut both sides at a 30-degree angle to leave vertical edge 1⅝" high at each bottom corner
2	2x3s	47⅛" long L.P. to L.P.	One end trimmed at a 60-degree angle and the other end trimmed at a 33-degree angle
1	2x3	24" long	
2	2x3s	14¼" long	

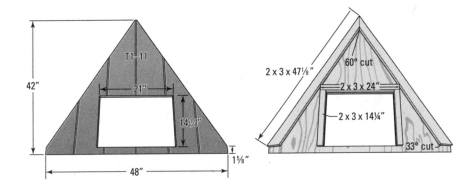

Gable 2 (run side, interior)

Quantity	Material	Dimensions	Notes
1	Sheet of T1-11	48" wide x 42" high	From the top center point, cut both sides at a 30-degree angle to leave a vertical edge 1⅝" high at each bottom corner
2	2x3s	47⅛" long L.P. to L.P.	One end trimmed at a 60-degree angle and the other end trimmed at a 33-degree angle
2	2x3s	16" long	
2	2x3s	14" long	
2	1x2s	13¼" long	
1	1x2	11" long	

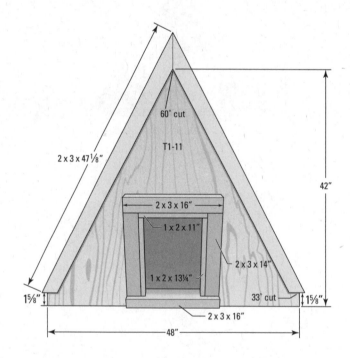

Gable 2 (run side, exterior) with run door

Quantity	Material	Dimensions	Notes
1	Sheet of T1-11	10½" wide x 13½" high	
1	Pressure-treated 1x3	17⅝" long L.P. to L.P.	Ends trimmed at a 15-degree angle
2	Pressure-treated 1x3s	17⅛" long	
1	Pressure-treated 1x3	10⅞" long	
2	Pressure-treated 1x3s	10½" long	
2	Pressure-treated 1x3s	9" long	

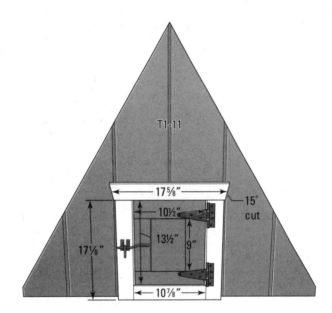

Roof panel 1 (fixed side)

Quantity	Material	Dimensions	Notes
1	Sheet of T1-11	48" wide x 48" high	
1	Sheet of T1-11	48" wide x 6¼" high	
1	2x4	44¾" long	Cut down both long sides at a 30-degree angle. (This creates a 44"-long board that's 3½ on the bottom and 1⅞ on the top.)
2	2x3s	44¾" long	

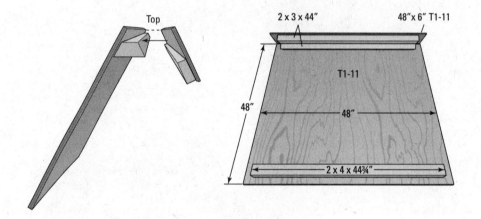

Roof panel 2 (hinged door)

Quantity	Material	Dimensions	Notes
1	Sheet of T1-11	48" wide x 41½" high	
2	2x3s	43¾" long	
2	2x3s	35" long	
2	2x3s	6" long L.P. to L.P.	Both ends trimmed at a 45-degree angle

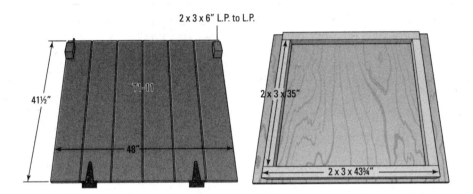

41½"

48"

T1-11

2 x 3 x 6" L.P. to L.P.

2 x 3 x 35"

2 x 3 x 43¾"

Nest boxes

Quantity	Material	Dimensions	Notes
1	Sheet of T1-11	23¼" wide x 13" high	Cut notches into back corners that measure 1" wide x ¾" high (nest boxes' lid)
1	Sheet of T1-11	20⅞" wide by 7½" high	Top edge trimmed at a 30-degree angle (nest boxes' front)
1	Sheet of T1-11	20" wide x 11½" high	(Nest boxes' bottom)
1	Sheet of T1-11	11¾" wide x 12¾" high (back) and 6" high (front)	(Nest boxes' divider)
2	Sheets of T1-11	11¼" wide x 14" high (back) and 7⅛" high (front)	(Nest boxes' sides)
1	1x3	11¾" long	(Inner blocking)
2	1x3s	10" long	(Inner blocking)
2	1x3s	6½" long	One end trimmed at a 30-degree angle (inner blocking)

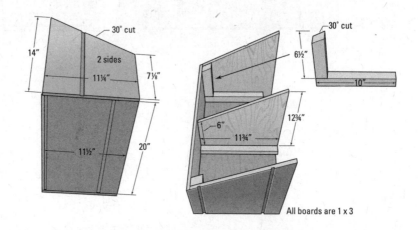

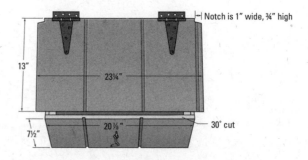

Roost

Quantity	Material	Dimensions	Notes
1	2x2	47" long	Not shown

Run panel 1

Quantity	Material	Dimensions	Notes
1	Pressure-treated 2x3	72" long	(Bottom)
1	2x3	72" long	(Top)
4	2x3s	48" long L.P. to L.P.	One end trimmed at a 60-degree angle and the other end trimmed at a 30-degree angle
1	Wire panel	48" x 71"	

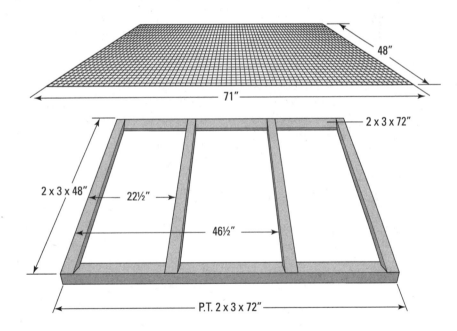

48"

71"

2 x 3 x 72"

2 x 3 x 48"

22½"

46½"

P.T. 2 x 3 x 72"

Run panel 2 with door

Quantity	Material	Dimensions	Notes
1	Pressure-treated 2x3	72" long	(Bottom)
1	2x3	72" long	(Top)
4	2x3s	48" long L.P. to L.P.	One end trimmed at a 60-degree angle, and the other end trimmed at a 30-degree angle
1	2x3	42⅞" long L.P. to S.P.	Both ends trimmed at a 22½-degree angle
2	2x3s	40" long	
2	2x3s	21" long	
1	2x3	7" long	(Blocking for latch)
1	Wire panel	24" x 48"	(Shelter-end panel)
1	Wire panel	23" x 48"	(Far-end panel)
1	Wire panel	20" x 40"	(Door panel)

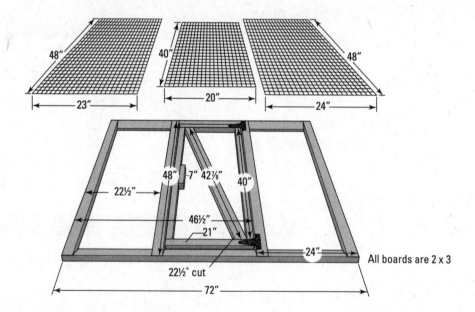

Run gable

Quantity	Material	Dimensions	Notes
1	Pressure-treated 2x3	46" long	(Bottom)
2	2x3s	44⅛" long L.P. to S.P.	Start with a 2x3 that's 46½" long. Trim the bottom end to a 30-degree angle. Trim the top end to a 60-degree angle, so that if you rest the 30-degree end flat on the ground, the 60-degree cut is plumb. Now measure up from the bottom of the 2x3 and mark the 44⅛" spot. Make a 30-degree cut at this mark (the cut should run horizontally, or parallel with the bottom cut).
1	Wire panel	47" by 40"	Cut to 40" high triangle

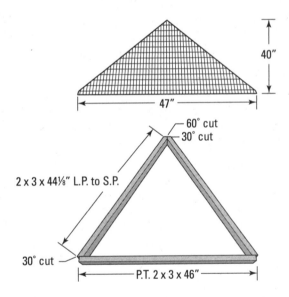

40"

47"

60° cut
30° cut

2 x 3 x 44⅛" L.P. to S.P.

30° cut

P.T. 2 x 3 x 46"

Assembling the coop

Rookie DIYers will appreciate the fact that each piece of the Alpine can be assembled as an individual unit. After all the pieces are created, it's simply a matter of putting them together.

1. **Begin with the shelter.**

   a. Secure the shelter floor to its 2x4 runners.

   b. Assemble the triangular gables. On the nest box side, cut an opening that is 21 inches wide and 14⅛ inches tall. The opening should be located 1⅝ inches up from the bottom edge of the T1-11 and centered. Attach the gables in place at the floor.

   c. Follow by building roof panel 1 (the fixed side). Then fasten the base to the shelter floor. The 2x3 bracing inside the roof panel and gables should help "lock" the pieces together while you screw everything in place.

   d. Assemble roof panel 2 and fasten to roof panel 1 with two T-style hinges; place the hinges about 10 inches from the door's edges, and use the screws provided. The base of the roof door shouldn't be attached to anything, so that the door may open freely. Two hook-and-eye latches screwed into small wooden cleats and the shelter floor can lock the door in the closed position.

TIP

   e. Our design features a piece of metal at the shelter peak to keep rainwater from running down into the coop. Use heavy-duty construction adhesive to glue the flashing to the coop. If the flashing is heavy enough to stay put on its own, you can simply allow it to rest in place — no permanent attachment is necessary.

TIP

   f. A short length of rubber is draped over the hinged door's seam in our design. This serves as a flexible strip of flashing that lets rainwater from the metal peak bypass the door's seam and shed right off onto the roof panel itself while still allowing the door to be opened. A scrap piece of rubber pond liner or a swatch of heavy-duty plastic sheeting should do the trick on your coop.

2. **Add the nest boxes and roost.**

   a. Use the diagrams that appear in the earlier section to cut and assemble the pieces for the nest boxes.

   b. Insert the box into the appropriate gable hole and fasten it in place.

c. Secure the nest box lid in place to the coop's exterior wall with two T-style hinges, fastened with the screws provided. A hook-and-eye latch, with one end threaded into the lid and the other end threaded into the front of the box, locks it shut.

d. Add the roost bar.

3. Assemble the run.

a. Build the run panels and door, along with the run gable, according to the diagrams that appear earlier. Then staple wire mesh in place at each section.

REMEMBER

b. The panel without the door can be covered by one large piece of fencing, but treat run panel 2 (with the door) as three distinct panels, each needing its own section of fencing.

c. Add a latch to the run's door panel. We used a self-locking model (which you would typically see on a fence gate, but almost any style you prefer (barrel bolt, hook-and-eye, hasp) can be made to work. Use the hardware provided to fasten it to the run's door panel.

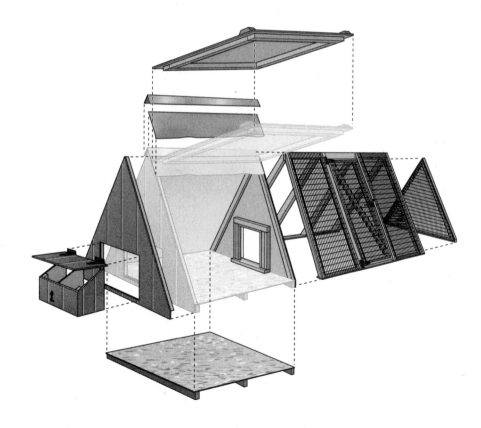

Index

Minorca chickens, 520
mint
  drying, 353
  freezing, 316
  uses for, 63
Mite Away Quick Strips, 506
molded candles, 445–447
moon phases, planting by, 151
mortises, 89
mothballs, 32
mother, for sourdough starter, 401
mound, 119
mouthfeel, 374
Mozzarella cheese recipe, 415
mulch
  about, 140
  choosing, 144–145
  for fighting weeds, 157
  inorganic, 142–144
  organic, 140–142
  plastic, 142–144
mushrooms, pressure canning, 244
muskmelons
  growing, 47
  harvesting, 152
  planting guidelines for, 122
mustard greens, for companion planting, 168

N

N (nitrogen), in fertilizer, 135–136
Nancy Jane's Stacking Planters, 25
nasturtiums, for companion planting, 168
nectarines
  canning, 212, 217–218
  freezing, 298
neem oil, for controlling pests, 166
nematodes, 163
nest boxes, in chicken coops, 527–528
netting, 28
New Hampshire Red chickens, 521

nightshades
  peppers, 49–50, 51
  potatoes, 55
  tomatoes, 49–51
nitrogen (N), in fertilizer, 135–136
nominal dimensions, 583–584
Nosema, 499–500
no-till gardening, 78
no-till layered garden technique, 68
nut-bearing trees, 59–60
nutrients, adding with cover crops and green manures, 145–148
nutritional needs, of chickens, 530
nylon fencing, for chicken coops, 611

O

oatmeal, as soap additive, 454
okra
  harvesting, 152
  planting guidelines for, 122
olives, 51
OMRI (Organic Materials Review Institute), 129
onions
  for container planting, 22
  growing tips for, 56–57
  harvesting, 152
  planting guidelines for, 122
  preparing for cold storage, 366–367
  pressure canning, 249, 262–263
  side-dressing, 139
  watering guidelines for, 128
open-pollinated varieties, 43
opposums, as predators to chickens, 548
oregano
  drying, 353–354
  uses for, 62
organic fertilizers, 136–137
organic gardening, 75
Organic Materials Review Institute (OMRI), 129
organic matter, adding, 75–76

S

white-egg layers, 519–520

whiteflies, 164

whole-grain mixtures, for chickens, 533

whole-wheat flour, 427

wicks, for candlemaking, 443–444

wide row planting, for seeds, 117–118

wide-mouth canning funnel, 190

wilting, 127

winter, beekeeping during, 476–478

winter rye, 147

winter squash

  freezing, 305, 315

  growing tips for, 48

  harvesting, 153

  planting guidelines for, 123

  side-dressing, 140

wire composter, 130

wire mesh, for chicken coops, 607

wood, for building beehives, 582

wood and wire thee-bin composter, 574–578

worms

  composting and, 134

  as pests, 160–161

wormwood, for companion planting, 168

Wyandotte chickens, 518

Y

yams, pressure canning, 249–250

yeast

  for baking bread, 425–428

  for homebrewing, 375–376

yogurt, 405

Z

zoning restrictions, for beekeeping, 459

zucchini

  drying, 341, 349

  growing, 47

Zucchini Bread and Butter Pickles recipe, 276, 282–283

Zucchini Chips recipe, 349

About the Authors

Todd Brock has written, directed, and produced more than 1,000 hours of television programming. His shows on topics ranging from landscaping to home renovations to organic gardening have aired across the US on major networks, including HGTV, DIY Network, and PBS, and locally in one of the country's Top 10 TV markets. The series "Growing a Greener World," for which Todd is scriptwriter and consulting producer, recently won a Southeast Emmy. As a freelance writer, Todd's work as a food writer has appeared on the popular website Serious Eats and in print in one of Atlanta's most recognized publications. He is a regular contributor to *Cowboys Wire*, covering sports news for fans of the Dallas Cowboys. He is the author of several *Dummies* books, including *Building Chicken Coops For Dummies*. When he is not writing, Todd competes in the sport of obstacle-course racing. He lives in the suburbs of Atlanta with his wife, Debbie, and their two daughters, Sydney and Kendall.

Bob Beckstrom is a licensed general contractor, living in northern California. He enjoys building things, spending time outdoors, and sharing what he's learned with other people. His first building experience was as a VISTA volunteer in 1968, as the coordinator of a self-help housing project in rural Alaska. He taught elementary school for ten years; has taught adult courses in house building and remodeling at The Owner Builder Center in Berkeley, California; and has written and edited extensively on home-improvement topics, including *Decks & Patios For Dummies*.

Howland Blackiston has been a backyard beekeeper since 1984. He's written many articles on beekeeping and appeared on dozens of television and radio programs (including The Discovery Channel, CNBC, CNN, NPR, Sirius Satellite Radio, and scores of regional shows). He has been a featured speaker at conferences in more than 40 countries. Howland is the past president of Connecticut's Back Yard Beekeepers Association, one of the nation's largest regional clubs for the hobbyist beekeeper. He is also the author of *Building Beehives For Dummies*, the companion book to this one, providing detailed instructions in how to build hives from scratch. Howland, his wife, Joy, and his bees live in Easton, Connecticut.

Cathy Cromell is the Southwest regional reporter for the National Gardening Association (NGA). She completed the Master Composter and Master Gardener certification programs at the University of Arizona Maricopa County Cooperative Extension Urban Horticulture Department in Phoenix, where she also absorbed abundant hands-on experience hoisting tons of organic matter while overseeing the composting area of the Master Gardener Demonstration Garden. As editor of Arizona Master Gardener Press at the Cooperative Extension, Cathy produced gardening books that received numerous awards. She was also a writer for *Better Homes and Gardens New Garden Book* and a contributing writer for *Gardening in the Southwest* (Sunset Books).

Rik DeGunther attended the University of Illinois as an undergraduate and Stanford University as a graduate student, studying both applied physics and engineering economics (some of this education actually stuck!). He holds several United States patents and is one of those nerdy guys who likes to take things apart to see how they work and then put them back together and try to figure out what the leftover parts are for. Rik is CEO of Efficient Homes, an energy efficiency auditing firm in Northern California. He also writes weekly op-ed columns for the *Mountain Democrat,* California's oldest and most venerable newspaper.

Suzanne DeJohn has worn a variety of hats during her years with the National Gardening Association, including work in the education, editorial, and IT departments. She coordinated NGA's online question and answer service for six years and has answered literally thousands of gardening questions. Convinced that gardeners are curious and love to learn, she was inspired to create the *Exploring the Garden* series of in-depth, online courses that teach the principles of botany in the context of the garden. Suzanne also does web- and print-based graphic design work for NGA, takes photos for the websites, and creates illustrations to accompany articles.

Owen Dell is an internationally recognized and widely admired expert in sustainable landscaping. He has written numerous articles for *Sunset Magazine, National Gardening Magazine, Southern California Gardener, Pacific Horticulture,* and many others. He's an international speaker who has presented hundreds of truly rousing lectures, classes, and workshops to homeowners and professionals. Owen is also the co-writer and co-host of the popular Santa Barbara, California, television series *Garden Wise Guys,* a sustainable-landscaping sitcom. His other book, *How to Start a Home-Based Landscaping Business* (Globe Pequot), has helped thousands of budding professionals get a healthy start on their careers. Owen's work has been featured on HGTV, Peak Moment Television, and NBC and in *The Wall Street Journal, Fortune* magazine, *Landscape Architecture Magazine,* the *Los Angeles Times,* and many other publications. He has won numerous awards for his work.

Kelly Ewing is a writer and editor who lives in the wonderful community of Fishers, Indiana, with her husband Mark, her daughter Katie, her son Carter, and furry canine friend Cheyenne. She has coauthored several books, including *The Internet All in One Desk Reference For Dummies, PCs All in One Desk Reference For Dummies,* and *Direct Mail For Dummies.* She has ghostwritten several books and edited more than 75 books on a variety of topics. She also writes articles on sports, travel, and human interest for several newspapers. In her spare time — when she can find it! — she enjoys spending time with her kids, reading, walking, writing, scrapbooking, cooking, and doing crafts.

Philip Giroux is a second-generation Californian who developed his desire for planting and his love of gardens watching his father, an avid gardener, and graduated from the University of Arizona with a degree in landscape architecture and ornamental horticulture. He established his landscape designing and building firm in 1978, specializing in custom residential installations, including the estates of Rupert Murdock and Henry Mudd. Philip is responsible for numerous large-scale commercial projects, such as the Los Angeles County Museum of Arts Sculpture and Japanese Pavilion Garden. Philip has served as L.A. Chapter President for the California Landscape Contractors Association and is a member of the Royal Horticulture Society.

Theresa A. Husarik is a writer, photographer, crafter, fiber person, and animal lover who lives on a small plot far away from the heart of the city. When she is not tending to her brood (which includes llamas, alpacas, angora goats, cats, dogs, peacocks, and chickens), she can usually be found either behind the computer writing something or in the craft room making something.

Amy Jeanroy has been canning and preserving foods for 20 years. She is passionate about filling the pantry with useful, delicious foods, and creating healthy meals from her own small farm. Amy is the Herb Garden Guide for About.com and also writes a weekly farm newsletter that provides homemade recipes to help her readers store and use their summer bounty.

Rob Ludlow, his wife, Emily, and their two beautiful daughters, Alana and April are the perfect example of the suburban family with a small flock of backyard chickens. What started out as a fun hobby raising a few egg-laying hens has turned into almost an addiction. Originally, Rob started posting his experiences with chickens on his hobby website, but when he realized how much his obsession with chickens was growing, he concentrated his efforts on a site completely devoted to the subject. Now Rob owns and manages www.BackYardChickens.com (BYC), the largest and fastest-growing community of chicken enthusiasts in the world.

The National Gardening Association (NGA) is committed to sustaining and renewing the fundamental links between people, plants, and the earth. Founded in 1972 as "Gardens for All" to spearhead the community garden movement, today's NGA promotes environmental responsibility, advances multidisciplinary learning and scientific literacy, and creates partnerships that restore and enhance communities. NGA is best known for its garden-based curricula, educational materials, international initiatives, and several youth garden grant programs. Together, these reach more than 300,000 children nationwide each year. NGA's websites, one for home gardeners and another for those who garden with kids, build community and offer a wealth of custom content.

Marty Nachel is a freelance writer on beer and brewing. As a member of the North American Guild of Beer Writers, in September 1996 Marty was voted one of the three best beer writers in the United States at the N.A.G.B.W. Quill & Tankard Awards at the Great American Beer Festival in Denver. A former President of the Chicago Beer Society and founding member of the Brewers Of South Suburbia (B.O.S.S.) home-brew and beer appreciation club, Marty has been brewing his own award-winning beers since 1985. In 1986, he was the first person in the state of Illinois to become a Certified Beer Judge. In addition to his homebrew judging duties, Marty served on the panel of beer evaluators at the prestigious Beverage Testing Institute in Chicago, home of the World Beer Championships, as well as the Great American Beer Festival in Denver, Colorado. His articles have appeared in *All About Beer* magazine, *Brew Magazine*, *Brew Your Own* magazine, *Celebrator Beer News*, *Drink* magazine, *Fine Cooking* magazine, *Zymurgy Magazine*, and Epicurious.com.

Charlie Nardozzi is a nationally recognized garden writer, speaker, and radio and television personality. He has worked for more than 20 years bringing expert gardening information to home gardeners through radio, television, talks, online, and the printed page. Charlie has written for national magazines such as *Organic Gardening* and contributed to many of the *For Dummies* gardening titles, authoring *Vegetable Gardening For Dummies*. He also authored the *Ultimate Gardener* (HCI Press) which highlights heart-warming stories about the trials and tribulations of gardening and *Northeast Fruit and Vegetable Gardening* in (Cool Springs Press). He also contributed to other book project such as *Vegetables from an Italian Garden* (Phaidon Press). Charlie's skills as a garden communicator extend beyond the printed page. He's the former host of PBS's *Garden Smart*, reaching more than 60 million households. He has also been a gardening expert on many national syndicated television and radio shows such as HGTV's *Today at Home*, Discovery Channel's *Home Matters*, Sirius Radio's *Martha Stewart Living*, and *Garden Life Radio*.

Emily Nolan has loved baking for as long as she can remember. Her earliest memories are of digging in her mother's huge tubs of flour as she put together pies and breads. Her mother handed Emily scraps of dough to keep her busy — even at that tender age, Emily had baking in her blood. Today. Emily does freelance editing, recipe writing, and recipe development.

Paul Simon is a nationally recognized landscape architect, public artist, horticulturist, master gardener, and urban designer. Paul brings a wealth of knowledge, skills, and abilities from various fields in the gardening, horticulture, and design industries. He holds a B.S. in Landscape Architecture from the University of Kentucky with a diverse curriculum in site design, urban design, community planning, geography, architecture, plant and soil sciences, forestry, and civil engineering. He is also an esteemed member of the American Society of Landscape Architects. In addition, Paul is involved as a horticultural editor for www.kidsgardening.org. Kids Gardening is a leading national provider of K-12, plant-based educational materials, providing programs and initiatives for plant-based education in schools, communities, and backyards across the country. Paul continues to provide unique articles underscoring the importance of kids gardening and outdoor learning.

Cheryl K. Smith has raised goats since 1998 when she got two Nigerian Dwarves. She published *Ruminations, the Nigerian Dwarf and Mini Dairy Goat Magazine* from 2001 through 2007 and published the book *Goat Health Care* (Karmadillo Press) in 2009. She has written for *Dairy Goat Journal, Countryside,* and other magazines. Cheryl served as legal counsel for the American Goat Society (AGS) from 2003 to 2005 and on their board of directors from 2005 to 2009. She has also served on the boards of the American Nigerian Dwarf Dairy Association (ANDDA), the Northwest Nigerian Dwarf Dairy Goat Association (NNDDGA) and the Northwest Dairy Goat Herd Improvement Association (NDGHIA). Cheryl lives in the community of Low Pass, located in the coast range of Oregon, with her herd of experimental miniature dairy goats, Mystic Acres Oberians.

Lance Walheim has been gardening most of his life. He got his start when his father forced him to turn the soil and plant tomatoes in the family vegetable garden as punishment for a deed he can't recall. Funny thing was, he found that he enjoyed working in the soil and has been doing it ever since. He has written or contributed to more than 40 gardening books on subject ranging from citrus to roses (including *Roses For Dummies*). He has also written extensively about lawns and lawn care – check out his book, *Lawn Care For Dummies*. He also has served as a writer for *Sunset* and *National Gardening* magazines and is part owner of California Citrus Specialties, marketers of specialty citrus fruit. But his true loves are family and gardening, the "composts" that enrich his heart and soul.

Karen Ward is the author of *Pickles, Peaches, and Chocolate* and a life-long home canner, home economist, and recipe developer. In addition to judging preserved food at the San Diego County Fair each year, Karen teaches canning and preserving to men and women of all ages. Karen has been a featured guest on many television shows, including QVC and HGTV's *Smart Solutions*. She is a founding member of the San Diego Chapter of Les Dames d'Escoffier International, a non-profit organization mentoring women and providing scholarships in the culinary arts. Karen is a native-born Southern Californian. She makes her home in San Diego with her husband, Chris.

Marni Wasserman is a certified chef and culinary nutritionist who uses passion and experience to educate individuals on how to adopt a realistic, plant-based diet that is both simple and delicious. She is dedicated to providing individuals with balanced lifestyle choices through organic, fresh, whole, and natural plant-based foods. As a prominent figure of health and nutrition in Toronto, Marni is a contributor to *Chatelaine, Huffington Post, Bamboo,* and *Tonic Magazine.* She has made several TV appearances on CBC and CTV, and has been featured in the *Toronto Star.* Marni has also consulted with the Windsor Arms Hotel for its vegan and vegetarian menus, and she participates in several live speaking and cooking demonstrations. If that isn't enough, she is also the author of several well-received plant-based e-books such as *Cleansing with Super Foods* and *Veggin' Comfortably.*

Ann Whitman earned a Bachelor of Science degree in Plant and Soil Science at the University of Vermont. She also completed a Master of Arts degree in Landscape Design from the Conway School of Landscape Design in Massachusetts. Ann is the author of *Trees and Shrubs For Dummies* (Wiley Publishing, Inc.) as well as *How-To Landscaping Basics* and *Water Gardens: Simple Steps to Adding the Beauty of Water to Your Garden*, both published by Time Life. She also contributes to several gardening magazines and websites. When she's not writing, Ann gardens on fertile river-bottom soil in Vermont where the winters are long and the summers are short but worth it.

Kimberley Willis lives with her husband, Steve, on a small farm in the thumb area of Michigan. She is now retired and enjoying her grandchildren, her chickens, and gardening. Kim worked at the MSU Extension office in Lapeer County Michigan for 18 years as a horticulturist and doubled as the resident chicken expert. She has raised numerous breeds of chickens and other poultry for eggs, meat, and showing for more than 40 years. She is a strong advocate of eating locally and shares her bounty of eggs with family and friends. Kim is a proud member of www.backyardchickens.com/ and is also a member of the Huron County Michigan Fowl Group on Facebook. In addition, Kim is a garden and country living writer for Examiner.com and has written more than 600 articles online.

Dave Zook, his wife, Suz, and their four children, Justin, Jordan, Jenika, and Javon, live on several acres in rural Lancaster County, Pennsylvania. He is the founder/owner of Horizon Structures, a manufacturer of pre-built storage sheds, garages, horse barns, and chicken coops. Dave and his family keep a small flock of chickens at home in one of his company's coops. He continues to improve the designs and develop new ones based on customer input as well as his family's experiences with their own backyard flock. Over the past nine years, Horizon's line of chicken coops has proven to be very popular with chicken fanciers — and their hens — throughout the U.S., with coops now in 48 states!

Publisher's Acknowledgments

Executive Editor: Lindsay Lefevere

Development Editor: Susan Pink

Copy Editor: Susan Pink

Editorial Assistant: Matthew Lowe

Sr. Editorial Assistant: Cherie Case

Production Editor: Magesh Elangovan

Cover Image: © Daxiao Productions/ Shutterstock

PERSONAL ENRICHMENT

Staying Sharp
9781119187790
USA $26.00
CAN $31.99
UK £19.99

Facebook
9781119179030
USA $21.99
CAN $25.99
UK £16.99

Guitar
9781119293354
USA $24.99
CAN $29.99
UK £17.99

Investing
9781119293347
USA $22.99
CAN $27.99
UK £16.99

Beekeeping
9781119310068
USA $22.99
CAN $27.99
UK £16.99

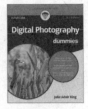

Digital Photography
9781119235606
USA $24.99
CAN $29.99
UK £17.99

Meditation
9781119251163
USA $24.99
CAN $29.99
UK £17.99

Pregnancy
9781119235491
USA $26.99
CAN $31.99
UK £19.99

Samsung Galaxy S7
9781119279952
USA $24.99
CAN $29.99
UK £17.99

iPhone
9781119283133
USA $24.99
CAN $29.99
UK £17.99

Crocheting
9781119287117
USA $24.99
CAN $29.99
UK £16.99

Nutrition
9781119130246
USA $22.99
CAN $27.99
UK £16.99

PROFESSIONAL DEVELOPMENT

Windows 10
9781119311041
USA $24.99
CAN $29.99
UK £17.99

AutoCAD
9781119255796
USA $39.99
CAN $47.99
UK £27.99

Excel 2016
9781119293439
USA $26.99
CAN $31.99
UK £19.99

QuickBooks 2017
9781119281467
USA $26.99
CAN $31.99
UK £19.99

macOS Sierra
9781119280651
USA $29.99
CAN $35.99
UK £21.99

LinkedIn
9781119251132
USA $24.99
CAN $29.99
UK £17.99

Windows 10 ALL-IN-ONE
9781119310563
USA $34.00
CAN $41.99
UK £24.99

SharePoint 2016
9781119181705
USA $29.99
CAN $35.99
UK £21.99

Fundamental Analysis
9781119263593
USA $26.99
CAN $31.99
UK £19.99

Networking
9781119257769
USA $29.99
CAN $35.99
UK £21.99

Office 2016
9781119293477
USA $26.99
CAN $31.99
UK £19.99

Office 365
9781119265313
USA $24.99
CAN $29.99
UK £17.99

Salesforce.com
9781119239314
USA $29.99
CAN $35.99
UK £21.99

Coding
9781119293323
USA $29.99
CAN $35.99
UK £21.99

dummies.com

dummies®
A Wiley Brand